ORGANIC
PLANT
PROTECTION

Some material in this book first appeared in **The Organic Way to Plant Protection,** edited by Glenn F. Johns and the staff of **Organic Gardening and Farming** and published by Rodale Press, Inc., in 1966.

ORGANIC PLANT PROTECTION

**A Comprehensive Reference on
Controlling Insects and Diseases
in the Garden, Orchard and
Yard without Using Chemicals**

Edited by Roger B. Yepsen, Jr.

and the editors of
Organic Gardening and Farming® magazine

Rodale Press, Inc.
Emmaus, Pennsylvania 18049

Library of Congress Cataloging in Publication Data

Main entry under title:

Organic plant protection.

    Bibliography: p.

    Includes index.

    1. Plants, Protection of. 2. Organic gardening.
3. Garden pests. I. Yepsen, Roger B. II. Organic
gardening and farming.

SB974.O73   632'.94   75-43829

ISBN 0-87857-110-8

OB-600

First Printing—May, 1976

Printed in the United States of America
on recycled paper

CONTENTS

How To Use This Book

First, take a look at how the book is arranged. It is composed of two sections. Section One is a series of chapters, written to be read from first to last, if you so desire. Although much of the material is background reading, you'll find many specific methods, recipes, and mentions of commercial products. The controls discussed in Chapters 3 through 10 are arranged in that order for a reason—to take you first to those measures with minimal interference with the garden or orchard environment (including correct plant feeding, interplanting, resistant varieties, garden sanitation, cultivation, and timed plantings) and then to controls that can have profound consequences on that environment (biological controls, physical traps and scares, and a succession of botanical repellents and poisons from water through garlic to pyrethrum and sulfur). When confronted with a problem, go only as far along this ladder of controls as necessary. Ideally you should stick with methods discussed in the first few chapters. These, you'll notice, are *preventatives*—ways to avoid trouble, while most of the methods further along are *controls*—things to do once trouble has hit. The final two chapters of Section One talk in depth about weeds and wildlife and how they affect crops for better and for worse.

Section Two can be thought of as an encyclopedia of plant protection. The entries are arranged alphabetically, and give concise information for specific pests and diseases. You'll find many references to other entries and to the chapters up front. To take you on a quick tour of this encyclopedic section, let's pick a pest—a yellow green beetle with black stripes that is devouring tomato foliage. Turn to the tomato entry, and scan it for a likely sounding insect. They are italicized and arranged alphabetically. After a bit of searching you'll come across the Colorado potato beetle, described in just enough detail to confirm its identity. In this case, the insect is better known as a pest of potatoes, and its life cycle and controls are discussed under potato—as indicated by "see POTATO."

If it's a disease you're after, skip over the insect subentries to the disease subentries. And following the diseases you'll often find a discussion of the most serious wildlife pests. If pests and diseases are of only occasional or regional importance to a crop, they are listed and cross-referenced at the end of the pest or disease paragraphs.

A very important part of this book is the Index. If you want to know all you can about the use of garlic as an insecticide, for instance, the Index will clue you in to all of the pertinent references scattered through the book. An index entry or subentry set in capitals (such as JUNE BUG) cues you in that it is also an entry in the encyclopedic section.

Appendix I lists plants known to have insecticidal powers that might make them useful as sprays or dusts. Appendix II tells how you find the sources of many commercial products mentioned in this book.

Where did all the information come from?

The information for this book comes from hundreds of sources, including many readers of *Organic Gardening and Farming* magazine who wrote in their observations, successes, and failures with organic plant protection. The magazine's editors and writers offer many articles on pest control each year. Of the dozens of books that have been used, both technical and written for the layman, several that proved to be exceptional sources are listed in the Bibliography. Most of the 50 state agricultural experiment stations and extension services have contributed books, bulletins, leaflets, and newsletters; while most of their publications suggest chemical controls, and plenty of them, these public agencies are becoming more aware of the debilities of hard chemicals, and references to biological and cultural control are cautiously creeping into their recommendations. Experiment stations offer up-to-date information on resistant varieties, and often recommend cultural controls suited for their regions. The USDA, too, is getting away from straight pesticides and offers a wealth of printed material, including their monthly *Agricultural Research*.

An important source of information has been the people whose very livelihoods depend on the viability of organic controls—those who grow organic fruit and vegetables for a living, those who market beneficial insects and pathogens, and those who offer pest management services.

The color photographs were selected from the USDA's considerable collection. The many line drawings of insects and disease symptoms that accompany the encyclopedic section are courtesy of the Connecticut Agricultural Research Station and the USDA.

SECTION ONE
AN ORGANIC PLANT PROTECTION PRIMER

The chemical-wielding gardener has it pretty easy. There's nothing to read but a label. But reading the 12 chapters that follow should enable you to understand what is going on in the garden and then to make an intelligent, rather than a knee-jerk, response.

1
Introduction:
What Will Be Your
Role In The Garden?

In 1962, *Silent Spring* burst a big hole in the thinking of a lot of people. Rachel Carson opened her book with an eery fable of a town in which spring did not come—plants blossomed, but no birds or bees were to be seen and farm animals produced no young. A fine white powder was observed falling from the sky. In time, fish disappeared from the streams, and roadside vegetation turned brown. The evil character behind these strange developments was man, and the white powder was synthetic insecticide.

In the years since *Silent Spring* was first published, this scenario has come to read more like a news item than a setting for a fable. And more and more people have taken a look around at the toll our way of life has taken on the environment. These people also looked inward, critical of the notion that man, as but one species out of thousands that share the Earth, is destined to be ecologically dominant. The notion is not original to us current occupants. Robert L. Rudd suggests in *Pesticides and the Living Landscape* that this high-and-mighty role was reflected in biblical allegory: man was seen as monarch of flora and fauna, a creature so unique and gifted as to be above the laws of nature.

Recent times have done little to temper this self-opinion. Indeed, the fruits of our technetronic society seem to confirm it. Cars, airplanes, televisions, computers, and man on the moon—all appeared within the span of a lifetime. And by all indications, the rate of change continues to increase. Few people have shaken off the gut thrill of acceleration long enough to take a look at the scenery. Ms. Carson was one of those

3

few. She saw that it was time for us to reconsider our attempts to tame the earth to our liking by the sheer force of will and wits.

For various reasons, many of her readers weren't ready to recognize the interrelatedness of all living things—that man is as dependent on bugs for existence as they are on him. And the use of insecticides has continued to increase. In 1964, two years after *Silent Spring* came out, 143 million pounds of insecticides were used for agricultural purposes in this country. In 1970, the United States sprayed, dusted, and dumped more than 500 million pounds on its fields.

If the allegations in *Silent Spring* and in the publications of other ecologically minded writers are true, then why are insecticides more popular than ever? One readily apparent reason is the lobbying and promotion of the pesticide industry. Another is known to anyone who has read the chemically oriented bulletins from state agricultural stations and the USDA. A more insidious reason is suggested by Paul DeBach, professor of Biological Control at the University of California, in *Biological Control by Natural Enemies*. Terming insecticides "the ecological narcotics," he draws an instructive parallel between the effects of narcotics use by humans and the effects of the exclusive use of chemical pesticides. In either case, immediate objective is usually reached, but sooner or later the dosages and frequency of use must be stepped up as tolerance or resistance to the chemicals develops. This cycle repeats itself, and in time a habit is developed. Even though the user comes to recognize the futility of his actions, the problem is not immediately solved. ". . . Withdrawal is slow, difficult and painful, and reattainment of normality a lengthy process both in humans and generally in agro-ecosystems."

It's hard to get hooked on biological controls. Because most such methods take time, organic growers miss out on the gratification of seeing instant results. Also, while chemical doses must be repeated and compounded, biological control is permanent; experience in the field has shown that pests rarely develop resistance to biological controls.

An even uglier reason for the growing use of pesticides—the value of the industry's annual product now exceeds $1 billion—is posited by Dr. Robert van den Bosch, chairman of the Division of Biological Control at the University of California at Berkeley. That reason is greed, "the age-old drive to squeeze all possible profit from a good thing."

> If human arrogance and foolishness were the only factors involved in pesticide misuse it might be a relatively simple matter to bring order out of chaos by identifying vain and stupid people and shunting them aside. But greed is another matter—virtually all of us are touched with it; once we lock onto a windfall we are reluctant to let go. In pest control the windfall was created by DDT, which catalyzed an

explosive expansion of the pesticide industry. The expansion
of the pesticide industry was so rapid and massive that it
simply overwhelmed pest-control technology.

So much for the chemically minded opposition. You won't find a
lengthy polemic against the use of chemical pesticides in this book. The
subject is complex, and involves much more than statistical evidence and
prediction. That is, it seems that neither side can be argued solely on the
basis of empirical fact, that our emotions and values figure importantly
in deciding what our course should be. On the one hand, Ms. Carson
says, "Future historians may well be amazed by our distorted sense of
proportion," and, "Future generations are unlikely to condone our lack
of prudent concern for the integrity of the natural world." But Wheeler
McMillen, whose argument is summed up in the title of his book, *Bugs or
People,* sees our situation differently. "Today's amazing chemical aids
. . . represent but a fair beginning. Unfettered scientific enterprise will
never be content with yesterdays nor even with todays." McMillen's goal
for tomorrow? "We should proceed to master our environment." But
perhaps *your* perspective is the clearest of all. As a gardener or farmer,
plants and animals are your intimates. How do you feel about them?

What will be your
role in the garden?
If you have grown and tended plants for any
length of time, you have no doubt acquired an awe for the myriad pests
and ailments that attack your mute, placid charges. Or perhaps "distaste"
or "hate" would better describe your feelings. You can't be blamed for a
shiver of revulsion at happening upon a fat, four-inch hornworm. And
the diseases that cause your plants to wilt and pulp into ruins—what
place could such maladies possibly have in the scheme of things? This
book will help to show that such grotesqueries do indeed have a place.
The tiny fleahopper may seem insignificant, and a chemical nostrum will
make him disappear for a time, but countless such creatures play roles in
even the most modest of backyard plots. These roles are important because they're all interrelated, and the diagram illustrates why this is so.
A balance of life in the garden is dependent on this cycle. Each part of
the cycle is dependent on the others; knock out any one element—such as
the balance of pests and beneficial insects—and your garden is in trouble.

Organic Plant Protection can serve as your guide to creating and
maintaining the balance of nature on your piece of land. This is an
on-going process, one requiring that you know something about the
dynamics of the balance. So, while you won't find many one-shot cures
between these covers, you will learn to discover what part of the cycle is
going amuck, why it is going amuck, and how to set things right again.
To assist you in putting a tag on the problem, black-and-white photo-

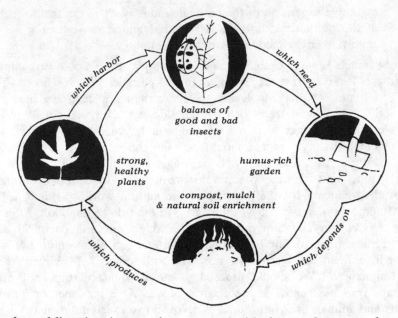

which harbor

which need

balance of
good and bad
insects

strong,
healthy
plants

humus-rich
garden

compost, mulch
& natural soil enrichment

which depends on

which produces

graphs and line-drawings are incorporated with the text for easy reference, and a section of color photographs shows the most important insects and disease symptoms.

Once the adversary's name is rolling off your tongue, the next step is to get to know him, so habitat, life cycle, appetite, vulnerabilities, and strengths are all described. (Incidentally, the best cure for entomophobia is to learn something about bugs.) Finally you will find a variety of controls—biological, cultural, botanical, and mechanical—and how to use them in an integrated program.

Possessed of a knowledge of these controls, you still have to decide whether or not to use them. Does the situation at hand warrant taking action? Are the plants suffering intolerable damage? Remember, plants can lose some leaf area or part of their root systems without damaging the harvest. Also, by planting for yourself and a little extra for the bugs, a bit of damage won't hurt your take. And most important, a variety of pests scattered about the garden is a good sign that at least the dynamics of *your* part of the environment is in working order. If beneficial insects are to stick around to guard the garden, there must always be a few pests around, and this will likely mean sharing a tiny portion of your crop with your little enemies.

But your beneficence can be expected to stretch only so far, and if, for example, cabbage is literally disappearing through the nocturnal ravages of the cutworm, you may safely conclude the plants are suffering intolerable damage. Take appropriate action, without a qualm of guilt.

However, as you administer the recommended controls, take a second to reflect on what went wrong. Why did the bugs, or pathogen, get out of hand? Could it be that the plants weren't growing vigorously to begin with, and thus were unable to sustain an attack? Perhaps they got that way from deficient soil, too much or too little water, or a chemical residue in the soil. Are you encouraging a build-up of pests by planting only one crop to a large area (monocropping) or by repeatedly growing the same crop in the same spot year after year? Interplanting and rotation help to discourage both pests and diseases. Are plants set too closely together? Most diseases are discouraged by plenty of light and a flow of air around plants. Could you have avoided trouble by setting plants earlier or later in the season? As you will see in many of the encyclopedic entries that follow, timing is important. Have you left piles of plant debris about the garden? These provide homes for wintering pests. Does your garden attract bug-eating birds, toads, and other wildlife? Chapter 12, "The Good and Bad of Wildlife in the Garden," will tell you who your allies are and how to interest them in your plot of land. Not until you have answered such questions can you effectively decide on a long-range solution to your problem.

You can see that organic plant protection involves more than home-made sprays and a tip of the hat to those good buddies, the ladybug and praying mantis. In fact, these well-known tenets of organic control have received a lot of criticism of late. Homemade sprays of garlic, soap, peppers and a kitchenful of other domestic ingredients should no longer be labelled "safe." They may be safe to humans, but can cause more insect problems than they solve if used indiscriminately. Helga Olkowski, a biological control specialist, and husband Bill, a research entomologist at the University of California at Berkeley, warn that, "if you think that disaster is caused only by commercial synthetic poisons, we have seen resurgence of aphids, for instance, after the excessive, ill-timed use of water sprays to knock them off trees. By knocking off, causing diseases in, or otherwise discouraging ladybugs, lacewings, spiders, and other important predators on these particular trees, the aphids remaining were able to resurge to even more damaging population numbers." As for that popular organic nostrum, garlic, "We shuddered to read, in the letters-to-the-editor column of one garden magazine, of a lady who was spraying garlic on her plants every three weeks. No wonder she was having to do it repeatedly—she was probably indiscriminately causing all kinds of eco-system disruptions. This would hardly lead to a stable situation."

Other iconoclasts have bagged the praying mantis, saying that it is not only voracious but also pretty unselective in its eating habits. That is, the mantis may eat good bugs, too. Ladybugs still reign supreme in gardeners' eyes as biological control agents, but the worth of importing them to the backyard has been questioned. It appears that the beetles you buy may not stick around to do much help. Beetles collected during the late spring and summer tend to have poor appetites, although some suppliers have a process that restores their appetites. Those collected during winter months tend to disperse rapidly.

With millions of people dying of starvation, should organic methods be regarded as an idealistic indulgence?   Critics of organic soil building and plant protection claim that, in this time of worldwide food shortage, we can ill afford to abandon chemical agriculture. Such an attack doesn't really impinge on your backyard practices, as it is doubtful that you have seriously considered exporting produce. But it is important that you not consider organic growing a luxury. It makes sense on a small scale just as it does globally.

The technological giant-steps of modern agriculture are taking us to dead ends. This can best be seen in our country, the most "advanced" of them all, the perpetrator of the so-called Green Revolution. With agriculture becoming big business, farms are fewer and bigger. This has forced the family farm into obsolescence, and led to the costly distribution of foods developed and picked with shipability, not taste or nutrition, in mind. New high-yielding varieties are more profitable but less resistant to bugs, and therefore depend on chemical sprays. These sprays and chemical fertilizers are expensive—increasingly so, as it takes much energy, now at such a premium, to produce them. Developing agriculture into a more energy-intensive activity hardly makes sense in view of our finite and dwindling petroleum supply. Mulch, compost, and manure have fed crops and forests for eons, and it appears the Arabs have no control over these commodities. But as it stands now, farmers in the energy-prodigal United States can hardly afford the sprays and fuel that are givens in our method of agriculture.

The consequences of modern agriculture don't stop at the hedgerow. Significant amounts of various agricultural toxins are showing up in our drinking water. In 1969, the Community Water Supply Study found measurable levels of pesticides in seven of 160 samples taken; small, unmeasurable amounts were acknowledged in about half the samples. In 1975, the Environmental Protection Agency reported that all but one of five city water supplies tested contained dieldrin, a proven carcinogen in humans. Other pesticides commonly found in water are DDT, endren, chlordane, aldrin, and lindane. Of these chemicals, dieldrin, DDT, and aldrin have been taken off the market after the danger they presented to human life was belatedly admitted.

Gardeners and farmers alike have examined and rejected many of the accoutrements of modern agriculture. Their answer?—to take the best that current experimentation in the field has to offer (resistant varieties, biological allies, and the like) and to incorporate it with ways that have worked in the past. This is not a head-in-the-sand retrogression, but an attempt to become reacquainted with an older, wiser agriculture, in which growers worked in harmony with nature instead of trying vainly to tame her to a median-strip servility.—*Roger B. Yepsen, Jr.*

2
Sizing Up The Enemy: Insects, Mites, Nematodes, Molluscs, And Others

To know them isn't necessarily to love them, but if you understand something of how bugs work, you'll be better equipped to handle them when they get into trouble.

First of all, let's take a look at that name "bug." It's a poor one, as you can see from the chart. True bugs, such as the lygus bug and stink bug, are but one of many insect families. And insects comprise one of six

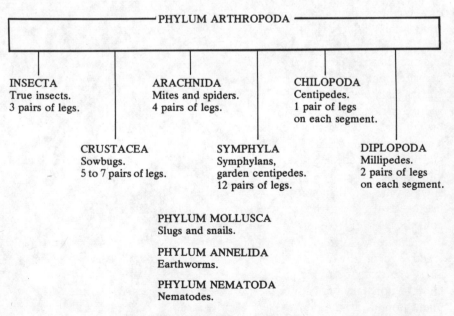

PHYLUM ARTHROPODA

INSECTA
True insects.
3 pairs of legs.

ARACHNIDA
Mites and spiders.
4 pairs of legs.

CHILOPODA
Centipedes.
1 pair of legs
on each segment.

CRUSTACEA
Sowbugs.
5 to 7 pairs of legs.

SYMPHYLA
Symphylans,
garden centipedes.
12 pairs of legs.

DIPLOPODA
Millipedes.
2 pairs of legs
on each segment.

PHYLUM MOLLUSCA
Slugs and snails.

PHYLUM ANNELIDA
Earthworms.

PHYLUM NEMATODA
Nematodes.

10

branches of the phylum Arthropoda: Insecta, Crustacea, Arachnida, Diploda, Chilopoda, and Symphyla.

Carrying this argument against the popular definition of "bug" a bit further, not all little garden animals are arthropods. Nematodes fall under the Nematoda phylum, earthworms are Annelida, and snails and slugs are classified as Gastropoda (or Mollusca). So you can see that calling a nematode a bug is something like calling yourself a wombat.

Given that not all pests are bugs or even insects, it can't be denied that these words are very convenient to use. There just aren't many catch-all terms for the variety of little creatures that live in the garden, and this book resorts now and then to the vernacular. Please pardon our phraseology.

How insects and
their relatives grow.
A curious thing about the way insects grow up is that the important changes usually take place *after* birth, which is not true of ourselves and the other so-called higher animals. After hatching from the egg, it is up to the larva to do most of the insect's growing. In terms of the insect's role in the garden, this means that larvae do a lot of eating. The most voracious feeders you'll run into, whether pests or beneficials, are larvae: the tomato hornworm transforms from a tiny egg into a fat, four-inch food tube in just a few weeks; the funny-looking larva of the ladybug is much hungrier (and more beneficial) than its well-known adult form, and can eat up to 40 aphids in an hour.

It is as a larva that you know most garden pests. Pupae are usually tucked out of sight, eggs are so small as to be nearly invisible, and many adults cause relatively little damage. Most of the control measures in this book are aimed at the larval stage, many of them taking advantage of the fact that larvae are typically soft-skinned, slow, and vulnerable to disease, parasites, and predators. The soft skin is susceptible to the osmotic workings of salt in water, to the tiny daggers of diatomacious earth, and to sharp barriers or mulches. Because most larvae are slow, they can be picked by hand and dropped into a can of water topped with kerosene or stepped on. Successful hand picking requires that you observe plants often and well, as it doesn't take long for larvae to become fully grown and go into hiding as pupae. The vulnerability of larvae to diseases and natural enemies has led to much research of late. The most useful and available pathogens for the gardener are *Bacillus thuringiensis,* milky spore disease, and nuclear polyhedrosis viruses. All work on the larval stage.

The third stage of complete metamorphosis is the pupa, an outwardly inactive form in which the insect develops into an adult. The pupa needs energy to make these big changes, and it coasts on the food stored up as a larva. Pupae are typically secreted away in bark crevices, plant refuse, or underground. In the orchard, a thorough scraping of rough, scaly bark will help to take care of several important pest species. Pupae in plant waste can be disposed of by keeping the garden tidy, particularly after harvest. Cultivation is the age-old means of dispatching underground pupae.

The final stage is the adult, typically a highly mobile form. It is important to their survival that they are good walkers and fliers: they can thus both find a mate quicker and spread their kind far and wide. And while some adults eat enough to be considered pests in their own right, those of many species nibble on nectar and pollen or are even without mouthparts and digestive systems.

Adults reproduce in any of three ways: sexually (involving male and female), parthenogenetically (females alone being responsible for reproduction), and a combination of both in the same species.

All told, the metamorphic process helps enable insects to succeed in a very competitive world. Take eggs, for example. Because they are tiny, fantastic numbers of them can be turned out by a single adult—a queen bumblebee is thought to be able to lay more than a million over its life span—and such numbers enhance a mother's ability to pass on life to a new generation. It figures that, even with egg parasites, predators, cannibalism, and adverse weather, a good number of eggs should still be around to become larvae. This larval stage has a specialized mission, existing only to eat, and the pupal stage launches a mobile adult that spends most of its time mating and looking for good places to stash eggs. Indeed, insects can be formidable enemies.

Incomplete (or simple) metamorphosis involves three stages instead of the four discussed above. The egg hatches into a nymph, which often looks like a scaled-down version of the adult. The adult stage is reached in a series of instars, or molts. There is no resting stage before the last molt.

About the only time insects aren't aggressively bettering their species' chances in the world is when the temperature drops and the food disappears. Factors such as shortening days and changing weather trigger their instinctual process of adjusting to winter. Insects winter in various stages, depending on species and climate. Their metabolic processes slow almost to a standstill in a dormant period known as diapause.

How insects are built.   Mature insects have segmented bodies, made up of head, thorax, and abdomen. Their bodies are tough. While man and the other vertebrates have internal skeletons, insects are held together by a strong exterior skeleton, or exoskeleton. This body wall completely covers the insect, and is often protected by secretions of waxes and other substances that exude from tiny pore canals. The outer layer of the wall is made of chitin (pronounced ky-tin) and presents a formidable barrier to the world: it is insoluble in water, alcohol, and diluted acids and bases, and cannot be broken down by the digestive juices of mammals. Snails, some insects, and certain bacteria can successfully attack chitin, however.

Of all the body parts of an insect, the grower is naturally most concerned with the mouth. The design of mouth largely determines what food the insect will go after—and the source of food determines whether an insect is labeled friend or foe. Mouth parts are either of the chewing or the sucking kind. Chewing insects have mandibles or jaws that move sideways to bite off and chew food. Sucking insects are equipped with a beak through which liquid food is drawn. Chewing mouth parts are considered to be the more primitive of the two.

The thorax bears the agents of locomotion—wings and legs. Pests that crawl or walk can be entangled in sticky barriers, held off by repellent plantings, or hand picked. Plant protection is somewhat more difficult for flying pests; baited traps and fine-mesh netting are typical controls.

Respiration is carried out by an intricate system of minute tubes, or trachea, that connect with openings (spiracles) in the exoskeleton. Circulation is accomplished with a simple tubelike heart. Blood circulates throughout the body cavity, and is not confined to veins. It is without the hemoglobin that serves in higher animals to carry oxygen, and is usually colorless or tinted pale green or yellow. Insect blood takes nutrients to the organs it bathes, and carries waste products away. The heart does not generate much blood pressure; in fact, blood pressure may be less than atmospheric pressure. New adult insects force blood into their wings by swallowing air to increase the pressure within.

Digestion takes place in a tube, often coiled somewhat, that extends from the mouth to the anus. Food matter is absorbed from this tube (known as the alimentary canal) by the blood, and muscles work to suck in food and move matter through the insect. Some insect diseases disable insects by paralyzing this canal.

The size of an insect's brain is relative to the complexity of its behavior. *An Introduction to the Study of Insects,* by Borror and DeLong, gives the ratio of brain volume to total body volume as 1:4200 for a predacious diving beetle, presumably an insect with few tricks, and 1:174 for a bee, an insect known for its complex social behavior.

Insects get by in the world not on strength of intelligence but by instincts and evolution. (Still, they can learn to improve their performance in mazes.) Instincts are automatic responses to stimuli that have survival value; if a behavior pattern works out to an insect's advantage, the insect survives and passes the trait on to its progeny. Evolution enables insects to adapt to changes in their environment. Their numbers are so great that individuals with genetic quirks are being born all the time, and some of these react better to the new situation at hand than the normal insects. These lucky aberrants survive, and pass the valuable quirks on to their progeny. It is this ability to adapt to changes that accounts for insects developing resistance to the most potent chemical pesticides that man can devise.

3
When Plants
Get Sick

Says the venerable USDA 1953 *Yearbook of Agriculture* on plant diseases, "Weather, insects, and plant diseases are the three great natural hazards of crop protection." Growers worry a good deal about the first of these, but can do little to stop the rains or ward off a frost. Insects are little bits of trouble that can be observed in action, and are quite easily identified—and it makes growers comfortable to be able to put a label on a problem. But it's hard to put labels on plant diseases—they are neither observable nor easily identified, much to the frustration of growers. You can see the *results* of a disease plainly enough—yellowing foliage, leaf spots, and so on—but the disease organisms themselves are invisible to the unaided eye. This makes it easy to confuse the effects of a disease with those brought about by insects or weather. For example, "A spotted or yellowed rose does not necessarily mean rose blackspot," says Dr. Cynthia Westcott in the introduction to her *Plant Disease Handbook*. "More than half the specimens sent to me as blackspot are examples of mite injury or spray injury or reaction to weather conditions."

**If you can't see it,
how can you tell what it is?** A simple question, but the answer eludes even such knowledgeable people as Dr. Westcott, a plant pathologist. ". . . It is not expected that anyone, amateur or professional, can read a brief description, look at an unfamiliar disease in the garden, and make a very reliable diagnosis. I certainly cannot. . . .I have written 'water-soaked' or 'reddish brown' too many hundreds of times for different diseases to make such symptoms seem very distinctive."

14

The color illustrations in this book will help you identify some of the more common diseases of the garden and orchard. But it will behoove you to learn a bit about the pathogens, or agents, behind these diseases—viruses, bacteria, fungi, nematodes, and environmental factors—before you attempt your own diagnoses.

Virus diseases.   Viruses are neither organisms nor inanimate molecules, and it's not even for certain whether they are living or non-living. In some ways viruses behave like living organisms, and in other ways like non-living chemicals. They can increase their numbers, but only when in the living cells of the host plant or animal.

Viruses are spread from plant to plant in a number of ways. Bugs often act as vectors, especially aphids, leafhoppers, mealy bugs, and white flies. Aphids are the worst offenders—the green peach aphid can carry more than fifty different plant viruses. Parasitic plants known as dotters pass on viruses through the graft unions they make with their hosts. You, too, can transmit some viruses just by handling plants or brushing them with infected tools. Occasionally, infested soil may be responsible. And because viruses can invade all parts of a plant, a new plant propagated from infected tubers, bulbs, seeds, or scions will usually be infected, too.

Although virus particles can only be seen with the aid of an electron microscope, there are several characteristic symptoms of virus infection to look out for. Typically, yields are small and of poor quality, and some strains can bring a quick death—spotted wilt and curly top on tomato are examples.

The largest group of viruses includes those that cause a yellow and green mottling of leaves, called *mosaic,* and spotting of leaves. Mottling results from chlorosis (the death of chlorophyll in cells) and it may be displayed on stems and blossoms, as well as leaves. Chlorophyll manufactures food for the plant through photosynthesis, and chlorosis therefore leads to stunting and poor yields.

The second group includes those diseases that cause yellowing (called *yellows*), leaf curling (or *leaf curl*), dwarfing, or excessive branching—but little or no mottling or spotting. Yellows and leaf curl block up a plant's vascular system (analogous to our circulatory system), thereby restricting the flow of water and nutrients. The task of identifying a virus is complicated when plants are infected with two or more viruses concurrently; the symptoms of one may be added to those of the other, or a new symptom may evolve.

Methods of control are directed at eliminating one or more of the conditions that enable viruses to spread. Once a plant has been infected, there is little you can do to restore it to health.

Bacterial diseases.   Bacteria are plants, invisibly small ones, that cause trouble when they make their lives in animals and other plants. They lack chlorophyll, and do not benefit from photosynthesis. Some bacteria live only on dead animal or plant remains, and are termed saprophytes. Those that cause disease in living organisms are parasites or pathogens. Many kinds of bacteria can live in either role, and thus plant pathogens are often able to overwinter or maintain themselves between successive crops by living saprophytically on plant refuse.

Each bacterial cell is an independent plant. Some even wiggle little hairs, or flagella, to move about. Although bacteria can't propel themselves very far, they are carried to plants in flowing or splashing water or in transported soil. They can enter a plant through wounds or squeeze through the tiny natural openings in the skin, cuticle. Once inside, bacteria flow with or swim short distances in the tides of sap.

Fortunately for the backyard diagnostician, bacterial diseases are often easily identified by symptoms. *Rots* attack leaves, stems, branches, and tubers; because of a bacterial enzyme that dissolves cell walls, the affected tissue becomes soft, slimy, and malodorous. Soft rots often follow other, less serious, diseases. For example, black rot of cabbage and late blight of potato would be far less serious if it weren't for the subsequent soft rot. Also grouped with rots are necrotic blights and leaf spots, which are areas of dead tissue that sometimes spread to kill leaves.

The second group of bacterial diseases is characterized by *wilting,* caused when pathogens block a plant's vascular system. Such a blockage may lead to such diseases as black rot of cabbage, ring rot of potatoes, and tomato canker.

The third group, *galls,* results from an overgrowth of the affected plant's cells. Problems begin when the galls interfere with the flow of food and water through the vascular system.

Bacterial diseases are generally favored by wet soil, high humidity, and high temperatures. A plant's nutrition may make it susceptible to disease—for example, too much nitrogen in the soil encourages bacterial wilt pathogens—so be sure your plants have the advantage of gradually available nutrients in the form of compost and mulch. Problems can also be avoided by using disease-free seed and resistant varieties, and by crop rotation. If you notice a few wilted plants in the garden or field, remove and destroy them immediately, as bacteria multiply by cell division and their numbers increase very quickly. There's no saving a plant once infected, and susceptible crops should not be returned to the immediate area of infection, as bacteria can lie in the soil for years.

Why hasn't someone come up with a safe, effective spray or dust to fight plant bacteria? Consider the unique power of the enemy: the continued natural selection of millions of little disease organisms makes pathogenicity—the ability to cause disease—possibly the most stable characteristic in nature. In other words, avoid the bacteria rather than cast about for a cure.

Fungi.   Like bacteria, fungi are plants that take their energy entirely from organic matter. Neither has the ability to turn the sun's energy into food, as both are without chlorophyll. If a fungus feeds on live matter, it is classified as parasitic; if the matter is not alive, the fungus is called saprophytic. It is the former that cause you trouble in the garden and orchard; the latter is beneficial, helping to break down wastes in the compost pile.

Fungi that affect plants are known and named for their appearance. *Downy mildew,* also known as false mildew, grows from within a plant and sends branches known as sporangiophores out through the plant's stomata to create pale patches on leaves. True or *powdery mildews* live on the leaf surface. They send hollow tubes into the plant to suck out nutrients. *Rust* fungi are named for the color their pustules impart to leaves. But a rusty area is not necessarily the work of a fungus; weather and spray injury are likely to be the cause. *Leaf spot* fungi cause round, yellow to yellow green spots that darken with time. If you've seen the grayish, downy patches that form on berries that don't get eaten soon enough, you know what *gray mold* looks like. This fungus disease affects many fruits, flowers and vegetables. *Soil-inhabiting fungi* cause damping-off, the dread disease of seedlings, and various root rots.

Conventional chemical sprays and dusts are widely used to fight fungus diseases, but the organic grower can safely rely on sanitation, eradication of diseased plants, and the use of resistant varieties.

Nematode diseases.   Nematodes are classified as pathogens because of the nature of their effect on a plant's health. As defined by Dr. Cynthia Westcott, a disease is caused by the *continuous* irritation of a causal factor, as opposed to an injury, which is of a transitory nature.

Nematodes are simple worm parasites that either stick their heads in a plant to suck the sap or actually spend their lives inside the plant. Control measures involve crop rotation, enriching the soil with humus, and planting pest-free stock.

Environmental diseases.   When gardeners behold a sick looking plant, they tend to jump to the conclusion that a parasitic disease is the agent. But a more probable cause of trouble is a physiological disorder, one that results from a less-than-ideal environment for the plant. Of course weather causes its share of problems; the vagaries of wind, rain, sunlight, and temperature combine to create such conditions as dieback, blasting, leaf scorch, hollow heart, and sunscald.

All too often, the well-intentioned gardener is his own worst enemy. This is especially true of those that use chemical insecticides, herbicides, and fertilizers, as these extremely concentrated substances are easy to misuse. The organic gardener has a built-in advantage—unless chemicals have blown or washed in from elsewhere, there is no need for him to worry about such things as bordeaux injury and copper injury. Some organic gardeners, however, take over land that has been saturated with pesticides and herbicides, and they inherit problems. For them, the soil can be purged with activated charcoal (see the first section of Chapter 8, "Naturally Occurring Predators and Parasites").

Growers are increasingly aware of the effects of polluted air and water on their crops. Ozone, soot, sulfur dioxide, chlorine, and escaping piped gas are as detrimental to plant health as they are to ours, and the symptoms are shown graphically on the greenery of our gardens, lawns, and trees. The cures for environmental diseases are often out of the hands of the individual, but you'll find some helpful suggestions for controlling them under individual entries.

4
"The Most Controversial Of All Organic Claims": Plants Fed Organically Are Less Attractive To Pests

"The most controversial of all organic claims is that plants grown on rich organic soil, without use of chemical fertilizers, and without being sprayed, will not be attacked by insects because insects won't like their taste."

So says Robert Rodale in *Organic Gardening and Farming* magazine. This claim does sound less than credible at first, but seeing is believing, he suggests. "Down through the decades organic gardeners and farmers have made that claim because they saw with their own eyes that plants often enjoyed an almost mysterious immunity to insect attack. Neighboring growers would have to spray several times a season, while organic gardeners and farmers could keep insects well under control by using a few biological controls plus some old-fashioned handpicking of beetles and insect egg clusters."

If you're not already convinced that correct plant feeding discourages bugs and disease, then it's not likely that testimonials from other growers will do the trick, so we will skip these—this *is* one cultural control that must be seen to be believed. Instead, here follows a brief explanation of why organic material feeds plants better than chemicals, and some possible reasons why unsprayed, well-fed plants are bothered less by pests and diseases. You'll also see how some soil amendments work directly to control pests.

The Claim, Part 1:
Organic Soil Grows Healthy Plants

Cheeseburgers
and sky-blue potions.
First of all, it seems that many tenders of domesticated plants and animals are all too readily convinced that our charges need a host of commercial preparations, and plenty of them. An ad now running on television does its best to convince us that for years the family dog has been trying to say through pantomime that he needs egg in his diet. Last year, millions of pet owners were sold the line that dogs, like other members of the family, need cheese in their diets. This same solicitous concern is extended to plants. Manufacturers of chemical fertilizers prey on gardeners' fears—that plants aren't getting enough nutrients, that the soil needs a synthetic boost to produce a good crop. The trouble with this line of reasoning is that man has yet to be able to duplicate in the laboratory the intricate processes that quietly take place underground. Pouring a beaker of sky-blue potion on the ground is little different than giving a dog cheeseburgers: both acts make *you* feel better, easing your concern that you've done the right thing; but neither act satisfies real needs.

If chemical soil potions don't really take the place of soil in feeding plants, just what do they do? Some critics see the role of chemical fertilizers in an insidious light. In *Pay Dirt,* J. I. Rodale refers to these fertilizers as a form of "dope"; Beatrice Trum Hunter uses the term "soil drugs" in *Gardening Without Poisons.* Indeed, feeding a plant with synthetic food is like feeding a person intravenously. In one case the digestive tract is bypassed; in the other, the soil is disregarded, serving only as a chemical reservoir and an anchor for the plants' roots.

The soil, as a living thing,
cannot be reduced to a formula.
It is beguilingly simple to think of the nutritional needs of plants in terms of a series of proportions, such as 5-10-10 or 4-8-4. Such formulas express the amount of nitrogen, phosphorus, and potash, respectively, in a fertilizer mixture, the numbers standing for the percent of each ingredient. Commercial brands promise these nutrients in big doses, and it would seem that plants receiving all those nutrients couldn't help but make it through the season in good shape. The fallacy here is that chemicals dumped on the ground aren't necessarily taken up by plants in the proper amounts. One problem is that the food elements in chemical fertilizers are almost all soluble, while in nature plants are accustomed to getting nutrients from many insoluble sources. Because the chemical fertilizers are so readily available, plants

tend to pick up too much of a nutrient. And too much can be as bad as too little.

It's not always easy to tell just what ails a plant that suffers from an imbalance of a nutrient. Appearances are very deceiving, and plants are slow to manifest the effects of a deficiency. Visual symptoms of nutrient deficiency may appear in any or all organs, including leaves, stems, roots, flowers, fruits, and seeds. A general note to keep in mind is that a deficiency of one element implies excesses of other elements; for example, too much potassium can block a plant's uptake of magnesium.

The consequences of using chemical fertilizers go beyond the garden fence and farmer's hedgerow. Their use is playing havoc with our environment. Environmental scientist Barry Commoner has pointed out that, as a result of our over-emphasis on nitrates and nitrites, these chemicals are leaching off to cause eutrofication and foul drinking water. This over-emphasis is part of the cheeseburger-for-dogs syndrome. Because nitrogenous fertilizer is relatively cheap, farmers put on extra amounts to be sure their crops are getting enough. Ralph E. Carstenseon, president of the Nu-Ag Company in Rochelle, Illinois, says that based on data accumulated through plant tissue tests over a three-year period, Illinois farmers have spent as much as $50 million on fertilizers for corn alone that wasn't really needed. And here's a timely consideration: as we become more acutely aware of energy as a finite resource, the practice of burning up to five tons of coal to produce one ton of nitrogen fertilizer deserves a critical look.

Chemical pesticides don't do
the soil any favors, either.
In a garden fed with humus, manure, and compost, the soil hosts a wide variety of beneficial microflora that quickly chew up and destroy, or keep in dormancy, disease organisms. These tiny bits of underground life include: bacteria, which are generally effective as scavengers and may produce antibiotics; actinomycetes, poor as scavengers but excellent producers of antibiotics; and fungi, valuable as competitors with disease organisms, as hyperparasites, and as antibiotic producers (some fungi that thrive on rich organic soil actually trap nematode worms). But when fumigants are applied to the soil, several deleterious things take place. The populations of some soil organisms, particularly fungi, are greatly lowered, while bacterial groups less affected by the chemicals multiply far beyond those in untreated soil because their antagonists and competitors are killed. Over a number of years, a new soil equilibrium is established, but it's marked by a less diverse microflora than before. Why is this bad? A parallel situation arises in the insect world when a severe control wipes out the delicate balance between species, allowing pests or potential pests to become rampant. There are pests and

potential pests underground, too, invisibly small but ready to come to the fore and cause trouble.

Chemicals can also interfere with nitrification—the conversion by nitrifying bacteria of atmospheric nitrogen into compounds that plants can eventually use. Herbicides such as chlorpropham, amitrole, 2,4-D, diallate, and propanil have all been found to inhibit nitrification, reports J. F. Parr of the Agricultural Research Service in Baton Rouge, Louisiana.

Applications of herbicide can trigger pest outbreaks. David Pimentel and I. N. Oka at Cornell studied how corn treated with increasing amounts of 2,4-D, the herbicide, reacted to insect and blight attack. According to their study in *Environmental Entomology,* the herbicide stimulated pests and increased their numbers as rates of application increased. Corn borer larvae were significantly heavier on treated corn, female moths raised on treated plants were more fertile, and the larvae survived better in treated plots than untreated ones. Corn leaf aphid populations rose from 30 to 80 percent on treated corn—the more herbicide used, the more aphid problems. Southern corn leaf blight produced more and heavier galls on treated corn.

In sum, soils highest in organic matter tend to be "the most suppressive of disease," say Baker and Cook in *Biological Control of Plant Pathogens.* Disease in soil is the exception rather than the rule. Pathogenicity is abnormal and perhaps occurs only when natural biological control is diminished by environmental disturbance, such as the application of certain hard chemicals.

Things you can do
to encourage a healthy soil.   Biological controls and cultural methods rarely wipe out a pathogen, but can reduce its numbers or its ability to produce disease. You can intensify the pathogen's antagonists by one or more of the following methods: using tillage methods that modify soil structure, crumb size, and aeration; rotating crops to lower the density of pathogen inoculum in the soil; adding organic amendments that stimulate antagonists; and using trap and inhibitory plants to reduce injury from nematodes and some fungus pathogens. Here are things you can do to encourage the beneficial organisms in your soil.

• **Tillage.**   Tillage practices that modify the environment so as to favor antagonists can be regarded as methods of biological control. It is well known that a diminished oxygen supply greatly reduces root growth, and the susceptibility of citrus roots to decay increases as aeration decreases. It appears that the no-till method used in conjunction with herbicides decreases soil aeration, while chisel plowing would enhance it. Subsoil tillage (chisel plowing) to break a hardpan at the plow sole reduces fusarium damage by permitting better root penetration.

Plant residues allowed to decay on the soil surface before incorporation in the soil are less susceptible to plant diseases than fresh residue plowed under directly. What's happening here is that when stubble is cut and allowed to lay, it is rapidly invaded by fungi. Then, when incorporated into the soil the vegetal matter cannot be used by pathogens as a food source, since possession is more than nine-tenths of the law in the soil.

• **Rotation.**   The association of microorganisms built up around plant roots is changed drastically when crops are rotated, as each crop has its characteristic microbial association. Thus, crop rotation is also a form of microbial rotation.

Crop rotation is our best method of control for soilborne pathogens of cereals, such as speckled and pink snow molds. Winter fallow works best here. Rotations have proved effective in the control of scab, black scurf, and verticillium wilt of potatoes, particularly when the rotation included two or more years of clover or alfalfa.

• **Trap crops and inhibitory plants.**   Research shows that marigolds inhibit root-knot nematodes; see NEMATODE. Stubby-root nematodes multiply rapidly on tomato roots but do not feed on asparagus roots, and nematode populations on the tomatoes were substantially reduced when the two crops are grown together.

In field trials involving potatoes grown continuously over 13 years, scab was controlled if soybeans were grown as a cover crop and incorporated green into the soil before planting of potatoes. The soybean residue evidently feeds the pathogen's antagonists, which produce antibiotic substances. Bean growers in California's Salinas Valley noticed that fusarium root rot was much less severe or nearly absent if beans were preceded by a crop of barley—evidently barley straw incorporated into the soil immobilized nitrogen needed by the pathogen for growth.

• **Adding organic amendments.**   The early attempts to use practical biological control were through organic amendments: potato scab was controlled by plowing under green rye, phymatotrichum root rot was checked by barnyard manure, and English scientists have controlled potato scab with grass clippings. After six years of tests in Kansas, chicken manure gave perfect control of take-all disease of wheat.

Studies show that when manures and crop residues are incorporated into the soil, the rapidly multiplying beneficial microorganisms cause oxygen to be in temporary short supply. This weakens pathogens, which are overwhelmed by beneficial bacteria and then digested. Some pathogens may germinate because of the added nutrients, but because of the intense microbial activity they are done in by antibiosis and digestion. The wetter the soil amended with manures, the greater percentage of digestion in a given time. Destruction of pathogens seems to be independent of the kind of manure used.

(Farmers take note:) Control of pathogens by adding plant residues to the soil depends critically on the time of planting relative to the time the materials are added. Control is generally best if you plant within a few days after amendment, providing that pathogen spores have had a chance to germinate and be digested and that general microbial activity is still intense. Planting at the time of adding plant residues can result in increased disease. Planting too long after amendment can also result in increased disease because microbial activity will have slowed down and pathogens will be less antagonized. In the case of straw and stubble and green manures, peak control generally lasts up to a month.

The use of cover and legume crops, particularly green legumes when plowed under, has been an especially effective means of control of various plant pathogens. Certain volatile substances released by decaying legume tissue may actually trigger germination of disease spores and at the same time prevent their growth, so that they germinate and are quickly digested by soil microorganisms.

• **Some general benefits.**   Ethylene gas, which can discourage growth of fungus is probably produced by species of anaerobic bacteria that multiply when the furious activity of beneficial organisms working on organic matter reduce the amount of oxygen in the soil. Soils high in organic matter and nitrogen produced more ethylene than was produced by infertile soils. Thus biologically active soils usually produce the greater quantities of ethylene necessary for fungistasis.

Spraying apple leaves with high-nitrogen urea just before leaf fall increases their microbial populations 170-fold, and the intense decaying plus increased activity of earthworms drastically reduces the number of apple scab organisms. It follows that a scab might also be controlled by spraying with liquid manure or manure tea instead of chemical urea.

Mud, because of the numbers of beneficial microorganisms in it, makes an excellent coating for freshly-cut pruning wounds to keep out infection, according to recent research. Pre-soaking pea seeds for 24 hours to remove exuded nutrients favorable to pathogens averted pre-emergence damping-off of seeds when planted in infested soil.

Finally, it's important to note that disease-free soil can often be added to inoculate an area in trouble from soil pathogens.

The Claim, Part 2:
Healthy Plants Resist Pests

Now for the second part of Robert Rodale's claim—that the healthy plants which sprout from organic soil are in some way repellent to bugs.

At first this statement appears to go against logic. Wouldn't a bug choose to pick on healthy plants, just as we instinctively look over the garden to select the most attractive vegetables for a salad?

Apparently not. Bugs and people have dissimilar appetites, as can be seen elsewhere on the homestead. It is the weak, underfed, rough-coated calves—and not the suckling, fat, smooth-coated ones—that are eaten up with lice. A weak, sickly hen in the flock will always carry most of the lice. Trees weakened by drought, leaky gas mains, or loss of roots due to excavation are more heavily attacked by borers than nearby healthy trees of the same kind. Chinch bugs tend to collect and breed more heavily on corn or wheat up on an eroded slope rather than down at the foot of the slope where eroded soil minerals and organic matter pile up to enrich the soil.

Judging by such evidence, bugs and diseases act as censors in nature. And it's all because insects thrive and reproduce better on unbalanced or inferior diets, as we think of them. While we are interested in proteins and minerals in our food, the bugs go for plants having excess carbohydrates. Other plant constituents figure in insect feeding habits, too. In his classic work, *Insect Resistance in Crop Plants,* Reginald Painter has prepared tables that show the relationship between levels of potash, nitrogen, and phosphorus in the soil and the amount of insect injury. High nutrient content *increased* insect damage in some cases, and *decreased* damage in others. It all depends on the particular crop and pest. So, the best way to make plants unattractive to bugs is to be sure that plants get a balance of nutrients, and this can only be brought about with a healthy soil, enriched naturally.

More evidence, from both researcher and casual gardener, is available, but the acid test will take place with your own plants. The following several pages give a crash course in plant nutrition and organic fertilizers. More detailed information can be found in a general book on organic gardening, and the second part of this book gives many specific suggestions for discouraging pests and diseases through correct plant feeding.

• Nitrogen.

The worst error you can make with nitrogen is to give the plants too much. Prof. J. G. Rodriguez of the University of Kentucky reports that "aphids respond positively to increased elements, particularly nitrogen"; in other words, put too much fertilizer on your soil and you will make aphids happier, including the bean, cabbage, cotton, and pea aphids. USDA tests show that spider mites raised on plants supplied with low levels of nitrogen laid an average of 5.4 eggs per day, while those grown on plants with high levels of nitrogen laid 10 eggs per day. And, growers who overdo the nitrogen may find their tomatoes drop blossoms without setting fruit. A balanced feeding program—applying natural fertilizers that make nutrients available *gradually*—will insure against too much stem and foliage growth at the cost of fruiting.

A number of pests are attracted to plants with high levels of amino acids, which can be caused by too much nitrogen in the soil. Professor Albert Schatz of Temple University reports that "whether insects prefer to feed on certain plants may be determined by the kinds and amounts of amino acids in those plants. And the kinds and amounts of amino acids present may, in turn, be determined by the mineral nutrients available to the growing plants. Thus, soil fertility can influence the resistance or susceptibility of plants to attack by insects." Aphids in particular will make tracks for plants high in amino acids.

The answer, as many growers have found out, is to get nitrogen from the gradual decomposition of organic matter. There are several natural processes that get nitrogen into the soil—quiet, unseen activities that make chemical fertilizers redundant.

Composted plant waste, manure, and even lightning supply nitrogen naturally. Many gardeners take advantage of the fact that legumes add nitrogen to the soil. Clovers, alfalfa, soybeans, fava beans, and other bean-type plants lock this element into the soil by the action of the nitrogen-fixing bacteria on their root nodules. In addition, there are other bacteria occurring free in the soil that extract nitrogen from the air.

Along with these tiny bits of life, several larger underground allies are at work in the soil. Earthworms add nitrogen to the garden both by converting unusable forms into usable ones and by contributing the nitrogen contained in their dead bodies. Nematodes, mites, snails, millipedes, centipedes, and others help too. Their excretia and dead bodies enrich the soil with nitrogen proteins. Although it's been said earlier, it's worthwhile repeating that pesticides and concentrated chemical fertilizers can make life hard or impossible for these soil creatures.

• **Phosphorus.**   Phosphorus has been called the "master key to agriculture" because low crop production is due more often to a lack of this element than any other plant nutrient. How can you tell if your plants need more phosphorus? Deficiencies are expressed somewhat differently in different plants: in corn and small grains the leaves assume purplish tints; legumes become bluish green and are stunted in growth; but in most plants the leaves become dark green with a tendency to develop reddish and purple colors. Too much or too little of this element can cause marked changes in pest behavior. The egg production of spider mites is encouraged by an imbalance, according to Dr. Floyd Smith of the USDA, and phosphorus deficiency can lead to problems with white flies both outdoors and in potting mixtures.

To give your plants just the amount of phosphorus they can handle, add it to the soil in the form of rock phosphate, a natural rock product containing 30 to 50 percent phosphorus. When the rock is finely ground, the phosphate is available to the plant as it is needed. Rock phosphate is especially effective in soils which have organic matter. Other phosphorus sources include basic slag, bone meal, dried blood, cottonseed and soybean meal, and activated sludge.

• **Magnesium.**   Imbalances of magnesium are increasingly causing problems for growers. The most common symptoms of deficiency include a yellowing, bronzing, reddening, and death of the older leaves, commonly followed by shedding of the leaves. Mites thrive under such conditions. Even though soil tests may indicate available magnesium in your soil, too much potassium can block the uptake of this element. This problem is often brought about by the use of commercial chemical fertilizers, which are high in potassium and usually lacking altogether in magnesium. In a good organic garden, the situation is not likely to arise, as these two nutrients are supplied as natural rock powders whose nutrients are made available to plants slowly, over a period of years.

• **Other important elements.**   Here briefly are the deficiency symptoms of several other important nutrient elements: A *sulphur* deficiency is indicated by yellowing of the younger leaves in the initial stages of the deficiency and finally by yellowing of all the leaves. (The yellowing of leaves is commonly referred to as *chlorosis*.) *Iron* deficiency is revealed by the chlorosis of the new leaves at the growing tips of the plant. A deficiency of *manganese* leads to chlorosis of the young leaves, as in iron deficiency, followed by an early death of the leaves; most manganese deficiencies occur in neutral or alkaline soils.

The principal symptom of *copper* deficiency is wither-tip, in which the leaves at the stem tip wilt without recovering overnight or during cloudy weather. *Zinc* deficiency, which is often caused by the use of chemical superphosphate, is revealed in a variety of ways, such as yellowing between the veins followed by the dying of the tissue in tobacco, little-leaf in pecans and citrus trees, and leaf spot in sugar bean and potato. Common symptoms of *boron* deficiency are the dying of the growing tip of plant stems, internal cork in apples, water-soaked areas and bitter taste of cauliflower, and cracked leaf stalk in celery.

Some Organic Fertilizers And Mulches

Here are descriptions of some organic soil-builders—what they are, where you can find them, and how to use them. Unless otherwise noted, these fertilizers can be worked into the soil in spring or fall, top-dressed around growing plants, added to the compost heap, or used as mulch.

How can you tell what your soil needs, without relying on dying plants to signal the problem? A soil test will tell you just what nutrients you have and have not. You can send a sample of your soil to a laboratory or agricultural extension service at your state college, or you can buy a testing kit and make many of the necessary tests yourself.

You might try making up your own fertilizer formulas—many organic growers have benefitted from experimentation—but don't get hung up on percentages. You can take some assurance in knowing that nearly all of the nitrogen and sulfur, and more than one-third of the phosphorus that become usable for plant use, are supplied by organic matter. Many other nutrients are present in organic matter, too.

• Aluminum foil.   This unlikely mulching material serves three purposes: it retains moisture in the ground, reflects an extra dose of light onto plants, and repels aphids. The repellent quality was studied by the American Rose Foundation, which made several discoveries. When aphids take off to fly, they head directly toward the sky, and when they decide to land again, they reverse their direction *away* from the sky. It is believed that the reflection of the sky on aluminum foil confuses the insects into constantly reversing their direction, and they never land on plants.

These tests also showed that aluminum is most effective for only the first foot or so of space above the ground. Controlling pests on tall roses may require structures to hold the foil well above the ground.

All types of aluminum foil can be used for insect control but a special paper-backed kind, sold in many lumber yards as insulation material, will do the best job of mulching directly on the ground.

Remember that aluminum, plastic, and similar inorganic materials do not add any humus to the soil, and success with these should not tempt you to do away with a regular program of incorporating organic matter.

• Blood meal and dried blood.   Although the plants in your garden aren't likely carnivores, they will benefit from sparing applications of these slaughterhouse by-products. Blood meal and dried blood contain 15 and 12 percent nitrogen respectively, and 1.3 and 3 percent phosphorus. Blood meal also assays at 0.7 percent potash. These materials can be used either directly in the ground or added to the compost pile. They should be used sparingly because of high nitrogen content—a sprinkling is enough to stimulate bacterial growth. Both are excellent for breaking down green fibrous matter in the compost pile. An added benefit is that deer will stay clear of gardens and orchards fertilized with blood meal or dried blood.

• Bone meal.   Years ago, mountains of buffalo bones were collected from the Western Plains for use as fertilizer; nowadays the main source is the slaughterhouse. Bones aren't all alike, and bone meal differs too—phosphorus and nitrogen content depends mostly on the kind and age of the bone. Raw bone meal has between 2 and 4 percent nitrogen, and 22 to 25 percent phosphoric acid. The fatty materials in raw bone meal somewhat delay its breakdown in the soil, and steamed bone meal (the most commonly used form) is made from green bones that have been boiled or steamed at high pressure to remove the fat. The steamed bones are easily ground into meal and are usually in better condition for mixing with the soil. Steamed meal contains between 1 and 2 percent nitrogen and up to 30 percent phosphorus. It is available in hardware stores, local nurseries, and wherever garden products are sold. You can also buy bone black or charred bone, which have a nutrient content similar to that of steamed bone meal.

Bone meal is most effective when used with other organic materials. It generally acts more quickly when applied to well-aerated soils, and works to counteract soil acidity. Gardeners report that freshly cut seed potatoes will have little trouble with potato bugs when rolled around in bone meal so that a little adheres to the damp cuts. Others have found that bone meal can serve as an insect repellent; sprinkle handfuls of it in borders and between plants to chase aphid-carrying ants from the lawn, flower beds, and garden.

• **Compost.**   Probably the best organic fertilizer, compost can include any or all of the other materials listed here. Leaves, grass, vegetable debris, waste paper, table scraps, manure and a good number of other possible ingredients all combine to make this an excellent fertilizer for flower beds, orchard, garden, trees, and ornamentals. The ingredients will decompose naturally, so there's no need to add lye or other chemicals. To speed the process up, you can add materials high in nitrogen and protein such as dried blood, bone meal, and manure. Avoid putting fat or meat in the compost pile, as they don't break down very well; soapy water is of no benefit, either. And if young children play anywhere near the areas to be composted, don't empty the cat box on the compost pile— a dangerously toxic by-product may be formed.

Aside from these cautions and limitations, just about any organic odds and ends will do. It's a good idea to shred materials before adding them to the pile, using either a rotary mower or a compost shredder. Generally, compost should be applied about a month before planting. If the mixture has evolved only to a half-finished state that is still quite fibrous, you can still use it right away or apply it in fall so that it will decompose sufficiently by planting time. If the compost is ready in fall and won't be used until spring, cover it and store in a protected place. If the finished material is to be kept for long periods during summer, water it from time to time.

In the garden, compost should be applied freely, from one to three inches thick a year. Flower beds need just a scattering. In the orchard, cultivate between the trunk and the drip line, and then work in a bushel of compost per tree; trees that bear heavily may be able to use more than this allotment. Shrubs and ornamentals are usually composted according to their size.

The physical condition of the soil has an important bearing on the prevention and control of diseases, and compost is the most important contribution you can make to your soil: a healthy dose of compost will keep tomatoes relatively free from blight and rots; fruit trees seem to become more resistant to disease when well fertilized with compost; and sowing seeds in a mixture of half compost and half sand will discourage damping-off of young seedlings. Tests conducted at the Connecticut Agricultural Experiment Station showed that root rot fungus had a relatively short existence in soil with a high organic matter content because of organisms which produce antibiotic substances.

The heat of a compost pile can be sufficient to kill weed seeds, grubs, and diseases on discarded vegetable matter, but the pile must be turned several times so that plants near the surface get a chance on the inside where peak heat is generated. It is all right to compost most diseased vegetable matter. For example, composting cotton plant residues following ginning operations destroys the verticillium wilt organisms and eliminates the disease as a possible source of infection in the next year's crop, according to tests at New Mexico State University. The experiment, described in the USDA publication *The Plant Disease Reporter*, indicated that temperatures developing in the compost piles (up to 155° F.) killed the wilt organisms in the gin trash.

Wireworms don't like composted soil, as organisms in the compost give the pests a hard time.

Because compost contains so many elements in proper amounts, it gives growers insurance against diseases prompted by any of several deficiencies. Take dieback, for example. This disease has been attributed to copper and potassium deficiencies, too much fertilizer, acidity, and so on. When properly made compost is used regularly, these problems are all alleviated.

Compost also tends to balance soil that is too acid or alkaline since it itself is generally neutral. This is important because, if bound up in too much acid, nutrients cannot reach a plant. The optimum pH level for purposes of nutrition is between 6.0 and 8.0. Counter an overly acid soil by adding ground or crushed dolomite limestone (not burnt lime), wood ashes, or ground oyster shells to the compost pile. Alkaline soil will be improved with compost buffered by acid material, such as leaf mold, pine needles, or acid peat. (It is notable here that well-fed plants can tolerate a wider range of pH.) If you can't arrange to have a compost bin or heap, these additives can be mixed right in with the soil around the plants in need.

There is evidence to suggest that some plants fertilized with their own composted residues may eventually become strong enough to resist disease. Some gardeners have found this to be true of black rot on grapes. They compost infected clusters of mummified fruit and then apply the decomposed material around the base of vines, digging some into the soil. Though not universally applicable, the principal behind this practice is valid: grape tissue is known to be able to build up resistance to disease in much the same way the human body does.

• **Cottonseed meal.**   This meal is made from cotton seed that has been freed from lints and hulls and then deprived of oils. Its low pH makes it especially valuable for acid-loving crops. Cottonseed meal analyzes seven percent nitrogen, and two or three percent potash. It is available commercially.

• **Granite dust.**   This is another excellent source of potash, containing an average of 3 to 5 percent (up to a content of 11 percent from one Massachusetts quarry). Granite dust is also rich in potassium. Commercially processed "fortified" granite dusts are now widely available, sold as complete natural soil conditioners. The added ingredients may include chicken droppings, fish meal, castor pomace, blood meal, greensand, or any of several other fertilizers.

Julius Hensel, the German chemist credited with discovering the value of granite meal as a soil conditioner and fertilizer back around the 1890's, noted that continued applications of "artificial manures," or chemical fertilizer, tended to go along with declining yields and increasing parasite infestations. He reasoned that the chemicals were failing to replace essential nutrients and were probably promoting parasites that flourish upon impoverished and sickly plant structures. He saw these parasites as scavengers evolved by nature to dispose of unfit organisms. He made his own fertilizer by grinding and stamping granite into a very fine dust and then mixing in three parts of lime and two parts gypsum to ten parts of granite dust. After applying this blend to his garden, he achieved spectacular yields.

• **Grass clippings.**   Because they're fairly rich in nitrogen, grass clippings are useful as a green manure to be worked into the soil, for adding to compost heaps, or for mulching. Most lawns produce over one pound of nitrogen and two pounds of potash for every hundred pounds of clippings in the dry state.

• **Greensand.**   This interesting mineral fertilizer comes from deposits laid down in what was once the ocean; at one time in short supply, it is now mined in New York, New Jersey, Maryland, and Ohio. Greensand contains more potash than granite dust—six or seven percent, as compared with from three to five. Because it's an undersea deposit, it contains most if not all of the elements occurring in the ocean; some of the major constituents are silica, iron oxide, magnesia, lime, and phosphoric acid.

Greensand does a good job of absorbing and holding water, won't burn plants, and is especially valuable in conditioning sandy and hard soils. It stays put better than rock powders, and you can spread some around plants as a sort of combined mulch and compost.

• **Herbs.** Any plant with repellent qualities, including herbs, peppers, and members of the allium family, can lend its repellency to a mulch.

• **Leaf mold.** To make this nitrogen-rich (up to five percent) fertilizer, shred the leaves if possible and compost them in a container made from wood, stone, or snow-fencing. Keep the leaves damp and apply limestone to offset acidity, unless you plan to use the leaf mold around acid-tolerant plants only. Leaf mold from deciduous trees has been found to be somewhat richer in potash and phosphorus than that made from conifers.

• **Leaves.** Just plain old leaves can work as a fertilizer; they are an excellent source of humus and mineral material, including calcium, magnesium, nitrogen, phosphorus, and potassium. Leaves, especially acid maple leaves and pine needles, are best used around acid-loving plants such as azaleas, rhododendrons, and hollies. (The leaves of a few trees, the sugar maple for one, are alkaline.) Leaves may be applied directly to the soil, decomposed in a leaf mold container or compost pile, or laid down as mulch. Some small-landowners find that a shredder is a very wise investment, while others make do with a power lawn mower. A mulch of oak leaves serves to control cabbage maggots on cabbage, radishes, and turnips. One upstate New York family found that leaf compost resulted in a virtually disease-free vegetable garden, and they had less trouble with bean beetles, too.

• **Limestone.** Several common plant diseases—including potato scab, beet rot, tobacco, tomato, and cotton wilts—thrive in acid soil and are consequently reduced by the alkalinizing action of limestone. The microorganisms that produce penicillin, streptomycin, and other soil antibiotics, which in turn kill or make harmless the microbes causing these diseases, must have calcium and magnesium to do their work. Liming acid soils supplies these nutrients, and therefore increases production of the antibiotic-producing microbes. Besides working to increase the fertility of the soil, crushed limestone can be built up around tree trunks to act as a shield against the tiny, sharp teeth of pine and meadow mice. Snails and slugs won't cross a line of lime.

• **Manure, dried.** Manure in this form is available at just about every fertilizer store. Pulverized manure of sheep, goats, and cattle have about 1 to 2 N, 1 to 2 P, and 2 to 3 K, while poultry manure analyzes 5 N, 2 to 3 P, and 1 to 2 K.

• **Manure, fresh.** This has been a basic fertilizer for many centuries. Horse, hen, sheep, and rabbit manures are considered *hot* manures because of their relatively high nitrogen content; rabbit manure, for example, analyzes 2.4 N, 1.4 P, and 0.6 K. Because of all that nitrogen, it's best to allow these manures to decompose into compost before applying them directly to plants. Cow and hog manures are relatively low in nitrogen, and are called *cold* manures.

Animal manures make things grow in the garden because they stimulate and release a lot of energy in the soil. They have been called the keystone of the compost program. If you don't have livestock on your place, you may be able to get manure from a local dairyman, egg farmer, or riding stable.

A South Dakota gardener, Charles P. Shryock, found a fringe benefit from using manure. His letter to *Organic Gardening and Farming* is worth repeating. "I found a way to keep bugs off my garden quite by accident. I was having a bad time with beetles and aphids. My cukes, melons and beans were not doing well, but as I had baby ducks, I didn't want to use poison.

"I have rabbits, so one day when I cleaned out the pens, I took the manure and put it between the rows in my garden. The plants really perked up, the bugs disappeared, and the manure didn't burn the plants.

"I figured that maybe it was the ammonia in the rabbit manure that drove the bugs away. I really don't know what it was, but it worked. Since then whenever I clean the rabbit pens, all the droppings go right into the garden. In winter I put it into sacks to dry and spread it on the garden come spring."

Manure is just a bit too rich for some applications. Fire blight, the dread disease of pears, is encouraged by manure mulch or liquid fertilizers that would cause rapid or late growth.

• **Mulches.** It has long been recognized that mulches are highly beneficial to plants because they help maintain uniform soil temperature: root systems stay cool and moist during the summer, and are protected from cold during the winter.

Research suggests mulches also serve to discourage diseases and pests by producing antibiotic agents that are picked up by a plant's root system (a process described earlier in this chapter). Heavy mulching reduces root-knot injury caused by nematodes. Organic farming pioneer Sir Albert Howard described a case in which nematodes were wiped out by one application. But it is the physical make-up of mulch that is most beneficial. A thick layer will help prevent black spot of roses, a disease spread by splashing water. Mulching can save the season for tomato growers plagued by blight, a viral disease that is signaled by yellow brown, curling leaves. The mulch's function here is apparently keeping the roots cool and moist. For detailed descriptions of special mulches for tomatoes, see TOMATO in the second part of this book.

Strawberry growers will find that mixing cedar and lime into a hay mulch discourages the emergence of many young pests. Spittle bugs in particular can be dealt with by mulching strawberries with straw, instead of hay, as is customary. Grasshoppers are stopped by a layer of mulch— hatching hoppers have a hard time making it into the world from their eggs.

Many troublesome weeds such as morning glory, thistle, and quack grass can be controlled by covering the entire area with a smother mulch made of organic matter and waste paper. This generally works well, but may be impractical in small gardens as the treated area must lie idle for a time.

Although it adds no nutrients to the soil, aluminum foil is used as a mulch material to discourage aphids and conserve soil moisture.

While it might seem at first that trees are just too tall to benefit from the pest repellent powers of mulch, many orchardists have found mulching invaluable in producing a presentable crop. To make the most of mulching, you should first weed the ground underneath the tree, to a foot or two beyond the drip-line of the branches. Then give the soil a good liming; this is especially helpful if chemical fertilizers have been used, as the soil will be quite acid.

Next, spade the compost into the top two or three inches of soil. Start a foot away from the trunk, as there are no feeding roots that close, and cover the cleared area. Finally, lay on straw to retain moisture and block light from any insurgent weeds.

Mulch can even serve to lure pests away from the crops above. Ruby M. Morris of Ames, Iowa, learned that oat hulls from a nearby feed mill made an excellent mulch for rabbit-prone raspberries—the rabbits prefer oats to raspberries. "In short order, we finished mulching our entire raspberry patch with 8 to 12 inches of these versatile oat hulls, in which there was apparently enough seed left to satisfy the chomping rabbits. The bushes stayed very much intact, with no evidence of rabbit damage. Now each time we wander out, it's pleasant to find the birds searching for their daily quota of the seed remaining in the chaff."

• **Newspaper and magazine paper.**   Newspaper serves both as a soil-builder and animal-repellent. It is mostly composed of wood cellulose, a natural product of the forests. Repeated use on the garden will tend to make the soil acid, and you should keep a record of soil acidity and apply lime at suitable intervals. Added nitrogen in the form of blood meal assists decomposition of newsprint, and blood meal serves as an animal repellent in its own right.

Two Harvard University biologists, Carroll Williams and Karel Slama, found that a hormone in American newspapers, magazines, and other paper products can be used to prevent certain insects from reaching the stage of development at which they can reproduce. The source of the hormone has been traced to the balsam fir. And in Louisiana, grower R. Batty found that a ½-inch layer of newspapers somehow prevented root-knots on his okra crops.

• **Peat moss.** Though it doesn't contain any nutrients, peat moss serves to aerate the soil and improve drainage, and ultimately helps plants absorb nutrients from other materials. It is made up of the partially decomposed remains of plants that have accumulated over the centuries in relatively airless conditions. Established lawns can be top-dressed with a ½-inch layer of peat moss twice a year, and an inch or more can be spread and worked into vegetable gardens and flower beds. Not everyone agrees that this is a valuable planting medium; some gardeners, Ruth Stout among them, have suggested that peat moss isn't worth the money.

• **Phosphate rock.** This is the commercial term for a rock containing one or more phosphate minerals of sufficient grade and suitable composition for use as fertilizer. It is often recommended as an antidote to onion rot and other underground diseases. Calcium phosphate is the most common of these minerals; the term also includes phosphatized limestones, sandstones, shales, and igneous rocks. Phosphate rock ranges from 28 to 39 percent phosphoric acid. *Colloidal phosphate* is a finely divided type of rock phosphate with an application rate about 50 percent higher than that of rock phosphate.

Tennessee orchardist H. L. Rushing highly recommends a rock dust mixture as a means to worm-free apples, even from trees that have been poor producers. This mixture is made up of one part ground limestone, two parts phosphate rock, three parts granite dust, three parts cottonseed meal, and four bushels of compost. Rushing applies one pound for each foot of the tree's drip-line diameter.

• **Sawdust.** This mulch material is often applied in a one-inch layer around plants that are about two inches high. Prior to spreading the sawdust, many gardeners side-dress with a nitrogen fertilizer such as cottonseed meal, blood meal, or tankage. You should use well-rotted sawdust only, as raw, pale-colored sawdust will mat and cake, thereby preventing proper penetration of rainwater.

A sawdust mulch can keep down the weeds in your vegetable garden, too. In most instances, a one-inch layer applied when vegetable plants are three to four inches tall will be enough to eliminate most of the need for cultivation, besides conserving soil moisture. Sawdust also can be used to a five- to six-inch band over rows after seeding to prevent soil crusting, but cultivation will be needed to control weeds between rows. A good supply of organic matter in your soil, or some nitrogen-rich materials like cottonseed or soybean meal, dried blood, or bone meal, will prevent the nitrogen shortage which sometimes develops while the sawdust mulch decomposes.

Sawdust is especially useful as a mulch for strawberries because of its acidic nature. By holding each plant's leaves and berry-producing stems in one hand, the mulch can be worked in and around the plants with the other hand. This layer also serves to hold the growing berries off the ground, and you'll find that the harvest is cleaner and damaged little by slugs.

• **Seaweed and kelp.**   Many seaweed users apply the stuff fresh from the sea, while others prefer to wash the salt off first. In either case, seaweed is high in potash and trace elements. It can be used as a mulch, worked directly into the soil, or placed in the compost heap. Dehydrated seaweed and liquid preparations are available commercially.

• **Sludge.**   Sludge is processed in two ways. *Activated sludge* is produced by agitating sewage with air bubbles. Bacterial action coagulates the organic matter, which settles out to leave a clear liquid. The nitrogen content of the product is between five and six percent, with from three to six percent phosphorus. Its value as plant food is similar to that of cottonseed meal, a highly recommended fertilizer.

Digested sludge settles out of sewage that is not agitated and has about the same fertilizer value as barnyard manure—two percent of both nitrogen and phosphorus. It often has an offensive odor that persists for some time if it is put on the ground in cool weather. Dr. Myron Anderson of the Agricultural Research Service suggests that the odor from digested sludges may be eliminated by storage in a heap during warm weather.

Sludge brings excellent results when applied to lawns, around trees, ornamentals, flower beds, and gardens. It's a first-rate compost ingredient, as well. To get some for use on your soil, call up your city hall or local sewage treatment plant. Many plants will deliver truckloads at a nominal charge, and you might even consider renting a truck and doing your own hauling.

• **Tankage.**   Meat tankage consists of waste processed into a meal which contains ten percent nitrogen and up to three percent phosphorus. Bone tankage has the same ratings.

• **Vinegar.** Flower gardeners have benefited from adding a little vinegar to flowers that like an acid soil, such as azaleas. Add two table-spoons to a quart of water and irrigate your plants with the mixture. Because it's acid in nature, vinegar helps keep cut flowers longer by preventing spoilage caused by fungi and bacteria.

• **Wood ashes.** This is a good alkaline fertilizer, containing 1.5 percent phosphorus and seven or more percent potash. If left unprotected in the rain, wood ashes will lose much of this potash.

Wood ashes can be mixed with other fertilizers, side-dressed around growing plants, or used as mulch. For best results, apply five to ten pounds per 100 square feet. Be sure that the freshly spread ashes don't come in contact with germinating seeds or sensitive new plant roots. By spreading a circle of wood ashes around the base of plants and then soaking the area, you can control maggots, cutworms, cucumber beetles, squash borers, red spiders, potato bugs, and slugs.

• **Wood chips.** In addition to doing a fine job of aerating soil and increasing its moisture-holding ability, wood chips have a higher nutrient content than sawdust.

A number of other soil-builders deserve your consideration: hoof and horn meal, dry fish scraps, feathers, brewery and cannery wastes, castor pomace, hay and straw, tobacco stems, lobster shells, molasses residue, and last but certainly not least, garbage.

According to Prof. L. F. Johnson of the Plant Pathology Department at the University of Tennessee, mixing mature dried crop residues with nematode-infested soil will reduce plant damage. In one test, certain crop residues, such as oat straw, clover, tomato stalks, and lespedeza hay, gave better control than sawdust and peat moss. A 95 percent reduction in number of galls per plant was obtained when oat straw was added at a rate of ten tons per acre.

Some materials may introduce pest problems of their own. One gardener, the wife of a fisherman, made good use of the fish heads and innards in the raspberry patch, but pets kept digging up the scraps. She countered by sprinkling the ground over the scraps with pepper, and hasn't had any pet trouble since.

One type of organic waste deserves some caution, as Alabama grower Frank Praner can attest. He came by a big sack of commercial broiler mash and added a thin layer of the stuff to the mulch around the fig trees in his orchard. "That night it rained a little. Next day the leaves on the fig trees started to curl. The reason puzzled me. On the third day, I placed my hand on the broiler mash below the trees and to my surprise it was very hot to the touch. By then the fig trees were all shriveled up and dead."

How proper soil moisture
can put off the bugs.   "With many plant-insect relationships, either an excess or a deficiency of soil moisture may cause the plant to tend toward susceptibility to the insects. . . ." So says Reginald H. Painter in *Insect Resistance in Crop Plants*. It appears that insects which feed by sucking plant juices are most affected, probably because available soil moisture changes the osmotic pressure in their food.

Prof. Rodriguez of the University of Kentucky explains the susceptibility another way. During dry spells, he says, some plants take up nitrates much more quickly than the drought-stricken foliage can reduce it. The imbalance can attract mites, which develop in high numbers in orchards and fields under drought conditions. In either case, organic methods are a big help; ample humus in the soil is one of the best protections against drought short of an irrigation system, acting as a perfect reservoir to balance out soil moisture reserves. Humus soaks up moisture during rains, and then meters it out slowly in dry spells.

Another benefit of using organic matter to increase soil moisture is that ants will find life unpleasant below ground, and ants are the agents behind much aphid damage. Many physiological problems will clear up, too. Blossom end rot of tomatoes is brought on by insufficient soil moisture, and one recommended remedy is to mulch the plants. If adequate moisture is not available in the soil, the plants will remove water from the tips of the fruit, bringing on the end rot.

5
Protecting Plants With Other Plants

An important, and interesting, facet of cultural control involves staying bugs and disease by growing certain plants next to each other. There are four different practices: *companion planting,* whereby crops are in happy combinations as learned by observation; *mixed cropping,* valuable because plant diversity has been found to foster a healthful mix of insect life; *repellent planting,* which makes use of odorous plants that keep insects away from neighboring crops; and *trap cropping,* using plants that are attractive to pests to lure them from valued crops.

Companion Planting

While the mechanics of repellent planting and mixed cropping aren't all that mysterious, the various benefits claimed by practitioners of companion planting aren't all that easy to explain. Seemingly innocuous combinations of plantings produce crops that not only grow better, but that are relatively free from insects and diseases as well. Many gardeners who follow this method just accept that it does work, without trying to come up with the reasons why. Some see companion planting as the product of witchcraft and wishful thinking.

But it's likely that companion planting is based on something more mundane than alchemy. The protection may be due to the increased health of vegetables growing near their friends (see the list of these friends, below). Insects typically pass by healthy plants (read Chapter 4, "The Most Controversial of All Organic Claims," if you don't believe this), preferring to pick on weak or sick plants. Why are companionate plantings healthier? Perhaps because the plants make complementary demands on the environment. For instance, the compatibility of celery and leek can be traced to the upright-growing leek enjoying the room and light near the bushy celery plant. Or, the roots of two friendly plants may occupy different strata of the soil, as do swiss chard and beans. Lettuce and kohlrabi get along well because the lettuce is harvested about the time the kohlrabi comes to need all the space in the row.

Unbeknown to the casual observer, the root exudates of a plant can affect the well being of its neighbors. Marigolds put off a substance that keeps nematodes at bay, and interplanting the flower with susceptible crops will show positive results over a year or two. Mustard oil released from the roots of mustard family members will sweeten an acid soil, helping out adjacent plants that suffer when the pH is too low. The secretions also inhibit the hatching of potato nematode cysts. Root exudates of some asparagus varieties resist nematodes. The roots of both oats and flax excrete compounds that inhibit the growth of some harmful soil fungi. Many deep-rooted plants, including certain weeds, have the ability to bring towards the surface many essential minerals, making them available to their neighbors. This is important to plant protection because plants with deficiencies are especially prone to disease and insect feeding. Associations like these can strengthen the vegetables, giving you better taste, better nutrition, and less insect damage.

When planting a companion garden, it's good to get the companions right in there together. One way is to plant zig-zag rows, with the zigs and zags of the beets and onions tucked into one another. Another method is to use the techniques of intercropping, and plant several companions in the same row. You'll find that your companionate garden breaks down into loosely defined sections. The corn, squash, cucumbers, pumpkins, etc. might be in one section. The strawberries, spinach, beans, etc. might be in another. It's best to place paths between these sections rather than between companions. Plant herbs in borders, and scattered throughout the garden.

Mixed Cropping

Take a walk along a hedgerow or through a patch of woods, and you'll notice a great variety of plant life standing branch to branch, likely more kinds than you can name. Why the fraternity of different species? Certainly not to please the bugs. In nature, as in the garden, plants have a better chance of survival if they are surrounded by plants of various species. Plants in a monoculture—for example a Midwestern field of corn—are more susceptible to their enemies. University of Chicago graduate student Helen S. Raizen suggests some reasons why an interplanted garden will do better. For one, many insects find their food through chemicals produced by their host plant, and it stands to reason that if plants of the same species are clustered together, the chemical signal will be much stronger. Therefore, more insects home in on your crops. It also figures that an insect finds it easier to track down one host plant after another if all are grown close together in neat rows.

Companion planting wouldn't work if insects weren't selective about what they eat. If all crops tasted equally good, aphids wouldn't be deterred by a wall of chives, and they'd just eat their placid way to maturity. Luckily, plants have evolved a chemical defense against bugs, producing substances detrimental to them. Some plants have been found to produce insect hormones that either cause developmental abnormalities or prevent metamorphosis into adults.

But nothing is static in nature, and bugs evolved sensory mechanisms to detect and avoid plants with defenses. Others developed metabolic mechanisms to cope with the poisons. For example, several tobacco pests rapidly excrete poisonous nicotine so that toxins do not build up within their bodies. Another pest, the tobacco wireworm, renders nicotine safe by transforming it into a relatively non-toxic alkaloid through the action of an enzyme. (In line with this last defense method, a study has shown that caterpillars eating a wide variety of plants had a hundred times as much of this enzyme activity as specialized feeders.) A third means of metabolic adaptation involves storing the poison as is within the insect's body. The handsome monarch butterfly stashes away the heart poisons manufactured by one of its important hosts, milkweed. Storing up toxic substances has an important side-benefit for the monarch, making it very unpopular among lepidoptera predators. The very distinctive wing coloration emphasizes the monarch's bad reputation—so effectively, in fact, that the entirely edible viceroy butterfly can successfully mimic its coloration and avoid being eaten.

While it's true that some bugs have learned to get around the defenses of some plants (in fact some bugs are even attracted by the protective chemicals), there is no single bug that will eat everything on your property. Aphids and the Japanese beetle may come close, but the limited appetites of most insects make them good subjects for companion planting.

In sum, a good mix of plants encourages a healthful variety of bug life. The principal mechanism at work here, say van den Bosch and Messenger in *Biological Control,* "is the perpetuation of natural controls, such as predators and parasites, which act as mortality agents for many plant pests." Whether mixed plantings involve garden rows or alternating fields of susceptible and non-susceptible crops, the effect is the same.

Beneficial insects typically need alternate hosts between surges of the pest you may have in mind, and if you arrange to have several different plants growing nearby, you'll have good bugs on hand in case of trouble.

Repellent Planting

While it may seem to the beleaguered grower that bugs are crawling over everything in the garden, chances are that a few plants are having no trouble at all. Garlic, marigolds, and mints are known for their built-in repulsiveness to bugs, and a number of other plants have this fortunate trait, too.

As many organic growers have seen for themselves, repellent plants bestow some protection on nearby crops, up to a distance of about three feet. While some turn off a whole variety of insects, others are effective against a particular pest: garlic is offensive to most insects you'll come across, but the herb borage is noted for repelling one, the tomato hornworm. The table below shows which plants bother which bugs. If a bug has been troubling you season after season, check to see if there is a protective plant that could be at work against it in your garden.

Repellent Plantings: Here's a list of more than thirty common pests of garden and orchard and the plants they can't stand.

Ants (and the aphids they carry)	Pennyroyal, spearmint, southernwood, tansy
Aphids	The above, as well as: garlic, chives, and other alliums; coriander; anise; nasturtium and petunia around fruit trees
Asparagus beetle	Tomato
Borer	Garlic, tansy, and onion
Cabbage maggot	Planted in adjacent rows: mint, tomato, rosemary, hemp (illegal just about everywhere), sage
Cabbage moth	Mint, hyssop, rosemary, southernwood, thyme, sage, hemp (look out for nosey neighbors), wormwood, celery, catnip, nasturtium
Carrot fly	Rosemary, sage, wormwood, black salsify, various alliums, coriander
Chinch bug	Soy beans

Colorado potato beetle	Green beans, horseradish, dead nettle, flax
Cucumber beetle (spotted and striped)	Tansy, radish
Cutworm	Tansy
Eelworm (*see* Nematode)	Marigold (French and African)
Flea beetle	Wormwood, mint, catnip; interplant cole crops with tomatoes
Fruit tree moth	Southernwood
Gopher	Castor bean
Japanese beetle	Garlic, larkspur (poisonous to humans), tansy, rue, geranium (white works best)
Leafhopper	Petunia, geranium
Mexican bean beetle	Marigold, potato, rosemary, summer savory, petunia
Mice	Mint
Mites	Onion, garlic, chives
Mole	Spurge, castor beans, mole plant, squill
Nematode	Marigold (African and French varieties), salvis (scarlet sage), dahlia, calendula (pot marigold), asparagus
Plum cucurlio	Garlic
Rabbit	Allium family
Rose chafer	Geranium, petunia, onion
Slug (snail)	Prostrate rosemary, wormwood
Squash bug	Tansy, nasturtium
Striped pumpkin beetle	Nasturtium
Tomato hornworm	Borage, marigold, opal basil
White fly	Nasturtium, marigold, nicandra (Peruvian ground cherry)
Wireworm	White mustard, buckwheat, woad

The onion family.   Chives, garlic, leeks, shallots, and allium—just reciting the list out loud is enough to taint your breath. And the aromatic power of the family is not lost on the insect world. *Garlic* is the mightiest of these, and is probably the most widely used living repellent. It helps out no matter where in the garden you plant it, and does so without taking up a lot of valuable space. (A fringe benefit you'll no doubt discover is that garden-grown garlic has a better-mannered taste than the cloves that come in boxes.) Garlic also does the job in the berry patch, grape arbor, and around fruit trees. It will not tamper with delicate fruit flavors, and the green garlic shoots don't assault the nose—while most protective plants work by scenting the air, garlic, the most powerful and helpful of them all, does not. So, if you haven't already, stick some cloves in the ground early next spring. What you don't eat will pop up again next year. Garlic sprays are popular bug chasers; for recipes, see the following section.

Slightly less potent but making up for it in appearance is the *chive*. The lavender flowers look good scattered about a rose garden. You can start them from seed or buy them by the clump. Some gardeners crush the leaves of chives, geraniums, petunias, and marigolds between their fingers and then hand rub each rose stalk to take care of rose chafers, leaf beetles, leafhoppers, and aphids.

Herb grower Marion Wilbur recommends decorative Oriental *garlic chives (Allium tuberosum)* for protecting ornamentals, roses, and young trees from aphids, red spider mites, and other pests. "We set out several rows of young citrus trees and planted garlic chives around all but one row. Those with the magic ring of garlic chives were completely pest free, while the row without this protective ring was soon badly infested with aphids and red spiders. This condition was quickly corrected when the garlic chives were planted at the base of the troubled trees. Around roses they are very effective and more attractive than regular garlic." These herbs can be started from seed in spring or by divisions. You'll find that the clusters of white, starlike blossoms last a good part of the growing season.

Next on the list is the *allium*, a colorful onion that displays a long-lasting, ball-like cluster of blossoms. More than a dozen varieties are available, in several colors and sizes. Plant the bulbs early in the spring, setting them at a depth of four times the diameter of the bulb, but never more than four inches down. These flowering onions thrive in soils both dry and well-watered, and are winter hardy, as well. Once alliums get a start, there's little need to buy more. They multiply readily, and you can collect and plant the seeds as you would onion seeds.

Egyptian onions find favor with some gardeners. These perennial bunching onions have the family's repellent aura, and may be used in place of young leeks or scallions in the kitchen. The Egyptian's coarse growth should be cut down in summer after the top bulbs have ripened; this produces an excellent mulch. Texas gardener Grace K. Williams protects her peach and apple trees by planting red onion sets around them. She uses a variety known as winter onions, because freezing temperatures do not injure them. "They were perfectly hardy and started growth again in the spring, with myriads of new sets. Never a peach borer in the peach bark—no aphids in the apple trees! Also, peach leaf curl was at a minimum."

Scattering onion sets here and there among the vegetables will remove potato bugs, bean beetles and stem borers from pest status. Many gardeners see to it that a few onion plants mingle with their flowers each year, too.

Protective herbs.   A variety of herbs can protect your plants, although they might not occur to you as being unusually virulent. These successful interplanting combinations aren't the result of disciplined research, but were discovered by observant gardeners. "Just planting tansy or setting in garlic won't get rid of pests overnight," says one. "It takes time to bring about a naturally healthier environment. But I've discovered it's much more practical in the long run and much easier to accomplish than many gardeners realize."

Tansy is so valued as a repellent that it was the subject of an article in *Organic Gardening and Farming.* Also known as bitter or yellow buttons, it is a tall, strong-growing and strong-smelling herb with jagged, fernlike foliage and flat clusters of orange yellow flowers that resemble the centers of daisies. Don't confuse this plant with look-alikes that have taken on similar names: silverweed or goose tansy grows in wet waste places; tansy ragwort is a low-growing invader of pastures and fields, and is reported to be a poison to livestock and a treatment for hemorrhoids; and one of the hedge mustards sometimes goes by the name of tansy mustard. But only *the* tansy, *Tanacetum vulgare,* has the fragrant power— it was used long ago as a substitute for pepper. You'll probably find the smell attractive, as did the old time Maine loggers who used tansy boughs for bedding. Perhaps the boughs also served to discourage bedbugs; insects can't cope with the plant, and keep a good distance.

Because of its size—in good soil, it may reach five or six feet—tansy is not suitable everywhere. Grow it with crops that can hold their own, such as in grape arbors or in berry patches to keep out Japanese beetles. Since flowers may have pests, too, tansy can be used as an ornamental perennial in the back of the border. If your vegetable garden is big enough, let tansy stand guard in several positions throughout the plot. To propagate it, sow seed or dig up a clump, then divide and reset. Herb gardens sell seed and young plants; you can occasionally get a hold of a curly leafed variety, *Tanacetum vulgare* var. *crispum,* which is shorter and considered more ornamental. Every few years, the woody center portion of a clump should be dug out and removed in order to let the new outer growth continue. Old parts can be chopped up and used as a pest-repellent mulch.

Once tansy gets a good start, you might try it as a tea or as flavoring for omelets and pancakes. A great fan of the plant, gardening writer Ruth Tirrell, says that "just a little chopped up makes a pungent substitute for cinnamon or nutmeg." However, "In large quantity, tansy may be toxic. I'd recommend only the fresh tips of spring growth."

One tansy look-alike can help your garden out—*yarrow*, an herb with a cool, clean smell a bit like lavender. It is also fernlike, but the yellow yarrow flowers appear much earlier in the season, usually around the Fourth of July. Although it's not as powerful as tansy, yarrow has a general rather than specific effect on insect varieties. It is certainly worth experimenting with, says Ms. Tirrell, and is more manageable than tansy. You can buy seed and occasionally plants from herb gardeners.

Borage performs two good acts, repelling the tomato hornworm and attracting bees in numbers. Once you scatter borage seeds, the blue- and pink-flowered annual will usually sow its own seeds. It grows to a height of two or three feet, and is often seen growing wild. *Thyme* also plays this dual role. Fruit growers benefit from growing *mother-of-thyme*, an herb which forms an aromatic, spreading mat.

Just as *rue* was once used to ward off pestilence, it now serves to repel the Japanese beetle. It has some use also as a salad herb. Because rue has attractive blue green leaves, it complements flower gardens and ornamentals. You can start it from seed or root division.

You'll find several appealing allies in the *mint* family: spearmint; peppermint; apple, lemon, orange and pineapple mint (more delicate in fragrance but effective just the same); pennyroyal; and hyssop. As a group, these plants are sturdy perennials with a knack for escaping the garden and reestablishing wherever the ground is rich and moist. Earthworms seem to be happy under a canopy of mint. *The Rodale Herb Book* relates the success one gardener had with spearmint: "Despite unfavorable growing conditions that year—a severe summer drought occurred—no pests came near the brussels sprouts, whereas a half-dozen purple cauliflowers in another part of the garden, not near to mints (or any strong-smelling plant), were attacked by aphids. Apparently the spearmint protected the sprouts." Indeed, mint is a valuable companion to any member of the cabbage family.

One member of the mint family takes the form of a ground-hugging vine. It is known by many names—ground ivy, gill-over-the-ground, creeping Charlie (or Jenny), and catsfoot to recite a few—and comes back year after year to produce pretty purple flowers and an aroma that protects nearby plants from insects. It spreads readily, sending down roots wherever it touches the ground, and prefers a partially shaded location. According to some sources, sniffing the crushed foliage will relieve headaches. Another mint that's easy to grow is pennyroyal. It spreads fairly rapidly and can be started from seed or by division, as it will put down roots wherever the stems touch the ground.

Coriander and *anise* are annuals that have a reputation for repelling aphids; coriander also works against the carrot fly if planted between rows of carrots. A border of *opal basil,* teamed with interplanted marigolds, will help to minimize tomato hornworm damage. A thick growth of *prostrate rosemary* will act as a border for snails and slugs; apparently the sharp foliage doesn't feel good next to their slimy, soft skin. Nematodes find life unpleasant when *calendula* (*pot marigold*), *salvis* (*scarlet sage*), or *dahlias* are grown in neighboring soil. If these unseen, underground pests are sapping the life of tomatoes, interplanting with *asparagus* can do the trick. And the asparagus beetles in your garden will shy away from the herby *tomato* aroma. A host of other aromatics deserve mention as bug chasers, even though not enough is known about them to associate them with a certain pest. Here are some good ones to experiment with: *marjoram, oregano, lavender* and *santolina* (both effective against moths), *blessed thistle, camomile* (used in teas, also), *lovage, chervil, lemon balm,* and *bergamot.* Instead of arranging these herbs in a stiffly formal herb garden, scatter them informally among crops. In time, you'll come up with your own favorites.

Ruth Tirrell recommends the Artemisia family as repellent herbs "with a touch of class." As a group, the artemisias display white or gray foliage, making them good company for aesthetic plantings. They bloom in August and September, and retain their foliage in good condition long after blooming. Most species take to ordinary garden soil, but will do much better in composted ground. Dried leaves or branches can be scattered about the garden to produce the same effect as the living plants.

Probably the best-known name in the family is *wormwood.* Actually, this name is often loosely applied to many artemisias, but it properly applies to *Artemisia absinthum*, a hardy perennial with wooly gray leaves and a strongly bitter odor. The Bio-Dynamic Farming and Gardening Association recommends spraying a tea of wormwood on the ground in fall and spring to discourage slugs, and on fruit trees and other plants to repel aphids.

Southernwood is a notable cousin. This shrublike plant grows to at least three feet high, displaying gray green, finely divided foliage. It does best in well-drained soils, and is propagated by root division. *Silky wormwood* (*A. frigida*) is anathema for snails. Marion Wilbur planted the herb around her Oregon flower garden, and "noticed that snails, which were very abundant in the area, did not venture through the border into the flower bed"—they were stopped dead at the outside edges. "It appears that they ate some of the wormwood and thus met their end, leaving their shells as evidence." Silky wormwood prefers full sun and a rather dry location. Other members of the family include *tarragon, mugwort, silver mound, fringed wormwood,* and *dusty miller.* While more moderate in smell than wormwood and southernwood, they all give a measure of protection to any garden graced by their silvered foliage.

Protective plantings can keep animals away, too. *Spurge* (also known as the *mole plant*) will discourage moles from trespassing. Seeds are commercially available (see source listings in the Appendix), and the plant is decorative and self-sowing. *Castor beans* will work too, but the beans are highly poisonous to humans and should not be grown where children might happen by. As a safety precaution, the large seed pods can be clipped off before the poisonous seeds mature. This plant is an annual in colder areas, perennial in the South, and is grown quickly and easily from seed. The effectiveness of the castor bean plant lingers on after it is yanked, as discovered one fall by Ms. Wilbur. In an area rampant with gophers and moles, she interplanted young trees with fast-growing castor beans that had been sown early in the spring. "By the time the plants were two to three feet high, we noticed that there were no more signs of the intruders. By fall the castor bean plants were quite large, and to avoid crowding our young trees, we removed them. The house was sold two years later and we could not determine how long the effect lasted, but up until that time there were no further signs of moles or gophers, even though they were present in very noticeable numbers in the yards of neighbors on either side of us." Plant a border of mint to repel mice and rats, and try a line of alliums if rabbits are giving you much competition.

Repellent flowers:
not just pretty faces.   Elmer G. Gustavson, a New Jersey gardener who uses flowers to repel bugs, says that, "in addition to the expected practical effect of the marigolds, asters, and nasturtiums, I was able to enjoy the added dimension of new arrays of color." Many vegetable gardeners have found *marigolds* valuable in keeping Mexican bean beetles away from snap beans; growing miniature varieties makes picking easier. Also, these flowers have been found to exude a substance into the soil that keeps down the nematode population in the immediate area. The experience of Bonnie Kappel, a Montana gardener, is typical: "Every strawberry plant in one bed where I hadn't planted marigolds was dead, while another bed, only 15 feet away, which was interplanted with marigolds, thrived. This year, *all* the strawberries will get the same protection." Researchers at the Connecticut Agricultural Experiment Station found that in five ounces of soil where a large marigold was grown there was only one meadow nematode, and only two in a plot with a small marigold, compared to from four to seven in soil where a tomato was grown. Rachel Carson mentioned in *Silent Spring* that the Dutch use French marigolds to reduce nematode damage in public flower gardens. Marigolds also bring good results when planted with potatoes and tomatoes, and will keep white flies off greenhouse tomatoes. The taller African marigold is just as effective, but don't expect bugs to shy away from the odorless varieties.

The *pyrethrum* flower is so potent that it is widely used as a commercial pesticide. Although most of the world's supply comes from farms in Kenya and Tanganyika, there's no reason why you can't plant some seed about your garden for the same effect.

The appearance of the flower belies its use—it resembles a daisy. An exhaustive study on the subject, *Pyrethrum: The Natural Pesticide*, relates that a "German woman of Dubrovnik, Dalmatia, who picked the flowers for beauty, threw them into a corner after they withered. Several weeks later, they were found surrounded by dead insects." No date for the story is mentioned, but pyrethrums were used in Europe more than a hundred years ago and by the Persians long before that. By 1885, the United States was importing 600,000 pounds of the flowers in a year. In this century, pyrethrums were overshadowed by the great popularity of synthetic insecticides. Rachel Carson helped to bring the flower into the public's eye with the publication of *Silent Spring* in 1962, and since then more and more gardeners have been introduced to this excellent alternative to dangerous chemicals.

You can either buy dried pyrethrum flowers as powders or sprays, or grow the plants from seed yourself; the same properties that make the commercial stuff an effective killer will work at this modest level, too. This perennial does best in soil with good drainage.

Feverfew is a daisylike flower that is sometimes called pyrethrum. Like the real thing, it works as a bug chaser and can be planted as a border around roses or scattered throughout the garden. Feverfew grows to about 1½ feet tall, has yellow green, ferny foliage, and self-sows readily. You can propagate it by seed (in February or March), root division (March), or cuttings (set between October and May). If you like to experiment with the effect of herbs on your own body, herbals abound with uses for feverfew.

The *nasturtium* has become a popular flower in the garden for its ability to attract some insects and repel others. Plantings draw aphids from crops, and put the white fly and squash bug to flight. Nasturtiums can be brewed into a potent spray, too. If you're bothered by wooly aphids in apple trees, try both planting a ring of flowers around the trunk and spraying the foliage with nasturtium tea.

According to *Companion Plants,* by Helen Philbrick and Richard Gregg, white *geraniums* serve as a trap plant for the Japanese beetle: the bugs eat it and die. Gardeners report that plantings of geraniums keep beetles from roses. *Nicandra* (or Peruvian ground cherry), a pretty plant with little pale blue flowers, is also said to mean death for any bug partaking of its foliage. It grows best in the shade, but produces more flowers in full sun. Set the seeds in fairly rich garden soil. Its blooming period (and its effectiveness) can be extended by keeping fading blossoms plucked.

Petunias can do a job, too, as discovered by Mrs. Robert Duell of Vermont. "I was given a number of surplus petunia plants this year. After running out of space in the flowers, I planted them around two of my dwarf apple trees which I had planted last fall. The third tree had none. I found on inspecting them one day that the two with petunias around them had no bugs or ants, but the one without was loaded with ants and black aphids. It would seem apparent to me that the petunia gives off a scent of some kind which repels them. This is the first year I have used petunias, but from now on they shall be around my fruit trees every year."

Other plants worth a try.   An interesting publication of the USDA, *Insecticides from Plants,* lists a great number of plants found to possess insecticidal powers. While these plants were tested as dusts, teas, or extracts, some might also be interplanted to protect nearby crops. In any event, this could be a fruitful area for the backyard experimenter. Some of the plants that grow domestically are listed in Appendix 2.

Trap Cropping

Not all companion plants earn their living by repelling potential trouble. Instead, many organic growers use plants that are highly attractive to pests to lure them away from valued crops. These so-called trap crops can be set either around plantings or between rows. Because pests congregate on them, handpicking is made easier. Trap crops also serve as breeding grounds for parasites and predators. Once again, here is a non-technical means of plant protection that has evolved from years of observation and experimentation by growers like yourself.

Not all growers subscribe to using trap plants, however. A logical argument against the practice is expressed by Dr. Charles H. Brett of North Carolina State University: "The fallacy is that very few, if any, insect pests would be present in the first place unless the principal crop itself was attractive, and if this were true, the presence of an even more attractive crop would only compound the problem. Flies are not present unless there is garbage, and the solution to their control is not to bring in more attractive garbage."

But the truth is, trap crops do work in many situations. On a large scale, cotton growers plant strips of alfalfa in their fields to attract and concentrate lygus bugs which would otherwise raise havoc. At the garden level, a number of happy combinations have been discovered. Dill attracts the tomato hornworm from tomato plants (and the fat larvae are easy to spot on the spindly herb stalks, facilitating hand-picking). Japanese beetles can be lured from valued crops with plantings of white or pastel zinnias, white roses, or odorless marigolds. Another combination is suggested by gardening writer Catharine O. Foster in the *New York Times*. She observed that "knot weed at the edge of the garden in a field was chewed by beetles right down to the stem. It was a perfect distractor, and I picked off beetles by the score and dropped them into kerosene." Japanese beetles are attracted to soybeans, too. By sacrificing this one crop to the beetles, you'll help liberate your cabbage, carrots, cauliflower, eggplant, lettuce, onions, parsley, peas, potatoes, turnips, and others.

Mustard, planted early as a catch crop, saves cabbage from the ravages of the gaudy harlequin bug. And you'll have less trouble with aphids if susceptible plants are grown near nasturtiums.

Once pests flock to the trap crops you can release purchased or collected beneficials on the plants to clean up. Thus, these plants can serve as little insectaries. With plenty of food at hand, your beneficials will be off to a good start.

6
Resistant Varieties: Plants That Protect Themselves

Garlic, marigolds, and the mints are very special plants—they seem to have an aura around them that keeps bugs away. And plants like sunnydew, pitcher plant, and Venus flytrap turn the tables, getting their food from insects. Most plants are not so fortunate, however, and seem to just sit there and take it without a fight. After all, plants have long been symbols of passivity.

But you may have noticed in your garden that one crop fares much better against insect attacks than an adjacent variety of the same crop. Such strains that consistently do well are called resistant varieties— varieties that either put bugs off or sustain damage that would lay another variety low.

Over great periods of time, the interaction of plant and insect—the eaten and the eater—have brewed changes in the natures of both. And organic gardeners are the beneficiaries. Using resistant varieties makes it easier to avoid reliance on chemicals, enables beneficial insects to go about their business, and fits in well with other controls. And, as C. B. Huffaker reports in *Integrated Pest Management,* interest in resistant varieties is picking up: "There are now about 150 varieties of 23 crop plants that are resistant to nematodes, more than 100 crops resistant to a total of 25 insects, and at least 150 that have inbred protection from a variety of plant diseases." The Council on Environmental Quality reports that by the mid-sixties, more than three-quarters of crops grown in the United States were planted to resistant varieties—in 1900, that figure was one percent.

You couldn't hope to find an easier, more effective means of pest control. Imagine a gardenful of vegetables that the bugs fly right past, or rows of crops that sterilize any insects that make the mistake of stopping to feed. While this vision isn't likely to become reality—not just yet, anyway—the growing list of varieties on the market is a step in the right direction. A list under RESISTANT VARIETIES in the second section includes many varieties that are readily available at this writing. (In time, this list is apt to become dated. Suppliers may drop varieties for a number of reasons, one of them being that some resistant strains don't have a very long useful life. Huffaker reports that, while some have lasted at least 30 years, other varieties lose their special power in only 5. Within a plant or insect species there are usually many slightly different forms, or bio-types. This means that, given local variations in climate and environment, plants and insects of the same name won't act the same. And hopefully, resistant varieties not included here will be made available soon.)

Why is it that insects will devour one variety of a crop while another goes relatively unscathed? Resistance comes about in a number of ways, writes Dr. John Todd in *Organic Gardening and Farming* magazine. "Throughout the course of its evolution, a plant will cope in one way or another with one kind of insect, then use a different strategy with another kind." Researchers have put these strategies into three categories: non-preference; antibiosis; and tolerance. Resistant varieties generally are protected by more than one of these.

Non-preference:
growing unappetizing plants.
Non-preference plants are those which either turn an insect off or lack the stimuli that would turn an insect on. That non-preference is working is evidence by fewer eggs on plants, and fewer bugs seeking shelter and food.

A number of things about a plant may turn bugs away. The colors of certain varieties earns them some protection: red cabbage shows resistance to the cabbage looper and imported cabbageworm, and yellow green pea varieties are more resistant to the pea aphid than blue green varieties. According to the late Dr. Reginald Painter, an important researcher in the field, "From what is known of the lack of response of insects to yellow and red, it seems quite possible that in these cases the insects concerned simply do not 'see' the yellow green or red-leafed varieties, finding them partly by chance; if that is so, leaf color in these cases is a part of the mechanism of resistance."

The downy hairs on some non-preference varieties offer some resistance, either because the hairs affect the way in which light is reflected or because the fuzz just doesn't feel good to insects. Wheat growers in Michigan gain protection from the cereal leaf beetle by growing varieties with fuzzy leaves. Hairy varieties of legumes and cotton have fewer problems with leafhoppers.

In seeking shelter, many insects prefer plants that they can snuggle up in, especially plants with leaves that are close together. Sorghum and milo varieties with loose-fitting leaf sheaths are attractive to the chinch bug, and thrips are drawn to onion varieties having a narrow (in other words, cozy) angle of contact between leaves.

Some varieties are safer from attack because they don't put off the good smells that pests home in on. The aromatic oils or esters in certain potato varieties render them resistant to the Colorado potato beetle. Damage that does occur is found on the lower, older leaves, which evidently give off less smell. In a test reported by Painter, the oil on leaves of some potato varieties collected on the feet of aphids, no doubt an unpleasant experience for the little pests. Plants that taste bad also have built-in protection, but to seedlings just one bite can be fatal.

Odors also guide egg-laying bugs to suitable plants. If the cueing odor is absent or disguised in a variety, the females spend much of their time finding a host. And with such short lifespans, many would-be mothers never get around to laying their eggs.

Antibiosis, and the case
of the missing Rocky Mountain locust.

A second type of resistance, antibiosis, is shown by plants that, in Painter's words, "have the ability to prevent, injure, or destroy insect life." The effects are sometimes difficult to detect, and sometimes dramatic. An insect that partakes of such a plant may vomit or go into a stupor, come to be stunted, have poor fertility, or die young.

Antibiotic plants contain volatile oils, known as phytoalexins, that repel insects or fungus. Some plants seem to produce these oils when under attack, while others, such as garlic and marigolds, always have a good supply. As put by P. R. Day in *Pest Control Strategies for the Future,* "It is well established that all plants show defense reactions after physical or chemical injury . . . usually [involving] synthesis of polyphenols that may be toxic to any organisms present and to the plant itself." While both susceptible and resistant varieties respond with defenses when attacked, Day says that resistant plants react quicker, and the development of the parasite is discouraged. Some plants even react by killing the tissue around the area of infestation, as well as finishing off the offending pathogen. Dr. Arthur Galston, who teaches biology at Yale University, suggests that plants may encase repellents in vacuoles—little packages within the cells—that rupture when bitten by an insect. Unfortunately, they would also rupture when bitten by man, leaving a bitter taste in the mouth. So, it's not likely that you'll find this method of resistance incorporated in food plants.

Antibiosis has been found to figure in a number of insect-plant relationships: aphids on beans, cantalope, peas, Northern Spy apples and resulting hybrids, and Lloyd George red raspberries and resulting hybrids; the European corn borer, southern corn rootworm, and corn earworm on corn; the potato leafhopper on potatoes; the wheat stem sawfly on wheat and barley; and the chinch bug on sorghum. A solid-stem variety of wheat, Rescue, gives sawfly larvae another sort of problem—after hatching, the worms have trouble boring through the solid stems to reach feeding areas elsewhere in the plant.

A dramatic case involving antibiosis has been studied by Charles H. Brett, Professor of Entomology at North Carolina State University at Raleigh. His paper on the subject might well have been called "The Case of the Missing Rocky Mountain Locust," for it concerns the gradual disappearance of this locust—considered the most destructive plant-eating pest ever to appear in North America. "The locust swarms darkened the sky, and when they descended they devoured almost anything including bark, paper, and dead animals," writes Brett. Outbreak peaks were recorded in 1818, 1855, and 1876, and resulting famine drove many Plains settlers from their farms.

And then for some unknown reason, the numbers of this pest dwindled. No action had been taken against them—indeed, there was little the early farmers of the Plains could do—but the Rocky Mountain locust had disappeared. Brett suspected that the increasing popularity of alfalfa in the region was responsible, through the mechanism of antibiosis. The locusts were attracted to the alfalfa but it played tricks with their bodies—much like people drinking whiskey instead of milk, as he puts it. So, the locusts hadn't really disappeared, but were still around in another form. To test his idea, Dr. Brett fed foods other than alfalfa to the small, modern-day grasshopper of the Great Plains, and sure enough, they turned into a phase resembling locust specimens collected a hundred years ago. Thanks to the inadvertent selection of alfalfa as a major crop, the descendents of the most dreaded pest of the 1800's are today small insects with short wings, prone to being malformed and very susceptible to bacterial disease.

Tolerance: plants that can
sit there and take it.
In contrast to the other two types of resistance, tolerance is a passive role. Instead of avoiding, repelling, or otherwise influencing the life of insects, a tolerant plant survives and produces a crop simply by regenerating tissue fast enough to remain healthy. That is, it can take the chewing and still come through at harvest time. "Some

plants lose up to 30 percent of their leaf mass without much lessening of yield," says Dr. Frederick R. Lawson, a Florida entomologist.

Unlike non-preference and antibiosis, tolerance does not work by keeping down the number of bugs. In fact, you may well find more bugs on tolerant plants than on ordinary varieties. The New Alchemy Institute found this to be so when they tested 20 cabbage varieties for resistance to the cabbage butterfly larva. The varieties that produced the greatest number of marketable heads did not necessarily do so by keeping the caterpillars off; in the context of this experiment, "resistance seems to involve some ability on the part of the plant to head, mature, and avoid destruction in the presence of feeding larvae."

Tolerant plants are characterized by their ability to replace leaf area or a large part of their root systems. Such growth is stimulated by the plant's output of growth hormone, and is dependent on the plant's ability to heal the wound and resist any diseases that may enter the affected area. And some tolerant plants survive bug troubles because of their structure. The tough, resilient stalks of some corn varieties can take the burrowing of European and southern corn borers without breaking.

It's important to remember that healthy plants of any sort are more vigorous and better able to stand up to insects and diseases. Dr. Painter, who identified the mechanism of tolerance, found that "the general vigor of a plant greatly affects its tolerance to insect attack." In fact, research at Kansas State University has shown that the health and nutritional balance of soil is as important in warding off insects as the variety planted.

How well do
resistant varieties work?

One disadvantage to resistant varieties— and a source of discouragement to plant breeders—is that the effective life of a good variety may last only five years. Day explains why: "If a parasite, as a result of a mutation, can avoid triggering the defense mechanism, its development will be unchecked. . . . This is one reason why new mutant forms of pest and disease organisms appear which are no longer controlled by existing resistant varieties." Painter found that, in time, these successful mutants may be able to replace the previously dominant bug or disease.

While it's true that breeders can introduce other genes to bring about new resistant traits, the pest or disease will usually undo these defenses, too. "In apples," says Day, "there are at least nineteen different ways of initiating what seems to be the same basic mechanism to resist scab fungus, and nineteen corresponding ways for the fungus to avoid tripping the alarm."

Another reason why resistant varieties don't always do the trick is that bugs are smarter than most people give them credit for. After biting into a foul-tasting plant, some insects will apparently remember their unpleasant experience and avoid repeating it for a time. Painter reports that monarch butterfly larvae were tested for memory by first letting them nibble leaves they don't like and then offering them a second try a bit later. The larvae declined up to about 1½ minutes after the first taste. "If offered after that period, the larvae would always take a few bites, then withdraw, snapping their mandibles and thrashing from side to side." Painter concludes that "apparently some kind of associative memory persisted for this short period."

Certain substances in plants are very attractive to insects, and work to undo resistant qualities. Researchers at the University of Kansas have found that insects prefer to eat plants with high concentrations of free amino acids, and that such concentrations are found in plants suffering from improper nutrition. Imbalances of both macronutrients (phosphorus, potassium, and nitrogen) and trace nutrients and minerals (such as calcium, iron, and sulfur), will drive up free amino acid levels. Chemical fertilizers cause trouble by supplying so much of the macronutrients that plants pick up little of the trace elements; free amino acid levels shoot up, and the bugs move in. The logical conclusion has yet to be scientifically tested, but organically grown vegetables will likely prove to have significantly lower levels of these acids, and consequently will be less tasty to insects.

You can plant varieties
that resist disease, too. Plant breeders find that disease-resistant varieties are easier to come up with than those resistant to insects. Painter suggests several reasons for this: diseases generally tend to stick to one species more than insects, while if an insect is turned off by one resistant crop, it can usually get by on another; diseases land on target more or less by chance, while insects can sniff out the target crop; and the digestion, reactions, and make-up of a disease organism is easier to comprehend.

It follows from this that the list of varieties resistant to diseases, given in the second section under RESISTANT VARIETIES, runs a bit longer than that of insect-resistant varieties. And by looking through seed catalogs and experiment station publications, you should be able to find many more varieties.

Keep in mind that new disease strains can get past a resistant plant's defenses. Ten years ago, the Martha and Mary Washington varieties were the answer for gardeners who wanted rust-free asparagus; today, the new rust strains that evolved in the meantime are kept in check by a second generation of varieties—Waltham and Seneca Washington, and California 500.

How do resistant
varieties come about?
Resistance occurs in nature, without man's help. Plants differ in their reactions to threats from the environment and, as expressed by Darwin's law of survival of the fittest, some plant varieties disappear while others survive to perpetuate their kind. Many of these survivors make it because they have developed ways of getting by the bugs—ways collectively called "resistance."

But natural selection isn't operating as it once did. Philip Luginbill, Jr., an entomologist with the Agricultural Research Service, explains why: "In agriculture today, natural selection is seldom allowed to take place. Man persists in moving plants from place to place so they are exposed to new pest species. Man is also responsible for the native plants spreading insects and diseases into new areas before the native plants can develop resistance."

Monoculture interferes with resistant varieties, too. While fields of uniform, high-yielding crops are needed to keep the wheels of agribusiness rolling, Day states that the lack of genetic diversity that is a part of this way of farming now "limits the capacity of a crop to respond to threats from pests and diseases."

The study of insect-resistant varieties of plants is still in its infancy. Use of pesticides and other chemical means of controlling insects has kept research to a minimum, and while some resistant varieties have reached the market, many more are in the wings as research picks up steam in the years ahead. Developing the varieties is a slow business. It takes at least ten years to come up with a plant resistant to one pest, and developing a plant that will discourage two or more pests takes twice as long. Another setback is that resistance to one bug is often linked with a susceptibility to another.

So, it seems unlikely that you will ever be able to go out and plant a totally bug-free crop. But resistant varieties do give you one more way in which to grow your food without poison.

7
Taking Advantage Of Bugs' Natural Cycles

Timing, Tillage And Mowing To Interrupt Bug Cycles

There's a lot you can do to make the agricultural environment less livable for pests. Cultural controls are anything but sophisticated—they were the first controls used by agrarian man—but determining proper timing requires that you know something of the pests' life cycles. As in determining optimum times for planting and harvest, it helps to keep a calendar of garden events: when the pests first appear, when they are at their strongest, and when their numbers subside. Life cycles differ from area to area. A pest may have only one generation in the North, while southern growers are hit with half-a-dozen. And you can't get all the clues from a book.

Robert van den Bosch's *Biological Control* mentions that fall plowing kills overwintering European corn borers, larvae of the wheat-stem sawfly, and cocoons of the grape berry moth. In *Beneficial Insects*, Lester Swann notes that "fall or early spring plowing of stubble will expose grasshopper eggs to freezing or drying, or bury them too deep for the nymphs to reach the surface after hatching." White grubs of the Japanese beetle, white-fringed beetle, and European chafer are killed by disking in summer. Corn will get off to a better start if the ground is either plowed or disked just prior to planting; this disturbs corn-root aphids and the ants that tend them. Pea crops benefit from plowing just after harvest, as the life cycle of the pea weevil is upset. Grain cutworms can be similarly con-

59

trolled. Swann adds that if you want to leave behind crop residues to protect the soil from erosion, you should till with a subsurface blade or shovel type of implement.

By reading a bit about the pests' life cycles in the second section of this book, you can in many cases anticipate trouble by tilling to catch the soil-borne stages. Most insect pests spend part of their lives below ground at some time or other. And at the end of the season, turn under crop residues to make them unavailable to pests overwintering in vegetation, while enriching the soil at the same time. Larvae that have made it through the winter can be dealt with in spring by passing over the garden with a heavy roller just before they are due to emerge.

Tillage as a part of good farming practice has seen its day in many parts of the country. My grandfather repeatedly disked his 150-acre Indiana farm to handle weeds and insects, but his son, my uncle, deals with the same problems chemically. For one thing, he cannot afford to lavish all his time on such a small farm and must supplement his income carpentering. On top of this, the price of gasoline has risen so that he cannot justify the many miles of back-and-forth plowing. So, he makes a single pass with an herbicide.

Disking in dry weather will raise up clouds of dust, which in turn could either aid or hinder the balance of pests and beneficials or nearby plants. It's up to you to note the effects of dust, and to remedy the situation if things are looking bad. Either refrain from plowing in dry spells (you might hose down sections to be cultivated) or wash dust from the plants to undo the effects of the dust bath.

Clean cultivation.   Writers on gardening and farming have a hard time coming up with a consensus as to whether crops should be closely weeded or allowed to mingle with the hoi polloi of the vegetable world. Once again, it's up to you to determine the proper course of action. But consider both sides of the matter first.

Proponents of clean cultivation argue that the destruction of weeds, escaped crop plants, and volunteers will remove the home bases of many pests. Indeed, there is research to support that such practice has prevented problems with the sorghum midge, squash bug, harlequin bug, cabbage bug, green peach aphid, and Japanese beetle. Theoretically, the checks and balances of biological control should see to it that pests don't often get out of hand, but then gardens and orchards in suburban settings are hardly ideal settings for the intricate interactions of biological control. Therefore, if the beneficials at hand don't seem to be winning the battle, by all means consider a weed blitz. The experience of several seasons should enable you to weed judiciously, where and when needed.

Clean cultivation should only follow a decision—that plants are in real danger of intolerable damage, and that the beneficials aren't keeping the pests in line. It is not a routine to be mindlessly performed each season.

Hopefully, though, your gardening practices have seen to it that your land, if not the land that surrounds it, is an ecologically sound habitat for helpful and troublesome bugs alike. By providing places for plant-eating bugs you are ensuring that there will always be a supply of free biological control on hand to intervene when trouble flies, walks, or crawls into the garden. Where the plant-eaters go, the parasites and predators will follow.

Gardens groomed of all nearby weeds are particularly prone to early and midsummer damage, as it is apt to be some time before the populations of beneficials can catch up with those of the pests who moved in with the appearance of the crops.

Beatrice Trum Hunter wonders, in *Gardening Without Poisons,* if birds aren't forced to plunder our orchards and gardens because of the spread of cleanly cultivated suburbs across the landscape. Where there once were all sorts of food sources, birds now face lawn carpet, dotted by occasional oases of garden or fruit trees. With suburban plots at such a premium currently, it's little wonder that vacant lots don't stay vacant for long, but gardeners and fruit growers are paying in crops for the dearth of wild food in their neighborhoods.

If you're in such a bind, the remedy could lie in planting fruiting ornamentals that are particularly attractive to birds about your property. Birds usually favor their accustomed wild foods to the crops that look good to you. Check Chapter 12 to find what food appeals to what bird. Such "trap crops" can also concentrate insects where they will do no harm.

The only possible conclusion to a discussion about clean culture is arrived at by van den Bosch: "Because there are both positive and negative values following the practice of clean culture, each pest situation must be worked out on its own merits." Once again, here's a way to work out garden problems instead of squirting at them.

Growing Crops When The Bugs Are Not

If you've spent much time in a garden, you no doubt have noticed that insects usually make their appearance at the same time every year, live their short season, and disappear from the scene. This leaves plenty of time to grow crops either before or after the bugs go through their hungry stage. The following table should aid you in your scheming.

Vegetable	Insect or Disease Avoided	Timing Recommendation
Cabbage (also broccoli, cauliflower, kohlrabi, and collards)	Cabbageworm, cabbage looper, aphid, and cabbage maggot	Plant as early as possible. In North Carolina, set plants out during the last week of May through the first week of June to avoid egg-laying flies.
	Cabbage maggot	In North Carolina, set plants out during the last week of May through the first week of June to avoid egg-laying flies.
Carrots	Carrot rust fly	Skip the early planting and don't plant until early summer, after the maggots have died of starvation. For this to be effective, celery planting should also be postponed, as this is an alternate host. In the metropolitan New York area, plant after June 1 and harvest in early September.
Corn	Cereal leaf beetle	Plant early.
	Corn earworm	Make several successive sowings, noting which one suffers the least earworm damage, and make that date your major corn planting in the future years.
		On the coastal plain of North Carolina, plan for a harvest between July 10-20.
	Corn leaf aphid	Plant early.
	European corn borer	In New York and southern New England, corn set in the latter half of May will usually mature between generations. In Missouri try to avoid having unusually late planted corn. The majority of first generation egg laying will be in the earliest fields in the neighborhood, while eggs of second and/or third generations are usually concentrated in later-planted fields. Therefore, try to keep planting dates about on the average with the rest of the corn in your community. In Ontario, very early and very late plantings are particularly susceptible.

Vegetable	Insect or Disease Avoided	Timing Recommendation
	Fall armyworm	In North Carolina, plan to harvest before the middle of July.
	Southwestern corn borer and lesser cornstalk borer	In Missouri, early-planted corn is not as attractive to second generation egg laying as is late corn. Corn planted prior to or by April 25 rarely suffers enough injury to justify the expense of chemical control.
	White grubs	In Missouri, delay planting until spring feeding by the two-year-old grubs has been completed. This is usually late May in southern Missouri and early June in northern Missouri.
Kale	Various pests	In the Midwest, harvest before or plant after the bad time, July 25–August 10.
Lettuce and leafy vegetables	A variety of pests that destroy leafy crops in warm months	Winter planting in areas where possible.
Pea	Cabbage maggot and seed-corn maggot	Avoid early planting.
	Pea weevil	Plant early.
Potato	Fusarium wilt	In Nebraska, avoid planting early.
	Verticillium wilt	Plant late in Montana.
Snap bean	Mexican bean beetle	Plant in early June near New York City.
Squash, gourds, cucumber, and muskmelon	Pickleworm	Plant early. Most damage occurs to late-summer and fall crops.
	Striped and spotted cucumber beetles; squash bugs; squash vine borer	Delay plantings to mid- or late-July.
Tomato	Cutworm	If possible, delay planting until after the spring wetness has left the soil; otherwise, use cutworm collars.
Turnip	Turnip anthracnose	Plant in cool weather.

You won't find information on every crop for every locale—research is sadly lacking in this area of cultural control—but by keeping a log of insect activity in your garden, you should be able to come up with your own timing schedule. As examples, here are the observations of several organic gardeners who take advantage of timed plantings. Says John Vivian, Petersham, Massachusetts, "If enough water is available for midsummer irrigation or deep watering, I advise delayed plantings (to June 15 or so) for most root vegetables to avoid the spring hatch of the carrot fly. Then let the weeds come up among the root crops in fall, and the fall hatch damage will not amount to much."

From Upper Sandusky, Ohio, Gene Logsdon reports that "sweet corn planted successively at three or four different times usually had one or two crops completely free of earworms. Observe the insect cycles closely in your own area, keep records and learn which planting comes between the earworm cycles, making that planting the largest. Also, cucumbers, cantalopes, and squashes must be protected from the cucumber beetle with screening from the moment they appear above the soil. Cantalopes grown in pots indoors and not set out until they reach good size is some help. Planting squashes, pumpkins, and cukes after July 1 (if you have the moisture) is some protection, too—but you probably won't get as good a crop because of the late start."

"We have the weather to fall plant squash here," says Louise Riotte of Ardmore, Oklahoma, "and I find fall-planted squash is remarkably free of insect pests. Bean beetles, while attacking early beans, are almost entirely absent in the fall. We note that almost all our fall-planted vegetables are free from insect pests." Another Oklahoma gardener, Ona Raney Shope, has been bothered by a small, black fly that attacks okra in spring when it emerges from the soil. Later plantings of okra, which really loves the hot weather anyway, assure a safer crop. And John Krill of North Lima, Ohio, has found that the cucumber beetle—and the bacterial wilt it carries—vanishes during the last week in June and the first two weeks of July.

How should you go about making your own plans? *Organic Gardening and Farming* suggests that you take note of three things: the kind of pests that cause problems, when they appear, and when they disappear. This is especially valuable if you are using biological helpers such as ladybugs, lacewings, and parasites. Release these beneficial insects several times at two week intervals, with the major release two weeks before the pest you're after makes its appearance. This gives the beneficials time to mature, so that they meet the enemy with full size and a big appetite.

8
Biological Control

Naturally Occurring
Predators And Parasites:
How To Make The Most
Of Free Biological Control

We react to bugs in different ways. The M&M candy colors of lady bug shells impress us with their beauty, the purposeful activity of bees and ants arouses our curiosity, and a large, unidentified black bug behind the toilet tank can make us recoil in fear. But it seems we are most moved by the "What if . . ." fantasies that make science fiction so popular: if ants can bridge water with their bodies and eat cattle on the hoof, if millions of flies can spring from one couple in just a summer, then couldn't insects take over the Earth? As the sensationalistic *Hellstrom Chronicle* made very real, there are two million different kinds of them and only one kind of us, and considering the variety, number, and adaptability of insects, it does seem amazing that bugs haven't already displaced every form of life.

On the other hand, nobody gets excited over the built-in controls that make sure such flights of fantasy remain nothing more than just that. A great number of factors in the environment work to keep things going pretty much the same, year after year. As several entomologists expressed it in *Biological Control* (Paul DeBach, editor), "That communities of plants and animals exhibit a high degree of homeostasis in their space-time features is a widely accepted ecological principal." It is this homeostasis—or balance between flora and fauna—that is so important in preventing ravages of plant life. As it is now, plants grow just about everywhere possible. The same species are found in the same places each season, and the populations of these plants and animals stick close to their characteristic densities. This balance is brought about by biological control.

While you are reading this, biological control is going on in your garden. But it is unlikely that you could walk right outside and watch it happening, and this helps to explain why nobody gets excited, why naturally occurring control means little to so many growers. Of all the characters that work to maintain the balance of nature, only a few are well-known. Everybody is familiar with the ladybug, and the size and peculiar posture of the praying mantis make this beneficial hard to ignore. But these two aren't even the most important to the grower, and there are hundreds of other predators and parasites whose work goes unnoticed. Most plant eaters have several enemies, and some are attacked by more than a hundred species. Almost 99 percent of all plant-eating insects— think of them as potential pests—are kept in check by their natural enemies.

So, without doing anything, you have an automatic head-start at getting your crops through the season, just by letting nature maintain itself as it has for millions of years. But you should compensate for the fact that your garden, yard, field, or orchard isn't just another piece of virgin earth. Beneficials must contend with poisons, monoculture, cultivation, harvest, and a number of problems that can be attributed to the grower's misdirected efforts.

Dusts and sprays
kill good bugs, too.   According to R. C. Doutt and R. F. Smith, in *Biological Control,* it is unlikely that there is a single square centimeter of the earth that has not been visited by a particle of man-made poison. And even though you've never administered a single drop of lethal chemical, your upwind neighbor may have. (Some growers have successfully contended in court that such a drift of poisons constitutes criminal trespass.) Also, chemicals remain active in the soil for varying lengths of time, and life in your garden could be affected by a dose from several years ago. Mixing activated charcoal with the soil will help to purge the garden of these chemicals, according to Dr. John F. Ahrens of the Connecticut Agricultural Experiment Station. The charcoal can also be used as a root dip for transplants or can be poured as a water solution into the transplant hole. Only one or two parts activated charcoal need be mixed to 100 parts water. However, because these methods are zonal in nature, they do not protect successive crops planted in the same area,

nor do they always do a good job of protecting roots that grow out of the area of application. A more effective treatment is to mix the charcoal directly with the soil. Rates of application vary with the pesticide to be removed and the nature of the plant to be grown; a general rate is 300 pounds per acre, and Dr. Ahrens suggests that it is better to err on the excessive side. The cheapest source of activated charcoal is a chemical supply house. Drugstore prices would be substantially higher, but the convenience of smaller packages may make up for this in the case of very small applications.

Tampering with nature.   If naturally occurring biological control isn't stunningly impressive, it does become painfully conspicuous by its absence from the field or garden. In recent years, the effects of chemicals on the environment have tampered with the balance of nature, upsetting the delicate interplay of beneficial and prey, and several serious phenomena have been the result. The foremost of these is termed *pest resurgence* of the target insect: populations of natural enemies are generally more vulnerable to pesticides, and the grower who uses chemical poisons is unwittingly knocking out one of the important restraints that keeps pests from coming back stronger than ever. For a number of reasons, the effects of such resurgence are often long-lasting. Once beneficials in an area have been killed, others are typically slow in getting to the treated crops, as they usually do not migrate and tend to stay where there is food. Also, when pests are nearly totally eradicated, beneficials that are still alive will either starve or leave in search of food. But the plants are still there, and phytophagous (meat-eating) insects can soon become re-established.

Pesticides sometimes enable those pests that can escape to infest and destroy nearby crops that weren't treated. Meanwhile, the beneficials, which tend to be more locally mobile in habit, tend to travel through the poisoned area and subsequently die in great numbers. Because beneficials are especially sensitive to small amounts of poison, pesticide drift has a greater effect on them, and this is another factor that contributes to an unfavorable beneficial-host ratio. Finally, resurgence of a particular pest can't be stopped by just any beneficial; research has shown that the most effective predators and parasites are those that specialize on one or a few host species.

Another malfunction of the natural clockwork is the outbreak of *secondary pests*—those insects that were innocuous and went unnoticed until doses of pesticide killed off the beneficials that had been keeping them at bay. This means that while the target insect is at least temporarily subdued, another insect blossoms into pest status. A case in point is several species of spider mite: before the greatly increased use of chemical pesticides that followed World War II, spider mites were considered only minor pests, but they are now the number-one arthropod enemy of crops all over the world.

A third problem effected by pesticide interference with biological control—and possibly the most insidious—is *pesticide resistance.* Because of their greater reproductive powers and better chances for evolutionary adaptation, plant-eating bugs are able to build up resistance faster than their natural enemies, and successively bigger doses only serve to set back these enemies and the humans who end up with the treated food on their plates. Paul DeBach reports that between 220 and 240 pests are known to be resistant to one or several pesticides, and that "resistance has been increasing in a geometric ratio since 1950 when less than 20 species were resistant."

Given that chemical pesticides and herbicides aren't present on your land, naturally occurring biological control can still be hindered by "safe" organic pesticides and even home brews mixed up in a blender. Such noxious dusts and sprays are usually just as discouraging to beneficials as pests, and many predators are actually more vulnerable—they are generally more mobile and encounter more poison as they hunt around to find their prey, and often reproduce slower. The aphid, on the other hand, often avoids sprays as it feeds on the underside of leaves, and can give direct birth to incredible numbers of active adults without mating. Even water sprays can do more harm than good, blasting away such beneficials as lacewings, ladybugs, and spiders, thereby leaving the way open for a serious aphid resurgence. Although spraying with water (or water made wetter with a little added soap) can be a benefit, it is not a panacea and should be done only when truly necessary. Rotenone is very harmful to ladybugs, and petroleum-based sprays hurt some helpful parasites, especially those that attack codling moth eggs. In general, any pest control method that rids the garden of all of a certain pest species is working too well.

How parasites and predators work.   Insect *predators* are the tiny meat eaters of the garden and field, as is suggested by the names of several: antlion, dragon fly, tiger beetle, and pirate bug. They are generally larger than their prey and are equipped with sturdy mouthparts adapted to their feeding habits. Some predators are built to tear and chew the prey into manageable swallows, and others have piercing mouthparts through which they suck the life out of their victims. The larvae must find and devour several insects in order to sustain themselves, and are sometimes of equal or greater importance to the gardener than the adult form.

Many helpful predators are active at night, and are virtually unknown by growers, who tend to assume that the most visible insects do all the work. According to specialists, however, this is not so, and lady-bugs and praying mantises have been somewhat overrated. Ladybugs sold commercially are collected in the Sierras when they are full of fat and in a dormant stage, so that when released in the garden they must fly off much of this energy before they're ready to feed and reproduce. This flight will likely take them right off your land. According to DeBach, growers who have released commercial ladybugs often mistake the naturally occurring helpers for the ones that were introduced. He suggests that growers should either rely on the ladybugs that are already present or purchase ladybugs that have been fed a special diet before shipping so that they will reproduce when released. Praying mantises present a different problem—they will eat bugs, all right, and at a steady rate, but their appetites are somewhat indiscriminate and they may attack bene-ficial insects and even an occasional frog. Many entomologists have recommended lacewings as excellent, if less impressive, alternatives.

The point is that some beneficials are better than others. The level at which a predator or parasite will keep a pest population is determined in part by the specificity of the beneficial's hunger. When the population of a given pest balloons, the bug with a broad number of hosts will not respond quickly to the sudden glut of easy meals, and its population is not likely to keep pace with the pest's. Another requirement of a good natural enemy is searching ability: if the hunter blunders around the garden, it is not likely to be able to keep the host population at a low level, and will fail to check a sudden upsurge.

Parasites reproduce at the expense of other insects by planting their eggs in or on any stage of the host, from egg to adult. The eggs of some species are placed on leaves so that they will be ingested by the feeding host and become active inside its body. Victims are always insects that have a complex (four-stage) metamorphosis. While some parasites use a number of species as hosts, many are host-specific, and this characteristic explains why they are generally considered more effective than predators in controlling a given pest problem.

Unlike predators, which consume a number of insects in their life-times, three parasite larvae may take life from a single host. Death comes slowly for the host, as the hatching larvae usually avoid feeding on its vital organs until near the end of their development. Of parasites that are commercially available, the tiny trichogramma is the most popular. It lays its eggs in those of two hundred different insect pests, and the wasp eggs are mailed to the consumer in host eggs. The Soviet Union makes the most of the trichogramma, putting different species and forms of the wasp to different tasks. Depending on their aptitudes, they now are released to attack eggs of pests in fields, orchards, and even the tops of forest trees.

Beneficials don't fare
well in a monoculture.   An important term in discussing biological
control is *monoculture,* defined as the growing of one crop in an area to
the exclusion of all others, and it is something to be avoided. Growing a
diversity of plants will bring about a diversity of pests and consequently
a variety of beneficials, thereby minimizing chances of a particular plant
eater overrunning the crops. On a large scale, this means strip-farming
two or more crops; in the garden, the traditional rows and patches should
be broken up. Predators that are general feeders are particularly attracted
to such an area, and they have a special value for growers—although they
won't reduce a pest population to the level possible with specific feeders,
they do serve to keep down sudden infestations of a variety of insects.

Certain combinations are very effective. Lester Swann, in *Beneficial
Insects,* suggests alternating strips of corn or small grain with strips of
meadow to avoid problems with chinch bugs, and strip-cropping alfalfa
and cotton to increase the effectiveness of natural enemies. Side benefits
of alternating crops are that birds find fields more attractive, the soil
tends to hold moisture better, and erosion is discouraged. In the garden,
interplanting lettuce and cantalopes will reduce leaf miner damage, and
planting Russian thistle with crops attacked by the beet leafhopper serves
to keep that pest away.

Because the adult forms of some worthy beneficials are not carnivorous and rely on high-protein foods such as nectar and pollen to sustain
themselves, you can keep them in your garden by planting flowers along
with the vegetables. Some ladybugs will turn to pollen if the aphid
population falls off, and this suggests the importance of growing pollen-
producing plants near crops or trees vulnerable to aphids; strawflowers,
for example, can attract ladybugs by the dozens. In California, citrus
groves are sometimes laced with pepper or olive trees that serve as breeding
places for both the black scale and its predator, *Scutellista cyanea,* a wasp
that lays its eggs within the eggs of the scale. This practice increases the
numbers of black scale but, more important, it ensures that the orchardist
will always have a supply of beneficials at hand. Black scale hosts can also
be perpetuated by planting oleander near citrus trees; the oleander should
be watered often to generate the humidity that favors the insect's development.

A parasite of the grape leafhopper needs a particular second species
to prey on in order to make it through the lean winter months, and when
it was discovered that this species feeds on wild blackberries, plantings of
the berries were set near the vineyards so that the parasite was able to
sustain itself through the year. Such protective plantings were effective
in providing parasites for vineyards more than four miles distant. These

instances are by no means exceptional, and a variety of plantings about your property will encourage many beneficials, whether set at random or for a specific purpose.

The bad side
of clean cultivation.
To the gardener, weeds are anathema. Clean cultivation is an accepted practice, as a tidy garden is assumed to be a healthy garden. Although weeds do harbor pests and can give crops competition, beneficials depend on them for both shelter and bugs to prey on. As with any means of control, weed-pulling should not be exercised arbitrarily, and only after deliberation on your part. Are the weeds choking out seedlings or sun-loving plants? Weeds around the periphery of the garden shouldn't necessarily be yanked. Are they serving as launching pads for pests doing serious damage to crops? Some weeds shelter and feed pests, while others (deadly nightshade, for example), are repellent to them. Do the weeds provide an alternative source of food or shelter for beneficials? Weeds help to maintain the natural balance between beneficials and hosts (especially between growing seasons of a crop), and those that produce pollen attract parasitic wasps.

You can help general predators—those that eat whatever bug is populous—by allowing pest-infested weeds to grow in the orchard. According to a study mentioned in Paul DeBach's *Biological Control of Insects and Weeds,* an unsprayed and uncultivated orchard has 4½ times as much larval parasitism as the average heavily sprayed orchard. It has been shown that eliminating weeds in orchards will substantially decrease parasitization of the codling moth. One victim of clean cultivation is the brachonid wasp, a parasite of the fruit moth; the brachonid overwinters in other hosts that include the strawberry leaf roller and the ragweed borer, and if you are to benefit from natural control, you should neither plow under second-year strawberry beds after each harvest nor destroy nearby ragweed, smart weed, lamb's-quarters, or goldenrod. In general, by letting the weeds around fruit trees go, you keep the population of beneficials high.

Clearing out wild vegetation from the edges of garden and fields so upsets the insects' habitat that a rapid buildup of pests can not be checked by natural enemies. The population of good bugs typically lags behind that of plant eaters, resulting in serious damage in early and midsummer. As you can see, organic growers are not immune to biological backlash.

It is common knowledge that thousands of pests overwinter in the soil, and that disking and plowing can do much to prevent problems. Few growers, however, appreciate the number of beneficials that also reside below ground. A parasite of the white apple leafhopper overwinters as a pupae near the soil surface, and is killed by disking in fall; apple growers should instead cultivate in June or leave plots of uncultivated ground beneath the trees. Parasites of the diamondback moth are destroyed by disturbing cabbage seedbeds after the seedlings are removed.

Harvesting affects bugs, too.   The time and manner of harvesting have a profound effect on insect life. Large-scale growers of grains can help beneficials by cutting and harvesting alternate strips. As explained in *Biological Control of Insect Pests and Weeds,* "When each set of alternate hay matures and is cut, the other strips are about one-half grown. Thus, strips of growing hay are always available to the pest species as well as the natural enemies, and a more satisfactory balance between each pest and its natural enemies can be obtained and retained during the entire growing season." And head counts of insects show that strip-harvesting can actually attract new species of parasites to fields.

A further word of caution: DeBach advises that the indiscriminate burning or burying of garden refuse can interfere with natural biological control by killing the weakened, parasitized pest larvae while permitting the healthy pests to get away and pupate.

Helping your beneficials help you.   Predators often emerge into the world at a time when little food is available for them, and they either starve or take off in search of prey. Ken C. Parmelee, a West Coast gardener, gets around this problem by collecting gallons of ladybugs from the mountains east of Carmel, California, and storing them in a refrigerator until pests appear in his garden. He also refrigerates clusters of praying mantis eggs that are gathered from branches at pruning time. In this way, Parmelee has free doses of natural control at hand to combat outbreaks of aphids, moths, butterflies, and thrips.

If the mantises are to be used to protect shrubs or ornamentals, tape or tie the cases to branches about three feet from the ground. In the garden, nestling the cases in a small bed of straw between rows will ensure a high survival rate. Place a board on top of the straw to keep it in place. This nest protects both the egg case before hatching and the $\frac{1}{4}$-inch-long young until they are ready to stake out a corner of the garden.

Although ladybugs are famous aphid eaters, ants that lug aphids about can give these beneficials more than they can handle. Ants feed on aphid honeydew and carry their tiny honeydew "cows" to the underside of leaves to feed. One gardener countered by putting a band of a nondrying sealing compound around the lower trunk of his cherry tree. Upon reaching this impenetrably sticky barrier, most of the ants dropped their aphids and backed away to safety. Ladybug larvae then crawled right over the barrier and devoured the abandoned cargo.

Another observant gardener noticed that his power rotary lawn-mower was wiping out great numbers of praying mantises by sucking them into the blades. Aware that the mantises hatch around the first of June in his area, he spares them by using a push mower from then until November. In other areas, mantises may appear at any time after the first warm days of April.

If yellow jackets make you miserable with qualms of paranoia, it may calm your fear to know that these insects often sting and then tear up hornworms for food. Some growers report that yellow jackets have all but ridded their gardens of hornworms. A gut reaction may also cause you to recoil at the sight of a tomato hornworm covered with small white knobs, but let the unfortunate creature be: this large, green worm is serving as a host for the eggs of the tiny brachonid wasp. If left alone, the worm will die and the eggs will hatch into more beneficial brachonids. And if you handpick the eggs, larvae, or pupae of pests, don't destroy them. DeBach suggests that they be placed in screened boxes so that any parasites present be allowed to develop and take off to do more good work. The wasps are tiny enough to escape through the screen.

Mulch has many benefits, but one of these may not be so obvious: the brown wood spiders that live in mulch eat a good number of grass-hoppers. Spiders have the ability to appear quickly in numbers to control sudden infestations, and one researcher believes that they account for eight times as many insects as do birds.

Dust has been found to encourage populations of California red scale, and DeBach recommends overhead sprinklers, cover crops, and road surfaces that are not dusty. In a field study, populations of this scale were almost halved by washing dust from citrus trees at weekly intervals.

The value of patient observation.   If you find a bug eating a benefi-cial, don't automatically assume that the attacker is a pest. A number of helpful predators will nibble good bugs from time to time, especially if other food is scarce. Your proper course of action in such cases depends on keen observation and some knowledge of the habits and appearance of beneficials. For example, the beneficial big-eyed bug is easily confused with its harmful look-alike, the leafhopper, and the best way to differentiate between the two is to watch them a while. The matter of identification is confused by the stages that beneficials and pests go through: many species come to man's attention only through the harm or good caused by the larval form. To give you some guidance, the following section lists profiles of the most important predators and parasites that you are likely to meet.

Also important to a successful partnership between you and your garden is patience with the processes of naturally occurring controls. Good bugs will not eliminate pests from the garden, and you can expect to lose up to five percent of your crop to the various plant eaters that remain on the loose. But without these few pests, the balance of life on your land would be upset—the meat eaters would leave for buggier pastures, and your plants would be open to big troubles.

Profiles Of Some Common Predators And Parasites

If you are to make the most of the good bugs on your land, you've got to be able to recognize them. By scanning these short biographies from time to time, you will be receptive to beneficials when they cross your path. For other descriptions, see the encyclopedic section later in this book.

Beetles

Ground beetles (also known as caterpillar beetles). Not to be confused with the June bug are several species of beneficial ground beetles. The good beetles aren't as rounded as the bad, and are large, shiny, dark, and live in the soil by day. One ground beetle, the green *Calosoma scrutator,* is aptly named the fiery searcher for its caustic secretions (handle him with gloves) and voracious appetite for hairy tent caterpillars. Another species, the European ground beetle (*C. sycophanta*), is the most important predator of gypsy moth larvae, eating up to 50 of these pests to sustain its development. You'll have little trouble spotting this one—it is iridescent blue and green with a gold caste. Where it can't find gypsy moth larvae, it climbs trees to stalk cankerworms. The large (over an inch long) and attractive (black with a border of blue around the forewings and thorax) *Pasimachus depressus* attacks armyworms and cutworms east of the Rockies; by day it hides beneath rocks and logs.

Ladybugs. Likely the best known of beneficial insect predators, the ladybug (or ladybird or ladybeetle, if you will) is becoming somewhat of a symbol for the entire process of biological control. The ladybug's appearance is paradoxical, in that its rotund, cheerfully colored adult stage looks anything but ferocious. On the other hand, the appearance of the spring larva matches its reputation for extended feats of avarice. These creatures are flat-bodied, tapered to the tail when viewed from above, and show blue or orange spots on a dark gray background. Even hungrier than the adults, they begin feeding the moment they leave their orange eggs, and can handle 40 aphids in an hour apiece. The species used most often to control aphids is the convergent ladybug. It is unfortunate that this beneficial and the destructive cucumber beetle should be look-alikes. Both have 12 spots, but you can tell them apart by looking for the converging marks that give the good beetle its name—they form a broken V on the dark thorax that points to the rear.

Some ladybug species are identified by the number of spots they carry: 2, 9, 13, and 15. The 16-spot Mexican bean beetle may look like a benign friend, but don't let yourself be fooled. It has no markings on its thorax, unlike the beneficial species, and it is larger as well.

For more information, see LADYBUG.

Stinkbugs.   While all members of this family put off a stink wherever they go, some redeem themselves by feeding on cankerworms, cutworms, and the Colorado potato beetle. Occasional prey include leaf roller moths and sawflies.

If you have a cold and your nose is out of service, identify stinkbugs by their shape—much like a medieval shield. Keep an eye out for the beneficial two-spotted stinkbug, a small black bug with red markings.

Blister beetles.   While these slender, ½- to ¾-inch-long insects are most often thought of as pests, the larvae of some species travel through the soil to feed on the egg pods of grasshoppers.

Checkered beetles.   Bark- and wood-boring beetles must contend with this brightly colored family of ⅛- to ½-inch-long beetles. They are covered with a thick coat of short hairs, and bear clearly visible patterns on their rounded bodies. The larvae are hairy, yellow to red, and horned. Adult checkered beetles prey on adult wood-borers, while the beetle larvae take care of pest larvae and eggs.

Soldier beetles.   Members of this family look much like fireflies, but lack the fire. The adults are typically found on flowers, while larvae are helpful predators. One common species with the ungainly tag *Chauliognathus pennsylvanicus* has yellow wings and a large black spot on its thorax.

Tiger beetles.   These ¾-inch beetles are distinguished by their flashy, iridescent hues of blue, green, bronze, and purple. The larvae spend their time at the bottom of tunnels, waiting for an insect to stumble in.

Rove beetles.   Looking somewhat like earwigs, these predators are credited with eating mites, bark beetle larvae, and cabbage maggots. They lack the earwig's long, curved appendages at the posterior, and are equipped with stink glands that are capable of propelling a noxious fluid whichever way the tail is pointed. When alerted to danger, the rove beetles typically lift their tails in readiness.

One member of the family is known as the red spider destroyer, a small, hairy black beetle whose yellow larvae hatch from orange eggs to eat larvae, at a clip of 20 or so a day. Another small black beetle, *Aleochara brimaculata,* digs tunnels in the soil to deposit eggs. The larvae seek out and destroy cabbage maggots and larvae of the cabbage fly. According to Swann, the beetle's brown, horned larvae may eat up to 80 percent of the cabbage maggots in a field.

Firefly (lightning bug or lampyrid beetle).   Known for their early summer pyrotechnics, fireflies benefit growers by feeding on slugs and snails. They feed only as larvae—apparently the adults eat nothing at all.

The larvae are flat, a toothed outline, and bear long jaws suited for their work. They ambush snails by climbing over the top of the shell and digging in with their jaws when the mollusc sticks its head out. The snail is paralyzed so quickly that it isn't able to retract its head.

Bugs

Ambush bugs.   The appearance of this small group of predators is variously described as "grotesque" and "odd shaped," and is best learned from an illustration. The front legs are suited for snatching up prey. You're most likely to find them hiding behind flowers or leaves, where they wait for passing insects. Although only $\frac{3}{8}$ inch in length, they will attack large fliers, including some beneficial bees and wasps.

Assassin bugs.   Some bugs of this group are known also as kissing bugs, a name that belies their true nature. These are voracious predators, known to take a bite out of caterpillars, Japanese beetles, leafhoppers, and even the fingers of gardeners. Assassin bugs are typically medium to large, black or brown in color, and have long, narrow heads. They take an occasional honeybee, but do far more good than harm.

Damsel bugs.   These small, dark, rounded bugs are entirely predacious, and are responsible for the untimely deaths of many aphids, leafhoppers, treehoppers, and small caterpillars. They are about $\frac{1}{4}$ inch long, with the body narrowed toward the head, and the front legs are well-suited for grasping small prey.

Flies

Although gardeners probably would vote flies least likely to help out in the garden, their numbers include many valuable predators and parasites. The predator species outnumber those that parasitize, but the latter group has proven more valuable for biological control.

Tachnids.   The most important parasite group, the tachnids, have little about their appearance that would suggest they aren't houseflies: both groups of flies are drab in color and bristly. But you're apt to see tachnids around foliage and flowers, where they feed on nectar and insect honeydew. Some tachnids have the ability to inject the caterpillar hosts with active maggots. Others place eggs or maggots on leaves.

One particularly important fly, *Lydella stabulans grisescens,* parasitizes from 16 to 75 percent of European corn borers in the Middle Atlantic states, southern New England, and from Ohio through Iowa. Like other tachnids, the female *Lydella* has the ability to hatch eggs within her own body, but this trick can turn against the mother. Swann notes that if she can't find a place to lay her young, they will try to find their own way out. "Larvae have been observed working their way out through the eyes of a dead female that had been normal and active a few hours before."

Other tachnids destroy the larvae of browntail and gypsy moths, the Japanese beetle, Mexican bean beetle, and sawflies.

Flower and robber flies.   Of the predacious flies, robber and flower (or hover) flies are best known. The flower fly does indeed hover, beating its wings so fast that they can hardly be seen, and "the fly looks as if it were suspended in midair," says Swann. Unlike the tachnids, these flies are brightly colored, and their black and yellow bands make them look much like bees. While the adult flies live on pollen and nectar (they are thought to be second only to bees as pollinators), the larvae's meals include aphids, leafhoppers, and mealybugs. Cynthia Westcott quotes an interesting statistic in *The Gardener's Bug Book* that suggests just how valuable these drab little maggots can be: individuals have been clocked at one aphid per minute for prolonged periods. Ms. Westcott suggests that if you find these legless, tan or greenish, sluglike maggots on flowers (particularly rose buds), hold off with the noxious sprays and dusts.

The robber fly is beneficial to growers both as an adult and larva. The big, powerful flies attack other winged insects (butterflies, moths, beetles, wasps, bees, and grasshoppers) when in flight, and the subterranean larvae eat grubs and grasshopper eggs that they happen to bump into. It is in this immature stage that robber flies are considered most useful. When on the wing, these sturdy flies sound much like bees.

Other flies.   Although many gall midges (gnats) do indeed produce galls on plants, some prey on aphids and mealybugs. Other fly predators include the snipe flies, found in the West, and predacious both as adult and larva, and the dance flies, widely distributed enemies of mites.

Nematodes

Fortunately for growers, some nematodes are cannibals. These helpful species may not look fierce—in fact, some are only $\frac{1}{25}$ inch long and hard to see at all. But their teeth and jaws are very evident under a microscope. Also important to their cannibalism is a stylet that protrudes from the mouth. This hollow tube acts as a hypodermic needle to inject paralyzing saliva into the victim, and also as a straw through which body fluids are sucked. Cannibalistic nematodes can drain up to 80 pests a day over their 12–week life span. See NEMATODE for more on this animal's habits.

Nerve-Winged Insects

Lacewings.   These are the most important of the several beneficial "nerve-winged" insects of the Neuroptera order. The brown lacewing is found in the West, and the green (or goldeneye) lacewing occurs east of the Rockies. Their delicate appearance and weak, erratic flight belie the fact that they consume great numbers of aphids and mealybugs. When at rest, the membranous wings are held upright like a tent, and the green species is distinguished by its iridescent eyes and foul odor. The spindle-shaped larvae are even more helpful to growers, imbibing the body fluids of a number of pests through curved, hollow mandibles. Their victims include thrips, mites, caterpillar eggs, scales, and leafhopper nymphs, as well as aphids and mealybugs. The appetites of these larvae have earned them the names aphid lion and aphid wolf.

To keep the ravenous young from feeding on their brothers and

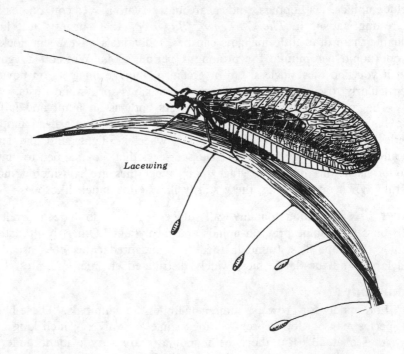

Lacewing

sisters before they hatch, the female lacewing lays each oval egg on the top of a delicate stalk projecting from the surface of a leaf or twig. In 6 to 14 days they hatch and in two or three weeks they spin yellowish pea-sized cocoons on a leaf. If the weather is warm, a mature winged adult emerges in a couple of weeks, completing the cycle of life and marking the beginning of another generation.

At night, bright lights attract the lacewings and they can be found smashed against automobile windshields and clinging to screen doors. Their main defensive weapon is an odorous excretion which is quite evident when one of them is grasped by an enemy.

Antlion. This nerve-winged insect is best known for the habits of the larva, sometimes called the doodle bug. You may have noticed their little cone-shaped pits in sandy or light soil without suspecting that a voracious creature lay hidden at the bottom. Once an ant stumbles into the pit, little landslides keep it from climbing back out. The antlion then pierces it, injects digestive juices, and sucks out its life through curved mandibles. If you're lucky, you may catch these beneficials at work mak-

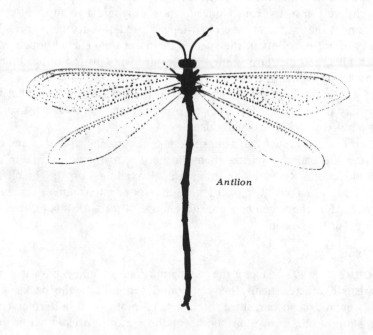

Antlion

ing their pits; they walk backwards in smaller and smaller circles, shoveling out soil with a flip of the head. The adults have two pairs of long, slender, veined wings, and resemble damselflies.

Damselflies and dragonflies are notable relatives; although they do not directly benefit the gardener, they do eat great numbers of mosquitoes and should be protected.

Praying Mantis

Thanks to its singular appearance, large size, and voracious appetite, this predator is known by just about everybody. Some growers can recognize the large, foamy, straw-colored egg masses, and harvest them to be relocated in the garden. The eggs are also available by mail (see Appendix 1).

If you want to stalk and store your own supply of mantis eggs, see PRAYING MANTIS.

Spiders

Maligned through the ages along with snakes and toads, the beneficial spider should instead be welcomed in the backyard garden. Spiders are exclusively insectivorous; indeed, they only eat live insects, since it is movement that attracts these eight-legged predators to their prey. Most spiders are not picky about the species of insect they eat, although wasps, hornets, ants, and the hard-shelled beetles are least preyed upon. Potential pests make up the mainstay of their diet.

If you will accept the spider's help in the garden, see to it that there is a variety of insect life for them to prey on. In other words, avoid the heavy-handed use of sprays and dusts.

Some species, such as wolf spiders and jumping spiders, run down their prey instead of snaring them in nets. Most spiders prefer dark, shaded locations where either moisture is available or the humidity is high. The new, naked spring garden offers a poor environment for spiders, but by the time the vegetables are tall enough to provide shade, they have moved in for the season.

Wasps

Braconid wasps.   Among the most important of aphid parasites, these tiny wasps characteristically leave a round exit hole in the backs of victims. Braconids also parasitize the larvae of moths and butterflies (gypsy moth, satin moth, browntail moth, codling moth, oriental fruit moth, strawberry leaf roller, sugarcane borer, tent caterpillars, and cutworms), and the larvae of many beetles.

If you've seen a fat tomato hornworm covered with egg like cocoons, then you have likely been the beneficiary of a braconid. These cocoons are usually the pupae of wasps that have gone through their larval stage within the worm's body. Swann cites an instance of more than 500 brachonid larvae being counted in the body of a hornworm that showed no signs of injury. But in time, the feeding of these tiny parasites will take its toll, and they will go on to lay their eggs in other larvae. "The gardener who picks these worms from his plants would do well to leave any that are parasitized," says Swann.

Another internal parasite of the braconid family specializes on the cabbageworm. When the larvae are finished feeding within the host, they exit the worm's body and form silky cocoons on a leaf. Although the affected cabbageworm does not die right away, it will not be able to pupate.

Satin moth larvae are the victims of an imported braconid, *Apanteles solitarios*. First introduced to New England in 1927, the wasps there now hit at least 60 percent of the overwintering larvae of this pest of shade trees.

The braconid parasites of the browntail moth have knocked this moth from pest status in New England and eastern Canada.

This family of wasps has also had a tremendous effect on gypsy moth populations, and includes both parasites of both pest, eggs, and larvae. Still, problems with this pest continue; P. B. Dowden suggests in a USDA pamphlet that "generally speaking there is an excellent sequence of insect enemies operating against the gypsy moth in this country, but the almost universal use of insecticides when defoliation occurs complicates an evaluation of the long-term results of this work." Now that DDT has been banned, there is a hope that braconids and other natural agents will be able to show us what they can do.

A braconid parasite of codling moth larvae, *Ascoqaster quadridentata*, would be more effective if it weren't for secondary parasites and broad-spectrum insecticides. In Nova Scotia—where the plant-derived ryania has been used instead of DDT and parathion, and where there are no secondary parasites—codling moths don't cause as much trouble to apple growers.

The most serious pest of peaches, the oriental fruit moth, is parasitized by a good number of braconid wasps, some species abundant and others quite rare. The numbers of these beneficials becomes rarer still when pesticides are used, according to H. W. Allen in a USDA Technical Bulletin (*Parasites of the Oriental Fruit Moth in the Eastern United States*): "In orchards that have been thoroughly sprayed for the control of the oriental fruit moth, few parasites will be found, since the insecticides greatly reduce the number of possible host insects and they also kill adult parasites moving about over the sprayed trees." This is unfortunate, as one wasp species, *Macrocentrus ancylivorous*, has shown great promise in controlling the oriental fruit moth. A USDA Farmer's Bulletin stated that growers in the region for which this parasite is known to be effective—roughly Massachusetts to Michigan and southward to eastern Missouri, Arkansas, and northern Georgia—can prevent nearly half the damage caused by the pest by making liberations when the second or first and second generations are present, without spraying. Another USDA bulletin stated that, in New Jersey, such liberations brought about a 50 to 80 percent reduction in fruit injury.

But you cannot buy *M. ancylivorous* today. This could be because consumers demand unblemished fruit, which biological control cannot promise, but Lester Swann suggests another reason—that the agricultural agents are also concerned with spotless fruit, and it is almost as difficult to say who started insisting first as it is to settle the question of the chicken and the egg. Did the USDA create the demand for perfect peaches, or were they simply expediting the consumer's wishes?

Chalcid wasps.   Mealybugs, aphids, scale, and larvae of beetles, moths, and butterflies are parasitized by these small ($\frac{1}{32}$-inch-long) wasps. Some chalcids are a metallic black, while others are golden. They are rated as even more important than ichneumonid and braconid wasps as biological control agents, and attack pest eggs, larvae, and pupae. The egg parasite of the trichogramma family are the best known to growers, and are commercially available (see TRICHOGRAMMA). Paul DeBach has tallied the chalcid wasps' worldwide use, and found that they have been successfully applied to control at least 38 pest species in 50 countries.

In this country, certain chalcids have been found useful in holding down scale populations, including purple, red, black, and yellow scale on citrus. The success of the wasps is dependent on favorable temperature and moisture, and is seriously affected by sulfur fungicides and niticides, road dust, and the use of chlorinated hydrocarbon insecticides. DDT had been a major threat to these beneficials.

Ichneumonid wasps.   These wasps are highly important as parasites of moth and butterfly larvae. Typically they are slender, have a long abdomen, and may bear a formidable-looking ovipositor. But this organ is used only for placing eggs, and not for stinging people.

Adult wasps feed on pollen and nectar, and often from puncture wounds made in host larvae; fly maggots often enter these wounds to infest larvae of the gypsy moth. Wasps deposit eggs either within or near hosts.

Several ichneumonid species were successfully used to control the spruce sawfly in eastern Canada and New England. Other species have been used to keep down populations of the European pine sawfly in New Jersey, the larch sawfly in Canada, and the European corn borer in the United States.

Making Bugs Sick
With Microbial Control

Microbial control enlists the services of insect pathogens, or diseases, to make bugs sick. These pathogens discourage pests either by killing them, by affecting their reproduction and development, or by making them more vulnerable to other insects, man-made controls, and even other diseases.

Several types of pathogens are at work in the garden: bacteria, viruses, fungi, rickettsia, nematodes, and protozoans. Different sicknesses bother different insect species, and this works to the gardener's advantage. By introducing a new disease or encouraging one that's already present, a specific pest can be controlled without endangering beneficials and bugs that are minding their own business. And while insects can develop a resistance to chemical controls, they are not thought to do so against diseases.

Before singing the praises of insect diseases any further, it should be pointed out that we are living in the Dark Ages of microbial control. This is due in part to the caution of the Environmental Protection Agency, which has served to discourage private industry from microbial research. What's more, the nature of the pathogens themselves has put a damper on private research. Because a particular pathogen works only on a few pest species, and because it is unlikely that patent rights could be granted on a pathogen—after all, they exist in nature—the commercial incentives just aren't there. Entomologist L. A. Falcon suggests in *Biological Control* that federal or state subsidies are needed to get the private sector involved.

So, while a great variety of microbial agents operating in nature have been identified and their use in controlling pests confirmed, only two are currently registered for use on food crops in the United States. By all accounts, however, this is an area that will soon come into its own. No one has written microbial control off as a pipe dream as yet. Here's a short primer on the subject, with particular attention paid to the couple of pathogens you *can* buy, and to one that you yourself can nurture and put to work.

Bacteria.   Of the various insect diseases, those caused by bacteria are the most numerous. Bacteria are simple, one-celled animals, little more than plants. They usually enter insects through the mouth, and then multiply in the bloodstream. Lester A. Swann describes the typical symptoms in *Beneficial Insects:* "As a rule, the infected insects become less active, cease feeding, and suffer from diarrhea; mouth discharges are also common. The tissues do not liquefy, or 'melt,' as in some of the virus diseases; generally the insect dries up and its color changes to dark brown or black."

Although you can't see bacteria at work, their modus operandi is interesting. Spore-forming bacteria produce endospores which enable them to live in a dormant state in an unfavorable environment. When a susceptible larva eats these spores, they blossom into rapidly growing plants that feed on the insect and occupy more and more of its body. After the insect's death, its decomposing body releases spores into the soil. Fortunately, larvae cease to eat long before dying because the bacteria produce toxic crystals that paralyze the victim's gut. While sick larvae will hang on from two to four days, their stomachs don't work and they are no longer a threat to crops.

Manufacturers of *Bacillus thuringiensis* (BT) have shown to the satisfaction of the USDA that this pathogenic bacterium is safe to man, other vertebrates, and plants. In fact, its use is exempt from tolerance limits on a number of food crops. BT is marketed by several companies under a variety of trade names—Dipel, Thuricide, and Biotrol—and it has been registered for use on more than 20 agricultural crops, as well as shade and forest trees and ornamentals. The disease is effective against an impressive number of common pests (see BACILLUS THURINGIENSIS), most of them moth and butterfly larvae.

One reason for the popularity of BT is that it is easily mass-produced by commercial firms. The bacterium is sold as endospores, in the form of a dust, wettable powder, or emulsion, and is stable during storage. However, experience has shown that BT is vulnerable to sunlight and temperature changes in the field, and care must be taken in spreading the preparation. Spray additives such as corn oil and other surface-active oils help to keep the BT on plant surfaces. Entomologist Falcon improved both the effectiveness and persistence of a commercial wettable BT powder by mixing five percent crude molasses with the prepared spray, but he found that the sweetness attracted egg-laying females to the treated plants.

The value of BT in integrated control programs has been confirmed by many investigators. For growers in the transition between chemicals and organic methods, this bacteria has proven compatible with most chemical pesticides. BT is not hard to come by. It is available by mail from suppliers, and can be found in many garden shops, nurseries, and department stores.

The only other pathogen registered for use in the United States is also a bacteria, *Bacillus popilliae,* marketed as Doom. The disease is used extensively against the grubs of the Japanese beetle, one of the most notorious pests in this country since its immigration in 1916. The spores that form within infected grubs lend a whitish cast to the victims, which explains its popular name, milky spore disease.

The marketed powder is made from ground-up, inoculated grubs, mixed with an inert carrier such as calcium carbonate (chalk). The powder can be applied to the soil at any time, except when the ground is frozen or a strong wind is blowing. Only mowed grassy areas are suitable for treatment. All you do is apply a teaspoon of the powder on the grass or sod in spots three to four feet apart. In time, the disease spreads out from the initial spots of application, carried by rainwater, travelling grubs, and insects and animals that feed on the grubs. Infected grubs do not immediately die, but their days are few. As they die and disintegrate in the soil, spores are spread through the soil and are ingested by healthy bugs. Only a single application is usually necessary, for as long as sufficient grubs are present, the disease will perpetuate itself in the soil. The worse the pest infestation, the faster the disease will spread—a good example of the way in which biological controls are self-regulating, adapting to the case at hand.

Just because milky spore disease is raging beneath your lawn does not mean that Japanese beetles won't fly in from elsewhere to cause trouble on ornamentals or garden crops. Because of the adult beetle's mobility, community-level applications of the disease have been found to be very effective. This pest is especially serious in new developments where large acreages of grass are planted at nearly the same time, and a developer can save his customers a good deal of trouble by discouraging the beetles from the start.

Garden pests are susceptible to a number of other bacterial diseases. Septicemia, an infection of the blood, causes squash bugs to lose muscular power and drop to the ground. This stiffening, called toxic rigor, is one characteristic of such blood diseases. Other maladies may give pests the runs, cause limbs to fall off, bring a discharge to the mouth, affect appetite, or discolor the insect. Obey your first reaction at seeing such ugly sights, and let the insects be. This will give them a chance to spread whatever is ailing them to their cohorts.

Viruses.   Of the six groups of microbial pathogens, the viruses are likely the most promising. They are termed "obligate parasites," which means they cannot live outside of living cells. It is this characteristic that makes viral pathogens so difficult to produce for large-scale applications—production must be done with live, infected insects.

Because no way has been found to mass-produce viruses, commercial production is expensive. Dead insects and the usual culture media like agar won't work. One way of getting around this problem has been to spray pest-infested trees with virus, collecting the larvae before they spin cocoons, and then trapping the emerging adults for release in infested stands. Viruses have the advantage of being passed on from infected adults to eggs.

The vehicle for viral pathogens is usually a water spray. Large-scale tests have proven such sprays effective in controlling the cotton budworm, cabbage looper, citrus red mite, and others. Forests of Canada and the northern United States were spared an infestation by the European pine sawfly in the 1950's by a spray made from infected larvae imported from Sweden.

Francis R. Lawson of Biocontactics in Gainesville, Florida, is researching means of producing the pathogens cheaply. But as things stand now, there can't be much of a market. Viruses can legally be produced and sold within a state if that state will grant a label, and can be produced for export to countries willing to grant permission, but no viruses can be legally shipped interstate for sale. These restrictions have led to various ways of getting around the laws. "I know for example that one small country is using virus on a certain vegetable," says Lawson, "and shipping that vegetable into the U.S. and western Europe." And several large food processing companies have resorted to bootlegging viruses.

Why doesn't the EPA permit interstate sales of viruses that have been tested and found safe to humans and other warm-blooded animals? The USDA has already gone through a whole battery of tests with two promising viruses, and all have proven completely negative. It doesn't make much sense to Lawson. "Every time the EPA grants a label for a new chemical insecticide they know beyond any doubt that they are in effect signing the death warrant of several people who will accidentally be killed. But if they were to grant labels for all polyhedral viruses the probability that any human or related animal down to and including snakes, lizards, toads, and fish would be injured or even become sick is so low that it cannot be calculated." After all, "humans have been eating plants with numberless viruses on them since we came down from the trees."

Why won't the EPA grant labels for the cabbage looper virus now receiving much attention from researchers? "I don't know," admits Lawson, "but perhaps the fact that the virus can be produced and sold with a very large profit to all concerned, for less than one dollar an acre, has something to do with it."

Lawson does not sell viruses in the United States, and knows of no place in the country where growers can buy viruses legally. Fortunately, there is a virus disease you can make use of in your garden. Called nuclear polyhedrosis virus (NPV for short), it is a scourge of cabbage loopers, especially in the South. The virus also infects the corn earworm, and has been used to protect cabbage, cauliflower, and a number of other crops eaten by the two pests. A solution made from just ten infected loopers will give complete protection to one acre, and a single application is often sufficient for a season. NPV spreads through a field rapidly. Two researchers, Thompson and Steinhaus, found that the caterpillar population of a whole field is struck almost simultaneously, while the pests in adjacent fields with similar conditions may go relatively unharmed. Predators and parasites serve as important vectors of the disease. Despite the speed with which the NPV can infect a field of caterpillars, you can expect the larvae to feed for at least three days before succumbing, and this delay should figure in your timing. The real trick is finding infected loopers. For Lawson's tips, see NUCLEAR POLYHEDROSIS VIRUS.

Lester Swann details a method suited for large-scale applications of the virus in *Beneficial Insects*. An infested field is sprayed with the pathogen and then swept with a net to collect the caterpillars one day before they die; normally, this would be three days after spraying. These worms are then crushed up and mixed with water. According to Swann, "One caterpillar in a gallon of water will give a standard concentration of about 5 million polyhedrons per quarter of a teaspoon; each polyhedron contains several hundred virus particles." In other words, a little caterpillar goes a long way.

The NPV of the beet armyworm occurs naturally in cotton fields, and has been collected and sprayed to prevent outbreaks. Important but less successful so far is the NPV of the bollworm; two commercial concerns have petitioned for its registration, but it is not yet on the market. This NPV is difficult to apply because the larvae feed on plant parts that are undercover, so that large doses of the virus are needed. Another problem is that ultraviolet rays in sunlight render the spray impotent. The virus may also be deactivated if leaf surfaces of cotton plants reach 8.5 pH or higher. Buffers added to the spray can counteract this alkalinity, resulting in improved performance, as do additives to improve wetting, dispersion, and adhesion. Still, not enough work has been done on the bollworm NPV to allow its effective use.

Fungi.   Although no fungal pathogens are as yet commercially available, a number of such diseases are at work in the garden. For example, there are 14 fungi known to attack aphids alone.

Fungal spores find their way into an insect's body between segments or around appendages, and then germinate and branch out into the body cavity. After a period of vegetative growth, strands extend through the insect's cuticle to the outside, where spores are released to infect new organisms.

One reason that these diseases haven't been put to much use by man is that few species can be grown outside of the host insect. Nevertheless, successes have been scored in field trials, and fungi should someday be agents of insect control for gardeners and orchardists.

Naturally occurring fungi are rated by entomologists as being very important in keeping insect populations in hand, serving as common causes of population crashes during outbreaks of many insect orders. Because fungal diseases are suited to warm and humid weather and cool, wet spells, they can only be used to best advantage in moist soil, during the rainy season, in geographical regions of high rainfall, and in individual orchards and fields that are notably moist. One fungus, *Beauveria bassiana,* proved more effective in controlling the Mexican beetle in New York State than rotenone, but this was during a period of frequent and heavy rains. Another difficulty with fungi as controls is that uneconomically high concentrations are often needed, unless conditions are nearly ideal. But, with all things considered, fungi appear to be second only to viruses as potentially important microbial insecticides.

Florida citrus growers have already enlisted the help of a fungus to disable the citrus white fly. The pathogen, known as red aschersonia, is obtained from infected white fly nymphs. These sicklings are swollen and secrete more than the normal amount of honeydew, and after death show a fringe of fungal growth that bears red, spore-bearing pustules. Lester Swann describes how the pathogen is prepared: Sterilized slices of sweet potato are inoculated and placed in bottles; in from 30 to 40 days the cultures are ready and the bottles are sent out to growers, or kept in storage if not immediately needed. Growers simply add water, shake the container, and filter its contents through cheesecloth to leave a suspension for spraying. One pint proved sufficient for an acre of orchard in the moist period of June and July.

Simple, cheap, and safe—hopefully other methods for using such pathogens will soon be discovered and refined. Field tests have shown that fungal control of a good number of pests is possible, the European corn borer, Mexican bean beetle, and mosquito among them. A fungus called white muscardine is considered likely to be the most important natural enemy of the chinch bug, and at one time the disease was propagated for distribution to large areas of the Great Plains. However, the disease is present naturally wherever there are chinch bugs, its effects waxing and waning with the weather, so there is little need for men to supplement this pathogen. Keep a look out for muscardine—affected bugs are covered with a white, cottony growth.

Another naturally occurring fungus that might catch your eye in the garden is *Spicaria rileyi,* a disease that holds down populations of the corn earworm (known also as the tomato fruitworm and true bollworm). Cotton grower Charles Denver reported at a Tall Timbers Conference on Ecological Animal Control that "when this natural biological control agent occurs," usually in September, "we are able to take advantage of it and reduce our chemical insecticide applications." This and other biological controls are under close scrutiny by cotton producers, says he, as insect resistance to conventional pesticides and environmental pollution may soon force them to abandon chemical poisons.

Scientists have hit upon a way to pit one fungus against another. In a recent experiment, their enemy was the fungus that caused the great chestnut blight, responsible for wiping out what had been the most prized hardwood in the eastern United States. The researchers found their answer in Europe. Although the disease is also found there, it was learned that in some sections of European forest the trees were affected with a much less virulent strain and were therefore much less sick. When the strong and weak strains are both injected in a diseased chestnut, the weaker robs the lethal strain of its virulence. Dr. Richard A. Jaynes of the Connecticut Agricultural Experiment Station cautions that it will be years before it can be seen whether or not the weaker strain can hold its own in the wild; he's concerned because this strain does not produce spores as readily as the other.

One reason for the EPA's reticence to approve any fungal insecticides is that there are reports of humans developing a reaction to the microbial agents. According to the USDA Corn Borer Research Unit in Ankeny, Iowa, such insecticides will not be generally available to the public until more is learned about their effects on vertebrates.

Nematodes.   While nematodes are tiny worms, often visible to the unassisted eye, they are usually discussed as diseases. This is because many of them live as parasites, passively draining life from their victims. While some of these victims happen to be crops, the nematodes we will consider here are beneficial.

It has recently been learned that nematodes serve man's interests by carrying bacterial pathogens about in the soil. The nematodes protect certain bacteria from the environment, and the bacteria prepare the nematodes' prey so that it can be eaten. Growers benefit when this team gangs up against such pests as Japanese beetle grubs. It's likely that nematodes are at work in your garden, but researchers are having trouble producing large enough numbers for use as applied controls. Entomologists at North Dakota State University recently found that grasshoppers eat nematode eggs on blades of grass and are killed when the nematodes hatch and grow. Entomologist Gregory Mulkern of that school is trying to mix the eggs with a grasshopper attractant and an edible carrier to see if the mixture can be used to control the insects. This method should prove relatively safe, as the nematodes appear to attack only grasshoppers and possibly earwigs.

Protozoans.   There have been few attempts to use protozoans as microbial insecticides to date. As is true with some other microbial pathogens, these tiny animals generally must be raised on living hosts. Another drawback is that few act with enough speed to save an ailing crop, so that trouble has to be anticipated by the grower. Protozoans have a gradual effect on their enemies, unlike the dramatic symptoms wrought by *Bacillus thuringiensis* and many viruses. Nevertheless, R. E. McLaughlin exhorts optimistically in *Microbial Control of Insects and Mites* that "biology today is a dynamic field, and the use of protozoans for control of insects should be boldly approached, learning from past failures and advancing to further successes."

Some microorganisms can be used to combat other microorganisms. Thor Kommedahl of the Department of Plant Pathology at the University of Minnesota believes it should be possible to coat seeds with "good" fungi and bacteria to discourage root infections. "When seeds and root surfaces of vegetables are examined microscopically," he says, "they are found to be colonized by microorganisms that can cause infection, and by others that feed from the nutrients that roots release into the soil. Some of these latter are antagonistic to the infectious bacteria and hold down the populations and activity of root-infecting fungi." Much seed is now commercially treated with chemicals such as captan or thiram, but the microorganism coating should be able to overwhelm the pathogens. Experiments have borne Kommedahl's theory out: suppression of seedling blight was as good as with captan, and even better than with that chemical under prolonged unfavorable conditions.

After researchers determine which fungi and bacteria work best, they must come up with coating materials that won't interfere with the biological agents. Until the day when seeds come coated with the beneficial organisms, organic growers will keep relying on healthy soil to protect untreated seeds.

A disease doesn't have to be lethal to be effective. One-celled microorganisms known as microsporidians are important parasites of insects, spending their lives in the cells of living bugs. The infected hosts either change in appearance—becoming stunted or swelling up grotesquely— or become sluggish. In any case, sick bugs have poor appetites and don't care much for sex either, which means less crop damage and manageable pest populations. Two highly susceptible insects well known to growers are the European corn borer and the cabbage butterfly. But, as Swann points out, artificial distribution of microsporidians is one more promising field for research that has yet to come to fruition.

Rickettsiae.   These are microorganisms that share qualities with both viruses and bacteria. Like the former, they are obligate parasites and thus can only be propagated in hosts or in tissue cultures. Like the latter, they have both a definite cellular structure and an active metabolism.

Masses of rickettsiae cause "a striking sign" in diseased larvae, says A. Krieg in *Microbial Control of Insects and Mites*—an opalescent discoloration that should be easy to spot. The disease was found to be more effective than a variety of *Bacillus popilliae* in controlling a beetle pest, but research has been handicapped by the pathogen's low host specificity and possible threat to warm-blooded animals. Overall, rickettsiae rank as the least important pathogen infection.

Pest Management Control Services: A Coming Trend

While backyard growers can organically handle their pests without much trouble, large-scale growers are often slow to abandon the pesticide treadmill. Given that the livelihood of farmers and orchardists depends on a good crop each year, their caution is understandable.

In fact, it's true that abandoning chemicals for pure biological control overnight could be catastrophic. One reason for this is that it takes some time for the insects of fields and orchards to resume a semblance of their natural roles. A second reason is that growers must become conversant with the cultural techniques that create favorable habitats for biological control. Dr. Everett J. Dietrick, head of a large insectary, recommends creating ecological niches to attract, raise, and conserve the natural enemy complexes. These niches can be made by supplying cover crops, trap crops, and other ground cover that serve as field insectaries. Growers should also employ different sequences in cropping cycles to take advantage of host-free periods of the season. And Dietrick points out that "strip-harvesting can attract and hold potential pest populations while biological controls increase, thus preventing the migration of potential pests into neighboring crops." To keep beneficials on the job, it's necessary to assure that nectar, pollen, alternative hosts, and water are available. Finally, after the grower has done everything possible to make a good neighborhood for the bugs, beneficials can either be collected from nearby fields or purchased for timed release.

Such natural techniques don't come naturally to growers, and they need help to arrive at integrated control (combining the most appropriate chemical, biological, and cultural controls) and to eventually abandon toxic chemicals all together.

Specifically, they need 1) expert advice, and 2) inexpensive sources of parasites, predators, and pest pathogens. This chapter details the ways in which private and public sectors are gearing up to provide both advice and the raw materials.

Expert Advice: From State Programs

To understand why growers in the transition often need expert advice instead of learning by the seat of the pants, it's necessary to know something about the intricacies of integrated control. We'll start with a working definition, used by Ray F. Smith, of the University of California's Department of Entomology at Berkeley, that describes integrated control as "a pest management system that . . . utilizes all suitable techniques and methods in as compatible a manner as possible and maintains the pest populations at levels below those causing economic injury." Can "suitable" in this context mean "chemical"? Smith explains, "implicit in this definition is also that imposed control measures, notably conventional pesticides, should be used only where economic injury thresholds would otherwise be exceeded."

This qualification brings in the crucial question of determining *intolerable damage* or, as Dr. Smith puts it, "economic injury threshold." Or, simply put, "to spray or not to spray?" This is a sticky question for growers hoping to both reduce the use of chemicals to a minimum and still produce a crop presentable to a public accustomed to pretty fruits and vegetables, and expert advice is needed to suggest the answers.

Washington State.   The need for good answers is especially acute for orchardists growing several fruit tree species, as orchards have a complex of pest and beneficial arthropod species that cannot be understood without several years of intensive training and field experience, according to Jack D. Eves, Pest Management Coordinator of the Cooperative Extension Service at Washington State University. For the time being, farmers' wives make many of the field observations in that state, including checking pheromone sex traps, taking leaf samples for mite counts, and sometimes making casual observations of pest population. But thoroughly trained personnel are needed. "We have found that a professional must still check each orchard at least once a week before recommendations can be made," says Eves. "Scouts can stretch the amount of acreage a professional can handle, but are not reliable information gatherers to base recommendations on until after at least three years of training."

"The growers like the scouts and the return of information on pest populations," Eves feels, "but often don't know how to interpret this information and must turn to a professional for interpretation and recommendations." He believes that the growers will in time pay for a "private pest-control-consultant service package" that would include scouts, materials, and professional recommendations on a fee-per-acre basis. Figuring out the interplay of beneficials and pests is extremely difficult, and it follows that pest management would be higher for orchards than row crops—three to five times higher, in fact. But this is compensated for by the results. In Washington, fruit growers can figure on pesticide savings of more than fifty percent.

New York State.   Trainees now patrolling upstate orchards will eventually become full-fledged pest consultants. Their training includes documenting growers' spray practices, surveying orchards, examining fruit at harvest time, and in-the-field training sessions—all under the auspices of the New York State Apple Pest Management Program. Initiated in 1973, this program has shown apple growers that they can get by with less chemicals and make better use of naturally occurring biological control. An interesting service of the program is a daily revised, 90-second telephone recording that gives growers the overnight temperatures, rainfall, leaf-wetting periods, relative humidities, and the weather forecast for the next 24 hours. The recording reports weather influences on the various diseases of apple, such as the infection period for apple scab, and the status and potential of mildew and fire blight trouble. The presence, emergence, and activity of insects is also noted. Growers are able to leave messages to the program workers at the end of the tape.

Other features of the program include: demonstration blocks used to establish that it is indeed possible to get by with less pesticide; postcards sent to alert growers to the phytophagous and predatory mite populations in their orchards and recommending a course of action; removal of thousands of wild and abandoned fruit trees to eliminate alternate hosts for insects and disease; calibration of sprayers for better coverage; and record-keeping for the 29 farms included in the program.

Although recommendations almost always involve what chemical to spray and when to spray it, they enable growers to spray more effectively, which means less chemical is used. And growers are learning that, in some cases, no sprays are needed at all. In the Integrated Mite Control Program for 1974, no summer miticide applications were needed in 14 out of 34 blocks surveyed because either existing mites were controlled by predatory mites or because there were none to worry about in the first place. When conditions did not warrant spraying, the field workers were able to get the word to growers in time to enable them to spare the environment a lot of toxic chemicals.

When asked to assess the growers' acceptance of this program, manager of operations James Tette admitted that it is too early to tell for sure. "Overall," he says, "we are talking of economics. If a grower can save $20/acre on pesticides, he might spend $10/acre for pest management." And these savings hang upon the variables of pest resistance and influence of environmental concerns.

Expert Advice:
From Graduates Of Special Programs

A big step in training people to carry through integrated pest management programs is a publication entitled *Integrated Pest Management— A Curriculum Report,* sponsored by the U.S. Office of Education. The book was written to give teachers, administrators, and counselors basic information about programs for preparing students for careers in this new and growing field. The various programs are geared for students in high school, community college or technical institute, four-year college, and graduate programs at the master's and doctoral level.

High school programs.   The message of integrated pest management programs at the high school level is that, "under integrated control, man acts as but one of the elements of the common ecosystem and functions with minimum impact upon the environment. Conversely, under conventional pest control practice, the role of man is often highly disruptive and economically and sociologically costly." The program is designed to ready students for jobs as operators of equipment used in integrated pest management, and involves the "application of agri-chemicals, biological agents, and the implementation of other techniques implicit to this type of strategy."

**Community college and
technical institute programs.**   The proposed curricula for this level involve either a two-year associate program, a one- to two-year certificate program, or programs for in-service training. The three available fields are: 1) Laboratory Services, 2) Application Services, and 3) Services and Supplies.

1) Springing from the Laboratory Services curriculum are six occupational choices: Laboratory Technician—Biological (works with many types of biological agents including microbial and virus organisms); Laboratory Technician—Chemical (engages in sampling procedures and assists in analytical procedures relating to pesticides and other chemical agents); Insectory Technician (raises, and assumes responsibility for, insects); Laboratory Assistant (performs laboratory duties as assigned by a laboratory supervisor or a technician); Environmental Monitoring Technician (samples specific components of the environment, to assure the integrity of pest management programs); and Scout-Field Sweeper (acts as a data collector in field situations). All require a two-year program, with the exception of Laboratory Assistant, which is a one-year program.

2) The second curriculum, involving Application Services, leads to four occupations: Integrated Pest Management Foreman (uses the disciplines required to perform the tasks of Integrated Pest Management and to supervise the application of pesticidal materials and biological control agents); Field Equipment Technician (advises and/or develops, adopts, maintains, tests, operates, and calibrates equipment used in integrated pest management); Aerial Applicator (applies pesticides or bio-control agents by aircraft); and Structural Applicator (operates equipment designed for pest control in structures). All are two-year programs.

3) Services and Supplies, the third curriculum, trains students for careers in sales of products used in integrated pest management.

Baccalaureate-level
programs (four-year college).

These programs lead to the position of Pest Management Specialist, with five possible areas of specialization: regulatory, pest management, support services, education-information, or business-marketing. The pest management program at Berkeley is one such program. According to the *Curriculum Report,* "Properly trained Pest Management Specialists are in short supply today and the outlook for employment in this important field is bright."

Post-graduate programs.

Students at the master's level can aim toward any of seven jobs: Extension Specialist for Pest Management (educating the public); Research Specialist in Pest Management (concentrating in either entomology, vertebrate pests, plant pathology, or weed science); Teaching Specialist in Pest Management (a faculty member in a post-secondary institution such as a community college or technical institute); Pest Management Advisor or Consultant (guiding growers, municipalities, industry, and others); Regulatory Specialist (interprets relevant laws and, if employed by a government agency, may enforce laws and regulations concerning quarantine, eradication, and other regulatory functions); Monitoring Specialist (known also as field scouts monitoring and sampling pest populations and other environmental phenomena for population trends for providing essential data to other specialists in pest management); and Manager/Supervisor in Pest Management (positions ranging from the middle-management to the very senior level).

The *Curriculum Report* has delineated four jobs that require preparation at the doctoral level: Extension Scientist, Research Scientist in Pest Management, Professor of Pest Management, and Senior Systems Analyst.

One program
now in the works:

At the University of California, Berkeley, the Departments of Entomological Sciences and Plant Pathology offer a curriculum that leads to a B.S. degree in Pest Management. A leaflet explains the program is based on the rationale that although "for decades we have depended heavily on chemicals to suppress pests of importance . . . attention now is focused on pest population management through integrated control systems. Traditional pest control and eradication has attempted the reduction or elimination of noxious species without full regard to the economic, biologic, or environmental consequences of such activities. Pest Management, however, implies the use of various methods of pest reduction, compatible with and in combination with one another, with full awareness of pest and damage levels and of ecological considerations."

The leaflet predicts a rosy future for graduates of the program. "Properly trained Pest Management Specialists are in short supply today and the outlook for employment in this important field is bright."

While publicly funded programs are training recruits and testing grower acceptance, a number of private insectaries and consultant firms have sprung up. And they report that business is good. "There is no doubt there's movement toward natural pest management," says Dr. Everett J. Dietrick, head of Rincon-Vitova Insectaries in Rialto, California, "but it is mostly in the talking and not in the doing stage." Nevertheless, his company, which produces insects for biological control, is going great guns.

Instead of just dealing in single species, Dietrick offers programmed packages that involve the release of several different insects. For instance, he sells a four-bug program to protect orange groves from the navel orangeworm. But the bugs he sells can't do all the work. "The backbone of any pest management system has to be the natural enemy complex already available on the land. We augment this, add other biological control to help the natural complex, and we find we don't have to spray."

A three-bug program allowed California grower Jack Hubbard to raise 70 acres of fine peppers, whereas just a few years earlier aphids had wiped out the crop—even though Jack was sinking $200 worth of chemicals into each acre. But before Dietrick's beneficials could go to work, pesticides were discontinued to allow both natural enemies and pests to revive. Since the spraying stopped, Dietrick spotted migrating predators and half-a-dozen natural parasites in the pepper fields, and releases of lacewings, ladybugs, and trichogramma wasps turned Jack Hubbard's tragedy into a success story.

"The biggest problem is convincing growers that they can get along without massive use of pesticides," says Louis Ruud, president of California Agricultural Services in Kerman, California. Although 90 percent of California growers are "spray jockies," to only 10 percent that use pest management specialists, Ruud sees these statistics in an optimistic light: "That means there's a development potential that includes almost nine out of ten farmers."

Mike Sipe, head of Pest Management Systems in Gainesville, Florida, agrees with Ruud's assessment. "The chief obstacle to the acceptance of biological methods of insect control lies in the minds of the farmers and their attitudes." He believes that field insect ecologists could reduce the amount of pesticides used to ten percent of its current level without using a single alternate method of insect control, just by timing applications properly. If, in addition, a farmer draws upon non-chemical methods of control now available, he could cut usage in half again, to five percent of its present level. Sipe says that one of the major functions of the pest management specialist is to reassure the farmer when he sees pests crawling on his crops. He uses as an example his experience controlling strawberry mites for six Florida growers, using the predatory mite *Phytoselius persimilis* as the natural control. Since the predatory mites eat the crop-damaging mites to establish themselves, it's self-defeating to wipe out all the pests and then release the predators. Sipe had success where he could persuade the farmer to accept small amounts of damage to allow buildup of the beneficial mites. But he ran into trouble when the strawberry farmers found another pest, the strawberry budworm, and sprayed without consulting him first. As a result, several of the farmers lowered the number of predatory mites to a dangerous level. From thereon, Sipe got the farmers to agree not to spray without consulting him. This was an important step, says Sipe, as the farmers tend to spray anything that moves. Several of the strawberry fields hosted the seed-feeding lygus bug, which seldom causes any damage. "In spite of this, the farmers wanted very passionately to spray for it." But Sipe was able to dissuade them. He believes that, eventually, the use of pesticides can be entirely eliminated, as he knows of no pest that has been thoroughly studied for which there exists no biological control agents.

A number of companies sell beneficials through the mails: lacewings, trichogramma wasps, praying mantises, and ladybugs. But Francis R. Lawson, who heads Biocontactics, a pest management firm in Gainesville, Florida, hopes that purveyors of beneficial bugs don't lead the public to think that mail-order help is a cure-all for pest problems. "Nearly all the biological control firms make releases of natural enemies, which may or may not be really useful. Most of them will admit that this is really a sales gimmick. What they're doing that is really valuable is selling expert advice, the most essential part of which is this: 'Don't use chemicals.' The release of beneficial insects helps, but that advice is at the heart of the matter." And he emphasizes the importance of field inspections on a regular basis during the growing season. Thus, the service is more valuable than the product. ". . . The most important thing now is to get farmers to accept expert entomological advice and pay for it, instead of accepting bad advice from pesticide salesmen, which they think is free, but is really not."

Lawson is concerned that biological control firms keep their reputations high. If people are found to be selling beneficial insects that may be worthless, he says, "the chemical companies may persuade the government to regulate us out of business. They've already done that in the case of pathogens (insect diseases), which now must be registered. It takes so much money to register a pathogen that only large companies can afford to develop them—and the large companies aren't going to do it."

What lies ahead? The changeover from chemicals to integrated control to straight biological and cultural control is moving at a slow but accelerating rate. Of the move to integrated control, the University of California's Ray Smith reports that the pace of these activities is increasing each year. For evidence of the move from integrated control to biological and cultural control we have the steadily rising sales of beneficial insects and insect diseases. Slowly but surely, American growers are being weaned from the practices of chemistry-set agriculture. The several commercial firms now offering control services in this country will likely blossom into an established service industry with openings for thousands of trained workers. Hopefully the curriculum report *Integrated Pest Management* will serve as a model for career development so that there will be people to fill these openings.

9
Physical Traps
And Barriers

Insect Traps,
Homemade And Commercial

The most obvious way to be rid of insect pests is to chase them from the garden with repellents or to nail them on the spot with insecticides. But pests can also be rendered harmless by luring them into traps.

Most traps work by appealing to an insect's need for food, shelter, or sex. Generally, the unsophisticated traps that you can rig up yourself are preferable to commercial contraptions, because simple traps are less apt to cause the mass killing of good bugs along with the bad. So before you invest in a blacklight trap or insect electrocutor, try a few simple remedies that other growers have come up with.

One of the most popular traps is nothing more than a shallow dish or jar lid containing a bit of stale beer. Snails and slugs will crawl scale-miles on their bellies to drown in the stuff. If you find these pests are taking a drink and then leaving, mix a bit of flour with the beer to make a sticky mixture.

This beer trap may be a naively simple device, but it incorporates the two things that make a good trap: an effective lure (fermented malt, in this case), and a means of detaining the pest (a pool of liquid made more treacherous with flour).

Most other homemade traps are just as simple. The Roarks of California came up with a way to catch earwigs using nothing but kitchen wastes. Pour hot bacon grease or hamburger fat into four to six ounce cans (tuna size) until one-fourth full. Place the cans outside where needed.

99

The earwigs crawl into the can and cannot get out. But one word of caution: racoons. Don't place the cans near corn, as coons are also attracted to the smell of grease.

An Ontario gardener, Ms. Reta Robertson, traps earwigs by appealing to their need for shelter. She says the method has been in use in her area for more than fifty years. "They may be easily trapped in a bit of dry moss placed in a small flower pot inverted on a stake. If this trap is examined every morning and evening during June and July and the earwigs destroyed, the pest will be kept down."

With a little time and effort, you can elaborate on the principle behind Ms. Robertson's trap. Take four pieces of bamboo a foot in length, each piece open at both ends, and tie them into a bundle at both ends with nylon yarn. Paint them a light green shade and set them under bushes, against fences, and in any other place you think earwigs might like to congregate. Early in the morning, shake the earwigs out of the tubes and into a bucket of water on which is floated a layer of kerosene.

An inverted cabbage leaf placed on the ground will attract snails, slugs, cutworms, and other pests that hide during the day and forage on garden plants at night. Earwigs and various beetles will hide under boards laid down along garden rows. Even a lantern placed over a tub of water will fool its share of bugs, but not necessarily all of them bad.

The Japanese beetle finds the scent of geranium oil, geraniol, or anethole, hard to resist, and is especially attracted to the color yellow. Put these two quirks together, and you've got a good idea for your own invention. (Geraniol is a rose-scented alcohol used to make soap and perfumes smell good; anethol is the chief constituent of anise and fennel oils, and is used to flavor perfumes and toothpaste.) Tests with such lures show that results went satisfactorily if the population is high or if the traps aren't placed close to plants to be protected.

Citronella oil attracts fruit flies, male only. Ants can be lured to small containers baited with sugar water, meat fats, or anything else that coaxes their cordons to march across your kitchen counters. Grasshoppers are attracted by all kinds of scents. Beatrice Trum Hunter suggests baiting hoppers with molasses, citrus fruit, lemon or vanilla extracts, apple flavorings, beer, vinegar, saccharin, salt, calcium chloride, and soap. Other attractants you might experiment with are anise and pine tar oil, casein, and even such kinky scents as auto lacquer, dry-cleaning fluid, and smoke.

Traps in trees.   When Ms. Murry Rice of Kansas found she could no longer tolerate the wormy fruit that disgraced her trees, she devised a trap to catch the codling moths that were causing all the trouble. She mixed up molasses, water, and a little sugar and poured the sticky stuff into little buckets. When the buckets were hung from the fruit trees, Ms. Rice reports she found "oodles" of the moths that had met their end.

This villain of the orchard can also be lured with sassafras oil. A solid bait for the codling moth is made by filling a small ice-cream cup two-thirds full of sawdust, stirring into it a teaspoonful of sassafras oil and a tablespoonful of glacial acetic acid, and then adding enough liquid glue to saturate the sawdust mixture thoroughly. When the cup is dry, after a day or two, suspend it in a mason jar partly filled with water. Another mixture calls for sassafras along with molasses and yeast. You can even add a little ryania, a botanical poison, but as few moths will ever escape the goo, anyway, this ingredient constitutes overkill. If you're storing a quantity of sassafras oil, it would be wise to heed the advice of the 1890 *Pharmacopeia of the United States:* keep the stuff in a well-stoppered bottle, away from the light, to preserve its potency. Other possible baits include a geraniol, methyl eugenol, terpinyl acetate, pine tar oil, linseed oil, soap, household ammonia, and protein material, such as powdered egg albumen, dried yeast powder or casein.

Vincent G. Dethier suggests in *Chemical Insect Attractants and Repellents* that baited traps and spraying work well together. Most of the codling moths that end up in traps are females, and chances are most of these are laden with eggs, so a lot fewer worms are around to eat holes in the fruit.

An enemy of ripening figs and dates, the small black dried-fruit beetle, can be lured to its demise with a bucket of fermenting fruit. According to Lester A. Swann, in *Beneficial Insects,* "the buckets are baited with peach culls, melon rinds, souring dates, and so on (with a little water to hasten fermentation) . . . . The bait is more attractive after it has become infested with larvae, which are prevented from escaping by greasing the top three inches inside the container."

Because insects follow a scent upwind, traps should be placed on the windward (upwind) side of a tree. Some growers find that two or three traps are needed per tree for adequate coverage. Hang traps at blossom time; codling moths emerge in late spring or soon after petal fall, flying at dusk if the temperature is over 60°F.

One of the most effective homemade traps is nothing more than a piece of plastic fruit coated and made sticky with Tanglefoot or Stikem, commercially available compounds that foul up the feet of insects. The innovator of this trap, Maine orchardist Eugene A. Carpovitch, was troubled by the maggots of the apple fruit fly, and reasoned that, "if he is a fly, he should respond to flypaper. The only question was in which form to apply the flypaper principle. It seemed logical to display a large, well-colored decoy as an attraction." He first hung up a few red plastic apples, without much success. The following season, he tried plastic oranges alongside the apples. "One fact became evident at once—the orange was much more effective than the apple; in one case the orange caught fourteen flies, while the apple one foot away caught none." Carpovitch then hung up several commercial traps, sticky cardboard containers baited with a feeding attractant known to draw apple flies, and compared the value of the three types of traps after a five-week period. The results: the plastic apples caught 17, the Sectar traps, 38, and the plastic oranges, 114.

What is it about the orange orbs that flies found so appealing? In a publication of the Connecticut Agricultural Experiment Station, Dr. Ronald J. Prokopy reports that apple fruit flies are much more highly attracted to spheres than to cylinders or rectangles. This agrees with Carpovitch's finding that the plastic oranges were three times as effective as the pagoda-shaped Sectar traps. However, Dr. Prokopy also found that under both laboratory and orchard conditions, the flies were most attracted by the blue or red spheres, less by green or orange, and least by the yellows: this is obviously at odds with the number of flies caught by the red and orange pieces of plastic fruit. Apparently there are other, unknown factors at work here.

So, if you have problems with the apple fruit fly or its relatives—the blueberry maggot fly, cherry fruit fly, and black cherry fruit fly—hang a sticky plastic orange or two in each tree. The fruit should be cleaner, although the results might not be so spectacular the first season because of a high initial infestation. To help reduce such an infestation, drop fruit should be picked twice a week and burned, and infested fruit should not be composted.

Commercial Traps And Attractants

For big pest problems, blacklight traps, electrocutors, and powerful synthetic attractants may be of help. Light and scent traps are also used by growers to monitor insect activity so that sprays and other controls can be applied more intelligently.

Light traps.   Flying insects can be drawn by lights into cul-de-sacs or electric grids. Some colors of light are more attractive than others, as you may have gathered from the use of yellow lights on porches. Night-fliers find blacklight particularly appealing. Although invisible to man, rays from the ultraviolet region of the spectrum will draw almost all important economic insect species that fly at night: the adult moths of the tomato and tobacco hornworm, codling moth, oriental fruit moth, corn earworm, European corn borer, cabbage looper, cotton leafworm, pink bollworm, European chafer, fall armyworm, bagworm, spotted cucumber beetle (carrier of bacterial wilt), cutworms, and hundreds more.

A clear blue light has been used to control grape leafhoppers in California vineyards. It was found that this color worked twice as well as white, according to Swann, and upping the wattage from 60 to 150 more than doubled the catch. Other important variables in the effectiveness of a light trap include its height, and the weather: humidity, temperature, and wind direction. Somewhat surprisingly, a blue light has been found to control early blight of tomatoes. *Frontiers of Plant Science* reports that the light inhibits the formation of disease spores, and that ". . . short exposures to red light revive spore formation." As yet, no practical applications for the gardener have been thought up.

Even regular light bulbs will draw some pests, including the adult European corn borer. Beatrice Trum Hunter says that pink or green fluorescent lamps work against the striped and spotted cucumber beetle, and an argon lamp appeals to the pink bollworm moth. Red, orange, and yellow lights are ignored or even avoided by almost all insects.

The Agricultural Experiment Station at Purdue University has experimented with blacklight traps. In one design, three fluorescent lamps draw bugs to the funnelled mouth of a cylinder, inside of which spins an electric fan to suck the insects down into a collecting chamber. Just one such trap protected a 50-by-60-foot garden of corn, potatoes, and cucumbers.

Light traps are easy to use. All you do is turn them on at dusk and off in the morning, and you can buy models with electric eyes to spare you even this little bit of effort. If they're to have an effect on summer larva populations, traps must be in operation early in spring, as soon as the adult moths and flies first appear. Be sure to inspect the traps often to see what kinds of bugs you're catching. For one thing, these inspections will tell you just when each pest appears in the garden and when it departs. This can help in timing plantings to avoid their egg-laying. But more important, frequent inspections of the trap will let you know when to turn the thing off. If the pests are few in comparison with innocuous insects, the trap is doing more harm than good. Chances are that many of these bugs would have otherwise ended up as meals for insect predators, fly-catching birds, toads, and fish. So, don't treat a blacklight trap as just another night-light.

Electrocutors.   Light traps often incorporate an electric grid that makes insects disappear with a pop and a flash. Such devices are often set up outside soft ice cream places to handle the flying clouds that hover about the fluorescent lights. While there's no denying the effectiveness of electrocutors in keeping the number of bugs down, your aims as a gardener aren't the same as those of the ice-cream man. He wants to kill bugs, any bugs, but you are only after those that may damage crops. With an electrocutor, there's no way of knowing if you're killing pests or just harmless bugs that happened by. All you hear is that little pop.

Another device that decimates night fliers is a blacklight combined with two rotors turned by a fractional-horsepower electric motor. The rotors are nothing more than two heavy strands of wire mounted on the end of the driveshaft. The wire should be rigid enough to pack a wallop, but not so heavy that it can be easily seen. This mangler has proven effective against codling moths in the orchard, but again, there's no way of discriminating between harmless insects and those that are really pests.

Protective Borders
And Barriers

Protective borders.   Instead of applying repellents and insecticides right on vulnerable crops, you can set up a miniature Maginot Line around patches of certain plantings or even an entire garden. Winged insects will aviate right over such barriers, but those that walk to lunch can be stopped.

If you have an active woodstove and live near a railroad yard, this recipe could be for you: set boards around lettuce and strawberry beds—they should stand five inches above the ground—and coat them from time to time with a paste made of train oil and soot. Slugs will not violate this boundary. If you're wondering what train oil is, you'd better talk to an old railroader, as this recipe is more than a hundred years old. But chances are that motor oil or fuel oil would do just as well.

A perimeter of wood ashes scattered around the bases of plants will block all sorts of crawlers and walkers. You can also sprinkle lines of bone meal, lime, powdered charcoal, coal ashes, diatomaceous earth, or any of several vegetative dusts such as sabadilla. A ring of mothballs placed on the ground will repel both bugs and warm-blooded animals. Washington orchardists keep deer from eating fruit by hanging small cloth bags of blood meal from branches. You don't need many of the bags—once the meal gets wet it releases an odor, and while the smell isn't noticeable to humans, to deer it signals trouble ahead. Hanging mothballs in mesh bags from trees will ward away deer, squirrels, skunks, and other animal pests of the orchard. *Farm Quarterly* reports the mothball method proved about 75 percent effective in Maine apple orchards.

The female cabbage moth doesn't care for the smell of tar, and you can capitalize on this dislike by cutting out square or disc-shaped collars of tarpaper for the bases of young cabbage plants. Slit the paper so that it can be slipped around the plants, and the cabbage will be safe from the moth's eggs. To protect cucurbits from earthbound pests, try soaking newspapers with turpentine and laying them over the ground as the plants vine out.

If the birds have been beating you to the berries and fruit each year, consider investing in a roll of mesh. One such mesh on the market is made of nylon, and has the advantages of being light and impervious to mildew and rot. To protect thorny or low crops with delicate stalks, the netting can be suspended on stakes. Gardener J. B. Reubens of Boulder, Colorado, has come up with another solution—he simply places 15-inch cones of wire screen over his berry plants.

Barriers. Barriers can be thought of as traps without the power of attraction. The insects just happen along and are somehow caught. Crawling insects, such as chinch bugs, armyworms, and wingless May beetles, are halted by plowing deep furrows between fields or around garden patches. The insects will fall into postholes dug at intervals along the bottom of the furrow, where they can be dispatched with a shot of kerosene, crushed with a stick, or simply buried.

Sticky bands can be applied to tree trunks and stems of large plants to halt the advance of a number of crawlers, including fall and spring cankerworms (you may know them as inchworms) on fruit and shade trees. The adult female moths are without wings, and have to crawl up trees to deposit their eggs. Lester Swann suggests that you can stop their seasonal treks by putting a strip of cotton batting two inches wide around the tree trunk (to protect the bark), wrapping a strip of tar paper around this, and applying a sticky substance to the paper. Put bands on in the middle of October to thwart the fall female moths, and again in early spring to catch the spring moths. Chances are good that you'll trap a few tussock and gypsy moths, too.

What sort of sticky stuff should you use? Commercial preparations, Tanglefoot and Stikem, are made for this purpose. A can of roofing tar works well enough, according to some growers. You can even make your own goo by mixing pine tar and molasses, or resin and oil. Such sticky preparations may damage tree trunks, so it's a good idea to lay down a layer of cotton batting or heavy paper before applying them. You might also cover a rope with the sticky material and wrap it around the tree a few times.

Sticky bands are also used to block wingless aphids, rose beetles, and ants on roses; codling moth caterpillars on fruit trees; the white-fringed beetle on pecan and other susceptible trees; and any other walking insects that use stems and trunks as aerial highways.

Barriers don't have to be messy to work. Burlap bands thwart the gypsy moth, which tries to pupate in the folds of cloth. Bands of corrugated cardboard or paper, wrapped in several thicknesses around a trunk, will attract hibernating codling moth larvae. This barrier should be put up in spring, and disposed of late in fall.

Flying insects can often be caught on a sticky surface of paper, cardboard, or wood—nothing more than an outsized piece of flypaper. This simple trap may be set up on a post, or hung from trees. Yellow traps seem to work best, especially against fruit tree maggots. White is also effective.

Other traps.   A contraption known as the hopperdozer can take care of grasshoppers on a large scale. This trap is nothing more than a long, narrow trough of boards of metal, mounted on runners so that it can be drawn across a field to scoop up the hoppers. A backboard is set up behind the trough to rebound even the best jumpers. At the bottom of the trough is a few inches of water, topped off with a thin layer of kerosene to kill the insects. The back and sides of the hopperdozer can be coated with sticky material to catch leafhoppers in clover and alfalfa fields. Such machines have caught up to eight bushels of grasshoppers an acre. A much smaller version—just a sticky box on the end of a stick—can be used to scoop flea beetles from the vegetable garden.

Some pests of fruit and nut trees play possum when frightened, falling right out of their trees to land motionless on the ground. The plum cucurlio and pecan weevil are two such insects. To trap them, jar tree limbs with a pole or board that's been padded at the top end to avoid injuring the bark. A sheet should be spread over the ground to gather the victims.

Pheromones:
Controlling Bugs With
Their Own Perfume

Judging by recent developments in the field of entomology, research entomologists share an evil inventiveness rivaling that of Dr. Frankenstein. With synthetic hormones they have created half-moth, half-worm monsters; they have sterilized male pests by the millions; and the paragraphs below tell how synthetic pheromones are used to make male moths fall in love with little cardboard traps.

The use of attractants for pest control is nothing new—the Chinese used them in an invaginated glass fly trap long before recorded history— but pheromones are the first attractants to tap the mighty reservoir of insect lust. Pheromone is an American word coined from the Greek *pherein* (to carry) and *hormon* (to stimulate, excite). The term describes an odorous secretion of an animal or insect that is emitted for the purpose of communicating with other creatures of the same species. Pheromones are complex compounds, and can signal danger warnings, discovery of food, mating calls, and so on. Many have been isolated, and certain of them are synthesized for use as attractants. Most are esters, a family of aromatic compounds.

What's been done with pheromones so far?
Conventional thinking has led to the use of pheromones to make conventional poisons sexy. Such a toxicant eradicated the oriental fruit fly from several South Pacific islands. This combination of poison and pheromone extends the effective life of the poison, reduces the amount of poison that must be used, and lures only certain species to their death.

More imaginative researchers have scattered pheromones throughout an area to distract males or totally foul up their ability to track down females. One recent test used the sex attractant of the cabbage looper, called looplure, to jam the senses of male moths so that they could not find females placed in traps. Even though the trial took place in an area adjacent to untreated fields, a 98-to-100 percent disruption of communication was achieved when compared with check plots. Good results have also been scored with disparlure, an attractant of the gypsy moth. Attractants such as these are said to be highly specific in effect, and turn on few non-target moths. Some scientists speculate that this is because females put off a second chemical that inhibits males of other species.

Other uses of sex attractants may soon come into their own. Researchers are considering the use of pheromones to distract pests from valued crops and to concentrate them in small areas for an easy kill by either man or beneficial insects. Attractants have also been used to collect males for mass sterilization. When released, the treated males go about their business as normal, except that their mating is an empty gesture: no progeny are produced. The effectiveness of such a genetic control program could conceivably be increased by scenting the sterile males with a sexy pheromone perfume to make them more attractive to females. Females would then waste their short adult lives in a frustrated wild goose chase.

Up to now, the assumption has been that female insects manufacture their own sex lures, and that there is a single attractant unique to each species to which the male will respond. But Dr. Lawrence B. Hendry and his co-workers at Penn State University discovered that the attractants originate in the plants on which the insects feed, says an article in *Organic Gardening and Farming*. The female, he believes, simply stores the pheromones and apparently does not change them in any way.

Dr. Hendry has found the attractants in plants in concentrations that correspond to the amounts found in females, and also has evidence that the males of a single species can be sensitive to as many as 20 different chemicals, depending on their diet. The females probably learn which pheromone to store and the male which one to seek while the insects are still in the egg or larval stage. He theorizes that the brain of the insect becomes imprinted or "programmed" to respond to whatever pheromone is present in its earliest food. Only male and female insects which feed on the same plants as larvae, he says, will be imprinted with the same attractant and mate as adults.

How can this finding be used in insect control? Hendry envisages a program based on spraying a field with some inexpensive compound which the insect larvae would eat and imprint. Later the same chemical could be used as a sex lure to confuse the males and prevent mating.

"We've opened up a lot of new doors," Dr. Hendry told *Organic Gardening and Farming.* "We're doing many experiments this summer on changing pheromones—feeding insects through plants to come up with different responses. With corn, for instance, we're employing a combination of food components which disrupt the borer's mating behavior—so that even if the insect is present, it won't produce successive generations." The European corn borer, costliest major pest of this crop, and the boll weevil hold the most promise for early success using this principle. "We already know the pheromones involved with the corn borer," Hendry said, "and development of different cottons for control of the weevil appears possible soon."

Breeding new varieties that turn off the worst pests of that particular crop is an excellent idea, Hendry says, although insects do adapt in time to such changes. He feels it is definitely feasible to develop much stronger resistance to serious pests by breeding specific attractant pheromones *out* of future varieties, and by developing alternate seed types which could be used on a crop-rotating basis to keep insects from adapting readily.

Defeating pests by deciphering their sex signals is also developing into a valuable tool for control of many costly troublemakers. In one advancement, scientists have broken the code for communication used by European elm bark beetles, the main carriers of Dutch elm disease. Researchers from the State University of New York's College of Environmental Science and Forestry, Syracuse, and the U.S. Forest Service station in Delaware, Ohio, announced they have isolated a combination of three attractants that have been combined in field tests to lure millions of the pests to their death. The powerful bouquet, released by females boring in elm trees, is termed an "aggregating pheromone" because it attracts both sexes for mass-attacking the host tree, breeding, and feeding.

What's on the market now?   As mentioned above, attractants have long been used to bait traps, and it is this application that will most likely benefit gardeners and small-scale orchardists. Traps are currently marketed for the purpose of monitoring the emergence and flights of adult insects, the idea being that the more a grower knows about the enemy's activity, the fewer the sprayings. And fewer sprayings mean a better chance for predators and parasites.

Other kinds of information can be divined if the traps are spread evenly over an orchard. By making frequent field checks, growers can see just where to concentrate their spraying, and can detect the invasion of pests from adjacent areas of infestation. After trap counts have been correlated with crop damage for a few seasons, the data may suggest whether or not to spray at all. And traps may eventually aid in timing the release of sterile males.

The traps you can buy are simply cardboard containers with adhesive surfaces, and come with attractants in pellet or capsule form and an illustrated guide for identifying the victims. No poison is necessary. You can get specific attractants for the codling moth, maggot flies (including apple and blueberry maggot, cherry fruit fly, and black cherry fruit fly), redbanded leaf roller, and oriental fruit moth.

According to Zoecon, a manufacturer, their monitoring traps can be put to good advantage by either large-scale orchardists or the grower with just a few trees. But interpreting the information you get isn't easy. "Tree fruits, particularly when you're involved with four or more fruit species, have a complex of pest and beneficial anthropod species that cannot be understood without several years of intensive training and field experience," says Dr. Jack Eves, pest management coordinator at Washington State University. To assist orchardists, Washington and several other states are training scouts to check pheromone traps and recommend best times for spraying (see "Pest Management Services" in Chapter 8 for a description of these programs). Eves estimates that effective tree fruit monitoring can reduce pesticide costs by more than 50 percent, and this means a lot fewer beneficial insects will meet their untimely end.

As research continues, new pheromones will likely hit the market; at least 25 are currently available for experimental purposes. A few of the more important ones now being worked on include attractants for the corn earworm, European corn borer, peach twig borer, San José scale, citrus red scale, and potato tuber moth—all of them pests, although Zoecon's director of product development, J. Antognini, suggests that pheromones of beneficial insects should also be given some attention. "The reason for this," he says, "is that the decision to spray depends not only on the population of the destructive insect, but also on the population of the beneficials in the area." Pheromones of beneficials could be used to rally these good bugs to meet pest infestations, and spraying wouldn't be necessary.

Using pheromone traps
to control pest populations. Eugene A. Carpovitch, a Maine orchardist, was intrigued with the idea of using commercial monitoring traps to snare codling moths en masse. From June 15 to September 20 of one year,

he hung up two traps to protect his ten apple trees. "Apparently, the traps did help in controlling moths," he reports, but then there weren't that many moths in the first place, thanks to spraying with ryania early in June and to the cool, wet weather that moths don't like. When Carpovitch queried the manufacturer about the effectiveness of their traps in keeping down moth populations, a spokesman cautiously indicated that they might help, providing that the infestation was low and every tree had a trap. This company has since gotten out of the trap business, and the man involved with the produce development concluded that the traps did not do an adequate job of protecting fruit; only one or two impregnated females from outside the treated area could cause big trouble, and commercial growers can't afford to risk that this might happen.

But Carpovitch feels that, "with some improvement in the trap design and with the accumulation of experience, codling moth control in home orchards can be achieved in a few years without chemical pesticides." For the time being, however, he takes care of the first wave of emerging moths by spraying two heaping tablespoons of ryania per gallon of water.

Looking ahead.   What of the future for pheromone traps? Predictably, Zoecon sees great things ahead. D. L. Chambers, of the ARS, agrees. He suggests their use can ". . . possibly provide control in time, place, and concentration of effect, precisely those factors provided by chemical pesticides that are generally absent in biological or cultural control practices." Others have pointed out that, unlike traditional pesticides, pheromones can't be scattered like one-shot bombs; instead, their use requires knowledge of the insect's strengths and weaknesses and of integrated control systems.

This knowledge is the key to the success of pheromone use. C. B. Huffaker advises putting these chemicals to new jobs only as we are able to foretell the consequences on the ecosystem. As for the mass-trapping of pests, he warns that some attractants might draw "certain natural enemies as readily, or more readily, than they do the target species. . . . Also, while some claim it is unlikely that the target species will develop a strain that will not be susceptible, this is by no means assured."

It appears we have a long way to go before pheromones can be intelligently used. Huffaker believes that "we know less about the importance of insect movements and how to quantify and predict them than any other basic principle of comparable significance." This lack of knowledge does not auger well for the future of biological control, and leads growers to fall back on pesticides. "The chemical horse again seems about to run away with the biological wagon," says Huffaker, "unless many more intensive behavioral studies are done."

10
Repellents
And Poisons

Natural Sprays And Dusts:
The Organic Gardener's
Last Line Of Defense

The previous chapters have suggested ways of saving your crops from "intolerable damage." *This* chapter will become of use at the point when you can no longer tolerate the chewing, sucking, and rotting that is going on out in the garden or orchard.

Your strict adherence to the principles of cultural and biological control and your strong back notwithstanding, chances are the little beasts will occasionally get the best of you. So, here are sprays and dusts that can serve as your last line of defense. The potions given below are basically of two sorts: repellents, that cause bugs to steer around treated plants; and insecticides, that kill or incapacitate offending bugs. It follows that if you believe there are a lot of good bugs running around with the bad, you'll want to start off with a mild repellent and move up to an insecticide only as necessary. The "-cide" means kill, and from the organic gardener's holistic point of view, a garden is better off if bugs are shooed away rather than killed.

It may come as a surprise to you, but even the tamest of sprays and dusts can be abused. One overdose or mistimed application can upset the delicate ecology of a garden or orchard, undoing many patient weeks of biological and cultural control. Beneficials flee the area, leaving the door wide open for a sudden pest resurgence. Please be aware that, even though you can brave a clove or two of garlic on your salad plate, insects don't share your tolerances. Use these aids only when other controls let you down; apply dusts and sprays locally, to take care of a specific problem, instead of blanketing the whole garden; do your best to avoid disturbing beneficials on the prowl; and as you stalk the garden rows with sprayer in

111

hand, try to figure out just what went wrong. Says William Olkowski, research entomologist at the University of California at Berkeley, "When you discover how the damage is occurring, then design a program to *modify the environment* and reduce the population size to the point where you can handle it. Adding flowering plants to the garden so there is a pollen and nectar source for beneficial insects is one way. Protecting predators, like predacious ground beetles, by giving them a home is another example. We use overturned flower pots for this. . . ."

Dr. Olkowski suggests that, "by studying the animal that is causing your problems, you can devise many such methods of managing the habitat that will reduce the pests and favor its natural enemies. Local snakes, toads, spiders, wasps, insect-eating birds (attract them with unsalted suet), all will help in insect control."

Make sure the control you pick matches the situation. Have you correctly identified the enemy? Even entomologists have trouble. "When our early spring lettuce was reduced to little nubs," says Dr. Olkowski, "we blamed the slugs. But careful observance at odd hours of the day showed that birds were doing the damage. A series of screen protectors solved that."

Stalking the enemy.   "If you do see intolerable damage on a plant," Olkowski says, "ask yourself, 'What is causing it?' It is really easy to be fooled! We found holes in our tomatoes during one season. This became intolerable when each one was damaged just as it was starting to ripen. Then it would shortly begin to rot around the holes. A close look showed a cutworm curled up inside. Nearby, tomato holes housed earwigs and sowbugs. However, a night-time check with a flashlight showed that slugs were creating the holes and the other animals were merely hiding in them during the day.

"There were no new holes in the tomatoes once we had handled the slugs with a program of handpicking at night, trapping during the day under overturned flower pots, and removing their habitat (they were breeding under the boards we had set out to walk on)."

Making your own

sprays and dusts.   There is a little of the experimenter in every organic gardener, and the result is a legacy of homemade bug potions. *Organic Gardening and Farming* magazine has received hundreds of recipes from growers who, when relying on their own resources rather than chemicals, went out and applied the scientific method to modest backyard experiments.

These growers have hit upon the same discovery: that hot-tasting or stinky things make the best ingredients. Garlic, peppers, and the more powerful herbs are among those most often mentioned as bug chasers. Of course, there are powerful organic sprays and powders available commercially—ryania, rotenone, and pyrethrum, for instance—but those you make at home are tamer, cost next to nothing, and encourage a bit of thinking about insects and their world.

With most recipes you'll find a list of insects or diseases observed to be vulnerable to the spell of that particular blend of ingredients. This isn't to say that there aren't other vulnerable species, but it's true that most formulations are somewhat selective in their effect.

As you read over the many recipes that follow, keep in mind that most are the product of trial-and-error work by other gardeners, and as such shouldn't be looked upon as sacrosanct formulae. Feel free to vary proportions and add or delete ingredients as you see fit. Keep an eye out for plants that aren't bothered by bugs, whether they be something you introduced or gardenside weeds—they might just be the stuff for a new recipe. But be prepared for failures. As Lester A. Swann explains in *Beneficial Insects,* "Since a repellent must in most cases compete with an attractant, and may be effective alone but not when the competition is present, an extract made from a plant avoided by a certain insect will not necessarily repel that insect when applied to another plant; its repellency may not be sufficiently strong to overcome the attraction. Actually, some repellents are deodorizers that counteract attractive odors."

Grow your own.   Most homemade sprays are derived from plants you can grow in your own garden, if they aren't already there. Be sure to read over the section on companion planting for other possible ingredients, as most plants that are potent alive are also potent when minced and sprayed.

Homemade botanicals have probably been used since there were gardens. *Dick's Encyclopedia of Practical Receipts and Processes,* published in the 1870's, suggested spraying cucumbers and melon plants with a decoction of elder leaves to kill thrips. This solution was also syringed over plants to discourage mildew. To bring the subject into the present, Dr. E. P. Lichtenstein of the University of Wisconsin is currently hunting for naturally occurring pest controls. He's found that parsnip roots contain a substance which effectively kills such pests as fruit flies, the Mexican bean beetle, pea aphid, and mosquito larva. You might try a parsnip root puree in your own experiments. The USDA has published the results of tests of 3,111 plant species of possible value in *Insecticides from Plants;* a list of domestic insecticidal plants and their uses is given in Appendix 2.

Hopefully, experimentation with domestic and foreign plants will offer new solutions. But for the time being, members of the allium family rank first in popularity with companion planters, and they are at the top of the list as spray ingredients, too. An interesting and very serious study has recently been made of the insecticidal properties of *garlic.* Entitled *Garlic as an Insecticide* and published by the Henry Doubleday Research Association in England, it is a ". . . summary of eight years' work on garlic as a non-persistent substitute for DDT and other organo-phosphorous and organo-chlorine compounds." The researchers were first led to experiment with garlic when they noticed that when planted between onion rows it seemed to reduce the attacks of the onion fly. In their report, the researchers conclude that essential oil of garlic (prepared by distillation) ". . . could be as effective as DDT or similar pesticides, with the advantage of being non-toxic at high concentrations to men and animals, while being lethal to certain pests, especially caterpillars and larvae." Tests of the toxicity of concentrated preparations led to the conclusion that ". . . garlic oil and its components can be safely regarded as non-toxic, even in very high concentration. . . ." In fact, the garlic proved to be a boon to the health of some experimental animals on account of its bactericidal action.

The antibiotic powers of garlic can be used to fight diseases in the garden. Researchers at the University of California found that garlic sprays effectively controlled downy mildew of cucumber and radish, cucumber scab, bean rust, bean anthracnose, early blight of tomato, brown rot of stone fruits, angular leaf spot of cucumber, and bacterial blight of beans.

An interesting sidelight that came up in the Doubleday experiment is that garlic bulbs nourished with chemical fertilizer ". . . grow well enough, but they will be lacking in the basic substances from which come the bactericidal and pesticidal properties of garlic." If you plan on growing garlic for bug potions, remember that the soil should contain ample amounts of humus and other organic matter. You can start your own stock by splitting up a purchased bulb into cloves, and planting them with their pointed noses just below the surface. The plants that come up will be far superior to store-bought garlic.

To make up a spray that the English researchers used in their experiment, take three ounces of chopped garlic bulbs and let it soak in about two teaspoons of mineral oil for 24 hours. Then slowly add a pint of water in which ¼ ounce of pure (not detergent) soap has been dissolved, and stir well. Strain the liquid through fine gauze, and store in a china or glass container, as it reacts with metals. Try the spray against your worst pests, starting with a dilution of 1 part to 20 parts of water, and then watering the spray down to 1 part in 100. You'll probably want to use as little garlic as possible if you depend on store-bought cloves, as they're quite expensive.

A variation on this recipe has been found to cause tree caterpillars to drop to the ground. Dissolve a half cake of Octagon soap in one gallon of hot water, add two mashed garlic bulbs, and drop in four teaspoons of red pepper for good measure.

Other alliums are nearly as powerful as garlic, and have their own special applications for the gardener and orchardist. *Onion* spray does bad things to disease organisms. California fruit grower Roger Dondero mixed up his own spray to see if it could do something about the leaf curl on his peach trees. He placed six onions (throwaways from a produce market) in a large pot of water and simmered them for several hours to make a fairly strong soup. He then sprayed each tree heavily for three evenings in a row. Within a few weeks, all the fungus on the leaves turned black, dried up, and fell off. No doubt a few onions sent through the blender and mixed with water would do the trick just as well, but the Donderos confess to liking the smell of simmering onions.

The simplest onion remedy of all was thought up by a gardener whose vegetables were disturbed by cutworms. He just ties the stems of wild onions to the vulnerable plants.

Should your roses be plagued by aphids, put *shallots* or *green onions* through a food chopper, mix with an equal amount of water, strain though cheesecloth, and spray on the affected bushes. Apply after every rainfall, if need be, to keep the population low. This spray will also keep aphids and fruitworms from tomato plants. *Feverfew* can be added to such recipes to good effect.

Next to the onion family, the most popular ingredients are *peppers*—hot ones. A typical recipe combines one clove of garlic, two or three red hot peppers, ½ mild green pepper, and ½ onion or the equivalent amount of onion flakes, blended in water; let the soup sit for a day or two, then strain and spray. Gardener Peggy Ede has tested the bug-chasing powers of several peppers in her Oregon garden. While Hungarian Wax suits her best for eating, Jalapeño has the necessary heat for her experiments. She picks the Jalapeños when they start to mature and then dries them on racks in the sun. Later in the season the peppers are frozen and kept for making spray. She says that the spray works well when made from either fresh or frozen peppers. "Put several in a large jar and fill with hot water. Let stand overnight. If you have a blender, it works especially well to put peppers, water, and garlic cloves all together in the blender and mix until smooth, then strain through a cheesecloth. You'll have a potent spray, good for all plants, and it's safe to use, cheap to make, and not harmful to the ground." The pepper juice spray can be frozen and used as needed for several months.

If beetles are the nemesis of your dahlias, try making a tea of ground red pepper and, when it has cooled, spraying it on the flower heads. According to gardeners who have tried it, some beetles are even killed by the hot stuff; considering these results, it's likely the remedy could work against other flower pests that feed in concentrated areas. Long red cayenne peppers are the favorite of some gardeners. The ground-up pods mixed with water and a little soap will give effective protection against ants, spiders, cabbageworms, caterpillars, and tomato hornworms. The pepper juice will repel a wider audience if garlic and onions are added; pests of flowers seem to find this mixture particularly noxious.

Pepper spray can rescue plants from a number of viruses, too; cucumber mosaic, ringspot, and tobacco etch are among those viruses prevented by the spray.

Illinois gardener Anita Stanley has come up with a quick and easy pepper remedy. To chase aphid-lugging ants from the ground near her grape arbor, she sprinkles red-hot pepper into their hills.

Herb and flower tea sprays.   In the section on companion planting you'll find a good number of herbs and flowers that protect nearby crops. Many of these companion plants yield their protective auras to water, making excellent botanical sprays. Oregon herbalist Marion Wilbur has concocted a tea of strong herbs noted for their insect-repelling qualities: 4 parts American wormwood; 4 parts desert sage; 2 parts erigeron; 2 parts eucalyptus; 2 parts silky wormwood; 1 part yerba santa; and 1 part wild buckwheat. Other herbs or combinations are also effective, but Ms. Wilbur says these work best for her. A tablespoon of the mixture is added to a pint of hot water and simmered for about 15 minutes. The resulting spray works against mealybugs, and the spent tea leaves are used as a mulch for extra measure. She also found this tea useful in eliminating fungus, damping-off, and insect troubles on flower seedlings, especially when the plants are watered with the solution once a week.

Carrying her experimentation a little further, Ms. Wilbur tried a mixture of herbs and soil as a repellent planting medium. Dry herbs are placed in a pan and scalded with boiling water and the excess water is squeezed out (to be used later as bug tea). The moistened herbs are then mixed 1:2 with soil. Seeds set in the mixture grew without damage from the sow bugs that were crawling all about at the time.

Next, she sprayed and mulched a dwarf lemon tree on her patio that had become infested with aphids and ants. She wasn't immediately gratified by the results, but when she checked the tree the next morning, the insects had gone. "In the past," says Ms. Wilbur, "when I used chemical sprays as a last resort on my plants, they seemed to kill the pests immediately—if they were effective at all. When I spray with the herb brew there seems to be no immediate effect, but hours later or the next day, no pests are to be seen."

Ms. Wilbur uses the herb brew to water transplanted seedlings and rooted cuttings. She reports that there is never any wilting or other sign of transplanting shock. "From these experiments and observations, I have come to the conclusion that the herbs act as a repellent to the pests and at the same time build up the internal resistance of plants to fungus and other diseases."

Here are some specific nostrums. *Chamomile* tea is as good for plants as it is for you. The Philbricks' *The Bug Book* says that the sprayed tea will preventing damping off on seed flats and in flower pots, and reduces the chance of mildew on cucumber seedlings. Among the other interesting suggestions from *The Bug Book* is a *tomato leaf* tea for dealing with green flies and caterpillars; *wormwood* tea against slugs, aphids, and other tender-bodied pests; and an interesting *stinging nettle* tea. This last-named solution is prepared by dropping the nettle plants into a barrel or keg of water and waiting about a week for the nettles to rot. The Philbricks recommend spraying the brew on plants plagued by aphids.

Recipes from
the kitchen and workshop.
Close to the alliums and herbs in popularity is *soapy water* or *soap suds*. Naphtha soap seems to be recommended most often, but any non-detergent soap should do. Soap will dissolve better if you add a tablespoon of alcohol to each quart of water base. Use this simple spray to chase away mealybugs, leaf miners, lacebugs, and when applied heavily to the underside of leaves, leafhoppers, mites, and aphids. To control leaf miners, it's best to douse your plants with suds about the time daffodils come into bloom; this timing catches the pest larvae that have made it through the winter. Soap sprays will cause various larvae to drop from trees; a capable wash for trees and ornamentals affected by bark-infesting larvae is made from *fish oil soap.* A super-powered solution for big troubles on ornamentals and flowers can be made from soapy water mixed with kerosene. In general, adding soap to a recipe will help keep the spray on the plants. This is important when going after pests that work on the underside of leaves, mites and aphids in particular.

Now and then, *buttermilk* comes in handy as a spray, especially against mites. A simple home cure for these pests is made by using buttermilk at the rate of ½ cup to four cups of wheat flour, added to five gallons of water. According to the bulletin of the Indiana Nut Growers Association, this spray destroys a very high percentage of both adult mites and their eggs. Dr. G. Edward Marshall, research entomologist at Purdue's fruit insect research orchard, explains that such a spray works by sticking mites to plants and enveloping them in the solution. Some of the sprayed mites appear to explode as the spray dries. Milk right out of the bottle or cow, diluted with nine parts of water, makes a spray that checks tomato mosaic. Tomato plants should be sprayed at ten-day intervals after transplanting. Milk and water sprays also prevent tobacco and sugarcane mosaic viruses.

Powdered sugar can be dusted on cabbage when the plants are wet to repel worms. *Flour,* too, will gum them up if sprinkled on plants in early morning when the dew is heavy. Usually one pint of rye or wheat flour will take care of all the plants in a small garden. Cabbageworms and moths get all gooky in the resulting dough, and as the sun rises in the sky they are baked into little pastries. Mustard seed flour, if you can come by it, mixes with oil to make a scale-smothering fall spray for fruit trees.

There are other ingredients in your kitchen. *Salt* is the simplest cure for slugs a gardener could hope for. A few shakes from a salt shaker will transform a slug into a harmless, if hideous, bit of slime. Don't use more than a shake or two for each pest, as salt does no favors for garden soil and will damage plant tissue. A cup or two of strong *coffee* left over from breakfast can be sprinkled over plants to save them from the red spider mite. Leftover asparagus can be whipped up and watered down to make a nematode repellent. Dr. W. R. Jenkins of the University of Maryland researched asparagus juice and reported that, "It gave considerable protection to tomato plants when we used it as a drench around the roots. But when we sprayed it on the leaves and it was carried down into the roots, we found that it did even better." Backyard alchemists find that volunteer *horseradish* mixed in water will repel potato bugs.

Just as a cedar closet protects clothes from moths, a tea made from *cedar chips* or *cedar sawdust* keeps away the Mexican bean beetle, potato beetle, red spider mite, mealybug, cucumber beetle, and squash bug. Or, you can just work the chips and sawdust into the ground as you plant the garden. Sifted cedar sawdust works well against chiggers in lawns. Blister beetles make tracks if a container of *boric acid* and water is set near their hiding places. A light sprinkling of *lime* will discourage sow bugs. Rags soaked in *turpentine* and laid in small trenches along vegetable rows somehow dampen the Japanese beetle's urge to reproduce. *Wood ashes* can be sprinkled around the bases of plants to block all sorts of crawling and walking pests, including beetles, mites, and aphids. Maurice Cote of New Hampshire reports that wood ash treatment against cutworms, slugs, deer, and rabbits is 80 percent effective. In fact, he finds the ashes more effective than rotenone. A Texas gardener, Ms. Norma Weidner, uses wood ashes in a gunk that is painted on oak trunks to block armyworms. She combines the ashes with sand, manure, soap, and red pepper, and has found the mixture also works to protect fruit and pecan trees.

Displaying an enviable spark of intelligence in their pin-head minds, insects recognize that *tobacco* does them no good and they do their best to keep away from it. You can take advantage of their good sense by putting a handful of tobacco or tobacco wastes in water to make a spray. Let the meal steep for 24 hours, and then dilute the solution to the color of weak tea. Stems can be purchased from florists and seedsmen, and store-bought plug tobacco works fine. Or, you can save a little time and effort by purchasing a tobacco extract and following the directions on the package. Tobacco sprays spread better if soap is added, but be sure to rinse the plants with clear water after each application so that foliage is not burned. This is potent juice, and should be used well before releasing beneficials in the garden. Tobacco sprays do funny things to roses, so unless the prospect of black roses piques your curiosity, use another spray.

The simplest spray of them all comes from the faucet. *Water* sprays work by knocking pests from their meals, and are particularly effective in dislodging aphids, red spider mites, and various worms. Again, use this spray only when necessary. Dr. Olkowski has observed resurgences of aphids after the excessive, ill-timed use of water sprays to wash them off trees.

Dormant oil sprays: safe and reliable protection for fruit trees.

For organic fruit tree growers, pest control is rarely a casual matter, and dormant oil sprays can play an important part in producing a good crop. An extremely thin layer of oil in many cases makes the difference between a harvest of good eating apples and scabby fruit fit only for the cider press. The oil layer works by suffocating pests, and unless adulterated, it is not poisonous to warm-blooded animals. Such sprays are cut with water, and usually contain only three to four percent oil.

A prime advantage of dormant oils is that insects apparently do not build up resistance to them—not yet, at any rate. "Theoretically, insects and mites should be able to develop resistance to any pesticide, including petroleum oils," says Dr. Paul J. Chapman, professor of Entomology at Cornell University. "However, in 85 years of use, no oil-resistant strain of a pest has appeared."

While dormant oils will not take care of all your orchard pests, they are especially effective in controlling those species of mites which over-winter in the egg stage, particularly the European red mite and San José scale. The sprays are also used with good results against the pear psylla, scale insects, aphids, thrips, mealybugs, and white flies, as well as the eggs of the codling moth, oriental fruit moth, cankerworm, and various leaf rollers. Fungus growth and a bacterial disease, fire blight, are cleared up with dormant oil.

Many other apple pests overwinter or lay eggs in the trash and leaves under the trees, and the oil treatments don't even touch them. Come spring, the adults fly up into the trees to make trouble. For this reason, it's wise to rake up leaves and keep the ground clear of fallen fruit. Although some of these insects may overwinter in a permanent mulch under fruit trees, so do many natural enemies, including the ladybugs that eat scale and mites. Dick Colburn, an entomologist at the Penn State Fruit Research Center at Biglerville, Pennsylvania, says, you shouldn't leave the ladybugs without a food supply by killing off all the mites and scale, and he recommends that you use dormant oil only every two or three years instead of every year. Such a program of reduced spraying should be of interest to growers who want to experiment with the delicate interplay of pests and predators in the orchard.

Without dormant oil or a healthy supply of natural enemies, infestations of mites and scale can severely damage trees. Mites destroy the chlorophyll in leaves, turning them a reddish brown, and the resulting poor production of carbohydrates can prevent the formation of fruit buds and reduce the size of the apple itself. Damage from scale will start killing off limbs and branches and can eventually kill the tree. Also, scale insects leave small reddish marks on apples, sometimes surrounded by a tiny whitish band, that lessen their keeping time and, in a commercial operation, knock them out of grade so they can't be marketed at top prices.

Stock preparations of dormant- (also called miscible-) oil sprays are sold by all garden supply houses, and come with instructions for dilution and use. Scalecide is one such product. Commercial preparations are sometimes combined with Bordeaux mixture, an arsenate of lead, or other strong chemicals that render the oil toxic. Without going into scary case histories, it should be emphasized that such chemicals are dangerous to handle and are to be avoided. Lime sulfur is also employed as a dormant spray, but it is intensely poisonous and can harm soil and plants.

You can make your own oil spray at home with a little trouble. Add one part light-grade motor oil (10 weight, without additives) to 15 parts water. Soap or detergent can be added to make the ingredients mix better. These ingredients are mixed together, brought to a boil, and poured back and forth from one container to another until thoroughly blended. Since all oil emulsions tend to separate back into oil and water, the mixture should be used as soon as possible after it is prepared.

Dormant sprays are so called because they are used when trees are in their dormant stage—before buds open in spring, and after leaves have dropped in fall. Organic growers emphasize spraying no later than the end of February to avoid injuring delicate opening buds and new twig growth. "I apply it when the leaf buds are just beginning to show signs of swelling," says Bill Hatfield, owner of the 30-acre Double Top Orchard in Franklin, North Carolina. "After the leaf buds open, or grow too soft and fat, the oil can penetrate the new tissue and kill it. I use it in the fall when the freezes are hard, the leaves are all off the trees, and when the temperature during the day has gotten above 40°." Hatfield thinks users should also wait for temperatures above 40° in the spring, as the oil spreads more easily. Apple and pear buds are the exception, being somewhat resistant to spray injury; for these trees, you can delay spraying a couple of weeks to make sure they get a good head start on the bugs.

Oil emulsions used on foliage are called summer sprays or white oils.

These are lighter in weight than dormant oils, but nevertheless can cause leaf burn and heavy leaf and fruit drop, as well as change the flavor of the fruit.

A thorough spring application usually should carry trees through the season. Some fruit growers use "superior dormant oils," highly refined oils that can be used later than regular sprays with safety. Later applications are especially valuable in controlling the European red mite, whose eggs become softer and increasingly susceptible to oil as their hatching period approaches. A three-percent concentration of superior oil will destroy many such pests that are normally resistant to oil; more mite eggs are killed with a two-percent superior-oil spray applied in the delayed dormant stage than by a four-percent spray applied when the apple trees are still dormant. As for apples, their delayed dormant stage is signalled when approximately ½ inch of leaf tissue is exposed in the blossom buds.

Thorough spraying is essential. Every part of every branch and every square inch of every trunk should be covered. Delay spraying if freezing temperatures are likely to follow, as the water-based mixture could freeze on the trees. You should also avoid spraying on windy days to ensure good coverage. Stir or agitate the oil solution frequently to keep it well mixed. It's hard to apply too much dormant spray, in that excess emulsion simply runs off. But moderation is the best policy, since the spray affects good bugs along with the bad. A tree should be sprayed in one shot, rather than a side at a time as happens when sprayers work down an orchard row; this is because coverages would overlap, and the resulting overdose could conceivably cause damage on citrus trees, especially in arid areas. The drier and warmer the air, it seems, the more likelihood of damage. It is safer to use a very thin mixture of a highly refined oil, such as vegetable oil. In fact, a report published by the USDA concluded that crude corn oil, crude peanut oil, and crude cottonseed oil are equal to or superior to petroleum oil against oyster-shell scale, Mexican mealybugs, and willow scurfy scale; the refined oils are somewhat less effective. Crude peanut oil was also found to be effective against San José scale, while linseed and cottonseed oils were of little use.

Other tree sprays.   Dr. John E. Bier, Professor of Forest Pathology at the University of British Columbia, has found a way to use nature's own method of preventing and curing tree disease. He found that the *bark* and *leaves* of healthy trees are covered with colonies of harmless fungi, bacteria, and yeasts that have the power of preventing the growth of pathogenic fungi—the source of most tree diseases. To put the harmless organisms at work in a spray, scrape healthy bark off a tree branch and shred small pieces of it in an electric blender. Healthy leaves also work. Use ¼ ounce of shredded material per pint of water. Keep the solution in a warm room for five days, pouring it back and forth between two jars several times a day to aerate it. After the five days are up, strain the solution and spray. You might also try standing the base ends of cuttings in the solution for an hour before setting them in a rooting medium. Dr. Bier has found that this treatment, along with watering the plants with the culture, will render the plants resistant to canker.

A Pennsylvania grower, Jerome W. Wagman, has come up with a fruit tree spray that can safely be used in summer—and the ingredients are in your kitchen. Dissolve two pounds of granulated *sugar* in five gallons of warm water. Let the mixture set for several hours before spraying. You can use it on any fruit tree, as well as on grapes, roses, cherries, and chestnut trees. These treatments should follow a dormant-oil spraying in early spring; you switch over to sugar spray after the blossoms start to drop.

A gallon of blackstrap *molasses* in 50 gallons of water does the trick in C. J. Gurttel's Washington State orchard. All you do is spray and then "let the sparrows do the rest. They sure like bugs sweetened with molasses," he says. A spray of *sour milk* can be used to loosen scale on small citrus trees so that the insects can be washed right off with water. The pear psylla is vulnerable to a spray of *liquified seaweed* and *onion juice*. A commercial spray, Banex, combines liquid seaweed with a petroleum distillate to make a barrier against mites, aphids, scale, thrips, and fungus spores on vegetables and trees. The one drawback to this product, admits the manufacturer, is that it must be applied in a fogger or micron sprayer so that every twig and leaf surface is covered with minute droplets.

Back in 1900, the report of the New York Farmer's Institute listed these ingredients to kill San José scale on trees: "3 pounds of common resin, 1 pound of caustic soda, 1 pint of fish oil, and 2 gallons of water." The mixture was heated to a boil, and then allowed to cool. It had to be diluted for spraying.

The high-powered botanicals:

rotenone, pyrethrum, ryania, and others.   On the island of Trinidad there grows a shrub called the *ryania*. This plant is the object of much attention of late because its roots are the source of a mildly alkaline insecticide that is considered quite safe to warm-blooded animals, including humans. Apparently, ryania works not by administering death to insects, but by making them good and sick. It incapacitates the oriental fruit moth, corn borers, cranberry fruitworm, codling moth, and cotton bollworm, among others.

Like the other botanical insecticides described in this section, ryania sounds good. The stuff won't kill the neighbor's dog, it works against a wide variety of insects, and it breaks down to harmless substances. But these potent botanicals aren't to be found in every organic gardener's workshed. One reason is that many gardeners see such insecticides as a crutch. If you find it necessary to call on such a powerful control, chances are the balance of life in your garden is out of whack. So, as you administer ryania or any of the other high-powered insecticides, ask yourself if the problem could have been prevented. These are "organic," "safe" insecticides, it's true, but that is not to say that they are a necessary part of growing organically.

To continue on the benefits of ryania, it is particularly useful for saving a crop that is very susceptible to a particular pest; a good example is control of the codling moth on apples. For this application, buy 100 percent ryania dust and mix it with water at the rate of about one ounce per two gallons of water. To make a stronger solution, use $1\frac{1}{4}$ ounces of the dust. About five sprays are needed during the season. Start spraying 10 to 14 days after the petal fall and continue at 10- to 14-day intervals until you have sprayed three or four times. When the second brood of codling moth larvae hatch, give one to three additional sprays at the same interval; your county agent should be able to tell you when the second brood is hatching. An ordinary hand sprayer holding two to three gallons of solution is good enough for the small orchard.

Rotenone is another plant-derived insecticide that has proven to be harmless to warm-blooded animals. It occurs in several tropical plants: derris (another name for rotenone), cube barbasco, and timbo, to name a few. When shopping for rotenone, you should read labels to see if the product has been adulterated with synthetic toxins. Pure rotenone can be safely used on all crops and ornamentals. It kills many types of insects, including certain external parasites of animals. However, it has little residual effect and the period of protection it offers is short.

A native weed, Devil's shoestring (*Tephrasis virginiana*), contains rotenone. It is a perennial with yellowish white flowers, growing to about two feet, and is found in the eastern and southern states. The plant was once used by American Indians as a fish poison. The roots contain up to five percent rotenone and you might, with the aid of an illustrated field guide to wild plants, find some roots to grind into your own powder.

Pyrethrum is a well-known insecticide that is made from the pyrethrum flower, a member of the chrysanthemum family. While pyrethrum is safe for warm-blooded animals, as natural insecticides go it's a heavy. Dozens of fruit and vegetable pests are controlled by it: all kinds of caterpillars, beetles, aphids, mites, leafhoppers, thrips, moths, and others. The esters (called pyrethrins) that give pyrethrum products their power are relatively non-toxic to bees and ladybug larvae, although adult ladybugs are killed at higher rates of application. A comprehensive work on the subject, *Pyrethrum: The Natural Insecticide,* (John E. Casida, editor), says that, ". . . although pyrethrins do have adverse effects on certain natural enemies the effects are probably fairly selective on different stages, and being non-persistent, the effects would not be long-lasting." Although offered in the book as a piece of good news, this statement should serve to caution the organic gardener; to use pyrethrum is to grievously tamper with life in the garden, insect enemies and insect allies alike. And as mentioned before, a temporary setback for the good bugs, brought about by an injudicious use of pyrethrum, could wipe out many patient weeks of biological and cultural control.

On the positive side, pyrethrum can save a seriously endangered crop; it is readily available commercially; although testing continues, pyrethrins appear to be readily metabolized by animals without ill effects, and rapidly break down into harmless substances in the environment; and the attractive daisylike flowers can be grown in the garden. To make your own pyrethrum spray, just grind up a few flower heads and mix with water. A little soap can be added to improve the consistency. In *Beneficial Insects,* Lester A. Swann tells how to repel the adult codling moth with pyrethrum extract. "Corrugated paper bands are impregnated with a five percent extract, to which a proportion of from five to ten percent of cottonseed oil, emulsified with blood albumen, has been added." He adds that pyrethrum mixed with vanishing cream makes an effective midge repellent for people, "providing the person does not sweat too much."

A review of the literature on this plant, compiled in Casida's book, highlights pyrethrum's strengths and weaknesses: the dust not only controls leafhoppers on potatoes, but acts as a growth stimulant on the crop as well; the dust is effective against the six-spotted leafhopper, which is a vector of lettuce yellows; pyrethrum is especially hard on the cabbage looper, but considerably less effective in controlling the imported cabbageworm; it little bothers the artichoke plume moth, while the artichoke aphid is very vulnerable; the tomato fruitworm and beet armyworm on tomatoes and aphids on spinach and commercial greens aren't controlled; pyrethrum can be mixed with oil and dropped in corn ears to check the corn earworm. This insecticide has considerable value to the beleaguered fruit grower, offering control of lygus bugs on peach; grape, flower, and citrus thrips; the grape leafhopper; and the cranberry fruitworm.

Recent tests suggest that pyrethrins are more useful in controlling adult populations than larvae. In either case, the insecticide is most potent when applied as a spray. As a last-ditch effort, you might mix up a spray containing the big three botanicals—rotenone, ryania, and pyrethrum, mixed with a colloidal clay and suspended in water. Pyrethrum quickly loses its powers when stored in open containers, but retains its effectiveness up to three years in closed containers.

If you buy pyrethrum, watch out for formulations that contain additives to increase its power and persistence. It is often combined with "synergists," things added to enhance its effectiveness. According to a report by New England Research, *An Evaluation of Potential Risks Resulting from the Use of Pyrethrins As Insecticides*, the most popular such additive, piperonyl butoxide, may affect liver microsomal systems.

Insects are paralyzed by pyrethrum, sometimes after a short period of jumping around. If a bug receives less than a lethal dose, it will revive completely. For this reason, insects that still show any sign of life after an application should be stepped on or otherwise destroyed; or, if you are so inclined, the stunned pests can be removed from the garden area to continue their lives elsewhere.

Of this group of lethal botanicals, *quassia* is perhaps the safest. It spares ladybugs and bees, while working against aphids, sawflies, and caterpillars. Quassia is purchased in the form of wood chips and shavings from a Jamaican tree. To make a solution for spraying, the wood is simply steeped in water. A century-old recipe for combatting aphids is made from quassia chips and larkspur seed boiled in water. The tea is syringed on plants.

False hellebore acts as a stomach poison for insects. It is especially useful against worm pests of the garden, sawflies, and chewing insects such as beetles, caterpillars, grubs, cutworms, and grasshoppers. Although grown domestically, false hellebore is not listed with the grow-it-yourself remedies because of its potency, both to the bugs and you, and it should not be ingested. If you decide to try this botanical, keep its original use in mind—at one time the tips of arrows were treated with false hellebore to make a slight wound lethal.

A commercial insecticide called Hellebore is made from the plant's roots and sold as a dry powder. It is most often used as a dust to protect ripening fruits and vegetables. As a dust the powder is mixed with flour or hydrated lime; a spray is made by mixing one ounce of Hellebore with two gallons of water.

You can grow your own false hellebore from seed sown in spring or early fall, or from root divisions in spring. The plant prefers light, sandy soil, and displays large yellow flowers.

Sabadilla dust is made from the seeds of a South American and Mexican plant of the lily family. The dust isn't mentioned much in current times, but it has been used as an insecticide since the sixteenth century. After studying sabadilla, entomologists at the University of Wisconsin patented a method for increasing the toxicity of sabadilla by heating the powdered seed in kerosene or other solvent to 150° C. (302° F.) for one hour. The seed dust has the interesting property of becoming more powerful during storage. It can be used to control a good number of insect pests, including the grasshopper, European corn borer, codling moth larva, armyworm, webworm, silkworm, aphids, cabbage looper, melonworm, squash bug, blister beetle, greenhouse leaf tier, squash bug, chinch bug, lygus bug, harlequin bug, and many house pests. Sabadilla seeds and dust are stocked by several suppliers, who caution users that the product can irritate mucous membranes and bring on sneezing fits.

Other plants have insecticidal powers, but aren't listed here because they are toxic to humans, difficult to obtain, or just because information on them is either non-existent or elusive. One such plant has buds that look somewhat like dolphins and was once used to consolidate wounds, as indicated by its Latin name, *Delphinium consolida*. Known as *field larkspur,* the plant grows in the wild and bears seeds that reportedly stymie aphids and thrips. These seeds are highly poisonous, and care should be taken that children don't eat them or any other part of the plant. A spray of two percent *oil of coriander* will kill the red spider mite; a spray of *anise oil* should do as well.

Diatomaceous earth.   About 30 million years ago, countless one-celled plants called diatoms lived in the sea and built little protective shells out of the silica they extracted from the water. When a diatom died, its tiny shell drifted to the sea floor; over the course of centuries, these shells built up into deposits, sometimes thousands of feet thick. When the ocean waters receded to leave the continents, the shells in these deposits were fossilized and compressed into a soft, chalky rock that came to be called diatomaceous earth. Today, the stuff is prepared for commercial use by quarrying, milling, grinding, screening, and centrifuging. The result is a fine, talclike powder that can be handled safely without gloves and even be eaten; however, it may cause silicosis if breathed heavily.

This tale is told here because the seemingly innocuous powder will kill insects on contact. Diatomaceous dust is not a poison, but works mechanically. Proper milling cracks apart the diatom skeletons to expose microscopic needles of silica that are razor-sharp daggers at the insect's scale of life. If these daggers pierce an insect's exoskeleton, the misfortunate creature dehydrates and dies. If the dust is eaten by an insect, the daggers interfere with breathing, digestion, and reproduction.

Fortunately, the tough internal and external tissues of warm-blooded animals make them immune to damage from the microscopic edges. Diatomaceous dust can be applied safely without requiring protective breathing devices, and only prolonged breathing of volumes more than 20 million particles per cubic foot of air, eight hours per day, five days per week (as would happen in grinding mills), requires the protection of a filter mask.

The use of protective dusts is not original with man. Birds and mammals have been taking dust baths, with the same effect, for millions of years. The Chinese picked up the idea over 4,000 years ago, but the method was then apparently lost, to be rediscovered in this country in the late fifties.

Diatomaceous dust also works inside animals, controlling worms and other internal parasites. Dairymen, cattlemen, horse owners, dog owners, and poultry men find that this method is gentle and natural. One interesting benefit of feeding animals the dust is that their manure seems to have a degree of built-in fly control.

Some bugs are more vulnerable to diatomaceous earth than others. It usually means death to the gypsy moth, codling moth, pink boll weevil, lygus bug, twig borer, thrips, mites, earwig, cockroach, slug, adult mosquito, snail, nematode, flies, cornworm, tomato hornworm, and even mildew. Also, on fruit trees the dust can handle aphids, spider mites, the oriental fruit moth, codling moth, and twig borer; brown rot can be controlled by dusting a day or two before harvest.

If diatomaceous earth sounds like an easy answer to your problems, it's not. Orchardist Fred Bracken of Palisades, California, says that if you don't know the life cycle of the insects on your trees, you'd better not try to use the dust; otherwise you might blitz the beneficials that are all-important to getting unpoisoned fruit through the season. This insecticide works about as well as the farmer or gardener using it works, and can't be regarded as a panacea. One point against the dust is that it performs less effectively in hot, humid weather, because the outside moisture balances an insect's internal moisture—and the insect doesn't dry up. Another problem is that a healthy and thorough application is needed to effect good control; unless an insect comes in contact with the tiny particles, it will go on its merry way.

In sum, early and conscientious applications can control a wide variety of destructive insects. Precisely what insects, how, and how effectively, requires more investigation and someone to do the necessary kind of research. However, to reduce a long story into one phrase, the USDA has interfered with testing and research.

Perma-Guard is the only firm presently processing and selling diatomite as a pesticide. The company has a patent, and is the only firm in the U.S. and Canada which can legally sell diatomaceous earth as an insecticide for grain storage. John Mansfield & Co., which mines in Lompoc, California, uses diatomite for roofing material, for concrete mixtures, and also for swimming pool filter systems.

Sulfur.   Sulfur has been used as a fungicide for thousands of years. It's a naturally occurring element that's needed in small quantities in the soil, but that doesn't mean that the vineyard, garden, or orchard can handle it in concentrated doses. Some organic growers won't touch sulfur, reasoning that as a fungicide it can disturb the soil microorganisms that work for the overall health of the plants. Entomologists point out that sulfur can have a negative effect on beneficial insects.

Many people cannot grow grapes without resorting to sulfur because they have planted grapes in areas of slow-moving air and high humidity concentrations—perfect for the development of mildew. Grapevines shouldn't be troubled by mildew if grown in sunny locations on slopes where the air moves, if properly pruned during the season for maximum air circulation and light penetration, and if cultured organically. In less than these optimum conditions, mildew may be a persistent problem, and growers usually have to choose between using sulfur or uprooting the vines.

Sulfur is used by fruit growers to get their trees by both fungal diseases and mites. Biological control research has shown that sulfur is lethal to many beneficials that, left to themselves, can keep down a number of important pests. So, in the orchard too, sulfur is a last resort. Another thing to keep in mind is that sulfur and oil sprays should not be used within a month of each other.

You shouldn't need to fall back on sulfur in the garden if plants are properly tended. This is just as well, as many cucurbits and roses may be severely damaged by this fungicide.

Are Hormonal Controls
The Coming Thing?

Hormones are compounds which trigger bodily changes in an insect, namely metamorphosis and moulting. These compounds occur naturally in the insect, and researchers seek to synthesize hormone "mimics" that can be used to play tricks with a pest's development, rendering it harmless.

At first glance, hormonal controls look good. Unlike conventional pesticides, they are not toxic to pests, but instead indirectly lead to control, either by death or interference with reproductive capability. Neither have they been found toxic to man and other vertebrates. Another point in their favor is their potential host specificity. While it was thought at first that the chemicals would be highly *species* specific, researchers now realize that they are *order* specific—which is less desirable, but still superior to most insecticides. A third consideration is that most growth-regulating chemicals degrade rapidly in the environment. The director of product development at Zoecon Corporation, a hormone manufacturer, explains that because these chemicals are not persistent in the environment, in some cases special formulations may be required to lengthen their residual life.

On top of this, hormonal controls are extremely potent. Only chemicals that show biological activity at one nanogram (a billionth of a gram) are seriously considered for further research. In 1968, Czech researchers learned just how little hormonal chemical was effective: less than one microgram (a millionth of a gram) applied to the body surface of a female linden bug at any time during the reproductive cycle sterilized the insect for the rest of its life. A dose of 100 micrograms administered to males is strong enough to sterilize the females they mate with, and these females, mating with other (untreated) males, can pass on enough hormonal chemical to sterilize the following generation of females. Considering the concentrated power of these chemicals, it should not be surprising that they are relatively cheap to produce, and this makes them doubly attractive to manufacturer and prospective user alike.

How hormonal chemicals work.   Two kinds of hormones are of interest: juvenile hormones and molting hormones. Harvard biologist Dr. Carrol Williams found that juvenile hormone (JH) is needed to stimulate an immature worm to grow larger, but that it must be absent if the worm is ever to become a sexually mature adult. So, a larva treated with synthesized JH will continue to molt into progressively larger worms instead of becoming an adult. In other cases, a half-pupa, half-adult monster is the result. If administered to an adult female during the reproductive cycle, the hormones disturb development of the sex apparatus, formation of the yolk, and maturation of the eggs within the female. Fiddling with an insect's hormones can also undo its ability to go into a resting phase (diapause), or wake it from diapause when the habitat is unfavorable.

While JH can only determine what sort of molt will take place, molting hormones (MH) actually cause the molt, disrupting insect development at any larval or nymphal stage. JH is the slower of the two, as it allows insects to continue to feed until their terminal molt. Thus, the grower does not reap any advantages until later, when the arrested development is reflected in less mating and a lower population density. Another disadvantage is that JH compounds must be applied during certain susceptible periods in an insect's development in order to take effect. Coupled with the fact that JH is unstable in the field, this means an application may miss an insect's vulnerable period.

MH compounds are not without problems, either: they are generally not as active as the better JH compounds; they don't pass as easily through an insect's cuticle; and because they have a more complex molecular makeup, they would probably be more expensive to produce commercially.

Primarily because of this last consideration, most hormone research today is concerned with JH compounds—synthesizing them and testing them in the field. This work goes on at several agricultural chemical and pharmaceutical companies (including Zoecon, which is an offspring of the company that developed the birth-control pill—juvenile hormones are a by-product of birth-control research). These concerns are also looking into anti-juvenile hormones, which work by stopping development of the insects at early molts. Such "hormonal insecticides" would be fast-acting and could be used much like conventional pesticides.

At this writing, no hormonal controls are on the market for commercial purposes, but producers are pushing for government acceptance. It's easy to understand their hurry, considering that the chemicals are cheap to make, are powerful even in minute amounts, and may appease some ecologically minded critics of traditional pesticides. Says Dr. Morton Grosser in an article written for Zoecon, "This combination of specificity, chain reaction, and absence of poison has never been achieved before in insect control." But that's not the whole picture.

Problems with hormonal control.   For organic growers and people in the biological control field, the initial enthusiasm for hormonal control has been tempered by the realization that this method might share the problems inherent in traditional chemical control. "There is danger that developments in this field could follow the pattern resulting from the almost exclusive reliance on conventional insecticides, with similar attendant ills," opines C. B. Huffaker in a background paper prepared for a 1973 conference on integrated pest management held in Berkeley, California. And one by one, the unique aspects of hormonal control that supposedly set it apart from conventional chemical control have been critically examined.

(1.) Although it is thought that hormonal chemicals disrupt processes peculiar to insects, and although insect hormones are structurally different from the hormones of vertebrates, we should not conclude that vertebrates are safe. Huffaker believes that "effects on vertebrates or other non-target species could arise through processes other than those with which they are associated in insects." While it's true that the compounds appear safe to vertebrates even when ingested in huge amounts, it comes to mind that developers and manufacturers of chemical products have been incredibly lax in the past in testing for long-term effects. If we'd known in 1945 what we know about DDT today, we might not have covered the earth with a layer of the stuff.

(2.) It had been thought that insects could not develop resistance to hormonal controls, as these chemicals mimic compounds in the insects' own bodies. But William E. Robbins suggests in *Pest Control Strategies for the Future* (published by the National Academy of Sciences) that the chemicals likely differ structurally from the insect's own hormones.

This means that the chemicals may well be handled by the insect as foreign compounds rather than its own metabolic juices.

(3.) To make their product more marketable, companies are coming up with new formulae that will last longer in the field and will knock out a bigger number of species. This undoes two advantages that hormonal controls could have, and to organic growers who believe that persistent, wide-spectrum chemicals wreak environmental havoc, the new formulae should be anything but attractive.

From the companies' point of view, however, a chemical that controls a good number of species is more marketable than a series of specific chemicals. "We're not too delighted when people suggest each substance must be specific for one species," says Zoecon vice-president Daniel Lazare. What does he see as the ideal compromise between selectivity and marketability? "We're hoping for moderate selectivity, to reach a family or group of insects while sparing some of the beneficial insects."

This juggling of priorities should sound familiar; the companies developing these so-called third generation pesticides are treating their product as a traditional chemical insecticide. And this approach is not going to earn them many friends from the ranks of organic growers.

Dr. Everett J. Dietrick, an entomologist who heads Rincon-Vitova Insectaries, has "very strong reservations" about the use of juvenile hormones. "They are out of step with nature. They could be one more useful tool in insect control if they are used sparingly and very specifically, and then only when absolutely necessary. But the companies making them plan huge sales, or they wouldn't be spending the money on them that they are. I'd say okay to them if they were very specific, but if using them widely is the way we make our food—no good. Nature resists single answers."

The use of hormonal controls, as invisioned by the firms now developing them, conflicts with organic practice in a number of other ways. As is true with conventional pesticides, broad-spectrum hormones can eliminate both the target pest and its natural enemies, paving the way for a resurgence of the pest and according to Dr. Barry M. Trost, a University of Wisconsin scientist doing research on such compounds, the result could be "an ecological disaster."

Researcher Francis Lawson sees broad-spectrum hormonal controls as just another chemical. "Any broad-spectrum chemical is going to kill pests *and* their natural enemies. . . . Who knows what effects you may get? The real problem is that for thirty to forty years we have sought only chemical solutions to insect control." Just as hormones seem to be the answer today, DDT was once looked upon as the perfect control.

(4.) Other concerns stem from the impressive power of hormonal chemicals. For one thing, their use could not very well be restricted to the area of application, as minute amounts might easily get carried by wind and water and end up biologically bombing a grower down the road.

(5.) And then there's the notion that any control that works too well poses a threat both to your plot and potentially to the earth around it. If it seems that we are overstating the problem, consider human nature for a moment. Hormones are a threat because their magical expediency appeals to us. They would enable us to turn our backs on the processes of biological control by encouraging monocropping (thereby undoing the diversity of insects that keep each other in line) and by encouraging growers to bypass the organic approach to insect control (through growing healthy plants from a healthy soil). "Hormones oversimplify the system," warns Dietrick. "They are a short-sighted answer."

In sum, hormonal control denies the interrelatedness of all the parts of our ecosystem, and appears at this time to be little more than the newest in a succession of increasingly sophisticated chemicals in man's arsenal.

11
Weeds As Pests And Allies

Weeds are the earth's natural covering. Many are edible, providing an inexhaustible supply of food for those who choose to harvest it. Their carcasses build the soil in yearly layers and their roots pull trace elements to the surface. If only garden vegetables were as rugged and tenacious— but they usually are not and must be nurtured along, with the stronger weeds kept in check.

Weeds have their uses and, properly employed, can be an asset to your homestead instead of a trial and a source of constant grief. Here are some of their good qualities that organic gardeners have come to appreciate over the years:

1. They can be used in the compost pile.
2. Shredded or just plain pulled, they can be used as mulch, particularly around trees.
3. There are lots of edible weeds, as anyone who has read Euell Gibbons knows.
4. Many of the deep-rooted varieties bring up minerals from the subsoil and make them available to crop plants.
5. Weeds with powerful roots can break up hardpan, permitting the crop plants to really take hold.
6. They protect the ground as a cover crop, keeping it from blowing away, and then add their organic matter to it.
7. Their root systems actually make room in the soil for the root systems of crop plants.
8. They improve the soil's aeration and water-soaking ability, thus providing a better environment for the soil microbial life.

Weeds can be used in the compost pile to advantage. Jane Stuwe of Great Falls, Montana, reports that she adds Russian and Canadian thistle to her compost pile—mainly because thistle was the one substance available to her. Bob Godwin, of Van Buren, Arkansas, works with Jimson weeds mixed with grass clippings plus table scraps and vegetable trimmings. Working with weeds this way is hard work, but worth it, he says.

Johnson grass is James Wood's affliction down in Albany, Texas. But he has found it to be a great soil-builder, containing 33 percent more nitrogen and 50 percent more phosphate than alfalfa, and 25 percent more potash than coastal Bermuda grass.

Believe it or not, using weeds as "mother crops" to nurse along your weaker vegetables should be given serious consideration. Joseph Cocannouer says in *Weeds, Guardians of the Soil* that right now there are many practical farmers in this country who are successfully employing weeds for this purpose. These growers consider weeds as good crop insurance, and realize that mother weeds invariably conserve soil moisture rather than use it all up.

F. C. King, British author of *Gardening With Compost* agrees that there is room for both crop and weeds, and has never found that controlled weeds interfere with the crop.

"Mothering hard-to-grow vegetables with the right kind of weeds will often solve growing difficulties," Cocannouer reports. This applies equally to leaf and root crops like beets, carrots, and turnips that need a deep, friable root zone. The mother weeds loosen the soil, permitting the root crops to grow large easily—to be savory and highly nutritious, they should not be forced to fight a dense, compact soil. The leafy vegetable crops also benefit from the intermingling of weed and vegetable roots.

Weeds also enter into the rotation of crops. On weak land, annual weeds used in rotation should be given two years to make a start. On abandoned or badly eroded land, it may take weeds four years to go deep enough to bring up valuable minerals to the surface. Because such soil is deficient in nitrogen, it is advisable to turn weeds under when they are in the flowering stage—the nitrogen content of leaves and stalks is greatest at this time.

If you really want to do a first-rate job of green manuring, permit the weeds to wilt before turning them under. This wise practice goes back to Roman days when Marcus Cato first observed that green materials should be cut and permitted to start decay before inculcating them into the land. The soil's work is to feed plants, and it cannot take on the extra work without lowering crop production.

Tobacco growers have long known that weeds can be used as a rotation link to bring productive fertility to the land. The weeds used include common and giant ragweed, thistles, and lamb's-quarters—all of which have penetrating root systems. According to the tobacco farmers, the weeds produce a superabundance of organic matter which is what tobacco, a rather exacting crop, needs.

A word of caution: green-manuring land with weeds may call for weed treatment—you just can't turn the weeds loose to grow any old way. Thick growths may have to be thinned to encourage strong root systems. However, Cocannouer advises, "with a dense growth of healthy weeds, many of the plants will fight their way down into the lower soils. Nature," he concludes, "will employ her soil builders constructively—if man gives her a chance to put her laws into operation without any interference from himself."

Weeds have one more great virtue—they can tell you what kind of soil you're working with. A beginning gardener or a new homesteader should find this a very valuable trait. Your soil is acid if it's got sheep sorrel, swamp horsetail, and cinquefoil standing on it. On the other hand, goldenrod, common spikeweed, salt grass, and pickleweed mean that it's alkali. Field mustard, horse nettle, morning glory, and quackgrass indicate the presence of hardpan. Smartweed, many of the sedges, hedge bindweed, and meadow pink tell you that poor drainage prevails.

Garden Weeding

In the organic gardens weeding mostly means mulching. You cover the soil so deep with plant residues or other impenetratable matter that weeds can't grow. This technique keeps weeds down in all the areas where crops aren't growing, such as garden paths and alongside rows or beds. All that's left for the gardener is to weed directly around the plants. As vegetables develop, the mulch can be pulled up to the stems. Long-time organic gardener Ruth Stout has developed a permanent mulch system. She keeps her garden well covered with yearly (or more) applications of hay or other mulch. She pulls the mulch aside to plant, and weeds just can't get started.

Catharine Foster, a Vermonter and organic gardener, uses several approaches to keeping her garden weeds under control. "While I drive around town or peer into my neighbors' yards, I often take note of the methods they use to control weeds. A few still use the old lengthy method of getting down on their knees and pulling the weeds out by hand—which is good exercise, it's true—but by now most other people use less arduous methods," she says.

"For several years I have been trying to figure out why the various gardeners in this Vermont town use the different methods they do. Perhaps those with a temperament for neatness are those that pile on peat moss, buckwheat hulls or ground bark between their plants so that everything looks very ship-shape and the weeds are mulched out of existence. In one such neat garden I saw that the mulch used was ground bark mixed with cocoa shells, a sensible mixture because cocoa shells by themselves are both expensive and likely to become very caked and moldly and horrible looking.

"Then there are the less fussy or slightly neat people who will use a hay mulch, newspapers covered with leaves, or half-finished compost which has undecomposed bits of twigs, peanut shells and even scraps of eggshell still showing.

"The least fussy—or those who like a mess—allow a riot of different plants to grow up all together, and then just use crowding as a weed-control method. One man I know who has such a riotous garden lets huge plants of lamb's-quarters grow up here and there among his vegetables because he likes to eat them as a pot herb. Another garden I stop to look at in June uses this method in the flower beds. During most of that month there are masses of lupines all through the garden, two kinds of poppies, and everywhere big lush plants of chives and other members of the allium family. What a good idea that was—to use chives as a ground cover and let the flowers take care of themselves and thrive with the protective alliums to ward off enemies."

Ground covers are helpful in smothering weeds. Pachysandra, myrtle, and vinca are good choices. Bigger plants that will crowd out weeds include ferns of many kinds, Siberian iris, day lilies, violets, feverfew, and catnip—all perennials. Artemisias or crown vetch will do, but they are inclined to take over if given half a chance. Lilies-of-the-valley are much nicer to encourage and the garden will grow in the shade, too.

Annuals that can be used as ground covers include marigolds, nasturtiums, snapdragons, petunias, and some of the herbs. These annuals can be planted by scattering seeds. One gardener plants lettuce this way, and the garden is handsome and absolutely weed-free as soon as the leaves get big enough to overshadow the whole plot.

One weed can be used to control other weeds: purslane. The low, thick-growing plants are pleasant to walk on, and they make it possible to go into the garden after a rain without compacting the earth. It also helps keep the earth cool in hot weather. Purslane is good to eat—in fact, the early settlers brought it over as a garden plant in the first place.

In other parts of the vegetable garden, the vegetables themselves can control weeds and protect the soil. Squash grown among corn serves both ends. Volunteer tomatoes do, too. Even the tomatoes you set out, if you refrain from staking them and let them spread, will discourage weeds. Of course tomatoes like a mulch, and some clean hay under the plant will keep the fruits clean and unattacked by pests, especially slugs who can't stand the prickliness of hay on their soft bodies.

Once in a while a discouraging abundance of some weed will get into a bed—it might be chicory in the asparagus, goldenrod near the rhubarb, or a big tough thing like horseradish where you do not want it—and if mulch isn't doing the job, you might consider salt. But it has to be applied very carefully, either as a solution you dribble on the leaves of the weeds to kill them, or sprinkled dry and then misted to form a film over the leaves. It is best to spread something on the ground if you are going to be careless or sloppy, because you don't want a lot of salt going down into the earth and injuring the delicate root hairs of your crops.

But other, harmless covers should suffice in most cases. In the vegetable garden, hay is preferred by many growers. In the flower garden, try ground bark. It does not dry out the way peat moss does, will not prevent water from going through it during a rain, and doesn't rob the soil of water the way peat moss does. Also, bark decays slowly and you can scratch compost through it without too much trouble. And it doesn't shrink up and let weeds come through the way peat moss does at times.

Stones work well around trees. They are handsome, effective, and do the job. Once there, that's that; they do not decay into the ground and never have to be replaced. Besides, they ward off any lawn mowers that could come bumping up against the bark. Also you don't have to worry about feeding between them, because trees are fed at the drip-line, out at the ends of the branches.

Mulch doesn't have to be plant residues—although organic mulches have several important side benefits that black plastic, newspapers, and stones don't have. Still, in particularly troublesome areas, or for certain jobs, you may want to cover the ground with black plastic. Plastic is not biodegradable, but if it has been used for something else and is to be thrown out anyway, your conscience shouldn't bother you too much. Cut big pieces of plastic into strips and put them between rows, weighing them down with rocks. Clear plastic will not work, however, as the weeds continue to grow under it. If you are interested in trying this method, you might check construction sites in your area. Painters often use it and then throw it away. Farmers that do not have enough room in their barns to store all their hay sometimes cover a stack with plastic, and when the hay is used up, they simply throw the sheets away. However, make sure you don't cover any of your vegetables with plastic as it kills indiscriminately. Also, if it is used around a vine plant, be sure to remove it when little vegetables start to appear. Moisture will form under them and cause blemishes and sometimes rotting. By the time the fruit appears on vines, there is usually enough ground coverage by the vine to smother most of the weeds, anyway.

If you are plagued with grass in the garden, you can consider a very natural control—geese love to eat narrow-bladed plants, and this makes them particularly suited for the keeping down of grass. When properly managed, their effectiveness will be greater than that of the most diligent gardener. Cotton, strawberries, corn, orchards, vineyards, and many other crop areas may be efficiently weeded by geese. Weeding geese must be contained if you want them to do a complete job, and three-foot chicken wire should do the job.

The economic value of geese has been shown in studies at the University of Tennessee Agricultural Experiment Station. Besides saving the expense of hand labor and chemical weed control, their manure is continually fertilizing the soil. The weed you hoe or pull will have its reuseable compounds and elements returned to the earth as quickly as that consumed by a goose.

Farm Weed Control

On the organic farm, weeds are controlled by cultivation primarily. Both farmers and gardeners know weed seeds are long-lived, and take care to cut weedy areas near the field or garden before seeds are made. The soil itself is a repository of billions of seeds from years past. Some seeds from weeds that grew in the first decade of this century are still alive in your soil, waiting for the right combination of depth, in the soil, moisture and temperature to sprout. Organic growers also give a thought to the manure they use. Cows and horses who eat weedy hay or are put to pasture in fields of ripened weeds produce manure so full of seeds that to spread it on a growing area is like sowing it to weeds. Many gardeners compost fresh manure with weed residues and garden trash—and the high temperatures of the working compost pile will kill the seeds.

While compost may be practical on a homestead or some parts of a farm, a farmer can't use it for mulch on big acreage. Ingenious organic farmers have not only learned to control weeds, but to get other benefits from doing it. Richard Thompson of Boone, Iowa, keeps down foxtail with a corn-beans-corn-oats-meadow rotation. The short growing time for the oats and hay allows him to get into the field and cut these crops— and any foxtail that's present before it can make seed. So, two years out of the five in his rotation he interrupts the growth pattern of the foxtail. If a farmer is in continuous corn or a corn-beans rotation, the longer growing times for these crops give the foxtail a chance to seed.

Foxtail will wait along fencerows and spread its seeds from there, so he also cut the rows with a fencerow mower before July 15, to get the weed before the seeds set. "It's harder than spraying herbicide," says Wayne P. Rogers, a New York State gardener, "but it does the job better."

But his weed problems didn't stop there. Here's how he gets a jump on weeds early in the season. Around April 1, he disks his fields. The disk is the proper tool for weeding, besides killing already-started weeds, it pulverizes the soil and makes a smooth, fine seedbed to get more weeds started. The idea behind the April 1 cultivation is to get as many weed seeds sprouted as possible so that you make the next cultivation worthwhile. Rogers recommends disking every two weeks until planting time.

He used to plant corn on May 1 or earlier, waiting three weeks for the corn to sprout, but the weeds would use those three weeks to grow an impressive size. Now he plants a couple of weeks later, when the soil is warmer, and goes over the soil with a spring tooth harrow just before planting. This harrow brings bigger clods of soil to the top and leaves a rough seedbed. The planter then sticks the corn seed two inches deep. This rough seedbed is fine for corn but poor for weeds. Rogers used to have a terrible problem with smartweed in the soy beans, but now plants late, between May 20 and June 1, using the disks and spring tooth as for corn. "My weed problems in the beans disappeared."

Weeds In Grain Farming

Organic farmers on the Great Plains have special problems with weeds. This tale of two organic growers in North Dakota shows how important ingenuity is to the natural farmers.

Weeds, adequate moisture and blowing are the main and related problems in the prairie land. Gordon and Curtis Overbo—and the organic farmers they work with around Webster, North Dakota—are tackling these problems.

Wild oats and mustard have been the biggest weed problems right along, and lately an import called Mexican fire weed is beginning to be troublesome. Weeds not only compete for space but take moisture away from the grain as well, and in dryland farming there is only so much water available.

The conventional method is to control weeds as much as possible by herbicides and by summer fallowing every third year. Fallowing also builds a reservoir of moisture, since uncropped, weed-free fields absorb the summer rains without having to provide water for plant growth. Trouble is, humus is depleted during the year, so the unprotected fields are defenseless against fall, winter, and spring winds. Even in the dead of winter, with ground frozen solid, granulated snow is driven abrasively across the land grinding away at the soil and humus particles so that the blowing snow becomes almost as brown as the soil itself. There is always a certain amount of water erosion each year, and by spring the ground is compacted and hard as stone.

Weeds can be controlled mechanically by holding off spring cultivation and planting time until the weed seeds germinate and begin to grow, but there is a certain amount of risk involved. The top few inches of moisture are gone and early spring rains are over, so that the probability of adequate moisture for germinating has been reduced. Unless planting is followed within a week or so by a good rain, the seeds are not apt to germinate and the field may have to be replanted. Unless the field is exceptionally clean, there will probably be a certain amount of wild oats and mustard to live with. In preherbicide days, children earned pocket money by walking through the fields and pulling out mustard plants by hand, and every so often a farmer would have so much wild oats that he'd have to plow everything back in. Later planting frequently lines up maturing grain with the hail season—and a situation where a few minutes can lose the year's crop. Generally speaking, the earlier the planting, the better. Putting all that together gives a fair idea of why farmers think carefully before they go organic.

As Gordon and Curtis see it, technology has been arbitrarily introduced without relating to the total picture and without taking into consideration everything that technology could accomplish if all the problems were to be approached together. In other words, they are trying to look at farming in North Dakota as if the slate has been wiped clean and the only thing to do is to use whatever works best.

Putting all the current solutions in a row and weighing their values, the Overbos eliminated herbicides for three reasons. First, they do contaminate, and are ecologically destructive to the environment and to the soil's organisms. Second, while herbicides provide a certain predictable control over a variety of weeds, the control represents a cost which cannot be related to overcoming all of the problems. Finally, herbicides represent a control—and a cost—which can only be improved by increasing the basic cost that has to be charged against one year's production. In other words, the benefits are temporary and do not carry over into the next year's crop.

Gordon and Curtis decided that the right type of mechanical weed control would provide a fixed basic cost, regardless of weed varieties, which would directly relate to soil and water conservation and to safe ecology. Since mobile equipment moves in a straight line, equipment would have to be adapted that would precision-plant grain in wide rows and be able to cultivate within close tolerances of each side of the plants.

Gordon is operating his 700-acre farm experimentally. One major trial was to see if it would be possible to adapt standard equipment to do precision farming. The idea was that it would be easier for farmers to convert to organics if they could easily convert their equipment. However, the project has demonstrated that such precision requires special equipment. Gordon is now using equipment originally designed for sugar beet cultivation. Planting and cultivating will be done with an ST series Howard Rotavator with a secondary tiller (a second rotating tiller following behind the first). The system will incorporate a planter and automatic fertilizer, using liquid seaweed, and will have the capacity to inter-row cultivate up to ½ inch on each side of the plantings.

The wheat rows will be planted 20 inches apart, and while the weeds are being controlled by cultivation, the soil will be turned and aerated, and the moisture will be conserved. Through fall and winter, the stubble will be left standing to protect the soil from blowing. The following year, new plantings will be made between the rows of old stubble. In the third year, the field will be planted into rows of one-year maturing clover and alfalfa, a cover crop that will be cultivated until fall.

Non-Toxic Ways
To Control Weeds

Declining soil fertility is a prime cause of weed growth. Fertile soil, especially soil well conditioned with organic matter, is not naturally conducive to weed growth. Many types of weeds appear to thrive only on soil that is low in some minerals and has an excess of others. As many farmers have learned, declining fertility encourages such weeds as broomsedge and tickle-grass to invade fields and pastures. Building up a soil organically, therefore, is one of the best ways to lick the weed problem.

Also, it is a fact that a soil rich in organic matter is more easily worked and cultivation and tillage can be timed most advantageously. Such soil is in good shape after a rain and can be worked without causing clods to form. Spring tillage on a good organic soil can prepare a fine seedbed.

Young grass plants in organic soil grow rapidly; their root systems tend to crowd out those of weeds, and their rapid vegetative growth often makes thick shade that helps suppress weeds. Too, weed seeds lose their viability sooner in a bacteria-rich soil than in one poor in bacterial life. With organics, ordinary management operations will usually go a long way toward controlling weeds.

Weed seeds don't originate only from seed you sow. Weeds can be borne by wind, water, or even carried on clothing of people walking from nearby weed-infested areas. If you have a nearby lot or field in which the weeds have run rampant, chances are good that you'll never obtain acceptable weed control in your own lawn. But you can get a head start if you have the weeds mowed at least twice a year to prevent them from maturing seed. If you live out of town, you may want to fence in such an area and turn loose some sheep. They're one of the most effective weed fighters known.

Maybe it's a bit more work, but hand pulling is one of the most effective weed preventives known. It's a good idea to know before hand whether the weeds at hand are annual, biennial, or perennial, as it will make your weed stalking chores a bit easier. Most annual and biennial weeds occurring in small patches can be yanked as soon as they are large enough to get a grip on and yet before they have begun to produce seed. Even if you pull out the tops of the weeds without getting the roots, you've done enough, since the piece of the root remaining in the soil will not sprout again. But that's not true with perennials. Often their roots get new shoots, and for complete eradication you may have to pull one weed several times or be certain that you get the entire root structure. It's best to pull such weeds when the soil is damp so that they can be removed easily. Don't neglect this chore, as weeds can rob your lawn of light, water, and mineral nutrients.

Undercut and cut around small patches of undesirable grass with a sharp spade. Lift the undesirable patch and use it as a pattern to cut a replacement piece the same thickness from an inconspicuous place elsewhere in the lawn. Make certain the replacement sod is firmed into place, and water it well until it becomes established.

Mowing is an effective method of keeping weeds in check because it allows the grass to crowd out the weeds. The best mowing height is usually from two to three inches. Although a lower mowing clearance will cut back the weeds decisively, it will also hamper the grass from growing. However, if you have an area of a lawn that is almost entirely weeds, you might want to take advantage of the physical makeup of some perennial weeds. Normally they store a reserve food supply in their underground parts; when the plants begin to blossom, their reserve food supply has been nearly exhausted and new seeds have not yet been produced, that's the time to lower your mower and cut back the weeds to severely weaken them.

In most lawns, however, a higher mower setting is needed. Mowing at a height of $2\frac{1}{2}$ to three inches shades the soil and protects the bluegrass roots from the damaging effects of summer heat. High mowing of common Kentucky bluegrass is an excellent deterrent to the germination and growth of many annual weed species. Some of the newer lawn grasses perform best when mowed at two inches or lower. Remember that the mowing technique you use on your lawn is one of the most critical maintenance procedures you can practice. Don't be misled by thinking that if you cut your grass tall that you will have to mow it more often. Regardless of the mowing height, the general rule of thumb you should follow is to cut it frequently enough so that you do not have to remove more than one-third of the green leaf area of the plant at each mowing. If you follow this rule, you should mow the low-cut turf more often. Also, increasing the mowing height from $1\frac{1}{2}$ to $2\frac{1}{2}$ inches greatly decreases the number of broad-leafed weeds.

Feeding programs that furnish lawn grasses with necessary organic plant food elements throughout the growing season tend to discourage weeds by enabling the grass to compete more successfully. Fertilize cool season grasses in the fall and spring and as needed during the summer months. Withhold spring fertilization of warm season zoysia, buffalo, and Bermuda until May 1; stop fertilizing them about August 31.

Most store-bought grass seed contains a certain percentage of weed seed, but there is something that you can do to avoid this—check the label to determine the percent of weed seed. Most often cheap seed turns out to be the most expensive you can buy because it is high in noxious weeds.

Weed control on the 305-acre Rodale organic farm at Maxatawny, Pennsylvania, involves strictly mechanical methods (cultivator and rotary hoe) and cultural practices (crop rotations, mulches, and fallow). Problem weeds include various species of sedges and mints in the wet areas, and giant foxtail, which seems to thrive everywhere.

Foxtail is by far the most serious weed problem. While sedges and mints respond well to drainage and fertilizers, foxtail has been favored by the system of cropping that is common in the area. On fields that have been treated with 2, 4D by previous owners, all of the native weeds have been severely weakened or entirely eliminated, leaving little competition for the foxtail. Consequently, the stands of foxtail have become stronger, more widespread, and have even developed resistance to herbicides that have been used to fight them. If allowed to grow up, many fields actually look at though they had been sown to foxtail.

Giant foxtail is a particularly noxious weed for several reasons. It is extremely tenacious, reproduces itself in fantastic quantities, and is suited to a wide range of conditions. In addition to competing with crops for light, moisture, and nutrients, foxtail secretes a phytotoxic substance which inhibits the development of corn. The severe infestations of foxtail on cropland are directly attributable to the widespread use of chemical herbicides that have eliminated native weed species.

One of the most effective ways to fight foxtail is to eliminate the row crops that favor its development. On the New Organic Farm there is no problem with weeds on the fields which have been sown to solid-stand legumes and grasses. The major weed problems exist in the row crops—soybeans and corn.

Row crops are cultivated mechanically, and the secret to mechanical cultivation is timeliness. If you let the weeds get ahead of the crop, you're in trouble.

The rotary hoe is a fine tool for organic farmers who are interested in row crops. Although it does not destroy all of the weeds, it slows their development until the crop can be cultivated more cleanly. The rotary hoe can be pulled at high field speeds, which means you can cover a lot of ground, a nice feature when those spring showers don't leave much time for the ground to dry. If you use the implement just when the weeds are germinating, and the tiny hair roots are still limited to the top inch or two of soil, it can be quite effective.

Workers at the Rodale farm have learned a lesson with the soybeans in this region of the country. Soybeans were planted in both solid stands and in the row. The beans are doing much better in solid stands, sown with a grain drill, and the weed infestation is much lower. Cultivating soybeans will not be attempted next year, as they will all be sown with a drill on the farm.

One of the goals on the New Organic Farm is to favor the redevelopment of weed species that have been eliminated or weakened by herbicide use, as it is felt that the species diversity will help assure that any one weed does not become a problem. To measure the accuracy of this hypothesis, they are working with biologists from nearby colleges who are doing a biological inventory of the new farm, and who will record any change in the number of species present now and in the future.

Weeds in the lawn.   Weedy lawns usually indicate poor management, or a mistake in establishment. Weeds become a problem because they are better adapted to conditions under which turf grasses perform poorly. These include low fertility, extremes of soil reaction, poor soil structure, low clipping or lawn seed mixtures. See LAWNS.—*Jeff Cox*

12
The Good And Bad
Of Wildlife
In The Garden

Despite the rape and sterilization of the environment wrought by bulldozers and chainsaws, many forms of wildlife have adapted to the change and are now actually thriving in the new microhabitats that we call suburbia. The garter snake, robin, and common toad may be encountered just as readily in the suburban garden as in a patch of deciduous woods.

Smaller and more adaptable, though, are the insects and other invertebrates. Their success is ensured by their tremendous reproductive capabilities and subsequent adaptability to change, to the point that the new habitats engineered by man have enabled the populations of many to blossom into status as pests.

Luckily, the animals that remain in built-up areas have kept their appetites for bugs. Unluckily, others prefer vegetables and fruits. But by encouraging beneficial wildlife to take up residence near your garden, you can go a long way toward managing your garden in cooperation with nature—and that's what organic gardening is all about.

Cold-Blooded Killers
Of The Garden:
Amphibians And Reptiles

Luckily, a few species of toads, snakes, and turtles have adjusted to a life in the crowded suburbs. While their lives and habits are often blanketed

145

by old wives' tales and superstition, these allies are worthy of your understanding.

Perhaps the most peculiar thing about reptiles and amphibians is that they are cold-blooded; that is, their body temperature changes with the environment. But they still need to regulate their body temperatures. When it gets extremely hot, a toad digs itself into the mud and a garter snake seeks the shade of a rock or board. In cold weather, such animals bask in the warmth of sunlight for short periods of time. In winter they hibernate beneath the ground, three or more feet under, to resurface in weather they can handle.

Amphibians

During the day, the *American toad* usually finds a moist, sheltered place beneath loose boards, under garden mulch, or in the shade of low-growing shrubbery. At night, with the safety of darkness, it hops about in search of cutworms, potato beetles, chinch bugs, ants, slugs, and a number of other small creatures. The toad's enemies are limited because of the distasteful slime that it exudes from its warty skin.

Although the typical backyard garden patch is hardly the ideal habitat for this rough-skinned amphibian, special provisions can be made to entice it to stay. Since the toad is an amphibian, it needs water. It not only breeds in water but also drinks through its skin while sitting submerged. Given enough fresh water, the female lays up to 15,000 small black-and-white eggs in paired jelly strings. The eggs hatch in 3 to 12 days into black tadpoles, which gradually transform into small toads in 6 to 9 weeks. Farm ponds, lakesides, and marshy areas yield tremendous numbers of these small toads in spring. A good rainfall sends them hopping across roads, lawns, and pastures, and this is a good time to collect a few for your own yard.

Once you have gathered or inherited toads, keep them happy by wetting down the shrubbery on a hot day, and provide a modest shelter so that they can rest out of the sun. You might cut a small entrance in a box or chip out a small opening in the side of a flower pot, and bury it a few inches into the ground, preferably in the shade of a tree or shrub. Since toads must have access to water, set out a shallow pan in the garden or in the box or flowerpot. Remember that the toad drinks through its skin, and the pan should be large enough to allow this.

If weather is moderate, toads remain active from March to mid-November. In that time, just a single toad can eat up to 15,000 insects—a substantial return considering your outlay in time and effort.

The large American toad (*Bufo americanus*) ranges throughout eastern North America. A variety of other smaller toads, such as the spadefoots, Fowler's, Southern, and red-spotted, range throughout practically all of the United States and southern Canada.

Although *salamanders* do not adapt as well as toads to backyard life, you should learn to recognize these tailed amphibians and understand that their diet consists primarily of small insects, spiders, sow bugs, worms, millipedes, centipedes, and other garden pests.

A rock garden with water nearby will encourage salamanders to stick around. At night they will come from beneath loose stones, boards, and crevices to hunt for food.

North America has more varieties of salamanders than the rest of the world combined, but their value as predators is underestimated, probably because they live secluded lives and are seldom seen at work.

Unless fresh water is available in a nearby pond, lake, or swamp, *frogs,* will probably not be present in your area. Unlike some of the salamanders, the frogs require an aquatic environment in which to spend much of each day.

If you have fresh water nearby, you might catch some tadpoles and stock them. While they're not likely to serve a vital role in the backyard ecology, the frog feeds on such a variety of insects that it should be considered a potential ally whenever proper conditions are available.

Reptiles

Reptiles are the second group of cold-blooded vertebrates that you should make friends with. Maligned down through the ages, snakes and lizards still inspire fear and mistrust among most people, and thousands of these beneficials are needlessly slaughtered each year. Turtles, on the other hand, have a more respected reputation but, with the exception of the well-known box turtle, they are not as common in the backyard as snakes and lizards.

Snakes have earned a grudging respect because a few species are poisonous to man: several species of copperheads and rattlesnakes, the water moccasin (or cottonmouth) in semi-aquatic habitats, and the tiny coral snake in the southern states.

The *garter snake* is probably the most common backyard reptile in the United States. A variety of species exist but all have relatively similar diets, feeding on mice, worms, caterpillars, and a variety of slow-moving insects. Although some garter snakes may strike viciously, especially when cornered, they are non-poisonous and should not be driven from the area or needlessly killed.

The garter snake mates in early spring, and 12 to 30 or more young are born alive in late summer. On cool nights they may seek the warmth of an active compost pile, much to the surprise of anyone chancing to turn the pile the following morning. One organic gardener from Colorado who wanted to get rid of them temporarily, while turning the pile, tried mixing in a couple of onions to shoo them away. The snakes disappeared within a few hours, but returned several days later. Other gardeners simply whack the top of the pile with a large board to make the snakes move out for a time.

The rat snakes, including the *black rat snake* and the *milk snake,* are also beneficial. As the name implies, these reptiles feed primarily on rodents, moles, and other warm-blooded prey. The black rat snake, however, will also take birds, rabbits, frogs, large insects, and even other snakes. Generally, however, it is a beneficial species and should be protected.

The milk snake is chiefly a rodent eater, and it is a wise farmer that makes sure at least a pair of these colorful reptiles live in the fields about the barns and outbuildings. Its close relative, the *corn snake,* plays a similar ecological role wherever it exists.

Lizards are found in many localities throughout North America, and where abundant they can be captured and set loose in the garden area. A noose-type knot on the end of a rigid fishing pole serves as a good trap. Common species include fence lizards, horned toads, six-lined lizards, and blue-tailed skinks; at least one species can be found locally from New England to California. The lizard's diet is primarily insects, including beetles, grubs, and caterpillars.

Another reptilian guardian of the garden is the common *box turtle,* described in Palmer's *Fieldbook Of Natural History* as "a useful destroyer of garden pests (that feeds on) plant material and worms, slugs, snails, and insects procured in (its) decidedly leisurely travels."

Gardeners occasionally take box turtles from the wild to serve as efficient predators in the backyard. Although painfully slow, these turtles are wanderers, and there's no guarantee that they will stay on the property unless it is fenced. What the box turtle pilfers in the way of an occasional lettuce leaf, bean, or berry is more than repaid by the many insects it eats.

Encouraging Birds To Help Out In The Garden

While not all species of birds can be attracted to the garden—woodland-breeding species will not nest in a suburban plot with only scattered trees, and wildfowl aren't inclined to dwell where no water is available—there are about a hundred species of birds that readily adapt to backyards. Here follows the profiles of a number of species of beneficial birds that can be enticed to become part of your backyard ecology. Of course not every bird will find conditions ideal in every garden area, but these species all can be attracted by food, water, nest sites, or plantings.

Before man began putting up houses for them, *purple martins* made their homes in hollow trees and rock crevices. Today, however, purple martins have come to depend on man to such an extent that they may not even nest if they fail to find suitable man-made quarters.

The first martins arrive from their winter homes in South America in January, and gradually make their way north with spring. By April they have reached the northern states and southern Canada. An advance troop of scouts shows up first, disappears for a few days, and then reappears with others. Females can be readily identified by their whitish underparts, while the males are a deep blue black all over.

Unfortunately, there isn't any one method that guarantees success in attracting martins. The two main drawing cards are a properly constructed and proportioned house, and a good location for erecting it.

The size of the dwelling seems to have little influence on a flock, but the size of each compartment could well determine whether or not the advance guard will decide to set up housekeeping. A single nesting pair will take to a room measuring six inches square and six inches high (inside dimensions), with a 2½ inch diameter opening one inch above the floor. The total number of compartments is up to you. One martin complex on the main street of Griggsville, Illinois, is reportedly 40 feet tall and contains 504 rooms.

Before investing either time or money in a martin house you should check with a local bird club, Audubon Society chapter, or college ornithologist to find out if martins regularly nest nearby. If the answer is "yes," chances of attracting some stragglers to your home grounds are good, especially if open fields and water are nearby.

If you're not handy with tools, you can purchase a ready-made dwelling. Some of the newer ones are made of aluminum and seem to wear better than those of wood. Should you make your own, be sure to paint it white. This is not only attractive to both people and martins, but also keeps the occupants cool by reflecting the sun's rays. A central air shaft and an air space beneath the roof allow air to circulate within and further cool the house. Openings other than the entrances must be covered with wire mesh to deter sparrows and wasps. To keep sparrows and starlings from moving in, either plug the entrances until the martins are due from the South, or take the house down each year.

The martin's nest is made up of grasses, leaves, twigs, and bits of shredded rags. An available supply of each nearby won't hurt matters any, especially if you're trying to establish a colony in midtown. As for food, martins eat great numbers of flies, mosquitoes, beetles, dragonflies, weevils, squash bugs, moths, and some wasps and bees. Because the birds glean insects from the air and return to their houses in long, gliding swoops, it's best to locate martin houses away from tall buildings and trees.

A close relative of the purple martin is the *barn swallow*. Although they may make a mess around barns and outbuildings during nesting time, their appetites more than make up for their indiscretions. Barn swallows are entirely insectivorous, eating flies, mosquitoes, codling moths, moths of cutworms, weevils, and wasps and bees (but practically no honeybees).

The best way to attract this bird is to provide suitable places for their mud nests. Around barns and older outbuildings it's usually not necessary to make special provisions, as the swallows build nests under the eaves or on rafters in open buildings. Otherwise, you can fashion a shelf or horizontal wooden plank beneath overhangs in a protected spot. It may be wise to hang a piece of burlap directly under the nest if the droppings of the young birds would mess up a heavily traveled area. Swallows also like available water and will tend to nest wherever open ponds or lakes provide them with aquatic insects and drink.

The *tree swallow* is also essentially an insect eater, but it will feed upon bayberries, blueberries, and fruits of red cedar and Virginia creeper. It is easily identified by its clean white underparts contrasted by a steely blue or greenish black back. The barn swallow's main field mark is a deeply forked tail, visible both when it's sitting on a wire and when flying.

The tree swallow will readily take to a bird box erected near a marsh or pond. The house should be placed on a pole about three or four feet above the water or along the shore. Make it five inches square with a 1½-inch opening placed three inches above the floor. Tree swallows also nest in gourds, mailboxes, and in the natural cavities of trees.

Bluebirds usually nest in tree holes, especially in old apple orchards, but will also move into suitably sized bird boxes. Because of the interest in restoring the territorial range of this beautiful and desirable songbird, bluebird boxes are often commercially available. If you're at all handy, the boxes are relatively simple to construct. They should be placed three or four feet above the ground, preferably on fence posts. This height often discourages starlings and house sparrows, which prefer higher nests. Face the houses to the south and, if possible, overlooking an open field.

The bluebird's food is about 70 percent animal matter, including grasshoppers, moths, crickets, beetles, bugs, ants, caterpillars, spiders, millipedes and centipedes, and earthworms. They are also fond of wild fruits such as wild grape, chokecherry, Virginia creeper, juniper, blackberry, bayberry, sumac, and mountain ash.

Many homeowners despise the *blue jay* for its aggressiveness at the bird feeder. It is also known to make frequent raids on the nests of other birds, sometimes opening and eating all the eggs in a single nest. But examination of the stomachs of several hundred jays showed that the bird is much more beneficial than harmful. About three-fourths of the jay's diet consists of vegetal matter, much of it nuts and acorns. They are also known to eat insects, spiders, snails, and even fish, mice, and amphibians, along with an occasional bird egg.

Blue jays seldom have to be encouraged. If they live nearby they will visit several neighborhood feeders and raise a family. They prefer coniferous trees for their nests but can adapt to tall, full deciduous trees.

The *brown thrasher* is a close relative of the catbird and mockingbird but is not quite as fond of wild fruit, preferring a diet of insect life. In fact, almost two-thirds of the brown thrasher's food is made up of insects such as May beetles, white grubs, cucumber beetles, cotton boll weevils, snap beetles, wireworms, armyworms, tent caterpillars, cutworms, cankerworms, grasshoppers, leafhoppers, and wasps.

The thrasher can best be recognized as a long, slim robin, rusty red above and striped below, with a long tail. It nests on the ground, in brush piles or in low, thorny thickets. You can attract it with certain plantings: hawthorn, honeysuckle, multiflora rose, viburnums, barberry, greenbrier and grape draw thrashers for both nesting and food.

Cardinals seem to live just as comfortably in mid-city parks as in country woodlands, nesting either in thickets or small trees. They are drawn to crabapple, multiflora rose, barberry, forsythia and spiraea, which serve as nesting sites.

The cardinal's diet is varied, consisting of 36 percent weed and other seeds, 24 percent wild fruit, 9 percent grain, 2 percent miscellaneous plants, and 29 percent animal matter, including potato beetles, cicadas, cotton worms, cutworms, codling moths, leafhoppers, cotton boll weevils, cucumber beetles, aphids, and ants. Someone has estimated that this bird does 15 times as much good as it does damage, so its beauty is more than feather-deep.

The *catbird* breeds throughout the United States, nesting in tangles of growth covered by vines. It has similar habits and nesting preferences to the brown thrasher, and the same plantings will attract both.

In spring the catbird's diet consists almost entirely of animal matter, such as ants, beetles, and caterpillars. In summer and fall, fruits and other vegetable matter become a more important part of its daily foodstuff, but as the young birds are being reared, 96 percent of the food given them is insect life. The catbird is especially notable as an important natural enemy of gypsy moths.

Chickadees of one species or another range throughout the entire United States. They nest in forests, open woodlands, parks, and orchards in hollowed out cavities in tree trunks and dead trees; you can attract them with nest boxes and feeders.

Better than two-thirds of the chickadee's diet is made up of insects and insect eggs, which are gleaned from tree twigs and branches. The stomach of one chickadee studied contained 450 aphid eggs, a favored food. Other prey includes bark beetles, weevils, scale insects, spiders, flies, wasps, and ants. Seeds of poison ivy, pine, weeds, and sunflowers top off the chickadee's diet.

For chickadees, a nest box or hollow tree should have an opening no larger than one inch in diameter. While the height above ground can vary from one to 50 feet, a range of 8 to 15 feet is probably best.

Few gardeners have reason to attract the *English sparrow* (house sparrow) because its very existence already seems to be dependent upon man. It is not really a sparrow but a species of finch, brought to this country from England in the early part of this century. Its food consists of everything from garbage and weed seeds to young garden plants and insects, especially harlequin bugs.

They may drive useful species such as martins and bluebirds from their nest sites. The only expeditious way of thinning their numbers from the vicinity seems to be shooting, but the benefit is usually temporary, as they will soon be replaced by others.

English sparrows nest as indiscriminately as they eat. Their structures of grass, trash, and feathers may be tucked on a feeding shelf, in a bird-house, rainspout, or hollow tree.

The dark bib of the male is a good field mark for distinguishing it from other sparrows. The female has no good field mark and is often confused with others of its kind. Most states consider the English sparrows an unprotected bird and tacitly advocate discouraging its presence.

Several species of finches inhabit the United States and all feed almost exclusively on seeds and dry plant foods. Redpolls, pine siskins, gold-finches, and the purple and house finches are members of this family.

The *purple finch* typically nests in pines but will also consider hedges and orchard trees. Its summer food is essentially insects, buds, and blos-soms, changing to wild fruits and weed seeds in fall and winter. The male is not really purple but shows a rosy red wash. Viburnums, dogwoods, and elders will attract this finch, and it readily accepts handouts at the feed-ing tray.

The similarly colored *house finch* was orginally native to the western states, but in recent years has extended its range eastward to Pennsylvania and into metropolitan New York. They nest in sagebrush, saltbush, mountain mahogany, cactus, tree cavities, and occasionally in buildings and nest boxes. Their food is almost totally vegetal with less than one percent being grain, and they eat great numbers of weed seed. Other preferred seeds include thistle, dandelion, sunflower, mistletoe, and, un-fortunately, mulberries and cherries.

The *goldfinch,* often referred to as the wild canary because of its distinctive yellow coloration and black crown and wings, feeds primarily on dried fruit and seeds of dandelion, thistle, burdock, mullein, sunflower, asters, goldenrod, birch, alder, hemlock, spruce, and sycamore. Its nest is bulky, cup-shaped, and lined with soft, downy plant material such as thistledown. They frequent hedgerows, wood margins, brushy fields, and flower gardens. The only destructive activity of the goldfinch might be to the crops of a commercial grower of garden flower seeds or plant seeds such as lettuce and turnips.

The *pine siskin,* as its name implies, prefers cone-bearing trees, such as the white pine, for both seeds and nesting sites. They also eat seeds of honeysuckle, lilac, maple, elm, and a variety of weeds, as well as aphids and other insects in summer.

The *redpoll* feeds primarily on weed seeds and seeds of pine, alder, and elm. In summer they too glean aphids from twigs and branches. The redpoll resembles a small brown sparrow with a bright red cap and black chin.

Several species of *flycatcher* inhabit every state in the continental United States. They are known for snapping up flying insects on the wing, and may occasionally feed on dried fruits.

The *phoebe* lives on boll weevils, gypsy moths, cucumber beetles, ants, grasshoppers, locusts, ticks, and caterpillars. It frequently nests beneath bridges and you can lure it to a nesting shelf, especially if the house is in or near a wooded area.

The *crested flycatcher's* menu consists of 94 percent insect matter, such as sawflies, stinkbugs, May beetles, weevils, grasshoppers, katydids, and caterpillars. Once in a great while it takes a honeybee. This bird is a cavity nester, and will take to a nest box placed 20 or 30 feet above the ground if it has an opening slightly larger than two inches.

The other members of the flycatcher tribe prey on similar insects. They all benefit growers' interests and are worthy of our complete protection.

Grackles breed throughout the United States west to Texas, Colorado, and Montana. They frequently congregate in parks and backyards and, when gathered in large flocks, are capable of inflicting serious damage to farm crops; growers have used sound cannons and guns to drive them from grain fields. In small groups, however, they are often beneficial, especially during nesting time.

Their food is one-third vegetable and two-thirds animal matter, including worms, carrion, sow bugs, frogs, and a variety of insects. In fall, grain, nuts, and fruits make up its diet. All in all, the grackle is probably more harmful than beneficial, but they should be credited with removing many of man's invertebrate enemies from lawns during the nesting season.

The common cardinal is a grosbeak and was known in earlier times as the "cardinal grosbeak." Its hefty beak is similar in structure to that of the *evening grosbeak* and *red-breasted grosbeak*.

Although their diets consist essentially of seeds, the red-breasted species also favors insects and is a well-known predator of the Colorado potato beetle. In fact, in some areas it is called the potato bug bird. It nests in farms and near gardens, usually 6 to 20 feet above the ground, and is more abundant in the Midwest than in the East. The male's black and white plumage is highlighted by a triangular red breast patch, accounting for its name and major field mark.

The evening grosbeak and pine grosbeaks feed on seeds and buds and are usually seen as winter visitors in the East. The yellow-feathered evening grosbeak is fond of sunflower seeds and seems to have extended its range in recent years because of the abundance of winter feeding stations. It's no big chore for a flock of these welcome visitors to clean up a pound of sunflower seeds in short order.

The *slate-colored junco,* commonly known as snowbird in the East, prefers to nest in woods or brushy pasture lands, usually on the ground under some cover. It is a beneficial bird, feeding in summer on insects such as click beetles, weevils, grasshoppers, leafhoppers, and ants, and in winter on ragweed, thistle, smartweed, wild sunflowers, and other weed seeds. They may also rob some grain, but most of the junco's hunting time is spent in open fields and woodland borders. Its plumage is dark slate-gray above and across the throat and white beneath. In flight the white outer tail-feathers flash conspicuously.

Formerly a bird of the Old South, the *mockingbird* is now a familiar resident from southern Mexico to Michigan, Maine, Wyoming, and possibly even further north.

Its incomparable ability to mimic other species of birds accounts for its definitive name. Popular in song and story, the mockingbird ranks high as a beneficial species, although it may damage fruit in some parts of the South. As with so many other birds, the mocker's diet changes with the seasons. In spring and early summer it devours myriads of insects, including ants, flies, wasps, boll weevils, grasshoppers, bugs, caterpillars, and spiders. It later feeds on the fruits of trees and shrubs such as sumac, mountain ash, wild grape, Virginia creeper, barberry, bittersweet, June-berry, and honeysuckle.

They typically nest near buildings in dense tangled, vine-covered brush, shrubbery, hedges, and low trees. Mockingbirds are year-round residents but will visit a winter feeder only when offerings include raisins, apple bits, currants, and nutmeats.

The common *mourning dove* is essentially a weed-seed eater. In one particular study, the doves were found to have eaten the seeds of crab grass, foxtail, panic grass, amaranth, purslane, ragweed, spurge, mallow, sedge and sorghum. The stomach of one bird contained 1600 purslane seeds.

The mourning dove is attracted to yards with coniferous plantings. They are early nesters, and build their crude structures in cedars, hemlocks, pines, spruces, and occasionally in rhododendron and holly. They typically raise several families a year and will visit winter feeding stations for free handouts of seed.

Many people make their first acquaintance with the *nuthatch* at the winter feeding tray. Its peculiar way of walking down a tree readily serves to identify either the white-breasted, red-breasted, or brown-headed species.

The nuthatch is both attractive and an important consumer of insects and insect eggs, especially in spring. One bird was found to have devoured over 1600 cankerworm eggs in one feast. Nuthatches do much good in orchards during the caterpillar season, and feed on codling moth pupae in the winter.

The nuthatch is a cavity nester, often claiming abandoned nests. It will also use nest boxes provided by man. The house should be about the same size as that for the bluebird, with a 1½-inch opening. The box should be placed from 12 to 25 feet above the ground.

Fortunate gardeners in the East host *Baltimore* and *orchard orioles,* while the *Bullock's oriole* inhabits the western United States. Their food consists primarily of insects taken in the treetops, and includes caterpillars of the gypsy moth, cankerworm, bagworm, brown-tail moth, and others. The one black mark against orioles is that they also like grapes, and when flocked for migration they may become pests by puncturing them. The Bullock also likes cherries.

The Baltimore oriole prefers to hang its nest from the drooping branches of elms or weeping willows, while the Bullock's oriole takes to cottonwoods, box elders, mesquites, or oaks. If suitable trees are not present, little can be done to entice these independent birds.

Of the many species of owls found throughout the countryside, the *barn owl* and *screech owl* have gotten along best with man.

The tiny screech owl, identified by its ear tufts, is more often heard than seen. It is common in towns and cities, where it patrols moonlit yards for insects and mice. Lizards, salamanders, and worms may also be taken during their nightly forays. This is one of the few owls that will nest in bird boxes; a large, eight-inch-square box with a 3¼-inch opening, placed 15 to 30 feet above the ground, will often attract a pair of nesters.

The barn owl is probably the most important predator of rats and mice in populated areas, rivaling the house cat in importance. While rats and mice make up the staple diet of these monkey-faced birds of prey, they will also take other small mammals, insects, birds, and frogs. As its name suggests it will nest in barns, but also adapts to other old outbuildings, bell towers, accessible attics, and large tree cavities.

Barn owls have been known to use nest boxes that are set high up in a secluded tree or atop an ivy covered wall. The barn owl is about four times larger than the screech owl, and a nest box should allow for this difference.

Although *robins* are typically pictured pulling a long, ductile earthworm from the yard, they also eat great numbers of grasshoppers, locusts, crickets, wireworms, leaf beetles, tent caterpillars, cutworms, and cankerworms.

Whether or not you'll want to attract more robins to your yard will likely depend on the presence of cherries, mulberries, elderberries or other berries, as the robin is known to enjoy pecking at them. You can encourage them to nest by setting up shelves or ledges.

The *towhee* (nicknamed chewink for its call) is a large, ground-feeding bird typically found scratching about beneath shrubbery for insects and seeds. Several species with various field marks inhabit practically all states on the continent. Their food consists primarily of beetles, moths, caterpillars, crickets, ants, and spiders, along with wild fruits and a variety of seeds.

They nest on the ground in a concealed spot, usually in a wooded area, and will also nest low in the dense shrubbery in the backyard.

A great variety of *sparrows* can be found in the garden throughout the year. A seasonal changeover occurs when those that nest in the Far North fly south to spend the winter. The *chipping sparrow, song sparrow,* and *field sparrow* are more likely to take up residence in the dooryard. Practically all the sparrows are useful as weed-seed eaters or as insect predators. The chipping sparrow, for example, feeds on aphids and plantain seeds—both backyard nuisances.

Ornamental evergreens, forsythias, berry patches, and woodland borders all attract at least one type of sparrow. Most species are also drawn to a well-stocked feeding tray—especially the winter-visiting tree sparrow, whose diet is almost entirely made up of seeds.

Like the English sparrow, the common *starling* is seldom encouraged as a backyard resident. Nevertheless, you can be sure that they'll be there.

Although they may be pests around buildings, airports, and bridges, they glean tremendous numbers of grubs from lawns and gardens. A study of over 2,000 individual starlings showed that better than half of their diets consisted of animal matter, including beetles, grasshoppers, millipedes, and caterpillars. Starlings also take grain, cherries, and other cultivated foods, and this trait, along with the fact that they often drive flickers, bluebirds, martins and other desirable species from their nest sites, makes them an unwanted species in most garden areas. But since there is little you can do to expel the starling, try to appreciate its contribution to natural control.

The *tufted titmouse* is one of the best-known and most welcome of the East's winter birds. In the West its niche is filled by the tiny *bush-tit* or the *plain titmouse.*

The titmouse feeds on both plants and insects. More than half of its animal diet consists of caterpillars, with the balance made up of wasps, scale insects, ants, beetles, and spiders. The western species also eat mealybugs, aphids, and leafhoppers. The nesting habits of the titmouses are similar to that of the chickadees.

The *red-eyed vireo* is very likely the most common nesting bird in the eastern forests although it is not a popularly known species. It migrates in fall to South America.

Homeowners living in forested areas will benefit not only from the bird's constant summer singing but also from its diet of caterpillars, moths, bugs, beetles, ants, and flies.

Warblers are insectivorous woodland birds that are most commonly seen and heard at migration time. More than 50 species of these diminutive birds enter the United States, but only about half-a-dozen overwinter here.

Warblers feed on caterpillars, beetles, wasps, ants, flies, aphids, cankerworms, and locusts. They prefer to build their nests in forested regions, and therefore are somewhat difficult to attract to the backyard. However, certain species of warblers may nest in small stands of conifers.

Twenty-three species of *woodpeckers* can be found at various places within the United States' borders. Each member of this family has the unique characteristic of a heavy, pointed beak, strong neck muscles, and a long barbed tongue, all of which aid in their probing and drilling for insects.

The *red-shafted flicker* of the West and its eastern counterpart, the *yellow-shafted flicker,* get much of their food on the ground; ants, ground beetles, cockroaches and caterpillars are their favorite prey.

Hairy and *downy woodpeckers* can be found practically anywhere in the United States as well as in the timbered regions of Canada and Alaska. Their main foodstuffs include the wood-boring larvae of moths and beetles, adult beetles, ants, caterpillars, aphids, scale insects, and snails.

Practically all woodpeckers make their nests in the holes of large branches and trunks, wherever plentiful insect food exists. If a yard is without old trees they may use nest boxes. You can attract them in winter through spring with suet.

Nine species of *wrens* are native to the United States. They have adapted their lives to a variety of habitats, including the backyard garden area. The wrens' food consists largely of insects, including ants, beetles, moths, weevils, flies, lice, snails, and various invertebrates. Backyard wrens will readily take to properly constructed nest boxes and may also nest beneath eaves, in drain pipes, or wherever small concealed openings exist.

How To Attract Birds To The Yard And Garden

Plantings.   The best way to draw birds to your dooryard is to plant species of hedges, shrubs, trees, and annuals that they are known to like for either food or nesting. Here is a listing of plantings that are notably attractive to both birds and humans, while being relatively easy to grow. The figure in parenthesis indicates the approximate number of bird species that utilize the plant in each region.

FOR THE MIDWEST	FOR THE EAST
autumn olive (15)	autumn olive (25)
Russian olive (31)	sumac (17)
crabapple (29)	gray-stemmed dogwood (16)
dogwood (47)	holly (22)
firethorn (17)	cherry (40)
elderberry (50)	highbush cranberry (34)
mountain ash (20)	silky dogwood (10)
sunflower (52)	mountain ash (15)
highbush cranberry (28)	bittersweet (10)
cherry (49)	amur honeysuckle (8)
wild plum (16)	crabapple (18)
cotoneaster (6)	firethorn (17)
tatarian honeysuckle (18)	flowering dogwood (36)
red cedar (25)	highbush blueberry (36)
bittersweet (12)	hawthorn (25)
holly (20)	red cedar (68)
hawthorn (19)	redosier dogwood (19)
	tatarian honeysuckle (17)
	Virginia creeper (37)

How effective can a change in environment be? According to Dr. William H. Drury, Jr., an ecologist with the Massachusetts Audubon Society, a single minor change in your landscaping plan can bring five to ten times as many birds as you now have. All you have to do is follow nature's lead by creating what's known as an edge effect, in either the backyard or garden. In nature this is the transitional zone between the woods and meadow. Birds find such zones attractive because it gives them three closely related environments—trees, brush, and the open. Luckily, birds can be satisfied by a realistic imitation of nature. Neighborhood birds tend to favor gardens bordered with a hedgerow. (English suburbs have more birds than ours, because gardens there are bounded by thick hedges, while the open stretches of lawn that prevail in suburban America serve to turn away many valuable species.)

To create an edge effect, place the taller trees along the outer boundaries and taper your plantings down to low shrubs facing the garden or yard. The background trees in a large garden may be any of the standard shade trees, such as maple, oak, poplar and sycamore. On a small site, begin the back area with such medium-sized trees as mountain ash or magnolia. You should plant two or three trees in a row, since the birds are at home when there's more than one. There should also be a solid line of shrubs to connect the widely spaced trees.

The species is important. Evergreens are best for shelter, with the red cedar at the top of the list, followed by spruce, hemlock, and pine. Recommended deciduous trees include birch, dogwood, hawthorn, box elder, mountain ash, red mulberry, cherry, quince, and crabapple.

In addition to establishing plantings for the birds, you can see to it that they have (1) housing during the spring and early summer nesting time, (2) supplemental food in winter, and (3) water all year-round.

Houses.   Although you have a variety of store-bought houses to choose from, you may prefer to fashion your own. It is important to note that different species have different requirements. For example, a bird house designed to accommodate the house wren will not appeal to the purple martin or flicker. Instead of houses, the robin and the phoebe prefer nesting shelves on which to construct their open nests. The diameter of a bird house opening is important in that it can keep the right bird out if it's too small and let in the wrong bird or predators if it is too large.

Below is a list of suggested dimensions for houses of a variety of beneficial backyard birds. Note that the house's location is very important, as some species prefer to nest low and others much higher from the ground.

Feeders.   Windowsill feeders are easy to make and easy to service. Almost any size or shape board can be used, as long as there is an edge around it to keep the seed from blowing off. Other features are optional. You might add a seed hopper or a branch on which suet can be attached. It's a good idea to have a drain hole in a corner and, in the event of heavy snow, a removable roof that can be placed over the feeder. If there are no bushes or trees nearby, it helps to attach some perches to the edge of the

Dimensions for Various Houses

	a×a' Size of floor (inches)	b Depth of birdhouse (in.)	c Diameter of entrance (in.)	Distance from ground to entrance (feet)
House Wren	4×4	6-8	1-1¼	8-18
Black-capped Chickadee	4×4	8-10	1⅛	8-15
White-breasted Nuthatch, Tufted Titmouse	4×4	8-10	1½	12-25
Tree Swallow	5×5	6	1⅜	8-30
Eastern Bluebird	5×5	8	1⅝	8-20
Crested Flycatcher	6×6	8-10	2⅛	15-40
Flicker	7×7	16-18	2½	10-35
Purple Martin	6×6	6	2⅛-2½	12-14
Sparrow Hawk	8×8	12-15	3	20-50
Saw-whet Owl	6×6	10-12	2⅞	15-45
Screech Owl	8×8	12-15	3¼	15-30

and for Nesting Boxes

Common House Finch	4½-6		Open	10-30

and for Nesting Shelves

	a' Width (inches)	a Length (inches)	Height from ground (feet)
Robin	5-6	8 or more	8-30
Phoebe	3½-4½	7 or more	3-20
Barn Swallow	6	6	8-12

feeder. In winter, suet is a mainstay for insectivorous birds and you can offer it, either melted or in chunks, in a hanging log bored with holes. Suet can be placed in woven string bags, chicken-wire baskets, or wire dishes fastened to a post or tree. When melted, suet can be poured into a pine cone or a hollowed-out coconut shell; bacon grease and melted suet can be rubbed on the bark of a tree or into holes bored into the tree to attract creepers, nuthatches, and woodpeckers.

Pheasants, cardinals, and jays like ears of corn stuck on nails in a board. A quart glass jar of whole or cracked corn can be inverted over a stick set into a flat board so that it feeds downward like a hopper.

Peanut butter, mixed with flour and cornmeal, can be spread on

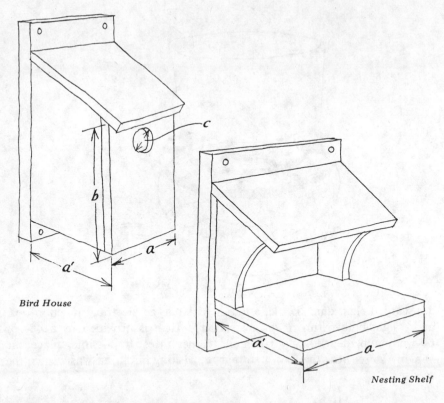

Bird House

Nesting Shelf

hardware cloth either stretched across a small board, stuffed in holes in a log, or placed in a can and hung from a limb.

You can stretch commercial wild bird seed mixtures very satisfactorily with a large percentage of fine-cracked corn, available at a reasonable price in 25-, 50-, or 100-pound bags. You can also add: millet and sunflower seeds; suet or melted bacon fat to which flour, oatmeal, and cornmeal have been added; chopped apples, softened raisins, currants, bread-crumbs, peanut butter, dried dog food, doughnuts, and slices of orange.

Water.   Summer and winter birds use birdbaths for both bathing and drinking. It's best to place birdbaths in somewhat shaded locations, as the water will stay cooler, evaporation will be slowed, and the growth of algae is discouraged.

Birds have a hard time drinking ice, and *Organic Gardening and Farming* reader P. E. Dorsey has come up with a heated birdbath to attract birds in the winter. If you can handle minor electrical repairs or do simple wiring jobs, this water heater should be easy to build. You need

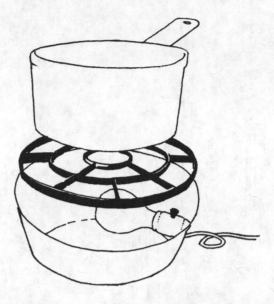

a discarded eight-quart kettle, a ten-inch skillet, an electrical junction box, and a light bulb fixture (see illustration). Heat is provided by a 40- or 60-watt bulb, depending on the air temperature. If possible, place the winter waterer near the feeder so that the visiting birds can wash down the seeds.

What About Birds That Eat Crops?

It would be blissful to tend a garden or berry patch in an arcadia where only helpful birds lived. But on your patch of land, living in harmony with birds may require the presence of a silent mediator—netting.

Large-scale fruit and vegetable growers sometimes construct long wire cages for each row or cages for entire patches or trees. But most of us do not need such complete protection, and cheesecloth or lightweight plastic netting will suffice. Choice individual fruits can be protected by draping a piece of transparent plastic over them. Leave the bottom open so that condensation can drain off, or the fruit may rot. You might also try plastic sandwich bags or paper bags to protect individual fruits. If such simple mechanical devices leave something to be desired, you might consider moving up to more sophisticated controls. The U.S. Fish and Wildlife Service at the Agricultural Experiment Station, Purdue University, has prepared a list of sources for various bird control materials. These materials include automatic exploders that ignite acetylene gas to make loud explosions at regular intervals. The acetylene gas is either generated by dripping water on calcium carbide (the same principle behind toy carbide cannons and old miner's lamps) or is supplied from a tank of compressed gas. The authors of the materials list thoughtfully point out that "the loud retorts may be objectionable in residential areas."

A number of companies market rope firecrackers that provide the same effect as the acetylene exploders but with less of an investment. The slow-burning ropes act as fuses, and firecrackers can be set at any interval to produce the desired frequency of explosions. In many states, laws prohibit the use of firecrackers for fun, but permits are sometimes issued to those with plant protection in mind. The authors of the list point out that "roman candles shot into roosts for a few evenings will effectively dislodge the birds," and they are doubtless right.

A number of companies offer "whirling, bright-colored, or shiny objects or owl replicas" that will instill fear for a few days, but the birds get used to these idle threats in time, and the scares must be changed frequently. Also listed are sources for recordings of distressed starlings, rotating light scares, and generators of high-frequency sounds that birds find unpleasant.

To keep birds from alighting where you would have them not, you can buy sticky materials, metal projections, and electric shocking wires for ledges; none is said to inflict serious injury. A couple of companies sell "specially designed 12-gauge shotgun shells that shoot an exploding charge about one hundred yards." Equally insidious are aluminum perches that feature wicks imbedded with poison. These last two seem to constitute dirty fighting, and aren't compatible with the message of this book; hence, they're not recommended.

For addresses of manufacturers and suppliers of control materials, see Appendix 1.

Ducks and geese
vs. slugs and weeds.   Some of the most valid tips on using ducks and geese in the garden come from *Organic Gardening and Farming* contributors who've given the domestic fowl a try.

Nancy Thornton of Oregon uses ducks to rid her garden of slugs. Ducklings, especially, are always searching for food, and eliminate slugs from both yard and garden, although the lettuce, zucchini, and green beans have to be fenced off from the wandering fowl. The Thorntons raise mallards and white Pekins for this task.

Wayne Rogers of northern New York State employs eight white Chinese goslings to patrol his strawberry patch and garden. These are preferred over the Toulose and Emden because of their smaller size, and their relative wildness makes them more active than most other species. They do little damage to the growing plants because they can move about much more nimbly than humans. For best results, however, the geese should be confined by a fence so that they do a thorough job.

Problems With Mammals

Although birds may cause some problems by damaging fruits and raiding berry patches, they are typically more beneficial than harmful. But mammals—mice, rats, gophers, rabbits, raccoons, deer and the like— deserve a little less compassion. Here is a variety of tips and tricks for taking care of raiding mammals, without resorting to poisons and pesticides.

Moles, voles, and rats.   Roy and Shirley Dycus of Blue Ridge, Georgia, have come up with a few ways of successfully protecting ground crops such as potatoes, onions, and carrots from rats and moles. They heavily mulch the potato patch with straw, hay, and leaves, and the moles that had previously eaten half the crop found it difficult to vent their air holes; thereafter, the pests tended to avoid these patches.

However, a straw mulch may have just the opposite effect on rats and mice. A mulch cover keeps them sheltered from the elements as well as hawks. Cats are likely the best answer to mouse control, whether in a small garden or a farm. Unlike hawks, which must see their prey before striking, a cat will patiently stalk a noise beneath a pile of cover mulch.

To protect newly set potatoes, the Dycus's soak the potato eyes overnight in a garlic water solution. The next day, while still wet, the eyes are rolled in dry wood ashes, set at least a foot apart on top of the ground, and covered with a one-foot-deep layer of leaves or straw. This family has also found that interplanting potatoes with castor beans (about four to a $40' \times 40'$ area) and edging with comfrey will keep rodent pests away. Moles, in particular, find castor beans repulsive. Mrs. Bjerstedt of Ohio came up with a castor oil solution that successfully takes care of her mole problems. She mixes two parts of oil to one part liquid detergent and whips the mixture in a blender to the consistency of shaving cream. A few tablespoons of this oil emulsion are added to a sprinkling can of warm water and then sprinkled over the troubled areas. Soil penetration is greatest following a rain.

Some mole remedies border on the ingenious. One simple method employs soft drink bottles set in the mole holes. The top of the bottle is left above ground so that a breeze passing across the mouth will make a whistle that vibrates throughout the mole's chamber. Some gardeners have successfully constructed small windmills that set up vibrations in the ground.

Field mice can cause much orchard damage by girdling young trees at the base. To help keep these pests away, do not mulch directly around the trunk—the mice won't want to come out into the open. Pine mice, however, burrow in the soil, and feed on root bark, causing underground damage that usually goes unnoticed until it is too late. To prevent trouble, dig a shallow ditch around the base of the tree and fill it with cinders. It also helps to spread some cinders in an area extending at least three feet around the trunk; the sharpness of the cinder particles deters the mice from pushing their noses into the soil.

Gophers and groundhogs.

While many people are averse to killing gophers and groundhogs, growers at times wield guns as a last resort. And a .22 caliber rifle is a more humane means of dispatching pests than slow-acting poisons. Flushing their burrows with water may make them move out, but they'll likely return.

Gophers will shy away from plantings of scilla bulbs. Scillas (sometimes called squills) are flowering bulb-type ornamentals with grassy leaves and clusters of flowers at the top of long stems. They grow readily with minimum care, adapt well to borders and rock gardens, and bloom in early spring. It's difficult to protect *all* vulnerable plants with scillas, as gophers nibble everything from vegetables to trees.

Groundhogs, or woodchucks, as they are often called, are a persistent problem for many gardeners. Anyone who has tried to keep these pests away with a fence soon discovers that the woodchuck climbs as well as it can burrow. Again, the only sure way to rid your garden patch of this animal is shooting or trapping.

If you feel compassion for the animals that would share your crops, traps are available for gophers, groundhogs, rabbits, squirrels, raccoons, mice, and others. Wire traps come in many sizes, and neither the animal nor curious children can get hurt. One drawback is that it is often difficult to get certain animals to enter the trap unless the bait is especially attractive.

Rabbits.

Rabbits plague almost every gardener at one time or another. The cottontail has adapted well to the suburbs, much to the dismay of backyard gardeners.

Unlike groundhogs, rabbits are not able to climb, and a good chicken wire fence of three feet or more in height will discourage them. Rabbits are considered game animals in most states and are therefore protected by law during certain seasons. Then, too, the discharge of firearms inside city and town limits may rule out shooting. If fences aren't doing the trick, it's best to call the local game warden, who will either trap or shoot the rabbits or come up with another method of getting rid of them.

Rabbits are often kept from seedlings with open-ended coffee cans, but once the plants get taller than seven or eight inches they again become vulnerable. Until plants get too tall, you can keep the clear plastic lid on the top end. Sunlight passes through the lid and the water droplets that condense inside keep the young plants watered sufficiently. One gardener hangs strips of aluminum foil on lines stretched across planted areas. Another, who lost 80 percent of her dahlias to rabbits, dusts the plants with talcum powder and an occasional dose of hot pepper. Blood meal has also been used successfully in discouraging rabbits, as they are strictly vegetarians and are turned off by the smell. If liquid blood is available, add a spoonful to two gallons of warm water and spray on tree trunks or around the garden. A sprinkling of powdered rock phosphate on seedling leaves will work, too.

To prevent rabbit damage in winter and early spring, fruit trees and ornamentals need a cloth or heavy paper wrapping, or even a wire cylinder. The shields should be 18 inches or more in height, depending on the depth of snow cover that you can expect.

Raccoons and opossums.   Other than shooting, the best control for coons is trapping them live. When the corn is sweet, however, it may be difficult to draw a coon into a trap as there's a smorgasbord all around him, so it's advisable to begin your control program before the corn ripens. The raccoon is notorious for having a sweet tooth, and honey-soaked bread, marshmallows, and peanut butter should work well. One farmer places a transistor radio (tuned to an all-night station, of course) in the corn patch with the volume turned all the way up. The only expense was the replacement of batteries every few days, and the coons stayed clear.

The opossum can also be caught in a trap baited with sweets. This animal isn't often thought of when gardeners find chunks missing from tomato plants or corn, but he's often the culprit. Opossums are scavengers and will also raid compost piles.

Squirrels.   Anyone who feeds birds in winter knows of the havoc a pair of squirrels can cause, not to mention the additional expense for sunflower seeds. Landowners with nut trees can also appreciate their appetites.

Unlike rabbits and raccoons, squirrels are easily attracted by peanut butter smeared on the trip plate of a live trap. They can then be released in a woodlot far from the garden.

Deer.   In recent years deer populations in suburban areas have increased so rapidly that the animal is now considered a pest in many regions. Since they're too large to trap and shooting is out of the question (the best control, say some, is an adequate harvest during the hunting season), the only solution is to repel them.

Fences work well, but may prove too expensive. Because deer are good jumpers, a four- or five-foot-high fence won't do. One Oregon gardener has found success with a four-foot-high mesh chicken wire fence and, about three feet outside of that, a single, parallel strand of wire $2\frac{1}{2}$ feet above the ground. The deer evidently have trouble leaping high enough to clear the mesh fence with the single strand wire in the way.

One inventive orchardist used a bit of psychology to take care of his deer problems. His young apple trees were being nibbled by the deer and the cost of fencing the entire orchard was out of the question. So, he drove to the nearest city zoo and asked for a truckload of various kinds of wild animal manure. He hung bear, lion, and tiger droppings from small bags in scattered parts of the orchard, and the deer keep their distance.

A Pennsylvania gardener tried a similar ploy, but instead of animal droppings he collected human hair from local barber shops and sprinkled it around the edge of his garden. The hint of human scent does the trick.

SECTION TWO
AN ENCYCLOPEDIA OF PLANT PROTECTION

To find an answer to your trouble, look up the plant, whether it be a vegetable, fruit, tree, or berry. General sections cover basic plant protection strategies; see FLOWER, FRUIT, LAWN, and TREES. Entries first discuss bug troubles, then diseases, and finally problems with wildlife. If you can't find what you're after, consult the Index; you'll be referred both to other entries in the encyclopedia and to the chapters of Section One.

The word color in brackets [color] following an insect or disease indicates that you will find that malady illustrated in the section of color plates, which are arranged alphabetically. References to other entries appear as such: see POTATO, or, see codling moth under APPLE.

Acerola

Root-knot nematodes can cause acerola considerable damage, especially when grown in soil lacking in organic matter. A deep, year-round mulch encourages the growth of a fungus that preys on the pests. If problems become severe, it may be necessary to graft plants on to resistant roots. See NEMATODE.

Scale may attack this fruit in some areas; a dormant spray can be used in serious cases. See SCALE.

Aphids

A great number of aphid (or plant lice) species are of economic significance to growers. There are violet aphids, green peach aphids, mint aphids, blackberry aphids, and dozens of other species named for a food preference.

Aphids are small, soft-bodied insects distinguished by their pearlike shape, long antennae, and pair of cornicles—tubelike appendages that project from the back end. A defensive secretion is given off by these tubes. Winged aphids hold their wings vertically when at rest.

Winged Aphid

Aphids suck plant sap, and cause withering of foliage and a general loss of vigor. Excess sugars and sap are emitted from the anus and are known as honeydew. This substance may make leaf surfaces sticky, and can support a black mold that blocks light from leaves. Ants feed on honeydew, and tend aphids like cows (see color plate). Control is made much more difficult when ants distribute aphids from plant to plant. Ants stroke and tap the belly of aphids to milk them of the honeydew. This must be a very delicate process: according to John Crompton's *Ways of the Ant,* Darwin tried in vain to coax drops from aphids by stroking them with fine hairs. In fall, ants carry aphid eggs into their nests, to be carried back out in spring and set on plants. To keep their charges from straying, ants may chew off the aphids' wings.

Aphid

Several parthenogenetic generations (produced by unfertilized females) of female aphids may be born alive in a season. After one or two generations, winged forms are born and fly off to other plants. Toward the end of the season, males and females mate to produce eggs that overwinter. This method of reproduction can generate great numbers of aphids within a short time.

• **Biological control.** Naturally occurring controls, if permitted to operate, will usually keep aphids from causing intolerable damage. The best-known enemy of this pest is the ladybug. Adults and larvae increase in numbers to meet infestations. If you don't use chemical sprays, chances are you have a sufficient number of ladybugs on hand to handle these pests. However, ladybugs can be purchased from a number of suppliers. Other important predators include soldier bugs, damsel bugs, big-eyed bugs, pirate bugs, spiders, assassin bugs, syrphid flies, and lacewings. The last-named is also commercially available. The principal parasites are brachonid and chalcid wasps. At least 14 species of fungus are known to attack aphids throughout the world.

*Wasp Laying Eggs
in Aphid*

The University of California imported a ladybug (*Exochomus quadripustulatus*) from Europe in 1921, and it has since caught on as an important predator of the wooly apple aphid. A parasite, *Aphelinus mali,* was introduced to West Coast orchards in 1929 and, with the above ladybug, reduced populations of the wooly apple aphid to manageable levels. Perennial apple canker, spread by the aphid, was eradicated. The widespread use of DDT and other hydrocarbons in the late 1940's set these beneficials back so seriously that both aphids and canker returned. But *A. mali* has persisted, and is now established in countries all over the world.

Agricultural Research magazine reports that a team of state and federal scientists are attempting to develop an economical control for aphids by using fungus diseases. The fungus spores germinate like seeds and produce threadlike stalks that spread through the insects' bodies, first weakening, then destroying the pests. The spores are raised on egg yolk and other constituents, and can be held in a dormant state in a refrigerator until needed. Just before the fungus is to be used, it is mixed with water in a blender and sprayed in a conventional manner in the evening. The *Agricultural Research* article says that, although specific control agents are usually not economically advantageous, aphids are such universal pests that such an agent would be of great value. One fungus, *Entomophthora exitialis,* has been distributed in California to help control the spotted alfalfa aphid. Another naturally occurring control is rain— hard, driving rains can kill large numbers of some species. Damp weather favors development of aphid diseases.

Professor J. G. Rodriguez of the University of Kentucky has found that aphids respond positively to increased elements in plants, especially nitrogen. In other words, the more nitrogen fertilizer you put on the soil, the happier the aphids. In particular, nitrogen has been found to favor the bean, cabbage, and cotton aphids.

• **Conventional controls.** Cultural controls include planting as far as possible from infested areas, clearing the garden neighborhood of aphid host plants, especially plantain, and seeing to it that plants are properly nourished and watered or irrigated as necessary.

Growers have come up with a great number of home remedies for aphid trouble. The simplest of all is to gently rub leaves between thumb and forefinger. These pests can be repelled by growing nasturtiums between vegetable rows and even around fruit trees. Other companion plants are garlic, chives, and other alliums, and coriander, anise, and petunias. Their effectiveness can be amplified by crushing a leaf now and then. As for sprays, aphids can be washed from the plants with a forceful jet of water. A tobacco water spray can be made by soaking tobacco stems, available from florists and seedsmen, in warm water for 24 hours. Dilute the brew to the color of a weak tea and syringe it on the foliage, being careful to hit the underside of the leaves. Or, you can just buy a tobacco extract and follow the directions on the package. A soapy spray is effective, but plants should be rinsed with clear water afterward. You may want to experiment with a mixture of crushed raw turnips and corn oil. An even more exotic spray is made by boiling $3\frac{1}{4}$ ounces of quassia chips and 5 teaspoons of larkspur in 7 pints of water until the mixture is reduced to 5 pints. A spray of strong lime water will also take care of aphids.

Red spider mites, scale, and mealybugs, as well as aphids, can be gummed up in a sticky mixture recommended in John and Helen Philbrick's *The Bug Book*. Dissolve $\frac{1}{4}$ pound of glue in a gallon of warm water, let the solution stand overnight, and apply with a sprayer to twigs and leaves of fruit trees. When it dries it will flake off, taking the pests along with it. In midsummer, several applications spaced seven to ten days apart may be needed to handle consecutive generations. Try mincing shallots or green onions in a food chopper for a spray to keep aphids off roses. From England comes a spray recipe using three pounds of rhubarb leaves, boiled a half hour in three quarts of water and mixed when cool with one quart of water in which an ounce of soap flakes has been dissolved. Elder leaves can be substituted for the rhubarb leaves, with the added attraction of discouraging mildew on roses.

Apple aphids can be discouraged by repruning a quarter of the length of leading shoots in July, and a like length of the side shoots after the second leaf (not counting the little leaves around the base). This helps on both apple and pear trees. Pruning shouldn't be necessary every year.

Aphids are attracted to the color yellow, and this can be used against them. Bright yellow plastic dishpans make a good trap when filled with slightly soapy water and set near infested or vulnerable plants. The extension service of the College of Agriculture at Washington State University suggests that such traps are also valuable in monitoring aphid activity. Winged aphids will usually appear in traps before they hit nearby crops. For monitoring on a large scale, cut the top off five-gallon lubricating oil drums, rinse them out well, and paint the inside yellow; the Washington Extension Service reports that a whitish yellow paint is less effective. Paint the outside of the can any color but red. Fill with water to within an inch of the top.

Winged aphids won't land on low plants if sheets of aluminum foil are placed around the base as a mulch. Apparently the reflection of the sky confuses them—they don't know which way is up. This simple method works against other small flying pests, too.

Years ago, the New York Agricultural Society suggested that aphids could be killed by placing a box over infested plants and burning tobacco in a cup underneath.

• **The role of ants.**   Ants aggravate aphid problems by lugging them about to feed on plants, and thorough control of aphids often requires that you do something about the ants as well. These aphid-tenders are best kept from trouble by setting up barriers. Ants are loath to cross lines of bone meal or powdered charcoal. A band of cotton, made sticky with Tanglefoot or Stikem, can be wrapped around the bases of some plants and trees. Ants are sometimes drawn to trees that are leaking sap, and the trees can be made less attractive by cleaning out the wound and coating it with shellac or some other wound dressing. If ants are carrying aphids into your house, track them to find where they are getting in and squeeze the juice of a lemon into the hole or crack. Then, slice up the lemon and put the peeling all around the entrance.

• **Root aphids.**   Aphids and mites damage bulbs by sucking out nutrients and causing wounds through which fungal and bacterial decay organisms can enter. Badly infested bulbs produce weak growth, and leaves are stunted and yellowish with brown tips. Those flowers that mature are usually small, streaked, and off-color. For control methods, see ASTER.

Apple

Producing a good harvest of apples isn't easy. Even orchardists who blitz their trees with carefully timed sprays have trouble— a pamphlet on chemical disease control in the orchard put out by the Indiana Cooperative Extension Service lists four important tips to remember, of which number four is, "If all else fails, fruit trees make excellent firewood."

But such pessimism is unnecessary if you follow a program of cultural and biological control, along with judicious dormant-oil spraying. You should be able to bring an excellent crop of apples through the season, without poisonous herbicides, pesticides, or fungicides. Chemically sprayed apples may be flawlessly complected, but then so was that famous prop in *Snow White and the Seven Dwarves*, and many orchardists want to do better by their customers. Dick Moore, a certified organic apple grower in California, is one of them; he made the transition from chemicals to natural control because he wanted "to do it right, give the land a chance, and give people decent food to eat."

It's true that orchardists of a traditional mind use all those chemicals for a reason—there are a myriad of insects, mites, diseases, and wildlife to contend with. "Being an organic farmer is not easy," admit Lowell and Freda Curtis, organic apple growers of Tanglewood Farm in Sonora, California. In the first year that they set out young trees, they lost 100 to codling moths and 196 to deer. The Curtises were able to get around such problems in time, but the answers did not come automatically. To keep down insect populations, they first studied up on the use of beneficial insects and then ordered trichogramma wasps, lacewings, and praying mantises. These beneficials, along with naturally occurring ladybugs, benefited from a nearby ditch that was left wild and a section of the property that had not been cleared. The purchase of a few bantam hens took care of earwigs that had been eating new shoots and nibbling at the fruit. The Curtises found that a band of Tanglefoot around the tree trunks thwarted codling moths and earwigs. After experimenting with strings of tin cans and flashing lights, they learned the only way to keep the deer at bay was to erect an eight-foot fence around the trees. But now, several years later, the couple enjoys modest success with their venture.

An organic orchardist has to begin from the ground up. Dick Moore's spring fertilization program consists of working manure and green manure into the soil out as far as the drip line of each tree. He then grows a cover crop of vetch between the trees. The Curtises use a variety of organic fertilizers: hoof and horn meal, bone meal, blood meal, fish emulsion, kelp meal, wood ashes, manure, compost, and anything else that will improve the soil organically. In reviving his old New England orchard, writer John Vivian mowed the weeds around each tree with a brush cutter, raked the cuttings under the branches for mulch, and let the stuff rot down for fertilizer. (Not all growers would go along with this practice, for fear that the weeds would harbor disease and pests, and they send off their weeds for a lengthy internment within the depths of the compost pile.) Some fruit growers suggest that mulch should be kept at least two feet from the trunk, so that rodents and insect pests such as the apple flea weevil are forced to live at a distance. You can keep mice and rabbits from girdling young trees by wrapping the trunks with a wire mesh barrier, veneer bands, or roofing paper.

The first thing in spring, remove all loose bark with a paint scraper, old hoe, piece of saw blade, or part of a mower blade. This will destroy overwintering eggs and larvae, and permit more thorough coverage with dormant spray. Scrape carefully so that the blade doesn't lay open the living wood. Put a sheet or piece of canvas under the scene of activity to catch all the scrapings, which should be carted away to the compost pile.

Old, decaying wounds resulting from broken limbs, poor pruning cuts, and woodpeckers, are a favorite hiding place for codling moth larvae and other destructive pests. John Vivian advises that as much as possible of the wet dark wood be dug out. Then, paint the newly exposed, healthy wood inside with tree-wound dressing. The dressing Vivian uses is made with roofing tar thinned as necessary with gasolene. He also applies the dressing on spots where limbs are removed during November pruning.

This late-fall pruning can have a lot to do with the way the trees produce fruit and resist diseases. The "cloverleaf method" is used to open up a tree so that air can circulate through the foliage; dry foliage is less prone to fungi that get their start on wet surfaces. Prune off all dead, split, or broken branches and stubs cleanly at the point of origin, beveling edges to encourage healing. Any running cavities and stubs that have rotted back into the tree should be cleaned out with a chisel to solid, live wood. This can be carried out in almost any season, except in wet weather. Trim the edges of cavities back to live bark and bring the cavity to a point at top and bottom; a straight chisel is the best tool for this. All cuts over two inches in diameter should be painted over with the tree-wound dressing described above. It's not a good idea to fill cavities with cement—the tree may look neater, but the filling will hide any further decay.

The danger of bacterial diseases such as fire blight can be minimized by cutting out cankers and diseased limbs during winter, and rubbing off any suckers and water sprouts while they are still very small. Bitter rot, blister canker, black rot, and blotch fungi also live in old cankers, and attack the tree through new, open wounds. The bark on old cankers should be removed to healthy tissue, and the wound must be painted over promptly.

As for sprays, a good blast of water will knock off mites and aphids, says Dr. Brian Beirne, director of Simon Faser University's entomology center in British Columbia. But many organic fruit growers rely on dormant-oil sprays to suffocate various pests; see FRUIT TREES for a description of a comprehensive spray program.

With these fundamentals behind us, we can now go on to the specific problems you're most likely to run into.

Insects

A number of **aphid** species may damage various parts of the tree. The yellow green apple aphid, trimmed with black, specializes on sucking the life from terminals in midsummer. Leaves may be curled somewhat, and young fruits are deformed. Black sooty mold tends to grow on the honeydew secretions of this pest. The shiny black eggs spend the winter on tree bark, and a thorough going-over with the scraper in early spring should take care of many of them. Spraying with dormant oil will catch most of those you miss. It also helps to remove suckers, and some gardeners claim excellent results when winter-hardy onions are planted around trees.

Apple/Apple Aphid

Another important species, the rose-colored rosy apple aphid, feeds on buds and opening leaves. If sufficient numbers are present, the leaves will curl around to protect the pests. Cynthia Westcott reports in *The Gardener's Bug Book* that a number of beneficials—syrphid flies, ladybugs, lacewings, and parasitic wasps —are of much help in keeping down populations of this pest, but that aphids go relatively unbothered in spells of cold and wet weather.

East of the Mississippi, the **apple curculio** injures young fruit by puncturing them. Unlike the marks left by the plum curculio, these punctures are not crescent-shaped. This is a brown snout beetle, smaller than the plum species, and distinguished by four humps on its back. There is one generation a year. Eggs are deposited in young apples, and larvae mature within June drops and in mummified fruit on the trees. Control measures are similar to those for the plum curculio (see PLUM).

The **apple maggot**, also known as apple fruit fly or railroad worm, causes brown tunnels or burrows inside apples. The unsuspecting grower may discover the presence of this pest the hard way—by biting into an infested apple. Maggots cause slight depressions on the surface and tiny holes where they emerge, but these external symptoms are often so slight as to go unnoticed. After an infested apple falls or is picked, the flesh may break down into a brown, pulpy mess.

The adult apple maggot is a fly, similar to the common house fly. In orchards throughout the Northeast and in northern parts of the Midwest, most serious infestations usually occur in July. Flies lay their eggs in the flesh of apples (usually sweet or subacid varieties that ripen during summer or fall), and legless white maggots develop in the flesh of the fruit. The insect passes winter in the soil in its pupal stage.

Collecting dropped apples may reduce the population of apple maggots. Dropped fruit of summer varieties should be collected twice a week, and those of later varieties, once a week. These apples can be fed to livestock, dumped into water to kill the maggots, or even made into cider if not too badly damaged.

You can catch this pest in the fly stage, before it has a chance to cause trouble, with a simple baited trap. Mix up one part black strap molasses or malt extract to nine parts water, add yeast to encourage fermentation, and pour the beery liquid into wide-mouthed jars. Once fermentation subsides, hang the jars up in the trees. To monitor apple maggot fly populations, the Cooperative Extension Service of New Hampshire suggests a bait made of two teaspoons household ammonia and ¼ teaspoon soap powder mixed in a quart of water. Fill quart fruit jars with the bait, and hang them shoulder-high on the outside of the sunny side of the trees. Ten or so jars distributed throughout the orchard should give a good picture of maggot fly activity. Examine the traps every two or three days to count flies and renew the bait if necessary; bait should be changed once a week or when diluted by rain.

Eugene Carpovitch, a Maine grower, took a different tactic,

figuring that "if he is a fly, he should respond to fly paper. The only question was in which form to apply the flypaper principle." For the evolution of his apple fly trap, see the section "Insect Traps, Homemade and Commercial" in Chapter 9.

If apple maggots have consistently been a big problem, the answer may lie in growing late varieties, such as Winesap, Jonathan, and York Imperial.

The **apple red bug** is an active red insect about ¼ inch in length, with bright red markings on the wing margins. The eggs spend the winter in bark lenticels on small twigs. Hatching occurs before blossoming, and the bugs mature in June. When the bugs feed on terminal leaves, distortion results. Feeding on fruit produces dimples or a series of small russet scars. A delayed spray of superior dormant oil should take care of these pests.

Green **buffalo treehoppers** are distinguished by a heavy spine on each shoulder. They damage young trees by puncturing the bark to deposit their eggs. Trees are sometimes stunted in severe infestations. There is one generation a year, and winter is passed in the egg stage. The nymphs hatch in spring and drop to the ground to feed on such plants as alfalfa and bindweed.

If treehoppers present a problem in your area, do not grow alfalfa cover crops nearby and keep bindweed out of young orchards. Overwintering eggs are killed by dormant sprays.

Cankerworms are small, striped measuring worms or inchworms. They are either black or green, and appear in one generation a year. Cankerworms hatch from eggs laid on the tree in late fall or early spring by wingless moths. The male moths are gray and have a wingspan of about one inch. You have two species to worry about: the fall cankerworm and spring cankerworm.

After fall frosts, the fall cankerworms leave their pupal stage in the ground and the wingless females crawl up tree trunks to deposit their gray eggs on the trunk, branches, or twigs. The worms appear just in time to feed on unfolding foliage in spring; they are colored brown on top and green below, and are marked with stripes along the length of their bodies. You will likely see them hanging from trees on fine silk threads.

These threads serve to complicate control of the worms. When winds catch a thread, the attached cankerworm may be lofted to a neighboring tree. This thwarts growers who band tree trunks with a sticky material to keep the females from making their egg-laying missions each fall, as one infested tree may spread trouble to those near it. Still, a sticky band around the trunk is the most efficacious means of control. Before applying the sticky compound, whether it be commercial or homemade, you should first lay down a layer of cotton batting or heavy paper to protect the tree bark. To catch this species of cankerworm, the bands should be applied in mid-October. You may catch a few tussock and gypsy moths, as well. Tree Tanglefoot is a commercial preparation made for snaring pests. A can of roofing cement works well enough, according to some growers. Or, you can stir up your own goo from pine tar and molasses, or resin and oil. In any case, the sticky band should be renewed from time to time to ensure its effectiveness.

You can also spray, safely and sanely, for cankerworms; see BACILLUS THURINGIENSIS. This bacterial control is sprayed in April or May. Nearby oaks and elms should be treated as well, as they are alternate hosts.

As for the spring cankerworm, the moths appear early in spring but are otherwise similar in habit to the fall species. The worms are colored green, brown, or black, and may show a yellow stripe. They have two pairs of prolegs, while the fall cankerworm has three. Control as for the fall species, except that sticky bands should be applied in February to catch the wingless females.

Codling Moth

The larva of the **codling moth** [color] is distinguished from other caterpillars by its color (white tinged with pink), its habit of tunneling directly to the core of the apple (see illustration), and its appetite. This worm is considered the most serious of apple pests. Fortunately, there are a number of effective ways of saving the crop without resorting to the poisons that many growers have unfortunately accepted as a necessary part of fruit growing.

Larvae develop from eggs laid in the blossom end of the apples in June, work their way into the core, and then tunnel out to the skin again. After leaving their trail through the apples, they spin cocoons in bark crevices to spend the winter. The gray brown moths, showing fringed hind wings, make their appearance in June.

A hundred years ago, orchards were the scene of huge bonfires in June evenings. Growers theorized that because moths were attracted to light, they would be drawn to their deaths. Today, one of the best organic controls involves banding tree trunks in spring with corrugated paper to draw larvae looking for a place to spin their cocoons. The bands should be wrapped in several thicknesses, and can be wired on. Keep the bands on at least until September, when the second generation of worms crawls across the bark to find a place to winter. Remove the bands later on in fall and burn them.

The codling moth larvae, like many other apple pests, are reduced in number by a careful scraping of rough bark each spring. If a water faucet is handy, a high-pressure spray from a short distance will dislodge some larvae from their hiding places in the bark. Eugene Carpovitch greets the first wave of codling moths in his Maine orchard with a spray of two heaping tablespoons of ryania per gallon of water. He's also tried keeping their numbers down with the pheromone traps now marketed by Zoecon, but these traps are best used for their intended purpose—as monitoring devices. For more information on pheromone traps, see Chapter 9.

Codling moths have been found to be vulnerable to several sprays. Soapy-water and fish-oil sprays seem to work best, causing caterpillars on the prowl to drop to the ground. Dormant-oil sprays will take care of many of the eggs. Nasturtiums can be planted around the trunks as a repellent barrier.

Perhaps the most promising means of control is the tiny trichogramma wasp, available through the mail as eggs. Making successful use of them depends on timing—the eggs should hatch just about the time the moths are layings their eggs, as this wasp is an egg parasite. If the number of wasp eggs seems paltry in comparison with the task at hand, keep in mind that trichogramma can have 50 or more generations in a favorable season.

Codling moths are attracted to blacklight traps. One grower used blacklight to draw moths to a homemade mangler consisting of two whips turned by a fractional horsepower motor. The whips are nothing more than two wires, attached to the end of the rotor at right angles to each other. The whips should be rigid enough to kill the moths, but not so thick that they can easily be seen.

It may well be worth your while to put out suet in winter and spring to attract woodpeckers to the orchard area, as these birds pick out a good number of pest larvae from tree bark.

The silken nests of the **eastern tent caterpillar** signal trouble for orchards. Also known as the appletree tent caterpillar, the black hairy larvae ravage foliage by day and spend nights and rainy weather in the nests. There is one generation a year. Overwintering eggs hatch very early in spring, and reddish brown moths appear three weeks after the dirty white cocoons are spun. Pest infestations usually occur in cycles of seven to ten years (the result of the effects of parasitism and disease), and the extent of damage ranges from none at all to complete defoliation. For controls, see TENT CATERPILLAR.

Tent Caterpillar

The **European apple sawfly** is brown and yellow in color and marked with numerous transverse lines. They are a little larger than houseflies. Larvae feed in the fruit just below the skin until they are about one-third grown, at which time they start boring directly through the fruit. They sometimes pass from one small apple to another, leaving a chocolate-colored "sawdust" on the surface. The winter is passed in the soil as mature larvae. Pupation occurs late in spring and the sawflies appear at about the time the trees blossom. Eggs are laid in the flesh of the calyx cup, and the young larvae feed there before beginning to tunnel.

Sawfly on Apple

If necessary to protecting a crop, spray trees at petal fall with rotenone; a follow-up spray a week or so later will ensure adequate control.

Populations of the **European red mite** has been increased by the use of high-powered insecticides, and this has become a serious pest of apple, pear, plum, and prune. The mature mites are very small, and can best be observed with a magnifier. The adult female is dark red with white spots; other stages may vary from red to green in color. Eggs laid in summer are brown, and those that pass the winter on bark are red. They are slightly flattened and stand on a delicate central hair. There are several generations to contend with in summer, the peak of infestation usually occurring in July or early August. Feeding causes bronzed foliage that may drop prematurely, and fruit from infested trees is likely to be small.

Superior dormant-oil sprays can be applied in early spring to kill the overwintering eggs. Ladybugs finish off up to 11 of them an hour.

The **flat-headed apple tree borer** is just that, excepting the fact that its appetite is much more catholic than the name indicates. Dr. Cynthia Westcott notes that this pest also mines the bark and wood of apricot, ash, mountain ash, beech, boxelder, cherry, chestnut, cotton-oak, currant, dogwood, elm, hickory, horsechestnut, linden, maple, oak, peach, pear, pecan, plum, poplar, prune, sycamore, and willow, as well as raspberry and rose. The borer typically feeds on the bark in a U-shaped pattern. Their feeding tunnels show through the bark as sunken areas, and it is in these tunnels that the borer passes the winter. Once the borers reach full size, they are ready to head into the wood. Tunnels are filled with a dry powdery substance known as frass. The adults are dark beetles with a metallic sheen. You may see them in May or June on the sunny sides of trees, where they lay their eggs in cracks or wounds.

"Preventative measures are best," says Dr. Westcott. Because the beetles are drawn to sun-warmed trunks, shade the trunks of young trees with any sort of shield. Trees that have just been transplanted should be protected by wrapping them up from the soil to the lower branches. Keep young trees pruned so that they have a low profile. If you have but a few young trees, you can control borers that have already got a start by digging them out with a sharp knife or a moderately stiff wire. Since the borer most often attacks trees in poor condition, seal up wounds with tree paint and make sure that the orchard has an adequate supply of organic fertilizer.

Fruit tree leaf rollers are small green caterpillars with black heads that damage fruit clusters, leaves, and buds. They may web together leaves and feed within. Apples are russeted as a result of their feeding. Control leaf rollers with a dormant-oil spray just before the buds break. *Bacillus thuringiensis,* a commercially available pathogen, has proved to be a very helpful spray.

Red-banded Leaf Roller

Two- or three-inch-long **gypsy moth** larvae ravage the foliage of apple trees. As is true with many other fruit tree pests, the gypsy moths start off life as overwintering eggs on bark. The gray or brown hairy larvae feed nocturnally through June and July. For control methods, see GYPSY MOTH.

Japanese leafhoppers start their feeding on water sprouts and later spread throughout the tree. The mature hoppers are about $\frac{1}{5}$ inch long and are colored dark gray. To reduce chances of an infestation, remove water sprouts early in the season.

Gypsy Moth

The pinkish white **oriental fruitworm** behaves much like the larvae of the codling moth, but enters apples through the stem and thus gives little external sign of damage. See PEACH for control methods.

Oystershell scale is elongate and enlarged at one end. It winters in the egg stage, to hatch in May and crawl about for a time before settling down on the bark. Eggs are laid under the scale, and a thorough going-over of the bark should reduce the population of this pest to an acceptable level. Dormant-oil sprays work to suffocate this pest.

Apple/Oystershell Scale

The **roundheaded apple tree borer** tunnels deep into the trunk of apple trees, usually near the ground line. The adult is a slender, long-horned beetle, colored gray and marked with two conspicuous, longitudinal white stripes. Infestations can weaken or girdle a tree; young trees may be killed. Adults may be seen

Roundheaded Apple Tree Borer

eating leaves and fruit, and lay their eggs in slits in the bark near the ground. Rusty brown material shows at the borer's hole.

Look for the telltale brown castings just above or below ground level. You can destroy some borers by snaking a wire into their holes; this should be done each fall and spring. A flood of boiling-hot water will go where a wire will not. A thick wash of soap can be applied to the lower trunk in order to discourage beetles from laying eggs there. Also see peach borer under PEACH.

Fruit Tree/San José Scale

San José scale sucks the sap from the wood, leaves, and fruit of apple, pear, peach, and other fruit trees. Serious infestations can lower the vitality of a tree, eventually killing branches and even the tree itself. The mature female insect is yellow and about the size of a pinhead. It lives under a protective covering that forms over it as it grows. Small, reddish discolorations often may be seen at the point of feeding, particularly on new, tender wood and fruit. Except for the first few hours of its life, and the short time that adult males are active, the scale remains in one place. The tiny, newly emerged young, called crawlers, move around on the tree and are sometimes blown or carried to trees some distance away.

To control, spray trees early in spring with an oil emulsion. An additional late-spring spraying should give even better results. Ladybugs feast on scale insects and can usually keep these pests under control. If your orchard is deficient in ladybugs, they can be purchased. See SCALE.

Peach/Shot-Hole Borer Damage

Healthy vigorous trees are rarely bothered by the **shot-hole borer,** known also as the fruit tree bark beetle, so an organic fertilizing program is the best way to prevent trouble. You may see shot holes in twigs of healthy trees and in the branches or trunks of weak ones. Black beetles exit the holes early in summer. For control, see PEACH.

Small, active **white apple leafhoppers** are only ⅛ inch long, but their feeding can remove significant amounts of chlorophyll, leaving foliage spotted or white. Nymphs are yellow or green in color. Leafhoppers feed on the underside of leaves, leaving behind dark dots of excrement. Adults cause spots on fruit by feeding, and mature fruit may be soiled by their excrement. Masses of these leafhoppers are known to descend upon rose gardens. Strong water sprays may wash leafhoppers from the bottoms of leaves, and sprays of quassia or ryania should prevent serious infestations.

The larvae of the **white-marked tussock moth** [color: tussock moth] are very noticeable pests of fruits and foliage. They reach a length of 1½ inches, are striped lengthwise with brown and yellow, and are hairy, bearing four upright white tufts on the front half, two long sprouts of black hairs near the head, and a similar sprout on the tail. Look for a bright red spot just behind the head. The female is ash gray and has no wings. The male moth has prominent, feathered antennae and gray wings marked by patterns of darker gray.

Fortunately, birds and parasites help out the organic orchardist with this one. You can do your part by scraping away the lathery egg masses that appear in fall. They may be found on bark, empty cocoons, or leaves.

Diseases

Apple scab [color] is one of the most universally destructive of all apple diseases. The leaves, fruit, and occasionally the twigs of apple trees are affected. Scab generally appears first on the underside of the leaves as diseased spots that gradually darken from dark green until they are nearly black. Both surfaces of the leaves may show numerous scab spots, and in severe cases curling and distortion of the leaves results in defoliation. Symptoms on the fruit are quite similar. As the spot on the fruit enlarges and becomes older, the velvety appearance in the center becomes brown and corky. Heavy infection may cause the dropping of young fruit and distortion and cracking of growing fruit. Infection on twigs will blister and rupture the bark to produce a scurfy appearance.

The fungus overwinters on the fallen infected leaves, producing a spore stage in spring. The spores are wind-borne and infect the young leaves and fruit during periods of rain. During summer, a different spore form is produced on the leaves and fruit, and these spores continue to produce new infections when washed onto leaves and fruit by rain. Infection may also occur during moist periods in fall. Summer spores are responsible for late fruit infection that will develop in storage either as typical scab spots or as small black lesions.

Damage to crops may come about in several ways: the premature dropping of young apples during or immediately following the blossoming period; the dropping of scabby apples before harvest; impairment of quality with a consequent reduction in value; the formation of "pin-point" scab at harvest or so-called storage scab, caused by late infection and responsible for lowering the quality of the fruit; and reduced vigor and health of the tree as the result of damaged leaves.

Because the fungus spends the winter on fallen infected leaves, these should either be raked up carefully or plowed under in fall or early spring. When pruning in winter, take off any twigs that show signs of scab. Varieties resistant to scab are available; check with your local extension agent. If your plants are in serious trouble, a sulfur or lime sulfur spray should protect them from infection. Ninety-five-percent sulfur is mixed up at a rate of 5 pounds to 100 gallons of spray; 2 gallons of lime sulfur are used per 100 gallons.

Baldwin spot, or **bitter pit** [color], is characterized by brown corky flecks in the flesh of the fruit. The flecks are most frequently found just under the skin of the apple, but may be scattered through the flesh as far as the core. Baldwin spot differs from drought spot in that the spots are sharply defined, whereas drought spot is a solid browning of the affected tissue. The name bitter pit derives from the bitter flavor of the corky tissue. While it is known that these troubles are not caused by an organism, the Connecticut Agricultural Experiment Station reports that extensive investigation has so far failed to establish the exact cause. It may be a nutritional disease, possibly caused by the ratio of calcium to other components of the fruit, coupled with certain moisture and temperature factors. Baldwin, Greening, and Northern Spy are the more susceptible varieties, while the McIntosh group is seldom affected. No control is known, but the Washington State Extension Service suggests several ways of lessening damage from bitter pit. Pruning and fruit thinning are important considerations. Avoid heavy pruning on vigorous trees; heading shoots will both stimulate growth and increase the chances of bitter pit. You should follow practices that encourage heavy cropping and delay thinning as long as possible. Cut down on fertilizers rich in nitrogen and potassium, and maintain a uniform level of soil moisture throughout the growing season. Fruit from overly vigorous or light-cropped trees should be harvested early, segregated, cooled rapidly, and marketed as soon as possible, especially with large-sized fruit.

Cedar-apple rust [color] is a curious disease, living one stage of its life on apple and the other on red cedar. Spores are blown from infected cedars to apple trees, where they cause bright orange spots on the foliage and to a lesser degree on fruit. The infections on apple foliage produce another spore stage, borne in delicate cuplike structures that reinfect the cedar and thereby keep the cycle going. A related fungus, quince rust, infects the fruit of Cortland, causing a hard green lesion on the calyx end.

If cedar rust presents a real problem, remove red cedars within a radius of one or two miles of the orchard—assuming this can be done legally—and cut down nearby susceptible varieties such as flowering crabapple. Resistant apple varieties are available; see RESISTANT VARIETIES.

Drought spot is a physiological trouble caused by boron deficiency and aggravated by drought conditions. The affected fruit has brown, corky areas in the flesh around the core which, in severe cases, may extend to the outside to cause cracking and distortion. Eventually the new growth fails to develop the side buds, resulting in naked twigs with tufts of foliage at the tips. The deficiency may be remedied by supplying each tree with finely ground glass, available commercially as FTE (fritted trace elements).

A variety of other **environmental conditions** lead to symptoms that might appear at first to be the work of a disease. Pits in the flesh of fruit may result from ozone in the atmosphere. Leaf scorch sometimes follows a deficiency of magnesium. Chlorosis is usually a sign of too little iron in the soil. Dry weather may bring on a condition known as Jonathan spot. Also see manganese toxicity, rosette, storage scald, water core, and weather (below).

Fire blight [color] is a serious disease of apple, pear, and quince. Hawthorne and other members of the Rosaceae are affected, including pyracantha, rose, flowering quince, and mountain ash. Affected blossoms and leaves wilt and collapse. Pear leaves turn black and apple leaves turn brown. Affected inner bark tissue is water-soaked at first and reddish. The inner bark of older branches becomes reddish brown in contrast to the normal whitish color. A milky ooze may appear on the surface of affected bark and turn brown in a few days. The surface of smooth-barked branches darkens, and cracks usually develop at the margins of the diseased bark area.

A bacterium is responsible for fire blight. It overwinters in the live bark at the edge of the cankers and in spring produces ooze containing the bacteria. Rainfall and insects, especially flies and ants, carry the bacteria to open blossoms. Infection may be evident within a week, and then rapidly progresses into the supporting twigs and branches. New shoots are inoculated by splashing rain and by sucking insects, especially aphids, leafhoppers, and plant bugs. Bark of twigs and branches may be inoculated through fresh wounds. Branches or entire trees, especially young, highly vigorous ones, can be killed within a few weeks, but often the infection is limited to twigs and small branches. Trees may be killed by root infection resulting from invasion through root sprouts.

Warm, moist weather is favorable for infection, and highly succulent growth favors development of the disease, as do excessive nitrogen fertilization, late fertilizer application, poor soil drainage, and other factors that promote succulent growth or delay hardening of the tissue near the end of summer.

The manner of pruning can go a long way to preventing fire blight. Generally, trees should be pruned every year so that only small cuts will be needed. On young trees, it is helpful to cut out infected twigs as soon as they can be seen, especially in early summer, making the cut at least 12 inches below evidence of infection as shown by darkening of the bark surface. The cutting tool should be disinfected after each cut; household bleach, diluted one part in nine with water, is satisfactory for this purpose. During winter, all infections from the previous year should be cut out, making the cut four inches below the basal edge of the canker or infected twig. This distance is adequate if careful examination of the inner bark is made to find the edge of the infection. There is no need to disinfect the cutting tools during the dormant season. Susceptible trees nearby, especially apple (including crabapple), pear, quince, hawthorn, and mountain ash, should be examined for cankers. These trees may be found in the wild as well as under cultivation. They are often planted as ornamentals. Good control of sucking insects helps prevent shoot infection. Most important are aphids, leafhoppers, and plant bugs, as well as psylla on pears.

Nothing is so essential in fighting this disease as avoiding susceptible varieties. The pear varieties Old Home, Kieffer, Seckel, and Winter Nelis and the apple varieties Delicious, Dolgo Crab, Duchess, Florence Crab, Gano, Haralson, Hibernal, Jonathan, McIntosh, and Northern Spy all have some resistance. These varieties are not immune to infection, but they are much more resistant than the pear varieties Bartlett, Bosc, Flemish Beauty, and Howell and the apple varieties Hopa Crab, Hylsop Crab, Transcendent Crab, Wealthy, Whitney Crab, and Yellow Transparent. The degree to which any one apple variety is resistant will vary from year to year, depending on local weather conditions during bloom, the proximity of pear trees with hold-over cankers, and the number of insect vectors.

Manganese toxicity, caused by the uptake of excess manganese from very acid soils, results in water blisters in the outer bark of the trunk that do not penetrate to the cambium. Usually these blisters burst and the brown liquid contents streak down the bark. Manganese toxicity in itself is not injurious to the tree, but the low pH it indicates leads to reduced growth and yield.

An obvious control method is to raise the soil pH. This can be done by adding crushed limestone or dolomite limestone. Wood ashes, marl, and ground oyster shells are all helpful. Any of these may be added to the compost pile.

Powdery mildew fungus [color] is a troublesome disease that overwinters in the apple buds. When the buds open in spring, the mildew fungus sends threadlike growth over the surface of the unfolding leaves and soon covers them with a mass of fungus filaments. The fungus growth robs the trees of nutrient material that the leaves normally provide for development of fruit. Spores are released by the fungus filaments, and these spread the infection to leaves, twigs, and fruits. Infected leaves have a white or gray powdery growth on both the upper and lower surfaces. In addition, the leaves may be curled, wrinkled, or folded. Leaves at the tips of twigs are small, distorted, and covered with gray mildew. Twig growth is stunted and the tip or terminal part may be killed. On one-year-old twigs, the fungus causes the same powdery white appearance, but by midsummer the powdery condition begins to disappear and the whitish growth turns into a brown feltlike covering in which numerous fruiting bodies are imbedded, giving the twigs a speckled appearance. On fruit, the injury appears as a network of fine lines of russet. In addition, the apples may be stunted, shriveled, or cracked.

For control, prune out distorted, badly mildewed twigs when you notice them, whether during the dormant season or the growing season. Although no variety is totally immune to powdery mildew, a few have shown some resistance, including McIntosh, Delicious, and Golden Delicious. Rome, Cortland, and Jonathan varieties are very susceptible.

Rosette, known also as little leaf, is most often due to a deficiency of zinc. This condition affects many plants, including pecan, apricot, peach, plum, grapes, and numerous ornamentals. Both homegrown trees and commercial orchards may sustain serious damage. A deficiency of zinc usually is found in alkaline, sandy soils low in organic matter, so the conscientious organic grower should have little or no trouble.

Symptoms are usually noted in pecan and fruit trees during either the second or third year after planting. When first purchased, most young trees have enough zinc stored in reserve to last for about one year. In its early stages, or on lightly affected trees, the disease appears as a yellowish mottling of the leaves, particularly in the tree tops. However, this symptom is sometimes absent in apple trees. In advanced stages, leaves are small, narrow, and crinkled. Foliage is often sparse. Reddish brown areas or perforations appear between the veins of pecan leaflets. New shoot growth ceases, and the internodes (distance between leaves) is shortened, giving the foliage a bunched appearance known as rosetting.

In the final stages of the disease, the shoots die back from the tips. Usually the dieback is confined to the current year's growth, but it sometimes extends to older branches of considerable size. When viewed at a distance in late summer, severely affected trees may have a bronze cast to them. Many branches will be seen to have only a small clump of leaves at the tips, and severely affected branches have no foliage and eventually may die.

Prevent trouble by laying down plenty of organic material. If only a few trees are involved, they can be protected by driving galvanized metal strips or nails into the trunk and limbs. For fruit trees, use six nails for each inch of trunk diameter.

The first symptom of **silver leaf** disease is the appearance of a metallic, silvery discoloration on the leaves of some branches, caused by an air pocket between the leaf tissues. The causal parasite is a wound fungus—that is, the spores can only infect living trees through fresh wounds or injuries. The fungus does not spread through the soil, unless roots are grafted from diseased trees, but is air-borne. Infected wood may show a brown stain. Infected branches gradually die. Vigorously growing trees are less susceptible to infection, and are sometimes able to recover from infection. The disease is most prevalent in cool, humid climates, and is encouraged by winter injury.

As branches begin to die, they should be pruned off, and seriously ill trees should be removed and burned. To make sure that the pathogen cannot enter trees, promptly cover pruning wounds with grafting wax; if possible, avoid large wounds by pruning often. Do not water trees excessively.

Storage scald is not the doing of a disease organism, but results from a breakdown of the tissue caused by absorption of volatile compounds. These compounds are given off by the fruit itself in the normal respiration processes incidental to ripening. This trouble may manifest itself in either of two ways: a browning of the fruit skin in varying patterns, or a complete breakdown of the flesh so that the apple looks baked. These two symptoms are sometimes known as hard and soft scald, respectively. Where control measures are necessary, oil-paper wraps and controlled air storage have proven successful. However, if fruit is not stored when overly green and proper attention is given to temperature and humidity control in storage, scald shouldn't be a problem.

Water core shows as translucent areas in the flesh of the apple; the affected areas may be confined to the flesh around the core, or encompass the entire fruit to give it the characteristic glassy look. Fruit affected with water core is heavier and harder than normal apples, and has a sweet, syrupy flavor. No responsible organisms have been discovered, and the omnibus term of physiological disease must be advanced as the cause. King and Fall Pippin are particularly prone to this trouble, but the common commercial varieties now in use are rarely affected.

Unfavorable **weather** and other environmental conditions can cause serious damage to an apple crop. If severe enough, hail injury is immediately apparent, but a slight bruising may not be evident until picking time. Harm to the twigs will be readily apparent in serious cases, but slight injury won't show until the following year, when a series of sunken eye-shaped spots will appear on the upper side of the twigs. Within a few years, these spots should be covered completely by new growth.

Prolonged winter temperatures below −10°F. can kill the bark and cambium on the lower side of those apple branches nearest the ground. Trees that have borne a heavy crop of fruit the preceding summer are most likely to be injured by low temperatures. Such trees are low in stored carbohydrates, and it is this that renders them vulnerable. Late frost may cause both fruit russeting and foliage injury. On young leaves, the lower side stops growing, and this results in a downward cupping and a loosening of the lower epidermis, which will be stretched across the cupped leaf like a drum head. Russeting on fruit may appear as a random pattern, often in the form of equatorial bands or as a random pattern of arcs and circles.

Sun scorch hits fruit on the south side of the tree and/or on the side exposed to the sun. The requisite conditions are air temperatures above 90°F. coupled with low humidity. The injury shows as circular areas varying in color from pale yellow through buff to brown. In extreme cases the areas are flattened and black with a light halo. (High temperatures do not often directly bring about foliage scorch, but cause irregular light brown areas.) Heavy deposits of sulfur on fruit or foliage will increase the severity of damage.

When old trees are pruned to expose formerly shaded areas to the sun, the bark on large branches may be sunburned; this occurs as anything from a roughening of the bark to a complete killing of large areas. The loss of entire branches may follow if wood-rotting fungi enter through these dead areas. See also drought and environmental conditions (above).

Wildlife

Mice can cause considerable injury to apple trees. Meadow mice feed on the trunks of trees at the ground level and may girdle trees. Pine mice gnaw at roots, and damage is not so easy to spot.

Wire guards can partially protect young trees. Place a cylinder of hardware cloth (three to four wires to the inch), measuring 6 inches in diameter and 18 inches high, around each young tree soon after planting. The cylinder should be set at least 2 inches into the soil. Paper bags or newspaper can substitute for wire, and plastic mouse guards are on the market. Mice are loath to leave protective cover, and it therefore helps to remove all vegetation within a three-foot radius of the trunk. Protective cover can also be reduced by mowing the grass and disking or chopping the sod. Some state agricultural extension services recommend setting out poisoned apple cubes to do away with mice, but the toxins used are poisonous to humans as well and would create an unnecessary hazard.

Rabbits also like the bark of the young apple trees. Although they will occasionally try plum, peach, or cherry, apple is their favorite. It is important to protect the trunks of young trees until they can bear fruit. Although rabbits rarely feed on tree bark during summer, they can be quite destructive from November through winter, especially after a heavy snow.

The trunks of young fruit trees can be protected in a couple of ways. An old, effective method is to fasten a piece of wire mesh around the trunk. It should be large enough to permit the tree to grow four or five years before the wire becomes tight around the trunk. When this happens, the wire should be removed to prevent girdling the tree. More recently, growers have been squeezing aluminum foil around the trunk of the tree. The foil, placed on the tree in November and removed in spring, expands as the tree grows. To avoid bark injury, do not wrap the foil too tightly around the trunk.

Apricot

When pruning apricot trees, be sure to remove all broken branches and diseased areas, and then rinse the trees with a naphtha soap solution to discourage bugs and fungus.

Insects

A small greenish insect covered with a powdery substance is the mealy plum **aphid**, occurring on apricot, plum, prune, and other fruit trees. Should it strike, the foliage will curl from loss of vital plant juices, the tree becomes weak and stunted, and the fruit is either split or covered with sooty mold that grows on excreted honeydew. See APHID.

Branch and twig borers are sometimes a problem to apricot growers. These brown or black beetles are about ½ inch long and cylindrical. They can be found burrowing into fruit buds or limb jointures, causing the branches to die and the trees to become weakened.

Prune off infected twigs from smaller fruit trees and remove all prunings from the vicinity of the tree as soon as possible. If infested wood is held for fuel, dipping it for a moment in stove oil will kill the larvae under the bark. A sound system of mulching and tree feeding will give apricots a built-in resistance.

Cankerworms (also known as measuring or inch worms) chew on the edges of leaves and occasionally drop down on threads of silk. See APPLE.

With sharp appendages at the back end, the **earwig** looks full of trouble. However, there's no need to be alarmed. "It is truly more beneficial than harmful," assures insect ecologist Everett J. Dietrick, especially if you ensure a good mix of insect life for them to prey on. They also feed on decaying plant material, and are active at night.

Earwig

You can keep earwigs out of the trees by luring them away with an organic mulch. Thorough plowing or disking in spring may drive them to hide at the base of tree trunks. Clarita Bumbaugh of Nordmont, Pennsylvania, suggests that they can be trapped by rolled up newspapers or jute sacking placed in the main crotch of the tree. The traps must then be collected and burned or placed in soapy water. Also, sticky barriers such as Tanglefoot and Stikem may be useful. See EARWIG.

The **plum curculio** is a brownish snout beetle that feeds in curved excavations and lays its eggs in the fruit. It also devours leaves and petals until the fruit appears. The curculio larvae leave fallen fruit to pupate underground. A good number of curculios can be knocked from foliage by jarring limbs with a padded board —the bugs play dead when frightened, and will land on a tarp or sheet placed below. To encourage his chickens to scratch for pupating larvae, one grower mixed wheat into the soil before

Plum/Plum Curculio

turning the fowl loose. You can interrupt this pest's life cycle by removing drops promptly, before the larvae can leave. See also BLUEBERRY.

Diseases

Apricot is one of a great many plants known to host **armillaria root rot.** The states west of the Rockies are most troubled, California in particular. Infected trees show a progressive yellowing and wilting of the foliage and stunted growth. Apricots are among the species that may live but one or two years after planting. Infected bark at the roots and lower trunk becomes moist and spongy. Characteristic whitish fan-shaped growths are formed in the bark and between the bark and the wood. After fall and winter rains, the mushroom stage may be seen around the bases of rotted trees. These honey-colored mushrooms appear only for a few weeks of the year. They grow to six inches or so in height, and the cap measures from two to four inches across. For controls, see PEACH.

Small purple spots on apricot leaves and black lesions on fruit are signs of **bacterial canker**. Resistant varieties have yet to be developed. Arrest the spread of the disease by pruning infected twigs and branches.

Black heart is a fungus disease that also causes verticillium wilt on the first hot days of summer, and the wood may show black streaks an inch below the surface. Trees may die of black heart, but often grow new foliage and recover.

No true cure is known, but proper feeding and watering should help to enable trees to resist disease. Do not plant tomatoes, cotton, potatoes, strawberries, or Persian melons near infected trees, as these crops are also susceptible to the verticillium fungus. This disease may be arrested by pruning affected branches.

Brown rot has become the most serious disease of stone fruit in the United States. The causal fungus withers and kills the blossoms in spring, and blighting of twigs follows as the fungus invades these parts through the bases of diseased blossom clusters. The affected blossoms are usually covered with ash-gray, powdery masses of spores which make it easy to identify the disease. Fungus causes ripening fruit to become brown, rotted, and covered with fungus. See PEACH.

Crown gall is a bacterial disease that girdles roots and crowns. It causes swellings where bacteria enter through wounds in bark. The swellings often occur at the soil line where cultivating tools have been carelessly used, and they may appear on branches damaged by ladders.

Do not purchase trees that show such protuberances, and set apricots in soil that has not previously hosted this disease. Remove the gall with a sharp clean knife and paint the wound with tree surgeon's paint to prevent further infection. If the gall encompasses most of the trunk, remove and treat only a portion of the gall at a time to prevent girdling the tree. Be certain to disinfect tools in alcohol so that contamination will not spread in this way. It is best not to perform this operation in the hot part of the summer; to prevent damage from sunburn after treatment, cover the affected parts with soil. Japanese apricots are resistant. Grafting can allow the bacteria access to trees, and budding is a safer means of propagation.

Apricot trees seem to be especially susceptible to **frost** and **freezing weather.** The fruit buds freeze and the entire fruit spur may be killed. If only the bud is affected, it turns brown and the flower never opens. Sometimes only the pistil (the central organ which ripens into the fruit) may be killed. You might try inspecting those flowers which will open to see if the pistil is still as it would be in the dormant bud. If it is, the fruitbud has been winter-killed, explaining the lack of a crop.

Deficiency of zinc in the soil causes the leaves to appear in spring as rosettes of small, narrow, stiff leaves mottled with yellow, a condition known as **little leaf**. In severe cases, twigs die and the tree may be lost. The disease is also responsible for fruit dropping, low yields, and delayed maturity.

One of the safest and easiest ways to supply zinc is sprinkling raw phosphate rock around the base of the tree. The use of plenty of manure, a natural source of zinc, will also help. A few zinc-plated (galvanized) nails can be driven into the trunk for a quick injection of the mineral.

Like peaches, apricots are subject to **pit burn**. When they ripen in very hot weather, the area around the pit turns soft and brown, as if the pit were heated. A thick mulch under the tree tends to keep the tree cool; if the heat is very bad, it may be helpful to sprinkle the mulch with water during the warmest part of the day.

Scab appears as small, dark greenish spots, $\frac{1}{16}$ to $\frac{1}{8}$ inch across, that become visible about the time the fruit is half-grown. The fruit may later crack. Yellow brown spots appear on twigs and branches.

If scab threatens a crop, consider using a sulfur spray or dust three to four weeks after the petals have dropped. Such applications prevent infection, but do not eradicate the fungus; new shoots and branches will likely be infected by the end of the growing season, showing yellow brown spots with blue or gray margins.

Another possible cause of cracking fruit is **sunburn**. This affects the skins most often in hot, humid weather. When the fruit is thinned, particular attention should be given to those growing on the exposed tips of the branches. If the leaves are lacking at the tips of the branches, it is better to remove the fruit. This will send the tree's nourishment to other fruit that is protected and likely to survive.

Arborvitae

Insects

Should aphids appear, a nicotine sulfate spray will control them. See APHID.

The **arborvitae leaf miner** may cause browning at the tips of leaves. The small greenish larva is a caterpillar that becomes a light gray moth as an adult stage. Eggs are laid on the leaves in early June, and late that month the larvae begin mining the leaves. Shaded plants are more heavily infested.

Burn any cocoons and any leaves that appear to be infested. Prune back the branches until healthy growth remains. The larvae can sometimes be repelled by spraying the tree with a strong soap solution in late June or early July. See EVERGREEN.

Another damaging insect of arborvitae is the **arborvitae weevil**, a small black insect with body and elytra covered with metallic green scales and fine short setae (hairs). It emerges from the soil sometime around early May and is present usually until late July. The larvae, which are legless and white with a light-brown head, pass through seven instars. During this time they feed on the roots of host plants—arborvitae and red or white cedar. The larval period extends from June or July to midwinter or the following spring. Adults attack the foliage of host plants, feeding lightly here and there so that no large area of plant foliage is consumed at one time. The foliage feeding scars may be observed for months after the adults have disappeared.

Control methods make use of the weevil's natural habits. When disturbed, it drops readily to the ground and remains immobile for a short period of time. Place a drop cloth under the tree and violently shake the main limbs until the bugs play possum and fall. Another method of control suggested by the habits of the pest is to place light traps in areas of extensive growth. The adult is not highly migratory, and will spend most of its time on the foliage of the host plant. Do not plant red or white cedars in the immediate area with arborvitae, as these trees may harbor the pest. Try to avoid excessive traffic through infested areas, since the weevils are easily transported on one's person. Carefully check balled nursery stock before planting to make sure it is not infested.

Small bags hanging from your trees are likely evidence of the **bagworm** on the prowl. This caterpillar lives in a silken cocoon that resembles a bag, often with bits of leaves attached to the outside. The caterpillar carries this bag with it as it feeds. A fully developed bag is about two inches long. Eggs are laid in fall and hatch in May or June of the following year. You can clear bagworms from your trees fairly easily by handpicking and destroying them.

Juniper scales may infest arborvitae; see JUNIPER.

Arborvitae may occasionally be troubled by **spruce spider mites,** but these can usually be kept off the trees by syringing leaves with water. See SPIDER MITE.

Diseases

The fungus that causes **twig blight** of juniper may also attack arborvitae, causing tips of infected twigs to brown and die back gradually. Old as well as new leaves and twigs are involved. Black pinpoint fruiting bodies of the fungus may be found on affected portions. During wet weather, disease-producing spores that ooze out of the fruiting bodies in long threads are scattered by wind, rain, and insects. This disease may be confused with a fall browning of the inner leaves that often follows unfavorable growth conditions.

Control by pruning out and destroying those twigs and branches that appear affected. The Dwarf Greenspike arborvitae is reported to be fairly resistant.

Twig browning and **shedding** (cladoptosis) may also appear on arborvitae. Whole twigs throughout the tree turn brown and later drop off. This is caused by dry soil, and trees located on lawns or along streets probably will require watering during summer. Soak the soil to a depth of about two feet by slow application of water through a porous hose or by sprinklers. Such watering should not be made oftener than at two-week intervals to allow necessary aeration of the soil between waterings.

Water injury causes a browning of the previous season's growth that shows on arborvitae, pine, and junipers in late winter or early spring. Drying winds and hot sun are the linked causes; trees in exposed locations and transplants are most severely affected. The discoloration is due to evaporation of moisture from the leaves or needles at a faster rate than the roots can pick up water. Mulching and a thorough soaking of the ground around the trees before the ground freezes will help minimize damage. Planting evergreens in protected places will prevent such drying. This reddish brown discoloration of the tips of the branches should not be confused with the browning and dropping of the leaves or needles on the inside of the tree nearest the trunk. This leaf fall may take place in spring or fall and is a natural shedding of old leaves. Individual trees vary in this natural leaf shedding: in some it may take place every year; in others every second or third year.

Ash

Insects

Larval **ash borers** tunnel into the trunk of trees at or below ground level, often damaging trees so badly that they can be easily pushed over. The adult moth is black with yellow bands and blackish brown wings.

The adult moth is drawn to light traps. Cut out and burn parts of infested trees, or even whole trees if necessary, to reduce infestation. The borer's damage renders trees vulnerable to disease. Keep the ground perfectly clear of grass and weeds, especially between mid-May and mid-August, so that birds can easily spot the eggs and worms. Other applicable controls may be found under peach borer in the PEACH section.

The injurious stage of the **mountain ash sawfly** is a small green caterpillar, ½ inch long, that is covered with numerous spines. These creatures strip the leaves by skeletonizing them into shreds, baring the ribs and veins. They particularly damage the leaves at the top of the trees. The adult is a ¼-inch-long fly with a wingspread of ½ inch. The body and wings are black, except for some body segments that are rusty or yellowish on the underside. The male fly is smaller than the female. The sawflies appear about the middle of May in the northeastern states and the female soon deposits her eggs under the skin of the leaf, forming white spots on the top surface.

If you can reach high enough, collect the egg clusters on the lower side of the leaves and destroy them. If not, sticky fly-paper or paper smeared with molasses will catch many flies.

The **oblique-banded leaf roller** is troublesome to many fruits, vegetables and flowers, as well as trees and shrubs. The greenish larvae roll the leaves and tie them together, feeding in the resulting protective cocoon. Eggs are often laid in branches and on rose leaves.

Where only a few plants are infested, the affected parts can be pinched off and destroyed. In infestation is heavy, dust plants with a mixture of equal parts of tobacco dust and pyrethrum powder. Or spray with a mixture of pyrethrum or rotenone. Dust or spray in two applications 30 minutes apart. The first drives the caterpillars from hiding, the second kills them.

Several insect pests of lilacs are also pests of ash trees— the lilac borer, the lilac leaf miner, and oystershell scale. For control, see LILAC. For carpenterworms, see TREES: INSECTS.

Diseases

A small mite is responsible for **ash flower gall,** a distortion of the staminate flowers of white ash that forms bunches or masses from ¼ to ¾ inch in diameter. These masses finally dry and remain on the tree over winter. To keep the mites at bay, spray trees with a mild dormant-oil emulsion in late winter.

There are three types of **leaf blotch** to which ash trees are susceptible. *Gloeosporium aridum* causes irregular brown blotches to appear on leaves in the midsummer of wet seasons, and leaves may fall. *Phyllosticta fraxinicola* makes small yellow spots in late summer, and some years *Piggotia fraxini* causes an epidemic of small purple spots with yellow borders. Burn fallen leaves to remove much of the source of inoculum for the following year.

Rust describes raised crescent-shaped or irregular swellings on leaves or petioles that burst open to release an orange powder. The infection then travels to a marsh grass which produces spores the following spring to reinfect ash. Control is not necessary, since the rust seems to do little real harm.

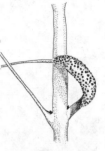

Rust

Asparagus

Generally, care should be taken to keep young plants free from grain and weeds. As soon as the needlelike seedlings emerge, hand weeding and mulching are called for. Continue to control weeds by timely cultivation of the asparagus patch. Mulching and composting will help to discourage both unwanted insects and disease.

Insects

The **asparagus aphid** has only recently come to the attention of entomologists. It is a tiny ($\frac{1}{16}$-inch), blue green creature. This aphid has been spotted in the mid-Atlantic states, feeding on asparagus and asparagus ferns. The young plant is damaged, and the bush may be severely rosetted. Protection is important in newly seeded plantings and young cutting beds. For control measures, see APHID.

The **asparagus beetle** is one of the most destructive insect pests of asparagus, attacking both garden variety and wild plants throughout the United States. The adult [color] is metallic blue black, with three yellow to orange squares along each wing cover, and is $\frac{1}{4}$ inch long. The larva [color] is $\frac{1}{3}$ inch long, colored olive-green to dark gray with black legs and head, and is soft and wrinkled. The beetle lays dark shiny eggs, no bigger than specks, that are attached at one end to spears. Both adult and larva eat foliage and disfigure shoots. The beetle hibernates in trash around the garden, and emerges in spring to eat the tender asparagus shoots and lay their eggs.

Asparagus Beetle: adult ; egg ; newly hatched grub ; fully-grown grub ; and pupa

It follows that an important means of control is garden cleanliness. If trash is removed, the beetle may have to leave the garden to find housing. Turning over the soil around the plants in fall serves to disturb the overwintering pests.

The beetle has a dislike for tomato plants, and interplanting serves a second purpose—asparagus is a natural nematicide, and will keep nematodes from nearby tomatoes. The beetles are also turned off by nasturtiums and calendula (pot marigolds). If beetles have already become established in your patch, you might turn to the old trick of letting chickens, ducks, guinea hens, or other fowl run in the asparagus planting. These birds invariably do an efficient job of wiping out the beetles and their larvae, but keep in mind that they may also take a swipe at nearby tomatoes, ripe or not.

A naturally occurring parasite, *Tetrastichus asparagi,* helps control the beetle in the eastern United States. Although not commercially available, the population of this chalcid wasp can be encouraged by your gardening practices. The USDA suggests: "Most insecticides applied to crops for control of economic pests reduce the population of parasites and predators; therefore, the elimination or reduction of insecticide use would favor the effectiveness of the beneficial insects." Another natural enemy of the asparagus beetle is the chalcid wasp, a very small, black or brown insect with nearly veinless wings. The wasps feed chiefly on larvae of harmful insects. Ladybug larvae also eat a fair share of beetle larvae. Bone meal can be applied to plantings with some success, serving both as a repellent and a fertilizer. Use it as often as needed. Many gardeners have found that dusting plants with rock phosphate is effective. And cloth or gauze netting helps to give young asparagus a good start; support the fabric with stakes between the plants and secure the ends so that no bugs can enter. As the plants grow larger, they become less susceptible to the beetle's attacks, and the protection can be removed. See also the discussion of the spotted asparagus beetle, below.

The **asparagus miner** is an insect which tunnels near the base of the stem and just beneath the epidermis. Some of the mines start a foot above the soil and work downward, often to below the ground. As a result, foliage may turn yellow and die prematurely. The adult is a two-winged fly. The miner passes the winter in a tunnel in the form of a pupa, resembling a flax seed. The miner afflicts asparagus in the Northeast and in California, and is considered a minor pest. Control is not usually necessary; pulling up and burning old stocks in late fall will destroy the overwintering puparia. Rust-resistant strains are also resistant to the miner (see asparagus rust, below).

The **garden centipede** (garden symphilid) is a fragile, white insect that grows up to ⅜ inch long. It is not actually a centipede, but is similar in appearance. Adults have 12 pairs of legs, the young have fewer. This pest travels rapidly through tiny cracks in the soil, constantly waving its antennae, and is rarely seen above ground. It eats numerous tiny holes, or pits, into the underground parts of plants. The roots of affected plants have a blunted appearance and the garden centipede's presence may first be made known by stunted growth. Besides asparagus, this pest damages flowers and a number of vegetables: bean, peas, sweet corn, beets, carrots, celery, spinach, lettuce, potatoes, and radishes. It's found throughout the humid areas of the United States and is particularly injurious to asparagus crops in California. All told, it is considered an important soil pest in 25 out of the 31 states in which it has been reported.

Control is difficult. You can take advantage of this pest's aversion to light by planting asparagus in a sunny area and by clearing out rocks or trash that the centipede might use as a hiding place. It is best to take these precautions early in the season, as the garden centipede is most troublesome in spring. Digging up the soil around the plants may also disturb its habitat and cause it to look elsewhere for a home. Large scale control of the garden centipede is affected by flooding asparagus fields with water.

The **spotted asparagus beetle** is slender, a bit larger than the common asparagus beetle, and is reddish brown or orange with six black spots on each wing cover. It occurs east of the Mississippi. The greenish eggs are glued singly by their sides to asparagus leaves just before the berries form. In a week or two, orange larvae appear and bore into the developing berries. Larvae pupate in the soil, and the mature beetles emerge in July to lay eggs for the overwintering generation, which appears in September. You may find this pest on a variety of plants, from asters to zinnias, and it is especially common on all cucurbits. Since the spotted asparagus beetle is unable to fly in the cool of morning, it may be controlled by handpicking. Inspect the shoots and berries daily, and pick and destroy affected berries. For further control measures, see asparagus beetle (above).

The **spotted cucumber beetle** (or southern corn rootworm) is another pest of asparagus, having similar habits to the asparagus beetle. The adult is slender and about ¼ inch long. Its wing covers are greenish yellow, marked with 12 spots varying in size. For habits and control, see CUCUMBER.

Asparagus is also bothered by the bulb mite (see GLADIOLIS and SNAPDRAGON), cutworms (TOMATO), harlequin bug (CABBAGE), JAPANESE BEETLE, several types of scale (including black thread, dictyospermum, latania, and lesser snow), stink bug (SNAPDRAGON), and yellow woolybear caterpillar (imported cabbageworm under CABBAGE). The asparagus fern may host the green peach APHID, beet armyworm (see BEET), onion thrips (ONION), and two-spotted SPIDER MITE.

Diseases

Asparagus rust is the most serious disease affecting asparagus. It is a fungus disease that appears as elongated, dusty orange red or reddish brown spots (blisters) on leaves and stems. Later these blisters darken and become firmer, and burst to release a fine, rust-colored cloud of spores. Plant tops turn yellow and die early. Depending on local conditions, an asparagus planting

Asparagus/Asparagus Rust

may become rapidly infected and die. The spores require dampness for germination, and therefore areas subject to heavy dews and damp mists are poor locations for asparagus; the disease is worst in moist seasons, and is found throughout the United States.

Asparagus rust has been eliminated in many areas by the use of rust-resistant varieties. Martha and Mary Washington were once very popular varieties, but new fungus biotypes have overcome them. Newer varieties that should work for you are Waltham Washington, Seneca Washington, and California 500. The New Roberts variety may be suited for the Midwest.

Since rust lives on the diseased plant tops from year to year, gardeners should cut affected tops close to the ground and burn them in fall. Also, rows should be planted in the direction of prevailing winds, as this will lessen the possibility of spores alighting on uncontaminated shoots. Cynthia Westcott mentions in *Plant Disease Handbook* that the rust fungus is parasitized by another fungus, *Darluca filum*.

Aster

Insects

Certain species of **aphids,** especially the corn root aphid, attack the roots of asters and a number of other plants, including brownallia, calendula, primrose, and sweet pea. An aphid attack results in little or no plant growth, and leaves turn yellow and wilt under bright sunlight. To check for this pest, examine the roots; the aphids are small and either white or pale blue green in color.

Ants are the agents of root aphid damage. They carry the young aphids through their tunnels to plant roots. If your flowers are in danger, see ANT for control measures. Once asters or another susceptible plant has been infested, you should rotate them. Thorough spading in fall will disturb the ant nests that often house caches of aphid eggs.

Aster flowers and foliage are often the target of the **blister beetle.** The black blister beetle, also known as the Yankee bug and just plain "blister beetle," is the best-known species. It is a fairly long (up to ¾-inch) and slender beetle, with soft, flexible wing covers. The entire body is black or dark gray, and the covers may be marked with white stripes or margins. Another species, the margined blister beetle, is distinguished by a narrow gray or yellow margin on the covers. Blister beetles are very active, and

Blister Beetle

frequently appear in large numbers in the latter part of June and through July.

Handpicking is effective in controlling this pest, but you should protect your hands with gloves, as the beetles discharge a caustic fluid that is harmful to the skin. Some growers achieve control by dusting with equal parts of lime and flour. This should be done at the warmest time of the day. For other controls, see BEET.

Brown areas on lower leaves signal the underground feeding of the **foliar nematode.** The discolored areas are wedge-shaped and occur between the veins, and the symptom progresses from the bottom of the plant upward. This wirelike pest also frequently affects garden chrysanthemums.

The best way to avoid nematode problems is to enrich the soil with plenty of organic matter. Unless the soil has been sterilized, don't plant susceptible flowers in succeeding seasons; these flowers include chrysanthemum, calendula, dahlia, and scabiosa. Interplanting with marigolds, on the other hand, may drive nematodes from flower beds. For other control measures, see NEMATODE.

Grubs of the Japanese beetle and Asiatic garden beetle feed on the roots of asters to cause an overall weakening of the plants. Milky spore disease is used to control both of these larvae; see JAPANESE BEETLE.

Small white larvae that trace pale, winding lines in leaves are probably **wild parsnip leaf miners.** Asters happen to be this pest's favorite garden flower. Eggs are laid in the leaves by tiny black or metallic blue flies. Handpick affected leaves.

The **six-spotted leafhopper** damages asters by sucking plant juices from leaves, which may turn brown and die. It is greenish yellow with six black spots, and grows to $\frac{1}{8}$ inch long. The young, or nymphs, are grayish. Look for leafhoppers on the underside of leaves, especially on the lower foliage. The pest is fond enough of asters to have picked up the alternate name of aster leafhopper, and it is the vector of a disease known as aster yellows (see below). The insects pick up the disease in the spring while feeding on infected wild plants.

Because this leafhopper prefers wide open spaces, asters grown near the house or next to walls will stand a better chance. If possible, do not plant the flowers near carrots or lettuce, two vulnerable crops. Six-spotted leafhoppers spend the winter on weeds, and growers with many asters occasionally burn over all nearby weed patches in early spring, before the pests can reach the garden. The only way to ensure that asters will make it through the season unscathed is to grow them under a shelter of cheesecloth, muslin, or fine-meshed netting.

The **stalk borer** is a long slender caterpillar that frequents flower gardens. It first makes its presence known by the effects of its boring: stems break over and leaves wilt. A close examination of the plants will reveal a small round hole in the stem from which the borer expels its castings. By splitting the stalk with a fingernail, you may find the caterpillar at work. It is brownish and is marked with a dark brown or purple band around the middle, with several conspicuous stripes running the length of the body.

Sprays are of little use in controlling the stalk borer, as it spends most of its life within plant stems. An effective, if time-consuming, remedy is to slit each affected stem lengthwise, remove the borer, and then bind the stem together. You can get quicker results by removing and destroying the stems. The best remedy of all is to discourage local borers before they get a chance to cause trouble. This involves clean cultivation and the burning of all stems and plant remains that are likely to harbor overwintering eggs. Adult borers (grayish brown moths) lay their eggs in weeds, especially ragweed, and a preventative program might include burning nearby weeds before the caterpillars can migrate to garden plants.

The **tarnished plant bug** is an active, brassy brown insect that sucks the life from young shoots and especially buds, leading to deformed or dwarfed flowers. The adults are small and roundish, and colored greenish yellow with black spots on the thorax and abdomen. Nymphs look similar, but are scaled down somewhat. While feeding, the bugs apparently inject a poisonous substance into the plant that kills the surrounding tissue. The adults hibernate under leaf mold, stones, or tree bark, or in clover, alfalfa, and whitetop. They appear in early spring, and are most numerous toward the end of summer.

Tarnished Plant Bug

Because these bugs are so active, sprays are of limited use unless used early in the morning; at this time of day, they are usually a bit stiff with cold. Prevention through clean culture is the best control. Sabadilla dust will take care of serious infestations.

Other insects that dine on asters include the spotted cucumber beetle (see CUCUMBER), four-lined plant bug (similar to the tarnished plant bug; see CHRYSANTHEMUM), SPIDER MITES, CUTWORMS, flower thrip (PEONY and ROSE), potato flea beetle (POTATO), and WIREWORM.

Diseases

Aster/Aster Wilt

Aster wilt is the most troublesome disease of the china aster (callistephus). The first noticeable symptom is a greatly reduced and blackened root system, which precedes wilting of the plant above. Brown streaks then appear on stems; this discoloration is most evident when a stem is cut. In time, entire stems become darkened, and a grayish pink fungal growth sometimes may form. Plants may be attacked at any time: young plants dry up suddenly, and older plants first show a pale green color and wilting of lower leaves on one side of the plant, followed by death of the entire plant. Wilting is most pronounced in heat of day, and plants seem to recover somewhat at night.

Prevention of aster wilt is the best medicine. The plants should not be grown continuously in the same soil, and crop rotation and changing seed beds will also help. The disease is aggravated by the use of nitrogenous fertilizers such as fresh manure that has not had the benefit of the compost heap. The disease hits hardest in warm soil, and you can counteract this by growing alternate rows of corn or other tall crops that provide shade. Similarly, greenhouse asters that receive some shade are less severely attacked than those that get direct sunlight. Resistant aster strains are available, but do not work well in all areas; consult with the local agricultural agent before selecting a variety.

Aster Yellows

Next to aster wilt, **aster yellows** is the most destructive disease. Young infected plants show a slight yellowing along leaf veins—a symptom known as clearing of the veins. As the disease becomes more severe, the entire plant is stunted and yellowed, and the unusual number of shoots that develop cause the plant to become very bushy and upright. Secondary shoots are usually spindly, and flowers are curiously deformed. Regardless of the normal color of the variety, flowers are often a sickly yellow green. This disease is carried by the six-spotted leafhopper (see above).

Damping-off hits aster seedlings and causes stems to collapse and rot off at the soil surface. The disease usually occurs in seedbeds and flats in which the soil is wet, the temperature high, and the plants crowded.

To control damping-off, water the seedbed only as needed.

Plant seedlings far enough apart so that air can circulate between them and carry away excess moisture.

Gray mold is a fungus that usually picks on white or light-colored flowers, showing first as a petal spot and then quickly rotting the entire flower. Leaves and stems are sometimes covered with a dirty gray mold. Cool, wet weather favors the development of and spread of this disease, and a change to sunny weather can save the flowers. Plant asters in a location that affords plenty of ventilation and sunlight. Unless the season is unusually humid, this precaution should save you from any trouble with gray mold.

Powdery mildew appears as a whitish dust or bloom on leaves, and flowers become dull-colored. This fungus disease is encouraged by hot, dry weather. While there isn't much you can do to change the weather, you can allow ample space between flowers and burn all above-ground refuse in fall. If asters are really in trouble, dust with sulfur in the afternoon.

Rust causes bright orange pustules on the underside of aster leaves. Common alternate hosts are the two- and three-needle ornamental pines, wild aster, and goldenrod.

Rust spores are easily carried about by the wind, so try to avoid planting asters on the leeward side of a possibly infected area. Rogue out infected plants, and consider long rotations if the asters are in trouble.

Avocado

Insects

Avocadoes, particularly in California, may be bothered by the **avocado caterpillar,** a leaf roller moth with brownish red forewings about an inch across. The larvae are yellow green and skeletonize leaves or web them together. They often damage the fruit also.

Rotenone or pyrethrum will take care of serious infestations. There is evidence that the moth stage of the insect can be lured to light traps. Install the traps near the fruit and light them during the evening. Natural enemies of the caterpillar may be employed to curb its destructiveness. The trichogramma wasp is available commercially as eggs. The wasps should be hatched before the pest larvae appear, as they are egg parasites.

Snails under the trees can be dispatched by allowing chickens and ducks to forage about the plants. See SLUGS AND SNAILS.

Diseases

Anthracnose or black spot is a fungus disease that may not be noticed until the fruit starts to ripen. It causes brown or tan colored spots to appear on green-colored fruit, and a lighter-than-normal spot on dark fruit. Depending on the amount of moisture present, spore masses may spread to form a pink layer over the surface. It does not take long for the rot to penetrate the entire fruit. Anthracnose can be prevented by using resistant varieties. Deprive the disease of its ideal conditions by locating plantings in relatively dry areas.

Avocado root rot is a fungus disease that appears in sections that have poor drainage or a combination of poor drainage and poor soil. It is the most serious malady of avocado in California. Symptoms include yellow leaves, sparse foliage, wilting of leaves with slight or no new growth, and a dieback of twigs. Eventually the larger branches or the whole tree dies. Seeds can carry the fungus if fruit is left on the ground for a period of time.

Prevention is the best means of control. Be certain the growing area has the proper drainage, and use disease-free plants. Resistant rootstocks include the Duke and Scott varieties.

Susceptible varieties of West Indian avocadoes may be greatly damaged by **avocado scab,** especially in Florida and Texas. This is a fungus that causes corky, raised, brownish, oval-shaped spots on fruit. As the spots become older they may run together and give the fruit a russetted appearance. Cracks sometimes develop, and open the way for other rot organisms. On leaves and twigs, scabby lesions are formed.

Lula is a particularly susceptible variety. Resistant varieties are available; check with the agricultural experiment station in your state.

The most important disease of avocado in Florida is **cercospora spot** or **blotch.** On fruit, look for small, scattered, brown, slightly sunken spots of definite outline but irregular shape. Gray spore-bearing structures appear on these spots in humid weather. In time, the spots crack, permitting other fungi to enter and decay the fruit. Small, angular spots are another symptom.

The disease is carried over on leaves, and a thorough clean-up after harvest may help reduce spotting.

There are several notable **environmental** or **nonparasitic diseases** of avocado. One of the most common is zinc deficiency, causing a condition known as little leaf. Fruit is often deformed, and if the deficiency is not corrected, branches may die back. Zinc can be supplied in the form of raw phosphate rock around the base of the tree. Zinc is also found in manure, an excellent natural source.

A chlorotic yellow pattern on leaves, with veins remaining green, is characteristic of iron deficiency. Fruit size and shape and leaf size are little affected. The USDA recommends reducing the amount of water given to trees in problem soils.

If avocadoes are irrigated with chlorinated water, the result may be tipburn of the leaves—a considerable reduction of green leaf area. This leads to a general weakening of the tree, and the dead areas may be invaded by fungi which then spreads to the fruit. Control of this condition depends on using water with a lower chloride content. Tipburn may also be a sign of salt in the soil, often the result of poor drainage.

Wildlife

In areas where irrigation ditches must be maintained, **gophers** sometimes tunnel in the ditches and destroy the system. One organic gardener has imported owls to prey upon the gophers. He supplies artificial owl houses in his orchards and the birds accept his food and shelter graciously.

Azalea

Insects

A pest of many ornamentals is the **azalea bark scale (azalea mealybug)** [color]. Plants growing outdoors show white, cottony or wooly masses fastened to twigs, usually in the forks of branches or close to buds. Both sexes are enclosed in a feltlike sac. The honeydew secreted by the scale may give rise to black, sooty mold on foliage and branches. Affected azaleas become weakened and do not produce healthy flowers, and may even die.

Cut out and burn weakened branches. Dormant-oil sprays in late winter and early spring are effective, because the nymphs spend the winter on the plants. Use a weak white-oil emulsion. For early blooming varieties, spray on a warm day in late fall to avoid injuring the early spring blossoms.

The **azalea lacebug** [color] (as well as the rhododendron lacebug) injures azaleas by sucking plant juices from the underside of leaves. The adult bugs have squarish lacy wings, are about ⅛ inch long, and have black markings. The nymphs are nearly colorless at first, and darken with time. Should the underside of leaves show a reddish orange discoloration, suspect this pest.

Strong detergent sprays have been used to good effect on the azalea lacebug, but if not many bugs are about, it may suffice to crush the bugs by drawing leaves between the thumb and forefinger.

Certain varieties of azalea are highly susceptible to the little **azalea leaf miner (azalea leaf roller)**. This is a garden pest in the South, and more of a greenhouse pest in northern states. The adult moths are about ⅜ inch in length, are colored golden yellow with purplish markings, and hide under leaves when disturbed. The mining stages of the larvae are flat, while the leaf roller stage has the characteristic caterpillar shape. The eggs are very small, white, and disc-shaped, and are found along the midrib or veins on the underside of leaves. The leaf miners typically winter in the leaf roller stage, sheltered by rolled leaves. Yellow-and-purple moths emerge from the latter part of March through April. The larvae make mines that are visible only on the bottom side, but keep an eye out for the topside blisters that result from their feeding. All stages of the pest can be found during summer months, which suggests that there are a number of generations each season. In the greenhouse, the leaf miner breeds continuously. Severe infestations may result in the complete destruction of foliage.

The surest and simplest control is handpicking and destroying any blotchy and anemic-looking leaves. Some gardeners burn them, but they can also be stashed in the depths of the compost pile, where the heat will kill the insects. Handpicking seems a laborious control at the season's start, but there will be fewer and fewer pests about as summer goes on.

Wilting tips on azalea twigs are evidence that **azalea stem borers** are at work somewhere within the plant. This is a small, yellow, cylindrical beetle. The bark is sometimes girdled below the wilted portion, and as the inch-long yellow grubs bore down into the trunk, they often push sawdust out of holes near ground level.

Should twigs wilt soon after blooming, inspect them closely for evidence of the borer. If you act quickly enough, it may suffice to cut off the stems two or three inches below the wilted portion. A delay on your part may make it necessary to prune the wilted twigs an inch or so below the point at which the pest is at work.

Azaleas held for a long while in the greenhouse may be severely damaged by the **cyclamen mite.** Although too tiny to observe in action, its feeding on new growth aborts or deforms both leaves and flower buds. Greenhouse temperatures of between 60° and 80°F. are favorable to the mite, and growers have much less trouble with plants grown under lath or outdoors.

Cyclamen Mite

Because the cyclamen mite has a fairly wide host range, it is hard to escape entirely. When the pest is particularly troublesome, growers find it can be more easily avoided if the azaleas are set out in the open garden rather than kept under glass. Frequent hosings will help to keep the mite from getting started on flowers. Don't place newly potted azaleas with others until you're sure they're free from mites. Most nurseries are able to control such pests, and you can buy mite-free plants from them.

For other insect pests of azalea, see RHODODENDRON.

Diseases

Among the diseases that may afflict azaleas is **azalea bud and twig blight.** The first sign of this disease is the dwarfing of flower buds followed by their browning and death late in summer or early fall. The fruiting bodies resemble tiny pins stuck into the buds. Picking and burning infected plant parts either in late fall or early spring will help to reduce infection. Seed pods can be removed as soon as flowers have withered.

Perhaps the most serious disease attacking azaleas is **azalea petal blight** (also known as azalea flower spot and Ovulinia flower blight). The disease is found primarily in the southeastern United States, where it is particularly severe on azaleas of the Kurume and Indian types. The fungus causing this disease attacks only the flowers of the azaleas and, infrequently, the flowers of closely related plants, such as rhododendron and mountain laurel.

Azalea petal blight appears as small pale spots on the inner surfaces of the petals of colored flowers and as brown spots on white flowers. These spots rapidly enlarge until the whole flower collapses. In the diseased flowers, small dark resting bodies of the fungus serve to carry the disease through seasons when the azaleas are not in flower. The resting bodies fall to the ground with the flower and remain there until favorable weather conditions return, at which time they germinate to produce little cups from which spores are shot. These spores, once on a moist azalea petal, germinate to produce an infection.

Azalea petal blight is controlled by avoiding overhead watering while the plants are in flower. Removing and destroying diseased blossoms and seed pods will help to keep the resting stage from perpetuating the disease. It also helps to cover beds with several inches of mulch. The disease is discouraged indoors by lowering the humidity.

Chlorosis is usually the result of environmental conditions rather than the attack of a disease-producing organism. Too much lime in the soil prevents plants from taking up certain elements, particularly iron. This is shown when leaves, particularly those at the tip of new growth, turn pale green or yellow. Leaf margins and the tissue between veins turn a lighter color, while the veins themselves stay dark green. The soil imbalance can be righted by adding plenty of organic matter to neutralize the basic soil.

Another soilborne disease is **cutting and graft decay,** which results from infection by a soil fungus. In cutting and grafting frames, this fungus primarily attacks the tops of plants, growing over the leaves and stems as a cobwebby growth. Under moist conditions, it will cause the decay of the infected parts; otherwise, it may cause a rot at the base of the cuttings. It is controlled by using sterilized soil or sand in the cutting beds and by avoiding overwatering.

Frequently **root injury** results from hoeing or cultivating the soil around azaleas. These plants are surface feeders, meaning that the roots which absorb water and nutrients are found very near the surface, and therefore it is best to disturb the soil around the plant as little as possible.

Shoestring root rot (known also as armillaria root rot) causes discoloration in both azalea and rhododendron. The disease is most easily diagnosed by cutting the bark of the crown and larger roots. If the fungus is present, there are large white fans or plaques between the bark and the hard wood and frequently small, dark shoestringlike strands on the outside of the bark of the infected roots. Mushrooms in late fall or early winter are another indication of the fungus.

Once the root rot fungus becomes established, it is very difficult to control. Exposing the crowns of infected plants to air may help, since the fungus cannot exist under dry conditions. Because the fungus thrives in wet, heavy soils, improve drainage and avoid overwatering.

Salt injury is a disease resulting from a soil condition that affects azaleas grown in containers. The symptoms include browning and death of the tissues around the margins of the leaves.

Frequently leaves yellow, and small, dark or warty growths may appear on the underside of the leaves. Give an occasional heavy watering to leach away excess salts that have accumulated in the soil. If the plants are in small containers and can be handled easily, soak them overnight in a tub.

Under extremely wet soil conditions, a group of soil fungi known as water molds will attack the roots and crown area of young plants to cause a disease known as **wilt, root rot,** or **water mold root rot.** Plants wilt and the leaves turn a dull green, followed by leaf drop and a permanent wilting. The main stem turns brown at the soil line, and a cut into this area reveals only dead bark and wood.

This disease only affects young plants growing in excessively wet soil, and it is easily controlled by providing good soil drainage before the plants are set out. In a heavy soil, avoid digging holes, even though they are filled with the proper soil mixture for the plant. Such holes act as a pocket to catch water, and thus provide the conditions that favor disease development. Planting too deeply also encourages trouble. See to it that the soil pH is between 4.5 and 5.5.

For other diseases of azalea, see RHODODENDRON.

Bacillus Thuringiensis (BT)

Bacillus thuringiensis is one of two pathogens registered for use in the United States. You'll find information on methods of application and commercial sources in the section, "Making Bugs Sick with Microbial Control," in Chapter 8.

Here's a list of the pests that have been successfully controlled with BT, arranged by the crops they are most apt to damage:

CROP	PEST	REMARKS
Almond	peach tree borer	
Alfalfa	alfalfa caterpillar	As effective as chemicals.
Apple	codling moth worm	Because worms feed on the surface only a short time before tunnelling, a good number of them won't ingest the pathogen and spraying will not result in flawless apples.
	tent caterpillar	
	fall webworm	
	eye-spotted budmoth	
	winter moth	

CROP	PEST	REMARKS
	tentiform leaf miner apple rust mite	Populations of predatory mites also dropped.
	red-banded leaf roller	
Artichoke	artichoke plume moth	
Castor bean	castor semi-looper	
Corn	corn earworm	Variable results; works best in encapsulated form and when mixed with standard clay formulations, as earworms crawl down into the whorl and are hard to get at.
	European corn borer	
Cotton	cotton leafworm cotton leaf perforator bollworms	Good control.
Crucifers	cabbageworm	Control offered is good to excellent.
	diamondback moth	Good to excellent control.
	cabbage looper	Variable results (poor to excellent); especially useful on pests that have become resistant to traditional chemical sprays.
Grape	grape leaf folder	
Orange	fruit-tree leaf roller orange dog	
Peach	peach tree borer	
Stored crops	various insects	BT has proven to be effective in controlling a number of insect pests of stored crops, but because the bacteria harm almost nothing but lepidoptera, its use has not yet proven practical.
Trees, various	gypsy moth, fall webworm, fall cankerworm, spring cankerworm, California oakworm, Great Basin tent caterpillar, linden looper, salt marsh caterpillar, winter moth	

From *Microbial Control of Insects and Mites*, H. D. Burges and N. W. Hussey, editors. Academic Press, 1971.

Banana

Insects

Nematodes may attack the roots of banana plants to cause root-knot. Keep plants well watered and grow them in fertile soil enriched with plenty of organic matter and mulched heavily with hay or straw. See NEMATODE.

Diseases

Dwarf Chinese bananas are subject to **finger tip rot.** This disease starts in the flowers and advances along the peel more rapidly than in the fleshy pulp within. The malady must be prevented by inspecting the plants at periodic intervals and removing diseased fruit or withered sterile flowers. The infected material should be burned or buried.

Freckle disease occurs commonly on the fruit and leaves of Chinese bananas, causing black spots to appear. The fruit can be protected by wrapping it with paper before it matures. This will prevent the spores on the leaves above from spreading to the bananas. Also, if fruit become ripe before they are harvested, wrapping them will prevent fruit fly damage.

Panama wilt is a soilborne disease that can be brought into a new planting area on diseased planting material. This disease causes the plants to decay internally and eventually die. Leaves gradually die, often breaking in the middle of the leaf stalk. Frequently only one central leaf remains on the stalk, and it too will die in time.

It is extremely difficult to control this disease once it gains a foothold in the growing area. Be certain not to use diseased plants, and not plant bananas in soil that is known to have been recently infected with Panama wilt.

Barberry

Insects

The **barberry webworm** webs together leaves and twigs, forming a nest within which it feeds. This webbing usually starts after midsummer, and the nests remain on the bushes during winter. The caterpillar is blackish with white spots, and is nearly 1½ inches long when full grown. A spray or dust of pyrethrum will control these webworms if applied thoroughly when the caterpillars are small. Some of the nests can be handpicked and destroyed.

Other pests include the APHID, JAPANESE BEETLE, and SPIDER MITE.

Diseases

Rust attacks European barberry and other varieties having saw-toothed leaves. (*Berberis koreana, B. mentorensis,* and most of the evergreen varieties are not susceptible even though they have saw-toothed leaves.) Japanese barberry is immune, but crosses of Japanese and European barberries may be susceptible. The fungus causes bright orange spots on the leaves in spring from which come spores that infect wheat, oats, rye, barley, and some grasses. The disease rarely does much damage to the barberry shrub. In many states, it is unlawful to grow susceptible varieties of barberries.

If there is a susceptible variety of barberry growing on or near your property, it is best to destroy it by applying salt or kerosene to the ground immediately surrounding the plant.

Wilt is caused by a soil-inhabiting fungus that apparently enters the plant through injured or healthy roots. Leaves of affected plants turn yellow or red followed by browning and premature defoliation. The sapwood of affected stems and roots is streaked with reddish brown lines. Older infected wood shows a brownish green discoloration.

Control by removing and destroying affected plants. Avoid replanting the location with barberry unless a volume of soil three feet square by one foot deep is replaced with new soil.

Basswood, see Linden

Bean

Ray McCraney, a Michigan grower, reports that pests attacking green beans will leave purple ones practically untouched. This is substantiated by various sources which suggest that odd-colored vegetables have a built-in resistance.

Insects

The tiny black bean **aphid** occurs on broad beans and, less frequently, on green and snap beans. They cluster on stems and under leaves, and cause leaves to curl and thicken. Plants become yellow and unthrifty. Aphids spread the virus of common bean mosaic (see below). Eggs are laid in autumn and, as typical with aphids, there are many generations each year. They over-winter on various shrubs. This species occurs throughout the United States, although infestations are local. See APHID.

The **bean leaf beetle** is an occasional pest. Adults vary greatly in color and markings, but are typically reddish to buff in color, with a black band around the outer wing margin and three or four black spots along the inner edge. They are ¼ inch long and over-winter in the adult stage. Adult beetles feed on the underside of leaves and on stems of seedlings. The slender white larvae work below ground, attacking roots and stems. See MEXICAN BEAN BEETLE for controls.

Bean Leaf Beetle

From Delaware through the South, the **bean leaf roller** damages early fall bean crops. This pest cuts slits in leaves and then rolls up the edge for protection. Look for a greenish yellow, velvety caterpillar, one inch long, with a broad head and con-tracted back.

Bean thrips are barely visible, thin, dark insects with long, narrow, black-and-white wings that appear to be fringed. Groups of them feed to cause blanched, wilted leaves, spotted with dark specks of excrement. Control is best effected by ridding the garden area of weeds, especially prickly lettuce and sow thistle.

The **bean weevil** is ⅛ inch long and colored brown with thin lengthwise stripes on its mottled brown wing covers. The legs and antennae are reddish. The adult lays eggs in holes chewed along bean pod seams. The small, fat, white grubs enter and feed in young seed, and will emerge when the beans are in storage. The exit holes are small and round. The beans can be cured by pulling up the plants with the pods on them at harvest time, and putting them on stakes to hold them off the ground. The curing process, which takes at least six weeks, involves certain biological changes, including fermentations and the production of heat. The cured beans may then be shelled and stored in a dry place without danger of weevil damage.

Beans/Exit Holes of Bean Weevil

Never plant infested seed. According to Cynthia Westcott in *The Gardener's Bug Book,* stored beans may be protected by either heating dry beans at 135°F. for three to four hours, or by suspending seeds in a bag in water, heating to 140°F., and then drying rapidly.

Several species of leafhopper attack beans. The **beet leaf-hopper** (commonly called white fly in the West) is dangerous as a carrier of curly top, a virus disease. This pale greenish or yellowish pest is found west from Illinois and Missouri, excepting the fog belt along the California coast, which is relatively free from infestation. It is ⅛ inch long, wedge-shaped, and becomes darker toward winter. Spending winter as an adult in uncultivated areas, the leafhopper lays its eggs in March, and the first generation matures on these wild plants. The adults of this new generation swarm to other areas from early May to June, spreading curly top virus, of which they are the only known carrier. The symptoms of this disease are: warty pronounced leaf veins; kinked petioles; rolled leaves that sometimes take on a cupped or bell-like appearance, becoming brittle; and stunted growth, often resulting in death. The disease is not transmitted by seed.

The best control is the use of resistant varieties. Rogue out afflicted plants as soon as the symptoms are spotted. You can control the leafhopper by eliminating winter weed hosts from nearby. Since these insects do not breed in perennial grasses (they actually tend to avoid them), it is advantageous to replace the neighboring weeds with grass. Once established, protect these grassy areas by watering or, if on a farm, by regulating grazing so that the areas are not destroyed. Remember that nature has provided this leafhopper with a number of enemies; encourage these helpers by using organic methods of protecting your garden.

Lima bean foliage is susceptible to the **cabbage looper,** a pale green measuring worm (inchworm), with light stripes on its back. See under CABBAGE.

The **clover root curcurlio,** a small robust beetle with a short blunt snout, may visit your beans. They vary in color from light to dark brown with shadings of gray and brick-red, and cut regular notches in the leaf margins. The larvae are tiny, gray, legless grubs with light-brown heads, and attack roots. Large-scale problems may be solved by crop rotation.

All types of beans are host to the **corn earworm.** The caterpillars grow to nearly two inches long, and vary in color from green to pink to brown, with lengthwise light and dark stripes and a yellow head. These pests help to keep their own numbers down—they're cannibalistic. Also in your favor are egg parasites, birds, moles, and cold moist weather.

Corn Earworm

The yellow-and-green-banded **cucumber beetle** shows three bright green stripes running across the wing covers. They grow no larger than ¼ inch, and feed on bean leaves throughout the South from South Carolina to California. For control, see CUCUMBER.

The **cutworm** is familiar to almost every gardener. These are the smooth, fat, soft larvae of night-flying moths. They feed close to the ground on the succulent bean stems. See TOMATO for more information.

The larvae of the **European corn borer** [color] occasionally bore into the stems and pods of beans. They are flesh-colored caterpillars, up to an inch long, with rows of small, dark brown spots. The female moth is yellow brown with wavy dark bands, and the male is slightly darker in color. These adults have a wing spread of one inch, and usually fly at night. Twenty-four parasites have been introduced to the United States to control the borer, and six of these have become established. A fungus disease and a protozoan are also helpful.

European Corn Borer

The **fall armyworm** [color] is an occasional pest. The larvae vary greatly in color, from light tan to green to almost black, and have three yellowish white hairlines down the back from head to tail. On each side is a dark stripe paralleled below by a wavy yellow one, splotched with red. The head is marked with a prominent white V or Y. They eat leaves, stems, and buds of plants. See armyworms under CORN for controls.

Small bean seedlings may be attacked by the **garden springtail,** a tiny dark purple insect with yellow spots. They have no wings, but use taillike appendages to hurtle themselves into the air. You will find springtails eating small holes in leaves near the surface of the soil. Clear the area of weeds, and spray a mixture of garlic and water on leaves.

Garden Springtail

The adult form of the **grape colaspis** (or clover rootworm) is a tiny, pale brown, oval beetle that is marked by rows of punctures. Telltale signs of this beetle are long curved or zigzag feeding marks on leaves. Plowing or spading in fall, rather than in spring, may give some control.

The **green cloverworm** is an occasional pest of beans from the eastern states to the Plains. The wriggling, green caterpillars riddle bean leaves for about one month, but control is rarely necessary.

The **green stink bug** does indeed put off a foul odor, but is more easily identified by its appearance: large (⅝ inch long), oval, and bright green with a yellow or reddish margin. It has a special liking for beans, and sucks sap from shoots and leaves, causing pods to fall and distorting seeds. Control measures are rarely necessary for this pest.

The **lima bean pod borer** can be a headache if you plant lima beans, particularly in the southern part of this country. The borer is a white to greenish or reddish caterpillar, has a pale yellow head,

Lima Bean Pod Borer

and grows up to one inch long. It wriggles violently when disturbed. The borer pierces through lima bean pods and eats the seed within, passing from one to another. While it usually devours many seeds from a small-seeded plant, it may obtain its entire nourishment from a single large seed. When the larva has finished feeding it goes to the ground and may crawl some distance to find a place to pupate. Its manner of crawling may attract your attention—larvae move rapidly and have been observed crawling up and down the walls of nearby houses. If the soil can be penetrated, the larvae attempt to spin their cocoons in the ground; otherwise, they enter leaves, trash, or other debris.

Eliminating these winter homes by cleaning the garden area thoroughly will offer some control. Crop rotation is recommendable for large-scale growers. Because the borer isn't difficult to spot, it should be easy to handpick them from leaves and pods. In addition, it has been discovered that damage is usually greater with beans that have been planted late, so a crop planted early may escape a good deal of damage from the borer.

Irregular sections chewed from bean leaves may be the work of the **margined blister beetle;** it is black with a thin gray or yellow margin around the wing covers. Handpicking with gloves and use of mosquito netting are recommended.

Mexican Bean Beetle

The voracious **Mexican bean beetle** [color] feeds on leaves, pods and stems the entire season as both a larva and adult and has a reputation as the number-one enemy of eastern vegetable gardeners. The latter form is ¼ to ⅓ inch long, broad domed, pale yellow to coppery brown, and oval, with eight small black spots on each wing cover. It will attack any garden bean, but has a particular fancy for the lima bean. The Mexican bean beetle spends the winter in rubbish or weeds, appearing late in March in the South and in June in the northern United States. Two weeks later, the adults deposit yellow clusters of eggs on the underside of leaves. The larvae are ⅓ inch long, yellow, with six rows of long, branching, black-tipped spines covering their backs. After skeletonizing bean leaves, the larvae attach their hind ends to an uninjured leaf and the pupae emerge from their crushed larval skins. In the North, there is one generation and a partial second; near New York City there are two generations; and further south, three to four.

Control of this pest becomes easier as the season progresses and the beetle moves to the upper side of the leaves. Keep an eye out for telltale skeletonized leaves, and destroy the yellow orange egg clusters found on the underside of leaves. Sanitation is also a help, depriving the beetle of a winter home. Clean up all plant debris after harvest. The praying mantis and several birds are a big help in bean beetle control. Time of planting can save your plants: early plantings have been found to be freer of the pest, so plant a heavy early crop for canning and freezing; near New York City, snap beans planted in early June will mature in July between generations of beetles. Interplanting works well for many gardeners. Some plant rows of potatoes between every two rows of green beans; not only do the potato plants repel the Mexican bean beetle, but the green bean plant is noxious to the Colorado potato bug. The bug is not however, put off by lima bean plants. Alternate rows of nasturtiums also are effective. A clove of garlic, planted in every hill of beans, will chase away this and several other bugs. Margaret Champie, of Sutherlin, Oregon, concocted a safe insecticide, as she was determined not to resort to chemical sprays. She made a tea of plants that bugs didn't bother—wormwood, two varieties of mint, matricaria, wild morning-glory (bindweed), mayweed, and the tops of Egyptian onions. These clippings were minced in a blender, diluted, and sprayed. "It was necessary to repeat the treatment a few days later and some were sprayed a third time, but while the bugs were not completely eradicated—they were few and far between from then on." A Tahlequah, Oklahoma gardener suggests using cedar water to repel the bean beetle. He boils cedar sawdust or chips in water, lets the mixture cool, and then sprays it on the bean plants. Bean varieties vary in their susceptibility to the Mexican bean beetle. See RESISTANT VARIETIES.

Finally, try companion planting to keep the Mexican bean beetle away. Savory has a reputation as the "bean herb," and young seedlings spaced at intervals in the furrow in place of a bean at planting time will protect the bean patch. Build protection into the bean patch at planting time by placing young savory seedlings in place of beans at regular intervals. Because savory is fine-seeded, it is best to sow it inside and then transplant seedlings at the time beans are planted. Strong-smelling marigolds also do a good job of keeping away these beetles.

Root-knot is a condition caused by **nematodes,** whitish, translucent worms barely visible to the naked eye. See NEMA-TODE.

The **pale-striped flea beetle** damages foliage by perforating the leaves. It is $\frac{1}{16}$ inch long and has a broad white stripe on the center of each pale to dark brown wing cover. See controls for flea beetle under POTATO.

The tiny ($\frac{1}{16}$-inch-long) black **potato flea beetle** is so named because it jumps like a flea when disturbed from its meal of bean leaves. See POTATO for control methods.

The **potato leafhopper,** considered the most serious pest to potatoes in the East, also visits bean patches, especially in the South, where it is called the **bean jassid.** It is small ($\frac{1}{8}$-inch-long), wedge-shaped, and green with small white spots on its head and thorax. It causes bean leaves to whiten and may stunt, crinkle, and curl them as well. For control measures see POTATO.

The **seed-corn maggot** immigrated to New York from Europe more than a century ago, and is now found all over the country. The yellow white, $\frac{1}{4}$-inch-long maggot has a long, sharply pointed head, and bores into bean seeds in the ground so that they will not produce good plants. Damage is greater in cold, wet weather, and when seed is deeply planted. The adult form, a grayish brown, $\frac{1}{3}$-inch-long fly, emerges in July to lay its eggs in soil or on seeds and seedlings.

Seed should be planted shallow when the ground is warm enough to enable the seedlings to get a good start. If maggot damage is heavy, the area should be replanted immediately.

Of the several species of **spider mites,** the two-spotted spider mite is probably the most common. These pests are tiny, oval, yellow or greenish specks, and but $\frac{1}{16}$ inch long at maturity. They live on the underside of leaves and branches and suck plant sap. Leaves take on a sickly appearance, with yellow or reddish brown blotches. Centers of infection often arise near roads or other areas where plants may be covered with dust. The mite population increases rapidly in hot, dry weather. Control is often not necessary, but see SPIDER MITE if things get out of hand.

Spider Mite

Bean growers east of the Rockies may be bothered by the **stalk borer.** When young, this caterpillar has a brown or purple band around its cream-colored body, with several stripes running lengthwise. The fully grown borer loses its stripes, and may take on a grayish or light purple color. For control, see ASTER.

The **tarnished plant bug** will likely retreat to the opposite side of its stem as you approach, but you may catch a glimpse of a flat, $\frac{1}{4}$-inch insect, colored mottled white and yellow with touches of black, giving it a tarnished appearance. A very close look will reveal a yellow triangle, with one black tip, on each side of the insect. The tarnished plant bug is found all over the country, and is a pest of more than 50 crops. For habits and control, see ASTER.

The **white-fringed beetle grub** lives in the soil and feeds on the roots of beans and a number of other vegetables and ornamentals. This larva is yellowish white, legless, curved, and grows to ½ inch long. It eats tender outer root tissues and may sever roots, turning plants yellow and limp, and finally killing them. This wormlike pest invaded Florida in the thirties and has spread through the South from Texas to Virginia. Along the way it acquired a taste for almost 400 plants. Less of a danger to the garden is the white-fringed adult, a ½-inch-long beetle, dark brownish gray in color, with a broad, short snout. It is covered with short hairs and has a light band along its side. Because its protective set of wing covers are fused together, this beetle cannot fly.

White-fringed beetles are particularly fond of legumes and large-scale plant growers shouldn't plant more than a quarter of their cropland in annual legumes, and shouldn't plant the same land with these crops more than once in three or four years. On a small scale, the home gardener can do much to control this pest. Be certain not to plant its favorite foods, the legumes, together. Clean cultivation can go a long way toward the elimination of this beetle. Also, it is essential to fertilize the soil heavily so that the plant may become strong enough to fight off the insects' attack; if possible, it is advisable to turn under a winter cover crop, and add the advantages of the crop's nutrients to the soil.

Wireworms may attack seeds and kill seedlings by eating underground stems of young plants. These worms are shiny, hard-jointed, smooth, yellow or brown, and grow to one inch long. For control methods, see WIREWORM.

Diseases

Among the diseases that may afflict beans is **anthracnose,** caused by a fungus. The most obvious symptoms are dark brown sunken spots on the seed coat that may extend through to the cotyledons. The spots darken and take on reddish brown margins. Under humid conditions, the centers of the spots may become pinkish. Brown to black ovals develop on the stems of the seedlings and may girdle and kill them. Veins on the lower surface of the older leaves appear dark red or dark purple, and in severe cases angular dead spots appear on the upper surfaces of the leaves. Bean plants are most susceptible in cool, moist summers. The fungus is carried on infested seed, and lives on the remains

Anthracnose

of diseased plant refuse in the soil; it occurs in the central north-eastern, and southeastern states.

The use of disease-free, western-grown seed has nearly eliminated the threat of anthracnose in some areas. Also, seeds that are discolored or that come from spotted pods should not be planted. Do not work in the garden when plants are wet, as the disease spreads more rapidly on wet foliage. There are a number of resistant varieties available; check with your seed store or state experiment station for the variety best suited to your area. As a final precaution, rotate crops and plow down old bean tops as soon as harvested.

If **bacterial blight** strikes your bean patch, you should have little trouble recognizing the symptoms. Look for leaf spots with a water-soaked or greasy appearance. One species causes a yellow halo to form around the spots (halo blight). The affected areas later turn brown and die. Similar grease spots form on pods, but these marks may turn reddish brown in drying. If a plant is afflicted early in the season, it may be severely stunted or even killed.

Sprays will not help you to combat this blight, as the bacteria occur *under* the seed coat. The above methods of control for anthracnose apply to blight. Use of California-grown bean seed has eliminated this disease from much of the Deep South. See RESISTANT VARIETIES.

Bacterial wilt is seed-borne and overwinters on both the bean seeds and on diseased bean plant refuse in the soil. This disease usually attacks and kills seedlings; if a plant becomes infected when taller than three inches, it may continue to live for some time. Leaves become limp, wilt, and then die. The wilting is at its worst during the warm part of the day, and if the disease is not too far advanced, the wilted leaves may temporarily regain some of their vitality in the cool of the night or during humid cool spells. The causal bacteria invade the plants' vascular elements and plug or injure the vessels which carry water from the roots to the plant tops. Plants are often afflicted with both blight and wilt con-currently.

To avoid problems with bacterial wilt, plant only seed that is certified wilt-free. Control measures are the same as for bean blight, as described above.

High on the list of bothersome diseases that plague the bean grower is **bean rust.** Its symptoms are easily recognized: look for numerous small, orange to brown pustules, found most often on the undersurface of leaves, but also occurring on petioles, stem, and pods. Badly affected leaves turn yellowish, dry up, and drop to the ground.

Control of bean rust involves cutting down or disking vines as soon as the last picking is made; this serves to prevent formation of the overwintering stage. Don't leave overwintering spores on stakes, and be sure to use new stakes if the disease was particularly developed during the previous growing season. Iain C. MacSwan, extension plant pathology specialist at Oregon State University, suggests using wire instead of stakes to support bean plants. Posts can be treated by spraying or dipping them with lime sulfur at one part in 10 parts of water. Also, there are several rust-resistant varieties available, including White Kentucky Wonder 191, U.S. No. 3 Kentucky Wonder, and Dade. Avoid susceptible varieties, such as Blue Lake, McCaslan, and Kentucky Wonder. This disease is not seed-borne, but the wind can carry spores a great distance; therefore, a long crop rotation is advisable. When choosing a planting site, remember that prevailing winds may blow spores in from an infected field. The fungus lives over winter in old stems.

Common mosaic is caused by a virus carried by aphids. Plants from seed that is infected with this virus and those that become infected in the seedling stage are severely stunted and set relatively few pods. The leaves turn a mottled light and dark green, become crinkled, and curl downward at the edges. Plants that become infected as they approach blooming time or later in the season may manifest mottling and a downward curling of the leaves only at the terminal growths, while in other cases the symptoms may not be at all apparent. Regardless of how affected the plants may seem, a few of the seeds in each pod may carry the virus inside.

Because mosaic viruses are carried in the sap of the plant, an afflicted plant cannot be saved. Prevent trouble by planting certified seed—such seed has a low inspection tolerance for common mosaic. See RESISTANT VARIETIES.

Curly top is a virus carried by the white fly (or beet leafhopper) and is not seed-borne. The disease dwarfs young plants, and leaves pucker and curl downward. Leaves may be cupped, or take on the appearance of small green balls. Plants infected when very young will usually die, while mature plants do not show the typical symptoms and usually live.

The best method of control is use of resistant varieties: the

Colorado State University Extension Service recommends University of Idaho, Great Northern, and Red Mexican.

Beans/Downy Mildew on Lima

Downy mildew attacks lima beans, and does its worst in the Middle Atlantic and North Atlantic states. This fungal disease causes irregular, white, cottony patches on bean pods; some patches may be bordered with purple. Affected pods shrivel, wilt, and die. The disease occasionally attacks young leaves, shoots, and flower parts. Wet weather, with cool nights, heavy dews, and fairly warm days, causes downy mildew to spread rapidly. During the growing season, it may also be carried to healthy plants by insects.

Avoid seed from an infected crop; to be safe, use seed from the Far West. Large-scale growers should use a two or three year crop rotation. Thaxter is a resistant lima bean variety.

Fusarium root rot, a fungal disease, first appears as a slight reddish discoloration inside the taproot. Gradually the entire taproot turns a deep red, then brown, and finally decays. Under favorable conditions, developed lateral roots may keep the plants alive.

Control is difficult. In serious cases, cultivation should be shallow and the crop should be irrigated more frequently, if possible.

Seed rot and damping-off (seedling rot) are caused by fungi which are present in nearly all soils. Seed rot is a semi-dry rot that occurs at the time of germination; it is apt to be a problem in cool, moist weather. Damping-off is a watery, soft rot of the young seedlings at or below the ground line, resulting in wilting of the unfoliate leaves and death of the seedling.

Although plants can be affected under a variety of moisture and temperature conditions, root rotting is not likely to occur in cool, moist soils. An effective treatment is to grow the beans in soils warm enough to encourage rapid germination.

Southern blight (or wilt) occurs in southern states, and is considered a minor disease. However, it attracts attention because of its striking symptoms: yellowing, wilting, and shedding of the leaves, and sudden wilting and death of the vine. Control shouldn't be necessary.

It goes without saying that **weeds** make trouble in the bean patch. Care should be taken not to hoe too deeply, as bean roots lie close to the surface and deep or extensive cultivation may result in undesirable root pruning. A heavy mulch can do the job of suppressing weeds, and also serves to preserve moisture in times of drought. Finally, remember that weeds provide homes for insect pests that are injurious to bean plants in their own right.

The first signs of **white mold** are dark watery spots on pods, stems, and leaves. These spots enlarge rapidly under cool moist conditions. The stems may be rotted through, causing wilting and death of part or all of the affected plant. Infected pods turn into a soft, watery mass, those that touch the ground being most susceptible. Very soon after the rot appears, you will notice a white, moldy fungus growth on the rotted area. These areas have the appearance of small patches of snow, unless darkened by soil. In a few days, the mold darkens and produces black kernels, called sclerotia, and may be seen in the drying fungus mass. The fungus carries over in the form of these sclerotia, which are resistant to drying and changes in temperature. Sclerotia in the soil may perpetuate the fungus for at least ten years.

The Connecticut Agricultural Experiment Station reports that the state's only recent serious problems with white mold occurred in a bean field in which lettuce had been grown the previous year. For control, the station recommends crop rotation and not following lettuce with beans. Some control may be effected by monitoring humidity and soil moistness around the plants; a field known to have white mold fungus should not be irrigated more often than necessary, and rows should be spaced wider to allow air to circulate around the plants.

Yellow mosaic is carried by aphids to bean plants from infected gladiolas, crimson, and red clover, as well as from other bean plants. Leaves of affected plants show much contrast between the yellow and green areas. The plants become dwarfed and bunchy. Follow control measures listed above for common bean mosaic. In areas where yellow mosaic is widespread, it is good practice to avoid planting beans very close to fields of host plants.

Beech

Insects

White **beech scale** is responsible for introducing a serious fungus disease to beech trees. As oil sprays may harm this tree, use a lime sulfur and water spray, mixed one part to ten.

Diseases

Leaf mottle or **scorch** appears in spring on young unfolding beech leaves as small, semitransparent spots surrounded by yellowish green to white areas. These spots enlarge, turn brown and dry, and are very prominent between the veins near the midrib and along the edge of the leaf. Later, entire leaves become scorched and premature leaf fall follows. In July, a normal set of leaves develops to replace fallen leaves. However, severe scalding of the bark on branches may occur as a result of premature defoliation exposing the branches to direct rays of the sun.

The causal agent of this disease is unknown. As a preventive measure, provide adequate fertilization. Where valuable trees have been defoliated, wrap exposed branches with burlap to protect them from the sun until the second set of leaves develops.

Beet

Insects

The **beet leafhopper** (commonly called white fly in the West) carries curly top, a virus disease, to table beets and a number of other vegetables and flowers. It is pale green or yellow, ⅛ inch long, wedge-shaped, and becomes darker toward winter. The symptoms of curly top are: warty, pronounced leaf veins; kinked petioles; rolled leaves that take on a cupped, or ball-like, appearance and become brittle; masses of hairlike rootlet growths on tap roots; stunted growth; and in many cases, death of the plant. See beet leafhopper under BEAN for control measures.

The **beet webworm** is found throughout the United States, but is especially harmful to beet crops in western states. It varies in color from yellow or green to nearly black, with a black stripe down the middle of the back and three black spots at the end of each segment. It feeds on leaves and constructs a protective hideout by rolling and folding a leaf and tying it together with webs. Sabadilla and pyrethrum are effective controls, but hand-picking should usually suffice.

Beet Webworm

Another damaging insect that gives headaches to beet growers is the **black blister beetle,** also called old-fashioned potato bug, yankee bug, and just plain "blister beetle." They are fairly long (½ to ¾ inch), slender, and have soft, flexible wing covers. The entire body is black or dark gray, and there may be thin white stripes on their wing covers. Blister beetles are usually found in swarms or colonies feeding on the blossoms and foliage of any of a number of garden and field crops—vegetables, vines, trees,

Blister Beetle

and flowers. They are so named because a caustic fluid in their bodies may blister the skin if the beetles are crushed upon it. (Cynthia Westcott notes that this substance was once used as a mustard plaster and as an aphrodisiac.)

To prevent damage, handpick the beetles as soon as they are discovered in the garden; because of the powerful, caustic fluid that they discharge, you should wear gloves. The blister beetle may be controlled with a safe insecticide made from sabadilla seeds. Entymologists at the University of Wisconsin report that when the powdered seed is heated in kerosene or other solvent to 302°F., a very toxic brew is formed. Sabadilla is available commercially from many seed and garden dealers. Perhaps because of the caustic liquid, hens will eat one blister beetle and no more. Some gardeners literally chase large swarms away with branches and shouts.

The **carrot weevil** may injure the roots of beets. It is a coppery colored or dark brown beetle measuring ¼ inch long. The larvae are dirty white, legless, curved grubs with brown heads. They grow up to ⅓ inch long, and tunnel into the roots of affected plants. For habits and control measures, see under CARROT.

Small seedlings may be attacked by tiny, dark purple, yellow-spotted **garden springtails.** They have no wings, but use a taillike appendage to hurtle themselves into the air. You will usually find springtails eating small holes in the leaves near the surface of the soil. Keep weeds down around the garden. A garlic spray on the vulnerable lower leaves may keep springtails away.

Garden Springtail

The tiny (¹⁄₁₆-inch-long) black **potato flea beetle** is so named because it jumps like a flea when disturbed. See under POTATO for control measures.

The **spinach flea beetle** emerges as an adult in early spring. This is a greenish black beetle with a yellow thorax and black head. It averages ⅕ inch long, and feeds on exposed beet leaves. The larval form is a dirty grayish purple, warty grub, ¼ inch long, that feeds on the underside of leaves. The grubs drop to the ground when they sense danger. For control, see SPINACH.

The **spinach leaf miner** is another spinach pest that attacks beets. The adult is a gray, black-haired, two-winged fly about ¼ inch in length. It lays white, cylindrical eggs on the underside of leaves in. clusters of from two to five. In a few days these eggs hatch into ⅓-inch-long, pale green or whitish maggots that eat leaves. For control, see SPINACH.

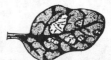

Spinach/Spinach Leaf Miner Damages

Diseases

A fungal disease that strikes gardens east of the Rocky Mountains is **leaf spot.** Small, circular, tan or brown spots with reddish purple borders appear scattered over leaves and stems. The spots later turn gray with brown borders. Heavy infection causes the leaves to become yellow and either scorch or drop off. Infection and dying of leaves and the production of new leaves result in a pyramiding effect of the crown. This fungus overwinters on seed balls and lives in the soil or on diseased remains of plants. Although not usually a serious threat to beets, it may be advantageous to ward it off by using a crop rotation of three years or more. Be certain either to cultivate deeply or to overturn beet refuse in the soil. This deep tillage will destroy the plant remains that usually harbor the fungus. The selection of resistant varieties depends upon your location; check with the county agent or extension service.

Beets will have a better chance of avoiding **yellows** virus if kept out of the wind—aphids are a prime vector, and are light enough to be blown about in a breeze. Oil emulsion sprays may keep aphids from transmitting this disease, according to Walter Carter in *Insects in Relation to Plant Disease.* Corn-oil emulsions stymie the aphid vector of beet mosaic virus.

Begonia

Insects

The melon **aphid** (and likely a number of other species) occasionally infest the begonia; see APHID. Other pests include the cyclamen mite (AZALEA), flower thrips (PEONY), fuller rose beetle (ROSE), MEALYBUGS, and SLUGS.

Diseases

Bacterial wilt often strikes begonias. Small light spots appear on the underside of the leaves and gradually enlarge and merge into water-soaked areas. The leaves then turn brown and die. Also look for wilting and browning of stems and leaf areas. A puslike bacterial slime fills the stems and midribs of plants and leaves.

Plants severely affected by bacterial wilt must be pulled out and destroyed. Those that aren't so bad may survive if the infected areas are cut out with a clean knife. Since this disease is highly contagious, it can be spread by direct contact with tools, boxes, pots, and even sprinklers that have been used on infected plants.

The disease thrives best in periods of high humidity so, if possible, keep the indoor area dry and well ventilated. Remove diseased leaves, stems, and plants from the growing area, as they are the springboards for the propagation of the disease. Set only healthy plants.

One trouble that may confront the begonia grower is **dropping of buds,** a malady with a couple of possible causes. Buds may drop if the begonias are exposed to high temperatures. Because tuberous-rooted begonias and gloxinias require temperatures between 65° and 75°F., they should be planted in a cool, shady spot of the garden. Indeed, begonias are a desirable ornamental for gardens that do not get a lot of sun.

Both begonias and gloxinias like well-drained soils, and if the center buds drop first, it is usually a sign that the soil has poor drainage. This does not mean that the soil should not be watered, for dried-out soil can also cause dropped buds, especially once the plants have formed buds. The best way to prevent such problems is to add plenty of well-composted organic material to the soil. This vital addition will allow the soil to soak up more water and nutrients, while enabling the soil to drain well without quickly drying out.

Begonias sometimes have too many leaves for the amount of flowers. **Excessive foliage** may result if too many shoots have been allowed to remain on the tuber. Leave just one shoot per tuber, and break off any others before they reach a height of two or three inches. Another possible cause of excessive foliage arises from soil that is too rich in nitrogen, often as the result of super-soluble chemical fertilizers. Too much nitrogen keeps plants in a vegetative state.

Gloxinias and tuberous-rooted begonias are both affected by **mildew.** The first evidence of this disease is a soft, grayish growth on leaves. Later stages of mildew are indicated by a soft, dark brown discoloration of the leaves. Mildew often occurs when plants get too much water. Water only as needed, provide good ventilation, and remove diseased plants.

Rotting plants are sometimes caused by coming in contact with decayed matter that hasn't been well composted. Also, be certain to remove all flowers when they have finished blooming.

Stem rot results from overwatering and the use of unsterilized soil. You can escape trouble by clearing the area of old plant rubbish and by being careful not to draw soil or mulch up too close to stems. As soon as a rotted spot is noticed on a stem, cut the infected area out with a sharp knife or razor blade.

Birch

Unless necessary for controlling a pest, prune birches as little as possible, and then only at a time when they are in full leaf, since these trees bleed profusely. The best time for doing the necessary pruning is late summer, for large wounds heal over rapidly in July and August when the tree is running less fluid in preparation for the coming winter season.

Insects

Two species of **aphids** are common on birches, the yellowish birch aphid and the waxy birch leaf aphid. Migration of winged aphids in swarms occurs in severe infestations. Control these aphids with a forceful spray of water. Also see APHID.

Birch/Birch Leaf Miner Damage

The adult **birch leaf miner** is a small black sawfly that measures $\frac{3}{16}$ inch long. It attacks most North American birches except the yellow birch, causing blotch mines and brown spots on the leaves, which come to appear blighted or scorched. Tender terminal leaves are most susceptible. The miner adult lays its eggs in newly growing leaves; it will not lay eggs in the older, hardened leaves. The larvae develop in mines in the leaves. At maturity they fall to the ground to pupate and overwinter as pupae in the soil. Adults emerge early in May (late May in Canada) and may continue to emerge for a two-week period. Depending on the length of the growing season, there may be three or four generations, the first two of which are the most injurious. The vitality of the tree is reduced because of loss of foliage, making it more susceptible to the bronze birch borer and other pests.

Sanitation is important in controlling the birch leaf miner. Be sure to gather and burn or compost all leaves that fall to the ground prematurely. As the leaf miner takes a liking to new foliage, it is a good idea to prune back all unnecessary new growth. This is especially true of water sprouts, which are not necessary to the proper growth of the tree. Pruning is especially important when new broods of the insect are seen to emerge early in the growing season. Proper fertilization according to the organic method will increase the vigor of the tree and give it more strength to fight off attacks from injurious insects.

The larvae of the **birch sawfly** sometimes feed around the margins of birch leaves, but as they seldom do serious damage, control measures have not been necessary. The larvae of another sawfly, the birch leaf miner, is much more important; see above.

The biggest enemy of birch is the **bronze birch borer,** a slender, bronze-colored, ½-inch-long beetle. The upper portion of the tree is often infested first, and shows spiral ridges on the bark of the branches. Although it consumes a bit of foliage, the adult causes little injury itself. After emerging in the latter part of May, the female lays her eggs upon or in the bark, and tunneling borers begin work at the top of the tree, giving it a stag-head appearance as the insects continue downward. Rusty red patches appear on the bark. When the tunnel network has expanded enough to cut off the flow of sap in the main trunk, death occurs.

Birch/Bronze Birch Borer Damage

Unfortunately, the birch borer often becomes entrenched before its presence is discovered. The small larvae hatch and tunnel through the bark to the sapwood, where the insect winters over in a dormant state. The only method of safe control is to keep an eye out for infestation.

To control these insects by natural means, slice out and burn all infested parts and suspect debris before the adult emerges in May. This will prevent a profuse hatching of young beetles. Birches should be properly nourished and watered in dry spells.

The **case bearer** is a light yellowish green caterpillar, about ⅕ inch long, that mines in the leaves and causes them to shrivel. Small cylindrical cases are formed on the underside of the leaves. The adult moth is brown, and the insect overwinters in cases on the bark. Kill the overwintering larvae by spraying with lime sulfur and water, mixed one to eight, before growth commences in spring.

Caterpillars of the **gypsy moth** feed on birch. See under TREES: INSECTS.

Oystershell scale is a common pest of young birch sprouts; see LILAC.

Diseases

Paper and yellow birch are attacked by the **European canker fungus.** Cankers are formed on branches near forks, sometimes appearing as concentric rings of callus growth. The main trunk, if infected, may be flattened and bent.

Pruning and burning of affected wood will help your birch trees. Cut out small cankers, and sterilize the wounds and paint them.

Rust is seen as reddish yellow pustules on the underside of infected leaves. It sometimes causes defoliation, but generally rust is not serious enough to warrant control measures.

Willow crown gall may strike birches. It is caused by a bacterium that invades the roots, trunk, or branches, stimulating cell growth so that tumorlike swellings with irregular rough surfaces are formed. The galls may be the size of a pea or larger, those on the trunk sometimes growing to one or two feet in diameter. Growth of the tree may be retarded, leaves often turn yellow, or branches and roots sometimes die.

To control crown gall, destroy affected trees and nursery stock. Do not replant the area with willow, poplar, chestnut, sycamore, maple, walnut, or fruit trees. Avoid wounding the stems of healthy trees, since infection occurs through wounds.

Nectaria canker, already described, may also affect birches. See TREES: DISEASES.

Blackberry

The best preventive for diseases and pests is a clean berry patch. Start with healthy certified stock from dependable nurseries. Keep the canes thinned out to let air and light circulate. Any leaves or fruit that drop out of season should be removed at once, since they may harbor disease or pests. All old canes should be removed as soon as they have finished bearing. When pruning, cut the canes all the way back to the soil level and destroy the prunings. Be sure to pick all the berries, even the few that turn small and dry toward the end of the season.

Since wild plants harbor many diseases and insects, it is best to eradicate those near cultivated plants. Rake and burn all nearby apple and cherry leaves. Keep a close watch on your plants for symptoms of serious troubles such as virus diseases or orange rust. At their first appearance, remove the entire affected plant, including all the roots, and burn it.

Insects

The **blackberry psyllid** is a jumping plant louse that occasionally injures cultivated plants, and is usually to be found on wild blackberry. The adult is yellow brown, about ⅙ inch long, and is marked with three yellow brown bands on each wing. The adults live through the winter in protected places and appear on the plants soon after growth begins. They lay eggs in leaf stems and tender shoots. Both nymphs and adults puncture the stems and leaves, causing stunted or distorted growth (sometimes called galls).

As damage from psyllids is usually not very great, control measures are seldom needed. They collect and breed on lycium, so elimination of this plant will help curb the psyllid population. This pest has many natural enemies, including ladybugs and about fifty species of gall midges. If further control is required, spray a soap solution on the plants.

Occasionally, blackberry leaves are devoured by the larvae of the **blackberry sawfly.** Adults appear in late May, and the females lay white oval eggs, placed end to end and fastened to the larger veins on the underside of leaves. The larvae roll the leaves, fasten them by a web, and feed within. In July they are fully grown, ¾ inch long, and bluish green in color.

When control is necessary, use pure pyrethrum or rotenone, applied early in summer to the underside of leaves. If the eggs are removed and destroyed in spring when first laid, sawflies should not be a serious problem. Fly paper, or paper smeared with molasses, will help eliminate the adult flies.

The larvae of the **leaf miner,** another type of sawfly, sometimes infest blackberry and dewberry leaves. There are two generations, the first in May and early June, and the second in August. Eggs are laid in blisters on the underside of leaves. The larvae mine the leaf edges, making blotched areas that give plants a scorched appearance. The adult is a blackish four-winged fly, about ⅙ inch long. So far, a satisfactory organic control has not been worked out for this insect. Infestations can be reduced somewhat by pinching feeding larvae.

The common brown **May beetles,** of which there are more than a hundred species, sometimes cause serious damage by eating blackberry leaves. In the larva or white grub stage they feed on the roots of bluegrass, timothy, corn, soybeans, and several other crops, as well as on decaying vegetation. Their pearly white eggs are deposited in spring, one to eight inches deep in the soil, and hatch three to four weeks later.

May Beetle

Populations of white grubs, and consequently of May beetles, can be reduced by rotating blackberries with deep-rooted legumes such as sweet clover, alfalfa, and other clovers that are unfavorable to them. Legumes are most effective if planted in the years of major beetle flights. The renovation of bluegrass pastures badly infested with white grubs may be necessary; the sod is thoroughly torn up in spring or late fall, treated with organic fertilizer, and sown in spring with a seed mixture consisting mainly of legumes. If you plant blackberries in fields that have been fallow for several years or on land that has been in pasture or grass sod, be especially watchful for white grubs. If they are in the soil, at least one intervening crop of legumes should be grown. Be sure to use clean cultural practices before the berries are planted. Other control measures should include deep plowing and frequent stirring of the land during the winter before cane fruits are planted.

The **raspberry cane maggot** is also a pest of blackberries. The white, ⅓-inch-long maggot causes the tips of new shoots to wilt and take on a purplish discoloration. Galls may appear on the canes. For more information and control, see RASPBERRY.

The **raspberry crown borer,** which hollows out canes, seems to prefer trailing blackberries to upright plants. See RASPBERRY for symptoms and control.

The **red-necked cane borer** causes blackberry canes to develop enlarged swellings, ½ to 1½ inches in diameter and extending for several inches along the cane in a cigar shape. If these swollen places are cut open in winter, slender creamy white grubs will be found, usually in the pith. In May, bluish black beetles with a coppery red thorax may be found on or in these swollen areas. Eggs are laid in June in the shoots, and the larvae hatching from them bore into the bark to cause the peculiar growth. These galls or swellings develop in late July or August and prevent the shoots from developing properly.

You can control the red-necked cane borer during fall or early winter simply by cutting out all canes having these abnormal swellings.

Rose scale, a common pest of both blackberries and raspberries, gives the canes a whitish, scaly, inflamed appearance. The scaly shell is secreted by a small reddish insect that covers itself with a waxy coating. Eggs are laid beneath the scale in fall, and hatch in spring to suck the sap from the canes. Rose scale is sometimes mistaken for anthracnose, but unlike anthracnose it appears only on the surface.

Rose/Rose Scale

Control by spraying with a miscible-oil solution. Remove and burn infested canes during the dormant season.

If the blackberry leaves are dull and pale, with yellow dots on the upper surface and webbing underneath, they may be infested by the **spider mite.** These pests are more prevalent in dry weather, but unless there is extreme drought they should not bother well-mulched berry bushes. Give your plants enough water and the mites will disappear. You can also dislodge them with water, as described in the RASPBERRY section. See also SPIDER MITE.

Tree crickets, especially the black-horned tree cricket, may be a problem for blackberries. These greenish yellow insects, with feelers projecting from the front of the black head, will attack red and black raspberries, trailing brambles, wild shrubs, and fruit trees. Since they usually lay their eggs at the edge of a field, they do less damage to a square field than a long, narrow one. Canes injured by crickets show areas of bark split in an irregular line. Inside these splits are a series of small holes extending into the pith. These holes or punctures are usually made in rows of up to 75 or 100. Frequently the canes break off at the injury. The eggs remain in the canes through winter, hatching in spring to pale green, slender young. The nymphs grow rather slowly, reaching maturity in late summer, mating in fall, and laying their eggs in the maturing shoots as the weather turns cold.

If infested canes are not too numerous, they can be removed and burned to destroy the eggs. Where infestation is heavy, many of the eggs can be destroyed by cutting back the canes to half their length. This should save much of the crop. The prunings must be collected and burned before the eggs hatch in spring. It helps to keep down weed growth as well as any wild raspberry, blackberry, and dewberry plants growing nearby. If a further measure is needed, an application of rotenone should help.

Diseases

Anthracnose, a fungus disease of a number of garden plants, is also a major enemy of blackberries. The most serious damage is to the stems of the fruit and to the berries, which wither early. Leaves may become infected and drop. The first symptoms appear in spring as small, purplish, slightly raised spots on the young plants. As the plants grow, the spots enlarge and their centers become gray and slightly sunken. Other spots appear on the leaves and stems. The lesions are often so close that irregular spots are formed over the cane surface. During the second year, when the fruit is to appear, the bark may crack, causing the plant to lose water and dry up.

Spores of this fungus disease are carried by rain, wind, and insects. As the buds open on the fruiting cane, new tissue becomes exposed and infected. The spores germinate and the fungus penetrates, often extending into the woody section of the plant.

Anthracnose is best controlled by careful sanitation practices. Remove old canes after fruiting and the stubs or handles of the trailing brambles after the plants are set. Be sure to cut your plants low when planting them, and to discard any showing severe, gray bark lesions. Although not entirely resistant, erect types such as Humble, Texas Wonder, Dallas, and Lawton are less susceptible. Since wild raspberries are usually heavily infected, it is best to eliminate them from the immediate vicinity. Avoid planting anthracnose-prone plants near your blackberries: this includes beans, cucumbers, grapes, sweet peas, and raspberries.

Moisture on the canes favors spore germination and infection, so provide air circulation to speed drying. Eliminate weeds and thin out weak and spindly canes. If necessary use a spray of lime sulfur, mixed ⅘ pint per gallon or 10 gallons per 100 gallons of spray, in spring when ¼ inch of green leaf is exposed from the buds. Do not use this spray after the delayed dormant period, or severe foliage injury may result.

Trailing varieties of blackberries may be affected by **cane dieback,** which causes buds to fail to break early in the growing season. The plant may produce both normal buds and some that grow only a few inches before they wither and die. The leaves may be mottled and small, and scorched areas often appear on the leaf surface.

Check to see that adequate soil moisture is maintained to a sufficient depth throughout the year. It is best to plant on sandy soil that runs eight feet deep and has a very high rate of water penetration.

Many plants, especially bramble fruits, are vulnerable to **crown gall,** a bacterial disease. Crown gall weakens the plant and ultimately may kill it. It is recognized by the presence of galls or knots on the roots and sometimes on the canes. The bacteria invade the plant tissue through open wounds and cause galls to form; even after the galls decay, the germ lives for some time in rotted tissue in the soil, and may reinfect the plant. Plants with numerous galls may be stunted and produce dry, poorly developed berries. Latham raspberries are particularly subject to crown gall.

Sanitation is the best control for this disease. Destroy all plants that show symptoms of gall. Order plants from reliable nurseries and carefully inspect each plant before it goes into the soil. Once a planting is badly infected, the only recourse is to plow up the entire field and grow corn or grass for several years.

A good planting site would be one where grain crops have been grown for several years, as they usually reduce the number of crown gall bacteria in the soil. Furthermore, there are as a rule fewer insects in the soil where small grain or sweet clover has been grown than in newly plowed bluegrass or old nursery and orchard land. Stay away from land where brambles have been recently grown and land receiving drainage from old bramble fields.

There is a fungus disease that causes double blossoms from which no fruit sets. It is called, appropriately enough, **double blossom.** If you spot any blossoms with crinkled multiple petals among the healthy blossoms of your plants, it is best to inspect all buds before they open. Buds affected by double blossom have chubby contours and are fleshier and redder than normal buds. Pick off and destroy all such buds before they can open and release the spores of the fungus. After the harvest, cut all canes close to the ground and destroy them.

Dwarf or rosette is a virus disease causing marked reduction in growth and productiveness. Affected plants usually become unproductive within a year, with a downward cupping and reddening of the leaves, dwarfing of the cane growth, and general unproductiveness.

Clear out any patches of wild blackberry in the vicinity, as they may contain the virus. Himalaya and Advance are very resistant to dwarf; Boysen and Young are relatively resistant.

One of the most serious diseases of commercial berry plantings is **orange rust.** Once infected with orange rust, a plant never recovers, as the rust reappears year after year. Usually the leaves are so heavily infected that the diseased plant will not bear a crop. Orange rust affects the leaves of the plant, causing yellow dots to appear on both sides early in spring. Two or three weeks later, light-colored areas develop on the undersurface of the leaf, and in a few days the epidermis is ruptured, exposing large, bright orange red, powdery masses of spores. These spores blow about and infect other plants. Infected plants are stunted and worthless for fruit production. The orange rust fungus winters in the roots and stems of old plants. In spring it grows up in the pith of the developing canes and out into the leaves, where it produces the spore masses. .

To combat orange rust, the infected plants must be dug out and destroyed, including all the roots and suckers. Since orange rust is a systemic disease that spreads through the plant, not even one cane should remain. If there are any wild berries nearby, be sure to inspect them too for disease—it is pointless to root out all of your own infected plants and ignore those just over the fence.

Better still, eradicate wild berries near your plants. Avoid touching healthy plants with diseased materials, and do not cultivate diseased plants when the leaves are wet. Give the berries a heavy mulch of straw and leaf mold and, when the season is over, a heavy dressing of compost. Add some extra potash and phosphate to your compost, because fungus diseases are often encouraged by malnutrition. Always try to plant resistant varieties, such as Eldorado, Boysen, Lawton, and Snyder.

Septoria leaf spot is a fungus disease that can cause serious defoliation. In early summer, small dots appear on the leaves of infected plants, purplish on the edge and tan or light brown in the center. When the spots are large enough, you may see several blackish dots in the center. These are the fruiting bodies, producing millions of spores that infect surrounding leaves and cause them to drop. In seasons of heavy rains, the leaves of an entire planting may be diseased.

Sanitary measures give the best control for septoria leaf spot. Preventing weed growth and training the canes will give the plant free air circulation. Remove old leaves and cultivate early. Remove and burn all diseased canes immediately after harvest.

Blackberries, like raspberries, are susceptible to **virus** diseases. While there is no control as yet, buying good stock from reliable nurseries is a preventive. Some nurseries offer registered virus-free blackberries and raspberries.

For botrytis fruit rot, cane blight, and powdery mildew, see RASPBERRY.

Blueberry

Small plantings, especially new ones, are seldom troubled by the pests and diseases that hit large-scale plantings. Blueberry bushes are benefited by mulch because they are not deeply rooted and can be harmed by drought. Oak leaves, peat, sawdust, pine needles, or even spent hops from a brewery are all good mulches for these acid-loving plants. Careful cultivation will also help keep the bushes pest-free.

Insects

The **blueberry bud mite** is invisible to the naked eye. An infestation will distort flower buds or even prevent buds from developing. These mites are rarely a problem in the North, although they sometimes cause trouble in the South. Control with a miscible-oil spray in late September or early October.

The **blueberry bud worm,** a type of cutworm that eats fruit buds, may develop in weeds under the bushes. Clean cultivation will control them.

The **blueberry fruit fly** can be a troublesome pest. It is about the size of a housefly, with black bands on its wings. This fly lays its eggs in ripe or overripe berries. In just a few days, tiny colorless blueberry maggots burrow into the fruit and cause it to drop. Early varieties appear to be less susceptible to the blueberry maggot than late ones.

Pick up and dispose of all dropped fruit, because it may contain the eggs for another generation. Cultivation around the plants also helps, as larvae drop to the ground under the bush and plowing exposes them to predatory ants and birds. Some growers have controlled the blueberry fruit fly with a flat, paddle-shaped piece of board that is brushed with a commercial sticky compound (try Tanglefoot or Stikem) and hung on each bush. Clean up all old trimmings, and pick ripe berries before the fruit fly can lay its eggs in them. Commercial growers have found a two-percent rotenone dust to be an effective control.

The **blueberry leaf miner** may eat a few leaves or roll up a few more, but it is not a serious pest and will usually not affect fruit yield. It has been effectively controlled by a parasite, *Aparteles ornigis.*

The **cherry fruitworm** hatches in late May in the North, and the pinkish larvae bore into the fruit and feed till mid-June. It is controlled by a parasitic fungus, *Beauvaria bassiana,* which also keeps the cranberry fruitworm in line. A tiny wasp parasite, *Trichogramma minutum* Riley, is effective against both the cherry and the cranberry species. The adult fruitworm is an ash-gray moth, marked with black spots, that lays eggs on berries in mid-July. They hatch as green caterpillars that eat into berries near the stem, shriveling them. A web is woven around a cluster of berries.

Commercial growers are forced to flood the growing area after harvesting, but the cranberry fruitworm is usually controlled in small plantings by handpicking, keeping the bushes free of weeds and trash, and frequent cultivation of the soil between plants. Ryania and rotenone can be used against fruitworms.

The **plum curculio** [color] is a brown-snouted beetle, ¼ inch long, that damages many stone fruits. It overwinters in pro-

Plum/Plum Curculio

tected areas around the garden and in early spring lays its eggs in the young fruit, later feeding on the fruit. The mark of the plum curculio is a small, crescent-shaped depression in new fruit. The larvae enter the soil to pupate. Late-ripening berries are less frequently bothered by this pest.

The best control is sanitation. Pick up and destroy any dropped fruit as soon as possible. Clean up rubbish heaps and other possible winter hiding places, such as old boards. If possible, try to avoid planting near wooded areas, since the beetles are more numerous there than out in the open.

There are two varieties of **scale** which may become a problem for blueberries. Putnam scale is the more common. It often occurs on forest trees and will infest older blueberry bushes, clustering on the rough wood and feeding on the fruit. It is dark gray to black and circular, and produces a reddish secretion. Terrapin scale is a dark reddish brown insect with dark bands radiating from its center back to fluted edges. It secretes a honeydew on which a sooty fungus develops. When scales are numerous, there may be a putrid odor.

The ladybug is a natural predator of scale. Pruning to remove dead, excess, and infested wood should keep both species well under control. Dormant-oil sprays also keep down scale infestations.

The **stem borer** or tip borer is a long-horned, ½-inch-long, slender beetle that girdles the tips of blueberry and other acid-loving plants in spring. It lays eggs in the stems, and the grubs bore into them and down into the trunks of woody plants. The stem borer is controlled by cutting out and destroying all dead and wilting tips.

Tent caterpillars are more damaging to large commercial plantations of blueberries than to small plantings. Wild cherry trees are their favorite host, so be cautious if there are any in your vicinity. See TENT CATERPILLAR.

Other occasional pests of blueberries are the European corn borer (see CORN), JAPANESE BEETLE, and rose chafer (ROSE).

Diseases

Bacterial or **stem canker** affects the canes of blueberry bushes, causing reddish brown or black cankers. All buds in the cankered areas are killed and sometimes the stem itself is girdled and dies. In other cases, the stem above the canker continues to grow, but it may be weak and unproductive. Eventually the plant will die.

Stem canker was formerly a serious problem in the South, but resistant varieties have been developed, such as Murphy, Wolcott, Angola, Croatan, and Morrow. The new rabbiteye varieties are also immune.

Botrytis blight affects growing tips, flowers, and newly formed berries. On canes, infected areas are brown or gray, extending down a few inches. The fungus, sometimes called gray mold blight, covers the flower with a dense, gray, powdery mass that quickly spreads to adjacent flowers and fruits. Young berries shrivel and turn purplish. Varieties that drop the corolla promptly are less susceptible.

Because succulent growth is most seriously affected, fertilizers heavy in nitrogen should be avoided. Prune out blighted twigs as soon as possible and burn them. Keep your pruning tools clean to avoid spreading the disease.

Cane gall or stem gall appears as rough, irregular, warty growths along the stems of plants. Older canes are more susceptible than young growth. Infected canes should be pruned out and destroyed; you're best off buying healthy nursery stock.

The fungus disease **mummy berry** causes berries to shrivel and dry out on the bush just before they should ripen. Under the dry skin of the fruit is a thin black layer. Leaves may wilt and blacken. The mummy berry fungus overwinters on the ground beneath the bushes, so kill it with an early spring cultivation. Like many fungal diseases, it is nurtured by overfertilization of the plants. Mummy berry is seldom a problem with heavily mulched plants.

Powdery mildew is very common with blueberries. This whitish mold on the topside of leaves appears after the harvest and so has no effect on fruit yield. Berkeley, Earliblue, and Ivanhoe are resistant varieties.

Stunt is a virus disease more common in the South than in the North. It is less troublesome than it used to be, although potentially present wherever there are wild blueberries. Stunt is spread by a leafhopper, and the reduced vigor of the plant results in abnormally small leaves that are curved upward and yellowish. The plant has a dwarfed appearance, with clusters of berries much smaller than normal. The plant may turn reddish in mid- or late-summer. Stunt-resistant varieties include Harding, Stanley, and Jersey.

Wildlife

Birds may take most of your blueberry crop unless you find a way to protect your bushes by screening or enclosure. Posts eight feet tall can be set around your planting and through it in rows, with wire screening nailed around the sides and on top. Fish netting also works well, and gives better ventilation than screening. The frame should hold the netting at least a foot away from the berry bushes.

Boxwood

Insects

Boxwood Leaf Miner

The **boxwood leaf miner** is the most serious insect enemy of boxwood in the United States. This pest weakens the plant by removing tissue from the leaves, causing the foliage to become yellowish green and stunting new growth. Twigs may die, giving the plant a ragged appearance. Most varieties of boxwood are susceptible to attack.

The larvae are yellow, wormlike insects, many of which may be present within a single mined leaf. Rake up and compost fallen leaves, and prune back succulent new growth, especially water sprouts, in early spring. The dwarf, or English, variety of box is immune to the leaf miner.

The **boxwood mite** is a common pest in most boxwood plantings. The adults are $\frac{1}{64}$ inch long and yellow green to reddish brown in color. The overwintering yellow, rounded flattened eggs on the underside of the leaves hatch shortly after the middle of April. The young nymphs feed on adjacent tissue. During the second instar, the mites feed on both surfaces of the leaves. On the upper surface, small patches are rasped from the outermost layer of cells, appearing as fine scratches. This gives the leaves a mottled appearance and serves as an early indication of the presence of mites. The third instar larvae go from leaf to leaf to feed. The adult mites feed mostly on the tender shoots and on the uppersurface of the leaves. As mites increase in number, the damage becomes more apparent. Leaves become bronzed, wither, and sometimes drop to the ground, leaving the plant looking scraggly.

Mites can be controlled by squirting the boxwood with water

several times during spring and summer. Apply the water by hose late in the afternoon.

The **boxwood psyllid** causes a cupping of terminal leaves. It is a small, grayish green sucking insect, the nymphs of which are covered with a whitish waxy material. Plants are seldom seriously injured, although their appearance becomes unattractive. If infestations are severe, growth may be retarded. Control with a pyrethrum spray at the first evidence of leaf cupping.

Diseases

Decline or **dieback** often follows winter injury or occurs on plants that are growing in a poorly-drained soil. Nematodes may also encourage this trouble. In spring the foliage of affected plants changes from the normal dark green color to gray green or bronze and finally to a straw color. Shoot growth is weak and old leaves drop prematurely. Entire branches die, especially in the middle or top of the plant. Sunken areas or cankers may appear in the bark of the trunk just above the ground line or on the branches in crotches where dead leaves and debris accumulate. The bark on the sunken areas may be brown or streaked with brown and often peels or splits away from the gray, discolored wood beneath.

Plant boxwood in well-drained soil and protect the plants from drying winter winds and severe low temperatures. Remove affected branches by cutting them back to healthy wood several inches below the cankers. On large branches, remove small cankers by cutting back to healthy wood on all sides of the canker and shape the wound to a point at either end. Paint all wounds with shellac and, when they dry, cover with a tree paint. Before growth starts in spring, remove leaves and debris lodged in the crotches. A strong stream of water will do an excellent job of removing this debris.

Leaf spotting on box is quite frequent and may be caused by any of several fungi. Infected leaves turn a strawy yellow color and their undersurface is thickly dotted with small black fruiting structures. Damage is limited to plants lacking in vigor, and it is important to enrich the soil and ensure good soil drainage.

Exposed boxwoods may suffer **winter injury** from severe cold and drying winds. Leaves may become grayish green or brown with dead twigs. Protect plants from exposure. Let the season's new growth harden off before the onset of winter, which means you should not overfertilize late in the season.

Broccoli

Insects

In general, the pests that injure cabbage also attack other members of the crucifer family, including broccoli, brussels sprouts, turnip, rutabaga, Chinese cabbage, mustard, and cauliflower. See CABBAGE for these pests of broccoli: cabbage aphid, cabbage looper, imported cabbageworm, cabbage maggot, flea beetle, and diamondback moth.

Diseases

Broccoli is plagued by the same diseases that afflict other crucifers. Look under CABBAGE for these diseases: blackleg, black rot, club root, damping-off (seed rot), downy mildew, rhizoctonia disease, watery soft rot, and yellows (or wilt).

Brussels Sprouts

Insects

Almost all of the enemies of brussels sprouts are shared by broccoli, cabbage, and the other crucifers. Under CABBAGE, see cabbage looper, imported cabbageworm, flea beetle, and diamondback moth. Other possible pests are APHIDS, and WHITE FLY.

Diseases

Brussels sprouts share many diseases of the other crucifers, including blackleg and clubroot; see CABBAGE.

Butternut

Insects

For insects, see WALNUT.

Diseases

For **anthracnose** of butternut, see TREES, DISEASES.

The fungus *Melanconis juglandis* infects small branches of butternut trees, producing a dark discoloration of bark and causing a **dieback** which progresses down the branches to the trunk. Severely affected butternut trees eventually die. Dead branches are covered with small, black, pimplelike fruiting bodies of the fungus. In wet weather, spores ooze out in a black, inky mass from the fruiting bodies and are splashed and blown about, infecting other branches.

Control by destroying severely affected trees. Where infection is light, remove diseased branches promptly, pruning back to sound wood.

Several of the wood-rotting fungi may attack butternut trees as wound parasites, causing **root rot** or **heart rot**, which contributes to the decline and death of trees. The only control for these fungi is the proper care of tree wounds by cleaning, shaping, and painting them.

Cabbage

The several members of the cabbage, or crucifer, family have two things in common—insect enemies and diseases. Therefore, these plants will be treated as a group and included under the cabbage entry: cauliflower, broccoli, brussels sprouts, turnips, Chinese cabbage, rutabaga, and mustard. Where differences do occur, they are so indicated. Generally, mints and monarda (bee balm, bergamot, and oswego tea) make excellent companions for cabbage plants. Not only do these perennials repel various pests, but they attract bees and hummingbirds to the garden as well. Growers have found that pests are less partial to red than green cabbage. The number of different cabbage enemies may be discouraging, but most of them are minor. Helga Olkowski's *Common Sense Pest Control* concludes with the question: "Do I really need to kill that animal?" If the object of your wrath is only taking a random nibble, either handpick and stamp him or forget him. There are better ways to spend your time in the garden.

Insects

Foremost among insects that attack cabbages is the cabbage **aphid**. This tiny green to powdery blue insect has a soft body covered with a fine whitish wax. Aphids cluster on the underside of leaves, causing them to cup and curl. They may also occur on flower heads. Broccoli is particularly vulnerable. Affected plants are stunted, and seedlings may die.

When cabbage aphids appear in cool weather, they can usually be discouraged by a fine, forceful spray from the garden hose. Try pulling up old, woody mint plants in late summer and laying them as a mulch under broccoli and cabbage. Mint can also be planted among crucifers to repel the aphids. Fine-ground limestone, sprinkled over cabbage and the heads and foliage of

Aphid

broccoli, can drive them away. While this powder makes aphids uncomfortable, sprinkling diatomaceous earth will actually kill them. If the damage has already been done, remove and destroy the plants as early in the season as possible, for they may be infected with mosaic, a virus disease that is often spread by aphids. You may be able to save later plants by removing only those leaves that have been affected. Because aphids winter in the North as small, dark eggs on the stems and old leaves of crucifers, a thorough garden clean-up at the end of the season could save you trouble next year.

The **banded cucumber beetle** is an occasional cabbage pest, from South Carolina to California. This beetle is yellow or green and shows three brighter green stripes running across the wing covers. They are small, no larger than ¼ inch, and feed on leaves of young cabbage plants and heading broccoli. See CUCUMBER.

All of the crucifers are open to damage from the **cabbage looper** [color]. This is a large, pale green measuring worm with light stripes down its back. It grows to 1½ inches long, and it's so named because it doubles up or loops as it crawls. The round, greenish white eggs are laid singly, usually on the upper surface of leaves. The looper overwinters as a green or brown pupa, wrapped in a cocoon attached by one side to a plant leaf.

Cabbage Looper Moth/Cabbage Looper

Biological controls have been effective in subduing the cabbage looper. The tiny trichogramma wasp is a parasite of several caterpillars, and is commercially available. Gardeners can also use the bacteria *Bacillus thuringiensis* to kill and infect the looper and other caterpillar pests that include the salt-marsh caterpillar, imported cabbageworm, beet armyworm, and diamondback moth. See BACILLUS THURINGIENSIS. If you raise large amounts of cabbage, especially in the South, loopers may be controlled by spreading a homemade virus potion. Entomologist Francis R. Lawson of Biocontactics, Inc., a Florida research concern, has found that a solution made from just ten loopers infected with nuclear polyhedrosis virus (NPV) will give an acre complete protection. The trick is finding a virus-infected looper in your cabbage patch. Lawson says to look for loopers that have turned chalky white and appear half dead. They may climb to the top of the plant and lie on the leaves, or hang down from the underside. These affected worms soon turn black and liquify. Capture ten of them and run them through a blender with some water. Then dilute to give the mixture a sprayable consistency. Once infected, loopers die within three or four days. In some cases, the application of NPV may control loopers for an entire growing season. See NUCLEAR POLYHEDROSIS VIRUS.

The **cabbage maggot** [color] infests the stems of early–set cabbage and other crucifers, and late in spring radishes and turnips may also be damaged. These larvae are small (⅓ inch), white, legless maggots with blunt rear ends. They attack stems just below the surface of the soil, riddling them with brown tunnels. The seedlings then usually wilt and die; most infested cabbage and cauliflower seedlings never produce heads. Also, the maggot earns more bad points by serving as a vector for bacterial soft rot and the fungus that causes blackleg.

Another potentially serious pest of cabbage is the **cross-striped cabbageworm**. Newly hatched larvae are gray with small black tubercules and large round heads; mature larvae are green to bluish gray with at least three distinct black bands across each segment. Long dark hairs grow out of the black tubercules, and the slender worms grow to ⅔ inch long. The adult is a small pale yellow moth, with mottled brown patterns on the forewings and partially transparent hind-wings. See imported cabbageworm, below.

The fat, smooth, pulpy **cutworm** is as bad as it is ugly. Of the many species, you are most likely to run into the black, bronzed, and dingy cutworms. The black cutworm (or greasy cutworm) is gray to almost black and has a broken yellow line down the center of its back with a pale line to each side. It grows to 1½ inch or even longer, and has a shiny, greasy appearance. As its name suggests, the bronzed cutworm is bronze in color and displays five pale lines from head to tail. It is a pest in the northern states. A northern cousin is the granulate cutworm, which has a rough, granulate-appearing skin and a dusty brown color. It burrows very shallowly in the soil, often exposing its back. The dingy cutworm, a northern species, is also aptly named —it is a dull, dingy brown, and has a wide, pale stripe running the length of its back, flanked by a thin dark stripe on each side. They sometimes crawl up the stems of plants to feed. For control measures, see TOMATO.

Cutworm

Although the larva of the **diamondback moth** [color] is a relatively minor pest, it at times can cause considerable damage to the cabbage family by eating small holes in the outer leaves. These caterpillars grow only to ⅓ inch long, are greenish yellow with black hairs, and when disturbed will wriggle and drop to the ground. The adult is a gray to brown, small (¾-inch-across) moth, with fringed back wings; when the moth is at rest, look for the diamond on its folded wings. See BACILLUS THURINGIEN-SIS for an effective biological control.

The **fall armyworm** is so called because it travels in veritable insect armies to consume everything in its path and because it does not appear until fall in the North. The larvae vary greatly in color, from light tan to green to almost black, and have three yellowish white hairlines down the back from head to tail. On each side is a dark stripe paralleled below by a wavy yellow one, splotched with red. The head is marked with a prominent white V or Y. They eat leaves, stems, and buds of plants. For control measures, see armyworm under CORN.

Harlequin Bug

The very visible **harlequin bug** [color] is black with brilliant orange to red markings. It is shield-shaped, flat and ⅜ inch long. Although attractive to the eye, the bug has a disagreeable odor at all stages. Some authorities consider it the most important pest of the cabbage family in the United States, as local infestations often destroy whole crops, especially in the South. The bugs spend the winter around old plants and other trash that accumulates in the garden. In early spring they lay their eggs on the underside of early blooming plants. The distinctive eggs are easy to spot—they look like small white pegs with black loops, standing on end, lined in two neat rows. Look for and destroy these eggs whenever possible; if allowed to hatch, the immature nymphs drain the juices out of the plants, causing them to wilt, turn brown, and die.

It is possible to plant a trap crop of turnips or mustard greens near or around the cabbage patch so that the harlequin bugs will be lured away from the desirable cole crops. Patrol the trap area, remove the bugs, and drop them into a jar of water topped with kerosene. To eliminate most of the harlequin bug trouble before it starts, keep down weeds in and near the garden. Sabadilla and pyrethrum, two plant-derived, commercially available bug battlers, will handle the pests.

Cabbage/Cabbage Worm

The bright green, velvety smooth **imported cabbageworm** [color] is covered with close-set hairs and grows to one inch or longer. No member of the cabbage family is safe from its appetite, although sea kale is rarely bothered. It eats huge ragged holes in leaves and spots the feeding area with bits of excrement. It also bores into heads of cabbage. The adult is the well-known white cabbage butterfly, whose white to pale yellow wings have either three or four black spots; the tips of the front wings are grayish. In the early spring, these butterflies may be seen depositing their yellow, bullet-shaped eggs at the base of leaves. The eggs usually take from four to eight days to hatch, depending on temperatures. After being laid, they are pale in color, turning to a straw-yellow just before hatching.

The weather has a lot to do with how much trouble these caterpillars will give you. According to Hilde Atema of the New Alchemy Institute, they can drown during heavy rains.

Companion planting may be used to advantage against the cabbageworm. Inez Grant of Columbia, Maine, has her own system: "We plant all our cole plants together for protection from insects. Simply by surrounding the row in plants such as tomatoes and sage which are shunned by the cabbage butterfly, we avoid pest trouble. This moth and resulting green worm that hatches from its eggs used to be a real problem for us until we read about and started using this method of control." Further interplanting methods are recommended by Beatrice Trum Hunter in her valuable book, *Gardening Without Poisons*. She suggests that tansy, sown around cabbage plants, can repel cabbageworms and cutworms. Also, plantings of rosemary, sage, nasturtium, catnip mint, southernwood, hemp, or hyssop will protect crucifers against white cabbage butterflies. Onions and garlic may be planted as borders around beds of cabbage and its relatives. D. J. Young, a southern Louisiana gardener, has devised a companion planting system to deal with severe looper damage. He prepares a fertile bed with a mixture of compost and manure worked in the ground, and marks with small stakes the spots where he will eventually transplant his cabbage plants. Between each stake he plants two garlic cloves about two inches apart. When the garlic has grown to a height of two inches, the cabbages are transplanted, giving the young vegetables immediate protection.

Insect predators and parasites claim a lot of these pests, but don't expect too much help from the birds around your garden; because of toxic body fluids, the caterpillars aren't favorite foods. Hilde Atema says that brown-headed cowbirds, song sparrows, and redwing blackbirds eat some cabbageworms. Yellow jacket hornets have been found to thrive on these pests, and their presence should not be discouraged. The braconid wasps *Macrocentrus ancylivorus* and *Agathis diversa* are extremely helpful control agents. They are small insects with short abdomens, and rank as important parasites of aphids too. Numbers of dead aphids about the garden with a round hole in the back testify to the presence of these wasps. You can encourage *M. ancylivorus* by planting strawberries near the garden, as it also feeds on the strawberry

leaf roller, and by avoiding poison sprays. Another friend, the
trichogramma wasp, is a commercially available parasite that
attacks many worms of the lepidoptera order, including the
cabbageworm. This wasp lays its eggs inside the eggs of harmful
insects by the use of a pointed egg-laying apparatus. When the
trichogramma egg hatches, the young parasite proceeds to eat out
the contents of the egg in which it lives, causing the egg to blacken
and preventing it from adding one more harmful insect to the
garden. See TRICHOGRAMMA. To supplement this natural
help, you can control the cabbageworm by the use of a number
of homemade, non-toxic sprays. Dorothy Schroede of Lyons,
Colorado, has made her cabbages distasteful to this pest and the
cabbage butterfly by spooning a little sour milk into the center of
each cabbage. "That for me was the perfect solution," she says.
"Skim milk soured with vinegar is cheap, quick to make, and easy
to apply; its effect endures for the greater part of a week; it
doesn't drive away friendly bugs or birds, and it keeps butterflies
off as well as do the sharper vegetable sprays." Another repellent
drench can be made by blending, in a mixer, spearmint, green
onion tops, garlic, horseradish root and leaves, hot red peppers,
peppercorns, and water. Add some pure soap, dilute, and pour on
each plant. Another organic gardener, Ms. Margaret Bean, makes
a powder of ½ cup of salt and one cup of flour and shakes it on
the cabbages while dew is still on the leaves. She sprinkles up to
an ounce on the worst heads. When the worms eat the mixture
they bloat up and fall off dead. These two ingredients can also be
mixed with water to produce a safe spray. Other gardeners get
by with just an occasional sprinkle from a saltshaker. This should
be done right after rain or when there is dew on the plants. A
simple dusting powder can be made by stirring up one quart
of wood ashes to one cup of flour. You can also try sprinkling the
cabbage plant with rye flour when dew is still on the plants.
Usually one pint will cover all the plants in a small garden. Inspect
the garden later in the day, and you'll find the cabbage moths and
worms all gummed up with dough. And when the sun bakes these
ensnared pests to hard pastries, they die.

Protective canopies of lightweight polyethylene or nylon
netting can keep egg-laying cabbageworm moths from tender
young broccoli and cabbage plants. The netting is easy to stretch
over rows and is available from most garden supply stores and
mail-order houses. Simple frames of wood can be constructed to
support the netting. Although the netting will keep butterflies
from laying eggs on the plants, the pupae spend the winter under-

ground and often surface around the plants to cause trouble. Tilling the soil several times in fall and early spring will expose these pupae to the air so that they will dry up and die. You should also relocate the patch to keep from perpetuating problems with these latent underground pests. Some gardeners trap cabbage loopers in sheets of colored plastic that are folded twice and placed on the ground every three days or so. The captives are then shaken into a bucket of water.

Not all of the many worm pests of the cabbage and its relatives can be discussed here, but a few of occasional or regional importance deserve mention. Control as for the imported cabbageworm, above. The yellow, purple-striped gulf white cabbageworm feeds on the leaves, stems, and the outer layers of leaves of cabbage heads; they also enjoy collards. In the Northeast and Utah, the larva of the purplebacked cabbage moth feeds from inside a silken web. The zebra caterpillar is a velvety black with two bright yellow stripes on each side and many thin, yellow transverse lines. The southern cabbageworm looks similar to the imported cabbageworm, but its appearance is distinguished by alternating longitudinal stripes of bright yellow and dark greenish purple, and it is scattered with black spots. The yellow woolybear caterpillar is bright yellow and very hairy.

You may find any of several species of the nocturnal **mole cricket** eating or flying about the garden at night or on very cloudy days. They may be drawn to lights near the garden. The northern and southern mole cricket are the species of most concern to gardeners. They are large (1¼ inches long) and have sturdy shovellike forelegs that are adapted for digging into the soil. The northern species is brownish gray above and paler underneath, while the southern is a pinkish buff. Both species are a problem only in the South, and are at their worst in warm, moist weather. Their tunnel cuts off the roots of seedlings, and some young plants may be totally uprooted. Moles may also chew off stems at the soil surface and pull the plants down into their tunnels. See GRASSHOPPER.

The **seed-corn maggot** also attacks young cucurbits, especially cabbage and radishes. They are dirty yellowish white, ¼ inch long, and have pointed head ends. For control measures, see cabbage maggots, above.

The malodorous green **stink bug** is smooth oval, bright green, and about ½ inch long. They are occasional pests of cabbage and mustard, piercing stems and leaves to suck sap and leaving tiny

Stink Bug

holes in the center of surrounding cloudy spots. Small affected plants are stunted and distorted. Control by keeping down weeds. See SNAPDRAGONS.

Vegetable Weevil

The **vegetable weevil** is a dull buff color with a pale V on its wing covers. The head has a short broad snout. They are ⅜ inch long, rarely fly, and attack cabbage, carrots, cauliflower, mustard, radish, and swiss chard. The adults devour foliage at night and hide close to the ground during the day. The green or cream-colored larvae are also destructive. They grow to ½ inch long, and their yellowish brown heads are patterned with brown dotted lines. Control by rotating crops, and destroy the underground pupae by cultivating; keep the garden clear of weeds and trash, as these provide homes for resting weevils, which become inactive as the summer progresses.

Diseases

Black leg is a fungal dry rot that affects most crucifers. Like black rot, this disease is seed-borne and can live over in plant debris for one or two years. Spots appear on the leaves, starting as inconspicuous, indefinite areas and becoming well-defined dark patches in which many tiny black dots are scattered. Similar spots appear on cabbage stems, and the plant may wilt or even topple over as the head grows. Edges of the leaves of affected plants will wilt and turn bluish or red. Seed produced by such plants is affected. The disease spores are spread by the action of dew and rain; consequently, blackleg damage is great only in humid, rainy weather. For control, see black rot, below.

Cabbage/Black Rot

Disease troubles are not unusual in the cabbage patch, and one of the more common is **black rot**, a bacterial affliction that appears on the leaves of any crucifer as yellow, wedge-shaped areas with darkened veins. The leaves then wilt, and severely affected young plants may not produce heads. Heads on more mature plants finally rot. There are some points of confusion brought about by the resemblance between black rot and yellows, described below. The chief points of distinction are: the veins and vascular bundles of leaves and stems in yellows tend to be brown while those in black rot are black and bad-smelling; and soft rot of cabbage heads commonly follows black rot but seldom yellows. Black rot is carried by insects, spattering rain, or surface water—it is primarily a wet-weather disease. The bacteria live over in the soil, in plant refuse, or in seed from diseased plants. After transplanting, infected plants may grow normally with little or no sign of disease for three to six weeks. Thereafter, in midseason, plantings of cauliflower or cabbage may suddenly show a rather large percentage of plants with black rot.

If black rot has been a serious problem, control by treating the seed with hot water before it is planted. Great care should be taken, however, for excessive heat is likely to somewhat reduce germination. Place the seed in a cheesecloth sack and immerse it in water held at a constant 122°F. for 15 to 20 minutes. Keep the water continuously agitated, and maintain the temperature by frequently adding hot water, being careful not to apply it directly to the seed. At the end of the treatment, immerse the seed in cold water, drain, and spread in a thin layer to dry. Seed that is produced in areas with little or no rainfall (such as California and some other Pacific Coast regions) is free of black rot infection, and need not be treated by the hot water method. You can also lessen chances of black rot infection by eliminating the conditions in which it can live over. Use clean seedbeds, removing plant refuse from the garden area. Because black rot can live in the soil for one or possibly two northern winters, grow non-cruciferous crops for two seasons on a former cabbage patch, or sterilize the soil between cruciferous crops. If the seedlings are watered artificially, avoid sprinkling the foliage, since this helps to spread the black rot bacteria. Irrigate in the furrows between rows, if possible.

Plants affected with **club root** have yellowed leaves that wilt on hot days and may recover at night. Eventually, the plants may become stunted or die. The roots are enlarged and grotesquely misshapen with club-shaped swellings that later rot and become slimy. Such roots are unable to absorb nutrients and water, and this causes the above-soil symptoms. The most susceptible cucurbits are cabbage, Chinese cabbage, brussels sprouts, some turnips, and mustard. Generally, most turnips and rutabaga varieties aren't troubled, but no member of the cabbage family is safe. The club root fungus is spread mainly on infected manure or plant refuse, and on soil clinging to shoes and tools. It's not seed-borne.

Club Root

To keep club root fungus out of your garden, use only healthy seedlings for transplanting. Club root is most dangerous to plants growing in acid or neutral soil (pH of 5 to 7.2); add lime or other basic substances as needed. Weeds related to the cabbage family may carry the disease. Cabbage maggot fly repellent, mentioned above, helps to prevent club root; mix old whitewash lime with wood ashes, and sprinkle around cabbage stems. The New York State College of Agriculture reports one available resistant variety, Badger Shipper, a globe-type cabbage.

Crucifer seedlings in the seedbed may be affected by **downy mildew** [color]; the disease rarely occurs in the field. Look for small, grayish or purplish lesions on leaves, petioles, and stems. Close inspection of these affected areas reveals the downy growth, either white or purplish in color. The affected areas later enlarge, turn yellow, and finally the leaves dry up and drop off. Downy mildew tends to spread very rapidly in cool, humid weather, and most seedlings in a seedbed may be ruined in a few days. Helen Philbrick and Richard Gregg, in *Companion Plants,* suggest spraying a tea made of dried horsetail leaves and stems. Called Equisetum tea for the plant's Latin name, it is brewed by boiling 1½ ounces of the dried herb for 20 minutes in one gallon of cold water. Horsetail is also known as meadow pine, because it looks like a small pine tree.

Leaf spot is a bacterial disease that causes small, gray to brown spots on cauliflower heads. These spots later develop into soft rot. Cabbage shows spots that first appear water-soaked and later grow in size and length, taking on a brownish or purplish gray color. The best means of control is to use seeds grown in western states where the disease does not occur. Seeds can be treated in hot (122°F.) water for 30 minutes, with fair to good results.

Rhizoctonia is a fungal soil disease that chiefly attacks young succulent tissue and dormant storage tissue. There are numerous strains, which vary in the hosts that they attack. Rhizoctonia disease has many effects on cruciferous crops, for it attacks them at different stages: damping-off and wire stem can attack young seedlings; bottom rot occurs in midseason; head rot develops between early head formation and maturity as a dark, firm decay at the base of the outer leaves and heads; root rot occurs before harvest and in storage. The important control measures are to sort out the plants that have wire stem and to avoid planting crucifers in short rotations where bottom, head, and root rot have occurred.

Cabbage seedlings in seedbeds are also apt to be damaged by **seed rot** (or damping-off), caused by soil-inhabiting fungi. Stems of young seedlings will show a water-soaked appearance at the ground line, and young plants soon topple over and die. Control can be effected by using only soil possessed of good texture and plenty of organic nutrients. It is also helpful to rotate the outdoor seedbeds, to avoid sowing too thickly, and to be careful to water no more than necessary.

Turnip anthracnose is primarily a disease of the turnip, although it affects other crucifers, including mustard, rutabaga, radish, and Chinese cabbage. Signs of this malady are many roughly circular spots on the leaves, first water-soaked and later drying up and becoming brown. The dead tissue in the center of the spots often falls out, giving a shot-hole effect to the leaves. The petiole may show elongated gray or brown spots. This fungus is seed-borne and starts from a few infected seeds. Plants set in cool weather are usually safe from turnip anthracnose. Southern Curled Giant is highly resistant, says Cynthia Westcott in *Plant Disease Handbook*.

Virus infection of cauliflower seedlings is minimized by growing three narrow rows of barley as a barrier crop, according to R. E. F. Matthews in *Plant Virology*.

Watery soft rot is a fungal disease common to many garden crops. It causes cabbage and cauliflower heads to collapse with a very soft type of rot. The first symptom may be a white, cottony growth; this gives rise to black, hard bodies called sclerotia. These growths then fall to the soil, where they lie dormant until the next season. It is a cool weather affliction, and the spores are encouraged by very humid conditions.

While there is no truly effective means of control for watery soft rot, removal of affected plants before the sclerotia can fall should help. Rotation is of little avail, since this fungus attacks so many other vegetables. Destruction is rarely widespread, however, affecting individual plants and not whole fields.

The **yellows** disease (also known as fusarium yellows or wilt) is somewhat notorious and appears in many backyard gardens. Yellows is a warm-weather problem, and is almost completely checked when the average soil temperature is below 60°F. As temperatures of soil and air rise, the disease becomes more virulent. However, when the average temperature reaches 90°F. or above, yellows development is retarded. It is caused by a soil-borne fungus, and affects cabbage plants at any age—seedlings wilt and older plants lose their vitality as leaves yellow. (Symptoms are similar for other cucurbits.) Lower leaves are the first to turn yellow, then brown, and finally drop, leaving the bare stem exposed. The heads may become stunted and bitter, but are usually not rotted. The plants become stunted, and the vascular bundles turn brown. The symptoms of yellows and the aforementioned black rot are very similar, and the two diseases may easily be confused: the most reliable distinguishing feature is that black rot turns leaf veins black, instead of brown.

Yellows has been known to live in the soil for as long as

20 years. As a result, crop rotation is usually not a satisfactory control. The rapidity with which the disease spreads depends on the degree of susceptibility of the host plant and the favorableness of the environment. In the area where yellows is most severe (from Long Island to Colorado, including the southern parts of New York, Michigan, Wisconsin, and Minnesota and southward as far as cabbage is grown as a summer crop), the optimum conditions for the development of the disease usually prevail during the first three or four weeks after the transplanting of the main crop of cabbage. On resistant plants or susceptible plants in cool weather, the disease may only cause a leaf or two to drop, after which the plants may very well recover and produce normal heads. Early varieties, although very susceptible, often escape the disease. The right conditions for yellows may not appear until the early crop of cabbage is reaching maturity. Fortunately there are a number of resistant varieties, and yellows has ceased to be a problem in some areas. Use only resistant varieties that are appropriate for your region.

Camellia

Camellias are subject to many pests and diseases. If your camellias have had trouble in the past, look to the condition of the soil as both the source of and solution to your problems. These flowers thrive best in a well-drained soil to which manure or other humus material has been added. Mulching camellias encourages the vigorous growth that gives plants the strength to fight insects and diseases. It's a good idea to plant them in light shade, where there is little danger of damage from heat reflected off walls or sidewalks.

Insects

Among the insects that attack camellias in the garden is the **fuller rose beetle** (or **weevil**), a grayish brown beetle with a cream-colored stripe on each side, growing to ⅓ inch long. It feeds on the edges of leaves at night, and spends the day hidden in twigs, foliage, and flowers. Since this pest is wingless, sticky barriers around the base of the camellia trunk or branches may be enough to keep them from crawling to the leaves. Also see ROSES.

In flower gardens east of the Rockies, the small, shining bronze **rhabdopterous beetle** makes itself known as a nocturnal pest. Adults eat long, narrow holes in young foliage. If you tend to be nocturnal yourself, try handpicking with the aid of a flash-light. Otherwise, use a garlic-based botanical on camellia foliage.

The **root-knot nematode** is a microscopic, wormlike pest that is best combatted by adding plenty of organic matter to the soil; some fungi that inhabit rich soil are lethal to this pest. Avoid growing susceptible plants near camellias. See NEMATODE.

Camellias suffer from a number of **scale insects**, including the camellia scale, parlatoria scale, and tea scale. When scales attack, foliage becomes weak and may drop from the plant. Some of the scale can be scraped off by hand, but the most effective control procedure is spraying with oil. Use any of the safe, refined oil emulsions at a strength of about two percent ($2\frac{1}{2}$ ounces to a gallon of water). It is best to spray in late winter and early spring. Be sure to cover all parts of the plant for thorough control.

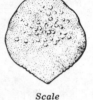

Scale

Other pests include the fuller rose weevil (see ROSE), MEALYBUGS, and SPIDER MITES.

Diseases

During winters, large numbers of buds may fall, with the edges of young petals turning brown and decaying. Some varieties suffer much more from **bud drop** than do other varieties. The cause has been attributed to severe frost in September and October, to severe freezing weather during the winter, and to an irregular water supply.

Make sure that the plants don't suffer from a lack of water. Cover them to give protection from sharp frosts and freezes. Avoid watering late in the season, so that little new (and vulner-able) growth will have to face the cold. Mulching will help to maintain uniform soil temperatures and a water supply through the winter.

Camellia dieback (canker) is a widespread disease that causes tips to die back and leaves to wilt and turn brown. Stems may turn brown and become girdled. Infection can occur on buds killed by freezing, so remove dead buds promptly. All dead twigs and stems with canker should be clipped off and burned.

Flower blight [color] is potentially the most serious disease of camellias. The first symptoms are small brown spots that quickly enlarge to cover the entire petal. The veins are usually darker brown than the surrounding petal tissue. Later, a hard, dark brown or black body forms in the base of the flower or in individual petals. These "sclerotia" may resemble a petal or miniature flower in shape. The sclerotia remain dormant during winter, and as the flowering season approaches they produce saucerlike objects from which the spores are shot into the air. Sclerotia can lie dormant in the soil for at least three years before germinating.

This disease has sometimes been confused with frost injury, which browns only the outer or marginal portion of flowers or petals. In the South, areas known to harbor camellia flower blight are often quarantined. Northern growers should be on guard against purchasing diseased plants. It's best to buy barefooted plants from which all buds have been picked; on balled plants, discard the upper two or three inches of soil. Once this disease hits, remove all flowers, both from the bush and those on the ground, and burn them. If flowers have already decayed on the ground, remove and discard the upper three inches of soil or mulch.

Leaf yellowing may be either an environmental condition or a disease caused by a virus. In the former case, the variegations usually follow a uniform and rather typical pattern that is more or less similar on all leaves. On the other hand, the yellow areas caused by virus are irregular and vary on different leaves, branches, and plants; affected plants grow rather normally, but the leaves are more susceptible to sunburn and frost injury than are normal leaves.

Rogue out any plant suspected of virus infection. Propagators should be extremely careful to use virus-free rootstock for grafting.

Root rot is a fungus disease that results in a gradual wilting, yellowing, and death of one or more branches. Affected leaves may fall prematurely. Small plants and cuttings succumb more rapidly than older plants, and varieties differ in their resistance. Diseased plants should be discarded and the soil prepared to provide good drainage.

Faded green or brown dead areas on leaves may be the result of **sunburn**. Symptoms are most common on the upper and exposed sides of bushes. If affected areas are subsequently attacked by fungi, they may change color and fall out.

Sunburn strikes when plants accustomed to partial shade are exposed to bright sunlight. This may come about by transplanting to a sunny spot, by turning bushes around so that the former north side is facing south, or by removing overhanging branches. In winter, bright days combined with cold soil may dry the leaves to produce similar symptoms; the problem here is that the leaves lose more water than is absorbed by the roots. You can help by providing partial shading in winter months.

Campanula

This flower is particularly susceptible to the foxglove **aphid**, a shining, light green insect with dark green patches around the base of its cornicles. Its feeding results in yellowed or blanched spots, leaf curling, and a distortion of leaves that resembles virus disease. See APHID.

Campanula may also be bothered by onion thrips (see ONION) and SLUGS AND SNAILS.

Canna

Insects

Two species of **canna leaf roller** fold or roll leaves, tie them up with webs, and feed within them. Foliage often becomes ragged and brown, and leaves may die. One caterpillar is pale green, set off by a dark orange head, and reaches a length of 1¾ inches; the other is greenish white and measures one inch when fully grown. They are a problem in the southeastern states, south of Washington, D.C.

The caterpillars can be killed by pinching rolled leaves. Clean up and burn plant refuse in fall, and remove affected plant parts.

Other insects that may cause trouble are the corn earworm (see CHRYSANTHEMUM), fuller rose beetle (ROSE), goldsmith beetle (ROSE), and saddleback caterpillar (ROSE).

Diseases

One of the most troublesome diseases affecting canna is **canna bud rot**, recognized by water-soaked leaves that darken and spread to form brown ragged areas. Flowers may be killed by the infection of young buds or the stem. Prevent this disease by buying healthy rootstalks, spacing plants, and watering carefully to keep new growth dry.

Cantaloupe (Muskmelon)

Insects

Holes in fruit may be the work of the **pickleworm** [color]. This is a white to greenish, ¾-inch-long caterpillar, marked with a brown head. Look for sawdustlike frass at the holes.

Late crops are most susceptible to the pickleworm. A trap

Pickleworm

crop of squash will lure away these pests, but be sure the vines are disposed of before the worms leave the squash blossoms. Clear the melon patch of all plant debris immediately after harvest, and cultivate at this time to destroy pupae.

High on the list of pests that bother cantaloupes is the **striped cucumber beetle** [color]. In the adult stage, it is yellow to black with three black stripes down the back, and grows to about ⅕ inch long. The larva is white, slender, brownish at the ends, and about ⅓ inch long. Adults not only feed on leaves, stems and fruit, but are responsible for spreading bacterial wilt as well. Larvae bore into the roots and also feed on the stems below the soil line; they usually attack young plants, causing them to wilt and sometimes die. The beetle is most common east of the Rocky Mountains.

Cucumber/Striped Cucumber Beetle

It is important that cantaloupes get a good start on the season. One gardener suggests applying directly to the plants a mixture of 75 percent colloidal phosphate and 25 percent wood ashes. The powder will adhere to plants better if they are still wet with the morning dew. The mixture can also be worked into the ground around the plants during hoeing and cultivating.

Radishes interplanted among melons will discourage the beetle. See also CUCUMBER.

Other pests include those that infest SQUASH, and APHIDS, the grape colapsis (see GRAPE), potato flea beetle (POTATO), and SPIDER MITES.

Diseases

Curly top of muskmelon is caused by the same virus responsible for curly top of beets. The young leaves of diseased plants are stunted and curled, but may be normal in color; the older leaves are often yellow. The stems are shorter than normal so that the plants are stunted and bushy. Infected plants usually fail to produce fruit, and under some conditions they may be killed. The virus is transmitted from beets to muskmelons by the beet leafhopper (see BEET). Where this virus is known to have occurred, keep down nearby weed hosts. Rogue out infected plants. Avoid planting muskmelons near sugar beets.

Fusarium wilt causes the vines to suddenly wilt away, sometimes almost overnight, and for no apparent reason. The disease is caused by a fungus that is spread by the yellow-and-black striped cucumber beetle; if the plants are protected from the beetles, they will be protected from wilt. Tender shoots can be protected by placing hot caps over the hills when the seedlings are young. Tents of cheesecloth or mosquito netting may be spread over the hills until the plants are large enough not to tempt the beetles. Resistant varieties include Golden Gopher and Iriquois.

Leaf spot is a fungus living on diseased remains of vines in the soil. It causes numerous brown spots on the leaves, many of which may be killed. There is no spotting of the fruit.

Be certain to destroy diseased vines so that the virus organism will not perpetuate itself. It is good practice to grow melons or cucumbers no more often than once in three years in the same soil.

Mosaic can be brought on by a host of viruses to cause chlorosis, stunting, and reduction of yield. The most commonly observed symptoms are mottled leaves which have dark green, light green, or yellow areas of irregular form. The leaves are often irregular in shape and portions of the veins may be killed. The vine tips are often stunted and yellowish. Under certain conditions, stem growth may continue while that of the leaves does not, producing a condition known as rat-tail. Less readily observed is the abortion of flowers of all ages. Flowers that appear normal to casual observation often have aborted anthers and scant pollen. Fruit may appear normal, or they may be mottled, small, or misshapen. Fruit not affected directly by the virus are often low in quality or sunburned, or they may have poorly formed net. These indirect effects result from lack of sufficient foliage to supply food and to cover the plants. Losses are slight if the plants are not infected until melons reach harvest maturity, but severe losses may result if infected earlier.

Although many varieties of muskmelons and cantaloupes are susceptible, Honey Dew and Honey Ball are less affected than others. Control in the absence of other sources of infection can be maintained by using seed that is free from the virus or by carefully roguing at the thinning stage. The virus can be transferred from one plant to another by your hands. Keep down weeds in the vicinity.

Powdery mildew [color] grows on the surfaces of the leaves and stems, sending minute feeding organs into the host tissues. This disease can be recognized by the powdery white growth on the stems and both surfaces of the leaves. Infected leaves and stems may remain alive for indefinite periods, or they may become brown and die. Severely attacked plants become weak and non-thrifty and produce few or no melons. The melons may be small or malformed or they may be normal in shape. Large melons often have poor net and poor flavor, and may be sunburned.

Resistant varieties are available; consult your extension agent for an up-to-date list. Dusting with sulfur will take care of mildew, but only certain varieties can be dusted without an adverse reaction. Cantaloupe varieties tolerant to sulfur have been developed.

Cape-Jasamine

Southern growers of this plant are often bothered by the **Florida wax scale**, distinguished by a thick, waxy covering on a reddish brown body; the covering is sometimes tinted pink. This scale lives on stems, and causes plants to become stunted. A dormant-oil spray, applied before growth starts in spring, should take care of this pest.

Other pests include the fuller rose beetle (see ROSE) and WHITE FLY.

Carnation

Insects

A number of **aphids** infest young leaves and buds. They do the most damage in greenhouses. See APHID.

The **variegated cutworm** is a common pest of greenhouse carnations in fall, when they climb stems and eat holes in the buds. The adult is a moth with a wingspan of up to two inches, and displays brownish gray forewings. The caterpillar is light brown, mottled with darker brown. Normally there are two annual generations out-of-doors, but there may be more in the greenhouse environment. For control measures, see CUTWORM.

Other insect pests include the cabbage looper (see CABBAGE), flower thrips (PEONY), fuller rose beetle (ROSE), celery leaf tier (CELERY), MEALYBUGS, SLUGS AND SNAILS, and SPIDER MITES.

Diseases

Whitish spots on leaves may mean a fungus infection, one that is capable of invading the branch and causing death of the plant above the infected part. Known as **alternaria leaf spot** and **branch rot**, this disease is controlled by watering the soil, not the plant, to keep foliage dry. Soil that is rich in organic matter will mete out water as it is needed.

Bacterial wilt causes wilting of plants and shoots, accompanied by splitting of the stems at the joints and by yellow streaks in the vascular system. Tissue just under the epidermis is sticky, and cutting across the stem shows discoloration and a bacterial ooze. The disease appears to spread rapidly at high temperatures. Although the parasite works internally, it is spread by splashing. Use clean cuttings, rogue affected plants, and water carefully.

Botrytis flower rot causes a brown spotting or rot of flowers. The gray mold you may see growing over these brown spots is the fruiting stage of the fungus. Since the fungus fruits on dead plant material at the base of the plants, it is nearly impossible to eliminate the sources of infection. Keep moisture from condensing on flowers by turning on the heat one-half hour before sundown, especially during late winter.

The fungus disease **bud rot** is carried by small mites. It causes buds to shrivel, and the resultant blooms are unhealthy and malformed. As this disease has been found to flourish under cool, wet conditions, it's advisable to hold off the planting of susceptible varieties until the warm weather has somewhat alleviated the danger of cold nights. Be certain to avoid overwatering, and provide plenty of compost. As the plant grows and takes the nourishment from the soil, it builds a resistance that can fight off most of the troubles associated with bud rot. Remember to remove and destroy any diseased buds, so that the disease does not have an opportunity to propagate itself. Buds should also be removed from the ground, because they carry spores that are responsible for the spread of disease.

The first symptom of **fusarium wilt** is a dull green color to plants, which then wilt and eventually turn the color of straw. Cutting across the main stem reveals brown discoloration, sometimes accompanied by a dry, punky rot. A pink mass of spores may be seen on the roots. This wilt is caused by a soil-borne fungus which enters through root wounds and then plugs the water-conducting system to kill the plant. Plants that have been outside are very apt to become infected. The disease may be carried in infected cuttings. It can show up at any time, but is particularly noticeable after rooted cuttings have been planted in flats or benches and in later winter when flower production draws on the strength of the plant.

Soil sterilization is of utmost importance in control of the disease. Use only clean cuttings and sterilized sand in the cutting bench.

Leaf rot is one of the most common diseases of carnations, causing discolorations on the stems and both sides of the leaves.

These discolorations appear most often on the tips of leaves. When most of the plant is afflicted, death usually follows.

Any plant that appears to be suffering from leaf rot should be removed immediately to avoid infecting healthy plants in the vicinity. Use cuttings from healthy plants only, and give the plants plenty of room to allow air to circulate. When watering, avoid wetting the foliage, as wet leaves render a plant vulnerable to the disease.

Pale tan **leaf spots** with purple borders are symptoms of fungal disease. Look for small black fruiting bodies on the surface of the spots to make sure of the cause. The disease is spread by splashing water; if water is syringed on plants, do so early in the day, and use a mulch to discourage splashing. Stick to healthy plants for cuttings.

Mosaic, streak, and **yellows** are virus diseases that may show as light mottling in the leaves (mosaic), red or yellow spots or streaks (streak), or yellows (a combination of both diseases). Streaks in the flowers are either due to mosaic or yellows infection. Use only healthy stock. Take care in disbudding, as these viruses are transmitted by mechanical contact. Keeping down the aphid population will discourage the spread of the viruses; see APHID for means of control.

Carnation **rust** is the agent behind numerous brown pustules that appear over various parts of the plant. The pustules usually start as water blisters on the lower leaves, and burst to discharge a brownish powder that spreads the disease to other parts of the plant as well as to healthy plants.

Rust-resistant varieties are available. Buy only those plants you know to be healthy, as one sickling can quickly spread its misfortune to neighbors. See to it that plants don't have excess moisture on their leaves—it's best to water the ground, not the plants, and to do so early in the day. A soil rich in organic matter will retain moisture around the roots without making puddles. Generally, carnations and dianthuses should be planted in a sunny part of the garden, far enough apart so that air can circulate between them.

Carrots

Insects

Carrots are prone to injury from several **aphids**: among these are the bean, green peach, and corn root aphids. Control is not usually necessary; if you do need help, see APHID.

Carrot Rust Fly
Maggot

The **carrot rust fly** is particularly destructive in the northeastern states and in coastal Washington and Oregon, and also is found in parts of Idaho, Utah, Wyoming, and Colorado. The larvae are yellowish white, legless, and grow up to ⅓ inch long. These maggots hatch from eggs around the carrot crowns, and burrow down into the roots. Their tunnels are rusty in color from the maggots' excrement, which explains the name. Plants may be stunted, and the infestation leads the way for soft-rot bacteria (see below). If this damage is slight, affected parts can be cut out and the carrots used for cooking. Some gardeners prevent maggot troubles by putting used tea leaves in with the carrot seed. If the infestation becomes serious and cannot be controlled by rotating the crop, skip the early planting and do not plant until early summer, after the maggots have died of starvation. This procedure requires that celery plantings also be postponed, as the maggots will otherwise live happily on the celery roots while they wait for the carrots. In the New York City area and similar climates, main crops planted after June 1 will escape the larvae if harvested in early September, before the second brood has hatched. To repel the slender, shiny green carrot fly, some gardeners have successfully tried sprinkling pulverized wormwood around plants. The flies will not lay their eggs at the crowns of plants protected with this homemade pesticide. You have other natural allies—the fly is repelled by adjacent plantings of leek, onion, pennyroyal, rosemary, sage, black salsify (or oyster plant), and coriander.

From Colorado east to Georgia and New England, the **carrot weevil** produces pale, legless, brown-headed grubs. The larval worms grow up to ⅓ inch long, and tunnel into carrot roots. Early carrots are usually the most severely injured. The weevil spends the winter in the adult stage in weedy or grassy areas immediately adjoining old carrot fields. The following May, these adults travel to the nearest host plants.

The adult usually reaches its goal by walking, and thus travels only a short distance; this suggests rotation as a means of control. Avoid replacing them with other crops that are attractive to the weevil, such as parsley, celery, parsnips, and many types of weeds. By cleaning out debris, high grass, and weedy, fallow fields, the pest will have a hard time finding a snug winter home. In spring, destroy any grubs in the soil by cultivating deeply around the area where the carrots are to be planted. Also, be certain to grow your carrots in well-fertilized, organic soil, as the weevil is likely to pass up a healthy carrot in favor of weaker prey.

Carrot Worm

The **carrot worm** (also called carrot caterpillar, parsley worm, and celery worm) is the larval form of the black swallowtail butterfly. The larval form is as bizarre in appearance as the winged adult is beautiful, and both are easy to spot. The two-inch caterpillar is green with a yellow-dotted black band across each segment; when disturbed, it projects two orange horns and emits a strong, cloyingly sweet odor. The well-known black swallowtail has large, black fore wings with three rows of yellow markings parallel to the wing edges, the rear wings also having a blue row, an orange spot each, and the projecting "swallowtail" lobe.

Because the carrot worm population is rarely very great, most gardeners find that early morning handpicking works well enough. Rotenone (or derris) dust is sometimes used in serious cases.

A serious mycoplasmic disease, aster yellows, is spread by the **six-spotted leafhopper**, also known as the aster leafhopper. (Mycoplasma are microorganisms that resemble both viruses and bacteria.) The first symptom you are likely to spot is a yellowing of young leaves as they emerge from the crown. Side shoots also take on a jaundiced appearance, and older outside leaves may become bronzed or reddened and twisted. Finally, near the end of the season, the crown becomes blackened and dead. The responsible leafhopper is greenish yellow with six black spots, and grows to $\frac{1}{8}$ inch long.

Because this leafhopper seems to prefer open areas, the planting of carrots near houses or in protected areas may help to prevent infestation. If this is not possible or practical, try enclosing your plants in cheesecloth, muslin, or plastic netting, supported on wooden frames. Pyrethrum can be dusted onto the carrot tops. Avoid planting carrots near lettuce or asters.

Vegetable Weevil

If southern gardeners find holes appearing overnight in carrot foliage, a prime suspect is the **vegetable weevil**. This pest is a dull buff color and has a pale V on its wing covers. The head has a sharp, broad snout. It is $\frac{3}{8}$ inch in length, rarely flies, and does its dirty work at night. The green or cream-colored larva is also destructive. It grows to $\frac{1}{2}$ inch long and its yellowish brown head is patterned with brown dotted lines. Control by rotating crops, and destroy the underground pupae by cultivating. Keep the garden clear of weeds and trash, which provide homes for nesting weevils as they become inactive as the summer progresses.

Many species of **wireworm** dine on carrots, puncturing and tunneling roots. They are so called because they resemble jointed wires. Color varies from white to yellow to brown—they get darker as they grow longer. For control of this ubiquitous pest, see WIREWORM.

Carrots also fall prey to a number of relatively minor pests: MILLIPEDES, onion bulb fly, THRIPS, webworms (see parsnip webworm under PARSNIP), and yellow woolybear caterpillar (imported cabbageworm under CABBAGE).

Diseases

In the South, carrots are grown during the cool months of the year when most of their parasites are not very active, and southern gardeners should therefore not have any serious problems with diseases of this crop.

Carrot seeds are vulnerable to **damping-off**, which causes the watery soft rot of stem tissue at the ground line. Roots may become infected, turn black, and rot, and the seedlings themselves later become yellowed and die. Adequate spacing of plants should prevent this trouble.

Fusarium root rot primarily affects cucurbits, but may also cause a spongy rot of carrots that are stored at temperatures above 45°F. The rot fungi enter through wounds and bruises in the root, causing shallow, scabby spots on the taproot. The following methods of control are recommended: crop rotations omitting root crops; avoiding injury to the roots at harvest; cleanliness of storage rooms or areas; and if possible, storage at approximately 32°F.

Leaf blight on carrot foliage first appears as yellow to white spots, irregular in shape, on the margins of seedling leaves. These spots quickly become brown, and take on a water-soaked appearance. Spots may also girdle slender taproots, resulting in the death of the root below the infected spot. Affected roots may appear water-soaked, and sometimes have lesions, dark spots, craters, or pustules. The flower cluster of seed plants may have both blasted seeds and seeds capable of germination that will transmit the infection. Infected parts of the flower cluster become discolored and may die.

To avoid blight, plant only seeds that have been treated by the hot water method, at 126°F. for ten minutes. There is no dust or disinfectant that will kill the bacterium of the blight inside the seed without injuring the embryo. A four-year schedule of crop rotation, good garden cultivation, and sufficient spacing between plants will all aid control. Also, good healthy soil encourages the root system to develop and feed nutrients that are used for fighting off the disease symptoms.

Tiny nematodes in the soil cause **root knot**. The small knots or galls form on the lateral roots and rootlets, and small pimplelike swellings in the taproot enlarge and roughen the surface. Plants are often stunted and chlorotic (yellowed or blanched in appearance), but the knots are the only dependable symptom.

Rotation of carrots with nematode-resistant crops will sufficiently reduce the nematode population so that at least one crop of carrots may be successfully grown. Such resistant crops include small grains, hegari, some cowpeas, and velvet beans. Sometimes they must be grown for three or four years before a satisfactory decline in nematodes is noticed. See also NEMATODE.

Vegetable soft rot is an infamous bacterial disease that affects many vegetables, causing heavy damage. The disease is characterized by a soft, slimy rot of the taproot that is distinguished from other rots by a foul, sulfurous odor. Infected tissues are discolored gray or brown, and either the tender lower end or the crown may be affected. Leaves often wilt or turn yellow in the late stages of the disease. Soft rot is favored by hot humid weather, and is caused by bacteria in the soil.

Rotation of the rows often prevent vegetable soft rot in the garden, but the disease can also occur in storage. For this problem, it is advisable to discard at harvest those roots which are bruised or otherwise damaged, and to store the crop in a cool, dry, clean place. Carrots should only be packed in containers that allow some ventilation.

Castor Bean

The castor bean plant is valued by gardeners for its lushly tropic appearance, as a means of discouraging moles from tunnelling in the garden, and as a companion plant that keeps insects from vine crops. Because of its size (8 to 12 feet high), the castor bean is better suited for field plantings of vine crops than small gardens. Children should be warned not to eat the toxic seeds. Castor oil concentrates the noxious properties of the plant. To make a repellent solution that can be sprinkled from a watering can, mix a tablespoon of the oil with two tablespoons of liquid detergent in a blender until the product has the appearance of shaving cream, and add to warm water in a sprinkling can. Sprinkle the liquid wherever moles are causing trouble. It penetrates the soil best after a rain shower.

Garden Webworm

Insects

Although the castor bean is used as a repellent, it has a modest list of its own pests. The hairy **garden webworm** spins light webbing over plants and feeds on the foliage underneath. It is a light green, inch-long worm with small, dark green spots, and hides within a silken tube on the ground. Growers in the Midwest and Southwest are particularly bothered by the garden webworm. Cut off and destroy webbed branches; handpick feeding webworms, and step on those hiding in their silken tubes.

The black-and-yellow southern armyworm may bring castor beans to grief; see CELERY. Other possible troublemakers are the corn earworm (see CHRYSANTHEMUM), potato leafhopper (POTATO), serpentine leaf miner (PEPPER), and SPIDER MITE.

Catalpa

Insects

Trees may be defoliated by the **catalpa sphinx**, a brown or green caterpillar about 2¼ inches long. There are two broods of the sphinx, one in June and another in August or September. If you find any caterpillars crawling on the limbs of trees, handpick and crush them. Generally, this is all that is needed, for there are many parasites of the sphinx that keep the insect under control naturally.

San José Scale

Presence of the **comstock mealybug** is often made known by patches of white in cracks in the bark. See MEALYBUG.

San José scale occasionally hits catalpa. See LILAC.

Diseases

Certain fungi may cause brown circular **leaf spots** on tree foliage. Infected tissue within the spots often drops, leaving holes in the leaves and causing premature leaf fall to follow. Good garden housekeeping is needed to aid materially in control. Collect, remove, and burn or compost all dead leaves that may harbor disease-producing fungi. If leaves are composted instead of burned, they should be piled in alternate layers with soil. Be sure that any leaves left exposed are covered completely with soil.

Verticillium wilt may cause one or several branches to wilt. Purple to bluish brown streaks in sapwood of wilted branches indicate the presence of this disease. For control, see TREES: DISEASES.

Cauliflower

In general, the insects and diseases that harm cauliflower are also injurious to cabbage; see CABBAGE. Insect pests seem to prefer green to purple cauliflower. Although the purple variety doesn't sell as well at the roadside stand because of its odd appearance, many have found its taste is superior to that of the green.

Cedar (White)

Diseases

When a white cedar suffers **foliage browning,** all the leaves on the inside of the tree turn reddish brown and fall to the ground either in spring or fall. This natural shedding often occurs after a dry season, or it may happen every second or third year, varying with the individual tree and conditions. The discoloration is distinguished from fertilizer burn in the way it hits the inside of the entire tree, whereas fertilizer burn or sunburn due to root injury start at the tip of the branch and work back, generally progressing up the tree from the lowest branches. Red spider mite injury differs too, causing a sudden bronzing of all the leaves on a branch during summer.

Foliage browning or winter bronzing is apparently due to physiological changes in the tree, and is tied in with the tree's nutrition in a way not yet understood. It disappears with the advent of warm weather.

Two types of **gall rust** may infect white cedars. One causes a good-sized spindle-shaped gall; the branch beyond the gall usually dies. The life cycle of this fungus is completed on the leaves of the serviceberry plant, from which come the spores that infect the white cedar. A second type of gall rust, *Gymnosporangium hyalinum,* causes a smaller spindle-shaped gall on white cedar twigs and branches. The infective spores come from the leaves of pears and hawthorn. Cedar-apple rust gall [color] may also damage apple trees in the area.

Pruning and burning of affected parts help control these fungi. If possible, eradicate the alternate host plants—serviceberry, pear, and hawthorn—within a half-mile radius.

Nursery blight is a condition causing tip dieback. It occurs occasionally on white cedar but is much more common and serious on red cedar. A small canker girdles the twig which eventually dies. Control by cutting and burning affected twigs.

A fungus may cause **witches' brooms** to appear at the ends of the branches of white cedar. On young trees the entire top may be broomed. Branches beyond the infection point usually die as soon as the fungus girdles the branch. Cross-sections of infected wood show wedge-shaped brown spots in the wood. In spring, brown horns grow out of the infected area and produce spores that infect bayberry and sweet fern, which in turn produce spores to reinfect the white cedar. The only control known is the eradication of the bayberry and sweet fern.

Celery

Insects

Of several **aphids** known to feed on celery, the green peach aphid is possibly the most common. It is yellow green and bears three dark lines on its back; see APHID.

The larva of the **carrot rust fly** is an occasional celery pest, feeding on the roots of early plants. These ⅓-inch-long worms are yellowish white, legless, and leave rust-colored tunnels as they eat their way through the plant. The adult is a slender, shiny green fly. For habits and controls, see CARROT.

The major pest of celery is the **celery leaf tier** (or greenhouse leaf tier), ravaging a variety of vegetables and ornamentals throughout North America. These caterpillars are initially pale green in color, with a white stripe running the length of their backs and a pale stripe centered within. As they grow to their full length of ¾ inch, their color changes to yellow. The worms eat holes in leaves and stalks, and have the peculiar habit of folding leaves and tieing them together with webs. The adult is a small, brown, nocturnal moth with wings crossed by dark wavy lines. The eggs are laid on the underside of leaves and look like fish scales.

Celery Leaf Tier

Since the leaf tier does not usually appear in gardens in great numbers, gardeners have relied on handpicking to prevent trouble. It's also a good idea to handpick and destroy any leaves that appear damaged or rolled, as a leaf tier may well be sequestered within. *Bacillus thuringiensis* is a commercially available pathogen of this pest. In serious cases, pyrethrum can be applied in its pure state; this botanical poison makes the larvae sick and they then leave their webs. A second dusting should kill them.

Carrot Worm

The **celery worm** is hardly a picky eater, which explains why it is also known as the carrot worm and parsley worm. The adult is the well-known black swallowtail butterfly. Its black wings are marked with three rows of yellow markings parallel to the wing edges, the rear wings having a blue row, orange spot, and characteristic "swallowtail" lobe. The larva worm is as bizarre in appearance as the winged adult is beautiful; reaching a length of two inches, it is green with a yellow-dotted black band across each segment. When disturbed, the worm projects two orange horns from its head and emits a strong, sweetish odor.

Because the celery worm population is rarely very great, most gardeners find that early morning handpicking works well enough. If your celery gets into bad trouble, consider a dusting of rotenone.

If your celery plants are stunted and yellowed and you can find no obvious cause, the plants may be victims of **nematodes** (eelworms). These tiny pests, some of which are too small to be seen with the naked eye, live in the soil and suck juices from celery roots. Roots develop root-knots, or galls, and affected rootlets turn brown. Finally the plants become chlorotic and may die.

Seedbeds should never be located on soil that is known to be infested with nematodes. If it is impossible for you to obtain clean soil, infested soil can sometimes be rendered safe by starving out the nematodes: keep the land fallow for several months and, if practicable, flood the fallow land for two or three months. Nematodes that hatch in such plots will starve to death in a few weeks. An alternative method involves planting the land to resistant cover crops, but this requires that the land be kept free of weeds, as a few weeds can sustain a considerable number of the tiny pests. For more information, see NEMATODE.

The **parsnip webworm** is a small black-spotted caterpillar that webs together and feeds upon unfolding blossom heads of celery. It grows to about ½ inch in length, and varies in color from greenish yellow to gray. When mature, the webworm leaves its web and burrows inside a flower stem to pupate. The gray moths appear late in summer. Damage is usually not serious; control by cutting off infested flower heads.

Gardeners and farmers from South Carolina to Florida may run into the **southern armyworm** at work on their celery. These caterpillars are black or yellow with black markings, and they are luckily susceptible to many natural predators and parasites, including birds, skunks, and toads. The armyworm is so named because in some seasons they attack plants in huge numbers, destroying everything in their path.

An easy, effective way of halting the advance of large numbers of armyworms is suggested in the Philbrick's *The Bug Book*: encircle the garden with a ditch, plowing so that the side nearest to the crops is perpendicular; the worms will be trapped in the entrenchment and may then be crushed, buried, or cremated.

Armyworm

Tiny, oval yellow or green specks swarming over celery leaves are likely two-spotted **spider mites.** They live on the underside of leaves, and suck plant sap; their feeding gives a sickly, blotched appearance. Control is often not necessary, but if you feel the plants need help, see SPIDER MITE.

The **tarnished plant bug** is a nuisance to more than 50 plants including celery. It is shy and will likely hide as you approach, but you may catch a glimpse of a flat, ¼-inch-long insect, colored mottled white and yellow with touches of black that give the wings a tarnished appearance. A very close look will reveal a yellow triangle, with one black tip, on each side of the bug. The nymph is very small, greenish yellow, and marked with black dots on the thorax and abdomen. As it feeds, the adult liberates a plant toxin that may result in black celery joints. Also, look for brown sunken areas on leaves and shoots near the top of the plant. For control methods, see ASTER.

Tarnished Plant Bug

Celery growers should also keep an eye out for the cabbage maggot (see CABBAGE), the white, brown-headed carrot weevil, which burrows into celery hearts (CARROT), various cutworms (see cabbage cutworm under CABBAGE), the flesh-colored European corn borer (CORN), the reddish brown carrot beetle (CARROT), jumpy, aphidlike six-spotted and beet leafhoppers (ASTER, BEAN), the potato flea beetle (also jumpy; see POTATO), THRIPS, and the yellow woolybear caterpillar (see imported cabbageworm under CABBAGE for controls).

Diseases

Perhaps the most serious diseases of celery are the early and late **blights.** Early blight first appears as small, pale green or yellow spots on seedlings in the plant bed or on transplants in the field. These spots enlarge, turn brown or gray, and gray or pale lavender spores are produced on the upper leaf surface. In severe cases, the spots grow together and kill the leaves.

Sunken, tan, elongated spots may mar stalks just before harvest, and growth is stunted.

The fungus is sometimes seed-borne; it doesn't live in the seed for more than two years, and newer seed should be disinfected by dipping for 30 minutes in water at 118°F. It has been found that the longer plants are left in crowded seedbeds, the worse blight is apt to be in the field.

Celery/Late Blight

Late blight begins as small water-soaked spots on the leaves of seedlings. The spots later darken and become dotted with tiny black dots which are the fruiting bodies of the fungus. Thousands of gelatinous threads of spores may be exuded from a single dot in wet weather. Infected seed can be treated in hot water at 118°F. for 30 minutes; while this treatment could be used on all seed sown late in fall for a spring crop, it is not so necessary for early plantings, since temperatures in early fall are probably too high to permit infection. If the disease cannot be controlled in the seedbed, it is better to destroy the seedlings than to plant them in the field where control would be very difficult and other plantings would be exposed to the disease. A good way to avoid problems is to select a blight-resistant variety.

Damping-off is the principal cause of losses occurring in seedbeds. It's particularly serious in beds sown in summer, and at times may destroy as many as 95 percent of the plants. Usually the first sign of damping-off is wilting or toppling over, caused by a watery soft rot that attacks the plants at the ground line. If the affected plants are scattered about the seedbed, damage may go unnoticed, but the disease may also attack groups of plants. During periods of high humidity and high temperatures, the threadlike mycelium of the causal fungus may lie on the soil like a spider web. It is during these periods that damage is greatest. Losses are highest in August and September, and are reduced sharply as weather becomes cooler and drier in fall.

Remember that crowding plants aggravates damping-off, as the dense mat of vegetation keeps the humidity high. Also, the use of double shades over the beds during the first month or until the first leaves unfold is a good practice. One shade can then be removed, and the plants are further strengthened by lifting the other shade a few minutes longer each day. Soil that has been used previously for seedbeds is apt to harbor the fungus.

Stunted, one-sided growth and yellowing are signs of **fusarium wilt,** a fungal disease. Vascular strands become reddish brown from the roots to the leaves. Avoid this problem by planting seed in clean, healthy soil and by discarding diseased plants. Green celeries are generally resistant.

When **pink rot** occurs, the stems become water-soaked in spots, and a telltale white to cottony pink growth appears at the base of the stalks. These spots of infection usually start in growth cracks or in wounds left by blight or insects. The stalks rot and take on a bitter taste. This fungus lives in the soil for many years, and may cause damping-off in the seedbed.

To control pink rot, you should rotate the growing area whenever possible, avoiding successive plantings of celery, lettuce, or cabbage in the same soil. Remove and destroy sick plants so that healthy ones will not become afflicted.

Chard (Swiss Chard)

Insects

Because chard shares most of its insect enemies with the beet and other vegetables, none is dealt with fully here. See BEET.

Tiny black dots may be bean **aphids.** See APHID.

Blister Beetle

The long, slender **black blister beetle** should be handled with care—that is, with gloves. If a bug is crushed while hand-picking, a toxic substance may blister the skin. See BEET.

An occasional pest of chard is the **European corn borer,** a flesh-colored caterpillar with dark brown spots. See CORN for means of control.

Garden Springtail

The **garden springtail** is a tiny, dark purple insect with yellow spots; it attacks chard seedlings. The springtail has no wings, but uses a taillike appendage to hurtle itself into the air. It is usually found eating small holes in leaves near the ground line. Clear weeds from the area; a garlic and water spray can be applied to the lower leaves.

The tiny ($\frac{1}{16}$ inch long), black **potato flea beetle** is so named because it jumps like a flea when disturbed. See POTATO for control measures.

Potato/Flea Beetles

The **spinach leaf miner** occasionally makes tunnels in chard leaves. The adult is a gray, black-haired, two-winged fly about $\frac{1}{4}$ inch in length. It lays white, cylindrical, reticulated eggs on the underside of leaves in clusters of from two to five. In a few days, these eggs hatch into the $\frac{1}{3}$-inch-long, pale green or whitish maggots that tunnel the leaves. For control see SPINACH.

As the **tarnished plant bug** feeds, toxins in the plant are

Tarnished Plant Bug

Vegetable Weevil

liberated and chard leaves may be deformed. The adult is small, mottled with white and yellow, and has a tarnished appearance. Look for a yellow triangle on each wing. See ASTER for control measures.

The nocturnal **vegetable weevil** does its dirty work at night. It grows to ⅜ inch long, is a dull buff color, and has a pale V on its wing covers. The head has a short, broad snout. See CABBAGE for controls.

Diseases

Chard may be spoiled by **chard blue mold,** which appears as large yellowed spots on top and bluish purple mold underneath. This disease also occurs as spinach downy mildew. According to Cynthia Westcott's *Plant Disease Handbook,* a week of humid (85 percent), cool (45° to 65°F.) weather is needed to introduce blue mold. She recommends planting in fertile, well-drained soil, avoiding crowding, and using a two- to three-year rotation with other crops.

Cherry

For an effective spray program, see FRUIT TREES.

Insects

Aphids, particularly the black cherry aphid, may be seen massed two-deep, standing on each other's backs as they try to stick their beaks into the leaves.

Nature provides natural enemies that handle aphids, particularly in the case of large infestations, but in some orchards it may be necessary to introduce ladybugs or lacewings to supplement low native populations. Sprays of soapy water have been used to kill aphids, and heavy local infestations can be controlled by dipping whole branches into soapy solutions. See APHID.

The **buffalo treehopper** may be a serious pest of cherry trees. Light greenish in color, this insect has a triangular shape that makes it distinctive. Two horns protrude at the shoulders. This insect causes its damage by laying eggs in the bark of the tree through a curved slit. Infested trees often appear rough and cracked, and the slits made by the treehopper's ovipositor can give entry to a variety of fungi and diseases.

Remove weeds from the immediate area if treehoppers are a problem. Large-scale growers should not grow alfalfa or sweet clover as cover crops.

The **cherry fruit fly** is usually to blame for wormy cherries. It looks something like a small housefly, but is distinguished by bold bars on the wings. The maggots develop from eggs laid in the cherries, and eat until fully grown, when they drop to the ground to pupate two or three inches below ground.

Once eggs are laid, the damage has been done, so the adults are the object of control measures. You should spray trees with rotenone as soon as the flies appear. They can best be monitored with a commercial or homemade trap. A simple trap can be made by painting a 10″ x 6″ plywood board a bright yellow and hanging a screen-covered jar below, to which has been added a mixture of ½ household ammonia and ½ water. The board is then covered with sticky tree-banding material, and the contraption is hung up at a height of six to eight feet, preferably on the tree's south side. If attached to young limbs, the traps can be pulled down for easy inspection. According to the Irrigation Experiment Station at Prosser, Washington, a minimum of four traps should be used in small orchards and about one per acre in larger orchards. Traps seem to work best when surrounded by foliage, in that more places are provided for the flies to alight in approaching the traps. Renew the ammonia and water bait each week, and check the board for stickiness from time to time.

The **cherry slug** (also called the pear slug) is the sluglike larva of a small, black, shiny fly (known as a sawfly) that appears in May and inserts its eggs in blisters on leaves. The larvae feed on the upper surface of leaves, especially on young trees, eating away the green tissue and skeletonizing the leaves. They have large head ends, and somewhat resemble tadpoles. Two or three weeks later, the mature larvae drop to the ground and pupate; a second batch of adults appears in July or August, and their larvae further devastate fruit tree foliage.

Cherry/Cherry (or Pear) Slug

Because the first generation of black-and-yellow sawflies emerges from cocoons in the ground just about the time cherries and pears come into full bloom, you might anticipate it by cultivating the orchard soil. Check with your local extension agent for some idea of best timing. You might also consider a second pass through the orchard after the first brood of slugs hits the ground. Botanical sprays of white hellebore offer some control; quassia and rotenone are other good bets.

A primary enemy of cherries is the **plum curculio,** a small (¼-inch-long) gray snout beetle with four humps on its back. Early in spring, shortly after the cherry trees bloom, the curculios move from their hibernating places in orchard trash to the trees.

Plum/Plum Curculio

They attack the fruit soon after it sets and deposit their eggs just beneath the skin of the cherries, making crescent-shaped slits around each egg puncture. The curculio larvae feed within for several weeks.

The curculio adults have a habit of playing possum and dropping to the ground when scared. This makes it possible to catch them by jarring the tree with a padded board. Start at blossom time and continue this simple control for about six weeks thereafter, being sure to spread a tarp or sheet out to gather the catch. See PEACH.

Tent Caterpillar

The **tent caterpillar** develops webs in spring and will eat every leaf in reach before dropping to the ground—unless you take action. Wild cherries are particularly vulnerable; in fact, cherry growers are often better off if nearby wild cherry trees are chopped down. While it seems a shame to destroy such beautiful trees, they may host infestations that could ruin a harvest. Once caterpillars have already attacked, a strong soap spray may help. See TENT CATERPILLAR.

Both wild and cultivated cherry trees are apt to be ravaged by the **ugly-nest caterpillar.** The ends of the branches are enclosed in large pointed webs or nests, with yellow larvae feeding on the leaves. The adult moth has a wingspread of about one inch; the fore wings are yellow with brown and blue markings. Female moths lay their flattened egg clusters on the bark of branches and cover them with a gluelike material for protection. Cut off and burn webs.

Other pests of cherries may be seen under PEACH and PLUM.

Diseases

Black knot may be a threat to sweet and sour cherries. The name describes the coal-black, hard swellings that are scattered throughout the twigs and limbs. This is a fungal disease that survives from year to year in the knotlike swellings. In spring, spores are formed on the surface of the knots and are released in rainy weather to be transmitted by air currents. Knots are first seen as olive-green swellings, and then blacken and cause a gradual weakening of the branch beyond the knot. The College of Agriculture at Penn State University suggests that all knotted twigs and branches that can be spared should be removed. Cuts should be made at least four inches below the beginning of the swelling, and should be covered with grafting wax or tree wound paint. The infected prunings should be burned before March 15 to prevent the release of spores. The college recommends that all neighboring wild plum and wild cherry trees (alternate hosts) be removed if infected. It is best to allow those infected branches or limbs that are essential for tree growth to remain until early or mid-summer. At this time, trim the knot growth with a knife and paint the wound. A publication of the Extension Plant Pathologists of the Northeastern States recommends that affected small limbs be pruned during the dormant period, at least three or four inches below the knot; on large main limbs and trunks, the knot and one inch of the healthy bark surrounding it should be cut out with a knife and chisel. Cover all wounds with grafting wax, and remove knotted tissue from the orchard and burn it.

Brown rot is the most serious fungus disease of cherry fruit east of the Rockies, particularly where fruit has been injured by curculios and oriental fruit moths, or cracked by hail or too much rain. The rot first appears as a small, round brown spot that quickly spreads to cover the cherry. Spores appear as gray or pale brown tufts or cushions. In time, the cherry shrivels up and may drop. In spring, mummified fruit may give rise to brown, cup-shaped growths that send spores off into the wind.

The Cooperative Extension Service of Montana suggests a number of control measures, applicable to the various stone fruit. Diseased, mummified fruit that stay on trees should be collected and destroyed. (Mummies of cherries very seldom stay on trees all winter, however.) The Extension Service recommends that no wild plum, peach, or other stone fruit seedlings be allowed to grow in orchards, because of their susceptibility to disease. Cultivation is said to reduce chances for the formation of the sexual and asexual stages of the fungus on mummies, so turn them under after a number have fallen. Moisture encourages brown rot, and ripe cherries should not be sprinkled with water. Proper pruning will allow better air circulation and rapid evaporation of rain water. When harvesting, do not pick cherries at the hottest time of day, and try to avoid wounding fruit during picking and packing, as wounds are ideal avenues of infection. Fingernail scratches and damage from rough containers will contribute to the start of trouble.

Once it is harvested, fruit should be kept cool and well ventilated. Orchard boxes should be constructed so that they allow ventilation when stacked. If cherries are overheated and begin to sweat, the chances of brown rot soar. The period between picking and placing cherries in a cool packing shed should be kept as brief as possible. It helps to provide some sort of forced ventilation in the cold storage room; openings in the boxes will help to knock down temperatures quickly, and the forced air will remove excess moisture.

The Extension Service of Montana points out that the optimum temperature for germination of brown rot spores is between 75° and 80°F. Spores have been found to germinate as low as the freezing point, but growth at this temperature is very slow.

If you grow garlic or onions, prepare a botanical brew and spray fruit well before harvest. If this doesn't turn the trick for you, consider applying an application of pure sulfur dust to ripe cherries several days before harvest.

Cherry leaf spot is sometimes known as yellow leaf, as bright yellow foliage develops soon after the purple spots appear. It has also been referred to as shot-hole disease because the dead areas of the spots often drop out. No matter what the name, this is the most common and serious of cherry leaf diseases. Early defoliation caused by this disease results in dwarfed, unevenly ripened fruit. The most serious cases occur in the season following extensive early defoliation. The results can be: cold injury (death of limbs or trees); small, weak fruit buds; death of fruit spurs; reduction of fruit set and size; and reduced shoot growth. The chief symptom of cherry leaf spot is found on the leaves, but symptoms can also be found on petioles (leaf stems), fruit, and fruit pedicels (stems). Small purple spots appear on the upper surface of the leaves about 10 to 14 days after infection. They may be pinpoint in size or up to $\frac{1}{4}$ inch in diameter. On the underside of the infected leaves during wet periods, whitish pink masses are found under the purple spots. These masses contain spores and a gelatinous substance. The spots usually dry, and a chlorotic (yellow) ring forms around the edge. The center of the lesion may shrink and fall out, causing a shot-hole effect; sour cherries are more prone to this damage than sweet. Older leaves turn yellow and usually drop prematurely. The fungus develops most rapidly under wet conditions and warm temperatures of around 70°F. Infection occurs at lower temperatures, but more slowly.

There are two stages in the life cycle of this fungus, and it helps to know something about them.

• *Primary cycle.* The fungus overwinters in dead leaves on the ground. Fruiting structures called apothecia develop on these leaves in late April, and spores mature at various times, depending on temperature and moisture. Generally, most of the spores are discharged from bloom four to six weeks after petal fall during wet periods. The infection early in the primary cycle is limited, because the susceptible developing leaves are small and most of the air pores (stomata) are too immature to be infected. Other factors are low temperatures and drying out of spores. Prevention of this early infection is crucial to eliminating early spore production on the leaves.

Upon germinating, the fungus enters through the stomata (air pores on the underside of the leaf), and the mycelium branches out inside the leaf to later form a fruiting structure (acervulus) on the underside of the leaf surface. Each acervulus contains thousands of spores (conidia).

• *Secondary cycle.* The acervulus appears as a pink to whitish pink mass on the underside of the leaves during humid conditions. In dry periods this mass is brown in color. The conidia are spread from leaf to leaf by water. The rapid spread of leaf spot fungus in summer and fall is usually due to rapid increase and spread of the fungus during wet periods by means of repeated generations of conidia.

The Penn State College of Agriculture recommends rotary mowing the orchard after leaf drop in fall, and a fall application of a nitrogenous fertilizer to hasten the decay of the leaves and thereby reduce the number of those on which the fungus can over-winter. A slight disking around the trees just before bloom also serves to decrease the spore discharge of the cherry leaf fungus, as well as the brown rot fungus.

Foliage browning may be traced to several causes. A natural browning and shedding often occurs after a dry season or may simply happen every second or third year without apparent cause. In this instance, all the leaves of the inside of the tree turn reddish brown and drop either in spring or fall. The discoloration is distinguished from fertilizer burn or sunburn due to root injury because the discoloration takes place on the inside of the tree. Fertilizer burn and sunburn start at the tip of the branch and progress up the tree from the lowest branches. Red spider mites bronze leaves, but they cause all of the leaves on a branch or tree to suddenly discolor in summer. Winter bronzing is due to some physiological changes that are tied in with the nutrition of the plant, and organic feeding should eliminate any trouble.

A deficiency of zinc in a cherry tree's diet brings about a condition known as **little leaf.** Leaves are crinkled, mottled, and may be bunched together at the tips. Fruit is sometimes mis-shapen. On a small scale, growers can get around this problem simply by driving galvanized nails or metal strips into the trunk and limbs of large trees. Use about six nails for each inch of trunk diameter, and make sure the nails or strips are zinc-coated.

When **virus yellows** comes to the orchard, leaves show green and yellow mottling with waves of defoliation starting three to four weeks after petal fall. Trees infected for several years will develop abnormally large leaves and few spurs, and bear small crops of large fruit. The tree gradually deteriorates. Yellows is transmitted by budding and through seed. In *Modern Fruit Science,* Norman F. Childers stresses that growers specify virus-free trees from the nursery.

Experiments in recent years have shown that **X-disease** is spread to cherry and plum trees from wild chokecherry bushes. Leafhoppers act as vectors; species in the western states may spread the disease from one cultivated plant to another, while those species in the East apparently do not carry it from one cultivated cherry or peach tree to another. Although trees cannot be saved once affected, spread of X-disease can be halted by destroying all chokecherry bushes in the vicinity of the orchard.

Infected trees on Mazzard rootstock make poor growth, bloom is delayed, leaves often become duller than normal, and some of the fruit never matures. Such immature fruit is light-colored and insipid. It tends to be triangular in cross section, and has less flesh in proportion to the pit than does normal fruit.

On infected red-fruited trees such as Montmorency, the fruit is pale pink in color, and sometimes is partly dull white. On a black sweet cherry such as Windsor, the fruit is usually red in color, and develops other symptoms similar to those on Montmorency. A sweet cherry such as Napoleon with light-colored fruit usually has dull white fruit when infected. On all varieties, the fruit is worthless.

Late in the season, bronze discoloration occasionally develops along the midveins of a few leaves. After several years of poor growth, dieback may develop on infected trees. The disease progresses more rapidly in peach and sour cherry trees than in sweet cherry trees; it may be five or more years after infection before large sweet cherry trees become unprofitable.

It is often difficult to identify X-disease on cherry trees propagated on Mahaleb rootstock because fruit symptoms rarely develop. In June or later, infected trees often suddenly wilt and become nearly dead by the end of the season. Other trees do not wilt but may decline slowly without characteristic symptoms. If no cause of decline can be found, such as girdling by mice, verticillium wilt disease, or dead roots from wet soil, check the

immediate neighborhood for diseased chokecherry. If chokecherries are found nearby, it can be assumed that the wilted trees
are infected with X-disease. Trees on Mahaleb rootstock that
produce roots above the bud union may develop X-disease
symptoms characteristic of trees on Mazzard rootstock.

Infected chokecherry bushes develop yellow to red foliage
and, in advanced cases, the shoots are short and rosetted. The
above-ground parts of the bushes ultimately die. Unfortunately,
the roots of infected bushes often are not killed and new sprouts
develop from roots of X-diseased plants.

X-diseased chokecherry bushes have been found in or near
all peach or cherry orchards in which X-disease has appeared. In
experiments conducted in western New York and the Hudson
River Valley, cases of X-disease could invariably be traced to
nearby chokecherry plants. In the few instances where the
disease occurred with none of these wild plants in the vicinity, it
was found that chokecherries had been removed only a few years
before. An extension publication of the New York State College
of Agriculture states that control depends on removing all chokecherries from the surrounding area, preferably for a distance of
at least 500 feet. Because it is difficult to diagnose the disease
in its early stages, all chokecherry bushes should be destroyed
whether or not they show symptoms. Before a new orchard is
planted, scout the area carefully for chokecherries. On open
ground, deep plowing will make it quite easy to pull out and burn
the plants. Subsequent cultivation will prevent sprouting. It is
important to check the orchard occasionally for new plants, as
birds carry chokecherry seeds.

The **yellows** and **ring-spot virus** complex causes the most
serious reduction of sour cherry yields in New York State, according to the New York State College of Agriculture. Fruit set is
reduced as soon as infection occurs; growth is reduced because
leaf efficiency is impaired; and, as the yellows disease develops,
buds that normally produce lateral shoots and fruit spurs produce
flowers instead. Once these buds have blossomed, no additional
growth occurs at the nodes where they are borne, and long bare
twigs and branches eventually develop. The only fruits on such
branches develop on the terminal shoots. The final result is a
small number of blossoms and an equally small number of leaves,
many of which drop in June because of the disease. In addition,
the weakened buds are more susceptible than normal to winter
injury, and the twigs finally become so weakened that dieback
occurs.

Ring-spot symptoms are most prominent during the two-week period following petal fall. Typically, they are produced by a given tree for only one or two years, when the tree is in the initial "shock" stage. Etch-type symptoms, characterized by darkened, depressed fine lines and rings, develop on the upper surface of the leaves. Dead tissue may develop on leaves in this stage of symptom expression. Sometimes the lines are broad, chlorotic, and not depressed. Yellows symptoms develop later in the year, commonly beginning three to four weeks after petal fall. Leaves develop yellow color in different patterns, and drop along with other leaves that do not turn yellow.

Sweet cherries also are infected by cherry yellows virus disease, although leaves on affected trees do not turn yellow. Most varieties of sweet cherries appear to be less susceptible than sour cherries, but they are damaged to a significant degree. The precautions in purchasing and planting of sour cherries should be followed for sweet cherries. It may not be wise to rogue out affected sweet cherry trees, however, because of the lack of diagnostic symptoms.

The practice of replanting trees in old orchards exposes new trees to large sources of nearby inoculum. The interplants become diseased quickly and, even before they show symptoms or suffer serious damage, provide inoculum for infection of subsequent replants.

More than ten years of research and many years of experience show that cherry yellows need not be so serious as it is at present. Spread of the viruses is reduced if new plantings are made in solid blocks isolated from other cherry orchards. Many old orchards that were planted in isolation are producing much better crops than those in which constant replanting has been practiced, or in which a high percentage of trees were diseased at planting. Replanting in old orchards must be stopped. All trees in old orchards should be removed at the same time. The block should not be replanted until all large roots have been completely removed and the soil has good tilth, proper nutrient level, adequate organic matter content, and suitable pH. Adequate soil preparation requires one year or more. Any factor unfavorable for growth will add to virus damage when the trees eventually become infected. The trees should be as virus-free as possible, for this is the only means of excluding serious forms of the diseases.

There appears to be a delay of a few years before the viruses begin to spread from trees that were diseased at planting to neighboring healthy trees. Therefore, it is suggested that any tree showing yellows symptoms during the first years after planting be removed at once. You should also remove those that show such severe symptoms of ring-spot that twigs are killed, that develop unusually poor fruit spur systems, and that grow very poorly without explanation. Once this is done, you can plant groups of trees in which a low percentage are infected by the less severe virus strains. Such trees are those most likely to be available in nurseries at the present time; because of the widespread use of budwood from isolated virus-free foundation plantings, trees have been greatly improved during the last ten years.

The New York State College of Agriculture suggests the following steps to reduce spread of the virus.

• *For orchards* less *than ten years of age:* 1) Remove all trees that grow poorly, fail to set up a good spur system, or show yellow leaf symptoms characteristic of the virus disease. This practice will remove a potential source of infection to other young trees and will eliminate boarder trees. 2) Replace trees only if the original planting is less than five years old. Replant with the best trees available, preferably with those having a certificate of freedom from viruses.

• *For orchards* more *than ten years of age:* 1) Destroy all trees that show many yellow leaves in June, produce a poor spur system, or have many dead twigs. Such trees do not pay for the care they receive and they endanger other trees in the orchard. 2) Do not replace old trees, as new ones will soon be infected by the remaining diseased trees. 3) Bulldoze complete blocks if the trees are so diseased that a normal crop has not been harvested for a few years. Such orchards cannot be returned to profitable production.

• *Planting for the future:* 1) Isolate new plantings, setting them as far as possible from existing cherry blocks and other stone fruits. At least 100 feet of isolation is necessary but distances of 500 feet or more are preferable. Open fields between plantings of different ages will provide suitable isolation, but may not be economical in areas of intensive fruit growing. An alternative is to plant apples or pears between cherry blocks or between cherry and other stone fruit blocks. Occasionally it may be necessary to reduce the size of individual plantings and to have more blocks of each kind of fruit. Smaller plantings will increase the cost of spraying and other orchard care operations, but increased cherry production will more than offset the added costs. 2) Make solid plantings, and avoid interplanting among older trees. When an orchard is prepared for replanting, all existing trees in the old planting must be removed to eliminate this certain source of yellows virus. 3) Purchase the best trees available. These should carry a certificate stating they were produced with virus-free buds. If such trees are not available, every effort should be made to obtain trees produced under a careful program designed to reduce the virus content of the trees. Horticultural inspectors will know whether sour cherry yellows is abundant in the different nursery blocks. A better plan is to contract with a nurseryman to produce virus-free trees two or three years in advance of your planting date. In many cases, the intervening time can be well spent in preparing the soil. 4) Profitable cherry production depends heavily on the careful selection and preparation of planting sites. Soil condition and cultural care also are important phases of a prevention program.

Because one aspect of the damage caused by cherry yellows virus disease is to increase susceptibility to winter injury, other factors conducive to winter injury must be taken into account. While one growth factor alone might not result in trouble, it may cause damage when compounded with virus yellows. A case in point is potash deficiency: pomologists recently found that potassium levels higher than those previously thought adequate will help to reduce winter injury. 5) In new plantings, follow the roguing programs outlined above. Most nursery trees contain a percentage of affected trees.

Wildlife

See Chapter 12 for ways of keeping birds and other wildlife from beating you to the cherries.

Chestnut

Insects

Several types of **aphids** may attack your chestnut trees; see APHID.

The most serious insect pest is the **chestnut weevil,** of which there are two species, both attacking the nuts of Asian chestnut trees. In years of heavy infestations the feeding of the larvae inside the nuts may destroy practically the entire crop.

The larvae in the nuts can be killed by immersing them in water kept at 120°F. for 30 to 45 minutes, depending on the size of the nuts. If the nuts are gathered from the ground daily, few worms will enter the soil. It helps to let chickens run beneath infested trees.

The white flat-headed grubs of the **two-lined chestnut borer** make torturous and interlacing galleries under the bark of chestnut and oak. The grub is about ½ inch in length, and the parent beetle is ⅜ inch in length, black with two narrow converging longitudinal grayish stripes on the wing covers. The beetles appear in May and June and deposit eggs. The grubs work in the inner bark and outer sapwood, pupating in cells in the wood. There is one annual generation each season. Mutilated, weakened, or dying trees are often infested and killed by this beetle.

Insects such as aphids and chestnut borers are commonly present when the tree has already been weakened, perhaps by drought or transplanting. Such trees should be given plenty of organic fertilizer and water.

Cankerworms, gypsy moths, lecanium scales, mites, and twig girdlers may occasionally be pests of chestnut trees. See TREES: INSECTS.

Diseases

By far the most destructive disease afflicting chestnut trees is **blight.** Within 15 years after it was first noticed in this country, blight had spread across the country. Few native chestnuts remain today. Even sprouts that arise from old stumps are hit, as the disease is still with us. On young wood, cankers appear as swollen, yellowish brown, oval or irregular areas. On older wood they are brownish, circular or irregular areas with slightly raised or depressed edges. Partial or complete girdling of stems by cankers causes leaves to yellow and brown. Dead leaves and burrs cling to diseased branches long after normal leaf fall. The surface of older cankers is covered with minute pinpoint fruiting bodies of the blight fungus. During wet weather, yellowish spore masses ooze from fruiting bodies. These spores are carried by rain, birds, and insects. New infection develops following the entry of spores through wounds.

As soon as the disease is definitely identified, cut down the tree and burn the branches and the trunk. Debark the stump to prevent sprout growth, and replace the tree with resistant hybrid chestnuts.

Breeding of resistant varieties is in progress. Chinese varieties, such as Crane and Orrin, and some Japanese varieties are resistant.

Though Chinese and Japanese chestnuts have some resistance to the blight disease, they are susceptible to the fungus that causes **twig canker,** also called **twig blight and dieback.** This fungus enters the tree through a dead twig. Once in the wood, it progresses rapidly, growing lengthwise in the wood and eventually girdling the branch. The trouble may be traced to winter injury in varieties not hardy enough for the area, to a lack of compatibility between stock and scion in grafted trees, or to some other adverse environmental factor.

Control this disease by planting varieties well adapted to the climate. Provide good air circulation. Trees should be protected from injury as far as possible, and should be periodically inspected. If any branches appear to have cankers, prune them one to two feet below the site of injury.

China Aster, see Aster

Chinese Cabbage

Insects

Chinese cabbage is preyed upon by a number of insects discussed under CABBAGE. The potato **aphid** (see APHID) and the yellow-striped **purple-back cabbage worm** (see imported cabbageworm under CABBAGE) have a particular craving for Chinese cabbage.

Diseases

Two crucifer diseases likely to strike this crop are **black rot** and **black leg;** see CABBAGE.

Chrysanthemum

Despite the awesome list of bugs and diseases that follows, chrysanthemums are relatively trouble-free. Remember that mums should not be planted in wet, shady places, and that it is best to water early in the day so that leaves have a chance to dry before nightfall, as fungus diseases thrive on wet leaves. Plants should be spaced well and staked to keep branches well off the ground.

Insects

The shiny, dark chrysanthemum **aphid** is a tiny speck that is often seen on stems, leaves, and flowers of this plant. They congregate in clusters on tender shoots of growing plants, stunting growth and causing a slight leaf curl. Plants sometimes die in serious cases. When cut mums are brought into the house, the aphids abandon them and crawl about. When crushed they leave dark stains. See APHID for control measures.

The **chrysanthemum gall midge** is a tiny, slender, orange, two-winged fly which lays eggs in the leaves and tender shoots of greenhouse plants. Each larval maggot forms a cone-shaped gall. A number of galls together often form knots, twisted stems or distorted buds. This tiny insect is so prolific in reproduction that it is difficult to tell just how many generations there are in a year. The midge is usually more abundant in spring and fall than during summer.

Damage can be reduced by bringing only clean cuttings or plants into the greenhouse. Because greenhouse plants are most bothered, think about moving your plants outdoors if you have trouble with this pest. Pick up foliage that appears galled or knotted and burn it, as the maggots are probably inside the leaf tissue.

Lacy wings are the key characteristic of the **chrysanthemum lacebug;** the nymphs are similar to the azalea lacebug. These pests bleach foliage and stems of mums, and leave dark spots of excrement on the underside of leaves. They breed on weeds, especially goldenrod, and are common wherever mums are grown. Strong detergent sprays have been used to good effect against this pest. If not many bugs are about, it may suffice to crush the bugs by drawing leaves between the thumb and forefinger.

The **chrysanthemum leaf miner** is a yellow maggot that feeds in petioles and between leaf surfaces, causing large, blisterlike mines. Leaves often dry up and drop off. Look for telltale specks of excrement in the tunnels. Control this pest by discarding affected leaves and stems.

At night, the mottled-brown **climbing cutworm** leaves the soil to climb chrysanthemums and eat tip leaves, flower buds, and blossoms. If only a few plants are involved, just scratch the soil surface and destroy the exposed worms; if you're in trouble with a lot of mums, see CUTWORM.

The **corn earworm** (also known as the **tomato fruitworm** and **cotton bollworm**) is better known for its ravages in the vegetable than in the flower garden. Nevertheless, it is a pest of annual and perennial flowers and attacks abutilon, ageratum, amaranth, canna, carnation, chrysanthemum, dahlia, geranium, gladiolus, hibiscus, mignonette, morning-glory, nasturtium, phlox, poppy, rose, sunflower, and sweet pea. The caterpillars show a marked preference for the opening buds and flowers of chrysanthemum, calendula, dahlia, gladiolus, and rose, although they also feed on leaves and may tunnel in stems of certain plants. Their injury to the buds is not unlike that caused by climbing cutworms,

Corn Earworm

with which they are often confused. The earworms gouge out the inner part so deeply that the flowers are a complete loss. When fully grown they are about $1\frac{1}{2}$ inches long, and their color may change as they mature from reddish brown to green, with brown, black, or green stripes. The parent is a fawn-colored moth with dark spots on the fore wings.

If the flower buds have been bored into there is little that can be done except to remove and destroy those that have been infested. Screen choice and valuable plants with cheesecloth to prevent them from becoming infested. See CORN.

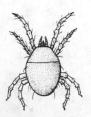

Cyclamen Mite

The translucent, microscopic **cyclamen mite** infests new leaf and blossom buds, causing them to become swollen and distorted. It is a pest of both garden and greenhouse. Plants may be stunted. See CYCLAMEN for this mite's life history and control measures.

The **foliar nematode** is a serious pest both in the greenhouse and garden. The first symptom you'll notice are darkened spots on the underside of leaves. After a few days, veins on the top surfaces of the leaves are discolored, and wedge-shaped spots appear between the veins until entire leaves become blackened and withered.

Once nematodes get inside leaves, there's no way to get them out, and control is aimed at preventing their trek from the soil to the foliage. They are so tiny that they can swim vertically in the water film on mum stems, so see to it that stems stay dry. Don't water from overhead, and use a mulch to prevent splashing on the plants. Remove and burn affected leaves, and discard badly infected branches. Cynthia Westcott suggests gardeners avoid crown divisions, and take tip cuttings instead. While most varieties are susceptible, Koreans are reported to be especially so. Be careful in selecting plants from nurseries, checking for damaged foliage.

Fourlined Plant Bug

Round, depressed tan spots on new leaves may be the work of the **four-lined plant bug,** so named because of the black lines running down its greenish yellow back. The nymphs are red in color. Handpicking should take care of most problems; rotenone is sometimes used as a last resort.

The slender, white **garden centipede (garden symphilid)** is found in moist soils that contain decayed humus, particularly near greenhouses. Look for twelve pairs of legs on the adults (fewer on larvae) and long antennae that are constantly in motion. See GARDEN SYMPHILID.

Several species of **spittle bug** suck plant juices from chrysanthemums, causing stunting and distortion. The adults look something like leafhoppers, are straw-colored or brown, and measure ¼ inch long. Pinkish to yellow green nymphs hatch from eggs in spring, and are usually found under the masses of white froth or spittle that they produce. It is this stage that causes damage; adults apparently cause no visible trouble. Spittle bugs are found throughout the northern states, and are particularly serious in regions of high humidity.

As for controls, you're on your own with this one. Almost every insect pest reference recommends a shot of chemical, with no suggestions for prevention or cultural control. Beatrice Trum Hunter mentions in *Gardening Without Poisons* that rotenone is effective against this pest, but you might concoct a milder botanical before turning to this powerful agent.

Thrip

Several species of **thrips** feed on mums, especially the flower thrip. They feed in the developing flowers, causing deformity and mottling. The adult of the flower thrip is brownish yellow and displays feathery wings; the young are lemon-yellow. See ROSE.

The larva of the **white-marked tussock moth** is a strange-looking, hairy caterpillar that grows to 1½ inches long. It has a red head from which sprout two hornlike tufts of long black hair. Another tuft projects from the tail. A black stripe is centered down the back, flanked by a wide yellow line. Usually a number of caterpillars feed together, skeletonizing leaves of many plants including geranium, German ivy, rose, and several fruit and deciduous shade trees.

Pick off and destroy infested leaves and groups of larvae. Scrape off the egg masses or paint them with creosote; these are very visible, lathery, and about an inch long. Fortunately, birds aren't put off by the worm's looks, and devour great numbers of them. This pest is preyed upon by many parasites, but nature has seen to it that the parasites have to contend with their own hyperparasites.

Another conspicuous pest is the **yellow woolybear caterpillar,** a hairy, yellow, two-inch-long food tube that attacks a great number of plants. Look for the black lines running down its back. Handpicking will take care of modest infestations; see imported cabbageworm under CABBAGE for other controls.

Diseases

Aster yellows is caused by a virus that is carried to chrysanthemums by aphids and leafhoppers. In general, the infected plants are yellow or mottled, and stunted. They tend to develop distorted flowers and many small, weak shoots. Flowers are deformed and often are colored green rather than their normal hue.

Control of aster yellows must involve the control of the aphids and leafhoppers that transmit the disease. See APHID and ASTER. Yellows can also be carried on garden implements or your hands. Take out any suspicious looking plants that may serve as a source of virus; no matter how valued a plant may be, it should be destroyed as soon as it is infected.

Dodder is a parasitic vine that is distributed by birds or in the seed. It appears as many strands of orange, stringlike growth, without apparent roots, that wind around mums. The little vines are not readily detached. Small clusters of whitish flowers produce abundant seeds for another year's crop. When seeds germinate, the dodder climbs up the nearest plant and sends little penetrating knobs into the host, through which it draws its nutrients. The dodder roots are dropped as soon as this attachment is made, and the plant becomes truly parasitic.

If the dodder is noticed early, the portion of the flower that has been attacked can be cut out and destroyed with the dodder. However, once this parasite has had an opportunity to become firmly established, it's necessary to remove and burn the infested plant.

Foot rot and **wilt** cause lower leaves to turn yellow and die, along with a general wilting of the plant. Near the ground the stem is greatly discolored and may show masses of pink spores; when cut across, it usually shows discolored vascular bundles.

Prevent foot rot by using cuttings from healthy plants. Any plants that appear to be affected should be destroyed. In the garden, it may be a good idea to grow mums in a new location.

Gray mold appears as flower spots that enlarge and rot the entire flower, particularly those of light-colored varieties. The fruiting of the fungus appears as a gray mold. This disease is particularly prevalent during wet or cloudy weather, and in greenhouses during late winter.

Avoid humid conditions by improving ventilation. In a greenhouse, turn on the heat an hour before sundown to prevent a sharp drop in temperature, which might condense moisture on the flowers and allow the fungus to grow.

Petal blight of chrysanthemums is a fungus disease. It may be expected during cool weather when excessive moisture remains on flower heads for several hours.

Ventilation is the key to preventing this disease, as it ensures that moisture can evaporate from the flowers even in cool, wet weather. Plants under cloth will be less likely to suffer from blight if intermittent openings are left in the roof to enable air to circulate.

Powdery mildew appears as a whitish powder on the leaves, and spreads rapidly during hot dry weather. See MILDEW.

Rhizoctonia stem and **root rot** hits the base of stems and roots, and causes plants to wilt slowly. The disease is encouraged by high soil moisture, and in warmer areas it may live on in the soil from one year to the next.

Plant mums in soil that has been free of disease, if possible. Where rotation is impossible, some growers have replaced soil. Composted soil discourages the rot fungus.

Stem rot (cottony stem blight) is a windborne disease that is hard to control in most gardens. In the soilborne phase, stems near the ground level are attacked, showing a white surface mold that causes the plants to wilt and suddenly die. In the windborne phase, the leaves, blossoms and stems are attacked by spores blown either from surrounding infected plants of many kinds, or from small mushrooms formed on the garden soil by the disease.

Be certain to plant in disease free soil, even to the point of replacing infected soil with good soil. Soil around plants should not be too wet. Wide spacing between plants allows air to circulate, reducing the moisture on plant surfaces. Diseased clumps should be removed and burned to prevent spread of the disease to healthy plants.

Stunt appears to affect part or all of mum plants, both in the greenhouse and garden. Infection is characterized by stunting of the entire plant or one or more branches, and early production of off-color flowers. Leaves on infected branches may be smaller than normal, flowers are small, and pink and bronze varieties are bleached. Greenhouse stunt appears to be mechanically transmissible and is often spread by handling, so break off buds instead of pinching or cutting them with fingernails or a knife. Take care in selecting healthy propagating stock, and rogue infected plants as soon as possible. Keep plants free from leafhoppers, as these insects also serve as vectors. For the first year, segregate new stock if at all possible.

The several species of **verticillium wilt** may bring about a number of symptoms. Leaves wilt at the margin and turn brown, and die progressively from the base of the plant upward. A cross-section of the stem near the ground may show a discoloration of the woody tissue, and many plants grow lopsided. Once plants are visibly stunted, they are usually beyond hope. Occasionally, wilted plants can be saved by providing very little soil moisture, but this is an emergency measure that is recommended only for valuable plants. A temperature of 60° to 75°F. is most favorable for this wilt, but once started, the fungus can persist outside this temperature range.

Because of the nature of verticillium wilt, protection measures are concerned more with prevention than control. Avoid planting chrysanthemums in the same spot continuously as this increases the soil's susceptibility to the disease, especially if the soil is kept fairly moist and at a temperature of 60° to 75°F. For garden and field planting, do not use soil where susceptible crops (such as cotton, tomatoes, and strawberries) have grown, and avoid soil that has previously hosted the disease. If space is limited and the same soil must be used yearly, select resistant varieties.

Cineraria

Insects

Both the adult and nymph leaf-curling plum **aphid** are flat-backed, a shiny pale green in color, and are found in the crevices of plant tips. They cause severe distortion and stunting of growth. Infested leaves are covered with white, crystalline droplets of honeydew. The winter host is typically plum; summer hosts include aster, mums, heliotrope, dahlia, erigeron, eupatorium, gerbera, cynoglossun, lobelia, mertensia, marguerite, and sunflower plants. See APHID.

Foliar nematodes cause water-soaked spots that appear first on the underside of lowest leaves and then work through to the upperside, where brown blotches become evident. Avoid splashing water from leaf to leaf or from soil to leaf; see CHRYSANTHEMUM.

The **greenhouse leaf tier** is a translucent, greenish white caterpillar that grows to about ¾ inch long; it is marked with a dark green stripe. When disturbed, they wiggle violently and often drop to the ground. They usually feed on the underside of leaves, but may web several leaves together. The adult is an inconspicuous, rusty brown moth with a wingspread of just under an inch. See celery leaf tier under CELERY.

The adult **greenhouse white fly** feeds in both the adult and immature stages by sucking plant juices. Heavy feeding gives leaves a mottled appearance, and may cause them to yellow and die. The adult is a tiny mothlike insect with a mealy appearance that's due to wax secretions. They also secrete sticky honeydew that glazes the lower leaves and encourages black, sooty mold. The nymph is oval, flattened, light green, and about the size of a pinhead. It looks somewhat like a small, soft scale insect, and spends its time attached to leaves until maturation. Don't bring infested cuttings or plants into the greenhouse. For controls, see WHITE FLY.

Whitefly

Other likely pests include the cabbage looper (see CABBAGE), CUTWORM (TOMATO), MEALYBUGS, six-spotted leafhopper (ASTER), SLUGS AND SNAILS, and SPIDER MITES.

Diseases

Powdery mildew gives cineraria leaves a whitish, powdered appearance. See MILDEW.

Citrus Fruit

Under this heading we will discuss insect and disease problems affecting oranges, grapefruit, mandarins, lemons, limes, and a number of hybrids and lesser species. Fortunately for citrus growers, significant advances have been made in understanding biological control of the most significant pests and diseases.

One beneficiary of biological control and organic practice is Robert S. Plimpton of Palm Beach Ranch Groves in North Palm Beach, Florida. Since buying the grove from a large corporate concern, he has shown his approach to be superior to the chemistry of the previous owner. Ethion was dropped when it was learned that this chemical aggravated the snow scale problems it was supposed to clear up. When Plimpton found that gumosis was caused or increased by the use of chemical fertilizers, he sold his fertilizer tank along with the liquid nitrogen preparation in it, and has since been using an imported seaweed fertilizer at the rate of 1 gallon per acre in 30 gallons of water. He was also fortunate in obtaining good supplies of cow manure from a local dairy, some hen manure, and plenty of clarifier mud from the local sugar cane mills. Clarifier mud is the result of precipitating the black muck soil, with its high plant-nutrient leaves, out of the sugar slurry with lime. He puts out five tons of this material per acre and soil analyses have looked excellent ever since.

Plimpton also got rid of the previous owner's sulfur and Chlorobenzalate, and now uses a commercial non-toxic barrier film made of polybutene and seaweed. He reports that, since using this product, ladybugs have made the grove their home, and it's likely that less and less of the barrier film will be needed as time goes on. The corporate concern also left behind herbicide and Plimpton abandoned that too, preferring to use choppers and hand hoeing to control weeds, vines, and other unwanted growth. The change to organic methods has paid off. Yields are well above those reported by the chemical-wielding corporate grower, having both better set and better size.

Insects

Brown, $\frac{1}{12}$- to $\frac{1}{8}$-inch-long Argentine **ants** are responsible for carrying around aphids, mealybugs, and scale insects. Cynthia Westcott observes in *The Gardener's Bug Book* that the slender workers give off a "musty, greasy odor when crushed." See ANT.

Black citrus **aphids** are usually kept down by a good variety of natural enemies and diseases. Growers who spray trees with nothing more severe than dormant-oil sprays will receive maximum benefits from this free help. These aphids are carried to leaves by Argentine ants (see above); see also APHID.

The **citrus mealybug** feeds on the juices of the plant, causing eventual death of the affected parts after they wilt and lose their color. The mealybugs coat the foliage with a sticky honeydew on which an unsightly black mold grows. Honeydew is also the natural food of certain ants that tend the mealybugs and carry them from plant to plant.

Mealybugs are usually found in clusters along the veins on the underside of leaves and crevices near the base of leaf stems. Since they multiply rapidly, all stages may be present at the same time. They have amber-colored bodies with short, waxy filaments. The eggs are laid in a protective cottony mass or sack that resembles a small puff of cotton. Each mass may contain 300 eggs or more that hatch in 10 to 20 days.

The first step in the control of mealybugs is to eliminate ants in and about the planting area. This can best be done by scattering bone meal about the ground. On plants that will not be damaged by frequent watering, syringe frequently with a forceful stream of water. Rotenone and pyrethrum are effective botanicals. Another species, the citrophilus mealybug, is kept in line by internal parasites that were imported from Australia.

The **citrus red mite** (known also as purple mite and red spider) is about $\frac{1}{50}$ inch long, and varies in color from deep purple to rose. This species infests leaves, fruit, and new growth. Injury appears as a silvery scratching or etching of the upper leaf surface. Leaves may turn brown and drop, and fruit becomes yellowed. Use a magnifying glass to check for the tiny mites and their red, stalked eggs on upper leaf surfaces, especially along the midrib, and in angular crevices on leaf stems and young, tender twigs. Although citrus red mites are most numerous from November to April, they can be seen at any time of the year. Regular dormant-oil sprays should control populations of this species, but natural enemies may well make spraying unnecessary. The drop in the mite population observed yearly around April is due in part to virus diseases. Two researchers, Gilmore and Munger, found that viral epidemics (termed epizootics) are influenced by population density. In summing up the considerable research aimed at control of the citrus red mite, J. J. Lipa reports in *Microbial Control of Insects and Mites* that a heavy virus epizootic may be spread in orchards by introducing diseased mites. "In all experimental groves an epizootic of the disease and a significant reduction of the mite population were observed." Best results were scored by mites collected from naturally infected populations, as opposed to mites infected in the laboratory. The virus spreads quickly through the orchard, probably because winds carry the mites from tree to tree. Lipa concludes that this virus ". . . has all the necessary features to become a valuable agent for biological control" of the citrus red mite.

Citrus rust mites are present most of the year, and their injury, while not materially affecting fruit quality, often results in rusty, rough patches on the skin. These pests are about $\frac{1}{200}$ inch long, and cannot be seen by the unassisted eye; in fact, they're even hard to observe with a 10X magnifying glass. Look for them on green fruit and both sides of leaves. A lime sulfur preparation, diluted 1 to 50 or 1 to 100 with water, will knock out this pest in serious cases. Sulfur dusts also work well. As with the citrus red mite, this mite is very vulnerable to naturally occurring diseases—in this case, fungus diseases. In one instance, a heavy epizootic decreased the percentage of infested fruits from 96 percent in August to 16 percent in November. Such epizootics are favored by heavy rains, and rise and fall to meet the density of mites.

J. J. Lipa states in *Microbial Control of Insects and Mites* that "the use of fungicides and some acaricides (or miticides) may interfere with natural control of mites as some of these preparations are detrimental to pathogenic fungi. In a detailed study of this problem, Giffiths and Fisher (1950) found that on trees sprayed with zinc sulphate ($ZnSO_4$) and copper ($CuOH_2$ and $CuSO_4$), populations of *P. oleivora* (the citrus rust mite) were much higher than on untreated trees." It has also been found that sulfur is toxic to the beneficial fungus.

The **navel orangeworm** is an important pest of almond, walnut, fig and citrus, especially in California. The worms are colored yellow to dark gray, with dark heads. The moth is distinguished by a line of crescent-shaped markings along the outer margins of its light gray wings. Plant and orchard sanitation, along with an early harvest, will prevent most damage.

Nematodes are responsible for two serious diseases of citrus, spreading decline and slow decline (see below). Soil that is rich in organic matter has been found to encourage fungi that prey on nematodes.

Californians have found the **orange tortrix caterpillar** to be of much trouble throughout the growing season. A host of other types of plants may also be subjected to damage from this brown-headed, brownish white caterpillar. This insect rolls leaves into a web and feeds within. If oranges drop before their time, suspect the caterpillar of boring into the rinds of the orange or scarring them near the bottom.

If gray moths with dark markings are seen in the vicinity of your citrus plants, chances are that the tortrix is laying its eggs on leaf surfaces. Look for these eggs (they are cream-colored discs, found on both leaf tops and bottoms) and destroy them. Pyrethrum has been found effective against this pest when either sprayed or dusted. Should you notice that the caterpillar has small white eggs on its back, do not pick it, as these may be the eggs of a parasite that will hatch to produce beneficial wasps. At least a dozen parasites of this caterpillar have been identified. Solicit their support by refusing to use sprays in your growing area. Such sprays often kill the beneficial insects and allow the dangerous insects to bounce back and spread unhampered. Light traps have proved successful when the tortrix is in its adult state.

Scale insects can be extremely bothersome to the citrus grower. There are several varieties of this small pest to contend with.

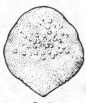

Scale

• *Black scale* is most easily recognized as a female, which is dark brown or black, hemispherical, and about ⅛ to ³⁄₁₆ inch long.

Most specimens have ridges on the back that form the letter H. This pest may be found on leaves, twigs, and sometimes fruit. It produces honeydew that serves as medium for the growth of a sooty mold; this mold reduces the effectiveness of the leaves and is difficult and expensive to remove from the fruit. A parasite shipped to California from South Africa in 1937 has made this species less of a problem.

• *Citricola scale* produces honeydew, which causes sooty mold to grow on the fruit. The female is gray, oblong, and about $\frac{3}{16}$ inch long. As is true of other scale species, this pest is victim of a variety of parasites.

• *Purple scale,* found on leaves, twigs, and fruit, produces a toxic substance that kills the more heavily infested parts of the tree. Its presence can often be detected at a distance by these dead areas. The scale can be recognized by the narrow, oystershell-shaped female, which is about $\frac{1}{8}$ inch long and purplish in color.

• *Red scale* is found on leaves, twigs, and fruit and produces a toxic substance that causes a more-or-less general killing of leaves and twigs. The scale is reddish brown, almost round, and a little over $\frac{1}{12}$ inch in diameter. On green fruit it causes a yellow spot somewhat larger than the scale; on leaves the spot extends through to the other side. Four chalcid wasp species give good control, according to Lester Swann in *Beneficial Insects.* A fifth was imported from Israel, and is now established.

The California Agricultural Extension Service says that, "In areas where no red scale is present the best way to avoid infestation is to prevent spread from infested hosts." Boxes, ladders, bags and other picking equipment used in harvesting require fumigation. Pickers' clothing should be well brushed to remove crawlers that might settle in uninfested trees. Although lemons may be sprayed with petroleum oils in April and May, the preferred timing of oil sprays on most other varieties of citrus is late summer or fall. The timing on navel oranges is critical, as this variety is most susceptible to injury. Oil treatments to maturing fruit are to be avoided—coloring of the rind and internal quality may be affected and fruit drop can occur. Timing of oil treatments varies for citrus varieties and areas. For specific information on timing of treatments, consult your local extension agent. High or subfreezing temperatures, low soil moisture, and low humidity can increase the susceptibility of trees and fruit to injury by oil sprays.

In California, discontinue spraying when it is evident that temperatures will reach 80°F. in the coastal areas, 85°F. in the intermediate areas, and 95°F. in the interior areas. Oil-sprayed trees may be injured if the spraying is followed by hot dry winds. Spraying should be discontinued if the relative humidity is 35 percent or lower in coastal areas, 30 percent or lower in intermediate areas, or 20 percent or lower in interior areas. You should spray as soon as possible after an irrigation so that the foliage will be as turgid as possible.

Red scale has been controlled biologically in a substantial number of orchards, reports the California Extension Service. Certain conditions are necessary for this method to be effective: favorable weather, control of ants, a minimal amount of dust or dirt on the trees, and choice of control measures that are least harmful to the red scale parasites. In California, weather conditions are most favorable for parasites in the coastal and intermediate climatic areas, and the possibility of biological control of red scale is good there if the other conditions are provided. The most important enemies of red scale are the parasites *Aphytis lingnanensis* Compere and *Prospaltella perniciosi* Tower in coastal areas, and *Aphytis melinus* De Bach and *Comperiella bifaciata* Howard in interior areas. The advice of a qualified entomologist should be sought in order to evaluate the possibilities for biological control in a given orchard.

• "Ethion is the common treatment for *snow scale,* along with dusting sulphur," says grower Robert Plimpton, "but a friend of mine in the citrus business told me his snow scale got progressively worse the more he used Ethion, and when he quit Ethion, his snow scale all but disappeared and was no longer an economic factor to him." Plimpton's reaction? "We sold our Ethion." A wasp parasite of snow scale has recently made the news. Importations have practically cleaned up the pest in several areas of Florida. Dr. Robert F. Brooks, the entomologist who is releasing the wasps, says that "eradication of the snow scale may not be possible, but this wasp should keep snow scale populations at such a low level that we can tolerate them and not worry about them."

• *Yellow scale* is often found mixed with red scale. It lives on leaves, where it produces a marked yellow spotting, and on twigs. It may cause heavy leaf drop, but not the serious diebacks that result from red scale. A chalcid wasp imported from the Far East handles yellow scale populations, as long as ants aren't bringing in great numbers.

Control scale insects with an oil-emulsion spray. This may be applied from petal fall in spring through September, but the preferred time is June 15 to July 15 in Florida, and June through

August in California. It is best not to spray trees that show signs of wilt, or to apply dosages less than six weeks apart. Although this spray is primarily for scale control, it will also remove sooty mold from the foliage and provide protection from other pests that attack citrus during midsummer. Important natural enemies include the Australian ladybug, twice-stabbed ladybug, and several predacious mites and parasitic wasps.

Six-spotted mites are about the same size as purple mites but are yellow white to sulfur-yellow in color. Adults usually have six dark spots that are barely visible on the back or abdomen with a 10X magnifying glass. These mites live in colonies on the undersurface of the leaves only, especially along the veins and midribs. Injury appears as yellow spots, often cupped toward the top of the leaf. Six-spotted mites prefer grapefruit, but are found on other types of citrus. They usually disappear with rainy weather. Oil sprays are effective. See SPIDER MITE.

The **white flies** [color] that infest citrus are not considered serious pests in commercial groves but are disliked by growers of ornamental citrus plants. The nymph, which is seldom recognized by the grower, infests the underside of the leaves and sucks sap from them, resulting in injury to some trees. Ornamental growers object to the dark sooty mold fungus that grows on honeydew given off by the immature stages of the white fly. If this pest is causing intolerable damage, consider an oil spray as recommended for scale insects (see above). It may help to remove chinaberry trees from the area. Given favorable weather conditions, red-and-yellow fungi grow on and destroy many of these pests. These colorful beneficial organisms are seen as brightly colored pustules on the underside of leaves.

Whitefly

Diseases

Anthracnose is a catch-all term for three citrus maladies—wither tip, anthracnose stain, and anthracnose spot. While it was originally thought that these conditions were caused by a fungus, the fungus is actually either a secondary invader of weakened tissue or a latent infection that only becomes noticeable after the fungus takes hold in dead tissue. Control of wither tip and anthracnose spot depends on maintaining tree vigor, and not on eliminating a fungus.

• *Wither tip* describes the gradual yellowing, parching and dropping of leaves, followed by dieback of twigs and branches. In some cases, the wilted leaves stay on the tree, giving portions of the canopy the appearance of having been scorched by fire, says

L. C. Knorr in *Citrus Diseases and Disorders*. If you look closely at affected twigs, you may see a light gumming and a distinct line of separation between healthy and killed tissue. Tiny black fruiting bodies of the secondary fungus appear as speckles on dead terminals.

Now that it is known that the fungus acts as a secondary problem and is not alone responsible for seriously damaging trees, wither tip is no longer held to be a serious problem. It has come to light that dieback usually results when injured roots can no longer support the leaves and twigs, which then wilt and die back until there is a balance between roots and tops. Root troubles are usually the result of deep plowing, fluctuating water tables, drought, fertilizer burn or soil deficiencies, oil spillage, and insects and diseases. Conditions up top may also lead to dieback—hurricanes, long spells of hot and dry wind, salty sea spray, and winged pests.

• A second condition once attributed to anthracnose fungus is *anthracnose stain*, which is a russeting and tearstaining of rinds. Researchers have found that these symptoms can be traced to the citrus rust mite and to melanose.

• *Anthracnose spot* is the third disease to be blamed on fungus. Lesions on rinds are round, brown or black, sunken, hard, and measure $\frac{1}{8}$ to $\frac{3}{4}$ inches in diameter, with tiny black fruiting bodies sometimes visible. These spots later serve as entrances for rot organisms, but pathogens are a secondary cause of damage and do not initiate spotting. According to Knorr, anthracnose spots usually develop at sites of mechanical injuries or in fruit that is overripe. Grapefruit is especially vulnerable.

In light of what is now known about so-called anthracnose diseases, control is a matter of maintaining tree vigor, as well as preventing mechanical injury to fruit.

If you have inherited an orchard in which chemical controls were practiced, trees may show signs of *arsenic toxicity*. Arsenic is sometimes sprayed on grapefruit trees to lower the acidity of fruit that is harvested early, and an overdose of the chemical shows up as chlorosis of the leaves. The affects are cumulative, and several years of spraying causes the most serious damage.

In light cases, chlorotic spots appear in a mottled pattern, extending to the leaf margins and often crossing veins. This symptom could be confused with manganese deficiency except that arsenic injury is first seen on mature leaves in summer and fall, usually on the south and southwest sides of trees. In serious cases, leaves become yellow throughout and drop, and fruit is misshapen, dwarfed, hard, and spotted within. Knorr points out that such symptoms on fruit are similar to those caused by boron deficiency, and it is likely that overdoses of arsenic are linked with boron deficiency. You can help trees out by supplying boron in the form of ground glass, commercially available as FTE (Fritted Trace Elements). This supplies the soil with the raw stuff necessary for natural chelation.

Blight is an umbrella term for several diseases, all having in common blightlike wilt and dieback in the tops. These diseases are orange blight, limb blight, go-back, wilt, dry wilt, leaf curl, roadside decline, and Plant City disease. Just as confusing as this maze of names is the disease itself—no one seems to know for sure its cause. As most people think of it, blight of citrus crops involves: 1) foliage wilting despite sufficient soil moisture; 2) dieback that is apparently independent of trunk or root damage; and 3) the appearance of water sprouts after the onset of decline.

This mysterious disease is terminal—once affected, trees never recover. The progress of infection in the orchard does not spread from tree to tree, but jumps around without apparent reason. You'll first notice an unusual dullness of the foliage that precedes wilting. Leaves may revive somewhat at night, but wilting becomes progressively worse, and rains and irrigation are of no help. Leaves then roll, droop, and drop, and dieback soon follows. An unusual number of water sprouts appear with the rainy season, and the new foliage is soon killed by the disease. In distinguishing this disease from others with similar symptoms, Knorr points out that, in early stages of wilt, trees appear to have normal root systems. This characteristic distinguishes blight from disorders having both similar above-ground symptoms and roots obviously damaged by water, excess fertilizer, nematodes, gophers, fuel oil spillage, or mushroom root rot. Also, blight seldom hits trees of less than 12 years.

While researchers debate the causes of this disease, your only recourse is to take out affected trees and stick in new ones. Chemicals, transplanting, and pruning are to no avail.

Brown rot gummosis, also called foot rot, is caused by a fungus that attacks and kills the bark at or near the ground level. Large quantities of gum are usually produced when the infection is above ground. Under some conditions, the fungus may attack the upper part of the trunk or even limbs and twigs at the top of the tree. Lime and lemon varieties are most susceptible to this fungus; orange, grapefruit, and mandarin varieties are somewhat resistant. Of the common stocks, smooth lemon, sweet orange, rough lemon, Cleopatra mandarin, Carrizo and Troyer citrange, and trifoliate orange are most resistant. Highly susceptible rootstock varieties include smooth lemon, Page, sweet orange, and grapefruit. Infection is favored when wet soil remains in contact with the bark.

To avoid gummosis, plant trees high enough so that, after settling, the point at which the first lateral roots branch out is at ground level. On heavy soil it is especially important to use stocks that are resistant to the disease. With older trees, all soil should be removed from around the trunk down to, or even below, the first lateral roots. Never apply water around the base of the tree, for this area should be as dry as possible. Nursery growers can treat seeds for ten minutes in 125°F. water.

Treatment consists of exposing the crown roots and cutting away the dead bark and about ½ inch of the live bark. No wood should be removed. Cover the wound with a tree surgeon's solution. If the disease has killed the bark more than halfway around the tree it is best to remove the tree and replant.

Canker is a bacterial disease that has been eliminated in the United States by burning infected trees and nursery plantings. However, relaxed quarantine practices may allow the fungus to re-enter the country on fruit from Japan. If growers are alert to the symptoms, an infestation could be wiped out before much damage is done. So, against that eventuality, the characteristics of this erstwhile killer are given here.

Canker may appear on any citrus variety. It is first seen on young leaves, twigs, and fruits as small watery spots that rise just above the normal tissue. These lesions later become grayish white and break open to show tan, spongy tissue. Once canker has struck, your only recourse is to destroy infected trees with flame throwers and disinfect workers' clothes and tools.

Lemon trees grown on sour orange stock are particularly susceptible to **citrus scab**, the principal lemon disease in Florida. The scab is caused by a fungus that attacks the new growth and young fruits of citrus trees. It seems to attack the growing parts of the treetop only while the shoots are very young and tender. Once the tissues have become developed and hardened, the disease cannot affect them; leaves more than ½ inch wide and fruits more than ¾ inch in diameter are immune. The scab develops its worst attacks in cool weather, when the foliage and fruit are growing slowly and it has an opportunity to gain a foothold. Dampness also favors the disease.

Scab is not a problem in dry, arid regions of the country. California plantings never suffer from it, though the disease has doubtless had many chances to reach California orchards in stock from Florida. For that reason, lemons have been grown with greater success in California than in Florida.

Scab fungus is carried over from year to year in infected twigs and leaves. It does not live over from season to season in ripe fruit. The fungus finds the most congenial conditions in sour orange sprouts that happen to arise from the rootstock and in water sprouts from rough lemon stock. These sprouts should be destroyed as soon as they appear in any citrus tree. Also, where the scab has appeared, all infected growth should be pruned out of the tree before new growth starts in spring. The strictest sanitation should be observed in the vicinity of trees which have been infected, and all fallen twigs and leaves should be removed and burned. A hybrid lemon, the Perrine, is very resistant to scab.

Green and blue mold first occurs as water-soaked spots of up to ½ inch across that rapidly enlarge to cover most of the fruit. Harvested fruit is most often affected, but may be occasionally struck while on the tree. Blue or green spores soon appear on the water-soaked area. There's no way to avoid the two species of causal spores, as they are always present in the air. Fruit should be handled carefully to prevent the injuries to the rind through which the spores enter. The blue species can spread from infected to healthy fruit by physical contact, and this means even greater care during harvest.

The false spider mite is responsible for spreading **leprosis**, a canker affecting fruit, leaves, twigs, and branches of citrus trees. Damage is worst on early and midseason varieties of sweet oranges, and sour oranges are also troubled. The disease first appears as chlorotic spots on green fruit. The spots eventually enlarge and turn brown, earning the alternate name of nailhead rust, and become cracked in the center. Spots on the leaves are somewhat long and ragged, not round as on fruit, and most are found near the margins. On the bark, thick reddish brown scales develop from tiny yellow spots.

Control of leprosis is dependent on control of the causal mites. A spray of wettable sulfur, mixed 10 pounds to 100 gallons of water, will do the trick.

Lightning is a spectacular and frequent phenomenon in citrus groves of Florida, reports Dr. E. P. DuCharme, professor and plant pathologist with the Lake Alfred (Florida) Agricultural Research and Education Center. Lightning damage usually covers an area in the shape of an irregular circle or oval, he says. The effects of lightning on citrus are much less dramatic than on other trees; there are no fires, no branches wrenched from the tree, and no bark torn loose. Usually the first symptoms are a permanent wilting of foliage, yellowing of the midveins and leaf veins, and defoliation. Wilting may start within four to six hours of the strike, according to Dr. DuCharme. The most characteristic symptom is a green bud surrounded by dead bark. Lightning typically hits one or two trees hard; those suffering a direct hit show narrow strips of injured bark running down the trunk. L. C. Knorr says in *Citrus Diseases and Disorders* that moisture-deficient trees suffer more than those well supplied with water. Deep-rooted trees are damaged more than shallow-rooted ones, and trees on clayey soils are more resistant than those on sandy soils. But there seems to be no way to avoid damage entirely, says Dr. DuCharme, unless each tree is equipped with lightning rods.

You can best discourage **mushroom root rot** as land is being cleared for the orchard by removing stumps and roots of the previous inhabitants.

Psorosis is the common name for a number of virus diseases that share the symptom of vein-banding chlorosis in immature leaves. The chlorosis may either appear as thin, pale bands bordering veins and veinlets, or as a leaf-shaped chlorotic area centered on the affected leaf. Other causes may generate these symptoms, but psorosis leads to patterns that are bilaterally symmetrical. In lemons, the virus may cause uneven growth in the leaves and fruit; this results in rough fruit and crinkly leaves.

As sweet orange, grapefruit, and mandarin trees mature, the virus causes local areas of outer bark to break away in small, irregularly shaped scales. Only the surface of the bark is killed; new bark forms under the old as it continues to scale off. Frequently pockets of gum are formed under the bark, and beads of gum appear in the affected areas. As the areas of infected bark enlarge, the wood becomes stained, the top begins to die back, and the trees gradually cease to produce. The virus may also cause yellowish, circular areas to develop on the fruit and mature leaves, occasionally resembling symptoms of ringworm.

The heartbreak of psorosis is transmitted mainly by means of buds taken from infected trees, and occasionally by natural grafts that take place between roots of adjacent trees. You can avoid the disease by propagating nursery trees with buds from virus-free stock. It is desirable to remove the bark on the outer, affected layer. This may be done by carefully scraping the bark with a garden tool. However, trees that develop bark symptoms of the disease within five to seven years of planting should be removed.

Nematode-free nursery stock should guard you from the effects of **slow decline**, caused by injury of the citrus-root nematode to the root system. Tree growth subsides, foliage turns dull green or bronze, and leaves become cupped. Later, leaves can be seen to be smaller and tops thinner than those of healthy trees, and fruit yield is affected adversely both in size and number. To make sure that nematodes are responsible, a visual inspection is necessary. Knorr observes that severely attacked feeder roots are typically more stubby, misshapen, and brittle, and they lack the usual yellow or white color of normal roots. Nematode nests and eggs are visible under $10 \times$ magnification. See spreading decline, below.

Nematode problems do not come about suddenly, but build up over a period of years. Even after affected trees are removed, the soil may harbor nematodes for several years, so replanting healthy stock in infested areas is useless. Be sure to plant nematode-free trees in soil known to be safe.

The University of California Extension Service recommends the use of resistant rootstocks—Trifoliate orange and Troyer citrange in some locations—while cautioning that citrus nematode races exist, and that it is important to determine if Troyer citrange roots are susceptible to the race of nematodes present in the soil. In 50 percent of the orchards examined, roots of this variety have been attacked by the citrus nematode.

Sooty mold is caused by aphids, mealybugs, certain soft scales, and particularly immature white flies. All secrete a sweet, syrupy material known as honeydew. This falls on leaves and fruit and supports sooty mold fungus. Sooty mold can blacken an entire tree, including the fruit. Control sooty mold by controlling these insects. Oil sprays will usually cause the mold to flake off, making the leaves bright and shiny.

Burrowing nematodes are responsible for **spreading decline**. The limits of infested soil are clearly demarcated in the case of this disease, whereas the borders of slow decline (see above) are less evident. Another difference is that the progress of spreading decline is clearly visible, taking in about two trees in a row each year. The roots of affected trees show half the normal number of feeder roots, and inspection with the aid of a lens will show the nematodes in the roots. Avoid tangling with this nematode by using only nematode-free stock in uninfested soil.

Water spot occurs during long wet spells, late in the season when water is absorbed by the white portion of the rind through openings caused by injuries. The resultant swellings cause minute splits in the rind, permitting more water to be absorbed. This condition, together with the oil liberated from the injured rind, causes the cells to break down. If dry weather soon follows, depressed brown scars result. Fruit so affected is usually subject to decay and is not suitable for shipment. If moist weather continues in the orchard, various fungi attack the fruit and cause rapid decay.

Susceptibility to water spot increases as maturity advances. It is greatly increased by mechanical injuries and by ice that forms on the fruit in cold weather. Early picking and orchard practices performed carefully to avoid fruit injury are also important in reducing loss from this condition.

Clematis

The **clematis borer** is a dull-white worm with a brown head, growing up to ⅔ inch long. It hollows out stems and tunnels the crown and roots, causing vines to become stunted and branches to die. Larvae spend the winter in the roots. To control, cut out and burn infested stems, and dig out larvae in crowns.

Other pests with a penchant for clematis include blister beetles (see ASTER), NEMATODES, and SCALE.

Collard

Collard is afflicted by many pests and diseases of the members of the cabbage family; see CABBAGE.

Collards were used in an experiment at Cornell University to test the value of interplanting in reducing insect populations. They concentrated on a particularly destructive species of flea beetle. In three plots, only collards were grown, while three other plots were planted to collards with alternate rows of tomato and tobacco plants. Said one researcher, "Most of the monocultured plots had from twice to three times the number of flea beetles as the interplanted plots." From such results, a general conclusion may be drawn: the greater the diversity of plants in any given garden area, the more pronounced the insect-repelling effect will be.

Columbine

Insects

The columbine **aphid** is one of several species seen on this plant. They cause stunting of foliage in late summer. See APHID.

The **columbine borer** feeds in the petioles and stems of both wild and cultivated plants in April and May; it later bores into crowns and roots. Infested plants wilt and die. Look for sawdust-like castings near entrance holes. The larva is a caterpillar, salmon-colored with a pale stripe down its back, and grows to 1½ inches long. To keep down the population of these borers, cut off infested stems or destroy infested plants. Clean up beds in spring, and scrape away surface soil or mulch to remove any overwintering eggs.

The **columbine skipper** is a butterfly with purplish wings. While pretty to look at, its larval form is a ¾-inch caterpillar that chews holes in leaves and rolls them up when not feeding for protection. This worm is green and has a black head. Control by handpicking feeding worms or crushing them when at rest.

Two species of **leaf miner** attack columbine. One makes serpentine mines and the other makes blotch mines. The pale, yellowgreen maggots eat their fill and then pupate on the under-side of leaves. Tiny brown, two-winged flies emerge in about two weeks. In the fall, fully grown miners drop to the ground and crawl into the soil to spend the winter. When infestation is light, pick off and destroy leaves; hoe the ground around plants in fall to expose the miners to the elements and birds.

MEALYBUGS, stink bugs (see SNAPDRAGON), and the WHITE FLY may feed on columbine.

Diseases

Wilt disease causes leaves and stems to wilt and dry up, followed by death of the entire plant. Inside the stem you may be able to see sclerotia (resting bodies) that look like mustard seeds. Cut out and dispose of affected plant parts, being careful not to let infected material come in contact with the soil.

Corn

Insects

Just as corn is a favorite crop for many gardeners and a major crop for many farmers, it is an important food for an impressive, or depressing, number of pests. While pests of corn have been the subject of much research, it still is vulnerable to insects in the garden and in the field.

Aphid

Of the several **aphids** known to damage corn, two are of particular concern to gardeners and farmers. The small, green blue corn leaf aphid infests the tassels, upper leaves, and upper part of the stalk. It is most prevalent in the South, and recently its numbers have increased in the American corn belt and Ontario. As the aphid feeds, it secretes a sticky substance called honeydew, which serves as a medium for a black fungus growth. This secretion also attracts corn earworm moths. Severe aphid infestations may prevent pollination and as a result the ears will have no kernels.

Growers have several natural predators on their side, including ladybugs and lacewings. Plant corn as early as possible, and encourage rapid growth by using fertile soil and good cultural methods. Find out which hybrid varieties are least susceptible to aphid damage.

Corn root aphids are similar in appearance to the corn leaf species. They feed on corn roots, but often rot on their own volition—they are carried to their meals by ants. Winged aphids that try to fly away are snapped up by the ants and taken below ground. Because these aphids would be of little harm without other insects to lug them to your corn plants, efforts should be directed at controlling the ants; see ANTS for methods of keeping them away from crops.

In some years, the **armyworm** is a fairly serious pest of corn. The larva is a green or brown caterpillar with several longitudinal dark stripes and one broken light stripe. It grows to 1½ inches long, and feeds chiefly at night and during cloudy days.

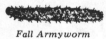

Fall Armyworm

Predators and parasites usually keep the armyworm in control —tachnid flies, egg parasites, birds, skunks, and toads. In most years, the outside rows along hay, pasture, or grain fields will absorb most of the damage. If vast numbers of worms make you feel helpless, try digging a ditch around the corn patch, with the side next to the corn plowed so that it is perpendicular. The armyworms will be trapped and at your mercy. You can reduce armyworm populations with the old-time practice of planting alternate rows of sunflowers. The efficacy of this method has recently been substantiated by researchers in Cuba, according to the British *New Scientist*. For many years, Greeks have grown alternate rows of maize (Indian corn) with cotton, and it is likely that the survival of this practice is partly attributable to reduced pest problems.

Several species of **billbugs** attack corn, occasionally causing serious damage east of the Great Plains in the United States and Canada. They are shaped like slender footballs and range in color from reddish brown to black. Billbugs typically play dead when disturbed. The larvae are humpbacked white grubs with a yellow or brown head. The adults eat small holes in the stems of very young plants and perforate unfolding leaves; the grubs attack roots and may tunnel up into stems.

To avoid problems with billbugs, don't plant corn on land that hasn't been cultivated for several years; these pests favor old pastures and reclaimed swamplands. Fall plowing, good drainage, crop rotation, and clean cultivation all help minimize danger.

A recent emigrant from Europe is the **cereal leaf beetle**; it bears watching as a serious threat to cereal crops and corn. This beetle was first discovered in the United States in 1962, and arrived in Canada five years later. It occurs from Wisconsin and Illinois east to the mid–Atlantic states, and in southern Ontario. Look for a ¼-inch-long beetle with a dark head, reddish thorax and legs, and a metallic blue back. The larvae are dark brown. Small yellow eggs may be seen near the midrib on the underside of leaves.

Parasites have been released, and may bring the cereal leaf beetle into control. Early planting is recommended.

The **chinch bug** is tiny, black, and has white wings and red legs. Nymphs are reddish in color. One positive way of identifying the chinch bug is by stepping on a few—they will put off a bad odor. They do their worst in the Mississippi, Ohio, and Missouri River valleys, in Texas and Oklahoma, and in extreme south-western Ontario. Chinch bugs and the nymphs climb the corn plants and suck juices from the stem.

Chinch Bug

The most effective way of dealing with chinch bugs is keeping the area around the garden free of weeds. Well-fertilized soil and early planting also help. Remember that small grains also appeal to this pest; planting wheat next to corn is an invitation it will find hard to resist. Interplanting soybeans will protect corn, as the broad soybean leaves shade the base of the corn stalk and make the stalks less appealing to the chinch bug. Some gardeners and farmers use physical barriers to keep the young, wingless bugs from crawling to the corn patch; *The Gardener's Bug Book* suggests turning up a ridge of earth with a plow and pouring a line of creosote on top. Finally, there are several resistant varieties available.

If you have grown sweet corn, you are probably familiar with

*Corn Earworm,
Adult and Larva*

the **corn earworm** [color]. It is found throughout the United States and eastern Canada. Early in the season, the eggs—dirty white, ribbed domes—may be seen glistening singly on host plants. These hatch to produce one of the most destructive of insects, a striped caterpillar that varies in color from light yellow or green to brown. They have yellow heads and grow to almost two inches in length. (Because of this pest's omniverous habits, it is also known as the tomato fruitworm and the cotton bollworm.) Early in the season, the earworm attacks buds and eats ragged patches out of tender, unfolding leaves. The most serious damage occurs later, when the larvae attack the ears. At first they feed on the fresh silky tassels, and may sever them. As the silks dry, the earworms shift to the kernels, starting from the tip. They frequently penetrate to the middle of the ear, leaving behind moist castings. Overall, trouble to the crop occurs in several ways: chewed silk prevents pollination; damaged kernels are prone to several diseases; and marred ears must be trimmed before they can be marketed, lowering value while increasing labor cost during production.

If you find earworms in the first corn that you harvest, prevent an outbreak by applying mineral oil into the silk just inside the tip of each ear—½ a medicine dropper's worth for a small ear, ¾ for a larger ear. Large-scale growers may find that a cheap oil can is easier to use. Do not apply until the silk has wilted and begun to turn brown at the tip, as earlier treatment will interfere with pollination and result in poorly filled ears. Mineral oil acts by suffocating the worms; it is tasteless and will not affect the flavor of the kernels. Another method of dealing with earworms already at work is to pull back the sheath a bit and gouge the pests out. This should be done after the silk begins to turn brown and when you are sure that pollination is complete. A third method of control is easier but not quite so effective. Simply walk through the corn patch every four days and cut the silk off close to the ear. Some growers plant marigolds around and among the corn.

Any corn variety with long, tight husks is physically safer from the earworm; see RESISTANT VARIETIES. The North Carolina Agricultural Experiment Station has found that clipping a clothes pin on the silk channel at the early silk stage will increase the effect of husk tightness and keep the worms from damaging the ears. Luckily, egg parasites, birds, moles, and cold damp spells of weather all are in your favor; even earworms, if hungry enough, will eat other earworms. The adult, a nondescript grayish brown moth, is attracted to lights and its numbers may be reduced with blacklight traps. The USDA reports that early plantings are least damaged in the Northeast and the north central states. However, early plantings are more susceptible to the European corn borer (below).

Soldier beetle larvae enter the pests' tunnel and eat the worm. Small black flower bugs eat both eggs and larvae; the beneficial's red nymphal form is also very helpful. As for the birds, Swann notes in *Beneficial Insects* that "the most important of these are the Brewer's and the California red-winged blackbird, the boat-tailed grackle, the English sparrow, and the downy woodpecker. The attack of the birds in their search for the earworms is sometimes so vigorous that they cause damage to the corn, especially sweet corn, by tearing open the husks."

The bacterial pathogen *Bacillus thuringiensis* has been found effective against the earworm, especially when applied as a dust. It is more lethal to the younger larvae that work close to the surface than to older larvae that are on their way into the ears. Pollination is not affected by this pathogen. See BACILLUS THURINGIENSIS. Another disease, one you can collect from nature, is NUCLEAR POLYHEDROSIS VIRUS.

Several species of the fat, smooth, pulpy **cutworm** attack corn, usually at night. You can often catch them in the ray of a flashlight. When disturbed, cutworms curl into a ring, and they spend their days resting in this position just below the soil around affected plants. The black cutworm (also known as the greasy cutworm) is black, or nearly black, and has a greasy appearance. Look for a broken yellow line on the back with a pale line to each side. They grow to 1½ inches or longer, and move restlessly about from plant to plant, cutting them off at ground level. The dingy cutworm is a dingy brown and is marked with a pale, triangular pattern on its back. They sometimes will climb to eat leaves, and become fairly inactive as summer progresses. Other species that feed on corn plants include: the variegated and spotted cutworms, which climb to the leaves at night; the glassy cutworm, a greenish white, translucent worm that feeds underground; and the claybacked cutworm, which is distinguished by a broad, pale stripe running down its back. For control measures, see TOMATO.

Another very important insect invader of corn is the **European corn borer** [color], a flesh-colored caterpillar that grows to one inch long and has brown spots and a dark brown head. You will likely find this borer on other crops as well—it is known to attack more than 200 plants. It has yet to spread to the Far

Cutworm

European Corn Borer

West or Florida, but farmers and gardeners elsewhere in the United States are vulnerable. According to the Canada Department of Agriculture, the borer is a serious pest of market sweet corn and canning corn from Quebec eastward; it is no longer a major pest of grain corn in southwestern Ontario, thanks in part to recent resistant varieties. The larva passes winter in corn stubble and pupates in spring. The nocturnal yellow brown moth appears in May, or early June in Canada. The male is much darker than the female, and dark wavy bands cross his wings. The eggs are laid in masses of 15 to 20 on the underside of leaves, overlapping each other like fish scales. These hatch early in June, and the borers immediately crawl to protected places on the corn plant, eating their way through the stalks and into the base of ears. Larvae may be found inside corn kernels. Broken tassels and stalks, and sawdust castings outside of small holes are signs that borers are feasting on your corn.

According to the Canada Department of Agriculture, "Cultural control should always be practiced because it is good agricultural policy. Shred and plow under cornstalks in or near fields where borers overwinter." This should be done in fall or early spring, before the adults emerge. It is generally advisable to plant as late as possible, but be certain to stay within the normal growing period of your locality. Another caution is that late plantings are especially vulnerable to the corn earworm; if this pest is an important one in your area, corn should be planted to come to silk when other plant hosts are up. In New York through southern New England, corn set in the latter half of May will usually mature between the two generations of borers. In Ontario, very early and very late plantings are particularly susceptible—moths of the overwintering generation are attracted to early-planted corn, and midsummer moths lay their eggs on late-planted corn.

Although there are no immune strains currently available, plant hybrids that are resistant or tolerant. Consult your county agent or state experiment station for help in selecting the best hybrid for your locality.

Handpicking is the oldest and simplest of remedies, and it can be very effective in controlling the borer. On plants showing external signs of borer activity, split the stalk a little below the entrance hole with a fingernail and pluck out the worm. For growers north of the Mason-Dixon line, shredding corn stalks from the ground up by April 1 and covering them with soil will go far toward discouraging a borer infestation. In fact, some gardeners believe that widespread use of this method alone would soon wipe out the pest. Also, cleaning up grassy or weedy areas adjoining the corn field will help prevent trouble.

There are still other methods of borer control available to the farmer or gardener who declines to use poison sprays. Since the corn borer lives from 10 to 24 days of its life as a nocturnal moth, it can be attracted to a light trap and then destroyed. A daylight-blue lamp will draw hundreds of the moths to their death. One gardener from New York's Hudson Valley has gotten excellent results with an electrocuting grid. Bruce Matthews sets the device high over the corn rows and installs a pair of 150-watt floodlights aimed through the grid to illuminate the rows on all sides. A timer turns the system on at 9 p.m. and off at 3 a.m. during the time of the moth's second appearance of the season. The results, he reports, are excellent.

Parasites have been used against corn borers with considerable success. The USDA has imported a parasitic tachnid fly, *Lydella stabulans grisenscens*, and this ally is now well established in southern New England and the Middle Atlantic states, and in Illinois, Indiana, Iowa, Kentucky, and southwestern Ohio. The adult fly deposits larvae, not eggs, at the entrance of borer tunnels. Lester A. Swann, in *Beneficial Insects,* describes what happens next. "As soon as the larva is deposited at the burrow opening it seeks out the host and enters it through a body opening or by puncturing the skin with its mandibles. Inside the host, it immediately seeks the main tracheal trunks of the breathing apparatus, cuts one of these, and forms a connecting funnel to supply itself with oxygen during development. When feeding is completed, the fly maggot leaves the host by puncturing its skin, and spins a cocoon alongside the host skin, or near by."

Other parasites of the borer include the gardener's good friend, the ladybug, which consumes an average of almost 60 borer eggs a day, and the trichogramma wasp, a commercially available egg parasite. Considerable work with diseases that affect the borer is being done at the USDA Corn Borer Research Unit at Ankeny, Iowa. In answer to a request for information on the status of the various borer natural enemies, the research unit named *Macrocentrus grandi,* a braconid wasp, as ". . . the most prevalent parasite collected throughout the Cornbelt. It will parasitize as many as 35 percent of the corn borer larvae in any given year in certain locations." Borers are also susceptible to a protozoan disease, *Perezia pyraustae,* that is found extensively in nature. This and other valuable protozoans are not available commercially, says the research unit, because there is as yet no satisfactory way to culture the disease organisms on artificial medium. You *can* buy the bacterium *Bacillus thuringiensis,* which is effective in controlling the borer and other lepidopteran pests; see BACILLUS THURINGIENSIS.

Flea Beetle

The small, dark **flea beetle** is so named because it jumps quickly when disturbed. Although it eats small holes in leaves in early summer, it is more important as a vector of bacterial wilt of corn, known also as Stewart's disease. This malady stunts growth of young corn plants and can kill them. It is most likely to occur after a mild winter and a cool, wet spring.

Plant varieties that are resistant to wilt; Canadians should be aware that North Star and Northern Belle are particularly vulnerable varieties of sweet corn. For other ways of combatting this pest, see POTATO.

Corn growing on the margins of fields is vulnerable to damage from **grasshoppers**. To help keep leaves, tassels, and stalks from being devoured, mow fields early in the season and keep them cut short. In *The Bug Book*, the Philbricks got good results in spring by knocking grasshoppers down with a long bamboo pole and letting their hens gobble them up. For other control methods, see GRASSHOPPER.

Grasshopper

Chainlike markings on the surfaces of leaves are probably the work of the **grass thrip**. Lowermost foliage may be killed, and larger leaves may take on a silvery sheen. Developing kernels are sometimes destroyed. Control by cleaning up plant litter where the pests hibernate.

The **lesser cornstalk borer**, a blue green worm with brown stripes, bores into lower parts of corn stalks. Although generally distributed, control is only necessary in the South. The borers make dirt-covered, silken tubes that lead away from stem tunnels in the soil. Stalks of young plants become distorted and may not produce ears.

Because the larvae spin their cocoons in plant debris, fall and winter cleanup of the garden area should reduce their numbers. Early planting and rotating corn with a resistant crop also are effective measures.

Several species of **sap beetle** attack corn. The adult is small ($\frac{3}{16}$ inch long), usually black, and active, and feeds on the ears of sweet corn, frequently making small round holes through the husk to enter the ear. The maggotlike larva is also harmful, eating into kernels of corn that is already damaged. It is white or cream-colored, grows up to ¼ inch long, and scatters over the ear when exposed to light.

The North Carolina Agricultural Experiment Station suggests that there will be fewer overwintering beetles if rotting plant material is kept from the area. The mechanisms that prevent damage to ears by corn earworms appear to operate somewhat against sap beetles, says the station, although corn earworms are rarely found in ears damaged by sap beetles. A number of resistant varieties are available.

The **seed-corn maggot** burrows its way into planted seeds, injuring them so that they produce sickly plants; also, soil organisms may thus gain entry to the seed and cause it to rot. The maggots are yellowish white, ¼ inch long, and have pointed head ends; the adult is a small, grayish brown fly. Damage is greatest in cold, wet weather and with shallowly planted seed. See BEAN for control measures.

The **stalk borer** is distributed generally east of the Rockies. It is a very active, slender caterpillar that grows up to 1½ inches long. The young insect is creamy white with a dark purple band around the body and several brown or purple stripes running down the back. The mature caterpillar loses the lengthwise stripes and takes on a grayish or light purple hue. It bores into the stalks of corn and works unseen. Plants around the periphery are particularly apt to be damaged.

Because the borer works out of sight, by the time you spot damage it may be too late to come to the plant's rescue. You can try slitting the stalk with a fingernail, plucking out the borer, and binding the stem. Keep weeds and grasses down in the garden area, since these serve as winter nurseries for eggs and newly hatched stalk borers.

Several similar species of **white grubs**, which are the immature forms of the common, large brown May or June beetles, may harm corn by feeding on the roots. They are white with brown heads and are found in the soil in a characteristic curved position. Because eggs are usually laid in grasslands, damage to crops is greatest when they are planted on newly broken sod land, especially if the soil is sandy or sandy loam. These beetles have a three-year life cycle, and outbreaks of white grubs occur every third year in the eastern United States and most of Ontario (in 1975, 1978, and so on); north of Montreal Island and around St. Jean, damage will be heaviest one year later in the same cycle,

June Bug Grub,
Adult and Pupa

while south of Montreal Island and in the Eastern Townships, white grubs will be troublesome one year earlier.

Most problems can be avoided by not planting corn on new sod land. Plowing in summer or fall kills or exposes the grubs to their predators.

Wireworm

Any one of several species of **wireworm** may cause poor development of plants. They are hard, wirelike worms, varying in color from white to yellow to brown and darkening as they grow longer. They may bore into corn seed and eat the germ, or enter the underground stem to cause young plants to wilt, discolor, or die. Damage is worst when corn is planted on soil that is the first or second year out of sod. See WIREWORM.

Diseases

Wilted leaves on dry days may be a sign of **bacterial wilt** or Stewart's wilt, a common disease of corn in the central, southern, and eastern states. Sweet corn is the most susceptible, especially the early, yellow, sweeter varieties. The wilting is caused by blockage of vascular bundles by the developing bacteria, and increased watering is of little use in saving plants. Leaves take on long pale streaks; when a severely infected stalk is cut after a rain or heavy dew, a sticky yellow ooze of bacteria exudes from the severed bundle.

The flea beetle (see above) is an important vector of this disease, especially after mild winters. Most white late-maturing varieties are resistant to wilt. Other control measures are destroying infected refuse and deep plowing of stubble in fall.

Ear rot [color], or diplodia ear rot, usually first occurs in the shank and then spreads into the ear. Rotting may also begin at the tip of the ear. Husks tend to become dry and bleached, and are often stuck together. You will see miniscule, black fruiting bodies embedded in the moldy kernels and husks—these create the spores that transmit the disease.

Use diplodia-resistant hybrid corn seed and don't follow corn with corn. Be sure to plow corn stalks under deep so that the disease is not spread.

Helminthosporium leaf spot [color] is a fungus disease that appears late in summer after wet weather as a sudden leaf scorch. Affected leaves look as though damaged by an early frost, and the fungus makes black threadlike growths on the injured tissue. To reduce the chances of infestation, avoid late planting and fertilize the plants properly.

Root rot is characterized by plants that are easily blown over and stalks that show a reddish tint when split open. The only known control measures are crop rotation and use of soil that is properly drained.

Corn **smut** [color] is a common fungus disease that appears as large, irregularly shaped galls on all parts of the plant. At first, the galls are grayish white, darkening as the season progresses until they burst to release masses of black fungus spores. Ripened spore masses have an oily appearance.

Preventative measures include instituting a three-year crop rotation, use of disease-resistant seed (see RESISTANT VARIE-TIES), turning under of garden trash or manure, and removal of old stalks in fall. As is true with many other maladies of corn, smut is less likely to affect healthy plants, and you should insure proper care and enrichment of the soil. After the fact, the only course left is to remove and destroy the galls. Spraying is of no help. If plants become too badly affected, they should be removed and burned. Be certain not to use diseased plants in making compost, since the fungus may affect the entire compost heap.

Another disease caused by diplodia fungus is **stalk rot**. After pollination time, look for reddish purple or dark brown blotches on leaf sheaths and stalks. Corn ears are rotted or chaffy, and many stalks will break after maturity.

Resistant varieties are available and a four-year (or longer) crop rotation will help you avoid this disease. Because the causal organism overwinters on injected stalks, crop residue should be plowed well under.

Several other rots affect corn; in general, good sanitation, crop rotation, and use of resistant varieties if available will help to keep your planting healthy.

A major problem for large scale corn growers is **weeds**. Richard Thompson, an organic farmer from Boone, Iowa, has found several ways of controlling foxtail in his fields. First, he uses a corn-beans-corn-oats-meadow rotation. The key to this method is the short growing time for the oats and hay. Foxtail is cut along with these crops, and isn't given a chance to make seed. Thompson points out that if a farmer is in continuous corn or a corn-beans rotation, the longer growing times will give the foxtail a chance to go to seed. He also cuts the fence rows before July 15 to discourage foxtail before the seeds set. Follow his schedule as the season progresses. Around April 1, disk the fields to kill young weeds and sprouting weed seeds so that the next cultivation is worthwhile. Thompson suggests disking every two weeks until planting time. He has found that a rough seedbed suits corn but discourages weeds, so he goes over the soil with a spring-tooth harrow just before planting in mid-May. At harvest time, Thompson has the satisfaction of a yield substantially above the national average—without herbicides.

Wildlife

The perceptive grower is grateful to the **birds** that are almost constantly at work in the garden for his or her benefit—but these benevolent feelings don't hold for crows, blackbirds, and starlings. Crows are fond of pulling up small corn plants in search of the tender kernels below. One way of getting around this problem is to plant untreated seeds through a permanent mulch that gives plants a chance to get off to a good start before the crows can spot them. By that time, any plant pulled will yield disappointing results to the average crow, and the flock will move on to another stand. The crow can be further discouraged by planting corn a bit deeper than recommended on the packet. After the plants are well established, pull the mulch back away from the plants. A Canadian gardener, Margaret J. Clark, has a solution for small-scale problems. She has found that crows will not bother germinating corn when three small twigs are stuck in the ground so that they lean together at the center of the hill. She points out, on the crow's behalf, that these birds do a good job of cleaning out cutworms early in the season. Some growers have diverted the crow's attention from the corn patch by setting out other food. This practice could have the negative effect of encouraging more hungry crows to visit your area—but crows are likely to prefer an easy meal to foraging for themselves. Netting around the corn plants gives protection at two periods in the season: until seedlings are well on their way, and for the two weeks preceding harvest.

Blackbirds raid corn plantings at dawn and dusk, stripping the ears. These birds do their worst when corn is in the silk stage. Bruce Matthew, a farmer from the Hudson Valley in New York, foiled the birds by placing seven–inch–high Dixie paper cups over each ear as the corn was pollinated. As mature corn was picked, he transferred the cups to less mature ears and eventually to the rows of a later planting. These inexpensive props should last more than one season. Dwight Stephenson of Ohio has come up with a novel, and effective, means of keeping blackbirds and starlings out of the garden. He cuts silhouettes of cats and snakes out of black tar paper, nailing the cats to a post and hanging the snakes on a string from cornstalks. He uses the cats for four or five days, and then replaces them with a shift of snakes, and so on throughout the season—the reason for this being that the birds will get used to a single shape and feel comfortable enough to enter the patch.

Raccoons are a serious pest for some corn growers. They may be fenced out of the garden area with chicken wire stapled to posts so that the wire projects a foot or so above the posts—raccoons climb fences rather than dig under them, and they will find themselves caught as their weight brings the slack top over onto them. Any that manage to get beyond that point may be kept from doing serious damage by tying a paper or plastic bag over each ear you want to insure, covered in turn with a piece of wire screening. The wire prevents the coon from tearing the bag, while the bag prevents him from reaching the corn through the wire. Although this scheme is virtually coon-proof, fencing is a lot easier.

A less time-consuming method has been suggested by Reverend Richard Wanke of Michigan: "About two weeks before the corn is ripe—the time that raccoons like to attack sweet corn—place one or two shakes of ground red pepper on the silk of each ear. The average garden can be protected in a few minutes, and a very large garden in half an hour. The cost is about ten cents per thousand ears." One treatment is sufficient, he reports, and the corn does not pick up the pepper flavor. The pepper can be mixed with lard so that it will adhere better. Another man of the cloth, Reverend Joseph C. Fleshman of Ohio, lashes a lit lantern on a six-foot pole set near the corn. As simple as this method is, it has worked for years. You might even try placing transistor radios between rows of corn or strawberries and dial a different all-night station on each radio. The raccoons evidently can't stand the discordant noise.

If, after these measures, raccoons are still getting to your corn, you might set up an electric fence. String 20-gauge wire at 8 and 16 inches above the ground, and use either a 6- or 12-volt battery or knocked-down house current for juice. Turn the fence on at night, since raccoons sleep during the day.

A final suggestion for outsmarting the coons: try planting pumpkin seeds with your corn, setting the seeds about four feet apart. The idea is that coons won't strip the ears because they like to be able to stand up and look around while they eat, and the big pumpkin leaves make that difficult.

If **squirrels** have been stealing corn seeds as fast as you can plant them, mix about one level teaspoonful of pepper to a pound of seed.

Cosmos

Insects

Among the insect pests of cosmos are the European corn borer (see CORN), LYGUS BUG, root APHIDS, six-spotted leafhopper (see ASTER), and SPIDER MITES.

Diseases

Sudden wilting of plants may be an effect of **bacterial wilt**, and is usually accompanied by a soft rot of the stem at the ground level. When stems are cut, a yellowish ooze appears. Infected plants should be destroyed and cosmos planted elsewhere, since the bacteria are soilborne.

The white, powdery appearance of leaves is a sign of **powdery mildew**. See MILDEW.

Stem canker causes dark brown spots to appear on stems. The spots later turn gray, rapidly enlarge, and girdle the stem to kill the plant. Burn old stems at the end of the season to reduce chances of the fungus overwintering.

Cucumber

Insects

Aphid

Melon **aphids** like nothing better than a meal of sap from the leaves of a cucumber. They are usually green but their color varies from yellow to black. Likely before you spot them feeding on the underside of cucumber leaves, you will notice the wilting and curling of the leaves. You may also see an unusual number of ants, bees, and flies swarming around, as they are attracted by the aphids' honeydew. If the aphids are numerous enough, the vine may either become too stunted to produce a crop or even die. The melon aphid is also dangerous as a vector of bacterial wilt.

Control is often not necessary, as parasites and predators do a good job of keeping populations down. These allies may have more than they can handle, however, if a cool, wet spring is followed by a hot, dry summer; for control measures, see APHID.

A particularly harmful pest of cucurbits in the Gulf States is the **melonworm**, a slender, active, greenish caterpillar that is identified by two narrow white stripes running the full length of its back. It feeds mostly on foliage, but may burrow into fruit. Control by handpicking.

Cucumbers in much of the country may be damaged by the **pickleworm** [color], which at first is a pale yellow with black spots that disappear as it matures. The full-grown worm is ¾ inch long and colored green or copperish. The pickleworm is especially serious in the Gulf States, but late in the season it is found as far north as New York and Michigan. They cause damage by burrowing into the buds, blossoms, vines, and fruits. Although very early spring plantings are seldom damaged, late crops may be ruined.

Pickleworm

Any hibernating pupae may be killed by plowing early in fall. At the end of the season, clean up all plant refuse from the garden. Pickleworms are attracted to squash blossoms, and squash may be planted as a trap crop. See RESISTANT VARIETIES.

The striped cucumber beetle's partner in destruction is the **spotted cucumber beetle** (also known as the southern corn rootworm). Like the striped species, this pest is rather slender, measures about ¼ inch long, and has a black head. The wing covers are yellow green, and 11 or 12 black spots are scattered on its back. This beetle not only has a big appetite, but carries the bacteria that cause cucumber wilt as well.

Spotted Cucumber Beetle

Control measures are generally as listed below for the striped cucumber beetle. The larvae, known as root worms, are easily controlled by rotating crops and prove troublesome only to growers who insist on growing continuous corn. See RESISTANT VARIETIES.

The yellow, black-spotted **squash beetle** looks something like a ladybug, and in fact is a member of the family. It is a minor pest, and you shouldn't find control measures necessary.

Although the **squash bug** prefers the taste of other cucurbits, it is an occasional pest of cucumber. The adults are dingy brownish black insects, are about ⅝ inch in length, and give off a very disagreeable odor when crushed. Immature bugs first have reddish heads and legs and green bodies, and later, black heads and legs and gray bodies. The southern squash bug, or horned squash bug, is a similar pest, and attacks cucumber north to Delaware. For control, see SQUASH.

Squash Bug and Nymph

East of the Rocky Mountains, the **squash vine borer** may tunnel in stems of cucumber and other cucurbits; you may see bits of yellow sawdustlike excrement around the holes or about the base of the plant. For control, see SQUASH.

East of the Rockies, the star insect enemy of the cucumber

*Striped Cucumber
Beetle*

is the **striped cucumber beetle** [color]. The adults are distinguished by yellow wing covers with three black longitudinal stripes, have a black head, and grow up to ¼ inch long. They enter the garden as soon as the cucumber seed germinates and you can usually find them on the underside of leaves. Other vine plants are also attacked; winter squash is particularly susceptible to damage throughout the growing season. The slender white larvae are up to ⅓ inch long, have brown ends, and damage plants by feeding on roots and underground parts of stems, sometimes destroying the entire root system. These wormlike larvae may also inoculate plants with bacterial wilt. The first and greatest damage results from the adults feeding on stems and leaves when the plants are just pushing through the ground and before they have developed true leaves. The beetle also is a vector for bacterial wilt and cucumber mosaic.

As an organic gardener, you have many means of control at your disposal. Perhaps the best of them is the time-tested procedure of heavy mulching. E. M. Watson of Chardon, Ohio, was treated to a graphic demonstration of the difference that mulching makes: "Last year I was setting out watermelon plants and was driven in by the rain before I could finish. I had all but one hill mulched with compost. I didn't get back for two days and the unmulched hill was literally destroyed by striped cucumber beetles; the others were not bothered."

Late planting is one of the easiest ways to avoid the worst beetle damage, although it is by no means fool-proof. If practicable, plant seed right after the first horde of beetles lay their eggs. *Organic Gardening and Farming* editor Gene Logsdon writes that he plants seed about June 15 on his Ohio farm. The trouble with this timing, he says, is that June 15 is just a little too late for good melon production. He gets around this problem by starting melons indoors in oversized pots around May 5. You might do so earlier or later, calculating on your juxtaposition from Logsdon's northern Ohio climate. He transplants the melons to the garden around June 15, and keeps them well powdered with rotenone.

Researchers have expended little effort in finding ways to control cucumber beetles biologically. Fortunately, nature provides a good measure of free control. The most effective enemies are a soldier beetle, a tachnid fly, a braconid wasp, and a nematode.

Israeli researchers have found that a straw mulch repels **white flies** near cucumber, reports R. E. F. Matthews in *Plant Virology*. See WHITE FLY.

Diseases

Among the diseases that may afflict cucumbers is **anthracnose** [color], a seed-borne disease caused by a fungus that lives in the soil. Leaves develop small, dark spots that may combine and destroy entire leaves. Fruits on young plants may turn black and drop off, and older fruits may be covered with irregularly shaped, sunken pits filled with salmon-colored growth. The disease is favored by warm, moist conditions.

A three or four year crop rotation is the best means of preventing anthracnose. None of the host plants—including watermelons and muskmelons—should follow each other.

Bacterial wilt is sometimes a problem to cucumber growers, particularly those living in north central and northeastern states. Plants with this disease wilt so quickly that leaves may be both dried up and still green. The bacteria are spread by spotted and striped cucumber beetles, and grow to plug the water vessels of stems and leaves; if you cut across a stem you may notice a sticky, white ooze.

Affected plants found early in the season should be promptly removed and destroyed. You might plant extra seed to ensure that there will still be enough plants left for a good crop. Follow the recommendations for the control of the spotted cucumber beetle discussed above. Covering other plants with cheesecloth is particularly helpful. There are several varieties with some resistance to scab.

Downy mildew is a fungus common in the Atlantic and Gulf states. The first symptom you will see is spots on leaves, yellow on top and downy purple underneath. The spots spread, killing the foliage and sometimes whole plants. Mildew is encouraged by cool, wet nights, and warm, humid days; if such conditions prevail in your area, use a variety resistant to mildew; see RESISTANT VARIETIES.

Mosaic virus is characterized by mottled or curled leaves that turn yellow and die, and fruits (often called white pickles) are warty and light-colored. It overwinters in perennial weeds that grow near the garden, such as milkweed, ground cherry, catnip, ragweed, pigweed, burdock, various mints, and horse nettle. The virus cannot overwinter in garden trash or annual hosts. The virus is usually spread by aphids, and occasionally by cucumber beetles or on implements.

The area surrounding the garden should be kept as free as

possible from perennial weeds. The New York State College of Agriculture recommends that this no-mans-land for weeds should be 100 yards wide in most seasons, although in cool, wet summers a 10-yard zone could be sufficient. There are several mosaic-resistant varieties available, including Spartan Dawn, SMR, and Salty; check with your county agent or experiment station to learn which varieties will do best in your area.

Scab is a fungus found chiefly in the northeastern and north central states. Symptoms include dark, oozing spots on the fruit that look like insect feeding punctures. The spots later dry up, leaving small pits covered by an olive-gray fungus growth. Small brown spots may appear on leaves and stems. This fungus lives in the soil and does its worst damage in cool, moist weather.

To avoid scab, do not grow cucumbers or squash in the same soil more often than once in three years. The USDA recommends growing cucumbers and muskmelons in areas and during seasons with few rains and with predominately warm, low humidity conditions. There are a number of resistant cucumber varieties available; see RESISTANT VARIETIES.

Currant

Insects

The currant **aphid,** sometimes called the leaf louse, is the most troublesome pest of currants, stunting the whole plant and diminishing fruit production. Look for distorted and yellowish or pale foliage that is rolled up and wrinkled by the yellow green pests feeding on the underside of leaves. Later in the season the injured leaves may drop, and this hinders fruit development. The eggs of the currant aphid are shiny black, cucumber-shaped, and attached in October to the bark of new growth near the nodes. Soon after the leaves open in spring, the eggs hatch and the aphids crawl to the leaves, feeding on them by sucking the sap.

The currant aphid is not easy to control. Eggs are often transported on certified nursery stock, and the sprocketlike cavities of curled leaves protect the aphids and hinder control. It is important to pluck off affected foliage if serious curling is evident. The shiny eggs can be rubbed off canes and destroyed in spring, or washed off with water when they are laid in October.

Currant borers can often be found and destroyed before they become a serious problem. In larval form the borer is a yellowish caterpillar measuring about ½ inch long. Adults are moths with yellow and black markings on their wings. Whenever you see a cane with wilting leaves at its tip, suspect the borer. Usually the damage occurs in spring.

Cut damaged canes back to ground level and quickly burn them before the moths can emerge. Light traps may be effective, and should be used before the moths lay their eggs in the canes, in June or July.

The **currant fruit fly,** or gooseberry maggot, is about the size of a housefly, with a yellow body and dark-striped wings. It emerges from the soil in April or May and lays eggs in the fruit. When the fruit drops the maggots enter the soil. Early varieties are less susceptible. Control by dusting with rotenone as soon as the blossoms have wilted, in two or three applications at weekly intervals.

In spring, the **currant sawfly** (or currant stem girdler) lays an egg in new shoots which are then girdled or cut partly off above the egg. After hatching, the larvae burrow several inches down into the cane, where they will stay until the following year. The sawfly can be controlled by handpicking on small plantings. Prune and destroy all the affected canes.

The **four-lined plant bug** is a pest of many plants, including currant and gooseberry. Like many berry pests, they winter in the canes, lay eggs there in spring, and hatch in mid-May or early summer to injure plants by sucking on the young leaves. Affected foliage shows spotted sunken areas and, later, holes. The nymph is bright red with black dots on the thorax; the adult is greenish yellow with four wide, dark stripes down the wings. If necessary, control this pest by dusting with rotenone at weekly intervals. A soap spray may also be effective.

Fourlined Plant Bug

The **gooseberry fruitworm** is a pest of currants and gooseberries that winters in the ground under dead leaves and trash. The following spring, the adult lays its eggs in the flowers and the larvae hollow out the fruit. The moth is ashy-colored with dark markings; the larva is ¾ inch long and yellow green with a pinkish cast. Control by spraying with rotenone at seven- to ten-day intervals. Destroy all the infested berries.

Currants are sometimes troubled by the **green currant worm** (or **imported currant worm**), which is black with yellow markings and devours foliage. Fortunately, they are rare.

Early in spring, check your plants for the white eggs on the underside of leaves. Unless you pick off and destroy them before

Red Spider Mite

the larvae hatch in late May, you may have to resort to a summer treatment of rotenone or pyrethrum.

Spider mites are an occasional pest of currants. For control, see SPIDER MITE.

Diseases

In the home garden, currants are often grown in the partial shade of trees, buildings, or fences. This practice makes them more vulnerable to disease than if grown in full sun with good ventilation.

Currants are susceptible to **anthracnose,** a disease of leaves and sometimes fruit that may occur if you work on the bushes while they are wet. You will see small reddish brown or purplish spots with masses of pink spores on the underside of leaves. There is not yet a cure for anthracnose of currants, but some varieties are resistant to it.

Both currants and gooseberries are host plants to the **blister rust fungus,** which is not so much a danger to them as it is to white pine trees. Blister rust is so destructive to white pines that there are federal and state regulations about planting gooseberries and currants in the vicinity of white pine nurseries or forests. You may need a permit to grow them. Currant and gooseberry bushes have to be planted at least 900 feet away from white pine trees. For more information, check with your local state agriculture extension service, the nearest USDA office, or the nursery from which you buy your plant stock. The rust disease shows as bright orange spots on the currant leaves in midsummer.

Sometimes a fungus invasion will cause **cane blight:** the canes suddenly wilt and die while loaded with fruit. Small black cushions on the canes will identify the disease. The best remedy is to remove all affected stalks and burn them.

Crown gall may be caused by ordinary soil bacteria. It is not always serious, and often the lesions or galls are not too severe and the bush continues to produce.

Mildew is a common malady of both currants and gooseberries. You will notice white cobweblike growths on the top surface of leaves. Mildew is most prevalent in wet seasons or in moist areas. Let your plants have good exposure to the sun and plenty of air circulation to help keep them dry. Promptly rogue out mildewed sections to prevent its spread.

Cutworms

There is little about cutworms that commends them. They are ugly to look at and unpleasant to the touch. Worse yet, they attack just about every plant in the garden. Young plants may be cut off at the soil line; this sort of injury is especially common in hot beds, cold frames, and of course in the garden early in the growing season. Larger plants suffer serious losses of foliage area.

Cutworm

Cutworms are typically plump, soft-bodied larvae, usually dull in color and scantily covered with coarse bristles or hairs. They are often to be found in the soil at the base of plants on which they feed. When disturbed, they commonly coil their bodies. Cutworms burrow down several inches into the soil to pupate, and grow up to be night-flying moths.

Many animals find cutworms a good source of food. Meadowlarks, toads, moles, and shrews claim many of the larvae. They also fall prey to braconid and tachnid wasp parasites.

• **Controls.**   Land on which garden crops are to be grown should be kept free of weeds and grass, especially during the fall months, in order to discourage egg-laying by the cutworm moths. Crops planted on sod land are especially subject to severe damage unless the land is plowed during late summer or early fall and is kept free of weeds and grass during the rest of the growing season.

Cultivate lightly or probe by hand around the base of the plant to find and kill resting worms. Place a stiff three-inch-high cardboard collar around the stems of young plants, pushing it one inch deep in the soil. Crushed egg shells can be scattered around plant bases and then covered with a thin layer of dirt. Cutworms will try to avoid brushing into the sharp particles. You might also put a ring of ashes around the plants and then soak with water. Chicken manure and a mulch of oak leaves are good preventatives. If you tie the stems of wild onions around vegetables, cutworms should be no problem. The variegated cutworm is vulnerable to *Bacillus thuringiensis*.

A simple bait can lure the worms to their death. Mix equal parts of hardwood sawdust (pine sawdust repels the pests) and wheat bran with a healthy dollop of molasses and just enough water to increase the bait's stickiness. Scatter a handful of it around each plant at dusk, or spread evenly along each field row of corn. The sweet molasses will attract the worms from the plants. As the cutworms crawl around in the bait, it clings to their bodies and hardens by morning, rendering them helpless. Since they will be unable to burrow back into the ground to hide from enemies and the elements, they are soon destroyed. Although this bait is not 100 percent effective, it should eliminate an amazingly large number of worms each night. Helen and John Philbrick, authors of *The Bug Book,* have come up with a beautifully simple means of thwarting cutworms that have saved many vulnerable transplants. They stick a toothpick or twig along the side of the plant stem, and this interferes with the worm's chewing. Cutworms are partial to sunflowers, and they can be planted in a border as a trap crop. Tansy, on the other hand, repels them.

On a large scale, all fields and gardens should be plowed or disked as soon as crops are harvested. This will leave no grass for the moths to lay their eggs upon. Large fields that had been in crops or grass the previous September should be plowed again in spring. A wise farmer might encourage his flock of chickens to follow in the furrow to snap up any of the worms that are brought to the surface. Or, he may turn several hogs loose into the plowed field, as they are capable of rooting up and eating large quantities of cutworms, grubs, and other destructive insects.

Cyclamen

The translucent, microscopic **cyclamen mite** often infests new leaf and blossom buds, causing them to become swollen and distorted. Infested plants give no satisfactory blossoms. If the mites hit early, no blossoms will form at all; later infestation leads to streaked or blotched blooms that fall before their time.

The mite is difficult to control when cyclamen is badly infested. Provide ample space between plants, and don't touch healthy plants if you've just been around ones in trouble—you won't notice the tiny pests on your hands. Rogue out plants that are in a bad way. Cynthia Westcott suggests that "valuable plants lightly infested can be immersed in hot water at 110°F. for fifteen minutes. Strawberry plants can be treated for twenty minutes in water preheated to 100°F."

Foliar nematodes cause leaves and stems to collapse, and the plant may not produce buds properly. Nematodes are sometimes carried in the dormant buds of the corms (underground stem bases) or in the soil, so the use of clean corms and clean potting soil is advisable.

Daffodil

Blast is fairly widespread and is characterized by flower buds which turn brown and dry up before opening. The cause is unknown, and bulbs behaving in this way year after year can be dug and discarded.

Ring disease can cause plants to fail to grow in spring. Leaves may be abnormal and twisted with small yellowish lumps called spikkels, which contain many nematodes. Flowers are not produced. This disease is so called because the bulbs show discolored rings when cut across. Yellowish pockets in scales contain numerous nematodes. Hot-water treatment of bulbs gives reasonably good control (110° to 115°F. for three hours for small bulbs and four hours for large ones). Plant in clean or sterilized soil and remove infected plants and bulbs, along with some of the soil around them.

Because of **bulb** and **root rots,** plants either develop poorly or don't even grow at all. An examination of bulbs shows rotted areas. Roots are brown and rotted, and you may find white or pinkish mycelium or spore masses. Rogue infected bulbs and remove soil from the area where the bulbs were planted. Narcissus should not be planted in an infected location for two or three years.

Dahlia

Insects

The **cocklebur billbug** is a weevil with a long, curved snout. It is ⅓ inch long, and has 13 black spots on its reddish back. The larvae are legless, curved, and white, with brown heads. They bore into the pith and hollow out stems for a foot or more near the base of the plant. Serious infestations are restricted primarily to the southeastern United States.

European Corn Borer

Stake dahlia plants to prevent breaking of stems. Postpone planting until June in order to escape the adult billbugs which emerge in May. In the garden area, destroy such wild hosts as ragweed, thistle, cocklebur, and joe pye weed.

The second generation of the **European corn borer** lays its eggs on dahlias and sometimes injures them seriously. See CORN.

When the **potato leafhopper** sucks plant juices, foliage is blanched. See POTATO.

Potato Leafhopper

Dahlia/Stalk Borer

Tarnished Plant Bug

The slender **stalk borer's** presence is usually first made known when its feeding causes dahlias to wilt, but by then it's often too late for help. The young borer is creamy white with a dark purple band around its body, and several brown or purple stripes running the length of its body. The full-grown larva is creamy white to light purple, and has no stripes. When young borers hatch early in the spring from eggs laid on grass and weeds, they first feed upon the leaves of the nearest plant and then gradually work their way to larger, stemmed plants.

Remove and destroy nearby weeds. Infested plants can sometimes be saved by slitting stems, destroying the borer, and then binding the stems and keeping plants watered.

The **striped cucumber beetle** is attracted to the pollen and petals of dahlia. These beetles are elongate, yellow green, and are marked with three black stripes. See CUCUMBER.

The **tarnished plant bug** is small, flattened, and brownish, with a somewhat brassy appearance to its wing covers. It causes deformity by puncturing buds and new shoots. See ASTER.

Diseases

Bacterial wilt is characterized by sudden wilting and death of plants. Cut stems will reveal a yellowish oozing from vascular bundles. Because bacteria overwinter in the soil, gardeners have found it important to sterilize soil and remove infected plant parts.

Wilting of a single branch or entire plant, followed by recovery at night, is symptomatic of **fusarium wilt.** The plant may remain alive for a short time, but it eventually succumbs. The fungus lives in the soil and in the tubers, so that once this wilt has struck, you must get new, healthy tubers and plant them in disease-free soil.

Gray mold causes flowers and buds to rot, especially in prolonged periods of cool, wet weather. There is no known control for this disease.

Mosaic (stunt) is a virus disease that appears as a mottling in leaf tissues, or as pale green bands along midribs and larger veins. Leaves are generally dwarfed or distorted, and infected plants are stunted, small, and bushy. Tubers are shorter and thicker than normal, and show reddish brown necrotic spots inside.

Promptly destroy infected plants to avoid spreading mosaic to other plants. Dwarfing may also result from the feeding of many leafhoppers, aphids, European corn borers, or thrips. In this case, plants should recover after the insects have been controlled.

Conspicuous light green or yellow concentric rings on leaves is a sign of **spotted wilt;** plants are not dwarfed. Rogue out affected plants, and control thrips, aphids, and leafhoppers, which serve as vectors of the disease.

Delphinium

Insects

The shiny orange delphinium **aphid** lives on the underside of leaves and between buds in flower spikes. Heavy infestations cause curling and cupping of leaves and dwarfing of shoots. Flower spikes become stunted, and florets fail to open. Damage is similar to that caused by the cyclamen mite, but is less severe and lacks the blackening symptoms of mite injury. See APHID.

Aphid

The most important pest of the delphinium is the **cyclamen mite,** a microscopic insect that causes distorted, brittle, thickened leaves and black, deformed buds that fail to open. This condition has become known as blacks, but the cause for the malady is not a disease pathogen but an insect.

Once established in a planting, mites are difficult to control. Destroy heavily infested plants. Mites on valuable plants can be destroyed by digging plants and immersing them in water at 110°F. for 15 minutes. Cut out badly infested shoots. Tools and hands are often the means of transportation for the insect—it rarely goes very far under its own power. Keep the garden free from weeds, and old plant parts should be removed and destroyed after the season. It may be a good idea to burn them on the spot, as digging and pulling may spread the mites. When planting delphiniums, give them enough room so that they will not be in danger of touching each other. Should mite damage become serious, repeated dusting with rotenone will give effective relief.

Cyclamen Mite

Delphiniums are vulnerable to the **red spider mite.** Flower growers have used a garlic spray with good results. See SPIDER MITE.

Red Spider Mite

Roots are often damaged by **slugs** and **snails,** and in some parts of the country plants are susceptible year-round. In Delaware, for example, January sees the worst damage to delphinium crowns. During late fall, before the first frost stiffens the ground, remove all soil above the plant crowns. Then cover the entire plant and fill the excavation up to ground level with coarse river sand. The sand is sharp and painful to the tender bodies of the slugs, making an effective barrier. When compost and pulverized rock fertilizers are added to the soil in spring, the sand will merge with the soil and improve drainage. Seedlings can be protected by placing the flats on inverted flower pots that are surrounded with ashes or sand. See SLUGS AND SNAILS.

Other common pests are blister beetles (see ASTER), cutworms (TOMATO), four-lined plant bug (CHRYSANTHEMUM), flower thrips (PEONY, ROSE), MILLIPEDES, and potato leafhopper (POTATO).

Diseases

Bacterial blight causes an irregular black discoloration and softening of leaves and stem which may extend nearly to the ground. When the stem is split, masses of bacteria ooze out and black internal streaking is visible. The bacteria appear to dissolve the cell membranes and the affected tissues, and give off a foul odor. The plants may be stunted or killed back severely. The causal bacteria appear to be caused by bacteria that overwinter in the soil on dead leaves and in the crowns of infected plants. In spring, the bacteria are splashed by rain to new leaves, where they produce the characteristic black spots. Starting on lower leaves, the disease will quickly spread upward during periods of wet weather until it finally affects the topmost leaves and the lower spike.

To reduce chances of trouble, clear away and burn all plant refuse in spring before new shoots emerge. In fall, cut off and burn dead plants in order to eliminate them as a source of infection for the next year's garden. If the disease is a real problem, obtain plants that are free from leaf spot and plant them in soil which has not grown delphiniums for many years.

Bacterial leaf spot is a common disease which causes the appearance of irregular, tarry black spots on leaves and sometimes on stems and buds. When infection hits young leaves, they frequently become distorted. This disease is carried both in the seed and in the soil, but is usually lethal only under very moist conditions. Excessive watering or irrigation intensifies the disease. Cracks in the stem at ground level also provide a means of entry for the bacteria.

Bacterial Leaf Spot

If leaves and flowers are badly deformed, or leaves are brittle and thickened with black or brown spots or streaks, suspect a condition known as **blacks,** brought on by cyclamen mites (see above).

A number of different fungi can bring about **crown rot** or **root rot** of delphiniums. The first sign of the disease is a discoloration of the lower leaves, which is quickly followed by a wilting of the young shoots. Within a few days the entire plant is dead. Roots of infected plants are black or dark brown, rotten and covered with white threads of the causal fungus. In wet weather, small cream-colored, egg-shaped bodies known as sclerotia are found on the crown and roots of infected plants and in the adjacent soil. These sclerotia are the durable seedlike bodies of the crown rot organism that carry the fungus through winter. It's not necessary to figure out which fungus is responsible, as these diseases occur infrequently and control measures are the same: remove and destroy diseased plant parts.

When **mildew** strikes, plants become small and deformed, and stems and leaves are covered with a mealy, white coating. Generally, the flower yield is low, buds are stunted, and the plant wilts. A plant that has been attacked by mildew should be cut down to the ground level to prevent the disease from becoming established. Resistant varieties are available.

Stunt (or greens) is caused by the aster yellows virus. Plants may be dwarfed, with small leaves showing mottling or chlorosis. Flowers are characteristically green, and a bunchy flowerhead is typical. This virus is spread by leafhoppers and has many plant hosts, including aster, ragweed, and chrysanthemum. Rogue out infected plants; controlling the six-spotted leafhopper will contain infections (see ASTER).

Dianthus, see Carnation

Dogwood

Insects

The most serious pest is the **dogwood borer.** Very young trees are frequently killed, and older ones are left reduced in vitality and with dead and dying branches. Borer-infested trees begin to show swollen, knotty, calloused or gall-like areas on the trunk, just at or immediately below the surface of the ground, or between the level of the soil and the branches above. Injury may also occur at the union of the trunk and principal branches. Young dogwood trees are attacked mostly at the crown.

The larva is white with a pale brown head. The adult dogwood borer is a clear-winged moth with a one-inch wingspan, colored blue black with some yellow markings. There is only one generation a year. The adults begin to emerge late in May and continue to do so throughout the remainder of the spring and summer months. They may appear as late as the end of September. The eggs are deposited on both smooth and rough bark, frequently near an injury. The larvae wander around aimlessly until an opening in the bark is reached, and then tunnel in. An infested tree four inches in diameter may be killed by a single borer in the course of a season, although under most conditions several borers would be required to kill a dogwood.

Once these borers are in trees, they are difficult to control, and prevention is a far more successful approach. Wrap the tree, especially if a new transplant, in kraft paper, and keep it wrapped for two years or until well established. Any entrances or wounds on the tree should be painted with shellac. It is equally important to maintain the vigor of the tree by organically fertilizing, watering, mulching, and pruning out dead wood. Trees planted more than 300 yards away from an established infestation will not become seriously affected.

Dogwood club gall is a grayish tubular swelling that contains a larva. The growths occur on the small twigs, often killing them back for several inches. The orange larva overwinters on the soil under the trees, protected by the sod and decayed grass and leaves. The adult is a small fly, or club gall midge, that emerges in May or June to lay eggs at the base of leaves. Upon hatching, the maggots work their way into the twigs and cause galls to develop. Usually the fastest growing and most vigorous twigs are heavily infested, as are water sprouts or sucker growth nearest the ground. Most of the flower and leaf buds that develop beyond the apex of the galls will die. While serious infestation of dogwood club gall stunts the tree, a light infestation hardly affects development.

Cut off and destroy the galls soon after they have formed, before the maggots leave them in late summer.

Trunks and limbs heavily infested with the **dogwood scale** have a whitish, scaly appearance. The female scales are grayish, pear-shaped, and about $\frac{1}{10}$ inch long; the males are narrow and pure white. Eggs overwinter under the female's protective shell. Infestations weaken trees and/or may kill encrusted branches.

To control, apply a dormant-oil spray in spring before new

growth starts. When the trees begin to leaf out, the young scales hatch and can be killed by brushing them with turpentine or, in serious cases, applying two or more doses of a nicotine sulfate and soap solution, spaced ten days to two weeks apart.

The larvae of the **dogwood twig borer** infest the terminal twigs of dogwood. Eggs are laid in June and July, hatch in about ten days, and the larvae tunnel downward in the twig, making several openings through the bark. The twig is girdled above and below the place where the eggs are deposited. There is apparently one generation each year.

Cutting and burning the infested twigs will help control this insect. Clip off the tips several inches below the girdle soon after wilting occurs.

The **flat-headed borer** deposits its eggs on the bark of dogwoods, and the larvae make irregular tunnels under the bark. When feeding is completed they bore into the wood to pupate. Larvae are white, have a flat head, and measure about an inch long when fully grown. The ½-inch-long adult is a wedge-shaped, metallic-sheened beetle. Control as for the dogwood borer. Since these beetles attack seriously weakened trees, the best preventive is to keep the trees growing vigorously.

Other insect pests of dogwood include cottony maple and lecanium scales (see MAPLE), and the oystershell and San José scales (LILAC).

Diseases

A generally unhealthy appearance of the tree may be the first sign of infection by **bleeding canker** fungus. Look for sunken areas in the bark, from which may ooze a reddish brown fluid. The bark eventually sloughs off, revealing wood with blue black or reddish brown streaks. Twigs and branches on the side of the tree above the canker die first, but the entire tree will die if the canker has girdled the trunk. Cut out infected wood back to live, normally colored sapwood, and seal the wound with good tree paint.

Crown or **trunk canker** leads to trees with an unhealthy appearance. The leaves are smaller and lighter green than normal and turn red prematurely in late summer. Later, twigs and even large branches die. Cankers are found on the lower trunk near soil level at spots where the fungus has invaded bark, cambium, and outer sapwood to cause a discoloration of infected tissues. The cankers enlarge slowly for several years until they extend completely around the base of the trunk or root collar, killing the tree. For a few years before their death, infected trees often bear large flower and fruit crops.

Since the causal fungus appears to enter only through injured tissue, avoid wounding the trunk during transplanting and when mowing. In case of an injury, trim the bark around the wound, shaping it to a point at the top and the bottom. Paint the edge of the wound at once with orange shellac and then cover the injured area with a wound dressing. If a small canker is found, cut out the infected area and all diseased bark. The edges should be painted with orange shellac and then covered with a wound dressing. If the canker is very large, destroy the tree and do not replant any dogwoods in that spot for several years.

Twig blight may be confused with the more extensive dieback of shrubs affected by crown canker. Control is usually not too difficult. Prune out the dead twigs until you reach sound wood. Improve the vigor of the tree by fertilizing and watering more heavily than usual.

Other diseases of dogwood include leaf spot and spot anthracnose; see TREES: DISEASES.

Douglas Fir

Needle cast is a fungus disease that infects developing needles. Mottled yellow spots appear, but may go unnoticed. In spring, the spots change to reddish brown, and elongated brownish orange fruiting bodies of the fungus develop in May or June. By July, spores from the fruiting bodies infect new needles and old needles fall. Trees that have been infected over a period of years have a thin appearance, with usually only one year's needles at the tips of branches. It's best to locate Douglas fir seedbeds away from older fir trees. Remove fallen needles.

For other diseases, see EVERGREEN and FIR.

Earwigs

Earwig

These brown, beetlelike insects are distinguished by a pair of sharp pincers at the tail end. Although these appendages are fierce looking, they do no harm to humans. Earwigs are usually beneficial in habit, acting as scavengers on decaying matter and predators of insect larvae, snails, and other slow-moving bugs. They are nocturnal feeders, spending the day under bark, stones, and garden trash. At times they may enter homes and feed on stored food, and they occasionally feed on foliage, flowers, and other parts of many plants, including dahlias, zinnias, butterfly bush, hollyhock, lettuce, strawberry, celery, potatoes, and seedling beans and beets. They damage sweet corn by feeding on the stalks.

The earwig is primarily spread by man, in bundles of plants and shrubbery, in cut flowers, and in florists' equipment. Left to their own resources, these insects cannot travel very far or fast. To fly at all they must take off from a high place, as their wings are not strong enough to lift them from the ground.

Earwigs are victimized in some areas by a parasitic tachnid fly brought to this country from Europe; *Bigonicheta spinipennis* is established on the eastern seaboard and in Idaho, Utah, and Washington, says Lester A. Swann in *Beneficial Insects*. Groundhogs and chickens are earwig enemies.

Earwigs fall for traps. Sections of bamboo can be set horizontally through the garden or flower bed; check the traps early each morning, and dump them into a bucket of water topped with kerosene. Or, try crumbling up paper into an inverted flower pot that's set up on a stake.

Eggplant

Insects

Among the insects most troublesome to the eggplant is the **Colorado potato beetle.** Both adults and larvae defoliate plants and are particularly destructive for the home gardener with small plantings. The adult is a yellow beetle with a broad convex back and is about ⅜ inch long. Running the length of both wing covers are five black stripes, and the thorax has black spots. The larval form is a humpbacked, red grub. For control measures, see POTATO.

Potato/Colorado Potato Beetle

The **eggplant lacebug** is grayish to light brown, flat, and has transparent, lacelike wings. They are a pest to crops in the South as far west as New Mexico and Arizona, feeding in groups on the underside of leaves, which they cover with brown spots of excrement. The leaves take on pale, mottled patches and plants often die.

If you observe either symptom or the lacewings themselves, draw affected leaves between the thumb and forefinger to kill any bugs present. This should be done as early in the season as possible, before a destructive infestation can build up.

Several **flea beetles** feed on the leaves of eggplant. They are small, brown or black, and jump like a flea when disturbed. For control, see potato flea beetle under POTATO.

Flea Beetle

Eggplant fruits may be marred by the feeding of the **pepper maggot,** which *The Gardener's Bug Book* describes as resembling "sharp-pointed pegs," at first translucent white, and turning yellow as they feed. The adult is a yellow fly with three brown bands across both wings, and lays eggs in fruit. You can arrest problems by keeping the flies away with a sprinkle of talc on each plant. This should be done during the egg-laying period in July and August. If an infestation has already occurred, remove and destroy the affected fruit.

The **tomato hornworm** and **tobacco hornworm** eat eggplant leaves and occasionally fruit. They are light or dark green with white stripes, and can grow to four inches long. The former has a black horn at the back end, and the latter's horn is red. Both species are often found in the same garden. See TOMATO.

Tomato Hornworm

Other possible culprits include APHIDS, the blister beetle (see BEET), cutworm (TOMATO), harlequin bug (CABBAGE), potato stalk borer (POTATO), SPIDER MITE, stink bug (SNAPDRAGON), WHITE FLY, and yellow woolybear caterpillar (imported cabbageworm under CABBAGE).

Eggplant/Greenhouse Whitefly

Diseases

Fruit rot, also known as phomopsis blight, may cause brown and gray spots in leaves, and large, ringed, tan or brown spots covered with small pustules on fruits. Damage is worst in warm, wet weather.

Organic gardeners and farmers should not be too troubled by the disease if they select rot-resistant varieties. A four-year rotation of crops is also helpful.

Verticillium wilt may cause leaves to wilt during the heat of day and then recover towards night. These leaves eventually dry up and fall off. The inside of the stem is discolored.

Avoid growing eggplant in soil that has recently grown tomatoes or potatoes, especially if the soil has previously harbored the disease, and rotate crops so that fungi cannot become established in the soil. Be sure to use only clean seed.

Elderberry

Insects

The elderberry is usually free of insects and diseases. The elderberry **aphid,** a blackish green insect found on the underside of leaves, may be controlled with rotenone or pyrethrum.

An occasional **elder borer** will visit the bushes, but they are seldom a serious problem. Control by removing and burning any infested stems.

Wildlife

Robins and **starlings** are fond of elderberries, but in a large planting they will not take enough berries to seriously affect the yield. If you have only a few bushes, keep birds out with netting.

Elm

Insects

The worst pests of elms are the **bark beetles** that transmit Dutch elm disease (see below).

The **elm borer** and the flat-headed apple tree borer lay their eggs in bark wounds on elm trunks. The larvae then burrow down to the cambium layer and may cause girdling of the tree. Borers are likely to attack trees weakened by drought, insects, and disease, and a good maintenance program will greatly reduce chances of trouble. Keep elms in a healthy, vigorous growing condition. Trees should be watered and organically fertilized. Repair bark wounds promptly, and remove dead, dying, or injured branches before April 1. Borers can sometimes be dug out of the bark by means of a wire.

The **elm leaf beetle** [color] is a yellowish to olive green insect, about ¼ inch long, with a black stripe along each wing cover. It devours elm leaves, especially those of Chinese or Siberian elms, reducing the tree's vigor. These beetles may become a household nuisance by migrating indoors in fall; normally, they overwinter in tree bark and outbuildings. In spring they fly to the elm trees and begin feeding on the new leaves, laying their eggs on the underside. When the ½-inch-long, yellow-and-black larvae hatch, they feed for several weeks and then drop or fall to the soil at the base of the tree where they pupate. Successive generations continue throughout summer and into fall.

Elm/Elm Leaf Beetle

To prevent their entry into the house, caulk cracks and other openings where they might enter. *Beauveria bassiara,* an important naturally occurring fungal pathogen, takes care of many of the beetles. Elms in California have been protected by releases of a tachnid fly and a chalcid wasp, both of which have become established.

Elm scurfy scale is found most often on the American elm, although it often kills other types of trees. The white scale is very small and may be found on both the leaves and bark. Scale spend the winter on the tree, and shelter purple eggs.

A dormant-oil solution gives the best control results, as it does with most other scale species that spend the winter on the tree. Apply a three-percent spray late in winter before the growth of the tree has started.

*Elm/European
Elm Scale*

The **European elm scale** is easily seen on the bark of elm trees during early summer when the scales reach maturity. The scales are oval, not over $\frac{1}{16}$ inch long, reddish purple, and surrounded by a fringe of white, waxy secretion. They are commonly found on the underside of limbs and branches. They are soft, and leave a reddish stain when crushed with the finger. Infested elm trees display a yellowing of the leaves on lower branches during July. Later in the season, seriously infested branches may become yellowish brown. When scales are extremely abundant, the foliage turns gray green and wilts.

Often it is possible to control the scale by merely washing the trees off with a forceful stream of water from the garden hose. Should a stronger control be needed, apply a mild dormant-oil spray early in spring.

Diseases

A fungus causes **dothiorella wilt,** or **dieback,** by infecting trees through wounds to cause a wilting and yellowing of the trees. When cankers form, they cause a dieback of infected branches. Diseased bark becomes shrunken and reddish brown with black, raised pustules appearing in the dead areas. A brownish discoloration of the sapwood may be confused with that caused by Dutch elm disease or verticillium wilt.

To control dieback, prune out and burn infected branches, making the cuts at least a foot below any evidence of brown streaking in the wood. Fertilize trees in low vigor so that they will have the strength to ward off the disease.

The greatest enemy of elm trees is **Dutch elm disease**, so named because it was first described by plant pathologists in the

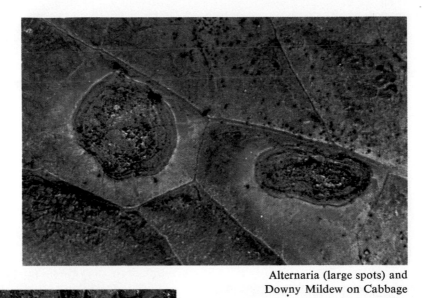

Alternaria (large spots) and
Downy Mildew on Cabbage

Anthracnose on Cucumber Leaf

Anthracnose on Tomato

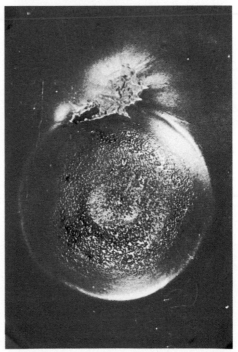

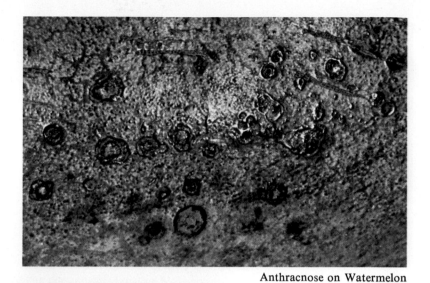

Anthracnose on Watermelon

Anthracnose on Watermelon Leaf

Aphids on Black Pecan

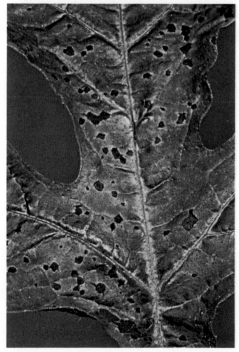

Aphids Tended by Ants

Asparagus Beetle — Adult

Asparagus Beetle — Larva

Azalea Mealybug

Bacterial Spot on Peach

Bacterial Spot on Pepper

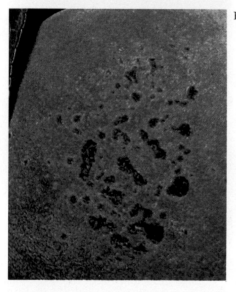

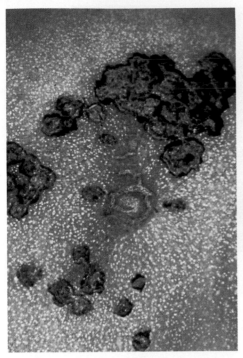

Bacterial Spot on Tomato

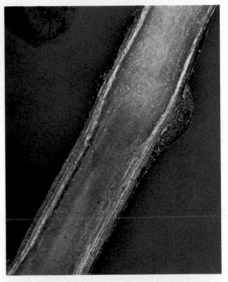

Bacterial Wilt
(Stem Damage) on Tomato

Bagworm

Banded Cucumber Beetle

Bitter Rot on Apple

Bitter Rot on Grape

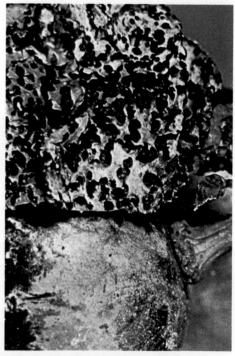

Black Knot on Plum

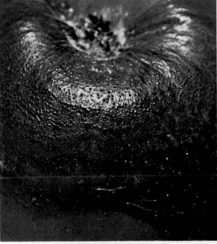

Black Rot on Apple

Black Rot on Grape

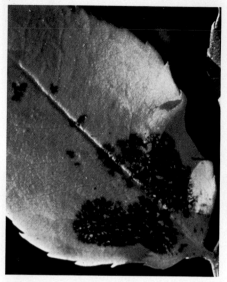

Black Spot on Rose

Blossom Blight on Peach

Botrytis Blight on Tulip

Boxelder Bug

Brown Rot on Peach

Cabbage Looper

Cabbage Maggot on Roots

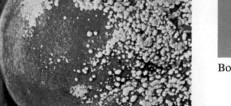

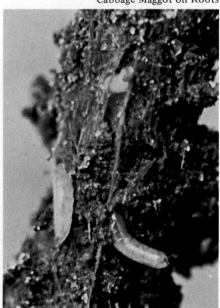

Cedar — Apple Rust Gall on Apple

Codling Moth — Adult

Colorado Potato Beetle — Adult

Colorado Potato Beetle — Larva

Corn Earworm

Cottony Cushion Scale

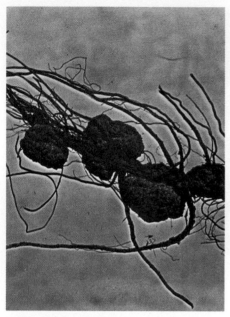

Crown Gall on Pecan

Damping-off Seedling Plant

Diamond Back Moth — Larva

Downy Mildew on Cabbage

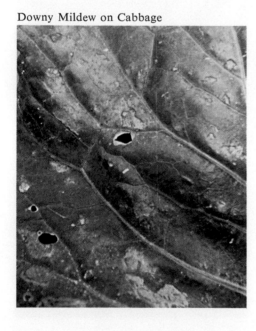

Downy Mildew on Grape

Downy Mildew on Soybean

Early Blight on Tomato

Ear Rot on Corn

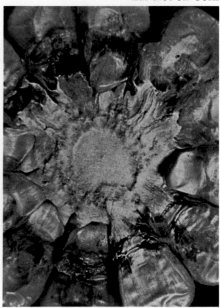

Earworm Damage to Young Corn

Eastern Tent Caterpillar

Elm Leaf Beetle — Adult

Elm Leaf Beetle — Larva

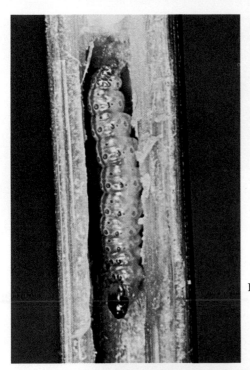

European Corn Borer

Fairy Ring — Turf

Fall Armyworms

Fall Webworm Damage

Fall Webworm — Larvae

Fire Blight on Apple

Flower Blight on Camellia

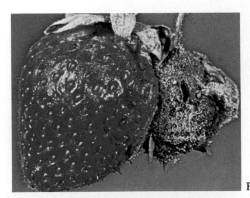

Fruit Rot on Strawberry

Fusarium Wilt on Tomato

Fusarium Wilt
(Stem Damage) on Tomato

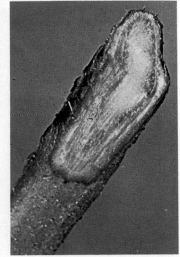

Gray Leaf Spot on Tomato

Harlequin Bug

Helminthosporium Leaf Spot on Corn

Hickory Shuckworm

Imported Cabbage Worm

Japanese Beetle

Lacebug Damage on Azalea

Larger Elm Leaf Beetle

Leaf Blister on Oak

Leaf Mold on Tomato

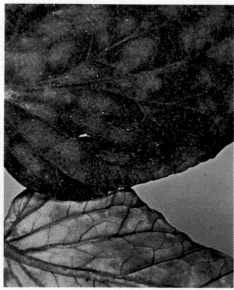

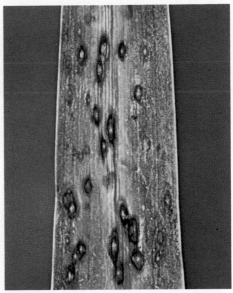

Leaf Spot on Iris

Leaf Spot on Strawberry

Locust Borer

Mexican Bean Beetle

Mimosa Wilt

Needle Rust on Pine

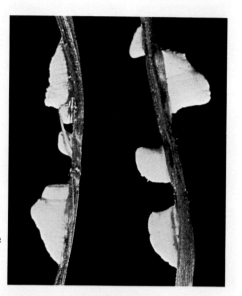

Oriental Fruit Moth Damage to Peach Twig

Pales Weevil on Pine

Peach Tree Borer — Adult Female

Peach Tree Borer — Larva

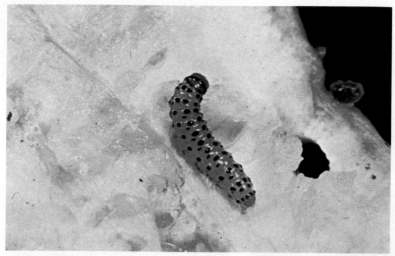

Pickleworm — Young Larva

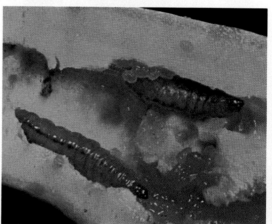

Pickleworm — Older Larvae

Plum Curculio — Adult

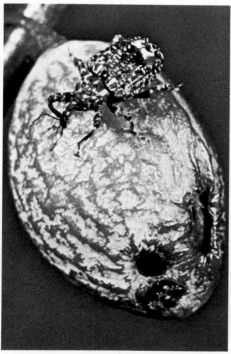

Plum Curculio — Larva

Powdery Mildew on Apple

Powdery Mildew on Cantaloupe

Root Rot on Peach

Rose Chafer

Rust on Bramble Leaf

Scab on Apple

Scab on Peach

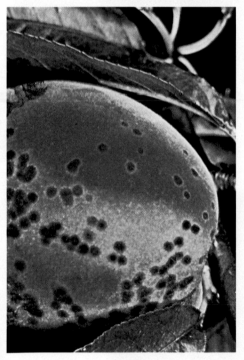

Scurf on Sweet Potato

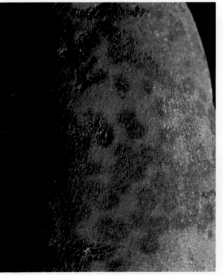

Shot-Hole Borer Damage

Smut on Corn

Soft Rot on Sweet Potato

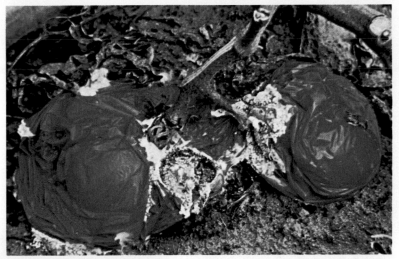

Soil Rot on Tomato

Southern Stem Blight on Peanut

Squash Beetle

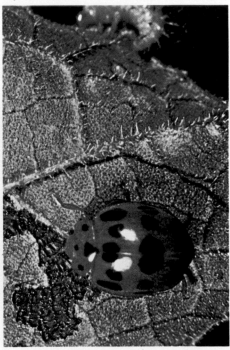

Striped Cucumber Beetle

Tobacco Hornworm on Tomato

Tomato Fruitworm

Tussock Moth Larva

Velvetbean Caterpillar on Soybean

Whitefly — Adults

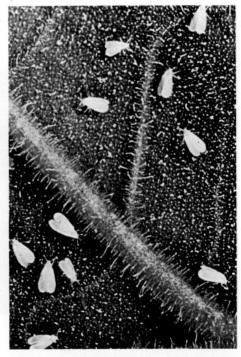

Wilt of Sweet Potato Stem

Wilt of Watermelon Stem

Wireworm

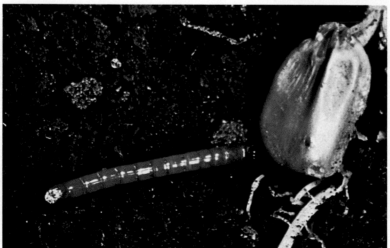

Netherlands. It first came to the eastern United States from Europe about 1930 and has since spread rapidly to most parts of this country and Canada. Many millions of dollars have been spent on control measures and on removal of diseased trees, not to mention aesthetic and other losses impossible to measure in terms of dollars.

Diseases are one form of nature's vast variety of checks and balances. The diversity of nature tends toward stability, whereas man is inclined to modify nature and reduce this diversity. The loss of street after street of elm trees is a result of this lack of diversity. Planting and replacement programs should consider interplanting of different species in order to avoid similar tree losses in the future.

Dutch elm disease control is a community problem. The wider the area over which controls are carried out, the better will be the results. Once an elm tree is infected with the disease, it never recovers. Therefore, as soon as infection is discovered, control measures must be promptly applied to keep the disease from spreading in a community. It is imperative to completely destroy all debris from diseased elms. A town in Massachusetts dumped its diseased elms in a river only to have the beetles survive the dunking and infect a community downstream.

The fungus that causes Dutch elm disease is *Ceratocystis ulmi*. Spores of this fungus germinate in the water-conducting tissues, causing the tree to wilt and die. Sometimes the tree is killed within a few weeks, and only a very few live longer than the second or third season following infection. All elms are susceptible, the American elm most of all. Chinese and Siberian elms are highly resistant to Dutch elm disease, as are some hybrid elms advertised as immune or resistant. However, some Asiatic species and hybrids are either not winter-hardy in northern climates or are very susceptible to diseases other than Dutch elm disease.

The danger of infestation is less common for young vigorous trees than for older specimens. Dutch elm disease grows rapidly in the direction of the length of wood fibers, and moves very poorly across the grain of the wood as it constantly encounters thick growth rings. In a young tree where a thick growth ring is formed every year, the fungus is walled off by a layer of healthy wood. But the fungus can easily keep pace with the slow growth rate of larger trees and readily infects them.

The disease is introduced through the holes made by European bark beetles as they feed on twigs and branches, and may also pass through natural root grafts between diseased and nearby healthy trees. If trees are 20 feet apart or less, they are likely to be united by a root graft, whereas elms over 30 feet apart are probably not connected. Two species of bark beetle in particular are important carriers of Dutch elm disease. The smaller European elm bark beetle is about $\frac{1}{12}$ to $\frac{1}{8}$ inch long and colored brownish to black. The female lays her eggs under the bark of dead or recently cut elm wood, in galleries that run *with* the grain of the wood, i.e., lengthwise. The hatching larvae bore small tunnels around the trunk or branch and away from the centrally located egg gallery. Adult beetles emerge in May or early June, fly to healthy trees, and feed in the crotches of the twigs. It is during this time—if they have emerged from the bark of diseased trees or wood—that they may introduce the fungus spores from their bodies into healthy trees. The fungus fruits abundantly on diseased wood and the sticky spores frequently adhere to the beetles. This habit of feeding on healthy trees after emerging from the bark of diseased elm trees makes this insect a major carrier of Dutch elm disease. It overwinters as a grub in the bark of unhealthy elm trees or of recently cut logs or firewood.

The native elm bark beetle is even smaller, $\frac{1}{16}$ to $\frac{1}{12}$ inch long. It is brownish, with a moderately stout body and wing covers coarsely punctured with small depressions. The female lays her eggs in galleries that run across (around) the grain of the wood.

The most noticeable symptom of Dutch elm disease is the wilting and yellowing of one or more branches of infected trees. There are several wilt diseases that attack elms, all of which produce symptoms that look very much alike, but if you see oval-shaped, depressed feeding holes at the crotches of one- and two-year-old twigs, you can be fairly sure of Dutch elm disease. Internally, a brownish staining appears in the annual rings, showing as discontinuous streaks when the bark is peeled away from the wood, or as small, shiny black or brown dots (or a partial to complete ring) when the branch is viewed in cross section.

The only way to be sure your trees have Dutch elm disease is to take twig samples for laboratory examination by plant pathologists. First, cut six twigs or small stems about seven inches long and $\frac{1}{2}$ to one inch in diameter from the diseased branches of each tree. Carefully mark the twigs or stems from each tree, and wrap securely in a cardboard box for mailing. Do not send material that has been dead for some time or that doesn't show the discolored ring under the bark. Send the samples to the laboratory of your state's agricultural extension service. It is very important that you mail the samples immediately after collecting, as the longer you delay in getting the twigs to the laboratory, the harder it is to identify the disease. Remember that a letter giving tree location, city, county, and date of collection should accompany each sample.

The only known method of Dutch elm disease control is to prevent the fungus from moving through root grafts and to keep the bark beetles from carrying the fungus from diseased to healthy trees. Sanitation is the basic measure in Dutch elm disease control. This means keeping all old and dying branches pruned. Promptly remove elms that are diseased, dead, or in low vigor from insect attack, flooding, soil fills, lightning, or other injuries. Any elm wood that might harbor bark beetles is a potential breeding place for the disease fungus. Destroy elm debris either by burning dead elm wood, peeling tight bark from elm wood and stumps, or by using mechanical branch chippers. Elm wood that has been cut and stacked should either be burned or buried at least six inches deep. Or, if you are using it for firewood, you should first remove and burn the bark from all pieces.

Heavy trimming involving the removal of healthy branches may increase the incidence of Dutch elm disease if carried out from July through September. This is because the trimmed trees are attractive to the smaller European bark beetle that invades the main trunk to lay eggs. Beetles introduce the fungus, and while the trees may appear vigorous in fall, they wilt and die rapidly the following spring. If trimming is necessary to shape the trees or to remove obstructions above streets, houses, or wires, it should not be done between July and September.

The Iowa State University College of Agriculture reports that extensive field trials are testing the effectiveness of an imported wasp in reducing elm bark beetle populations. Methods of artificially rearing the wasp are being investigated, and it someday may be practical to rear and release large numbers of wasps. Other predacious and parasitic organisms including fungi, bacteria, insects, and nematodes are also being investigated.

Elms, like all living things, should be kept in vigorous growing condition. Keep them fertilized and watered. Trees have heavy nitrogen needs, so use a high-nitrogen fertilizer such as blood meal or cotton seed meal. Repair bark wounds promptly, and remove dead, dying or injured branches to prevent beetle infestations.

Phloem necrosis is a virus disease transmitted by leafhoppers that affects a considerable part of the root system to eventually kill the tree. It is common in the midwestern and south-central states, and seems to affect primarily the American and winged elm. After the tree is infected, it takes a year for symptoms to appear. In midsummer, leaves of infected trees roll and turn yellow, then wither and fall. In later stages of the disease, the thin layer of inner bark that is in contact with the sapwood becomes butter-scotch in color and may be flecked with brown or black. A faint wintergreen odor can be detected when the bark is placed in a closed container in a warm place for a few hours, according to the Iowa State University Cooperative Extension Service. Once the external symptoms appear, the diseased tree will die within a period of from two weeks to two months.

Since diseased trees cannot be cured, protect healthy trees by following rigid sanitation measures. As soon as infection is noticed, diseased trees should be destroyed.

Slime-flux, or **wetwood,** inflicts the wood of elms and other hardwoods such as maple, birch, oak, poplar, sycamore, and willow, causing an increase in internal sap pressure. The sap seeps out of infected areas through cracks, wounds, and pruning cuts and flows down the trunk, soaking large areas of bark. The seepage often becomes contaminated with bacteria and yeasts, resulting in a foul-smelling substance called slime-flux. The slime-flux may prevent healing of the wounds and kill bark and wood over which it flows for some time. Toxic sap from infected wood is sometimes carried to branches to cause wilting and defoliation, and the tissues between veins and along edges of leaves are browned. Wood under the bark of wilted branches often shows grayish brown streaks similar to those caused by Dutch elm disease.

At the present there is no cure or preventive for wetwood. Drilling holes into infected wood to relieve sap pressure may correct the fluxing condition and prevent the spread of toxic sap into the branches. The holes should be drilled 6 to 14 inches below the fluxing area and slanted upward into the heartwood to within a few inches of the other side of the tree. It may be necessary to drill several holes at various locations on the trunk or branches before the infected wood area is located. A short piece of pipe screwed into the hole will carry the dripping sap clear of the tree.

When tapping and drainage of infected wood areas has reduced sap seepage, healing of wounds may be hastened by cutting the bark around the wound to a football-shaped form, pointed at the top and bottom. Shellac exposed bark around the wound, and paint the whole area with a tree dressing.

Other diseases of elm trees include verticillium wilt, black leaf spot, various twig cankers, and wood decay. See TREES: DISEASES.

Endive

Endive is especially vulnerable to aphid damage; several species are responsible. For control methods, see APHID. Other possible pests are dealt with under LETTUCE.

English Ivy, see Ivy

Euonymus

Insects

Euonymus is chiefly bothered by **scale** insects, including greedy, San José and euonymus species. The euonymus scale is perhaps the most serious pest of euonymus, often killing entire branches. It also affects bittersweet and the pachysandra. The female shells are gray and pear-shaped, and the male shells are smaller, narrower, and whiter. There are two broods each season, and the winter is passed in a nearly mature condition. Eggs are formed during May and hatch later in the month.

To control scale, cut and burn all infested and injured branches, and apply a dormant-oil spray in late winter or early spring, before growth starts.

Euonymus is also attacked by the bean APHID and cottony maple scale (see MAPLE).

Diseases

A bacterium causes rounded galls with an irregular rough surface on the stems or roots. This condition is known as **crown gall.** The bacteria enter through wounds made during cultivation. *Euonymus fortunei radicans, E. f. vegetus,* and *E. patens* are susceptible to this disease.

To avoid crown gall, do not plant euonymus having galls on the roots or stems. Avoid wounding stems or roots in cultivating. If the disease appears, prune and destroy affected parts. Badly affected plants should be removed and destroyed.

A powdery appearance of the leaves means that one of the **powdery mildew** fungi is present. Blast plants with a forceful water spray.

Evergreen

Insects

One organic gardener on Long Island has for many years counteracted insects on his evergreens by sprinkling moth crystals around the tree, and occasionally sprinkling soap flakes on the branches, especially if rain seemed likely. These simple control methods have resulted in tall, vigorous trees.

Many evergreens are troubled by the same pests. **Aphids** are among the most universal. See APHID.

Bagworms appear frequently on arborvitae and junipers. These insects pass the winter in the egg stage within the bags on the trees. To prevent bagworms from chewing up the evergreens next year, you should pick the bags during winter and burn them.

If your evergreen tree appears to be dying and fine wood dust or shredded wood particles are forced from holes in the bark, **bark beetles** or wood borers have probably struck. There are no direct control measures that are applicable, but since the insects usually attack dead or dying trees, keeping plants in a healthy, thrifty condition and preventing mechanical injury are the best insurance against trouble. If the tree is dead already, it is best to cut and burn it so that it does not provide a home for other insects.

Spider mites infest evergreens and cause severe damage. The mites are small creatures, scarcely visible, that suck sap from the needles, weaken the tree, and cause needles to turn yellow and die. Older and lower branches are usually attacked first, but eventually the entire tree may become infested. The mites' webbing appears around the base of the needles, and the branches take on a dusty or dingy look.

A good way to check for spider mites is to hold a sheet of white paper under a branch and rap the branch sharply. If mites are present, they will fall onto the paper where they are seen as tiny reddish specks moving about.

Perhaps the best method of control is simply to wash the tree or shrub with a forceful spray from the garden hose. Get the water up through the center of the plant. Inspect frequently through the hot months for an infestation. See SPIDER MITE.

FIG   351

Fern

Insects

The fern **aphid** is a tiny black speck that often infests the underside of Boston fern fronds, but it seldom causes much harm. Spray with soapy water; if the plants are in small pots, just dip them in the mixture.

The armored **fern scale** infests Boston fern in greenhouses and dwellings. The female scale is about $\frac{1}{12}$ inch in length, pear-shaped, and light brown in color. The male is smaller, white, and narrower. A white-oil spray will suffocate this pest.

The **Florida fern caterpillar** is 1½ inches long, and starts life colored a pale green that turns to velvety black as it matures. It hides by day along the midrib or in the fern crown, and feeds at night. The chief hosts are nephrolepis and adiantum ferns. The caterpillar eats young leaves and strips leaflets from old growth. Although a tropical species, widely distributed in Florida, it has been introduced into northern greenhouses on infested plants. These caterpillars are quite visible, making handpicking a practical means of control.

Florida Fern Caterpillar

Other pests include flower thrips (see PEONY, ROSE), MEALYBUGS, SCALE, and WHITE FLY.

Fig

Figs enjoy a greater range than many people would expect, growing north into New Jersey, but in colder climates they must either be planted in sheltered places or on southern slopes with good air drainage.

Insects

One rather prevalent pest is the **long-tailed mealybug.** This insect infests a good number of plants, including avocadoes. It has two long strands that extend from the rear, accounting for the insect's name. These pests are usually brought into the garden by ants, and the control of ants will probably eliminate mealybug trouble.

Ants can be kept off fig trees by banding the trunk with cotton and roofing paper with Tanglefoot or Stikem. You can also control them by sprinkling bone meal on lawns, flower beds, and in the garden. Two chalcid wasps, one from Australia and the other from Brazil, were successfully imported in the thirties. Ladybugs are also effective. For further controls, see ANT, MEALYBUG, and PINEAPPLE.

Another serious pest is the **root-knot** (or garden) **nematode.** This minute worm penetrates the fibrous roots and causes small knots or swellings to develop. Root growth and functioning is impaired. Severely affected roots usually die, and infested trees are usually stunted or weakened. See NEMATODE.

Also look for black scale, citrus mealybug, and navel orange-worm under CITRUS.

Diseases

Fig mosaic shows as chlorotic mottling and severe leaf distortion. Light or rusty spots occur on fruit, which are sometimes misformed and drop from the tree. The fig mite is a vector of this virus. The Mission variety is especially susceptible.

Fig rust is a fungus disease that attacks young fig trees without injuring mature leaf tissue. Leaves affected by fig rust fall prematurely, and affected trees are more susceptible to cold injury than are healthy trees.

You can recognize fig rust by the small yellowish green spots that appear on leaves. These spots enlarge and turn yellowish brown and the leaves often become distorted. The best control for fig rust is to rake up and burn all the old leaves.

Smut of figs is not a true smut but a mold. It is caused by a strain of the common black mold that grows on many kinds of spoiled fruits. The fungus produces spores in a black smutlike mass. Some of the spores are introduced into the healthy fig fruits through the eyes by the same insects that transport the yeast that causes souring (see below). The control measures for smut, like those for souring, are based on sanitation and control of the insects by destroying the waste fruit in which they breed.

Souring is used to designate spoilage of fresh figs that is accompanied by a sour odor or taste or by a dripping from the eye. Souring is caused by the action of yeast and bacteria that are carried into the fig by insects such as the fig wasp, thrips, mites, and dried-fruit beetles. The condition is less of a problem on scattered trees than in fig orchards located in the vicinity of melon patches, tomato fields, mulberry, or other fruit trees in which the dried-fruit beetle finds abundant breeding material. Mission, Celeste, and Kadota figs are somewhat resistant to this form of spoilage, as the eye is small and not easily penetrated by beetles. Decaying fruit and vegetables near the fig trees should be destroyed.

Filbert

Insects

Immature filbert **aphids** are of a light green color, while mature or winged forms are darker. Heavy infestations may damage the nut crop. The damage caused by aphids is cumulative, and the benefits of control measures may therefore only become evident after two or more years of aphid control. Aphids overwinter as small, dark-colored, oval eggs attached to twigs and small branches of filbert trees. The eggs hatch in March, and the aphids move to the unfolding leaves to feed. For control, see APHID.

Aphid

The **filbert bud mite** is microscopic in size but can be easily recognized by the damage it causes. The buds swell into an oversized, puffed shape, and deformed red flowers fail to produce fruit. See SPIDER MITE.

The larvae of the **filbert leaf roller** feed on the leaves and roll them for protection. The most serious damage occurs to young fruit buds, which are often severely damaged or cut off entirely. Heavy infestations can cause a serious reduction in nut production.

Adult filbert leaf roller moths have a wingspread of about ¾ inch and are usually buff-colored with darker, irregular markings on the wings. The mature larvae are approximately ¾ inch long, light green to dark green, and have a dark head. This insect overwinters in the egg stage. Eggs are laid in silvery masses looking somewhat like overlapping fish scales. Each egg mass contains about 50 eggs, and they are found on limbs and trunks of filbert trees. The eggs hatch in spring, usually in early April. Mature larvae pupate within rolled leaves and emerge as moths during the latter part of June or in July. Control as for the oblique-banded leaf roller, discussed under ASH.

The adult **filbertworm** moth has a wingspread of about ½ inch and is marked by two golden bands across each fore wing. The larvae feed within the nuts. Filbertworms overwinter in silken cocoons found in the soil, leaves, and debris on the ground. Adult moths usually begin to emerge in early July, and may continue to appear through late August and early September. Egg-laying begins soon after emergence. Eggs are laid singly on leaves, usually on the upper surface, and hatch in about eight or nine days. The newly hatched larva moves about until it finds a nut to enter and devour. To avoid tangling with this pest, harvest nuts as early as possible and immediately dry them.

The larval **omnivorous leaf tier** occasionally causes damage to young filberts by feeding on buds and leaves. When fully grown, larvae are about ½ inch in length and grayish yellow, with two light stripes and a darker central stripe on the back. Damage occurs during late April and May. For control, see the oblique-banded leaf roller under ASH.

Fir

Insects

Firs are susceptible to various **aphids,** including the balsam twig aphid, which feeds on shoots of fir and causes the needles to bend upwards. For control, see APHID.

Vigorous trees may be attacked by the **balsam bark beetle,** which causes a bleeding of the sap from the trunk and an eventual reddening of the needles and dieback of the upper parts of the tree. To control, prune and burn the affected parts.

Fir trees may be damaged by the **spruce budworm,** an insect which has caused severe injury to spruce and balsam fir in the northern forests at several times in this century. The young caterpillars feed upon needles of the new growth on terminal shoots and those of the preceding season, usually webbing the needles together and eating them off at the base. The webs holding the severed leaves and bud scales give the trees a sickly appearance, and in fact weaken the trees to such an extent that they become the prey of bark beetles and other secondary destroyers. At maturity the caterpillars are about ¾ inch in length, dark brown, and bear cream-colored tubercles. The adult moths have a wingspread of about ¾ of an inch and are brown marked with gray spots. They are most abundant in June and July and the females lay clusters of pale green, flat eggs upon the needles. These eggs hatch in ten days and the caterpillars hibernate in a partially grown condition. There is one generation a year.

If you are planting a great many seedlings, it is advisable to plan on stands that are mixed with a reduced percentage of balsam fir to cut chances of infestation. Should trouble occur, cut off and destroy the infested tips. If the spruce budworm has been a problem, encourage birds by providing bird houses and alternate sources of food.

Other natural enemies of the budworm have proven their value. In *Beneficial Insects,* Swann mentions wasp predators (observed in Canada), red squirrels, spiders and spider mites (both very susceptible to pesticides and slow on the rebound), and a trichogramma wasp parasite. *Bacillus thuringiensis,* when suspended in water and sprayed, effected an 80 percent mortality of budworm larvae in tests in eastern Canadian forests. Eighty grams of spore dust were used per gallon, and full effects were reached in eight days. Because the preparation washes off trees with rain, it should be renewed from time to time.

The method of harvesting can get lumbermen around the spruce budworm. It's best to cut the oldest stands first, as these are most susceptible.

For control of the dark green or black, pink-legged **spruce spider mite,** see SPIDER MITE.

Diseases

Among the diseases that afflict firs is **gray mold blight**. In cool, wet seasons it causes the new growth to curl, wither, and die. The grayish mycelium and fruiting bodies appear if the cool, wet weather continues.

It is best to improve ventilation to keep down the dampness that encourages this disease. Avoiding crowded planting sites will also help to prevent the blight.

There are several **needle cast** diseases of fir trees. Needles affected by these fungi turn brown the spring following infection, and may persist on the tree. The infective spores are usually discharged about July. Pruning and burning badly infected branches may help control needle cast.

The orange yellow or white stages of **needle rust** appear on the upper or lower surface of the needles. The alternate hosts include blueberries, willows, and several ferns. The usual way to control needle rust is to remove alternate host plants in the area.

Twig blight causes needles of new growth to yellow and twigs to die. Prune and burn affected parts.

Yellow witches' broom is a stem rust infection that causes dwarfing and yellowing of needles beyond the point of attack, and dwarfing and browning of twigs. The alternate hosts are chickweeds. This fungus may kill saplings if the trunk is affected. To control the disease, prune and burn all infected parts, and eliminate all chickweed from the immediate area.

Firethorn (Pyracantha)

Insects

The **webworm,** prevalent in the southwestern part of the country, is a major pest of the firethorn. The full-grown webworm is a yellow green caterpillar, about one inch long, that is covered with numerous black spots along its back and sides. A chewing insect, the webworm eats holes in the leaves and stems of plants. It is usually protected by a thin silken web that it spins about the food plant, webbing together both leaves and twigs.

Keep down weeds and other wild plants along the margins of the garden to prevent injury. Should damage from the webworm become too extensive, consider investing in trichogramma eggs. An effective spray can be made from fresh cow manure and clay, diluted in water sufficiently to pass through a spray nozzle. If cows don't live in your area, dried cow manure is available from most supply outlets.

Diseases

Fire blight bacteria cause a sudden wilting, dying, and browning or blackening of new shoots. Leaves on these shoots die, hang downward, and cling to the blighted twigs. The variety *Pyracantha koidsumii* is susceptible and *P. crenulata* is moderately susceptible. *P. coccinea lalandii* is relatively resistant.

Destroy any nearby diseased and neglected pear, quince, and apple trees, since they may harbor the fire blight organism. Between November and March, cut off affected branches at least three inches below the affected area. Before each cut, disinfect the pruning saw or shears with alcohol.

Flowers

Of the several types of plants dealt with in this book, flowering ornamentals are least likely to cause you trouble. Perhaps this is because bugs and diseases, like humans, find flowers less appetizing than vegetables, fruits, and berries. Or, perhaps flowers as a group have come up with ways of dealing with their problems that other domesticated plants lack. But the best explanation probably lies in the way we use flowers. We look at them, but rarely eat them, and so we are less sensitive to their flaws. There is still beauty in a bug-tattered rose, but a worm-eaten tomato does little for the appetite. In other words, anyone save a florist can tolerate more damage on flowers than on plants raised for food, and this makes organic flower protection a relatively easy matter.

• **Garden sanitation.** Preventative maintenance goes a long way in the flower garden. Keep the immediate area free of plant debris—in most cases, you can put the stuff to work in the compost pile. Many growers clear the garden of dead stalks at the season's end. This makes good sense for several reasons: the material is more useful if composted, rather than left to sit as a mulch; there will be fewer places for pests to overwinter; and many hollow plant stalks serve as subterranean turnpikes that give bugs and disease pathogens easy access to the rootstocks and bulbs below. If yanking a stalk leaves a hole in the soil, just sprinkle a little dirt to seal it up.

It's best to rogue out diseased or infested plants as soon as they're spotted. While this may leave an unsightly gap in a chorus line of flowers, experience shows that sicklings can quickly pass on their ills to neighbors. However, experience has yet to bring growers to a consensus of opinion on what to do with the rejected plants. Should they be burned, or submerged in the hottest spot of the compost pile? As you'll find in the flower entries, the answer depends on the virility and contagiousness of the particular disease.

• **Proper nutrition.**   Perennials that show up year after year may suffer from the eroding effect of heavy rains. Keep an eye out for plants on high ground that might be in trouble and, if necessary, come to the rescue with an occasional top-dressing of garden soil mixed with a bit of compost.

As is true of other types of plants, healthy flowers resist damage. Be sensitive to the particular needs of each flower variety you grow—an overdose of a nutrient can be as harmful as too little.

Forsythia

Though forsythia is seldom infected by diseases, **dieback** hits flowers and then twigs. Black sclerotia (fungal resting bodies) may develop on the surface or inside of infected twigs. Control by pruning and burning infected branches and by improving aeration around the bush.

Fruit Trees

Protecting fruit trees from insects can be tough. Unfortunately, there is no carefree way to produce unmarred fruit—the bugs just won't permit it. But if you follow a yearly program of prevention and control, as outlined below, you should be rewarded with a presentable crop.

• Laying the groundwork for a successful season.

A presentable crop begins with proper plant feeding. Orchardist H. L. Rushing of Tennessee uses a rock dust mulch made of 1 part ground limestone, 2 parts phosphate rock, 3 parts granite dust, 3 parts cottonseed meal, and 4 bushels of compost. He spreads one pound for each foot of the tree's drip-line diameter. If the tree is 15 feet across from tip to tip, he broadcasts 15 pounds of fertilizer out from the trunk to the drip-line, and then tops the application with a three-inch layer of mulch. A good mulch is old or spoiled hay, laid on at least six inches thick in a three-foot band around the drip-line. Use approximately 200 pounds for a standard tree, and 100 pounds for each dwarf or semidwarf. Keep the mulch away from the trunk, as such a covering will enable pests like mice, rabbits, and insects to sneak up to the trunk and do their dirty work. If mice have been a serious problem in the past, this year try pulling the mulch out past the drip-line in October.

It is important that trees be pruned in such a manner that sunlight reaches every leaf. This involves removal of more wood than most people are inclined to do. Another purpose for pruning is to keep trees down to a size that can be properly covered by spraying.

Most of the various rots inoculate in diseased limbs and twigs, and any dead plant parts should be removed and burned. It also helps to remove and compost fallen leaves from beneath trees.

The rock or "fortress" planting method can effectively guard against the pine and meadow mouse. Place an open-ended barrel in the planting hole over a six-inch rock or gravel layer at the bottom. Next, put a three-inch layer of soil over the rock, fill the barrel with topsoil or compost, then fill the six-inch space around the sides with more rock up to the top of the hole. Now remove the barrel by sliding it up carefully; add another three-inch soil layer, plant the tree, and finish with a surface of rock mulch. Put a wire-mesh band around the tree base to keep rock from the graft. About 1,000 pounds of rock takes care of a standard tree, while 500 pounds is sufficient for a dwarf or semi-dwarf. Orchardists typically use limestone rock for this planting technique, but any other type of rock will do. Besides stopping rodent damage, the method does a tremendous job of encouraging capillary action for a healthy circulation of water and air. Other advantages (although the rock method is not essential where mice present no major danger) include greater anchorage against strong winds, absorption of heat from the spring sun to help late frost protection, and a source of minerals as the rocks gradually weather.

• **What and how to spray.**   Thirty-five years of experience have gone into the following apple spray schedule used by Ontario orchardist Alvin Filsinger. For pears, cherries, plums, or grapes, use about half of the recommended proportions. If micro-fine wettable sulfur is not available, you can substitute lime sulfur. Neither form is compatible with oil sprays. Diatomaceous earth will stick better if you add a pound or so of white pastry flour to 100 gallons of mixture.

• 1) At the delayed dormant or silver-tip stage, apply a superior dormant-oil spray at 2 gallons oil to 100 gallons water. Wet the tree well, and you should take care of most scale, codling moths, leaf rollers, and mites.

• 2) Approximately one week later, apply micro-fine wettable sulfur, mixed 3 pounds to 100 gallons water; also apply diatomaceous earth, mixed 10 pounds to 100 gallons water.

• 3) If the weather is warm, repeat sulfur applications at weekly intervals.

• 4) At the pre-pink stage, apply the sulfur as before, as well as liquid seaweed to help control mites and aphids, to feed trees through the foliage, and also to offer some frost protection. If you spot fruitworms, cankerworms, tent caterpillars, or other pest larvae, spray rotenone (3 pounds to 100 gallons water), *Bacillus thuringiensis* powder (1½ pints per 100 gallons water), or diatomaceous earth (10 pounds to 100 gallons water).

• 5) At the pink stage, no insecticide should be needed, says Filsinger. This is just as well, as bees are busy pollinating at this time. If you do have pests at the pink stage, use either BT or diatomaccous earth, as they won't harm the bees. If the blossom period is a long one, it's best not to let the trees go for more than seven days without a sulfur spraying.

• 6) At the time of petal fall (the calyx stage), apply sulfur for scab, and diatomaceous earth or BT mixed with liquid seaweed (1 gallon to 100 gallons water).

• 7) Repeat step 6 after 12 days.

- 8) After another 12 days, repeat step 6; if scab is not a problem, cut the sulfur application in half.

- 9) Repeat step 6 again, if scab or insects are noticed.

Filsinger takes full advantage of commercially available biological helpers, keeping lots of praying mantises, ladybugs, lacewings, and trichogramma wasps about his orchard. He plants chives around trees to keep a variety of pests away, and recommends setting peppermint or spearmint at the base of trees if ants are carrying aphids up into the foliage. If rabbits are a problem, he paints the main trunk in late fall with ten pounds of resin dissolved in a gallon of wood alcohol. Filsinger also uses blacklight traps to catch night-flying moths, and sets up baited traps to monitor pest activity in the orchard.

If codling moths are particularly threatening, you might use ryania, a plant extract made from the pulverized wood of a Trinidad tree. A spray should be applied about May 1, when the first brood of moths appears. Traps baited with molasses will cue you in to their activity. A second brood appears about July 10, and a third in late August. Ryania is effective for only ten days or so, as it washes off the trees with rain.

Dormant-oil sprays should be applied in still air. Stir or agitate the oil emulsion frequently to keep it well mixed. It's wise to start a dormant-oil spraying program as a regular precautionary practice, tapering off after several years of observing its effects. Don't wait for a heavy infestation before spraying.

• What can be done for trees that won't bear fruit?
First of all, be certain there is a pollinating tree (a different variety) that blooms at about the same time. If there is, and the tree still is nonbearing, carefully break the bark in several places along a limb (at least 1½ inches thick) with a hammer or other tool. This will help stimulate hormones and shock an occasionally lethargic tree into setting blossoms and fruit. Of course, a late frost will sometimes kill the pollen germ even when blooms are already present.

• Light traps.
Lights of various colors are used to draw insects to traps, both for monitoring populations and for control. Blacklight, or ultraviolet light, is attractive to many species, while red to yellow lights have the least effect and may even repel insects (as witnessed by the color of many porch lights). For more information on light traps and what they catch, see the section "Insect Traps, Homemade and Commercial" in Chapter 9.

Gardenia

Insects

The **root-knot nematode** causes swellings or galls on the roots which prevent uptake of water and nutrients. Plants become weak and stunted, and are often yellowed. Young plants usually do not show the effect of nematode infestation, but older plants show marked symptoms.

Prevention is the best cure for root-knot. Infested plants should be burned or removed to the compost heap. Revitalize the soil with a good helping of organic matter, as microorganisms in rich soil make life unpleasant for these pests. See NEMATODE for more information.

Other insect pests of gardenia are flower thrips (see PEONY, ROSE), fuller rose beetle (ROSE), MEALYBUGS, SCALE, and SPIDER MITES.

Diseases

The cause of **bud drop** is physiological, connected to a change in a plant's environment. Buds discolor and drop before opening. Troubles arise from moving plants, too much heat or dry air, or waterlogging or dryness at the roots. No cure is known, and until one is discovered, surround gardenias with constant high humidity and a temperature close to 70°F.

Stem cankers start as sunken brown areas on the stem. The bark then splits, exposing the wood. The leaves of infected plants turn yellowish green, then yellow, and finally drop. Bud drop is increased, and plants generally appear sickly and stunted, dying when the canker girdles the stem.

The fungus gains entry through wounds made by leaf pruning at the time of taking the cutting. Avoid wounds during handling, and always use a sterilized rooting medium. Badly infected plants should be rogued. If the cankers are on smaller stems, it may be possible to cut off the stems below the canker. Bathe the cut with alcohol immediately after cutting. Sometimes the plant will gain new roots and progress nicely if soil is heaped over the canker so that new roots can develop above it.

Garden Symphilid (Symphylan)

Often confused by gardeners, symphilids, millipedes, and centipedes are all long, segmented, many-legged creatures, but

Centipede

Millipede

each is in a different class and has distinguishing habits. Centipedes are beneficial predators, feeding nocturnally on soil insects and millipedes. Millipedes are anything but beneficial, and are discussed in a separate entry.

Symphilids have bodies broken up into 14 segments, and move about on 12 pairs of legs. Because of their superficial resemblance to centipedes, they are sometimes called garden centipedes. They feed on young plant roots, and are capable of downing their own weight's worth in a day. Affected plants tend to wilt in strong sunlight and are prone to fungus and bacteria root rots. Lettuce leaves may be eaten full of holes if they rest on infested ground. On tomatoes, stunted plants show bluish stems, yellowed lower foliage, and dark green upper foliage.

To check garden soil for symphilids, try this simple method explained by Hussey, Read, and Hesling in *The Pests of Protected Cultivation*: "Confirmation of suspected attacks can . . . be obtained by removing plants, with the soil surrounding their roots, and immediately placing them in a vessel of water. The symphilids, released by gently breaking up the ball of soil, can be counted on the surface of the water, taking care not to confuse them with collembola (springtails)."

On a large scale, fields can be flooded for a time to wipe out the symphilid population. A safe, non-chemical control for the gardener has not been devised, but you might try drenching the soil with garlic or tobacco teas. It's best to move the compost pile some distance from the garden if symphilids have been troublesome.

Geranium

Insects

A number of **aphids,** including the green peach and foxglove species, feast on plant juices. See APHID.

At night, **slugs** leave their hiding places under rubbish to eat notches in the tender leaves of greenhouse geraniums. They leave a telltale slimy trail. See SLUGS AND SNAILS for control measures.

Termites have a widespread reputation as household pests, and their appetite for living plants has earned them a bad name in the garden, too. Worker termites that damage plants are sometimes known as white ants. They are wingless, about $\frac{1}{16}$ inch long, and are found in injured plants and in pieces of wood beneath the soil surface. Termite colonies can be found in old stumps, fence posts, or the structural timbers of buildings. The pests tunnel out the stems of geraniums both indoors and out-doors.

Clean up stumps, roots, and other woody material in contact with the soil. Use redwood or other termite-resistant wood for stakes and posts. Kerosene can be poured on colonies.

Several species of **white fly** cause leaves to become pale, mottled, or stippled. Plants eventually loose vigor, turn yellow, and die. Leaves often are sticky with honeydew and may be coated with black, sooty mold. The adults are white, wedge-shaped, and fly about like snowflakes when disturbed. The young are rounded, flat, and look much like scales. They have waxy threads on their spines, and stay motionless on the underside of leaves. White flies live outdoors in warmer parts of the country, and in greenhouses in the North. For control, see WHITE FLY.

Whitefly

Other pests to keep an eye out for include the corn earworm (injures geraniums in fall in the North; see CHRYSANTHE-MUM), cyclamen mite (occasionally curls leaves; AZALEA, DELPHINIUM), and celery leaf tier (CELERY) and MEALY-BUGS (both greenhouse pests).

Diseases

Bacterial leaf spot and **stem rot** may seriously affect either greenhouse or garden geraniums. Bacteria invade the vascular tissue of cuttings or plants to cause a variety of symptoms. Leaf spots vary from scattered, minute, translucent dots to brown, papery, wedge-shaped areas. Leaves may wilt and drop, and branches turn black, collapse, and rot. The bacteria are very infectious, and plants can pick up infection from splashing water, contaminated soil, or handling.

Control has been achieved by using only thoroughly cleaned and disinfected cutting tools and pots. Propagate only those plants known to be free of leaf spot. Lightly infected plants should be kept well-spaced; with careful watering of the soil so that leaves and stems don't get wet, the plants may survive. However, heavily infected plants must be rogued.

Botrytis blossom blight and leaf spot describe a fungus dis-ease that causes petals of entire florets to turn dark and wilt prematurely. If the fungus persists, a gray mold appears on infected tissues and falls on healthy leaves to spread the infec-tion. Leaf spots are brown and irregular, becoming dry, wrinkled, and surrounded with yellow tissue.

In the greenhouse, this disease is easily controlled by lowering the humidity and raising the temperature. Trouble usually occurs in late winter or early spring when a sharp drop in temperature at sundown causes moisture to condense on the plants. Turning on the heat a half-hour before sundown and opening vents a bit will prevent this temperature drop and subsequent infection. Avoid any wounding, crowding, or mishandling of the plant, as this encourages the disease. If the plants are planted outdoors, give them plenty of room. Rogue out infected plants.

The virus infection **crinkle** shows as irregular or circular spots on crinkled or dwarfed younger leaves. Symptoms show only during the spring months and disappear during summer. Even though plants have apparently recovered, cuttings taken from them will show virus symptoms the following spring. Roguing and control of insects through proper soil nutrition are the only known methods of control.

Mosaic is a virus that causes a light and dark green mottling of foliage in late winter or early spring. Leaves and plants are usually small. Symptoms are masked during summer, but cuttings taken from these plants will show the disease when temperatures are optimum. Control by roguing and insect control.

Oedema or dropsy is a physiological problem. Small, watery swellings appear on the leaves, and corky ridges develop on the petioles, stems and petals. This trouble occurs when over-watering or high humidity accompany cloudy weather, often in late winter. Plants are improved by withholding water and providing good ventilation and light.

Gladiolus

Insects

The **bulb mite** attacks bulbs of gladiolus and other bulb flowers. It is very small ($\frac{1}{50}$ to $\frac{1}{25}$ inch long), whitish, and is often marked with two brown spots. The mites are reared on onions and potatoes, and later congregate beneath the scales of the gladiolus. Luckily, their feeding doesn't usually sap a plant's strength, but mites may enable decay organisms to get a start. The usual treatment for the bulb mite is to dip the bulbs in hot water for about 20 minutes. Clean up rotting bulbs and decaying plant material. It's interesting, if unessential, to note that under unfavorable conditions the mite goes into a stage in which it develops a hard shell, ceases to eat, and searches about for a free ride to greener pastures. This ride may be aboard a mouse or fly, says Cynthia Westcott.

Gladiolus thrips can cause injury to gladiolus. The flower buds may be injured so that no good blossoms result. The minute insect hides in the sheaths of the flower stem, where it is difficult to reach with a spray. Adult thrips are milky white to dark brown; for a short time, the younger thrips are light orange. The insects are very slender, with their lacy wings folded back over the abdomen. They are large enough to be seen crawling about on the palm of the hand.

Since thrips like to hide in a narrow space, you can massage the flower spikes to kill any thrips found beneath the leaves or bracts. However, such a method is of practical value only on a limited scale in a small garden. If home gardeners leave the bulbs in the ground from one year to the next, they may well be host to a population of gladiolus thrips. No corms should be left in the ground from one year to the next, particularly in an area where neighbors grow gladiolus.

Gladiolus thrips also feed on iris, calendula, lily, dianthus, sweet pea, potato, cucumber, dahlia, aster, delphinium, hollyhock, and white clover; the presence of these host plants nearby complicates control. Generally, trouble with gladiolus thrips is much less serious when bulbs are planted early than late. It helps to dig early in the fall, before the corms are quite mature, and to cut off the tops. The pests will be carried away in the cut portion. As a final measure, burn these decapitated tops. See also THRIPS.

Other prominent insect pests include cutworms (see TOMATO), tarnished plant bug (ASTER), APHIDS (hibernate on the stored corms and damage new growth), and zebra caterpillar (see imported cabbageworm under CABBAGE).

Diseases

If you grow gladiolus for their beauty and not for a living, you shouldn't be troubled much by diseases. Select varieties resistant to fusarium yellows. **Dry rot,** recognized by small circles of decay on the lower section of the corm, can be prevented by using soil with adequate drainage and removing husks before planting. Aphids are vectors of several diseases; see APHID. Infected corms should be burned and not composted.

Dry Rot

Gloxinia, see Begonia

Gooseberry

Gooseberries are subject to most of the diseases and insects of currants. See CURRANT for full information.

Gooseberry witchbroom **aphids** are yellow green insects that cause the leaves to curl tightly. Control by applications of rotenone or pyrethrum if infestations are severe.

Gourds

Gourds are attacked by the same insects that plague CUCUMBER.

Grape

You won't find every pest of grapes listed below—far from it. Most of the insects that trouble grapes are general feeders, with few classified as specific to grapes. Small plantings and backyard arbors are likely to host a diverse mix of insects, although recent grape plantings may go for several years without insect troubles if vineyards and wild vines aren't nearby.

Good sanitation goes a long way toward preventing disease. Inspect the vines regularly and often, and remove any grapes showing dark spots (indicative of fungus) or red or purple spots (entry holes of insects). Discolored or mined leaves should also be removed. After the fruit has set, prune back excess growth ruthlessly in order to facilitate air circulation and thereby discourage fungus. This pruning prevents a second fruiting, which will not ripen before frost and may keep the first bunches of grapes from reaching their full potential.

While hybrid varieties win favor because they yield the highest quality fruit, most are less winter hardy than the native American species. The New Hampshire Cooperative Extension Service recommends planting on a slope having a southeastern, southwestern, or southern exposure. Such a slope creates excellent air drainage in spring (thereby decreasing the risk of late frosts), tempers the cold winter winds out of the northwest, and provides more early- and late-season sunlight to speed the growth and maturity of the crop. The air circulation on such sites discourages fungus diseases such as downy and powdery mildew. Flat or valley bottom sites are to be avoided, the Extension Service says.

In the first year, clean cultivation involves keeping the middles well pulverized and free from grass and weeds. You can use a cultivator, disk harrow, rotivator, or rototiller, and then follow up several times during the growing season by hoeing around and between the plants.

For an effective spray program, see FRUIT TREES.

Insects

Several species of **climbing cutworm** may damage grapes. These pests hide on the ground under weeds and trash by day, and climb the grape trunk on warm nights to eat the primary grape buds. According to the Ohio Agricultural Research and Development Center, the damage usually takes place in only a short period each year, as the vulnerable buds grow quickly. Serious damage is usually limited to areas of the vineyard in which there are weeds or grasses under the trellis. However, the University of California Division of Agricultural Sciences cautions against removing vegetation from around the base of the vines when buds are swelling, ". . . as destroying weed hosts at this time leaves only grape buds for the cutworms to feed on. However, a thorough reduction of the weed cover a month before bud swell will greatly reduce cutworm population." See TOMATO for other control measures.

The **grape berry moth** is likely the primary pest of grapes. It occurs in almost all grape growing areas east of the Rockies, including Ontario's Niagara Peninsula. Growers generally have to deal with two generations a year. Young larvae are white to cream in color at first, and become green and then purple if they feed on deep blue berries. They reach a length of ⅜ inch when fully grown, at which time those of the first generation form a cocoon by folding over a section of leaf and securing it with silk. Second generation larvae typically drop to the ground and form pupae in dead leaves. The adult moth is distinguished by tan fore wings with sharply distinguished areas of dark brown.

Grape/Grape Berry Worm

As the larvae feed, they tie the berries and flowers together with a silken webbing. Red spots show where larvae have entered a berry; later, the spots often turn purple and berries may split as they grow. About the time the berries touch in their clusters, the second brood of larvae is due. Affected green berries of blue varieties will sometimes turn red prematurely. Eggs for the second generation are laid from late July through August.

As the grape berry moths pupate and spend the winter on the ground, an early cultivation (before mid-May in Pennsylvania) will bury them and halt the first generation of larvae. Pupae fall prey to several species of ants and ground beetles, and the eggs are parasitized by a tiny wasp.

Early in June, a row of tiny holes may be seen around grape shoots. These are chewed by the **grape cane girdler** with the object of placing a single egg in each hole. If the eggs are allowed to hatch, the larvae feed within the cane and the shoot breaks and falls over, leaving the infested section still on the cane. The adult is a small black snout beetle that overwinters in trash in or around the vineyard.

Damage is not usually serious, as the stems are girdled beyond the grape clusters and there is seldom any loss of fruit. If infested canes are to be pruned, do so before the beetles emerge, in late July or August. The cuts should be slightly below the girdle. Damage is usually confined to vines closest to border or trashy areas. Clean the vineyard of long grass, rocks, and corrugated paper.

Grape/Grapevine Tomato Gall

Grape galls are caused by several species of small adult flies or midges that lay their eggs either on or in leaves, stems, tendrils, and canes. After feeding within the galls, the full-grown larvae emerge and drop to the ground to pupate and emerge as small flies. While galls look like trouble, they rarely cause economic damage. If the larvae are still within (a small hole indicates that they are not), it may be to your advantage to cut the galls from the vine and destroy them.

In the home vineyard, you should be on guard against the **grape leafhopper.** The adults of this insect pest are about ⅛ inch long and lay their eggs on the leaves. When the eggs hatch into nymphs, both adults and nymphs may be found feeding on the underside of leaves, causing whitish spots that later turn brown. If this injury is extensive, fruit may be seriously affected. There is a tiny microscopic wasp parasite, *Anagrus epos,* which becomes established early in the growing season and can produce three generations in a summer. By the time that the last generation has developed, the leafhopper is all but eliminated from the vineyard. During the early part of the year, the parasites breed on a noneconomic leafhopper that feeds on blackberries. As the family grows, the first brood of leafhoppers beckons the parasites to the grape vines, where *Anagrus* feeds and continues to produce offspring. With the advent of winter, the leafhoppers find a home on the vines or in nearby weeds but the beneficial parasites must overwinter in blackberry vines, which are often a great distance from the vineyards. By the time summer arrives and the parasites find their way back to the vineyards, the leafhoppers are already established on the grapes and have begun to feed. It's good practice to grow blackberries near the grape vines so that the parasites are able to move quickly from their winter home to the vines.

Pyrethrum has been found to be effective against the grape leafhopper. You might try a control method used by grape growers of the last century. The vineyardist would saturate a sheet with tar or kerosene and carry it, stretched on a frame, along a row while a partner walked down the row and disturbed the grape vines so that the insects flew into the homemade trap. The result? Fewer insects on the vines and a better-looking crop.

Insect-electrocuting light traps, using a clear blue light, will draw significant numbers of grape leafhoppers to their deaths. Preventative measures include keeping the area cleaned and raked so that the insects will be exposed to the weather, particularly during the autumn months. Avoid planting thin-leaved varieties such as Clinton and Delaware, as they are more susceptible to the leafhopper than are varieties whose leaves are more leathery.

The **grape phylloxera** causes leaf galls on the underside of leaves. These growths are wartlike and about the size of a pea. Heavily infested leaves become distorted and may eventually die. The responsible phylloxera stage is a plump, orange yellow, wingless insect. Five hundred yellowish eggs are laid in the galls. Nymphs leave the galls to feed on new leaves at the shoot tip, and galls result.

While nearly all grape varieties are susceptible to this pest, some varieties fare better than others. Consult your local extension agent.

The adult **grape sawfly** is a small, black, wasplike insect that lays its eggs in clusters on the underside of terminal grape leaves. The larvae line up side to side and strip leaves from the underside, leaving only the heaviest of leaf veins. Full-grown larvae drop to the ground to form cocoons and pupate. Infested leaves should be removed and burned.

The iridescent adult **Japanese beetle** feeds on the foliage and sometimes fruit of both wild and cultivated vines. The larvae (grubs) occupy themselves primarily with grass roots. The beetles seem to prefer vines with thin, smooth leaves to those with thick, pubescent leaves.

Japanese Beetle

Since Japanese beetles are very mobile, absolute control is difficult. Your best defense lies in inoculating nearby grassy areas with milky spore disease. See JAPANESE BEETLE. On cool evenings, the beetles turn sluggish and can be shaken into coffee cans containing kerosene.

In a pamphlet entitled *Nematodes and Their Control in Vineyards*, the California Agricultural Experiment Station Extension Service states that **nematode** damage is not always easy to spot. "Vines may produce satisfactory yields for long periods, even though nematode populations are increasing, if other factors such as soil, water, and cultural factors are favorable. Even old and heavily infested cane vines may remain productive under optimum cultural conditions. However, the high nematode populations will attack, stunt, or kill young vines when such soils are replanted."

Nematodes are slender, wormlike creatures that are often too small to be seen with the naked eye. A single gram of root may host from 2,000 to 10,000 pests. They suck plant juices through a sharp mouth part called a spear or stylet. Some nematode species that prey on grape work from within the roots and others feed externally. While their feeding naturally saps a plant's energy, the feeding wounds can aggravate problems by admitting pathogens. In addition, so-called root-knot nematodes produce swellings or galls on roots, which work to block the flow of water and food to the plant. These nematodes are especially severe in light, coarsely textured soils.

If nematode injury is so subtle, how can you tell what's going on underground? Root galls are concrete evidence that root-knot nematodes are at work, but other species are not as easy to detect. Laboratory examination of both roots and soil is usually necessary to establish what species of nematodes, if any, are present. The species must be determined because a number of harmless or beneficial nematodes also reside in the soil. The California pamphlet recommends that samples should be collected from several spots within the vineyard, and that roots and soil be taken from a depth of at least 8 to 12 inches below the surface. So that the nematodes do not die before reaching the microscope platform, place the soil samples in plastic bags and avoid setting them in the sun. Some states will examine the samples for you; in other states, California being one of them, you should take the samples to a commercial laboratory.

To prevent nematode problems, use resistant rootstocks and set them in planting material that is free of virus and nematodes.

Crop rotation and fallowing of the land will help. Rootings can be purged of the pests by submerging them in water heated to 125°F. for exactly five minutes. Cool the rootings immediately after the treatment and keep them from drying out.

The California pamphlet suggests several resistant varieties to growers in that state. In general, "wine and raisin grape varieties have been more readily adapted to the use of nematode-resistant rootstocks than those of table grapes, since appearance of the mature fruit is of minor importance." Growers in California should consult their local extension agent for up-to-date variety recommendations. See also NEMATODE.

The ungainly, light brown **rose chafer beetle** measures about ⅝ inch long and looks something like a dull Japanese beetle. They fly in from surrounding grassy areas about the time of grape bloom, especially in vineyards located near areas of sandy soil. Chafers reduce the crop by feeding on grape blossoms or small grape berries, during an active span of only five or ten days out of the season. The larvae are grubs that feed on grass roots, and apparently do not damage the roots of grapevines.

Rose Chafer

Adult chafers rarely cause significant damage. Milky spore disease will kill off the grubs (see JAPANESE BEETLE). Heavy infestations can be removed from vines with a good shake and collected in a sheet spread below. The chafer is very partial to the Clinton variety, which may be planted as a trap crop to concentrate the beetles for easy disposal.

The **snowy tree cricket** lays its eggs in a series of tiny holes that run the length of a cane for a short distance. The eggs are laid in these holes in early autumn and hatch into nymphs in spring. This stage feeds on other plants in the vineyard, and the only damage caused is by diseases that occasionally enter the site of injury. The adult is much like a cricket in appearance, but is more slender, has very long antennae, and is a very pale green in color. The Ohio Agricultural Research and Development Center says that vinelands having overgrown natural ground cover or cover crops are the most susceptible to infestations, as they afford cover as well as food for the feeding nymphs. Control measures are not required if the ground cover is reduced or eliminated.

Wasps occasionally beat growers to the grapes. To foil these pests, tie or staple small paper or plastic bags around each cluster. Clear plastic bags aren't necessary, as the sugar stored in grapes is made in the leaves.

Diseases

Black rot [color] is a fungus disease that attacks leaves, blossom, and fruit. About the time the berries are half grown, light spots may appear on them. These spots enlarge rapidly until the whole berry is affected. The berry becomes a shriveled, hard black mummy bearing small black pimples that contain the disease spores. A few or all of the berries in the bunch may be affected. Grapes thrive best where there is good soil drainage and good ventilation.

Pick off the dried fruit in which the fungus overwinters and remove it to the compost heap. Compost made from diseased fruit can give vines the ability to resist the black rot fungus, as the grape tissue will build up resistance to disease much as the human body does. Varieties vary considerably in their susceptibility to black rot. The Pennsylvania Agricultural Extension Service names Catawba, Concord, Niagara, and Duchess among those most apt to be troubled. Campbell Early, Delaware, Moore Early, Norton, Portland, Sheridan, and Worden are somewhat resistant.

Rounded, reddish brown galls on roots are symptoms of **crown gall.** Galls occasionally appear on aboveground stems as hard brown or black growths. When the galls are numerous, growth of the vine is adversely affected.

There is no known cure for this disease, and care should be taken not to injure roots or to plant grapes in soil known to be infected with crown gall. Do not plant infected stock in a vineyard.

Dead arm is a fungus disease that kills the shoots and branches (or arms) of grape plants. Control depends upon your ability to recognize symptoms so that affected parts can be removed.

Most new shoot infections occur before the shoots are 12 inches long. All parts of the shoots are subject to infection. New lesions are dark. The lesions eventually become elongated, and split to expose the inner fibers of stem tissue. Dark specks of the spore-forming pycnidia can be seen on the infected stems. The rotted tissue is not as dark as black rot and the pycnidia are larger, but less numerous. Spores are dispersed early in the season and infections are usually limited to the first six or seven nodes. Symptoms of trunk infection are most easily detected in June. The shoots from infected arms and trunks that are not killed are very much stunted. The leaves are small, crinkled and yellow— especially at the margins. They cup upward or downward and the margins are ragged and irregular. The fungus enters the trunk and supporting arms through pruning stubs or breaks caused by winter injury, and invades all portions of the wood. A cross-section of the trunk reveals a V-shaped section of darkened wood that extends toward the ground line. Affected shoots occur on either or both sides of the vine, depending on the location of the infected trunk tissue. Affected canes may die at any time during the year, but most die during the winter months. If the disease girdles the trunk, all above portions die.

Dead arm is most effectively controlled by removing infected trunk and arm cankers the first year symptoms appear. This should be done before June by cutting off all affected parts and removing and destroying them to reduce danger of spread of the disease. When in doubt, cutting off the trunks at the ground line is the most certain way to get all affected parts.

Although **frost injury** does not come within the scope of this book, it is a danger worth a mention—many growers find that spring frosts are as harmful as mildew and birds. In advance of heavy frost warnings, hang four or so thicknesses of newspaper over tender shoots or blossoms. The paper can be held in place by stapling. When the danger is past, the paper is easily removed in the morning when still damp. Avoid leaving it on more than a few days, as the foliage will become so tender that strong sun may burn it.

Mildews are a big headache for many grape growers. Downy mildew [color] is particularly harmful to European varieties; the *Pennsylvania Grape Letter* reports that the disease has attacked the clusters of Rougeon, deChaunac, and Chancellor before bloom, severely depleting crops. Leaf spots appear pale yellow on top, downy below, and turn brown in time.

Powdery mildew seriously affects the berries of French hybrids Rosette and Aurore in the East, and affects the foliage of most other French hybrids. Native American varieties are not very seriously damaged in the East, but the disease is considered a major problem in California. White patches are visible on leaves, fruit, and canes, and turn brown or black toward the end of the season.

Commercially, mildew is blitzed with a variety of sprays, ranging from sulfur on powdery mildew to insidious chemicals on the downy species. But these palliatives ignore the root of the mildew problem, according to Floyd Allen in *Organic Gardening and Farming* magazine. "Mildew ought to be looked upon . . . as a symptom that we are doing things which work detrimentally against ourselves and nature," he believes, and he has come up with hundred-year-old references to support his point. It appears that mildew was not a problem in the California of the 1860's—one source of that period claimed that "mildew cannot exist upon a healthy vegetable surface"—and Allen is led to wonder if sulfur must be a necessary part of successful grape culture. While most California orchardists that he talked to were dependent on it, a number of organic growers told him they do not use sulfur and do not have mildew. One gentleman wrote, "I have three or four acres of grapes and never heard of using sulfur on them. I don't have any mildew now nor did I have any in the last ten years." Allen got the impression that the practice of sulfur dusting perpetuated itself, just as insecticides triggered new pest problems and forced growers to go to new and stronger chemicals.

The question of the role of sulfur in instigating mildew is still unresolved, but don't use it if you don't need it. It occurs in a pure state in nature, but then so do a lot of things that can make you good and sick. It is mild relative to chemical potions, but even the mildest of botanical sprays has its consequences on the surrounding habitat. If you aren't a commercial grower, frequent washdowns with strong streams of water might take the place of sulfur. One grower, Harry Carian of Coachella, California, installed overhead sprinklers on all of his organic vineyards. Will Kinney, of Vita Green, believes proper nutrition can stave off trouble: "Should there be a deficiency of sulfur or copper nutrients in the soil, we can expect a deficiency of these fungicidal and germ-defensive elements in the plants and leaves; thus grape plants are more vulnerable to the invasion of the ever-present soil and airborne spores of mildew, both powdery and downy types."

Other growers suggest that the practice of over-fertilization, in league with big-scale monoculture, is just asking for trouble. One man reports that, while his moderately watered, unfertilized grapes are not impressive in size, they are sweet, highly flavored, and not at all bothered by mildew. But he suggests another highly important variable that can predispose a vineyard to trouble—climate. His ranch lies in the dry foothills of Tulare County, but coastal grape culture may be quite a different thing. Indeed, foggy areas seem to be most troubled, and mildews are at their worst when rainfall is heavy and the days are hot and humid. Good air circulation is important to prevention, and sites affording free movement of air are least prone to mildew. Pruning the vines can encourage air circulation through the plants.

Wildlife

It's no news to grape growers that **birds** have a penchant for fruit. Short of shooting them, there are a number of scares and barriers that should afford control. In Britain, where growers are loath to killing birds, much success has been had with the Merry-down Hawk, a plastic falcon held aloft by a gas-filled balloon. But many growers in this country get by with paper bags, slipped over maturing fruit bunches. The bottom corners are cut off to provide ventilation and let any accumulated moisture drain out. Keep a small pair of pruning shears handy to clip off any tendrils that get in the way. Staple the top of the bags, leaving just enough of an opening to allow ventilation without giving access to birds. Virginia grower H. C. Mathews warns that as the season advances you should see to it that the bagged bunches are shaded by leafy vines during the hottest part of the afternoon, or else fruit on the sunny side may be cooked.

Grapefruit, see Citrus

Grasshopper

A number of species of hopper are found in this country, not all of them of economic importance. Those that do harm crops and rangelands cause damage far beyond the amount of foliage they eat, as they chew through stems and leaves to cause large portions of plants to fall to the ground.

Grasshopper

Grasshoppers are a concern to growers over most of the continent, but are most serious in areas having an annual rainfall of from 10 to 30 inches—particularly the midwestern United States and Canada, including the High Plains and Mountain States. Most troubled are rangeland, wheat, corn, barley, oats, rye, and alfalfa, but there are plenty of grasshoppers left over to attack vegetable crops.

The eggs are vulnerable to cultivation, and the nymphs, which start feeding within a day of hatching, are susceptible to weather, disease, predators, and parasites. Most species deposit their eggs in the ground late in summer and in fall. The common pest species spends six to eight months of the year in the egg stage in the top three or so inches of soil. Cultivation compacts the surface layer, and discourages the newly hatched hoppers from emerging into the world. Working the soil also exposes the egg pods to parasites, predators, weather, and dessication. Fall tillage, right after harvest, is preferable, as it makes the soil unattractive to egg-laying females, as well as stirring up any eggs already deposited. The extension service of the University of Nebraska suggests that large-scale growers either plant such resistant crops as sorghum or border susceptible crops with a resistant planting. After reaching a height of eight to ten inches, such varieties as sorgo and kafir are practically immune to grasshopper attack. They can be planted rather late in the season to provide valuable feed for livestock.

Weedy margins, such as roadsides and fence rows, offer ideal places for overwintering grasshoppers, and it helps to replace them with perennial grasses, such as crested wheatgrass. An added benefit is the increased farm returns gained by growing grass along what would otherwise be unproductive field margins.

• **Natural enemies.**   A good layer of compost or mulch will keep many grasshoppers from surfacing in spring. Those that do make it are game for crows, sparrows, hawks, killdeer, flycatchers, bluebirds, mockingbirds, catbirds, brown thrashers, and meadowlarks—to name a few of the birds—and a wide variety of insect, mite, and nematode enemies. An impressive number of animals, including coyotes, skunks, cats (both domesticated and wild), snakes, toads, and spiders, also contribute their appetites. Guinea hens do a fine job of patrolling for hoppers.

Some enemies of grasshoppers attack the immature and adult stages, while others prey on the eggs. Some attack at one season, some at another. In combination they carry on a destructive action that never ceases. Flesh flies deposit active maggots on grasshoppers even while the latter are in flight. The tiny maggots work their way into the body and feed on its contents, leaving the more vital organs for last. When flesh flies are abundant, they frequently kill large numbers of grasshoppers by midsummer, and infest so many of those remaining that egg laying is greatly reduced.

Tangle-veined flies are similar in color to honey bees but are slightly smaller. Unlike flesh flies, the adults pay no attention to grasshoppers. Upon emerging from the ground, the egg-laden females fly to the nearest wooden fence post or other upright object and start laying eggs in cracks and holes in the wood. Eggs are laid very rapidly and in great numbers: one female was observed to lay 1,000 eggs on a single post in 15 minutes; another female, confined in a pillbox, laid 4,700 eggs in seven hours. Eggs hatch in about ten days, and the tiny maggots are blown away by the wind. Just how they find grasshoppers is a mystery, but the large numbers of grasshoppers in which they are found proves that many are successful. When a maggot gets on a grasshopper, it bores into its abdomen, lives on the contents, and thus eventually kills it. Once fully grown, it forces its way out of the grasshopper and goes into the ground, where it changes to a pupa the next spring. The adult fly emerges several weeks later. There is only one generation a year.

Bee flies, blister beetles, and ground beetles lay their eggs in the soil close to grasshopper egg pods, or even in them. Larvae hatching from the eggs work their way into the egg pods and usually consume all the eggs of the pods they enter. These predators have been known to destroy 40 to 60 percent of grasshopper eggs over considerable acreages.

Red mites feed on grasshopper eggs early in spring. They burrow into egg pods and suck the eggs dry. Later in the season larval and adult mites attach themselves to immature and mature grasshoppers of almost any species. Infested grasshoppers may live normal life spans but their egg production is often greatly reduced.

In some states, hairworms are common parasites of grasshoppers. They are long, whitish, extremely slender, and frequently are found coiled within the body cavity of living grasshoppers. Grasshoppers thus infested may live one to three months but are retarded in their development, and the females are rendered sterile. When the worms complete their growth in a grasshopper, they kill it by forcing their way through the body wall. They then enter the ground.

Surprisingly large numbers of immature and adult grasshoppers are trapped by spider webs. Even the largest grasshopper is securely bound with silken strands within a few seconds after it becomes entangled in a web.

Ground squirrels, field mice, and other rodents eat grasshoppers and dig in the ground for their eggs. No figures are available on the percentage of eggs destroyed by rodents, but it must be high, since evidence of their digging can be seen wherever grasshopper eggs are abundant. The Fish and Wildlife Service has found that birds play a part in the natural control of grasshoppers. All birds, except the strictly vegetarian doves and pigeons, feed on these insects. Some eat the eggs after scratching them from the ground. Birds are of value in holding grasshoppers in check when the pests occur in moderate numbers, but they cannot prevent outbreaks.

• **Controls.**   Seedlings can be protected by laying cheese-cloth over the rows. If your crops are in trouble right now, a hot pepper spray might come to the rescue. The ingredients are hot pepper pods, pure soap, and water; the proportions of each are up to you. It's likely that there are other ingredients with repellent powers, but grasshoppers are not so easily turned away as other insects. When Helen Philbrick, co-author with her husband John of *The Bug Book*, was asked for an effective recipe, she wrote back, "We tried everything for our Missouri grasshoppers, partly by observing what they didn't eat: horehound, castor bean, etc. . . . I brewed up castor oil and strong soaps and urine and turpentine. Nothing stopped them except to make silage of the crops, hoppers and all."

A few well-placed traps will do much to rid the garden of grasshoppers. Half-fill two-quart mason jars with one part molasses in ten parts water, and put several where the grasshoppers are at their worst.

Some traps are designed to catch the insects that hop or jump when disturbed. One trap known as the hopperdozer is merely a long, narrow, shallow trough of boards or metal and mounted on runners that can be drawn across a field to catch grasshoppers. At the back of the trough a vertical shield, about three feet high, is partly filled with water. Sometimes enough kerosene is added to cover the water with a thin film. The grasshoppers fly up to avoid the hopperdozer, strike the vertical shield, and fall into the kerosene-coated water.

Guava

Insects

The **broad mite** is a pale pest of foliage, usually to be found on the underside of leaves. Water sprays should dislodge most of the mites. They are vulnerable to sulfur dust.

The **guava white fly**, a minute sucking insect that looks like a tiny white moth, attaches its eggs to the underside of guava leaves. The eggs, $\frac{1}{100}$ inch long, hatch in a short time and the young suck the sap from leaves. Use oil emulsion sprays in fall when foliage begins to harden, or after fruit set in spring. The spray should contain $1\frac{1}{4}$ percent oil. This spray will also control the numerous species of scales that attack guavas.

Nematodes sometimes attack and kill wild plantings of guava. They should not menace any planting fed and mulched with organic matter, however, for a fungus that kills nematodes is present in decomposing organic fertilizer. See NEMATODE.

Diseases

Crown or **root rot** will sometimes destroy a planting that is made on soil containing tree stumps and old roots, particularly if the trees were oak. It is best to plant guavas where the land has been cleared long enough for all of the old roots to have decomposed.

Hawthorn (Flowering Crab)

Insects

Several species of **aphid** frequently infest hawthorn. The rosy apple aphid sometimes curls the leaves, and all species secrete honeydew, which supports sooty fungus. See APHID.

Several species of **lacebug** commonly attack the foliage of hawthorn. These tiny sucking insects feed on the underside of leaves, where they deposit small spots of dark excrement. When numerous, they cause foliage to discolor and drop prematurely.

Control by spraying or dusting the underside of leaves with nicotine or pyrethrum.

The **thorn limb borer** has been known to attack hawthorns. In the smaller branches and twigs of hawthorn, it causes swellings about an inch long with four or five longitudinal scars. Infested twigs may break off in the wind. The beetle is ½ inch long, brown, and decorated with two white crescent-shaped spots near the middle of the wing covers and two smaller circular spots near the apex. The thorax has a white stripe on each side extending onto the base of the wing covers. There is one annual generation, and the beetles appear in June.

Control by removing and burning the infested twigs. For further control methods, see peach twig borer under PEACH.

Other occasional pests of hawthorn are cankerworms (see APPLE), the round-headed apple borer (APPLE), San José scale (APPLE), cottony maple scale (MAPLE), gypsy moth, tent caterpillar (TREES: INSECTS), and two-spotted mite (SPIDER MITES).

Diseases

Fire blight is a bacterial disease that causes a sudden wilting and browning or blackening of new shoots. The leaves on these shoots die, hang downward, and cling to the blighted twigs. The disease rarely becomes serious unless the trees are planted near pears that harbor the disease-causing bacteria.

Avoid overfertilization. Cut out infected branches and twigs between November and early March, pruning at least a foot below the edge of the diseased bark.

During mid-May, leaves may show signs of **leaf blight** and **fruit spot**. Single blossoms or entire flower clusters wilt, die, turn brown, and hang on the twigs for some time before falling. All or part of the leaf may turn brown, with a fruit rot generally following leaf infection. The disease may be confused with bacterial fire blight, although fire blight causes tissues to be more blackened. The causal fungus overwinters on fallen, mummified fruit that has been partly buried in the ground. To control the disease, rake and burn all the mummified fruit.

Leaf rust appears as brown or orange spots on the upperside of leaves. Long, slender, whitish tubes break open on the underside to shed orange brown spores. Infected leaves fall, but the damage to hawthorn is slight. Since the alternate host is cedar, it helps to remove these trees from the area within a one-mile radius if possible.

Powdery mildew appears on hawthorn as a white mold that covers leaves and new growth, often deforming or killing them. Control by spraying or dusting with sulfur as soon as it appears. Affected new growth should be pruned out and burned. If infection has been serious in previous years, sulfur sprays may be applied three times at weekly intervals beginning the first of May.

Stem rust is similar to leaf rust, and also attacks twigs and fruit, sometimes deforming them. Spores that affect the hawthorn are produced on cedars during long spring rains; infection does not spread from hawthorn to hawthorn. The fungus is perennial in the cedars so that infected trees remain a threat to hawthorns year after year. If possible, control by removing all cedars in the vicinity for a radius of a mile.

Heliotrope

The **greenhouse white fly** causes leaves of plants to become pale, mottled, or stippled. The pests secrete a honeydew which may leave a black, sooty mold to grow on leaves. Plants lack vigor, turn yellow, and die. The adults fly about like snowflakes when disturbed; the young look much like scales, staying motionless on the bottom of leaves. See WHITE FLY.

Other common pests of heliotrope include APHIDS, celery leaf tier (see CELERY), MEALYBUGS, SPIDER MITES, and termites (see GERANIUM).

Whitefly

Hemlock

Insects

The larva of the destructive **hemlock borer** does damage under the bark of living, injured, and dying hemlock and spruce trees. The adult beetle is about ⅜ inch long, flattened, and dark brown in color with three small whitish spots on both wing covers. The larva is one of the so-called flat-headed borers. They make sinuous, interlacing, flattened galleries in the inner bark and sapwood, thus girdling the tree. The beetles appear from May through July. There is only one brood a year.

Prune affected branches; cut infested trees and burn the bark late in the winter or in early spring. Keep your trees in a vigorous condition of growth by applying organic fertilizers and adhering to a well-planned watering program.

Hemlock scale is a dark gray, circular species that occasionally infests the underside of leaves and causes them to turn yellow, giving the tree a sickly appearance. Young trees may be killed. See PINE.

The **hemlock webworm** webs together a few leaves and feeds upon them inside the web. The larva is less than ¼ inch long; some are bright green, others are brown. The moth is whitish with pale brown tips and a wingspread of less than ½ inch. Eggs are laid in June, and there is one brood each season. The larvae apparently live over winter in the webs in a nearly full grown state. Prune and burn twigs bearing clusters of these caterpillars.

The **red-banded leaf roller** may skeletonize the leaves of hemlock trees, causing them to turn brown and drop in late summer. The larva is green with a brown head, reaching about ¼ inch long when mature. The winter is passed in the pupal stage in trash under the trees, and the moths appear in spring. See control measures for the oblique-banded leaf roller under ASH.

Other insects may from time to time bother your hemlocks:

pine leaf scale (see PINE), spruce budworm (FIR), spruce mite (SPRUCE), and strawberry root weevil (STRAWBERRY).

Diseases

There are several forms of **needle rust**. Hemlock-blueberry rust causes long white tubes that discharge orange spores, which form on the lower side of needles in early summer. Often only a single needle will be infected. Alternate hosts are members of the blueberry family such as azaleas and rhododendrons. Control is best effected by removing the alternate host to break the life cycle and eliminate the rust from the environment. Rust does not often bother hemlocks, and it is more damaging on members of the blueberry family than on hemlocks.

When rust pustules form on both the upper and lower side of needles, the hemlock-poplar form of needle rust has struck; all other needle rusts on hemlock fruit only on the underside of the needles. Infection also occurs on young twigs and cones, which are distorted as the clustercups form and burst to discharge orange spores.

Control by removing the alternate host, the poplars. Damage is usually slight to hemlocks. If necessary, the infected twigs can be pruned and burned.

When **tip blight** affects hemlock, new growth curls and dies and may be covered with a gray mold of the fruiting stage of the fungus, especially during prolonged cool, wet springs. A change in weather conditions will stop the ravages of this fungus, but there is little you can do to control tip blight.

Phomopsis twig blight causes needles to turn brown and fall from affected twigs. The wood is dead, and small black fruiting bodies of the causal fungus may be found on the twigs. These fungi are usually found on trees growing under unfavorable conditions. Pruning and burning infected twigs removes the source of future trouble.

Hibiscus (Rose Of Sharon)

Melon Aphid

The melon **aphid** causes severe leaf curling, distortion of young leaves, and stunting of growth. The honeydew that these insects secrete supports the growth of sooty fungus on leaf surfaces. Damage is worst in the South; see APHID.

Other pests include the corn earworm (see CHRYSANTHE-MUM), fuller rose beetle (ROSE), JAPANESE BEETLE, and WHITE FLY.

Hickory

Insects

The **hickory bark beetle** is an extremely destructive pest of hickory trees. In July, the female makes a vertical tunnel about an inch long in the inner bark and sapwood, with a row of pockets along each side. An egg is deposited in each pocket. Upon hatching the grubs commence to tunnel in a direction at right angles to the parent gallery, and the larval galleries at the ends of the parent gallery are deflected so as not to run into the other galleries. A few such brood galleries may girdle the branch. The adult is a small brown or black beetle, ⅕ inch long, with four short spines on the abdomen. The beetles emerge in June and July through round holes resembling shot holes and eat at the bases of the leaf stems, causing many leaves to turn brown in July. Some drop and others hang upon the trees. There is one generation annually. As this pest does most damage to weak trees, fertilizing and watering may help to prevent infestation. Cut and burn seriously affected trees between fall and spring.

The **hickory gall aphid** forms galls in June on the leaf stems and new shoots. The hollow galls contain young aphids. In July they reach maturity and leave the galls, which then turn black. These globular galls cause much distortion to the shoots. Aphid eggs remain over winter in old galls and in crevices of the bark. If galls are very serious, control with a spray of nicotine sulfate and soap, just before the buds swell. Less severe controls are given under APHID.

There are several types of **hickory leaf galls**, most of them caused by midges or two-winged flies. They are seldom destructive enough to require control.

The larva of the **hickory leaf roller** is yellowish green and measures about an inch in length. It rolls hickory leaves and feeds on them from inside the rolls. The moth is dark brown with darker oblique bands on the fore wings. The hickory leaf roller has not been a serious pest and does not require control.

The **hickory tussock moth** feeds upon hickory and foliage of other trees. The full-grown larva is about 1½ inches in length, covered with white hairs, and is decorated with a stripe of black hairs along the back and two narrow tufts of black hairs at each end. The adult moth has a wingspread of about two inches, showing light brown wings marked with oval white spots. Eggs are laid in patches on the underside of leaves in July. The tussock moth

Hickory/Hickory Tussock Moth

hibernates in gray cocoons fastened to trees, fences, and other objects. There is one annual generation. Naturally occurring parasites help to keep this insect from getting out of hand.

The **painted hickory borer** tunnels under the bark and in the sapwood of hickory. The ¾-inch-long beetles emerge in May and June and are blackish with yellow markings. Eggs are laid in crevices or under the edges of the bark. Larvae become mature in 10 to 12 weeks and then pupate in the wood in September where they remain until spring.

Vigorous healthy trees are seldom injured by the painted hickory borer. Cutting and burning infested trees and all slash (logging debris) is the usual means of control.

Other pests of hickory include APHIDS, the fall webworm (see WEBWORM), and the walnut caterpillar (WALNUT).

Diseases

Hickory trees are subject to a fungus that causes **cankers** to form around dead branch stubs. Even though stubs appear to be nearly healed, brown fungal threads may be found within. This wood-rotting fungus will eventually spread through the tree.

Clean and scrape the canker and remove all discolored wood. Wounds should be treated with a good tree paint.

For anthracnose and witches' broom, see TREES: DISEASES.

Holly

Insects

The overwintering eggs of the **holly bud moth** begin hatching late in March, and small greenish white to gray green caterpillars appear between the terminal leaves of young holly shoots late in April or early May. About the middle of May, they begin to tie terminal leaves together to form compact cases. The caterpillars feed within these shelters, eating back the shoot so that the mass of leaves spun together dies and turns black. These black unsightly objects usually do not drop until pushed off by subsequent growth. At maturity the caterpillars are a little more than ⅜ inch long. When disturbed, they wiggle out of their shelters and drop to the ground. Many of the larvae leave the shelters when fully grown and spin loose cocoons among the dead leaves or rubbish on the ground. Others pupate within the shelters used by the larvae.

Destroy leaf shelters. A light summer-oil spray has been

found to reduce the population of the moth. This spray must be applied late in March, before the eggs begin to hatch. Apply to the underside of leaves. Garden sanitation will go a long way toward reducing the number of holly bud moths in your garden since they often spin their cocoons in plant refuse.

The **holly leaf miner** adult is a tiny two-winged fly, grayish black and about $\frac{1}{10}$ inch long. It makes its initial appearance during late May or early June, and may be seen flying about the newly developed holly foliage or walking over the surface of the leaves. Approximately three weeks are required for all the flies to appear.

Holly/Holly Leaf Miner Damage

Shortly after their appearance, female flies insert their eggs into the newly developing leaves. The eggs hatch in June, and larvae feed inside the leaves until the following spring. Although the maggots begin their feeding in June, leaf injury does not become evident until mid-August, when small, irregular, linear, serpentine ridges appear on the upper surface of leaves. Each irregular ridge indicates a maggot mining beneath the surface. At first, the ridges are darker green than the remainder of the leaf surface. Later, they become tinged reddish or reddish brown. By mid-September the mines increase in size, one end becoming blotch-shaped. If infested severely, the entire upper surface of the leaves may be covered with coalesced mines, giving the surface a blistered appearance.

Leaves showing the symptoms must be removed and burned. Severely damaged bushes should be removed. It is not a good idea to plant winterberry or inkberry in the same location as the holly, because these two plants are alternate hosts for the leaf miner.

The **holly scale's** covering is oval, light brown to tan in color, and extremely small, while the scale itself and its eggs are lemon-yellow. This scale overwinters in a partially grown condition. Feeding begins in the latter part of March or early April, and eggs are laid in June and July. There is usually only one generation a year. Symptoms include plant devitalization, yellow spotting of the leaves, and smutting of leaves due to fungus growth on secreted honeydew. The scales usually congregate on the lower side of the leaves.

Ladybugs offer free biological control. Natural populations can be supplemented with mail-order beetles. Excellent control has also been obtained by the use of a three-percent dormant-oil spray applied late in April.

Diseases

Leaf rot fungus is found in contaminated sand and on the boards of the cutting bench. It enters the cuttings through leaves that touch the sand. The disease first appears as a cobweblike growth on the leaves, a combination of the fungus threads and grains of sand sticking to the underside of leaves that touch the sand. Leaf drop usually begins two to three weeks after the cuttings are set. In some cases, targetlike spots from ¼ to ½ inch in diameter are found on the leaves.

Control of leaf rot may be accomplished by setting the cuttings in clean, fresh, or sterilized sand. If the disease has already been present in the bed, wash the bench thoroughly with a cleaning solution. Avoid taking cuttings from holly branches that touch the ground.

Leaf spot is nonparasitic in nature and causes light tan, ¾-inch spots on leaves in early spring or summer. The spots are often covered with tiny black bodies of fungi.

Spots are caused by sunscalding in either winter or summer. In summer, they may occur when a sudden rain shower is immediately followed by bright sunlight. The presence of ice on the leaves often results in a similar scalding in the winter. All that is necessary in the way of control is to pick off the affected leaves so that the appearance of the holly is not impaired.

Spine spot (or **purple spot**) is nonparasitic and causes grayish brown spots ranging from the size of a pinhead to a pea. These spots develop on leaves in late winter or early spring, and may appear on either surface. In most cases they are surrounded by a purple halo. The spots are the result of the wounds inflicted by the spines of nearby leaves as they are blown about in heavy winds. In other words, the holly actually wounds itself. Black fruiting bodies of a fungus may occasionally be found near the center of the spots, but these fungi are secondary, since they come after the leaf tissue was wounded.

Holly should be planted in sheltered locations so that the wind won't whip the leaves. If it is impractical to plant the holly in such a position, or if the bush has already been planted, you can construct simple wind barriers of burlap nailed to stakes set around the bush.

Tar spot is a fungal infection of holly leaves characterized by raised black spots resembling tar. The disease may be reduced by picking and burning infected leaves.

Twig canker causes brown areas to appear on the green wood of new growth. Eventually these cankers enlarge to girdle the twig. Small black fruiting bodies of the fungus can be seen on the dead wood. Prune and burn infected twigs.

Horsechestnut

Insects

The **white-marked tussock moth** overwinters in frothy white egg masses on the trees. There are two generations a year. One brood of larvae matures about July 1 and a second brood in August. These caterpillars reach a length of about 1½ inches. They are striped lengthwise with brown and yellow, and are hairy, with four upright white tufts on the front half, two long tufts of black hairs near the head, and a black tuft on the tail. The adult moth is ash-gray. The female is wingless and the male has a wingspread of about 1¼ inches.

Because the females cannot fly, control may be achieved by banding tree trunks with Tanglefoot or Stikem as described in TREES: INSECTS. This is effective only if the tree is not already infested and if the branches do not contact other infested trees.

Other pests of horsechestnut trees are the JAPANESE BEETLE and scurfy scale (see ELM).

Diseases

Leaf blotch may infect horsechestnut leaves with large reddish brown blotches surrounded with yellow tissue. Curling of infected leaves is common, and the fruiting bodies of the fungus appear as black specks in the discolored areas. To cut down on the source of infective spores, rake and burn fallen leaves.

Nectria cinnabarina causes roughened cankers on branches that bear reddish brown fruiting bodies. Prune and burn affected branches, cutting well below the infected areas.

For anthracnose and powdery mildew, see TREES: DISEASES.

Horseradish

Insects

The flat, brilliantly colored **harlequin bug** withdraws plant juices, resulting in foliage discoloration, wilting, and death. They are easy to spot, with bright orange to red markings on black. For control measures, see CABBAGE.

The **horseradish flea beetle** is small, shiny, black, and has yellow wing covers bordered with black. Control is rarely necessary, but some helpful measures can be found under POTATO.

Horseradish is also plagued by several crucifer pests. Under CABBAGE, see descriptions and control methods for cabbage looper, curculio, diamondback moth, imported cabbageworm, and webworm.

Diseases

Leaf spot appears as large dark spots on leaves. This disease is not serious enough to warrant control.

White, somewhat circular blisters on horseradish leaves are likely the first symptom of **white rust**. Later, these blisters break open to expose the white, powdery fungal spores. Control is not necessary.

Hyacinth

Insects

At least three species of the **lesser bulb fly** make their presence known by injuring rotting bulbs. Seventy-five or more larvae may be found in a single bulb. The flies are ⅓ inch long, and blackish green with white markings on the abdomen; the larvae are a dirty grayish yellow. Destroy infested or rotting bulbs, and use only healthy bulbs and rhizomes.

Other troublemakers are the bulb mite (see GLADIOLUS), NEMATODE, and yellow woolybear caterpillar (see imported cabbageworm under CABBAGE).

Diseases

Gray mold blight causes flowers to shrivel up suddenly and become covered with mold. This fungus thrives in cool, wet seasons, and a change in the weather will halt its progress. Destroy infected plant parts.

In the case of **soft rot**, plants fail to flower or buds open irregularly, and the plants can be easily pulled out of the ground. Rotted parts give off a foul odor. Trouble is aggravated by repeated freezing and thawing, and by heating bulbs in storage. Avoiding such unfavorable conditions will likely prevent this disease.

Yellow rot gives a water-soaked appearance to flowers and causes yellow, longitudinal stripes on leaves. The yellow stripes eventually turn brown and ooze bacteria if cut across. Bulbs show rotted pockets. Since bacteria are spread by splashing water, take care when watering. Plant disease-free bulbs, and rogue out infected hyacinths.

Hydrangea

Insects

The **hydrangea leaf tier** webs terminal leaves tightly around buds, and feasts on the buds from within this shelter. The responsible larva is a green, ½-inch-long caterpillar with a dark brown head. A mild garlic spray on buds may make them less appetizing to the leaf tier. Once the pest is at work you can squeeze the webbed leaves to destroy it; you should then tear open the web to allow the flower bud to develop.

Stem nematodes cause hydrangea stems to become swollen and split. Leaves drop off as a result. Cut potted plants back severely, wash off all old soil from roots, and put the plants in clean soil.

Other insect pests include the rose chafer (see ROSE), LYGUS BUGS, SPIDER MITES, and tarnished plant bug (ASTER).

Diseases

Bacterial wilt infects flowers and young leaves. Affected parts will turn brown and wilt, and if the weather is extremely hot the disease may kill the plant.

Remove any infected leaves and flowers as soon as they appear. If a plant becomes badly infected, it must be removed from the garden before other plants become infected. Be certain that the disease is not transferred to other plants by the indiscriminate use of pruning or cultivating tools.

Yellowed leaves are a sign of **chlorosis**, a condition thought to stem from too much lime in the soil. It may also be correlated with very high levels of nitrates and calcium. Organic growers should rarely be bothered by chlorosis, as imbalances are usually the result of concentrated chemical fertilizers.

Powdery mildew appears as a gray mold on the underside of leaves. Buds and new growth may also be attacked. Prune and burn old leaves. See MILDEW for other suggestions.

Iris

The iris is fairly untroubled by pests. Weeds may present a problem, but an easy answer lies in the use of a mulch in the flower beds. If cultivation is necessary, keep it shallow to avoid damaging root stems.

Insects

One insect that can cause serious damage is the **iris borer.** The feeding of this voracious larva paves the way for bacterial soft rot, which has the potential to cause more trouble than the borer itself.

Iris/Iris Borer

The borer spends the winter in the egg stage on old iris leaves, stalks, and debris. Larvae appear in April or early May, and can be seen crawling over the plant for the first few days, but they soon enter the leaves to feed. The first injury you're likely to see is slender feeding channels in the leaves, somewhat resembling the burrows of leaf miners. Leaves may also appear water-soaked. The larvae gradually make their way to rhizomes, arriving there early in July in most cases, and it is then that they grow to a length of 1½ to 2 inches. They are quite corpulent at this time, and colored pinkish with brown heads. As the larvae approach full growth, injury becomes conspicuous. This is particularly true if the rhizomes are destroyed and the plants tend to collapse.

Control depends on a thorough garden clean-up to remove the overwintering eggs on old leaves, stems, and debris. Hidden worms can be lanced with a pointed stick or, lacking a pointed stick, you can pinch them in the leaves. Transplant infested iris clumps in August.

The small, milky white larvae of **iris thrips** feed on the inner surface of leaf sheaths and on the young leaves of many iris varieties. This injury leads to russetting, blackening, stunting, weakened growth, and the death of tops. Russetted or blackened flower buds and stem buds often fail to open. This insect is found in new garden plantings in the basal leaves of plants. It damages Japanese iris seriously, and attacks most other types. The adult thrips are usually wingless, very dark, and slow-moving. See THRIPS.

When the **iris weevil** breeds in the seed pods of iris, the pods show many small holes. Eggs are deposited on the iris ovary, and the thick-bodied, white larvae then feed on seeds. The adult weevil is ⅕ inch long, and colored black with white and yellow scales. The pest is locally abundant wherever iris grows.

Destroy all flower heads after the flowers of affected plants fade, or destroy seed pods before the young weevils emerge. If seeds are to be saved for breeding, cover blossoms with cheesecloth.

When bulbous iris fail to grow or growth appears distorted, examine bulbs for brown patches or longitudinal stripes indicative of **nematode** infestation. Diseased plants should be rogued and the soil sterilized before reuse.

A number of other insects occasionally cause trouble, SLUGS AND SNAILS, and the two-spotted SPIDER MITE in particular.

Diseases

Botrytis rhizome rot causes iris to fail to grow in spring. Rhizomes may be affected by a hard, dry rot, without a foul odor. The gray mold fruiting stage is generally present, and shiny black convoluted sclerotia may be found on or in rotted tissues.

To control the rot disease, rogue and burn infected plant parts and take the infested soil from the garden area.

Crown rot usually appears in overcrowded beds. Leaves and flower stalks die back from infections at the base where white cottony mycelium, containing mustard-seed-size sclerotia, may be found. The sclerotia vary in color from cream to reddish brown. This fungus is pathogenic on many other flowers (including delphinium, aconite, and columbine) and may be spread by scattering the sclerotia during cultivation. Preventative maintenance involves thinning the plants to admit light and air. Remove infected plants along with the infested soil to stop progress of the disease.

Iris/Crown Rot

Occasionally, translucent **leaf spots** [color] of irregular shape appear on iris leaves. Control calls for removing and destroying spotted leaves early in the season and removing tops in fall. Be careful not to overwater, especially in wet weather, as leaf spot thrives on dampness.

Leaf Spot

Mosaic is indicated by light and dark green mottling of leaves, early flowering, and color breaking in flowers, along with stunting. Bulb sheaths may be marked with blue green or yellow streaks. This disease most often strikes bulbous iris; it occurs also on rhizomatous iris, but the symptoms are not so noticeable. Aphids carry the disease, and their control is important. Rogue infected plants as soon as the above symptoms are observed; see APHID.

Rust is known by the rusty pustules that appear on leaves of susceptible varieties (German iris is immune). Roguing and burning of infected plants breaks the continuity of the rust's life cycle. Resistant varieties are available.

Probably the most serious disease of German iris is bacterial **soft rot**. The bacteria enter the plant through wounds in young leaves made by the young larvae of the iris borer. The bacteria multiply rapidly in the soft leaf tissue and cause a water-soaked appearance around the entrance holes. The leaf is destroyed as bacteria make their way toward the rhizome. Once the rhizome is infected, healthy leaves fall over and collapse at the base. The foul odor of the rhizomes is a telltale sign of this disease.

Control of soft rot is dependent on control of the iris borer (see above). Remove any rotting leaves by cutting well below the water-soaked areas. Dip the shears in 70 percent alcohol after each cut to disinfect them.

Ivy (English)

Insects

The **nasturtium aphid** is one of several species that feeds on English ivy. When aphids suck juices from leaves and stems, these parts become curled, dwarfed, and yellowed. Other susceptible plants include globe thistle, dahlia, oleander, poppy, zinnia, and nasturtium. This aphid overwinters on euonymus. See APHID.

Another miniscule pest, the **two-spotted mite,** causes leaves to become gray and mealy. Mites and their webs can be washed away by squirting plants with water from a syringe. See SPIDER MITES for other control measures.

Two-Spotted Spider Mite

You may also run into MEALYBUGS and any of a number of SCALE species.

Diseases

Bacterial leaf spot is identified by irregular water-soaked spots with yellow or translucent borders. It usually appears on lower or inside leaves of densely crowded foliage and on greenhouse ivy. Infections on petioles produce black lesions that crack longitudinally. Stem infections may result in yellowing and reduction of growth. Improving ventilation will usually correct the trouble; it also helps to pick and destroy infected leaves and to water greenhouse plants without splashing.

Fungus Leaf Spot (left), and Bacterial Leaf Spot (right)

Dodder is a parasitic weed that looks like many strands of orange string with no apparent roots. The strings wind around ivy stems and cannot be easily detached. Small clusters of white flowers produce seeds for another year's crop. When seeds germinate, the dodder climbs up the nearest plant, sends little penetrating knobs into the tissue of the host, and lives on the host's sap. The dodder roots are dropped as soon as this attachment is made, and it becomes a truly parasitic plant. If possible, detach and burn this weed. Otherwise, rogue the affected plants.

Large tan spots that may show the concentric rings of fruiting bodies are known as fungus **leaf spot.** Remove and destroy infected plant parts.

Japanese Beetle

The Japanese beetle [color] causes extensive damage in many of the eastern states. A native of Japan, it was first found in this country in 1916 near Riverton, New Jersey. It has continued to spread, and is now present from southern Maine southward into South Carolina and Georgia and westward into Kentucky, Illinois, Michigan, and Missouri. Japanese beetles are a little less than ½ inch long, and are a shiny, metallic green. They have copper-brown wings, and six small patches of white hairs along the sides and back of the body, under the edges of the wings. Males and females have the same markings, but males usually are slightly smaller than females.

The Japanese beetle spends about ten months of the year in the ground in the form of a white grub. This grub is similar to our native white grub, but it is usually smaller—about an inch long. It lies in the soil in a curled position.

Japanese Beetle

Adult beetles first appear on their favorite food plants in late spring or early summer, depending on locale. If you live in eastern North Carolina, for example, expect them in mid-May; in the Philadelphia area, about June 15; in New England, about July 1 or later. In the Midwest, they show up about June 15 in the St. Louis area and July 1 in Michigan. They fly only in the daytime, and are especially active on warm, sunny days, moving readily from one plant to another.

The period of greatest beetle activity lasts from four to six weeks. The beetles then gradually disappear. In eastern North Carolina, most of them are gone by early August, but in New England some are present until frost. From time to time, the females leave the plants on which they have been feeding and burrow about three inches into the ground, usually in turf. There they lay a few eggs from which grubs will later hatch. After laying these eggs, the females return to the plants for more feeding.

Populations may be lower in some localities than in others as the result of one or more of the following conditions: a dry summer season, suppression by milky spore disease and other natural control agents, cultural factors, and intensive chemical control measures.

New housing developments are especially subject to high local beetle populations. Turf infested with Japanese beetles, but not containing the beetles' natural enemies, is often imported into these areas. In addition, adult beetles often fly into housing tracts having soil that contains no beetle enemies, and the pests can then become established easily.

Grubs feed on the roots and underground stems of plants, particularly grasses. Often this feeding goes unnoticed until the plants fail to make proper growth or die. When grubs are numerous, they can cause serious injury to turf.

Adult Japanese beetles feed on more than 275 different plants, and often congregate to feed on flowers, foliage, and fruit of plants and trees exposed to bright sunlight. Beetles feeding on leaves usually chew out the tissue between the veins, leaving a lacy skeleton. They may eat many large irregular areas on some leaves. A heavily attacked tree or shrub may lose most of its leaves in a short time. The beetles often mass on ripening fruit, and feed until nothing edible is left, but seldom touch unripe fruit. They seriously injure corn by eating the silk as fast as it grows, which keeps kernels from forming.

• **Natural controls.**   Nature itself exerts many controls on Japanese beetle grubs and adults. Weather, disease, and natural enemies are essential to keeping their numbers down.

Summer weather has a lot to do with determining Japanese beetle populations. Extremely dry spells destroy many of the eggs and kill newly hatched grubs; wet summers are favorable to the development of eggs and grubs, and are usually followed by seasons of increased numbers of beetles.

Of the several naturally occurring diseases known to affect this pest, milky spore disease is the most important. It kills grubs after turning their normally clear blood to a milky color. The disease is harmless to humans, other warm-blooded animals, and plants. Because of its safety and effectiveness, milky spore disease is now produced in dust form and sold commercially by mail order (see Appendix 1) and through many garden supply centers. If your local dealer does not handle it, your county agent can tell you the nearest source of supply.

The spore dust is made by collecting grubs and inoculating them with the disease. Treatments are most effective when applied on a community-wide basis. (The USDA suggests that if you and your neighbors wish to cooperate in buying and applying milky spore disease dust in your area, you should contact your county agricultural agent, as he can help coordinate the effort.) The dust is applied at any time, save when the ground is frozen or a strong wind is blowing. It is usually applied at a rate of two pounds per acre in spots ten feet apart. Use about one level teaspoon to each spot. The disease will become established more quickly if the dust is applied in spots only five feet apart; in this case about 7½ pounds of spore dust will be needed per acre. Do not expect immediate results, as several years may elapse before the milky disease becomes fully effective. It's useless to apply the disease dust and a chemical insecticide to the same turf; insecticides keep the grub population at a very low level and will prevent buildup of the pathogenic bacteria.

Of the parasites imported to control the Japanese beetle, the two most important are the wasps *Tiphia vernalis* and *Tiphia popilliavora*, according to Lester Swann in *Beneficial Insects*. The most valuable of the two, says Swann, is the first-named, known as the spring tiphia. It overwinters in the adult stage within the beetle's underground cocoon, and shows above ground in May, about the time the grubs are fully grown. The second wasp, called the fall tiphia, occupies the host's cocoon over winter as a larvae and appears in August. Its eggs are laid on the grub. The spring tiphia occurs in the mid-Atlantic states, and parasitizes an average of about 43 percent of the beetles through much of this area, according to the USDA.

In the thirties, Swann relates, state and federal teams got together with the Rockefeller Institute of Medical Research to find a way to economically raise a species of parasitic nematode to control the beetle; a resulting colonization program was considered responsible for lowering the pests' numbers in areas of New Jersey. Long, hair-thin nematodes are important in many areas today.

• **Other controls.**   If only a few plants are bothered, you may be able to get by with handpicking the beetles. Drop them in a can holding a bit of kerosene. It is more efficient to shake them out of trees or branches early in the morning, before they are limbered up. Place a sheet or tarp on the ground to catch them as they fall, and drop them into a bucket of water topped off with a layer of kerosene. You should repeat this every day, as beetles are apt to fly in from elsewhere.

Many problems can be prevented by following a few basic cultural controls. Remove prematurely ripening or diseased fruit from the trees and ground. Delayed corn plantings often get by without damage. It's best to remove susceptible wild plants from the immediate area, including brocken, elder, evening primrose, Indian mallow, sassafras, poison ivy, smartweed, wild fox grape, and summer grape. These plants are often a continuous source of infestation for other plants.

Gardeners have found that larkspur has a fatal attraction for the Japanese beetle; the pests nibble at the foliage and keel over. Others report that roses will be spared if interplanted with geraniums, as this pungent flower is noxious to the beetle. Two trap crops worth a try are Wilson soybeans, set every 15 or 20 rows to protect corn, and smartweed around the periphery of the garden or flower bed.

W. J. Crawford of Vista, California, has come up with an effective trap for this pest. In a large glass jug ferment a wine of sugar, water, and odd pieces of mashed fruit. A bit of yeast may be necessary to get the mixture started. Place the jug in the yard, and strain out the day's catch each evening. Other beetle baits are geraniol (a rose-scented alcohol used to make soap and perfumes more pleasant to the nose), and anethol (the main constituent of anise and fennel oils, and used to flavor perfumes and toothpaste). Traps seem to work best when the beetle population is high and when they aren't placed close to the plants to be protected.

Juniper (Red Cedar)

Insects

Although **juniper scale** is primarily a pest of juniper, it also attacks arborvitae and cypress. The scale covering of this pest is circular and colored white with a yellow center. The eggs and young are pinkish to yellow in color.

This scale overwinters as nearly fully grown, fertilized females. The eggs are laid during late May and throughout June. There is one generation a year. The scales may be found on the younger twigs, needles, and cones of infested plants. When infestations are severe, the plants look as though hit by extreme drought. Due to the secretion of honeydew by the scales, the plants often are blackened by a fungus that grows on the honeydew.

A three-percent dormant-oil emulsion sprayed during the last week in March or the first week in April will give satisfactory control. To control the young scale insects that hatch in late spring, use a nicotine sulfate and soap solution, sprayed at ten-day intervals.

The **juniper webworm** picks on low juniper plants in particular. The light brown caterpillar webs together leaves and twigs for protection and feeds on the leaves inside its web. The ⅝-inch-long brown and white moth appears in June.

A pyrethrum spray will kill many of the caterpillars if applied with enough force to penetrate the webbed nests and wet the insects. Penetration can be improved by first separating the webbed tips. If only small branches are infested, they can be cut out and destroyed.

Other pests of juniper are APHIDS, bagworms (see EVERGREEN), and spruce mites (SPRUCE).

Diseases

The Agricultural Extension Service of Purdue University reports that several species of juniper, especially the native red cedar, are affected by **rust diseases.** Rust diseases of juniper are generally more unsightly than destructive, but if severe infestations occur year after year, red cedars may be seriously damaged. There are three common rust diseases: cedar-apple rust, cedar-hawthorn rust, and cedar-quince rust.

On red cedar leaves the cedar-apple rust [color] disease causes chocolate-brown, globular to irregular shaped corky galls, measuring ⅛ inch to two inches in diameter. These galls are often referred to as cedar-apples and require two years to complete their development. In the second spring after the red cedar originally became infected, the cedar galls produce gelatinous, fingerlike, slimy orange spore horns during rainy weather in May and June. The galls then die. Spores produced from these gelatinous spore horns infect leaves of apple, causing bright orange spots. Spores produced from these infections in turn produce spores that cause infection of leaves and twigs of juniper in late summer.

Cedar Apple Gall

Cedar-hawthorn rust results in the formation of galls on juniper and leaf rust on hawthorn and cultivated apple. On juniper

Cedar Hawthorn Rust

(red cedar), the galls are often small and irregular in shape but may be as large as those produced by the cedar-apple rust; they differ in being perennial and more woody. Orange, wedge-shaped gelatinous spore horns are produced in May or June. Spores from these horns infect the leaves of hawthorn and apple.

Cedar-quince rust is responsible for the slightly swollen, elongate cankers that appear on the branches of red cedar and other junipers. During rainy weather in May and June, orange, gelatinous, cushioned-shaped spore masses break through the rough, diseased bark. Spores from these sources infect twigs, leaves, and fruit, or less often, quince, apple and hawthorn. Re-infection of cedars with cedar-quince rust disease occurs in late summer by spores produced from infections of quince, apple, and hawthorn.

Since the rust diseases of red cedar and other junipers require an alternate host for the completion of their life cycle, the logical control for these troubles is to avoid growing susceptible junipers within a mile of the alternate hosts—apple, hawthorn, and quince.

Avoid planting varieties of juniper that are highly susceptible to cedar rusts. The eastern red cedar and all its horticultural varieties are very susceptible to cedar rust diseases. The western and Colorado red cedar are much less susceptible. The columnar Chinese juniper, pfizer juniper, prostate juniper, and andorra juniper are rarely seriously troubled by cedar rust diseases. If you have the time and can go to the trouble, prune out galls during the first week in April before the spore horns develop.

Twig blight is caused by a fungus that makes the tips of infected twigs turn brown and gradually die back. Small, black pinpoints of fruiting bodies may appear on the leaves and stems of affected twigs. During wet weather, spores ooze out of the fruiting bodies and are spread by wind, rain, insects, and pruning tools. The disease is especially severe on nursery stock.

Twig blight may be avoided by planting resistant varieties. The spiny Greek juniper, Keteleer red cedar, and hill juniper are reported to be resistant. Susceptible apple varieties to avoid include Baldwin, Delicious, Franklin, Melrose, Red Astrachan, Stayman, and Transparent. When the plants are dry, prune and burn affected twigs and branches. Late winter is the best time for this.

Kale

Insects

In general, kale is bothered by pests mentioned under CABBAGE. The several that you are particularly apt to run into are listed here.

The turnip **aphid** has a penchant for kale, especially in the South. It is little more than a pale green speck, although a close look may reveal a black head and black spots on the winged form. Its resemblance to another kale pest, the cabbage aphid, has earned it the alternate name of false cabbage aphid. For control, see APHID.

The **celery leaf tier** starts off life a pale green, but becomes yellow as it reaches its full length of ¾ inch. Running down the back is a thin dark green line centered in a wider white strip. They make webs out of leaves, and if one takes a disliking to you it may either toss about in this protective shelter or drop to the ground. See CELERY for control measures.

Under CABBAGE, see cabbage looper, cabbage webworm, diamondback moth (adult of a destructive, green caterpillar), and imported cabbageworm.

Diseases

Black leg may cause spots to appear at the base of stems; at first these spots are merely pale blemishes, but they later turn black, girdle the stem, and can cause the plants to die. On the dead tissue can be seen many tiny, black, pimplelike bodies. Before the plant succumbs, leaves wilt and develop bluish red edges. For control, see methods for preventing black rot under CABBAGE.

Kohlrabi

In general, pests and diseases of kohlrabi may be found under CABBAGE. Kohlrabi and tomatoes do not fare well together in the garden, as this proximity invites insect pests to the former crop.

Ladybug

The story of the ladybug's services to growers in the United States began toward the end of the 19th century, when the destructive cottony cushion scale appeared in the citrus groves of California. The entire citrus industry was on the verge of extinction. About that time a USDA entomologist in Australia discovered a tiny spotted beetle feeding on some cottony cushion scale in a garden—the vedalia or Australian ladybug. A few beetles were sent across the sea and soon proved their worth by eliminating the scale on some test trees. More were imported and released in the orchards. The total cost of the transplantation amounted to $1500, a pittance considering that an entire industry, which flourishes today, was saved.

Palmer's *Fieldbook of Natural History* lists the food of the ladybug larvae as aphids, asparagus beetle eggs, Colorado potato beetle, grape root worm, bean thrips, alfalfa weevil, and chinch bug. While the adults also devour aphids and insect eggs, the immature larvae do the most good. Like most insects that undergo complete metamorphosis (from egg to larva to pupa to adult), the ladybug begins its life in spring as one of 200 or so eggs in the crevice of tree bark or on the underside of protected leaves. From these eggs emerge tiny tapered larvae which immediately begin feeding on aphids. So insatiable is the appetite of the lizardlike larva that it has been known to consume 40 aphids in a single hour, a capability that has earned it the nickname aphis wolf.

The larva becomes full grown—about ¼ inch long—in about 20 days. It then attaches itself to a leaf or stem and pupates. Finally it transforms into the familiar black-spotted adult. In fall, ladybugs gather in great masses to spend the winter beneath loose bark, under boards or rocks, or in some other protected place. On the Pacific Coast these hibernating beetles are collected in great numbers to be either distributed in crop areas or kept through the winter in captivity and sold commercially. The *Brooklyn Botanic Gardener's Handbook on Biological Control of Plant Pests* says that the reddish orange beetles generally feed on aphids, while the darker ones eat scale, mealybugs, white flies, and spider mites.

Although ladybugs fend for themselves quite well, there are a few precautions to be taken when stocking your garden.

1) Don't stock too early. If there are not enough pests in your garden patch to sustain them, they will either feed on what is there and then fly away in search of more insect food, or else starve to death. If pests are evident but not plentiful, place some ladybugs in the garden and store the rest in the refrigerator (not in the freezer) until needed. They will hibernate in the refrigerator for several more weeks.

2) It is best to release the beetles late in the afternoon or, better yet, at sundown. This encourages them to stay in your garden for the night and find suitable food and protection.

3) Beetles are usually shipped in boxes of straw or excelsior. Carefully place them at the base of plants about 15 to 20 paces apart, depending on the size of your garden and the number of beetles you've purchased. The beetle's instinct compels it to climb the nearest plant and hunt for food.

4) It's a good idea to dampen the ground in the areas to receive the beetles. A good mulch will help keep the garden floor moist and cool, and gives ladybugs a place to hide. Don't scatter them as you would sow grain, but gently place handfuls of them at the base of plants, spaced 20 to 30 paces apart. Rough handling, especially in warm weather, may excite them to seek safety in flight.

About 30,000 individuals are considered adequate for protecting ten acres of crops. To bring this number into perspective, the beetles are so tiny that it takes only 1500 of them to make an ounce. If the weather is warm and sunny, your stocked beetles will mate and lay eggs in a day or two. In 15 more days you should already have a second generation of larvae hard at work.

If you need a source, see Appendix 1.

Larch

Insects

Outbreaks of the dark larch woolly **aphid** are infrequent, but if control is required, see APHID.

The **larch case-bearer** is a pest of larch foliage. The larvae mine the insides of needles, forming protective cases attached to a twig, often seen in clusters. They spend the winter in the cases, dislodging them in spring to go to the buds and feed on new leaves. The moths emerge in May or June.

Natural predators usually keep this case-bearer under control. Five parasitic wasps have been imported into Canada. The case stage is preyed on by chickadees and other birds. Moths appearing in spring are pursued by birds. The hibernating caterpillars may be controlled by a dormant spray of lime sulfur before the tree's growth starts in spring.

The worst insect pest of larch is the **larch sawfly,** whose larvae can so seriously defoliate that growth is noticeably affected. In June, the female sawfly cuts into the underside of new twigs to deposit 50 to 100 eggs, leaving the twig curled downward like a fish hook. The emerging green larvae feed greedily on the needles, stripping the trees if very abundant. In midsummer they drop to the ground to spin the cocoons within which they live until the following spring.

A variety of natural predators prey on the larch sawfly. Birds and needle-billed stink bugs feed on the larvae, and when the worms drop to the ground they are devoured by skunks, shrews, and mice. Whatever is done in the larch's environment to encourage these natural predators of the sawfly will help control it. The area beneath the trees should be raked clean each autumn.

Diseases

Canker appears as a depressed area in the bark, often exuding resin at the edges and accompanied by considerable swelling of the branch or trunk on the opposite side. White cups with orange linings open and close with wet and dry weather; these are the fruiting bodies of the fungus. Infection can kill small trees and branches of large ones, but more often it merely weakens branches so that ice or wind cause them to break easily. The European, American, and golden larch are susceptible to this canker, but Japanese larch is relatively resistant.

Inspect trees frequently for trouble. Cankered limbs can be removed by pruning; burn the cankered material.

New leaves of larch are susceptible to **frost injury,** but new growth or secondary buds often replace them. Frost can also cause cankers or death of young trees by killing the cambium in stems of less than two inches.

Needle cast causes needles to turn brown in spring or early summer and remain on the tree over the winter. At a distance, trees look scorched. The infected needles bear long black fruiting bodies. Needle cast may be a serious disease in nurseries.

As soon as it appears, spray new growth with lime sulfur at intervals of two weeks apart until August.

Although two types of **needle rust** fungi affect larches, they are not serious enough to warrant control measures. The alternate hosts of these rusts are poplars and willows.

Larches are occasionally attacked by **shoestring fungus.** It is a sudden and spectacular attack, rapidly causing wilting and even death of one or several vigorous trees. Then, just as quickly, the outbreak will subside. Since attacks are sporadic and losses are not repeated, this disease is hard to predict. The risk is greatest when larch trees are planted on cut-over land where oak trees were once prominent. See TREES: DISEASES.

Laurel

Insect pests and diseases of laurel are similar to those of RHODODENDRON.

Lawns

Like all plants, lawn grasses need light, air, moisture, and nutrients. While they are never free of the possibility of pests and diseases, the quality of care you give your lawn can greatly help to reduce trouble.

Begin by providing good surface and subsurface drainage when establishing a lawn. Fill in low spots where water may stand. Where air movement is restricted, problems can develop, so thin or remove surrounding shrubs and trees as necessary to increase air flow and allow sunlight to penetrate.

Choose grasses that are adapted to your area, and be wary of inexpensive seed mixtures, as they may contain a high percentage of weed seeds. The severity of diseases can often be reduced by growing a compatible blend of two or more locally adapted, disease-resistant grass varieties. A mixture of Kentucky bluegrass and fescues have become popular—the bluegrass is hardy and undemanding, while the fine fescues, with their tolerance for shade and dry sites, broaden the bluegrass's adaptability. Bentgrass, often used on golf greens, requires more attention than other grasses. It needs frequent fertilizing, mowing, and watering.

The Cooperative Extension Service of Montana State College notes that temperature affects grass development: bluegrass and fescues grow best in cool temperatures, and Bermuda grass and zoysia types thrive in warm temperatures; Merion Kentucky bluegrass is more heat- and drought-tolerant than other bluegrasses, although it requires more care in maintenance than ordinary Kentucky bluegrass. For home lawns in Montana, use either Merion bluegrass or ordinary Kentucky bluegrass, mixed with a small percentage of perennial rye and white Dutch clover as a nurse crop. Because creeping bentgrasses require such close mowing, careful watering, and frequent applications of fertilizer, they are best used on putting greens and are unsuited for the average home lawn.

In the South, several turfgrasses are widely used—Bermuda, centipede, St. Augustine, and bahia, among others. The zoysias are very durable grasses that serve well in most areas.

As for turfgrass mixtures for prairie regions, the Canada Department of Agriculture recommends Kentucky bluegrass and creeping red fescue for lawns and fairways, and creeping bentgrass for golf and bowling greens. They advise against red-top or colonial bentgrass in turf mixtures because they are susceptible to most diseases and tend to choke out more desirable species. Seed for lawn and athletic fields should be guaranteed free from annual bluegrass and bentgrass.

Pure stands of Merion bluegrass were once widely popular in Canada, but proved not to have sufficient cold hardiness. Also, the tendency of this variety to build up thatch predisposed it to several diseases of the prairie region that caused it to die out. If Merion is used in Canada, the Department of Agriculture recommends mixing it with other bluegrasses or with creeping red fescues. The Merion grass should not make up more than 30 percent of any mixture.

Cultural Control

Your grass will be healthier if it is not mowed too closely. Upright grasses such as Kentucky bluegrass and fescues should be clipped to two inches or even higher in the summer. Creeping grasses such as bentgrasses, Bermuda grass, and zoysia may be mowed more closely, but not under $1\frac{1}{2}$ inches. Mow grass frequently, so that no more than $\frac{1}{4}$ to $\frac{1}{3}$ of the leaf surface is removed at any one time. If too much leaf is cut away, food manufacture is drastically reduced, resulting in poor root development and weak, thin grass that is more susceptible to infection by disease.

A good rule of thumb is to mow when the grass reaches a height of three inches. Except where winters are very severe, continue mowing the grass through fall until growth stops. The University of Alaska advises that grass will survive hard winters better if allowed to grow to a height of three to four inches before the first severe frost.

Thatch is a tightly intermingled layer of living and dead stems, leaves, and grass roots that develops between the soil surface and the green growth. Too much thatch keeps water, sun, and air from penetrating the soil, aggravates some diseases, and seems to prevent the grass from developing a deep root system. Excess thatch should be removed in early spring or early fall if $\frac{1}{2}$ inch or more has accumulated. At seeding time, too much thatch prevents new seeds from coming in direct contact with the soil for proper germination. On large lawns, thatch can be removed with a lawn renovator, power rake, or a powered thatch remover that goes over the turf and breaks up the clogging mat.

The way you water your lawn can make a great difference in its greenness and health. Deep watering to a depth of six or eight inches, once a week or every five days, is better than frequent shallow waterings. This is especially important in summer. Lawns that are watered too often are more disease-prone and they develop shallow root systems that cause them to brown easily. The common practice of watering in the evening is not recommended, since grass that stays wet during the night is much more prone to the diseases and fungi that thrive on moist conditions. You'll have better results if you water early enough in the day so that grass will dry out before nightfall.

It is not always necessary to apply lime to lawns. Where organic matter and humus content in the soil are high, they act as a pH buffer and make liming necessary less often, if at all. Naturally alkaline soils, of course, should receive no lime. Many homeowners damage their lawns by feeding them unnecessary lime, and it is best to have your soil tested to determine if the lawn needs this supplement.

The best pH for a healthy lawn is slightly acid, about 6.5 or just under neutral (7.0). If your soil is too acid, top-dress with natural ground limestone, preferably dolomite, as it supplies magnesium as well. Pulverized oyster shells, wood ashes, or any calcium-rich wastes may also be used. To raise a soil one full pH unit—say from 5.5 to 6.5—apply approximately 50 pounds of lime per 1000 square feet. Use 10 to 15 pounds less for light, sandy soils, and more for heavier loam or clay types. If a large amount is needed, you can apply one half in early spring and the other half in fall.

While many of the highly acid chemical fertilizers increase the need for lime, organic fertilizers seldom lead to overacidity. In addition, they are long-lasting and don't burn grass. The best choices are cottonseed meal, soybean meal, screened compost, and well-decayed animal manures used at approximately 100 to 150 pounds per 1000 square feet. Dried blood or blood meal is also excellent, as it has a high (8-to-14-percent) nitrogen content, plus other elements necessary to grass growth. Use ground phosphate with potash rock, greensand or granite dust, and bone meal for mineral nutrients, applied at 50 to 100 pounds per 1000 square feet. Rock fertilizers such as granite dust and rock phosphate are best applied in fall, so that winter snows and rains can wash them well into the soil.

Sludge has proved to be another excellent organic fertilizer for turf. It can be mixed with the soil when starting a new seedbed in September. Open up the soil to a depth of five or six inches and mix sludge and compost in thoroughly with the topsoil. After seeding, top-dress with more sludge, topsoil, and compost and cover with a thin straw mulch. For well established lawns, sludge may be applied in a ½-inch-deep layer during winter when the ground is frozen. Not only is it a luxuriant plant food, but the sludge cover will also insulate the grass roots from alternate thaws and freezes.

A few elements of winter care for your lawn will help prevent spring problems. Avoid a great deal of traffic on the lawn in winter, especially when snow is on the ground, as ice will form and kill the grass. Low spots on the lawn are especially subject to winterkill because water accumulates and freezes there. Remove all dog manure before the last snow melts to avoid burning the lawn. If the grass is not covered with snow, it may even need to be watered in winter months. If the soil is thawed down to three inches it may be watered anytime during the winter, but watering when there is frost in the topsoil will encourage heaving.

Insects

Many people find **ant hills** unsightly, especially in lawns where the grass is kept short. Actually, these natural aerators are beneficial to your lawn, and if you allow your grass to grow a little longer, the ant hills will be hidden.

Three **beetles,** the Asiatic garden beetle, Japanese beetle, and Oriental beetle, cause the same type of damage to lawns. A heavy infestation may cause spots of the lawn to die in August or September. If you pull up tufts of grass from these areas, you will see that the roots have been cut just below the surface of the ground. Beetles seem to flourish on poorly nourished grass and plants. The odor of prematurely ripening or diseased fruit often attracts them, so remove fallen fruit from the lawn area.

The Asiatic garden beetle feeds on many kinds of plants. They are attracted to lights, but in the day they hide in the soil around plants and are seldom seen. The Asiatic garden beetle is about ¾ inch long, dull cinnamon brown, and has finely striated wings.

The Oriental beetle [color] adults emerge in late June and July. The females lay eggs about six inches deep in the soil. Several weeks later the grubs hatch and work their way toward the surface, where they feed on roots of grass. In late autumn they descend a foot deep in the soil to hibernate, and come to the surface again in April to resume feeding. There is one generation a year. Oriental beetles are ⅜ inch long and have varied markings and colors. They do not fly much, and are often found in roses, hollyhock blossoms, and in the turf.

The most widely known means of safe control for the Japanese beetle is milky spore disease. See JAPANESE BEETLE.

Hairy chinch bugs are serious lawn pests. These bugs hibernate during winter in dead grass, leaves, and other litter. They emerge in spring, mate, and lay eggs on the grass or on the soil surface. Lawn damage is caused by the young bugs or nymphs, which are about ⅕ to ¼ inch long, reddish at first, and then changing to black with a white spot on the back between the wings. Lawns infested with chinch bugs may first show small spots of yellowing grass, then large irregular dead patches where the bugs have injured the lawn by sucking out the plant juices. Chinch bugs have an offensive odor, especially when crushed, and a severely infested lawn has an odor that can be detected by walking across it. As the life cycle of the chinch bug takes but seven or eight weeks, there may be two or more generations a year in the South. They are particularly damaging to St. Augustine grass, reports the Agricultural Experiment Station of Auburn University.

To test for chinch bugs, first select a sunny spot along the border of a yellowed area of lawn. Cut out both ends of a large tin can, push one end into the soil about two inches, and then fill with water. If chinch bugs are present, they will float to the surface of the water within five minutes.

These insects prefer hot, sunny lawns such as football or baseball fields. You can discourage them by shading the lawn with trees or shrubs. Another control is to seed your lawn in soil made up of ⅓ sharp builder's sand, ⅓ crushed rock, and ⅓ compost. Experiments at the University of Missouri have shown that well-fed lawns will discourage chinch bugs. When deprived of nutrients, the bug not only lives longer but lays more eggs.

When chinch bugs have severely infested a lawn, a natural predator called the big-eyed bug may move in and feed on the adults, according to research at the Connecticut Agricultural Experiment Station. The big-eyed bug also preys on insect eggs, spider mites, plant bugs, leafhoppers, aphids, and larvae of several

Lepidoptera species. They won't repair the bare spots in lawns damaged by chinch bugs, but they will control the pests so that you can reseed in late summer.

Cutworm

There are several species of **cutworm** that cause lawn injury. Most species are smooth grubs of greenish, brown, or dirty white coloring, either with or without striping. Presence of feeding larvae is likely if the adult moths have been seen in the area; they have a wingspread of from one to two inches and are usually multicolored with dull hues such as brown, black, gray, or dirty white.

Cutworms are among the earliest insects to begin feeding in spring. Most species have one generation a year, occasionally two. The generations usually overlap so that moths appear throughout the summer. Cutworms injure grass by cutting off the blades at the base, leaving closely cropped, small, elongated or irregular brown spots in the turf. The larvae generally remain concealed just below the surface of the ground or in clumps of grass during the day, coming out at night to feed.

Successful control of cutworms has been achieved by flooding lawns with water until they are puddled. This treatment, which is only practical on a small scale, brings the cutworms to the surface so that they can be collected and destroyed. See also TOMATO.

Earthworms, sometimes called night crawlers or dew worms, usually come to the surface at night. These purplish tinged worms may be as long as eight inches when fully grown. They often leave casts on the surface that make the lawn bumpy and difficult to mow. You're likely to see them after a heavy rain.

Since earthworms, like ants, are natural aerators, they are beneficial to the soil. Let your grass grow a little longer so the castings will be hidden. If an absolutely smooth surface is necessary, the use of a vertical slicing machine will help to break up the casts and smooth the turf.

The **European crane fly** has become established in western Canada and the northwestern United States. The adult crane fly looks like a large mosquito, with a body about one inch long. Often large numbers of these flies gather about a house, but they do not bite or sting and will not damage houses.

Crane flies come from the soil of lawns and pastures from August to September. They lay eggs in the grass, which hatch into small gray brown larvae with tough skins that earn them the name of leatherjackets. These leatherjacket worms feed on the root crowns of clover and grass during fall, remain in the larval stage through winter, and resume feeding in spring. Damage from leatherjacket feeding is most noticeable in March and April. About mid-May, they stop feeding and go into a nonfeeding pupal stage just below the soil surface.

According to the Agriculture Extension Service of Washington State University, many of these leatherjackets can live in the soil without seriously damaging lawns. Birds will feed on them, and no other control is required. Even highly infested lawns have shown recovery without the use of insecticides.

The **fall armyworm** is a brown-striped caterpillar that feeds on grass blades before becoming a large yellow-and-brown-striped moth. See armyworm under CORN for further description and control.

When turf is heavily infested with **nematodes,** it lacks vigor and may appear off-color, yellow, bunchy, and stunted. Grass blades dying back from the tips may be interspersed with apparently healthy leaves. Injured turf may thin out, wilt, and die in irregular areas. Symptoms of nematodes are easily confused with soil nutrient deficiencies, poor soil aeration, drought, insects, or other types of injury. Nematode-infested grass does not respond normally to water and fertilizer. Damaged roots may be swollen, shallow, stubby, bushy, and dark–colored.

Nematodes are slender microscopic roundworms. There are many types, most of them harmlessly feeding on decomposing organic material and other soil organisms. Some are beneficial because they are parasites of plant-feeding organisms, including other nematodes.

Control nematodes by keeping your grass growing vigorously through proper watering and fertilization, as outlined above. See NEMATODES.

The **sod webworm,** which becomes the lawn moth, has caused considerable damage in western Canada. The larvae feed on the shoots and crowns of the grass but not the roots. Irregular brown patches appear on the turf, and the grass dies back from the shoot. The larvae are slender, gray with a brown head, and about ½ inch long. They are readily seen when the brown or dead sod is lifted. You can control them with milky spore disease; see JAPANESE BEETLE.

White grubs of the Japanese beetle and June bug can cause serious damage if present in sufficient numbers by cutting off grass roots. They are the favorite food of moles, and attract these rodents to lawns. Sod affected by grub damage can be rolled back over the spots where the grubs have been at work. If the lawn shows brown patches and loose sod in late spring or late summer, rake off all the loose turf and turn over the soil under it. Continue to turn it up at intervals of a few days until late fall. Birds will make short work of the exposed grubs. If you have chickens or ducks, they will make an even better job of it. See JAPANESE BEETLE.

Diseases

By and large, good lawn practice will prevent or limit disease attacks from the start. Disease is encouraged by: 1) poor soil drainage; 2) excess moisture; 3) poor circulation of air because of surrounding trees, shrubs or buildings; 4) incorrect mowing; 5) stimulation of grass with fertilizer during the summer; and 6) high soil acidity.

Correcting poor soil drainage and maintaining adequate soil aeration will build your lawn by permitting stronger root and top growth. On the other hand, a soggy water-soaked soil is an ideal environment for disease. Pathogenic organisms need an abundance of moisture for the early stage of spore development and infection of the plant.

Watering late in the evening is a cause of much lawn disease because the grass remains wet through the night so that mold and fungus growth are encouraged. Anything that favors the undue and prolonged presence of moisture, such as a heavy mat of grass clippings, contributes to the incidence of fungus growth. So, if you leave heavy clippings on the lawn for their mulch value, be sure to rake them over lightly to break them up and permit circulation of air. Turf areas that are completely enclosed by buildings, trees, or shrubs may suffer from poor circulation of air. As a result, the grass will remain wet for long periods and may be excessively warm. These two adverse factors, excessive humidity and warmth, not only inhibit sound lawn growth but favor the development of grass disease as well. The remedy is simple: restore adequate circulation of air by pruning or removing some of the trees and shrubs.

Close mowing of bluegrass lawns weakens the grass and helps produce the succulent or tender leaf growth that is vulnerable to fungus. On lawns cut higher than 1½ inches, new leaves can be formed as fast as the lower ones are infected and no permanent damage will occur.

The bentgrasses, because of their ability to obtain moisture and nutrients from the soil due to their prostrate type of growth, can stand to be cut down to half an inch. Given favorable conditions the bents will successfully resist heat, drought, insects, and fungus attacks.

Applying fertilizer to speed midsummer growth can lead to lawn trouble by stimulating fungus growth. Instead, fertilize in early spring and fall, when the danger of disease is reduced. Strongly acid soil is more disease-prone than a slightly acid or neutral soil, and proper liming can help keep your grass healthy (see the introductory section above).

An effective way to inhibit the development of disease is to plant a mixture of grasses. Different diseases attack different varieties. For example, brown patch affects the bentgrasses while leaf spot hits the bluegrasses. If only a single grass is planted, the disease can easily spread from leaf to leaf, but in a mixed turf the disease organisms soon reach a type of grass that is resistant and further progress is halted. Where possible, plant disease-resistant varieties.

Try this three-step remedy if fungus diseases hit your lawn. First, use lots of compost, as it contains microorganisms that will ingest the disease spores. Second, inoculate affected areas with angleworms; they will eat the compost and grass clippings and provide rich fertilizer droppings. Third, irrigate the lawn with a canvas soil soaker (the soaker should be canvas, not the type made of plastic and pierced with tiny holes, which throw up a fine spray mist). The canvas soaker is laid across the lawn and water is run for 15 to 20 minutes, or until the soil is soaked to a depth of one foot.

Brown patch is a common turf disease of lawns and golf greens. It causes irregular spots of varying size, first colored a light yellow green and later turning to brown as the grass dies. The dead grass stays erect and does not mat down. All grasses are susceptible to brown patch. The responsible pathogen is a soil-borne fungus that attacks the roots, killing the fine feeding roots and then the entire root system. In periods of wet weather or when lawns are watered frequently, the fungus may grow up on the lower stems and leaves.

Brown patch flourishes under conditions of excess moisture and high temperatures. It occurs chiefly in acid soils, and is encouraged by constant watering and heavy fertilizing with high nitrogen fertilizers. According to the Montana State College Cooperative Extension Service, brown patch is less likely to occur when the available nitrogen supply in the soil is low and phosphorus and potassium levels are high.

To control brown patch, be careful not to overwater the lawn. Set the mower high, for close cutting makes the grass more disease-prone. Remove the clippings after you mow, and avoid using nitrogen-rich chemical fertilizer.

Chlorosis, or yellowing of turf, is a symptom of iron deficiency. Iron is essential for the production of chlorophyll, the green pigment necessary for manufacturing food in plants. Of the turfgrasses, centipede is the one most sensitive to the lack of necessary iron. The three factors that most commonly contribute to iron-deficiency chlorosis and dying out of centipede in spring are overfertilization, extended dry periods during the previous fall, and too much lime.

Overfertilization results in luxurious growth of the grass and effects a deficiency of the form of iron that can be absorbed and used by the centipede grasses. Chlorosis may develop immediately. During the latter part of the previous growing season, iron deficiency may have reduced the amount of food manufactured, causing the grass to enter the winter in a weakened condition. The result is that the turf is slow to reestablish an adequate root system in spring and consequently shows severe chlorosis during this period. If chlorosis is not too severe, the grass may regain color and recover. However, in the more severe cases the grass may actually starve to death as a result of failure to manufacture adequate food to maintain life.

Damage from late-fall drought often goes unnoticed because home owners assume that winter dormancy rather than drought is responsible for premature browning of the turf. Drought-damaged turf is badly weakened and enters the winter with a low food reserve that is inadequate to develop a sufficient root system. A poor root system will not be able to supply the plant needs during early spring.

Symptoms of iron deficiency in centipede, as well as other southern turfgrasses, sometimes result from too much lime. Have the soil tested for pH and treat according to recommendations. You can prevent iron deficiency chlorosis (yellowing) by maintaining centipede lawns under relatively low levels of soil fertility and at a pH below 6.0.

Copper spot is characterized by small, light copper-colored spots in the turf. The color is produced by masses of the fungus on the stems and leaves. Because it confines itself to the lower leaves and stems, the spots are not readily seen except just after mowing. Copper spot rarely causes serious injury, and control measures shouldn't be necessary.

Another disease of minor importance is **corticum red thread,** also known as pink patch. Round or irregular patches of blighted grass, light tan to pinkish and one to six inches in diameter, develop during cool, moist spring and fall weather. Where it becomes severe, the spots may merge to form large, irregular areas with a reddish brown cast. On Bermuda grass, the disease resembles winterkill. Bright coral pink or red threads about ¼ inch long protrude from diseased leaf tips and leaf sheaths. These fungus strands appear gelatinous in the early morning, and brittle and threadlike as the grass blades dry later in the day. Corticum red thread is most prevalent in fescues, Manhattan ryegrass, and bentgrasses.

Follow the preventive disease control practices suggested above. Maintaining a balanced high fertility level is important; remove thatch and collect grass clippings after mowing.

Dollar spot appears as round, brownish or bleached-tan spots, from two to six inches in diameter depending on the type of grass. It is more often seen on golf greens than home lawns. If left unchecked, the spots may merge to form large, irregular, straw–colored patches of dead grass. Individual blades are girdled by light tan lesions with reddish brown borders. All the widely used lawn grasses are susceptible, particularly bentgrasses, Bermuda grasses, and zoysias. New seedlings of tall fescue are often attacked.

Dollar spot develops during moist periods of warm (60° to 85°F.) days and cool nights. It is most active and damaging if there is a deficiency or great excess of nitrogen in the soil, or too much thatch. Injured turf recovers quickly if treated promptly. If left untreated, it may take weeks or months for new grass to fill in the sunken dead areas.

For control, keep thatch to a minimum, water only when needed to a depth of 8 to 12 inches, mow high, and rake vigorously. Maintain adequate soil fertility by use of the proper organic fertilizer.

Fading-out, also called Helminthosporium leaf spot, foot rot, and melting-out, attacks bentgrasses, fescues, and Kentucky bluegrass. Pure stands of Kentucky bluegrass favor the development of this disease, whereas recommended mixtures usually contain some naturally resistant species. It occurs in all parts of the country, and is most destructive during hot, humid weather. Diseased areas appear yellow or dappled green, as though the grass were suffering from iron deficiency. When the disease is not controlled, the grass fades out, leaving dead, reddish brown patches. Eventually, large irregular areas of the lawn may be killed.

Close examination of infected leaves in the early, or leaf spot, stage usually reveals brownish lesions, shaped oblong, and parallel to the leaf blade. The disease progresses to leaf sheaths, crowns, rhizomes, and roots, causing them to rot until the entire plant is killed. During hot weather, the disease may cause the sudden death of large areas of lawn; dead plants appear to have died from drought. Weeds and crabgrass usually invade these areas. As moist conditions favor this disease, it first appears in shaded areas. Fading-out is most severe on closely clipped turf.

To combat fading-out, follow good cultural practices to ensure healthy grass that will resist the fungus spores. Reduce shade in the yard and improve soil aeration and water drainage. Mow at the recommended height, and avoid excesses of nitrogen in the soil, especially in spring. Merion and Newport are leaf spot-resistant varieties, as are the Tifton turf Bermuda hybrids.

Fairy ring [color] appears as a circular ring of fast-growing, dark green grass, often with a ring of thin or dead grass inside or outside. The rings (they are not always closed, and some look like arcs or horseshoes) vary in diameter from a few inches to 50 feet or more. The strip of thin or dead areas may be three to six inches wide. After rains or heavy watering, mushrooms often appear in the dark green grass ring.

All turf grasses are subject to fairy ring, a disease caused by fungi of the mushroom family. Growth starts at a central point and spreads outward at the rate of a few inches to two feet or more per year. The fungus grows throughout the soil, forming a dense, white, threadlike growth to a depth of eight inches or more that keeps water from the roots of the grass.

The condition is controlled by aerating the ring with a spading fork or hand aerifier, making holes two inches apart and as deep as possible—at least four to six inches. Begin about two feet outside the ring and work toward the center. (Do not use the spading fork again without washing it thoroughly.) The aeration will allow water to penetrate the soil, and deep soaking every other day will help improve the condition and allow the soil to regain its health. This deep soaking is essential to speedy recovery.

It may be necessary to dig out the fairy rings, a laborious procedure. Remove all infested soil, digging two feet below the deepest extent of the white mold. Replace it with fresh soil, making sure that the top of the hole is covered over with a rich layer of properly composted humus. If you have been applying any commercial fertilizers to your lawn, particularly those high in nitrogen, discontinue their use.

Fusarium blight may affect lawns more than two years old. Light green patches several inches in diameter appear first, changing to a dull reddish brown, then to a bleached tan color. Patches of brown and thinning grass may be round or irregular, up to two feet or more in diameter. Apparently-healthy green grass may grow within the center of these patches.

Temperatures over 75°F. with high humidity favor the development of fusarium blight. Its severity appears to be related to drought stress; the disease may appear in one or two days in summer if night temperatures remain high. Bentgrasses, fescues, ryegrasses, and bluegrasses are all susceptible, but some varieties are more resistant than others. Merion bluegrass is especially susceptible to fusarium blight.

To control, water deeply to avoid drought stress. Avoid excessive nitrogen, especially during hot summer weather. Mow at the suggested height, and keep thatch to a minimum.

Lawn rot is caused by a fungus that attacks the stems and leaves of the plant to cause a soft rot of the tissue. This rotting gives a matted appearance of the affected areas, unlike brown patch. Newly seeded grass is more likely to be affected than older established turf. On new seedings, diseased areas look as though soaked with gasoline. The causal fungus requires plenty of moisture and warm temperatures, and therefore is destructive only during periods of warm, wet weather or when the grass is watered frequently on warm summer nights.

To prevent an outbreak of this disease, water infrequently and in the forenoon. Bentgrasses usually suffer more from this disease than other types.

Powdery mildew causes leaf blades to appear dusted with flour or lime. Close inspection reveals patches of a whitish, powdery growth. Infected leaves often turn yellow and wither. New plantings may be killed when mildew is severe; established plantings resist it better.

Mildew is most severe on Kentucky bluegrass grown in the shade, and occurs chiefly when nights are damp and cool, in late summer, fall, and spring.

Control powdery mildew by increasing air circulation, and

pruning dense trees and shrubs to reduce shade. Keep the lawn vigorous by organic fertilization and good drainage, while avoiding an excess of nitrogen. Mow your grass frequently at the prescribed height. Some varieties of Kentucky bluegrass are more resistant to mildew, and you may find it helpful to plant one of these if conditions in your lawn seem to favor the disease.

Pythium blight, also called greasy spot or cottony blight, causes round or irregular spots from a few inches to several feet in diameter during very hot, wet weather. The spots are first water-soaked and dark, and then fade to a reddish or light brown as the leaves dry out and wither. A greasy border of blackened, matted grass blades, often covered with a cottony mass, is seen when the pythium fungus is active. The patches may merge and form streaks, since the fungus is spread by flowing water and mowing. It is most common on newly established turf, although if conditions are favorable it occurs on established grass too.

The disease may spread very rapidly, killing out large areas of turf overnight. Dead grass lies flat on the ground, rather than remaining upright like grass affected by brown patch disease. New grass does not grow back into the diseased area. The fungi are most active at daytime temperatures of 85° to 95°F. (night temperatures falling no lower than 68°F.), when humidity is high, growth is dense and lush, and soils are poorly drained.

For control of pythium blight, avoid watering methods that keep the foliage and ground wet for long periods of time. Maintain a proper balance of nutrients, being careful to avoid the excess of nitrogen that stimulates lush growth. Improve surface and subsurface soil drainage. Where feasible, delay seeding until the weather is cool and dry.

Rust does not usually become a problem until summer, when extended dry periods slow the growth of grass. Heavy dew favors rust development. Some varieties of Kentucky bluegrass, particularly Merion, and the newer ryegrasses are very susceptible to the rust fungi. Close examination of rust-infected grass shows powdery rust–colored or yellow orange spots. The powdery rust will rub off easily on your fingers or a cloth. Continuous heavy infection of rust causes many grass blades to turn yellow, wither, and die. Severely rusted lawns are vulnerable to winterkill.

Damage from rust is less severe if Merion Kentucky bluegrass is mixed with common Kentucky bluegrass or with red fescue in a 1:1 proportion. Frequent mowing at recommended heights, organic fertilizing, and correct watering in hot, dry weather will help eliminate rust.

Seed rot and damping-off are diseases caused by soil-inhabiting fungi and are troublesome during the cool, wet weather of spring. The seeds rot in the soil, just after the seed coat is broken. Seedling grasses on new lawns appear water-soaked, turn yellow or brown, and rot off at the surface of the soil. Surviving plants are weakened, and affected areas are often heavily invaded by weeds. Damping-off is most severe on heavy, moist, or water-logged soils, and where seeding rates have been excessive.

To control seed rot, sow top quality seed at suggested rates in a well-prepared, fertile seedbed. If possible, seed in later summer or early fall. Provide for good surface and subsurface soil drainage when establishing a new lawn. Fill in low spots where water may stand; properly graded lawns usually do not suffer from this disease. Water only when necessary.

Lawn injury from **septoria leaf spot** and tip blight resembles that caused by a dull mower. Leaf blades are light yellow from the tip downward. Close inspection usually shows black dots (the fruiting bodies of the septoria fungus) embedded in the diseased tissue. Smaller lesions, $\frac{1}{8}$ inch or more in length with red or yellow margins, may also be present.

The septoria fungus is active during the cool, wet weather of spring and fall. During spring rains, the spores are splashed to healthy leaves where infection occurs, often in the cut ends of grass blades. Septoria leaf spot is usually of minor importance during the summer.

Control by following cultural practices that maintain a vigorous, healthy turf.

There are two species of **slime mold** that commonly appear in lawns. One of these molds appears as a bluish gray, sooty growth on the grass, the other as large masses of a dirty yellow growth. When the molds dry, they form powdery substances that easily rub off the grass blades. Neither of these organisms do any harm to lawns, although they may appear to smother or shade otherwise healthy grass. They are soil-inhabiting microorganisms that feed on decaying organic matter, and are not parasitic on the grass. Slime mold soon disappears, but if you wish to remove it, rake, brush, or hose down the grass with a forceful stream of water. Reduce thatch accumulation, as it favors the growth of the mold fungi.

There are two prevalent types of **snow mold:** gray snow mold and fusarium patch (or pink snow mold). Both diseases are most serious when air movement and soil drainage are poor and when grass stays wet for long periods at near-freezing temperatures. Snow mold is more common in northern areas. Damage often conforms to footprints, paths, snowmobile or ski tracks, because snow compaction and plant injury favor the disease. Snow mold may be especially severe in low places and on north slopes that have a deep snow cover for a long time. Most lawn grasses are susceptible to snow mold diseases; bentgrasses are more severely attacked than coarser lawn grasses. When warm weather arrives and the grass dries out, these diseases make no further progress.

Gray snow mold appears as grayish or straw-colored spots several inches to two feet or more in diameter. Some spots may merge to form large, irregular areas; where severe, the entire lawn may be affected. As the leaves are killed they turn brown and frequently mat together.

Fusarium patch causes bleached tan or light gray patches of indefinite shapes, one to eight inches in diameter, sometimes enlarging to one or two feet. At the advancing edge of melting snow, the spots may have pinkish margins. Snow is not necessary for the development of fusarium patch. It can occur anytime in cool (below 60°F.), wet weather in fall, winter, or spring. Diseased areas under snow cover may be covered with a dense, slimy mat of fungus filaments that turns a faint pink when exposed to light.

To control both types of snow mold, avoid overfertilizing with nitrogen, especially in late fall. Where winters are severe, lawns should not enter cold weather in an actively growing condition. Promote air circulation and good soil drainage. Mow frequently at suggested heights and rake vigorously to prevent a heavy mat of grass from forming. The Canada Department of Agriculture recommends the selection of winter-hardy grass species such as Kentucky bluegrass and creeping red fescue.

Stripe, or flag smut, is most noticeable during spring and fall because it is favored by cool temperatures. Infected plants may occur singly or in patches of a few inches up to a foot or more in diameter.

Infected plants are often pale green to yellowish and stunted. Individual leaf blades may be curled and show black stripes with black powdery spores. The stripes run parallel with the leaf veins. When first developing, they are yellow green; later the stripes turn gray and finally black. The leaf twists, curls, and shreds from the tip downward. Infected plants may die during hot, dry weather. In other cases, the symptoms disappear.

Spores of the smut fungi germinate in the soil and thatch. They grow throughout the plant tissues and remain within the plant until it dies. Smutted plants in newly seeded lawns are rare. Watering and high fertility encourage their buildup. Varieties of grass differ greatly in their resistance to smut.

Sunburn and drought injury are very similar in appearance but may occur independently. Sunburn sometimes occurs when a hot spell follows cool, cloudy weather. Drought causes the same brown discoloration of sunburn but over larger areas, first in the open sunny areas and later under trees if the drought is prolonged. Watering before the serious browning appears will forestall drought injury if you soak the soil several inches deep. Neither sunburn nor drought cause permanent injury, and grass will recover as soon as fall rains and cooler weather arrive.

Other Troubles

Algae may form a greenish or blackish scum on bare soil or thinned turf, especially in damp, shady, heavily used and compacted areas. The algae, which are a mass of minute green plants, dry to form a thin crust that later cracks and peels.

Improve air circulation and soil drainage to correct this condition. If it persists and becomes serious, upgrade your soil's fertility, and reseed the area.

Buried debris may cause disease-like symptoms in the grass. A thin layer of soil over rocks, lumber, bricks, plaster, concrete, or other building materials will dry out rapidly in summer weather. Eliminate the condition by digging up suspicious areas, removing the cause, and adding good topsoil.

Thin turf or bare spots resulting from heavy use result in **compacted areas** on the lawn. Waterlogged and heavy-textured soils will easily become compacted, especially if they are walked on constantly. Water flows off these areas and plants may die of drought.

Compaction can be remedied by aerating the soil (you can rent an aerifier at garden supply stores) or by installing drainage tile for seriously waterlogged soils. You can also core compacted areas, using a hand corer or power machine. Coring is a type of cultivating which uses hollow tines or spoons to remove soil cores. The resulting holes allow water and air to penetrate the soil. If necessary, fertilize and reseed compacted areas. Foot traffic on lawns can sometimes be reduced by putting in a walk, patio, or parking area, or by planting some shrubs.

Dog injury from urine often resembles brown patch or dollar spot. In affected areas, grass turns brown or straw–colored and usually dies. These injured areas, up to a foot or more in diameter, are often bordered by a ring of lush, dark green grass.

Chemical fertilizers applied on wet grass may cause serious **fertilizer burn.** Rugs, rubber mats, or metal dishes left on the grass in the hot sun will also leave their mark. Heavy watering helps injured spots to recover.

Moles raise ridges in the lawn as they burrow through the soil in search of grubs and worms. Because they eat soil insects, moles are considered beneficial. However, the grass above the raised tunnels will die if the roots are exposed to the tunnel air, and intruding mice may nibble on roots and bulbs.

If you can get rid of grubs in your lawn, mole troubles will decrease; see the discussion of white grubs, above. You'll find several types of mole traps in hardware stores. The Cooperative Extension Service of Iowa State University suggests the following procedures for trapping moles. Locate the main runway by rolling or tramping down all of the raised runways. Watch carefully at hourly intervals to determine which one is raised first—this is probably the main runway and the one over which the trap should be set. The trap may be placed anywhere along the runway, but a straight section of burrow is preferable. If you loosen the soil where the trap will be set with a fork or trowel the trap's action will be easier and faster. Tramp down the main runway again before setting the trap. If only the short section of runway where the trap is set is tramped down, the mole may go around it; if the entire runway is flattened, he will be less cautious.

If the mole is not caught in 24 hours, it has probably abandoned that runway. Tramp down all the runways again and reset the trap on another that is being used. In many cases, moles use their own and other burrows interchangeably. It may be possible to catch several moles by resetting the trap in the same place after each dead mole is removed.

If **moss** appears on your lawn, it probably indicates plenty of moisture in combination with a lack of phosphorus and potash in the soil. Sometimes excess shade, poor drainage, and soil compaction will aid moss growth. Moss can be removed by hand raking. Improving the soil with organic fertilizers, followed by reseeding, will eliminate moss permanently.

Mushrooms and toadstools can be an annoyance. Some have an unpleasant odor, and some may be poisonous and hence a menace to children and pets. They do no harm to the grass, however. Mushrooms are the above-ground growth of certain fungi that grow on decaying vegetable matter in the soil. In lawns, this might be buried stumps or tree roots, logs, boards, or a thick thatch. Mushrooms often pop up following heavy rains or watering, and may indicate a too-acid soil.

No compound will kill mushrooms and toadstools without injury to the grass, but they can be removed by raking or sweeping. They will not completely disappear until the buried material has completely decayed, and in some cases it may be best to dig up these pieces of rotting debris. Test your soil to check its pH; if necessary, follow the procedures for liming as described above.

Salt damage to lawns and shrubs may result if salt is used to remove winter snow from paths and sidewalks. As the snow or ice melts, it carries a salt solution to plants, causing roots to lose large amounts of water. The responsible phenomenon is osmosis, a process whereby water already existing in roots will move out through root membranes in order to dilute and create a balance with the salt concentration in the soil. Without the necessary water in its root system, the plant dies or is damaged.

Use minimal amounts of salt, and exercise care in its application near grass and shrubs. Use other methods to rid walks of snow or ice if possible.

Along the shore, salt spray or flooding with high tides causes serious injury to lawns. The injury from spray is temporary, but if the area is flooded for several hours the damage is likely to be permanent. If the flooding is of short duration, flushing with fresh water immediately afterwards will minimize the injury.

Skunks may dig holes in your lawn in search of grubs and worms. If you kill the grubs in your lawn, skunks will probably go elsewhere. Read the controls for white grubs, above.

Lemon, see Citrus

Lettuce

Insects

A number of species of **aphids** occur on lettuce, some feeding on leaves and a few on roots. See APHID.

The **cabbage looper** is a large, pale green measuring worm with light stripes down its back. It grows to 1½ inches long, and doubles up as it crawls. The looper usually feeds on the underside of leaves, producing holes that are ragged and unsightly. It occurs

Cabbage Looper

through the United States and is particularly troublesome in Florida, Arizona, and California. For habits and control measures see under CABBAGE.

Cutworm

Fat, smooth **cutworms** may be kept from new lettuce plantings with loose collars of tar paper or cardboard placed around the seedlings when set out. The collars should be 1 to 1½ inches in diameter and wide enough so that ½ inch lies under the soil and at least an inch remains above ground. See TOMATO for other measures.

Fall Armyworm

The **fall armyworm** attacks foliage of lettuce. It grows up to 1½ inches long and varies greatly in color, from light tan to green to almost black. Three yellowish white hairlines run down the back, and on each side is a dark stripe paralleled below by a wavy yellow one that is splotched with red. The head is marked with a prominent white V or Y. See armyworm under CORN.

Two **leafhoppers** are responsible for much damage to lettuce: the six-spotted (or aster) leafhopper is yellow green with six black spots and the potato leafhopper is green with white spots on its head and thorax. Both are small (⅛ inch long), wedge-shaped, and apt to go unnoticed until the damage is done. They feed by sucking plant sap, and this causes areas of leaf tissue to turn pale. In addition, the six-spotted species transmits a serious disease, aster yellows. For control measures see fusarium yellows, below, and potato leafhopper under POTATO.

Tender lettuce leaves are very vulnerable to the ravages of **slugs**. These are mollusks, not insects, and are closely related to snails. They hide during the day, and their night travels are recorded by silvery, slimy trails. A number of control measures are described under SLUGS AND SNAILS.

Tarnished Plant Bug

You'll have to look sharply to catch a sight of the **tarnished plant bug**—this flat, ¼-inch-long insect is very shy and will likely retreat to the opposite side of its stem as you approach. Its back is mottled white and yellow with touches of black, creating a tarnished appearance. A very close look will reveal a yellow triangle, with one black tip, on each side of the insect. For habits and control of this pest, see ASTER.

White grubs are white with brown heads and are found in the soil in a characteristic curved position. See under CORN for a description of habits and control measures of this root pest.

Wireworms may also attack the roots of lettuce. These worms are shiny, hard, jointed, and range in color from yellow to brown. See WIREWORM.

Diseases

Rotting of the edges of lower leaves is an early symptom of **bacterial soft rot**. The leaves of the head finally dissolve into an unappetizing, slimy rot. The bacterium that causes this disease lives in the soil and is splashed up on the leaves by rain; hilled-up rows and well-drained soil should protect the plants.

Lettuce doesn't show the telltale signs of **big vein** until the plants have developed several true leaves. From five to six weeks after the seed or plants are set in diseased soil, the symptoms become apparent: the leaves yellow along the veins and the entire leaf becomes thickened, crinkled, and brittle. Although no tissue is actually killed and the plant may well go on to produce a normal head, the head is smaller and less firm and the leaves are of inferior quality.

Once affected with big vein virus, soil may remain capable of causing the disease for a number of years. Either grow lettuce in virus-free soil or discourage the disease in infested soils by rotating lettuce with crops that don't carry the virus. Lettuce should not be planted on the same land more than once in three or four years. Rogue and destroy scattered afflicted plants.

Although not generally widespread, **bottom rot** is regularly destructive to lettuce in some localities. It is at first characterized by rum-colored, sunken lesions on the petioles and the midribs and a slimy rot on the lowest leaves. The disease then spreads upward, leaving the head a slimy mass. The main stems and midribs remain solid.

The bottom rot fungus enters the plant through bottom leaves that touch the soil, and varieties that have an upright habit of growth (such as the cos varieties) are less susceptible than others. The only practical means of control is rotation with crops not attacked by the causal organism, such as sweet corn or onions. In areas plagued by bottom rot, only well-drained soil should be planted to low-growing varieties.

If yellowish or light green areas appear on the upper surface of older leaves, your plants may be victims of **downy mildew**. As these areas enlarge, whitish to gray tufts of mold appear on them. The spots later turn brown, and infected heads are apt to break down with secondary rots, especially in transit. Downy mildew is most likely to be a problem in damp, foggy, moderately warm weather.

Wild lettuce near the garden or greenhouse should be eradicated as a precautionary measure. Several strains of Imperial lettuce are highly impervious to downy mildew.

Drop, or sclerotiniose, is caused by a fungus that may exist in the soil for several years. Young seedlings grow few leaves, and these quickly wilt and die. Older and larger plants may be affected in either of two ways: some tend to wilt quickly and take on the appearance of a dull green, wet, folded rag; others may show a few water-soaked leaves at first, with brittle stems that either appear glasslike when cut across or show a reddish discoloration, and the head eventually becomes an odorless, watery, brown, rotted mass.

Because this disease develops rapidly under cool, moist conditions, it is best to use on the surface a well-drained soil that dries out quickly. It sometimes helps to ridge the soil to prevent water from accumulating around the plants. Plants should not be crowded, as the fungus may otherwise spread from plant to plant. If weeds are kept down, the disease will be deprived of hosts and ventilation and surface drying will be improved. Rotation with crops other than cabbage, beans, celery, tomato, and cucumber may be helpful. Large-scale growers can plow deeply to cover the fruiting bodies of the fungus, and pasturing sheep in lettuce fields after harvest helps to clean up refuse.

When seedlings are attacked by **fusarium yellows**, they wilt and growth is stunted. Older plants often do not form heads, have white hearts, become lopsided, and their vascular system turns brown.

This disease is carried by leafhoppers, and control depends on keeping these insects away from the lettuce. Keep weeds down in the vicinity of the garden, and avoid planting lettuce near carrots or asters, two other plants susceptible to yellows.

Mosaic causes leaves to appear a mottled yellow and green, and plants take on an over-all yellowish cast. Growth is clearly stunted, and usually no head is formed. The effects of the disease are most marked in warm weather when leaves may brown at the margins and then die. The disease is spread by various species of aphids. The chief source of trouble in lettuce fields is from seedlings from infected seed; unless removed as soon as symptoms are apparent, they may infect an entire field within a short time after the aphids make their appearance.

You should therefore be familiar with symptoms of mosaic, and be sure to water seedlings carefully. Clean up weeds in order to eliminate possible host plants or lodging for aphids. Large-scale lettuce growers will benefit by disking out lettuce beds and fields immediately after harvest, as this reduces chances of mosaic spreading from these older areas to healthy young fields. It also helps to plan on avoiding interplantings of young and old growing areas. Several tolerant varieties are available. See also APHID.

The first disease that lettuce plants are exposed to is likely **seed rot** (or damping-off), caused by soil-inhabiting fungi. Seed decays and the stems of young seedlings show a water-soaked condition near the ground line. Plants eventually topple over and die. Occasionally, damping-off causes some damage to plants in the field, but it is primarily a disease of seedbeds. It often appears in small localized spots, but may spread rapidly and destroy an entire bed if ventilation is poor and the bed is kept too damp.

Avoid excessive moisture and let air get to the plants. Chances of afflictions are further minimized by using a light, sandy soil that dries out rapidly, especially for the surface covering of the beds. If your seedbeds have a history of trouble, either change the soil or move the seedbed to a new location.

Tipburn is a widespread disease of lettuce, occurring everywhere lettuce is grown in both greenhouses and in the field. The first signs are small, yellowish translucent areas near leaf margins. As these enlarge and become more numerous, tissues near the edge of the leaf die, thus forming an irregular brown border along the perimeter. Veins of the affected areas of the leaves often turn dark and may become infected with soft rot bacteria. Symptoms are aggravated on hot, dry summer days following cloudy weather or heavy irrigation, as these conditions cause rapid loss of water from the leaves.

Plants that have become succulent from rapid growth are particularly susceptible, and you should avoid conditions that favor such growth, especially in the late stages. A crop grown with a uniform moisture supply at a fairly high level is more likely to escape injury than one with irregular growth caused by a fluctuating water supply. Excessive fertilization, especially with readily available forms of nitrogen, should be avoided in areas where crops mature during warm weather. Several lettuce varieties are resistant to tipburn, including Slobolt, Summer Bibb, and Ruby.

Lilac

Insects

The **lilac borer** attacks lilac, privet, and other ornamental shrubs by tunneling under the bark and into the wood, thus girdling the stems and causing foliage to wilt. Roughened scars showing the old borer holes may occur on larger stems at places where the borers have worked for several seasons. This creamy white caterpillar is about ¾ inch long when fully grown. It passes the winter in tunnels in the stems. The adult, a clear-winged moth, emerges in spring and usually lays its eggs on roughened or wounded places on the bark.

Make a thorough examination of the bush before the spring season arrives and cut and burn any dying and unthrifty stems that may contain borers. During the summer season, check to see if fine boring dust is being pushed from small borer holes. Such holes should be cut out with a sharp knife. If the tunnels are fairly straight, the borer can be killed by probing with a flexible wire, or pulled out by means of a hooked wire to make certain it is destroyed. Further damage can be avoided by using care so that the limbs are not damaged.

The small **lilac leaf miner** mines and rolls the leaves of both lilac and privet. Where this little pest is abundant, bushes appear scorched. The adult moth shows fore wings that are brown mottled with silver with two silvery bands across the middle. Winter is spent in debris-covered cocoons in the ground under the plants. The moths usually emerge during May, and the larvae mature in July. During the latter part of July and August, another batch of eggs is laid, and the larvae from these eggs mature in September, drop to the ground, and form their overwintering cells. During the first stages, the greenish white larvae mine between the epidermal layers of the leaves to form a large, unsightly blotch. There are generally from three to eight larvae in a mine. When the larvae are nearly fully grown, they emerge from the mines and roll down the leaf tips and feed.

Remove any rolled leaves that are on the bush and burn them. It may be necessary to prune back the leaves until healthy growth remains. Spraying with a strong soap solution in July, before the insect grows out of the larval stage, may help.

Oystershell scale is distributed widely over the United States. The common name is well chosen as the shells of this scale look very much like a miniature oyster. The scale cover is about ⅛ inch long and colored ash-gray to black. The body of the female is yellowish white. Eggs are pearly white to yellowish. The scales overwinter in the egg stage on twigs and branches of the host. There is usually one generation of this scale insect in a year. Injury consists in devitalizing the plant by sucking the plant juices. In cases of severe infestation, plants are often killed outright.

Control the oystershell scale with the gardener's two primary weapons against insects of the scale line—ladybugs and a dormant-oil spray. Use a three-percent oil emulsion applied in late winter before the plants begin to bud. If the garden is stocked with ladybugs, you will find that the scales decrease drastically in number, for scales are the ladybugs' favorite food. Since the scales overwinter on the plants, you might also choose to use a dormant-oil spray, which is not dangerous since the spray does not poison the scales but kills them by suffocation. It is also a good idea to obtain clean planting stock if you are considering starting lilac plants in your garden. Also see San José scale, below.

Shrubs and trees heavily infested with **San José scale** cover the twigs, branches, and stems with a grayish layer of their tiny, overlapping, waxy shells. Injury occurs as dead or dying branches, thin foliage, and a weakening of the plant. The waxy scale covering the female is circular, grayish, and about $\frac{1}{16}$ inch in diameter; the male is smaller and more oval. Scale insects pass the winter in a partly grown state that is nearly black in color. From two to six generations are produced annually, depending on the length of the season.

San Jose Scale

Since San José scale winters in a partly grown condition, it is more easily killed by dormant-oil sprays than oystershell scale. Spray in spring before the buds open; a strong soap solution can be substituted. Before spraying, remove whatever dying and heavily infested parts of the plant that can be spared. During late spring and summer when the young scale insects are in the crawling stage, many of them can be killed with a white-oil emulsion.

Diseases

Bacterial blight infects leaves, causing brown to black spots that may cover the whole leaf surface. Bacteria may enter the twigs directly or pass from blighted leaves into the twigs. When girdling takes place, the shoot turns black and dry black leaves cling to the twigs. Flower buds also become blackened and flower clusters turn limp and dark brown. The bacteria overwinter in diseased twigs. Blight is most severe during moist, mild weather and appears as the young shoots develop. White-flowered varieties are more susceptible to the disease than those with colored flowers.

Prune out dense growth so that the lilac will devote its strength to a few limbs. If the lilac bush does become contaminated, prune again; cut out and destroy affected shoots as soon as they are noticed. Tools should be disinfected with alcohol after they have been in contact with infected twigs.

Shoot blight is caused by a fungus that is responsible for symptoms similar to those of bacterial blight except that the diseased stem areas are dark brown instead of black and killing of the shoots is more extensive. Blossoms and tender growing tips are blighted and turn brown. The shoots may be killed back four to five feet. Root sprouts that come up under the shrubs often are killed.

Control for shoot blight is much the same as it is for bacterial blight. Do not plant lilacs and rhododendrons close together, since the same fungus attacks both shrubs.

Lily

Insects

A number of **aphids** feed on lily, and one is fond enough of the plant to be named the purple-spotted lily aphid. This ⅛-inch-long pest feeds on the underside of lower leaves, later on stems, and finally on buds and seed pods. It most frequently infests regal, formosanum, speciosum, and other late-flowering garden lilies. Feeding causes yellowed foliage, and the new growth of some varieties is killed prematurely.

Other possible enemies of lily are the bulb mites (see GLADIOLUS), fuller rose beetle (ROSE), GARDEN SYMPHILID, striped and spotted cucumber beetles (CUCUMBER), and the yellow woolybear caterpillar (see imported cabbageworm under CABBAGE).

Diseases

A fair number of diseases prey on lilies, and most are discouraged by: (1) thinning plants to improve ventilation, (2) providing adequate drainage, and (3) roguing infected plant parts. To be sure of disease-free plants, grow them from seed in an isolated part of the garden.

Botrytis blight is a fungus that principally attacks foliage, damaging or killing it. Small round or irregular orange red spots appear on leaves, and in severe cases the spots may run together and kill the leaves. The fungus spends the winter in the form of small fruiting bodies that produce spores in warmer weather.

Many gardeners have found that botrytis can be controlled to some extent by cleaning up the garden borders where fruiting bodies may have accumulated.

Bulb or **basal rot**, a fungus disease, attacks bulbs through the roots and causes the bulbs to degenerate. Plants often eventually die. Symptoms may resemble tip-burning and root rot. Dig up and inspect the bulbs if trouble is indicated, and rogue out any infected plants. Because this disease persists in the soil, you should move the lilies to another area.

Gray mold is responsible for oval or circular spots which are reddish brown at first and develop pale centers and purplish margins. These spots may run together and rot the entire leaf, progressing into the stem and causing the stalk to fall over. If the spots dry out, they turn brown or gray. Buds or flowers may turn brown and rot, often showing the gray mold of the fruiting stage. This disease shows up and spreads rapidly under humid, cool conditions, especially if plants are crowded.

The usual control methods apply here: thinning, sanitation, and roguing. In the greenhouse, the disease is discouraged by warmer temperatures and a drier atmosphere.

Perhaps the most dangerous disease of lilies is **mosaic**, and it is this malady that has given the plant a reputation for being hard to grow. Mosaic is caused by a virus that lives in the plants, not in the soil or in dead plant tissue. When the disease first appears in the flower garden, it causes leaves to show a mottling of light or dark green. Leaves start to die from the ground upward, and the stems of the flowers often have crooked necks.

Mosaic is often transmitted by aphids, and their numbers should be managed (see APHID). The disease is also spread when lilies are propagated by bulb scales.

Aphids are also responsible for transmitting **necrotic fleck**, a virus that causes yellow flecks to appear on leaves. These blemishes change to gray or brown, and the surface is depressed but unbroken. Plants are dwarfed and have curled leaves. Flowers are small and develop brown streaks by the time they are fully open. See APHID.

Lime, see Citrus

Linden (Basswood)

Insects

Small linden trees are often injured by the larvae of the **linden borer**. The eggs of this beetle are laid in the bark, and the hatching larvae eat out a large cavity near the base. Decay follows and the tree may die. The white larvae, nearly an inch long, usually burrow near the ground, sometimes going into the roots below the surface. The adults are long-horned black beetles, about ¾ inch long and covered with a dense, greenish downlike hair. These beetles emerge late in summer and feed on leaves and tender shoots before laying eggs in the bark. Prune and destroy affected plant parts.

Other insects that trouble linden trees from time to time include APHIDS, JAPANESE BEETLE, oystershell scale (see LILAC), WHITE FLY, and white-marked tussock moth (defoliates linden trees, especially in cities; see HORSECHESTNUT).

Diseases

For diseases likely to trouble linden trees—anthracnose, leaf spot, and powdery mildew—see TREES: DISEASES.

Locust

Insects

The dwarf flowering locust or rose acacia is sometimes infested by **aphids**. See APHID.

Locust Borer Damage

The **locust borer** [color] is very destructive to black locust. Trees are usually attacked in their fourth or fifth year by larvae boring into the trunk and branches, but once the trees reach a trunk diameter of about six inches the locust borers leave them alone. Evidence of infestation is sawdust falling on the bark of the trunk and wet spots around the holes where the sawdust was ejected. Later, ugly scars show where the wounds have partially healed. Branches are weakened and may break, foliage becomes yellow and dwarfed, and entire trees are sometimes killed.

The eggs are deposited from August to October in bark crevices or wounds. Hatching larvae bore into the bark to overwinter, and bore into the wood the following spring. The adult beetles, which resemble the painted hickory borer, emerge during August and September and are very abundant on goldenrod blossoms in September.

If a tree is so badly damaged as to make it useless or is too limby to be used as a post, it should be cut off at ground level and the stump left to sprout. Localized infections of the bark can be removed, provided the tree will not be girdled in the process.

Individual borers can be killed with nicotine sulfate. Dip a small piece of absorbent cotton or soft cloth into a solution of one part nicotine sulfate to four parts water, stuff it into the borer's hole, and seal the opening with putty. It helps to maintain tree vigor with organic fertilization and frequent watering.

The **locust tree hopper** sucks sap and appears in three or four generations a year. As an adult it is an active brown insect of less than $\frac{1}{4}$ inch in length. If their damage is considerable, control by a spray of pyrethrum or nicotine sulfate, or dust once a week with a mixture of nine parts sulfur and one part pyrethrum powder.

The **locust twig borer** is particularly troublesome to black locust. The larvae tunnel into the small new twigs, causing galls or swellings measuring one to three inches long that crack open and disfigure the branches. The branches then weaken, and the tree's vitality is reduced. In its adult stage this insect has ashy brown fore wings marked with a pinkish white patch and several small blackish spots. The hind wings are mouse gray. The full-grown larva is about $\frac{1}{2}$ inch long and reddish to straw-yellow. Its head is brown and its thorax yellow.

The adults deposit their eggs on twigs in May and June. The eggs hatch within a week and larvae bore in twigs for a month. Larvae leave twigs when fully grown and spin a cocoon on the ground to pass the winter until they emerge from their cocoons in spring.

To control this destructive pest, a diligent pruning program must be undertaken. All branches that show evidence of the presence of the borer should be cut and destroyed in early summer before the larvae escape. A blacklight trap may prove effective in whittling down the population of the borer if employed in May or June when the insect is in the moth stage. Maintaining the tree's vigor helps keep borer damage to a minimum.

For control of the carpenterworm, see TREES: INSECTS; the mimosa webworm is a pest of honey locusts (see MIMOSA).

Diseases

Brooming disease is a virus that causes an abnormal development of black locust buds into short, spindly shoots having abnormally small leaves. Buds on these spindly branches also develop abnormal branches, giving the tree a broomlike appearance. The brooming typically occurs late in summer and the shoots often die during winter. Roots of infected trees are shorter, darker, and more brittle than normal. Excessive rebranching of the roots gives the appearance of root brooms.

There is no effective control for this disease. Remove and destroy affected trees.

Sometimes **cankers** appear on the small branches of locust, causing a dieback or wilt of branch tips. The first sign of trouble is small depressed areas that may enlarge to girdle the branch, and are usually covered with a gummy substance. Prune and burn the infected branches.

Lygus Bug

Several species of small, flat plant bugs are known as lygus bugs. They attack many field and vegetable crops, and are a major cause of catfacing injury on peaches and apricots. Young nymphs look something like aphids; older nymphs are smaller versions of the adults, which are shaped like footballs when viewed from above. They feed by sucking plant juices.

Lygus bugs overwinter as adults in crowns of plants and in plant debris. Large thick leaves of mullein form a fine blanket for these insects; Russian thistle, smotherweed, horseweed, sweet-clover, wild mustards, and nettle are other important reservoir host plants. Adults become active the first warm days of spring. They mate soon after emerging and begin laying eggs immediately. Eggs are inserted into plant tissues with just the caps raised slightly above the surface. They take from one to four weeks to hatch, depending on temperatures. There are five nymphal instars (immature stages) requiring about three weeks altogether. Newly emerged females begin to lay eggs in about ten days.

Lygus bugs are frequent victims of big-eyed bugs, damsel bugs, assassin bugs, and crab spiders. Two particularly beneficial big-eyed bugs look something like small lygus bugs, but their eyes are large and prominent, sticking out from the sides of the head. Damsel bugs are larger, about $5/16$ inch long, and are more slender-bodied than either lygus or big-eyed bugs.

Cotton grower Wilbur Wuertz and several University of Arizona entomologists came up with a way to control lygus bugs that plays on the bug's penchant for alfalfa. Wuertz planted narrow strips of alfalfa amid his rows of cotton, and the pests made for the trap crop in a hurry. This was the last move many of them ever made, as alfalfa is a friendly habitat for many natural enemies, including ladybugs and lacewings. Wuertz found that two percent alfalfa was enough to control the bugs; he plants it a month earlier than the cotton in order to have the alfalfa growing well by the time his money crop is sprouted.

Magnolia

Insects

Soft brown **magnolia scale** can kill trees if abundant. They overwinter as partly grown young, and suck the tree juices in spring and summer. Young scales are small, flat, and inconspicuous. Adults may be brown or mottled orange, with shallow wrinkles. A honeydew is produced on which an unsightly sooty fungus grows.

To control, spray the tree in late March or early April before buds open with lime sulfur or a dormant oil (½ pint oil to three gallons of water). Apply the spray on a warm, sunny day.

Diseases

For **leaf spot** of magnolias, see TREES: DISEASES.

Mango

Insects

A small brown **ambrosia beetle** is often found on mango trees. The cylindrical insect bores into the major limbs of the tree and into the trunk, carrying fungi along with it. Once this fungi is in the core of the tree, it multiplies to cause the wood of the tree to stain, rot, and die. To prevent the spread of fungi, it is recommended that the diseased and dying portions of the tree be pruned. Remove the infested branches from the vicinity and burn them.

A frequent pest of the mango tree is the **red-banded thrip,** a small black insect with a reddish band around it. The larvae are yellowish with a reddish band around the middle of the body. The thrip feeds on the leaves and causes them to turn darkly stained or russeted. It excretes over the leaves and fruits a reddish fluid that becomes hard and rusty brown or black in color.

The oil emulsion spray used for scale insects is good treatment for the red-banded thrip. It is best to use 1 to 1½ percent oil in the spray. See THRIP.

A considerable number of **scale** insects may find their way to mango trees. Red, mango, wax, and shield scale are among the offending species. Some scales secrete a substance known as honeydew that supports the growth of sooty mold fungi. The best remedy for scale insects is a mild dormant-oil spray. Natural enemies, including ladybugs, offer a good degree of control.

Diseases

The most common and widespread disease of the mango is **anthracnose.** This fungus causes small circular spots on flowers and fruits, and fruit often is russeted and cracked. The organism sporulates abundantly in wet weather, and the disease is common in extended periods of wet weather before the fruit are half grown.

Since the causal organism is also responsible for wither tip and ripe rot of several citrus fruits, it is best not to grow mangoes in the same immediate area. On a small scale, it may be practical to control this disease by pruning out infected twigs and branches. Don't overwater the fruit, particularly in the early periods of growth when the disease is most likely to occur. Perhaps the best way to control anthracnose, especially in areas of high rainfall, is to grow resistant varieties such as Paris and Fairchild.

Stem rot is a blackening of the stem end of fruit. The skin around the stem may show small blackened spots that show as slightly depressed just as the fruit is ready to be harvested.

It is believed that this disease hits fruit trees suffering a lack of moisture. Proper watering of the mango is the key to preventing both stem rot and anthracnose. Good ventilation will protect fruit in storage and in transit.

Tip burn can affect leaves by causing them to dry at the tip and turn light brown. Often the disease may involve more than half the leaf area. Severely affected trees are more often found in dry, arid regions.

It is best to avoid salt sprays and irrigation with salt water. Deep cultivation practices may damage the root system. See to it that trees have proper moisture. A heavy mulch of straw or hay is advisable. In severe cases, check the soil for potash. If deficient, the soil can be fixed up by mixing in banana residues or wood ashes, two potash-rich materials.

Maple

Insects

Boxelder bugs both act as household pests and cause injury to foliage and twigs of boxelder, maple, and ash. Being plant feeders, they do not damage buildings, clothing, or food, but they may cause alarm and annoyance by their presence. Full-grown boxelder bugs are about ½ inch long and resemble the squash bug in body shape. They have a reddish body marked with broad, shaded areas of brown on the lower surface. The thorax is marked by three longitudinal red lines, one down the center and one on each side. There are also red markings on the front wings. The young are bright red. These insects are true bugs and are equipped with sucking mouth parts.

The insect is most noticeable in fall when the adults seek hibernating quarters. They go to any place that affords protection, including houses and barns. On warm winter or spring days they come out into the open and return to the trees where they spend summer. In fall the boxelder bug congregates on trunks of trees, fence posts, and exterior surfaces of buildings.

Reduce their numbers by removing any nearby unwanted boxelder trees. If the trees are valued try handpicking or dusting with rotenone, or spraying pyrethrum indoors. Inside the house, seal any cracks in the exterior walls.

The **cottony maple scale** is a brown, oval, soft scale on the bark of the branches of maple and other trees. In June, large egg sacs are formed, their wax covering resembling a tuft of cotton. The best control is a spray of miscible oil (1 part oil in 15 parts water) applied in early spring before growth begins. Sugar maple trees should not be sprayed with oil mixtures because of possible injury. Many natural enemies help keep scale insects under control.

Maple/Cottony Maple Scale

The **maple bladder-gall mite** causes galls that first are green and later turn blood-red. Leaves become deformed if the mites are numerous, but the tree is not seriously damaged. A favorite host of this mite is the silver maple.

To control the maple bladder-gall mite, it may be necessary to spray the trees in early spring with an emulsion of highly re-fined white mineral oil prepared for use as a summer spray. Be certain to follow the manufacturer's instructions on diluting and care in handling. Sprays should be applied no later than the start of the blossoming period. It is useless to spray after the leaf damage has occurred and the galls have been formed.

Several other types of mites cause galls on maple leaves, and all can be controlled by a dormant-oil spray in early spring.

The **maple leaf stem** (or maple petiole)**borer** tunnels into the stalks of the leaves and cuts off the lower part of the leaf. The key to the control of the yellowish borer is to gather up and burn all fallen leaves promptly.

Maple/Maple Borer

The **maple sesian** (or maple callus borer) is a clear-winged moth whose brown-headed larva bores into maple trees, especially around wounds. The amber moth has a wingspread of about an inch, and there is one generation a year. Preventing injury to the trees is the best way to keep the larva from causing trouble. In the *Gardener's Bug Book,* Cynthia Westcott recommends smoothing off roughened bark, digging out borers in spring, and painting wounds.

The **sugar maple borer** is the most destructive pest of the sugar maple. It is a beautiful black beetle with brilliant yellow decorations, including a W-shaped mark across the base of the wing covers. It is about an inch in length and emerges in July. The female lays eggs in slits in the bark, and the young larvae tunnel in the inner bark and sapwood, hibernate in a chamber excavated in the sapwood, and the following spring cut large galleries in various directions, though usually in a spiral course upward and partly around the trunk. Sometimes two or more borers in a tree completely girdle the trunk and the tree breaks over. They hibernate the second winter in chambers four inches from the bark. Two years are required to complete the life cycle. Tree growth over the wound generally shows as a series of scars and ridges that show prominently on the trunk.

Examine trees carefully at least twice a year for evidence of the borer. If you see sawdust on the bark, chances are that it has infested your tree. If you find any burrows, cut them out or run a wire into the burrow and kill the grub. Close the opening with any of the accepted tree patching materials. Keep trees properly fertilized and watered to encourage vigorous growth.

Terrapin scale is a small, reddish, oval insect that occurs on the small twigs of hard and soft maple, often killing them. It is $\frac{1}{16}$ to $\frac{1}{8}$ inch long, with a black mottling on its reddish brown shell. Eggs are deposited in June under the old shells, and there is one generation a year. Control with a miscible-oil spray in early spring.

The **woolly maple leaf scale** shows as masses of white wax, resembling tufts of cotton or wool, on the underside of leaves in summer. Later these become white cottony wax cocoons. As cold weather approaches, the scales crawl into the crevices of the bark and there secrete a waxy protecting case in which they pass the winter. They often emerge on warm days and crawl about the bark.

The best control for this scale is a dormant-oil spray in late winter or early spring. When the young are crawling about, a spray of nicotine sulfate and soap will stop an infestation, but should be used only if necessary.

Other insect pests of maple trees include APHIDS, canker-worms (see TREES: INSECTS), oystershell scale (LILAC), and white-marked tussock moth (HORSECHESTNUT).

Diseases

Bleeding canker describes a wet spot appearing anywhere on the trunk from which sap oozes and dries to resemble blood. Cankers on young trees are long, with indefinite margins, and hardly show in the rough bark of older trees. Leaves above the canker wilt, and branches may die. In chronic cases leaves are small, dieback appears slowly, and the tree may die in from two to four years. Sapwood beneath cankers contains reddish brown radial streaks with olive-green margins.

For control, it is a good idea to prune out any infected tree parts and improve the soil drainage. Apply orange shellac or tree paint to any infected tree sections. Do not over-fertilize.

Nectria cankers start as depressed areas that quickly girdle branches on which cinnamon-colored fruiting pustules are abundant. Leaves beyond the point of attack wilt but remain attached to the tree. Eventually the branch dies. If one branch of a tree turns red in fall before the rest of the tree, suspect canker. Discovered in time, cankers can be scraped out and painted to prevent further infection. Prune well back of the cankered area and burn infected wood.

Purple eye is a fungus disease causing grayish tan leaf spots with purple borders. Tiny black dots in the spots are the fruiting bodies of the fungus. Control is the same as for anthracnose (see TREES: DISEASES).

Tar spot is a fungus that produces raised black tarlike spots on leaves. Silver maples are highly susceptible. This disease is unsightly rather than serious. Control by raking and burning fallen leaves.

Verticillium wilt of maple trees is recognized by a wilting and dying of leaves on one or more branches. Development may be slow, over a period of several seasons, or it may be so rapid that the entire tree is affected within a period of a few weeks. Bluish or blackish green streaks are often apparent in the sapwood, and may either be limited to a single affected branch or extend from the roots of the tree to a wilting branch.

Maple wilt seems to follow drought. The disease is noticeably reduced when trees are watered. Pruning can save trees, but some maples may have to be cut. Do not follow affected maples with either maples or elms.

*Anthracnose on
Sugar Maple*

Other diseases of maples include anthracnose, leaf scorch, leaf spot, and shoestring rot; see TREES: DISEASES. Norway and sugar maples are sometimes affected by rots; see TREES: ENVIRONMENT.

Marigold

Insects

Marigolds go relatively untroubled by pests, as might be expected—this flower is used to repel a number of pests, including nematodes (both French and African varieties work), the tomato hornworm, and white flies. But a few pests have strong stomachs and occasionally trouble marigolds: APHIDS, the JAPANESE BEETLE (found on African varieties), leafhoppers (see ASTER, six-spotted leafhopper), SLUGS AND SNAILS, SPIDER MITES, and stalk borer (DAHLIA, ZINNIA).

Diseases

Aster yellows is a virus signalled by greenish flowers and a witches'-broom appearance of the plant. Immediately rogue and burn infected plants and nearby weeds and ornamentals that have simliar symptoms. The aster leafhopper spreads this disease; see ASTER.

Stem rot causes dark lesions which may penetrate to the pith near the soil line. Roots are sometimes decayed. Plant marigolds in soil that has not previously hosted the disease.

Fungal **wilt** rots plant roots, and brown vascular bundles can be seen if stems are cut across. Plants may die. Set marigolds elsewhere, roguing and burning those that are infected.

Mealybugs

Mealybug

Mealybugs are well-known pests of house plants, vegetables, and fruit trees. Generally, they are an indoor pest in the North. The most common mealybugs look much like tiny tufts of cotton on the underside of leaves. They are soft scales, relatives of the hard-shelled scale species. Mealybugs, like their scale relatives, feed by sucking sap. Their secretions of honeydew attract ants and often support growths of dark sooty mold.

The simplest control, and the one least damaging to the local ecosystem, is a strong stream of water directed at the underside of foliage. In the house or greenhouse, mealybugs can be killed by touching them with a cotton swab that has been dipped in alcohol. The alcohol dissolves their protective coat of wax. Lacking swabs, you can administer the alcohol drop by drop simply by using a twig. Quassia is a venerable mealybug killer. If fruit trees are in serious trouble, try spraying soapy water; should this fail, you might resort to a spray of kerosene emulsion or fir-tree oil. Such sprays are effective, but interfere with naturally occurring biological control.

An important enemy of the mealybug is the lacewing. Eggs of this beneficial are commercially available. Two species of wasp parasite effected complete control of the citrophilus mealybug in California in the late twenties. A chalcid wasp from Japan has controlled Comstock's mealybug in Virginia and Ohio orchards. World-wide, 38 species of scale and mealybugs have been partially or completely controlled by introductions of their natural enemies.

Lacewing

Mexican Bean Beetle

The Mexican bean beetle [color] is the black sheep of the ladybug family. Adults are copper-colored and round-backed, and are marked with 16 black spots on their backs, arranged in three rows. You'll find no markings between body and head, the telltale sign that a beetle of this family is up to no good. The female lays orange yellow eggs in groups. Larvae are fuzzy, lemon-yellow, and covered by six rows of protruding, branched spines.

Mexican Bean Beetle

Adult Mexican bean beetles survive though the winter. In spring they leave their winter quarters and feed on bean foliage for a week or two. Females then begin laying their eggs in groups of 40 to 60. These are deposited on the lower surface of bean leaves. The tiny young grow into larvae that become longer than the adults, molting or shedding its skin a few times in the process. When full grown they attach themselves to the plant, usually beneath or inside a curled leaf. After the light yellow adult beetles emerge from the pupae, their shells harden and darken and the 16 black spots appear. Development from egg to adult requires about a month. One or two generations are produced each year.

Handpicking is the organic gardener's first line of defense; drop the beetles in a can of water topped with kerosene. Immediately after harvest, eliminate gardenside debris that could serve as an overwintering place. It has been found that earlier bean plantings are relatively free of trouble, so plant an early crop for canning and freezing. Destroy any orange yellow eggs you may find on the underside of leaves. Try interplanting with potato, nasturtiums, savory, and garlic. Some gardeners have had success with a spray made from crushed turnips and corn oil. A cedar-water spray, made by boiling cedar sawdust or chips, should also work. Derris is a potent repellent for this species. Rotenone can be used for serious infestations.

A USDA pamphlet on this pest says that other species of ladybug prey on the eggs and young larvae. Other beneficials are the anchor bug, preying on larvae, pupae, and adults, and the spined soldier beetle, attacking all stages. Heavy spring and summer rains help to keep down populations of the bean beetle, and a few days of drought and extreme heat may destroy an entire infestation without seriously damaging the crop. Several varieties of bean show some resistance to this pest: Wade, Logan, and Black Valentine. State, Bountiful, and Dwarf Horticultural rate as susceptible.

Mignonette

Among the most troublesome pests are the cabbage looper (see CABBAGE), corn earworm (CHRYSANTHEMUM), flea beetles (POTATO), flower thrips (PEONY, ROSE), six-spotted leafhopper (ASTER), and SPIDER MITES.

Millipedes

Millipede

When you happen upon these "thousand-leggers," they characteristically coil up like the mainspring of a watch. They don't actually have a thousand legs, but start off with three pairs and gradually grow up to 200 pairs. The number of body legs and body segments is increased with each molt. Sexual maturity is reached after seven to ten molts, taking place over a two to five year period. Full-grown adults no longer molt. Millipedes generally feed on decaying plant material, but may attack roots and stems of plants to obtain water in dry spells. Once they start feeding, they may not stop, as the weak sugar solution in sap is appealing to them. Seedlings are sometimes eaten clean through, and fungus diseases may follow attacks on larger plants.

Peat composts are less favorable to this pest than those containing leaf mold or rotted manure, say Hussey, Read, and Hesling in *The Pests of Protected Cultivation*. Millipedes can be brought to the surface by drenching the soil with nicotine preparations and raked off and destroyed.

Mimosa

Insects

The leaves of mimosa and honey locust trees are fed on by the **mimosa webworm.** This insect has come into prominence with the increased use of mimosas in landscape plantings and because honey locusts are often used to replace elms lost to Dutch elm disease. The webworms pass the winter in cocoons in bark crevices, cracks in the weatherboarding of a house, trash on the ground, or any other protected place near the trees. The moths emerge in late May or early June and lay their eggs several weeks later. The hatching larvae feed on the leaflets, webbing them together. There are two generations a year, and the larvae of the second generation are often numerous during late August and cause extensive damage, skeletonizing the trees and leaving their webbing over most of the limbs. At maturity the larvae are slender, about one inch long, and grayish brown with light-colored stripes the length of the body. Adult moths are grayish, with a wingspread of about ½ inch.

Most sprays do not have the pressure to force the insecticide into the web and growers must resort to physical destruction. You can tear down the webs with a stick, destroying any that fall on the ground.

Diseases

Mimosa wilt [color] is a disease caused by a soil-inhabiting fungus. Symptoms are easily seen: leaves wilt, hang down from the twigs instead of standing straight out, and in time become dry, shriveled, and then fall off. Usually, symptoms show first at the ends of the branches, followed by a progressive dying back of the branch. A cut into the sapwood may reveal a brownish black discoloration, while pink-colored masses of the fungus often appear on the surface of the dying wood.

Plant pathologists explain the fungus is an internal parasite in the tree, and therefore it cannot be controlled by spraying or dusting with fungicides. Cut down infected trees, burn the wood, and remove the roots to prevent spread to other trees in the same area. It's best to use resistant varieties, such as the USDA's Charlotte and Tryon.

Mint

Although mint is usually thought of as a pest repellent rather than a victim, a few insects and diseases may cause trouble.

Insects

Aphids feed on almost every plant that man does, and mint is no exception. In fact, the plant has its very own species, the mint aphid. This is a tiny, yellow green insect, mottled with darker green. In the event of severe infestations on mint foliage, see APHID.

Fourlined Plant Bug

The insect most likely to come to your attention is the **fourlined plant bug.** This greenish yellow creature has four black lines on its back, the inner ones thin, the outer two quite thick. They suck juices from young mint leaves, causing black spots. If damage is very serious, use rotenone; however, control is rarely necessary.

Diseases

Thorough garden clean-up in fall should protect mint from **anthracnose.** This disease is characterized by brown sunken spots that turn pale tan with dark red borders; serious cases may kill plants.

Early in the summer, crowded plants may be hit by **rust.** Light yellow or brown spots appear on stems, leaf stalks, or veins on leaves. Clean up plant refuse in fall, and thin plantings if necessary early in spring.

Plants affected by **wilt** grow slowly in spring and take on a bronze cast. The lower leaves yellow in warm, dry weather, and plants often eventually die. Do not plant mint in soil that is known to be infested; soil sterilization is sometimes necessary because the organism can live underground for years.

Morning-Glory

The **morning-glory leaf cutter** cuts through leaf stalks, causing the leaves to wilt. The greenish caterpillars hide during the day and feed only at night. You may also find holes eaten in leaves. The adults are yellowish moths with some light brown markings.

To control the leaf cutter, clean up the rotted and folded leaves in which they hide during the day.

Morning-glory leaf miner larvae make serpentine mines and, later, blotches in leaves. When mature, they suspend slender cocoons from leaves by a few silk threads. In a few days, small gray moths emerge. Handpicking of infested leaves and cocoons should reduce the leaf miner population to an acceptable level.

Mulberry

Many berry gardeners like mulberry trees because they decoy birds away from more choice berries. Mulberries are seldom troubled by many insects or diseases, but there are a few to watch out for.

Insects

The **mulberry borer** can be especially destructive in the South, but it is also found in the North. It is a black, long-horned beetle covered with gray hairs and bearing a light brown stripe along the edge. The larvae tunnel into the wood and may kill large branches or even entire trees.

Pruning and burning infested parts helps to control this borer, but seriously damaged trees may have to be cut down.

The **mulberry white fly** sometimes infests leaves, but since it does no significant damage, control is not required.

Diseases

Bacterial blight causes dark sunken spots on mulberry leaves. Young leaves may be deformed and brown, and watery streaks often appear on new shoots. Prune and burn infected parts to keep the blight from spreading.

Powdery mildew gives a whitish appearance to the underside of leaves. Some leaves may be lost, but the tree is not seriously harmed.

Muskmelon, see Cantaloupe

Narcissus

Narcissus are relatively free from diseases and insects because commercial growers take care to sell only sound bulbs. You should, however, observe a few precautionary measures:

keep the beds clean; avoid crowding plants, as this limits air circulation; and make sure that newly purchased bulbs are hard and plump—any with soft spots should be burned.

Insects

Narcissus Bulb Fly

The maggot of the **bulb fly** infests bulbs and ruins them. One larva hibernates in each bulb, and pupation occurs in the spring in the old burrow or nearby in the soil. The adults appear in early summer and lay oval white eggs near the base of the leaves or on exposed portions of the bulbs. The maggot is a yellow or dirty white larva without legs, and grows to about ¾ inch in length. The fly is about ½ inch long, hairy black with yellow or gray bands, and resembles a bumblebee.

Destroy all infested bulbs after digging. One-and-a-half hours of hot-water treatment at 110°F. will help guard against infestation. Small, stunted, and otherwise obviously infested plants should be dug up and burned.

The **bulb mite** injures nearly all kinds of bulbs, and Easter lily plants in greenhouses have been severely injured. The mites breed continuously in greenhouses or wherever the temperature and moisture are sufficiently high, and it is possible for ten or more generations to mature in a year. See GLADIOLUS.

When the leaves of plants are dwarfed and distorted and the time for flowering has passed fruitlessly, suspect the **bulb nematode.** To confirm its presence, cut across a bulb and look for dark brown rings that contrast with healthy bulb tissue.

The best preventative for bulb nematodes is to closely inspect the bulbs before planting. Any bulbs that appear soft or mushy should be quickly discarded. To be entirely safe, any bulbs already planted when the malady is discovered must be carefully pulled out and destroyed. Nematodes are apt to linger in the ground, so it is best not to plant susceptible flowers in the same locality.

Lesser Bulb Fly

The **lesser bulb fly** has a special fondness for narcissus. The flies appear in May and June and lay eggs at the base of leaves. The larvae find their way to the tip of the bulb and then go downward into the interior; as many as 77 larvae have been found in a single bulb. When fully grown, these maggots are between ⅓ and ½ inch in length, wrinkled, and dirty grayish yellow in color. They pupate in August in the bulb or in the surrounding soil. The fly is about ⅓ inch long, and has gray wings and a black abdomen marked with three white, crescent-shaped bands.

For home gardeners, it is best to discard any bulbs that feel soft. Plants that are grown outside can be protected by covering them with cheesecloth or gauze during the May and June egg-laying periods. Any plants that appear to be already infested should be discarded. Some growers prevent trouble by treating bulbs for 1½ hours at 110°F.

Other insects that you might come across are MEALYBUGS and onion thrips (see ONION).

Diseases

Basal rot is caused by a soil-inhabiting fungus. The decay usually begins in the root plate at the base of the scales, and spreads from there through the inside of the bulb, showing as a brown discoloration. Examine the root bases of bulbs and burn those which are obviously diseased. Bulbs that are in perfect condition in August or early September will sometimes become soft if kept too long out of the ground, and this also suggests early planting. Commercial growers control basal rot by providing good drainage and by destroying infected bulbs. It is best not to grow narcissus in soil that has previously hosted basal rot. Find another area of the garden to grow these ornamentals.

Blast is a fairly widespread trouble characterized by the appearance of flower buds which turn brown and dry up before opening. The cause of this malady is as yet unknown, but affected bulbs should be dug up and discarded.

Brown-tipped leaves in spring indicate **frost damage;** the quality of the flowers is not seriously affected. If bulbs are dis-colored or show withered, stunted growth, you should lift them up with roots intact and burn them.

Narcissus mosaic or **gray disease** is a mosaic virus. Plants lose vigor, and the key characteristic is an uneven, streaked distribution of green coloring matter in the foliage. Streaks also show in the flowers. Burn infected bulbs, roots, and foliage, and keep down the aphid population.

Nasturtium

Insects

Bean aphids frequently infest nasturtium plants; see APHID. The velvety green imported **cabbageworm** feeds on the underside of leaves, producing ragged holes; see CABBAGE. The **serpentine leaf miner** makes winding mines in nasturtium leaves. Usually no control is warranted; see PEPPER if your case is exceptional.

Occasional pests include the cabbage looper (see CAB-BAGE), corn earworm (CHRYSANTHEMUM), flower thrips (PEONY, ROSE), celery leaf tier (CELERY), LYGUS BUGS, and SPIDER MITES.

Diseases

Bacterial **wilt** causes plants to yellow, wilt, and die. Stems show black streaks, and bacterial slime oozes from cut stems. Bacteria are carried in the soil and infect nasturtiums through the roots. Plant in clean soil, making sure that nasturtiums don't follow other susceptible plants: tomatoes, potatoes, eggplants, zinnias, dahlias, chrysanthemums, and marigolds.

Nematodes

Most plants, both cultivated and wild, are prey to one or more species of microscopic thread or roundworms called nematodes (or eelworms). These pests spend most of their lives closely associated with host plants. Some are endoparasitic, spending their lives within plants. Others are classified as ectoparasites, and obtain their nourishment through plant walls. Unlike many other pests, nematodes have a wide host range and are seldom considered pests of just one or a few plant species. Symptoms of nematode injury include malformed flowers, leaves, stems, and roots; dwarfed plants with poorly developed floral, foliar, and root structures; and a variety of other conditions such as dieback and chlorotic foliage. Some endoparasitic nematodes cause tissue abnormalities in plants—known as galls or root-knots—that block the flow of nutrients through the plant. Feeding wounds provide an entrance for many disease organisms.

Despite their tiny size, nematodes are complex animals and contain most of the body systems found in higher animals, such as a digestive system, nervous system, reproductive system, and several kinds of muscles. However, they lack organized respiratory and circulatory systems. In many nematode species, functional males and females occur, but in a large number of species, females are the predominant sex found and males are scarce or unknown.

Soil samples almost always contain many kinds of free-living (nonplant-parasitic) as well as plant-parasitic nematodes. Usually, several genera of parasites are present in the same soil although only one or two may be causing the major amount of plant damage.

Because of the diversity of nematodes found in most soils, it is necessary that someone trained in nematode identification examine soil samples. The mere presence of nematodes in soil does not automatically mean that they are causing plant damage—the nematodes must be identified in order to determine if control measures are needed.

Should plant symptoms suggest that nematodes may be responsible for unsatisfactory plant growth, collect a sample of soil and roots for examination. The soil should be taken from several places around the plant within the root zone, including soil from the surface to a depth of about six inches. A one-inch diameter soil sampling tube is a convenient device for collecting such samples. Combine sufficient soil cores to make a composite soil sample of at least one-half pint. The soil and roots should be placed in a plastic bag to prevent drying. Samples may be taken at any time of year but preferably during active plant growth, from May to October. Check with the county extension agent to find where samples can be tested.

• **Controls.**   The standard controls for nematodes are avoiding infested plants, sterilizing soil, disinfecting tools, use of resistant varieties, rotation with immune or resistant crops, selecting uninfested fields, fallow, and enhancing biological control by fungi, predators, and parasites.

Soil sterilization is practical only on a small scale, such as for seed beds or greenhouse soil. Soil-filled flats can be dipped in water that is kept at the boiling point; pouring boiling water on soil doesn't seem to be effective. Steam heat and flame pasteurizers are also used by commercial growers. Tools can be disinfected in boiling water.

According to M. Oostenbrink in *Economic Nematology,* the cultivation of a resistant variety may suppress a nematode's population to 10 to 50 percent of its harmful density. New resistant varieties must continually be developed, however, as nematodes adapt to them and make them worthless in from 10 to 20 years.

If crops are rotated so that a susceptible crop is grown only once every 12 years, nematodes will be almost totally absent. Less effective but more practical is to grow for a few years a plant that nematodes don't like, or to interplant with such a plant. Many growers report success with interplanting with marigolds to keep nematodes from damaging crops, and research shows that pests both in the soil and in plant roots are affected. Indeed, a bulletin of the Connecticut Agricultural Experiment Station, *Marigolds—A Biological Control of Meadow Nematodes in Gardens,* says "the technique appears made to order for use around the home." These plants give both protection and flowers. They control nematodes by producing a chemical in the roots that kills nematodes when released in the soil. The Connecticut report notes that this chemical is produced slowly, and marigolds must be grown all season-long to give lasting control; real benefits may not be seen until the second season. However, marigolds have a residual effect, and can suppress nematodes for up to three years after having been grown.

Interplanting with these flowers may give crop plants competition—strawberries are an example. Therefore, you might either rotate plantings of marigolds with susceptible crops, or interplant marigolds with susceptible crops, or interplant marigolds two or more weeks after the other plants to lessen competition. If the pungent marigold odor covers up the delicate smell of neighboring flowers, just snip off the buds. White and black mustard plants exude an oil that nematodes can't stand. A study by Rohde and Jenkins (1958) demonstrated the worth of interplanting asparagus with tomatoes; juices from the roots of the former are toxic to root pests on the latter. Hairy indigo, velvet beans, and species of crotalaria (a yellow-flowering pea) are good cover crops for discouraging nematodes. You might also try interplanting with salvias and calendulas.

Organic amendments have proved helpful in biological control of root-knot on vegetables, reports a recent issue of *Agricultural Research,* a USDA publication. Indian scientists experimented with both oil cakes made from sawdust and the concentrated residues of the seed-oil extraction process. Since sawdust is very low in available nitrogen, this element must be supplemented. As these materials decompose in the soil, nematode toxins such as volatile fatty acids and phenols are produced. The tests suggest that rich organic soil matter may also encourage changes in root physiology to put off the pests. Some gardeners simply stir in sugar around plants.

Nematodes can be starved by growing immune or resistant crops for two or more years and by fallow cultivation, especially during May and June. Chupp and Sherf, professors of plant pathology at Cornell, report in *Vegetable Diseases and Their Control* that small gardens in the South are sometimes split up into three plots of equal size for this purpose. In one part the vegetables are grown, in the second chickens are kept, and in the third sweet corn is planted. Each year these plots are rotated so that the vegetables are preceded by one year of corn and one year of fallow ground. The effect is to greatly lower nematode damage. Trap crops have been traditional controls in Europe, say Chupp and Sherf. A highly susceptible crop, such as cucumber, tomato, or mustard, is sown densely and pulled three or four weeks later. Three or four such crops may be grown and pulled in a season. This is a tricky practice, as the nematode population may actually be encouraged if the trap crops are not pulled in time.

Flooding has been used as a control, but land must be underwater for about two years in order to kill nematode egg masses.

Hot-water treatments will disinfect roots, but germination is adversely affected. Sweet potatoes are treated at 116°F. for 65 minutes and finger-sized yams at 122°F. for 30 minutes.

• **Biological control.** Fungi are considered to potentially be the most useful biological control agents against nematode parasites. Predacious fungi capture nematodes by either of two methods, according to J. M. Webster in *Economic Nematology*. Some trap their prey with sticky appendages, while others have developed mechanical ring traps, one type of which is made of cells that suddenly enlarge to squeeze the nematode in a tight grip. Some fungi also administer a toxin that quiets the struggling captive. Other fungi simply ride on nematodes and send germ tubes into the host's body.

Even fungi that do not attack nematodes may nevertheless discourage them by putting off exudates that the pests dislike. In one study, James (1966, 1968) showed that the exudates of the fungus that causes brown-root rot of tomatoes serve to interfere with the development of the potato root nematode.

How can growers enhance biological control by fungi? Webster reports that the usual course taken by researchers is to supplement the soil with organic matter in order to stimulate fungal growth and trapping. While incorporating plant material with the soil may be followed by a rapid rise in the nematode population, predators soon catch up, including predacious nematodes and mites, as well as fungi.

Fortunately for growers, predacious and parasitic nematodes take a good many plant-parasitic nematodes out of circulation. And there is a number of other species of soil fauna that eat nematodes, from mites down to tiny amoeboid organisms.

• **Some types of nematodes and what to do about them.** *Root-knot nematodes* stimulate injured plant tissue to form galls; these growths then block the flow of water and nutrients to the plant above, leading to stunting, yellowing, and wilt. Plants typically limp through the growing season, but fruit production is poor. Although individual nematodes are invisible to the naked eye, egg masses can be seen as pearly objects. Roots appear scabby, pimpled, and rough to the point of cracking.

What crops can be safely grown on soil infested with root-knot nematodes? Chupp and Sherf list broccoli, brussels sprouts, mustard, chives, cress, garlic, leek, groundcherry, and rutabaga as fairly resistant. Others that may get by include globe artichoke, Jerusalem artichoke, asparagus, sweet corn, horseradish, some lima bean strains, onion, parsnip, rhubarb, spinach, sweet potato, and turnip.

Cyst nematodes cause plants to appear unthrifty or malnourished. Tops are smaller than normal, and consequently appear to be spaced further apart between and in the rows. Foliage may wilt and curl. Underground, look for clumps of roots and white females extending from the root surface. Skin on roots becomes thick, tough, and red or brown. Cyst nematodes have trouble hatching in very acid soils (pH 4.0) or alkaline soils (pH 8.0). A neutral pH of 6 suits them. So, potatoes may do best in an acid soil, and alkaline soils can be used for cabbage and beets. Most plants, however, do best at the pH that favors nematodes.

In the South, the *sting nematode* attacks a wide variety of vegetables and grasses. The first indication of trouble is areas of stunted plants in the field. As these areas enlarge and combine, the earliest-affected plants begin to die at the margins of older leaves. This nematode is at its worst in sandy soils low in organic matter. Chupp and Sherf recommend long rotations with watermelon or hot peppers and turning under crotalaria as effective controls. Important weed hosts, including crabgrass, ragweed, and cocklebur, should be eradicated. No resistant varieties have been developed.

Meadow nematodes, which cause internal browning in potato tubers and roots of corn, members of the cabbage family, lettuce, peas, carrot, and tomato, can be controlled by rotating with immune crops, such as beets, curled mustard, rutabaga, yam, and radish. Following injury, plants recover better if supplied with nitrogen-rich fertilizers.

• **Not all nematodes are pests.**   It should be noted in the nematode's behalf that some are important parasites of insect pests, including chafers, the alfalfa weevil, cucumber beetle, grasshoppers, and earwigs. Nematodes have been experimentally applied to turf to control the Japanese beetle, with success, and Dutky (1959) has used aqueous sprays containing nematodes to reduce populations of codling moth larvae in apple orchards. Most such trials employ a strain labelled DD-136, and this may soon become an important biological insecticide.

A recent issue of *Agricultural Research* reports that a new genus of a nematode that parasitizes the boll weevil has been found for the first time in North America. This parasite penetrates the body cavity, and causes the weevil to emerge early from hibernation because the parasites eat up the weevil's stored fat. The weevil feels hungry and emerges from hibernation early in search of food—too early, for they find no cotton and starve to death. In examining weevils from Louisiana floods in 1973, researchers found that almost three-quarters were infested. Work is now under way to learn more of the nematode's life cycle so that these beneficials can be mass-produced.

Nuclear Polyhedrosis Virus (NPV)

If you raise large amounts of cabbage, especially in the South, loopers may be controlled by spraying a homemade virus potion. Entomologist Francis R. Lawson of Biocontactics, a Florida research firm, found that a solution made from just ten infected loopers will give an acre complete protection. The trick is finding a virus-infected looper in your cabbage patch. Lawson says to look for loopers that have turned chalky white and look half-dead. They may climb to the top of a plant and lie on the leaves, or hang down from the underside of leaves. These infected worms soon turn black and liquify. Gather ten of them and run them through a blender with some water. Then dilute to give the mixture a sprayable consistency. Once infected, Lawson says, loopers die within three or four days.

In some cases, one application of NPV may control loopers for an entire growing season; however, cold spells will slow down the spread of the pathogen. In one experiment, mentioned by Swann in *Beneficial Insects,* "the mortality of the cabbage looper sprayed with the suspension was 100 percent on the ninth day at a temperature of 22°C. A drop of 6.5°C. doubled the time for the same effect." In comparing the effects of *Bacillus thuringiensis* and NPV on the alfalfa caterpillar, Swann notes that while BT is less potent and knocks out fewer pests, it has the important advantage of a shorter incubation period—death comes in one day instead of five or six (at variance with Lawson's figure of three or four days).

The NPV of the beet armyworm occurs naturally in cotton fields, and has been collected and sprayed to prevent outbreaks. Important but less successful has been the NPV of the bollworm. Also see the section "Making Bugs Sick with Microbial Control" in Chapter 8.

Nut Trees, see Butternut, Filbert, Hickory, Oak, Pecan, and Walnut

Oak

Insects

There are several **leaf miners** on oak, one of the most conspicuous being the white blotch leaf miner. Because these insects hibernate over winter in fallen leaves, it helps to rake and burn leaves in fall.

Oak gall scale appears as gray or yellow globular growths on oak twigs, usually in the axils of leaves or buds. Control these scales with a dormant-oil spray applied in early spring.

When the **twig pruner** strikes the oak trees, small twigs constantly drop upon the ground through July and August, and some hang with dried leaves. The eggs are laid on the smaller twigs in July; the young grubs work for a time under the bark and then tunnel along the pith in the center of the twig. The insects hibernate in the twig and the beetles emerge the following summer. The beetle is grayish brown, about ⅝ inch in length, and has long slender antennae. Gather and burn the fallen twigs promptly.

Many other common insects rate as pests of oak trees. The carpenter worm, cankerworm, gypsy moth, and tent caterpillar are discussed in TREES: INSECTS; see also APHID, SPIDER MITE, and two-lined chestnut borer (see CHESTNUT).

Diseases

Basal cankers on oak trees may superficially resemble a crack in the bark, but underneath the bark a fungus has killed the wood and may girdle the tree. Fruiting bodies of this fungus are distinctly stalked cups or saucers, colored dark brown and black, and are seen in the cracks in the bark. Control this canker by removing infected bark and wood and painting the wounds.

Leaf blister [color] causes light green or whitish puckered areas on oak leaves in midsummer. A spray of lime sulfur is an effective control, but should be resorted to only if necessary.

A number of different species of **oak galls** are found on these trees, many of them caused by wasps. They may appear as globular or rough swellings, one to two inches in diameter, or woody swellings at the ends of twigs. Damage is rarely serious, and in any event there is little you can do.

Leaf Blister

Until recently, oaks were considered one of the most healthy trees, being little bothered by pests and diseases. But since 1942, a fungus known as **oak wilt** has spread alarmingly through some of the best oak-growing states. The disease started in Indiana and has since spread through Illinois, Iowa, Minnesota, Missouri, Virginia, and Wisconsin. Diseased trees were found a few years ago as far east as Pennsylvania and as far west as Kansas and Nebraska. According to a leaflet issued by Purdue University Agricultural Extension Service, the disease attacks all species of oak. However, the red oak group (which includes northern red oak, black oak, scarlet oak, pin oak, shingle oak, and chestnut oak) is most susceptible. Most of the white oak group, though they can become infected, may linger a few years.

The first symptom of oak wilt in trees of the red oak group is a slight curling of leaves near the top of the tree or toward the tips of lateral branches. Affected leaves become pale in color, then turn to bronze and finally to brown, and then tan progressively from the tip to the base. Property owners unfamiliar with the symptoms of oak wilt are first concerned by the premature defoliation of infected trees, which necessitates repeated raking of leaves. But worse trouble soon follows. Once trees of the red oak group become infected, wilt symptoms progress rapidly over the entire crown of the tree, affecting the lower branches last, and death of the tree usually occurs within a few weeks. Peeling back the bark of twigs and branches affected with oak wilt may reveal diffuse tanning, stippling, or intermittent streaking of the sapwood. Trees can be observed in all stages of the disease at any time from May until September.

On white oaks, bur oaks, and other types within the white oak group, leaf symptoms of wilt are more localized than in the case of the red oak group. Usually, entire trees do not wilt immediately, and twigs with dead and dying leaves occur on only a few branches of infected white oaks. Some branches show leaf symptoms while others remain apparently healthy throughout the season. Defoliation is less pronounced, and withered, dead leaves tend to remain on the tree. Discoloration of the sapwood is generally more common in the white oak group than in the red. Since the symptoms of wilt develop relatively slowly on white oaks, infected trees may survive for several years, appearing perfectly normal for one or more seasons following infection before the "staghead" characteristic becomes evident.

Control of oak wilt involves preventing spread of the causal fungus. Infected trees should be cut and either burned or hauled away as soon as possible after infection is spotted. Usually, spores will not be produced until September or October on trees that wilt in July. As an additional precaution, oaks should not be pruned in fall or spring since the wilt fungus can gain entrance through wounds of this type. All oaks within 50 feet of an infected tree should be killed, as the fungus can travel underground from tree to tree through natural root grafts.

If valuable trees occur adjacent to an infected tree, it may be possible to save them from infection by digging a trench between the diseased and healthy trees to cut all roots that might serve to carry the fungus between them. The trench should be 36 to 40 inches in depth and can be refilled immediately.

The life of infected white oak trees may in some cases be extended by removing infected or dead branches. This is possible because of the slow spread of the fungus in the white and related oaks. It is not applicable to red or black oaks, because the disease will have spread too far before the first symptoms become visible.

Strumella canker is a fungus that occurs most frequently on forest trees but may become important on ornamental red and scarlet oaks. Infection usually is first noticed as a depressed area at the base of a branch stub that enlarges in a targetlike fashion, with concentric callus ridges, until the trunk is either girdled or considerably bowed on the side opposite the canker. The original infection on the branches, appearing as yellowish brown depressed or raised areas on the bark, usually passes unnoticed. The fungus travels rapidly down the branch and into the trunk, forming the canker which then withers, deforms, or kills the tree.

Remove trees as soon as infection is noticed to help protect remaining trees. If cankers are small you might try to cut them out, cleaning away all discolored wood, pointing the area at the top and bottom, and applying a good tree paint.

Other diseases of oak trees—anthracnose (see illustration), powdery mildew, leaf spot, twig canker, and shoestring rot—are discussed in TREES: DISEASES.

Anthracnose on White Oak

Okra

Insects

The green peach **aphid** occasionally visits okra for a meal. See APHID for ways of controlling this tiny pest.

The **corn earworm** is likely responsible for holes in okra pods. This caterpillar has stripes, a yellow head, and varies in color from light yellow to green to brown. It grows to almost two inches in length. The best and easiest way to control the earworm is by handpicking and destroying any worms on damaged pods that you can find. For other methods, see under CORN.

The large, oval **green stink bug** is both green and stinky. The nymphs are more rounded in shape, and are red with blue markings. It damages okra by puncturing the plant in order to feed. Keep down their numbers by clearing out weeds in and around the garden. It is best not to plant okra near legumes, eggplant, potato, and sunflowers, as the stink bug takes a particular fancy to these crops. Once the insects have invaded your garden, handpicking will prove helpful. Unless your hands are especially nimble, picking should be done early in the morning, before the stink bugs limber up. Sabadilla dust has been found effective against this pest, and in its pure form it is not toxic to either man or animal.

Shiny, metallic green **Japanese beetles** may swarm over okra; they occur from southern Maine down into Georgia and west to the Mississippi River and Iowa. Milky spore disease is a highly efficient means of control; see JAPANESE BEETLE.

Another okra pest is the **nematode,** a parasite of plants that works underground. The visible signs of its activity are stunted growth and galls or swellings on the roots. Although the galls on the smaller roots are tiny, the compound galls on large roots sometimes reach an inch in diameter. The pearly white specks within are the nematode egg masses. For control of this pest, see NEMATODE.

Diseases

Okra is grown extensively in the South, and is a popular choice of gardeners. The Louisiana Experiment Station says that although okra is generally considered a fool-proof crop, it is subject to several diseases, the three most important of which are discussed here.

Okra is highly susceptible to the formation of **root-knots,** or galls, caused by the root-knot nematode. The knots rot and the damaged root system cannot support the plant. See NEMATODE.

Southern blight is common in sandy soils of the Central Plains, and kills entire fields of okra. The disease, which is most active in hot weather, causes plants to lose their leaves and die suddenly. A small mass of pinkish fungus bodies can often be found around the base of the diseased plants. A number of crops are vulnerable to this fungal disease, and should not be transplanted with okra: soybeans, peanuts, tomatoes, peppers, and watermelons. Instead, plant okra on new land or in rotation with corn and small grains. Another helpful practice is to plow deeply under all plant debris on infected land.

Wilt describes a yellowing of the lower leaves, followed by gradual wilting and eventually the death of the plant. Stem tissue shows a dark brown discoloration under the bark. Once the wilt fungus is introduced to soil, it can live there indefinitely, and there is yet no means of purging the infected areas. Plant okra in soil that has no history of wilt.

Oleander

Oleander scales are circular, flattened, and live on stems and leaves. The females are pale yellow, tinged with purple, and the males are white. Infested plants lose color and vigor, and may die. This scale is found throughout the warmer states, and survives in greenhouses in the North. Prune out all encrusted branches, and apply a white-oil spray in winter.

Oleander is also visited by APHIDS, MEALYBUGS, and termites (see GERANIUM).

Olive

Insects

The **branch and twig borer** is a brown-and-black cylindrical beetle, the larvae of which are white. Usually the beetle bores a small hole at the base of the fruit or in the fork of a small branch, causing the twigs to break at these holes. The beetles do not normally breed in live olive wood, but prefer the dead wood of madrone, oak, and old grape canes. Consequently, it's best to eliminate dead wood by pruning often. Cut back the girdled portion a few inches as soon as it is noticed. See also APRICOT.

The **olive bark beetle** is quite diminutive, and colored black with white scales. The holes from which it leaves the bark appear as shot holes. Damage is worst on weak, sickly trees. Consequently, you should prune and fertilize carefully to encourage the plants' vigor. Prune and burn infested parts.

A variety of **scale** insects prey on olives. Black scales infest the trees to cause a black sooty appearance on leaves and fruit, and may greatly reduce vigor and productivity. Female black scale adults are small, dark brown or black insects with a very tough outer skin that has ridges on the back in the form of an H. The young are yellow to orange and are often found on leaves. Dead scales may remain attached to twigs for as long as three years. The scales secrete a sticky honeydew which supports the growth of a black fungus. Often black scales can so reduce the vigor of a tree that many leaves drop, and the next year's crop is reduced.

Scale

Olive scales may not disturb a tree until harvest, when sharply outlined, dark purple spots appear in marked contrast with the yellow green fruit.

Beneath the coverings, the bodies of male and female scales are reddish purple. Both may be found on any part of the tree above ground. On leaves, they cause a slight chlorosis, and on small twigs the wood is often a bit deformed and darkened. In heavy infestations, scales settle on the fruit as soon as it is formed in spring, often resulting in badly deformed olives at harvest. In early June the scales make their characteristic dark purple spots on the small fruit, which then tend to fade out as the fruit grows rapidly. By mid-August, the very small scales may be on the fruit without causing any change in color.

Natural enemies of scales offer effective control. One such parasite is a chalcid wasp imported from Persia in 1951 that deposits an egg beneath the armor of the host. The egg hatches, and the larvae feed within. The performance of this wasp has been inconsistent, however, because it only flourishes in relatively mild summers; dry, hot conditions usually hold down the population so that it is not of much help. Ladybugs contribute as well. See SCALE.

Other pests include the long-tailed mealybug (see MEALY-BUGS), bean thrips (BEAN), and WHITE FLY.

Diseases

Olive knot is a bacterial disease that is particularly present after long periods of rain. The olive knot bacteria are abundant in knots with live tissue, and are spread downward on the branches by rain. It is necessary for wounds of some sort to be present in order for infection to occur; these wounds may be freezing cracks, pruning wounds, scars from dropped leaves or flower clusters, and injuries from ladders or from cultivation and harvesting implements. The disease is carried by wind-borne rain, infected pruning tools, or diseased nursery stock.

When olive knot occurs, the trees take on rough roundish galls or swellings, sometimes two inches or more in diameter. They are likely to occur on twigs, branches, trunks, roots, or even leaf petioles and fruit stalks. The disease may kill much of the fruit-bearing area.

If the disease has already occurred in the orchard, it is a good idea when practical to remove all knots from the trees. Disinfect tools after each cut. After the knots are pruned, paint the exposed surface with a tree surgeon's solution. If the number of trees makes this solution impractical, the only other answer is to use resistant varieties, such as Mission and Ascolano. California growers find Manzanilla to be particularly susceptible. Since the disease is especially apt to spread in rainy weather, all pruning should be done during the dry summer months.

Soft-nose appears late in the season, during or at the end of the harvesting period. The fruit starts to color at the apex end and then shrivels and softens. It is believed that this trouble is caused by the addition of strong nitrogen fertilizers, especially unrotted manure, to the olive tree. Remember that the use of manure is generally beneficial as long as it has been properly rotted, as the nitrogen has then been fixed by microorganisms. These microorganisms build the soluble nitrogen compounds into their own bodies.

In **split-pit**, the pits split along the suture during fruit growth, resulting in bluntly flattened fruit. Although the fruit is of normal size and seems to progress satisfactorily, it is undesirable because the pit comes apart when the fruit is eaten. The cause of the condition is not known, but some growers believe that it is the result of an uneven watering system that allows the fruit to become dry early in the season and then overwaters it in compensation.

Verticillium wilt is a fungus disease that infects trees through the root system. It is common in soil that has recently been planted to potatoes, tomatoes, cotton, and other truck crops. This disease is generally fatal to younger nursery trees. Often wilt is sharply confined to one area of the tree, killing very small trees immediately. If verticillium is present, the tree will have dead leaves and dead flowers, often until midsummer and beyond.

To avoid this disease, do not plant olive trees in soil that has recently hosted susceptible crops such as tomatoes, potatoes, and cotton. Be certain to avoid interplanting such crops in the olive orchard. If any branches become infected with this disease, they should be pruned away immediately and burned. Also see TOMATO.

Onion

Insects

The foliage of young onion seedlings may be attacked by the **garden springtail**, a tiny, dark purple insect with yellow spots. They have no wings, but use taillike appendages to hurtle themselves into the air. Spray the foliage with garlic and water, and remove weeds from the area.

Garden Springtail

The larvae of the **lesser bulb fly** hatch from eggs at the base of the leaves and eat their way into the bulb through the tip. They grow up to ½ inch long and are wrinkled and dirty grayish yellow in color.

In some gardens, plants can be protected from the adult fly by covering plants with cheesecloth during the May and June egg-laying periods. Stunted and sickly plants may harbor the worms and should be dug up and burned to prevent spreading the infestation.

Lesser Bulb Fly

The onion **maggot** is a pest of onions chiefly in coastal areas. The full-grown maggot is legless, pearly white, and about ⅓ inch long. Like the cabbage maggot, these pests taper to a point at the head. The onion maggot is the more serious of the two, damaging onions by feeding in the lower part of the stem or bulb. Plants are susceptible at any age; one maggot is capable of destroying many seedlings by destroying their underground parts, and several maggots will team up to render large onions unfit for use.

The maggots usually gain entrance to the larger onions through the base where they attack the roots and burrow upward as far as two inches. When damaged onions are put into storage, they decay and cause surrounding healthy bulbs to rot. The destruction of seedlings not only reduces the stand but causes the remaining plants to lose their uniformity as well; this lack of uniform size is of considerable importance where onion sets are grown. Another species, the seed-corn maggot, confines its appetite to germinating seeds and the succulent stems of seedlings. Onions planted for sets are more susceptible than large onions, white varieties are more susceptible than yellow onions, and red varieties are least likely to be damaged.

Perhaps the best control method lies in the manner of planting. Home gardens are usually arranged in rows, but this plan only serves to help the maggot travel from root to root. Growers can thwart the pest by scattering onion plants throughout the garden. Since each maggot needs several young seedlings for nourishment, it will likely starve to death after its initial meal. Other plants will benefit from the scattered onions, since the strong onion smell is repulsive to many garden pests. Another frequently used method is adding sand or wood ashes to the top layer of planting rows. Or, radishes or cull onions can be used as an effective trap crop when planted at intervals near the seeded crop of field onions. The trap crops attract the egg-laying fly of the maggot, and are then destroyed to keep the main crop clear.

The **onion thrip** is perhaps the most damaging and widespread of the several pests that attack onions. The adult is an extremely active, pale yellow to brown insect with wings that measures only $\frac{1}{25}$ inch long. The larval form is a still tinier, wingless version that can barely be seen with the naked eye. They cause plant tissue to wither and collapse by puncturing plant cells to feed. A sign of feeding thrips is small, whitish blotches that run together to form silvery areas. Heavily infested plants become stunted, the leaves are bleached and die back from the tips, necks grow abnormally thick, and the bulbs fail to develop as they should. There are several generations a year, and injury is at its worst during dry, hot seasons.

Onion Thrip

Onion sets should not be planted next to a field of large onions, since thrips from the early maturing sets will migrate to other onions in the vicinity and may destroy the crop in hot dry summers. If thrips are a problem in your area, eliminate their winter homes by pulling weeds around the garden or onion field. Check closely any stored onion bulbs for evidence of thrips. Resistant varieties may come to the rescue—resistance to thrips is bred into several strains, and Spanish onions often show considerable resistance. Although severe infestations may wipe out even the Spanish varieties, your chances are better than with ordinary flat or global onions.

Shiny, hard, jointed worms about the roots of onion plants are **wireworms**. They range in color from yellow to brown. See WIREWORM for control measures.

Diseases

Damping-off is a fungal disease of seedlings that may occur in plant-beds or in fields that have been seeded directly. Seedlings are attacked at the soil line or just below, causing the adjacent tissue to shrink rapidly. The seedlings then fall over. Good cultural practices should discourage damping-off: frequent cultivation, providing good drainage, and planting in humus-rich soil.

Downy mildew is a fungal disease that overwinters on diseased plant refuse in the soil. The best time to examine plants for this disease is early in the morning while dew is still on the leaves. The first symptom is sunken, water-soaked spots on leaves, either yellow or grayish in color. These spots later become covered with a downy purplish mold growth, and may eventually be blackened by a second fungus. To combat this disease, use a three- to four-year plant rotation and destroy or plow under deeply all plant refuse. Some resistant varieties are available.

Neck rot, or botrytis rot, gives little sign of its presence until harvest time—most of the telltale signs develop in storage. The scales at the neck soften into sunken, spongy tissue, and one or more leaves of the bulb take on a water-soaked appearance. Often a gray to brown mold growth appears on the surface of the affected bulbs and between the diseased fleshy leaves. The mold growth produces numerous spores and black, kernellike resting bodies, or sclerotia. White varieties are extremely susceptible to neck rot.

Should neck rot afflict your onions, remove any that show the above symptoms so that the disease does not spread. Try to keep plants as dry as possible, and should watering be necessary, water the soil and not the plants. If you're sure to use plenty of organic nutrients in the soil and a liberal amount of humus, your onions' chances in storage will be greatly improved.

Stunted onions with withered tops may be victims of **pink root**, a fungal disease that lives in the soil and is encouraged by heavy, wet soils. Infected roots turn pink or reddish and then shrivel and rot. New roots are attacked as they form.

Onions should be planted on well-drained soil that has not recently grown ladino clover, ryegrass, or corn, as these crops leave a residue in the soil that is harmful to onion roots. If possible, do not plant onions, shallots, or garlic in soil that is known to have previously harbored pink root; wait at least four or five years before planting onions again. Although diseased sets and bulbs are difficult to detect, try to make sure that yours have come from disease-free fields. To gardeners harassed by pink root, the Louisiana Agricultural Experimental Station suggests planting varieties of the summer shallot derived from the Japanese Nebuka; as an alternate crop, these plants have a high degree of resistance to both pink root and yellow dwarf. Other resistant onion varieties are available; see RESISTANT VARIETIES.

Smut is evidenced by black areas on leaves and in between the segments of bulbs of white onions. These patches are filled with black pustules and loose spores of the fungus. Young diseased plants have twisted, curled leaves and may be killed outright. The disease is found throughout the northern states. Onions should not be planted in infested soil, and be sure to purchase undiseased sets. Evergreen has been found resistant.

Sunscald is not a disease but a name for damage that often occurs to onions when they are harvested on very hot, bright days. Immature bulbs, especially of the white varieties, are most prone to injury. The damaged tissue appears bleached, and becomes soft and slippery. Serious sunscalding will prevent bulbs from making United States grades and will result in a reduced price to the grower. A more serious problem, however, is that bacterial soft rot and other decaying organisms may gain entrance through the damaged tissue, sometimes causing complete loss of the bulb.

Sunscald can be prevented by protecting bulbs from direct exposure to the sun while curing. This may be done by pulling the onions with the tops intact and placing the bunches on the row so that the tops of each bunch will cover the bulbs of the previous bunch. This process is often called shingling.

For a list of varieties resistant to fusarium rot and smudge, see RESISTANT VARIETIES.

Orange, see Citrus

Orchid

Insects

Foliar nematodes cause brown or blackish spots delineated by veins; eventually leaf drop results. These tiny pests swim to leaves in the moisture on stems, and you can control them by improving ventilation around plants and by careful watering.

In the greenhouse, orchid growers may be bothered by the **orchid fly**, a small, black, wasplike pest. It lays its eggs in young leaves and causes them to swell. When the larvae hatch, they feed on many parts of the plant, including the bulbs. An early sign of trouble is swollen leaves. Cut off such leaves and destroy them.

The brightly colored **orchid plant bug** causes irregular, white stippling on the underside of orchid leaves. This insect is orange to red, has steel-blue wings, and is ⅛ inch long.

Here's a pest to experiment with. Conventional directions call for a shot of malthion, and then dismiss the problem, but organic orchid growers rely on botanical sprays. A mild garlic spray should keep the bugs away. If they get past the smell, try crushing the bugs between the thumb and forefinger.

There are several kinds of **scale insects** known to attack orchids. If infestation is heavy, consider a light oil spray. Use one percent of a summer oil to 1¼ gallons of water. Heavier sprays can injure plants that aren't tolerant. Scales can be also discouraged by removing sheaths from orchids. If a plant is badly infested, segregate it until it can be cleaned up.

Other pests you might see are APHIDS, flower thrips (see PEONY, ROSE), MEALYBUGS, and SPIDER MITES.

Diseases

Anthracnose is known by spots, on either leaves or tubers, that are soft, sunken, and somewhat circular. Spore pustules are pinkish or reddish orange and often arranged in concentric circles.

Since syringing spreads the spores to cause new infection, take care when watering. Reduce humidity around plants by improving ventilation. Cut and burn infected leaves.

Spots on leaves and tubers are often symptoms of bacterial diseases. Affected plants should be isolated. Do not water from overhead, as splashing water can transmit trouble. Provide good ventilation, ample mulch, and disease-free soil.

Some **virus** diseases can cause either "breaking" (variegation of flower color) or mottling of leaves with yellow and green patterns. Other viruses can lead to ringlike, concentric patterns in leaves, either yellow or brown, and necrosis may follow. Viruses invade all parts of the plant, from roots to flowers, and new plants derived from a diseased orchid by division or by backbulb propagation are almost certain to carry virus with them. Vegetative propagation in orchids is therefore a source of much disease in commercial and private plantings.

It appears that orchid viruses are not carried through seed, and seedlings should therefore be free of virus until they become infected from some outside source. Infection is usually introduced by insects (the green peach aphid transmits the virus causing breaking of flower color) or by cutting knives and shears contaminated with juice from diseased plants. It follows that there are several methods for preventing orchid viruses: 1) Keep aphids from plants (see APHID). While these insects are not often seen on orchid foliage, they feed and reproduce on flowers and flower buds. 2) Disinfect cutting tools between use on different plants. 3) Segregate diseased plants; keep healthy plants in a separate greenhouse or different area of the greenhouse. 4) When taking off flower spikes, use a "hot knife" attached to a torch.

Polluted air dries out the sepals and leaves of commercial varieties, spoiling the plants so that they are of little value. There is no easy solution: either move out into the country or build a small greenhouse to shield the plants.

Pachysandra

Insects

The female **euonymus scale** resembles a dark brown oystershell, while the male is slender and white. In heavy infestations, stems and leaves become covered with scales, leaves turn yellow, and vines die. This scale is found throughout the United States, but is less numerous in warm regions. Apply a dormant-oil spray before growth starts in spring. Cut off and burn any badly infested shoots before spraying.

Another occasional pest is the SPIDER MITE.

Diseases

When **leaf blight** and **canker** strike, leaves turn brown with irregular blotches and shrivel up. Lesions on stems may show pink masses of spores. Thin out thick plantings, and clean up dead plants and leaves.

Pansy

Insects

Leaves of pansies and violets are eaten by the **violet sawfly**, a bluish black or olive-green larva marked with white spots. They are smooth, to ½ inch long, and are found in the eastern United States. Feeding at night, the caterpillars skeletonize the lower surfaces of leaves, and later defoliate and eat holes in plants. Handpicking should take care of modest populations.

Other pests of violets include cutworms (see TOMATO), celery leaf tier (CELERY), flea beetle (POTATO), MEALY-BUGS, NEMATODES, SLUGS AND SNAILS, SPIDER MITES, and WIREWORMS.

Parsley

Insects

Aphids occasionally bother parsley; at least three species have been identified as pests. For control, see APHID.

Another caterpillar pest, the large, pale green **cabbage looper**, may be identified by the way it travels—it is a measuring worm and doubles up as it crawls. For a variety of control measures, see under CABBAGE.

Cabbage Looper

The yellowish white, legless grubs that occasionally attack the parsley roots are larvae of the **carrot rust fly**. For control measures, see under CARROT.

Parsley leaves are vulnerable to the ravages of the **celery leaf tier**, a caterpillar that changes in color from pale green to yellow as it reaches its full length of ¾ inch. Look for a white stripe running along the back with a pale strip centered within. For control, see under CELERY.

Because it is partial to parsley, the celery worm is also known as the **parsley worm**. This is a two-inch, green caterpillar with a yellow-dotted black band across each segment. When disturbed, it emits a strong, sweet odor and tries to look impressive by projecting two orange horns from its head. The adult is the well-known black swallowtail butterfly which has large, black fore wings with three rows of yellow markings parallel to the wing edge, and rear wings with a blue row, an orange spot on each, and the projecting "swallowtail" lobe.

Carrot Worm

Because the parsley worm population is rarely very great, most gardeners find that handpicking early in the morning is sufficient control. In serious cases, rotenone (or derris) may be used.

The underside of parsley leaves may harbor numbers of tiny green or straw-colored **strawberry spider mites**. These pests can cause stunting or even death of plants. See SPIDER MITES.

Diseases

Parsley is relatively free from diseases. A fungal affliction known as **leaf blight** (or septoria blight) may cause small, tan leaf spots, but control should not be necessary. Paramount is a resistant variety.

Parsnip

Insects

Most garden plants are susceptible to damage from **aphids**, and parsnips are no exception. See APHID for methods of control.

The larvae of the **carrot rust fly** may injure the roots of parsnips. These worms are yellowish white, legless, and grow up to ⅓ inch long. They are particularly destructive in the northeastern states and in the coastal areas of Washington and Oregon; growers also contend with them in parts of Idaho, Utah, Wyoming, and Colorado. For control, see CARROT.

Carrot Worm

The catholic tastes of the **celery worm** have earned it the names carrot worm and parsley worm. Both larva and adult are easy to spot. The former is a green, two-inch caterpillar with a yellow-dotted black band across each segment. When disturbed, it projects two orange horns from its head and emits a strong, cloyingly sweet odor. The adult is the familiar swallowtail, a butterfly with yellow, blue, and orange markings on its black wings. Each back wing bears a characteristic "swallowtail" lobe.

Because the celery worm population is rarely very great, most gardeners find that handpicking early in the morning works well enough. Rotenone (or derris) dust is sometimes used in serious cases.

The larval form of the **parsnip leaf miner** occasionally causes blotching of leaves, especially the lower ones. These worms are greenish, about ¼ inch long, and pupate to form a pale yellow fly with a green abdomen and brown curved bands on the wings. Control should not be necessary.

A small, black-spotted caterpillar, the **parsnip webworm**, may web together and feed upon the unfolding blossom heads of parsnips. It grows to about ½ inch long and varies in color from greenish yellow to gray. When mature, the webworm leaves its web and burrows inside the flower stems to pupate. Damage is usually not serious. Control by cutting infested flower heads.

For identification of pests not mentioned here, see CELERY and CARROT.

Diseases

Canker is a fungal disease that shows as dark brown, slightly sunken pits on parsnip roots, especially on the shoulders and crown. The causative fungus is kept at bay by good drainage and rotation. Chances of trouble are greatest in wet, cool weather. Model is a resistant variety.

Pea

Insects

Aphids, especially the large green pea aphid, are sometimes a problem to the pea grower. On a large commercial scale they often cause the plants to wilt and die. Home gardeners usually do not have such serious infestations. In addition to the general control measures listed under APHID, try repelling these insects by planting chives or garlic next to the peas. A variety that is listed as being resistant to aphids is Pride.

Yellowish white seed corn and cabbage **maggots** bore into sprouting seeds and prevent development of plants. Roots and stems are tunneled out, causing plants to wither and die. Early plantings are particularly vulnerable to these maggots. See CORN and CABBAGE for methods of control.

The **pea weevil** is a troublemaker in pea patches across the country, and is especially damaging in Utah, Idaho, Washington, Oregon, California, and New York. The adult is a brownish, chunky beetle, with scattered white, black, and gray markings. It is quite small ($\frac{1}{5}$ inch long) and feeds on pea blossoms. Eggs laid on young pods produce white larvae, $\frac{1}{3}$ inch long, with small, brown heads. The worms burrow through the pod and into a pea, which they eat and then pupate within. If peas are to be used as seed, they may be heated from 120° to 130°F. for five to six hours. This heat treatment will not damage the seed.

Pea Weevil

Most pea weevils meet their doom at summer's end. In addition to being preyed upon by other insects, birds and animals, many die as a result of ordinary culture practices. Government researchers have found that deep plowing or packing of the soil kills them in great numbers. You can reduce the possibility of infestation by destroying any vines and garden trash that the weevils could use for hibernation. This may be accomplished with little work by placing livestock or poultry in the pea patch after harvest. This pest has a tendency to settle from flight at the first scent of a pea blossom. Thus, fields of peas will likely have a greater infestation at the edges than at the center, and the center of large pea fields (over 100 acres) may be virtually untouched. For this reason, you should concentrate your watchfulness at the periphery of the field in the early part of the season. Plants may be dusted with rotenone between the time blossoms first appear until pods are formed. Because warm weather will cause an increase in mating and, consequently, in the number of weevils, early-planted peas are generally the least susceptible to attack.

Diseases

The combined effects of three fungal diseases that attack peas is called **ascochyta blight**. An easily recognized symptom is the small purple lesions, no more than specks, that form on leaves and pods. Stems develop elongated, purplish black lesions that may grow and girdle the stem, weakening it so that it is easily broken.

Affected leaves eventually shrivel and dry, taking on a resemblance to freshly cured clover hay. Stems and roots at ground level may be afflicted with a bluish black foot rot. The three disease organisms that collectively produce ascochyta blight infect seeds and overwinter in pea straw. In regions with very mild winters they may remain active on infected volunteer plants.

You should plant seed that is free from blight. Since infestation is rare west of the Rocky Mountains, western-grown seeds bring good results. According to the USDA, it is unwise to plant seed grown in humid sections of the East and Midwest. Large-scale growers are advised to plow down all pea stubble and vines immediately after harvest and to plant the field to a crop (such as grain) that would not require cultivation the next season. Staggered planting dates should be avoided, as this would only serve to spread disease from the stubble of the early planting. A three- to four-year rotation will reduce the possibility of peas picking up the fungi from the soil. After the crop is harvested, remove the diseased vines. Despite the efficacy of these precautions, it is important to locate new plantings as far as possible from areas that may harbor the disease.

Bacterial blight strikes peas in almost every area of the country except the semiarid regions of the West. Several symptoms may catch your attention: stems near the ground line turn purplish or nearly black, with irregular, discolored areas on the nodes; small, water-soaked spots appear on the leaves; and yellow to brown water-soaked spots develop on the pods. In time, the leaf spots turn golden brown and become papery, and a thin layer of dried bacterial ooze collects on them.

Control by planting western-grown seed that is free from bacterial blight, and by practicing a three- or four-year rotation. Because the bacterium enters through either the stomata or wounds, care should be taken to avoid injuring plants, especially when they are wet. Injury from hail storms often renders whole areas open to severe infection.

Fusarium wilt (pea wilt) is responsible for yellowed leaves and wilted plants. Affected plants may not wilt if the soil temperature is low. The interior of stems is of discolored lemon-yellow. The disease, which lives in the soil and enters through roots, may kill plants. Good, wilt-resistant varieties have been developed, and fusarium wilt is no longer a formidable threat; see RESISTANT VARIETIES.

In a wet season, peas may fall prey to **powdery mildew.** Leaves, stems, and pods become covered by a white, powdery mold. Late in the growing season, black specks (fruiting bodies of the fungus) appear in this mold growth. Infected vines are somewhat stunted, and in severe cases the vines dry out and die.

It is unlikely that you have anything in your power to hold the rains in abeyance, but you can confine overhead sprinkling to early in the day. If mildew has infected a planting, dig under all remnants of the vines as soon as the last peas are picked to prevent the mildew from perpetuating itself from year to year. For other methods of controlling powdery mildew, see MILDEW.

Root rots are characterized by yellowed, unthrifty plants with rotted and discolored underground stems and roots. Plants often die at flowering time.

Since excessive moisture favors this disease, avoid watering the plants more than is necessary and use well-drained soil. Also, peas should not be grown continually in the same soil.

Peach

See FRUIT TREES for ideas on a spray schedule.

Insects

Several species of **aphid** occur on peach trees. The black peach aphid lives through the winter on the roots, and migrates to the leaves and tender shoots in spring. The green peach aphid infests a great number of plants, sucking their juices and spreading mosaic, beet yellows, leaf roll, and other virus diseases; the yellow green pests appear as peaches go into bloom. Healthy ladybug populations will keep these and other aphids under control. Failing this, a spray of nicotine and soap will prove effective, according to the Connecticut Agricultural Experiment Station.

The **oriental fruit moth** [color] starts its life of destruction as a larvae tunneling in tender peach shoots early in the season; it later enters the fruit. Those hatching late may go directly to the fruit. This pest is the cause of most wormy peaches. Mature larvae are pink and about ½ inch in length. They are very active, and move about rapidly when disturbed. The first indication of an infestation is the wilting of the terminals of rapidly growing shoots. The wilted tips turn brown in a few days and die. Since the first brood usually confines its feeding to the terminal shoots, it is the later broods that are most harmful to the fruit. This fruit injury is not as easily recognized as twig injury. The worms enter the fruit and feed on the flesh, usually next to the pit. There may be a gummy exudate on the surface of the fruit as evidence. Sometimes the larvae enter through a tiny hole in the stem, leaving no outside evidence of the presence of worms in the fruit.

Peach/Oriental Fruit Moth Damage

It has been determined that survival of the fruit moth larvae is low when fruit of late ripening peaches is not available. This would suggest that if the fruit moth is a consistent pest in your orchard, it would be advisable to grow only those varieties of peaches that ripen early. No fruit will be available to the dangerous later broods, and the pest will not thrive as well. In many areas, control has been achieved by using parasites to eliminate infestation of orchards. Injury is most serious on trees that have made a rank growth, and this condition is to be avoided. Because full-grown larvae may overwinter in cocoons on trash and weeds, it helps to cultivate the soil to a depth of four inches, one to three weeks prior to blooming. Remove culls from the orchard and destroy them. A research bulletin from Rutgers University suggests that a tiny hymenoptera wasp known to parasitize the strawberry leaf roller can aid in the control of the oriental fruit moth as well. To introduce the wasp (*Macrocentrus ancylivorus*) to the orchard, just plant strawberries in or near the peach orchard. But chemicals have interfered with the wasps contribution to biological control. "Large scale colonizations in the peach-growing areas, in combination with native parasites, gave fairly good control until DDT came into use," says Lester Swann in *Beneficial Insects*. H. W. Allen, in a USDA Technical Bulletin (No.

1265, *Parasites of the Oriental Fruit Moth in the Eastern United States*), explains why: "In orchards that have been thoroughly sprayed for control of the oriental fruit moth, few parasites will be found, since the insecticides greatly reduce the number of possible host insects and they also kill parasites moving about over the sprayed trees." Fortunately for the organic grower, "despite heavy spraying in bearing peach orchards, parasites of the oriental fruit moth continue to be abundant and they serve to reduce moth populations in areas that are not sprayed, such as young peach interplanted with truck crops, abandoned peach, or apple orchards." Another piece of good fortune is that DDT has been taken off the market since Swann's book was published, so that *M. ancylivorus* and related wasps may be able to resume their full roles in the orchard.

These wasps don't get a lot of credit for the good work they do, partly because they are so small and some work only at twilight or at night. In size and shape they look something like mosquitoes, and are amber to yellow in color. Altogether, the six known species may often destroy 85 percent or more of the moth larvae, providing the orchard is unsprayed.

Another important parasite is *Trichogramma minutum* Riley, a widely distributed parasite of eggs. In one year, these and other parasites accounted for destroying an average of 32 percent of the moths in six Virginia counties. Even field mice help out, eating cocoons that overwinter on tree trunks. Swann reports in Canada, lacewings have been observed to finish off from 20 to 60 percent of oriental moth eggs.

Of all the beneficials, *M. ancylivorus* has been found to be the most effective, and mass releases of them were used in the forties to control the moth in California. The pest population subsided in time, and H. W. Allen concludes that "mass liberations of *M. ancylivorus* in combination with a reduced number of spray applications were as effective as a larger number of spray applications without the parasites." Swann laments that "today, however, parasites have given way to pesticides, and so far as we know Macrocentrus wasps are no longer being mass produced for commercial use. The oriental fruit moth investigation at the Moorestown [New Jersey] laboratories came to an end in 1958."

The **peach tree borer** [color] is one of the major pests growers have to contend with. The white, 1¼-inch-long larva feeds beneath the bark at or below the surface of the soil, and trees may be partially or completely girdled, with young trees occasionally being killed outright. Productivity is reduced and trees are less

Peach Tree Borer

able to withstand adverse weather conditions and attacks of disease and other insects. Larvae usually complete development in late July or August and go into the pupal or resting stage in the soil nearby. Three weeks later the adult emerges as a blue black, wasplike moth with clear wings. The female has a wide orange band around the body, while the male has several yellow stripes. Egg laying, which begins a day or so after emergence, is done on trunks and branches or on weeds, leaves, and clumps of dirt. The eggs hatch in ten days and the young worms bore into the bark just below the surface, starting the cycle all over again.

Examine each newly bought nursery tree and destroy every borer. When the trees are planted, force a piece of tin into the ground completely encircling each trunk, leaving a space of about two inches between shield and bark. In mid-May, fill this space with tobacco dust. The dust will become soaked by rain and make a potent barrier. Repeat this treatment each May. The tobacco in time becomes humus and will cause no harm to the tree. After examining nursery trees, some growers swab each one, from the roots up to the lowest branches, with Tanglefoot or Stikem. This sticky material will ensnare many moths and larvae before they can do damage. It should be renewed as necessary. By the time the trees are five or six years old, the bark will be so tough that the little worms can do little if any damage.

It often helps to plant garlic cloves close to the tree trunk. A ring of moth balls in the soil will do as well. Nuggets of soft soap can be tied around the tree base and up to the crotch; rains wash it down the trunk and into the ground, and the soapy taste repels both the moth and larva. If you have few trees, and they are under three years old, you might try the time-tested remedy of poking up borer holes with a wire. Do not remove the gummy exudate that forms around the holes, as it serves to seal the injury. Keep all trash and refuse away from the base of trees, and avoid damaging tree bark with cultivators.

The larval **peach twig borer** attacks twigs and occasionally enters the fruit. It can be distinguished from the larva of the oriental fruit moth by its reddish brown color. The larva is less than 1/2 inch long when mature and constructs a loose cocoon under the curled edge of the bark. Ten to twelve days later, the steel gray moth emerges. It has a wingspread of about 1/2 inch. There are four broods each season. The presence of the larva in the twig is made known by the reddish brown masses of chewed bark webbed together in the crotch. Entrance is often through wounds or breaks in the bark. Trees with wide-angled crotches and smooth bark are seldom attacked.

Keep trees in a vigorous growing condition by enriching the soil with liberal amounts of organic matter. Avoid mechanical injuries, as they offer the borer an entrance to the tree.

Follow the controls given for the peach tree borer (above). On the West Coast, where damage may be severe, dormant lime sulfur sprays (mixed 1 to 15) are used. Normally, however, controls aren't necessary.

The **plum curculio** [color] is an important pest, injuring peaches in a number of ways. The adult feeds on fruit and also makes punctures for laying eggs. Feeding punctures on small fruit result in scars known as catfaces. In addition, punctures make an opening for the entry of the causal organism of brown rot. The larvae that develop in small fruit cause it to drop from the tree. In the ripening fruit, larvae generally move to the seed and feed in that area. The damage inflicted is greatly in excess of the amount of peach flesh eaten, since the larvae generally travel around the entire area on at least one side of the peach. At harvest, wormy peaches are generally classified as culls and are practically worthless.

Plum/Plum Curculio

Sanitation is important to control. At harvest time, remove all rotted fruit to the compost heap. Mummies hanging on the trees should be removed before spring. If there are any left on the ground, they should be disposed of before blooming time. It is important to remember that the fungus can survive for years in mummies on the ground and can continue to produce spores. Wild plum thickets, abandoned stone fruit orchards, and fence row seedlings are all a source of mummies that produce brown rot spores in spring, and they must be eliminated from peach-growing areas. See the discussion of brown rot, below.

The larvae are yellowish white, legless grubs with bow-shaped bodies. The only other larva commonly found in peaches is that of the oriental fruit moth, which has true legs. The Arkansas Agricultural Experiment Station recommends a number of cultural controls that, used together, should go a long way towards protecting trees. Jarring trees with padded boards will cause curculios to play dead and drop to the ground, where they can be gathered up in a sheet. Infested fruit normally drop from the tree before larvae have completed their feeding, so drops should be collected and destroyed before the pests leave for the soil. The peaches can best be disposed of by boiling, burning, or soaking in oil.

Pupae usually rest within the top two inches of the soil, and sometimes deeper in periods of drought, and disking during the pupal period will lower pest populations. Cultivation before curculios begin to pupate is of little value, according to an Arkansas Experiment Station Bulletin. If the pupal cell is broken before pupation occurs, another cell is made by the larva. It is best to commence cultivation about three weeks after the infested peaches begin to drop from the tree. Remove any drops from the scene beforehand, as the curculio's chances are actually improved by burying the peaches. Cultivation should continue at weekly intervals for a period of several weeks. Parasites and a fungus help out considerably.

The **shot-hole borer** [color] is a little dark brown beetle that breeds under the bark of peach trees, among others, and emerges through small circular holes resembling shot holes. The larval galleries nearly girdle the stems and branches, and on stone fruits you will notice gum exudating from the exit holes. The adult beetle is about $\frac{1}{10}$ inch long, and appears in early spring. There are usually two generations a year in the northern states. This pest seeks out injured and weakened trees, and it is advisable to keep trees as vigorous as possible.

Other insect pests include red mites (see APPLE), rose chafer (ROSE), and San José scale (APPLE).

Diseases

Bacterial spot [color] is a serious disease caused by minute bacteria that infect leaves, stems, and fruit of peach. It is also a serious disease of plum, and may sometimes affect other fruits. The disease first appears on leaves as small, circular, pale green spots that later turn light brown. The tissue around the spots fades to a light yellow green and soon becomes purplish and angular in shape. Frequently the diseased tissues tear away from the healthy part, leaving the condition known as shot hole. Shedding of infected leaves is common. Often the bacteria exude in sticky droplets on the lower surface of the leaf; this exudate serves to distinguish bacterial spot disease from arsenical injury or other troubles causing spotting and shot-hole on peach leaves.

Bacterial Spot

Bacterial Leaf Spot on Fruit

On peach fruit, bacterial spot disease causes small circular sunken spots, and later cracking, in a variety of patterns. The bacterial spot disease also attacks stems of the current year's growth, causing small elongated cankers. It is important not to accept nursery stock showing cankers of any sort, since they may carry diseases.

Bacterial spot disease is much more dangerous to the peach orchard than is commonly supposed. Leaf infections cause serious shedding or defoliation, which results in serious weakening of the trees, making them unfruitful and more subject to winter injury.

Use healthy, vigorous nursery stock, free from bacterial spot cankers. There is a growing number of good cultivars highly tolerant to the bacterial spot disease. Plant in well-fertilized soil and keep the trees in a vigorous growing condition. Nitrogen fertilization is of great importance in bacterial spot disease control. One of the best ways to enrich the nitrogen content of your soil is to add plenty of compost, especially if manure was one of the compost ingredients.

On fruit, **brown rot** [color] appears as a medium-hard brown rot that spreads rapidly through the fruit. The rotted areas soon develop light gray masses of spores which are readily scattered by wind and rain to cause a rapid spread of the disease. The rotted fruits eventually dry into hard mummies that can carry the fungus over winter and produce spores in spring. If there is warm wet weather at blossom time, the spores from the mummies can cause extensive blossom infection, and from these blossoms the fungus grows back into the twigs to cause shallow cankers that will occasionally girdle and kill the twigs.

Brown Rot

Brown Rot Cankers

As this fungus infects fruit largely through insect injuries, the control program should involve keeping down populations of such insects as the plum curculio and oriental fruit moth (see above).

The peach brown rot fungus has difficulty penetrating the skin of uninjured peaches, but any break in the skin opens the way to infection. All types of mechanical injuries to the fruit should therefore be avoided.

The brown rot fungus grows rapidly at warm summer temperatures and may destroy infected fruit in a relatively short time, especially if the fruit is kept unrefrigerated. When a peach rots in a container, it is relatively easy for the fungus to pass to other fruits in contact with it. Thus, a high percentage of the fruit may be destroyed if peaches are kept for very long at temperatures over 65°F. This is especially true if there has been much rot in the orchard or if the fruit has been roughly handled.

Just a bath of plain hot water has been discovered to be an effective means of preventing brown rot. Placing freshly picked peaches in hot water will kill the fungi causing brown and rhizopus rots—without harming the peach, says Wilson L. Smith of the USDA's Agricultural Marketing Service. Smith gives the peaches a hot water bath just before sending them through the hydrocooler. He explains that it's the heat, not necessarily the water, that eliminates the fungi. He and his group have reduced post-harvest decay by dipping peaches in 120°F. water for seven minutes; in 130°F. water for three minutes; and in 140°F. water for two minutes. They made sure that they were killing the right organisms, too. They inoculated fresh peaches with both brown and rhizopus rots, and then dunked a sample of the inoculated peaches in 120°F. water for seven minutes. After six days in a room maintained at 70°F., only a fourth of the hot water-treated peaches showed traces of rhizopus rot and less than a tenth showed brown rot, while none of the untreated peaches were marketable. Hot water treatment is effective even when you can't give the peaches their bath until 24 hours or more after harvesting, Smith finds.

Recent peach varieties are generally somewhat resistant to brown rot. Check with the local extension agent.

Cytospora canker (known also as peach or perennial canker) is the work of a fungus that attacks the woody parts of stone fruit trees through bark injuries, pruning cuts, and dead buds. A small canker forms at the base of the bud in late winter to late spring. By summer, the canker girdles the twig and the growth beyond it wilts and turns brown. The bark of the dead twig soon becomes peppered with tiny gray black pimples, which are the fruiting bodies of the fungus. The first symptom on limbs is a wilting or yellowing of new shoots and leaves, which later turn brown. The older, visible cankers are oval to linear in outline, and are usually surrounded by a roll of callous tissue. The bark in the center of the canker becomes torn. The lesser peach tree borer often invades the cankers that girdle limbs or trunks. Smooth sections of the bark in the cankered areas become peppered with the pimplelike fruiting bodies of the fungus. During rainy periods, these pimples ooze a white or orange mass of spores, described in a Penn State correspondence course as looking like toothpaste.

Do not set stone fruit trees in soil having poor internal soil drainage. Wet spots should either be avoided altogether or drained. Trees on these sites often suffer cold damage and have a considerable amount of dead wood in them. Because severe infections of canker can provide a source of inoculum for nearby trees, new orchards should not be planted near cankered old ones —especially not on the down-wind side. It is best not to plant on ridge tops, as winter winds can dessicate dormant buds so that they die and provide an entry for disease.

Select stone fruit cultivars that are winter hardy. Attempts to transplant, train, and prune large trees from nurseries often result in canker at an early age. Trees of about $9/16$ inch in diameter provide the potential for branch selection and tree form, without the necessity of making large cuts to balance the tops with the root system. Nitrogen levels and cultivation practices that induce terminal bud set by September allow trees to become cold hardy early in the season. This minimizes the chances of early-winter bud kill, thereby reducing those entry points. Pruning is a necessary operation, but it does create entry points at the cuts and has a dramatic influence on cold hardiness. The operation should be delayed until as near the beginning of bud swell as possible. An unpruned tree is more resistant to injury from sharp drops in temperature, the vast common cause of cold injury. If pruning is delayed until near bud swell, this risk is minimized. After bud swell, the growing tree is more resistant to the disease, even though the fungus may penetrate the bark or pruning cuts. Midsummer topping and hedging with mechanical equipment will avoid danger from pruning. You can paint the trunks and lower scaffold limbs of cold-susceptible cultivars with a white latex paint to moderate the temperatures under the bark and greatly reduce cold injury and cytospora canker in the critical trunk and crotch area of the trees.

Twigs killed by the oriental fruit moth and twig cankers that result from brown rot blighted blossoms or rotted fruit often are entry points for the cytospora canker fungus. Proper attention to the control of these problems will in turn reduce the incidence of cankers; see discussions of this moth and brown rot, above.

Often the importance of **peach blossom blight** [color] is not simply the loss of blossoms, but the fact that the blighted blooms serve as a connection between the overwintering fungus in the mummies and the fruit rotting stage that develops in the last month before harvest. The fungus in peach mummies is active for only a few weeks in spring; consequently, if it were not for the fact that the blighted blooms and twigs continue to produce spores after every wet spell throughout spring and summer, there would be little infection of maturing fruits.

Leaves infected with **peach leaf curl** show symptoms soon after they unfold. They become crinkled or puckered, thicker than normal with a leathery feeling, and light green, yellow, red, or purple in color. The entire leaf or any part of it may be infected. In severe outbreaks of leaf curl, nearly all the leaves on a tree are infected. More often, only the leaves of occasional buds scattered throughout the tree will be diseased. By late spring or early summer, their upper surfaces turn grayish and take on a powdery appearance due to the production of fungus spores. Dry, warm weather soon causes the leaves to turn brown to grayish black and fall from the trees. Infected new shoots grow slower than normal, and are somewhat swollen and pale yellow in color. Severely infected young fruit become misshapen and seldom remain on the tree. Lightly infected fruit mature normally, although they will have one or more wartlike, irregular growths on them. These have no fuzz and are usually reddish in color. They are similar to the irregularities that occur along the suture of some cultivars, such as the Rio Oso Gem peach.

Spray with a three-percent dormant-oil spray. As soon as the new leaves show curling, they should be removed to the compost heap. Remember that fruit trees are more resistant to diseases and pests when they are well fertilized with compost. One organic gardener found that the onion water spray he was using for his aphids also worked for leaf curl. When applied to the affected areas, the leaves revived surprisingly and returned to normal health within a month.

The Penn State University College of Agriculture says that, while peach cultivars vary some in the susceptibility to leaf curl, none of good quality are immune.

When the roots of your trees become infected with tiny galls, **root-knot** has struck. This condition is caused by tiny nematodes. One control is to plant oats as a cover crop in the spring and *Crotalaria spectabilis* in the summer. Where this method was used, nematodes were controlled and tree growth equaled that of trees grown with clean cultivation and trap crops. Trap crops can be used to destroy nematodes. Susceptible cowpeas are planted from time to time, allowed to grow for two or three weeks, and then destroyed by plowing under. Thus the nematodes in the plant roots are destroyed before they develop sufficiently to reproduce.

Experimental tests and farm demonstrations have indicated that nematode injury to peaches can be substantially reduced by use of crop rotations and by planting root-knot resistant stocks. Some crops that can be planted on the land prior to peaches are crotalaria, rye, oats, and Bermuda grass. The following crops, however, are susceptible to root-knot and should not be grown on land before planting peaches: cotton, lupines, clovers, lespedeza, winter peas, vetch, cowpeas, tobacco, and most vegetables. See NEMATODE.

Rusty spot of peach can cause considerable damage to fruit.

The earliest symptoms are small, orange or tan areas. These spots slowly enlarge and develop a fuzzless, smooth center spot that in time turns into a brownish or reddish patch of hard, smooth skin looking somewhat like a bruise from limb rub. Very red varieties may not show injury until after harvest, while fruit that is not highly colored is quite unattractive.

So far as is known, some peach cultivars are not attacked by rusty spot; Triogem is one of these. The following are known to be susceptible to varying degrees: Redhaven, Washington, Loring, Goldeneast, Belle of Georgia, Redskin, Elberta, Jerseyqueen, White Hale, Jefferson, and Rio Oso Gem. The cause of this disease is not known.

Verticillium wilt is a soil-borne fungus disease affecting cherry, peach, nectarine, apricot, and plum trees. The disease first appears as a wilting or drooping of the leaves during midsummer or later. Leaves later may yellow, curl upward along the midrib, and finally drop. These symptoms develop on the older part of the shoot first, and progress toward the youngest growth. A few normal green leaves sometime remain at the tip of the shoot. In the following year, twig dieback may result, and shoot growth on the surviving twigs is shortened. It is somewhat difficult to distinguish verticillium wilt from winter injury (see below). In the case of winter injury, the wood just under the bark of the larger branches is discolored a dark brown, with less streaking of color than found on trees affected by wilt. Also, winter injury is responsible for killing all the tissues of the affected areas, including the inner bark.

The Penn State University College of Agriculture recommends that stone fruits not follow susceptible crops: tomatoes, potatoes, eggplant, peppers, strawberries, raspberries, and such weeds as pigweed, lamb's quarter, horse nettle (nightshade), and ground cherry. Once trees are planted, these susceptible weeds must be kept down. Soils high in organic matter tend to reduce the levels of the fungus, and trees benefitting from proper nutrition have a good chance of recovering from infections. It is fruitless to replace a diseased tree with another tree, as the wilt fungi inhabit the soil.

Winter injury is manifested in a variety of symptoms. Low winter temperatures, especially sudden drops to below-zero temperatures, will kill the fruit buds and late-growing tip growth. In extreme cases, the wood may show an abnormal darkening of the center of the branches, sometimes extending nearly to the last ring of growth. This injury is usually followed by considerable exudation of gum in the following summer.

On peach trees, **X-disease** first makes itself known late in June or early July, when the lower leaves on shoots develop water-soaked areas of various sizes. These leaves soon become blotched with red, and sharp margins develop around the discolored areas. Eventually these areas drop out to give the leaves a tattered appearance. Unlike similar spots caused by nitrogen deficiency and other weaknesses, the margins of the discolored and tattered areas usually cut across lateral veins. The reddened spots caused by nitrogen deficiency typically are exactly halfway between the lateral veins and affected leaves usually persist; but leaves on trees infected with X-disease soon drop, eventually leaving only a small tuft at the extreme tip of affected shoots. In severe cases, sucker growths often develop the same symptoms. See CHERRY for control measures.

Wildlife

Mice may completely girdle peach trees. Aside from the standard tree wound paints, you might try covering wounds with white Karo syrup and then wrapping with aluminum foil. It works, according to Mildred M. Luce of Falmouth, Maine. You can read more about wildlife pests under APPLE and in Chapter 12, "The Good and Bad of Wildlife in the Garden."

Pear

Insects

A simple mechanical barrier will keep many pests of pear from damaging fruit—the paper bag. Just staple small paper bags (sandwich size) around the fruit, and snip off the corners to allow rainwater and moisture to drain out and to encourage ventilation. The bags don't have to be transparent, as the plant makes its food in the leaves.

See FRUIT TREES for a description of an effective spray program.

The **cherry** (or pear) **slug** often defoliates young pear trees. See CHERRY.

Cherry/Cherry (or Pear) Slug

The **codling moth** may injure the fruit of the pear, especially of those varieties that are harvested late in the season. See APPLE for control.

The **fall webworm** [color] forms white webs or nests on the ends of branches. The eggs are laid in white masses of 400 to 500 on the underside of leaves. These hatch in ten days and the larvae from each egg mass leave together as a colony. They feed inside the nest, extending it to include more foliage as needed. When nearly fully grown, the worms leave the nest and crawl about in search of a place to make their gray cocoons. They often select rubbish, fences, and crevices in bark.

The fully grown caterpillar is about 1¼ inches in length, and is marked with a broad, dark brown stripe along the back and yellowish sides thickly peppered with small blackish dots. Each segment is crossed by a row of tubercules bearing rather long, light brown hairs. Keep down infestations by cutting off and burning the nests when they first appear.

Fruit becomes knotty, deformed, and gritty in texture when the **false tarnished plant bug** (also known as pear plant bug and green apple bug) punctures it. The adult looks much like the bona fide tarnished plant bug, although somewhat smaller and paler. The winter is passed by the egg stage in the bark, and the eggs hatch at blossoming time. The nymphs are green at first, and begin to puncture the fruit as soon as it sets. Damage may be serious in some years and trifling in others. If your trees are in trouble, nicotine sulfate may save the season if sprayed just after the blossoms fall. A second application can be made a week later.

Adult beetles of the **New York weevil** sometimes cause severe injury to young pear trees by eating off the leaf buds in early spring. They may also eat the bark of the new growth and cut off the leaf stalks and new shoots. They feed chiefly at night, so you may notice the damage they have done and never see the responsible insect.

The beetle is ash gray in color with spots that are darker, and it is about ⅝ inch long. The only known method of control is handpicking and jarring the insects onto sheets placed under trees, a control also used for the plum curculio.

The unfolding leaves of pear and apple are often disfigured by greenish yellow or reddish blisters that later turn brown. In severe cases the leaves may drop in midsummer. Colonies of microscopic **pear leaf blister mites** live within the tissues of the leaf. They pass the winter beneath bud scales. Control by applying a dormant-oil spray just before the buds open in spring.

In June small pears often drop in great numbers, some of them split open. Open examining them, you may see maggots of the **pear midge.** This midge, looking much like a mosquito, lays its eggs in blossoms. On hatching, the maggots work their way down into the core, gradually hollowing out a large cavity that may occupy the entire interior of the young fruit. The maggots reach maturity in June. The fruit usually cracks open and falls to the ground, and the larvae enter the soil, where they pupate and hibernate.

A strong botanical spray, such as pyrethrum, will offer some control; nicotine sulfate has been mentioned as a high-powered, last-ditch spray.

Pear psylla nymphs are small, dark green creatures that feed on the top side of leaves until only the veins remain. As adults, psylla are small flies, orangish yellow in color, with transparent wings. They hibernate under the edges of rough bark on the trunk and branches, emerge during the first warm days in April, and soon deposit eggs in old leaf scars, in cracks and crevices, and around the base of the terminal buds. Most of these eggs are laid before the buds open, and nearly all have hatched by the time the petals fall. The nymphs go to the axils of the leaf petioles and begin to suck the sap. Much of the sap is excreted as honeydew which drips upon the lower leaves and supports the growth of a black sooty fungus. About a month is required for the complete life cycle and by midsummer a badly infested tree is blackened on leaves and fruit. Some of the leaves will fall before the fruit ripens.

Although they may be killed by dusting limestone over them, the best preventative is a thorough dormant-oil spraying in spring. If the psylla are already established, try syringing the tree with a strong solution of soapsuds. This invariably does the trick. Pear psylla have a good number of natural enemies to contend with. Two small, dark chalcid wasps parasitize psylla nymphs. The parasite pupates within the body of the dead nymph and the adult form emerges through a hole chewed in the abdomen. According to the Washington Agricultural Experiment Station, one of these beneficials, *Trechnites insidiosus,* may parasitize up to 90 percent of the nymphs during July and August in unsprayed orchards. Earlier pest generations are less bothered, however. Pirate bugs are among the most valuable predators, and along with other true bugs can reduce psylla populations to below the level of economic significance. However, these predators, like the wasp parasite, build up in numbers slower than does the psylla in spring and early summer. Other common predators are ladybug larvae and adults, lacewing larvae (or aphid lions), and snake fly larvae and adults. These helpers do best when pest populations are high, as they do not have the searching ability to hunt down scattered psylla.

Pear thrips cause injury to the blossoms of pear and some other fruits. The black adults emerge from the ground in spring, work their way into the swelling buds, and soon lay eggs in the stems and midveins of the unopened buds. The eggs hatch in two weeks and large numbers of the white nymphs feed upon the unfolding buds. Heavily infested orchards appear as if a fire had scorched the trees, and the blossoms are destroyed.

A heavy mulch around trees can prevent the adults from making their way out of the ground. Cultivation may not effect control, as the thrips go as deep as three feet to spend the winter.

San José scale is a small, circular dark gray scale that infests the bark of nearly all kinds of fruit trees and many other trees and shrubs. It hibernates in a half-grown state and there are three broods each season. The largest scales are females, measuring about $\frac{1}{16}$ inch in diameter, and circular with a raised center or nipple. The males are smaller and elongated, with an off-center nipple. This scale does not produce eggs, but gives birth to living young which crawl about for a few hours and then settle upon the bark. The usual control treatment is to spray the dormant trees in spring. See APPLE.

The grub or larva of the **sinuate pear borer** tunnels in the branches to cause ugly scars and some breakage. The adult is a slender, glossy bronze brown beetle, $\frac{1}{3}$ inch long. The females lay eggs in the crevices and under the edges of the bark during June. In early July the eggs hatch and the young grubs excavate narrow sinuous tunnels in the sapwood just beneath the bark. They are partly grown when winter arrives, hibernate in the burrows, and continue their destructive work the following season. The galleries are then larger and their course shows through the bark. By the second September the grubs are about $1\frac{1}{2}$ inches in length. They tunnel deeper into the wood and excavate the pupal chambers in which they hibernate. They pupate the following April and the beetles emerge a month later. Two years are required for the complete life cycle.

Severely injured branches should be cut off and burned, and the trees fertilized and kept in a vigorous condition.

Diseases

Pear blight or fire blight is the most destructive disease of pear in many areas, and is nearly as injurious to certain varieties of apple. Quinces and a number of ornamentals are also affected.

The disease is caused by a bacterium that enters the plant at blossom time through the specialized flower cells that produce nectar. Bees are often responsible for carrying the bacterium about. Once inside the plant, the pathogen can move great distances within living tissue to kill twigs, branches, or even entire trees. A tree may be destroyed by a single infection in one season. Affected blossoms become blackened and shriveled, soon followed by the leaves on the spur. When infected from direct inoculation, terminals and water sprouts usually wilt from the tip downward and the leaves and surface of twig bark become brown to black. Affected leaves tend to persist, frequently remaining attached throughout the winter, and serve to call attention to cankers on the supporting branches.

As the infection progresses into the supporting branches, the bark surface (if smooth) becomes darker than normal. Affected tissues are at first water-soaked, later develop reddish streaks, and finally die and turn brown in color. A milky, sticky ooze containing bacteria may form on any affected part, and will turn brown on exposure to the air. Girdled branches soon die. Fruit becomes sunken and discolored, with necrotic cankers often forming.

Symptoms of fire blight are often confused with those of winter injury. An extension bulletin published by the New York State College of Agriculture, *Fire Blight on Pome Fruits and Its Control,* lists the following differences: 1) dead bark is brown in blight infections and gray mixed with white flecks in winter injury; 2) the wood is more likely to be discolored with winter injury than with blight; 3) winter injury is more likely to extend downward from cuts, to be centered in crotch areas and at the base of the trunk, and to be located in weaker parts of the trees; 4) the bark may become separated from the wood in winter-injured areas; and 5) there is usually an obvious symptom of infection, such as a fruit spur or water sprout, within the blight canker.

According to this publication, "the most important considerations are to prevent sudden increases in nitrogen supply at any time and to prevent late growth." Don't supply more manure than needed. In selecting an area for a planting of pears or susceptible apple varieties, look for fertile, well-drained soil, as tree growth stops earlier in the season on dry soil. Trees should be mulched in late fall or very early spring. Avoid late cultivation; in young orchards, it is best to abandon cultivation altogether in favor of a sod-mulch system of culture using either alfalfa or grass as a cover crop. Grass or alfalfa sod should be mowed early in the season and then allowed to grow in midsummer in order to check late-season growth of the trees. If the weather has been drier than normal, you may have to keep the sod mowed closely throughout the summer, and extreme drought often necessitates disking the soil lightly. The alfalfa mowings should be removed from the orchard or used as mulch around the trees.

Test the soil around pear trees to check for a deficiency of potash, and use lime if necessary to bring the pH up to 5.5 or 5.6. In existing orchards, it may be wise to change to a legume cover crop or sod-mulch type of culture, or a combination of the two.

Dormant sprays will help to keep down numbers of aphids and leafhoppers, two sucking insects that make many inoculations to growing terminals and water sprouts. Because a single site of infection can destroy an entire tree, it is important to cut off infested twigs on the ends of small branches. You should remove at least 12 inches of healthy-looking bark below the lowest evidence of disease to make sure of doing a thorough job. The extent of lesions can be determined on smooth bark by looking for the darker color that is symptomatic of trouble. If there is any doubt, make small cuts with a knife to see if the affected inner bark tissue is water-soaked. The knife should be thoroughly disinfected in a formalin solution between each cut.

The New York State College of Agriculture reports that no pear variety in that state is both desirable for its fruit and resistant to fire blight. The most prized variety for canning, Bartlett, is very susceptible. Other highly susceptible varieties include Beurre, Bosc, Gorham, and Clapp Favorite. Seckel, Kieffer, and Anjou are somewhat less susceptible. The Penn State College of Agriculture says that most of the high-quality varieties commonly grown in that state are very susceptible to fire blight. Bartlett, Bosc, Clapp Favorite, Flemish Beauty, Idaho, Parker, Patton, and Sheldon are listed as most susceptible. Anjou, Comice, Duchess, and Mendel are susceptible, and fairly resistant varieties include Garber, Kieffer, LeConte, Lincoln, Lincoln Coreless, Seckel, Tyson, and Winter Nelis. The Rodale Experimental Farm in eastern Pennsylvania reports success with Kieffer, Bosc, and Seckel pears. The Montana Cooperative Extension Service lists Old Home, Kieffer, Seckel, and Winter Nelis as having some resistance. While not immune to infection, they are much safer than Bartlett, Bosc, Flemish Beauty, and Howell. Louisiana growers are advised by their Agricultural Experiment Station that Pineapple and Richard Peters are the most resistant to blight, but that the former is a poor quality fruit and the latter is good quality but self-sterile and will not set fruit if planted by itself. Other varieties given as being more or less resistant to blight are Ayres, Baldwin, Carnes, Dabney, Douglas (acts as a pollinator for Richard Peters), Garber, Hood, Hoskins, Kieffer, LeConte, Maxine, Mooers, Old Home, and Orient.

Pear scab appears as velvety, olive-green spots on the fruit, becoming black and scabby at maturity. On leaves, the scab makes black spots. The disease is favored by warm, damp weather. Remove any leaves or fruit infected with scab, and keep the area under the tree free of fallen leaves and fruit. Resistant varieties are available and you should check to see which varieties are suited for your growing area. Pennsylvanians are advised by their extension service that Bartlett and Kieffer are partially resistant, while Bosc, Duchess, Seckel, and Flemish Beauty are quite susceptible.

Stony pit, a virus disease, is one of the most common problems for pear growers. The Bosc pear is considered very susceptible and most of the work on stony pit has been done with this variety. Occasionally, however, a Kieffer or Bartlett fruit will be affected. The symptoms appear soon after petal fall; look for dark green areas under the epidermis of the fruit. At maturity, the fruit is pitted, gnarled, and deformed. The flesh becomes woody, or stony, as the name implies. Leaves may show veinlet chlorosis or yellowing. Once a tree becomes infected, it continues to show typical symptoms every year. The only effective control measure is to destroy infected plants.

Pecan

Insects

Many insects, including **aphids** [color], will attack pecan trees if weakened through a lack of water. While pecans will survive in a region that gets 25 inches of rainfall annually, they need 50 inches a year to really thrive. If pecans are grown in a dry western or southwestern state, they must be irrigated. Too much light and superficial watering prevents the tree from establishing and maintaining a deep and healthy root system, making it more susceptible to insect attacks. A deep watering—three to six hours for each tree—is recommended in March or April prior to leafing out, again in late June or early July, a third time a month later, and a fourth in late August. Avoid using a sprinkler that sprays water on the leaves, as this encourages aphids and may lead to mildew. See black pecan aphid photo [color].

The **case-bearer** and the **hickory shuck worm** [color] are two notable pests of pecans. Although they do not bother the tree itself, they may seriously reduce the nut crop. Both insects are controlled by the trichogramma wasp. Release the beneficial's eggs two or three times per growing season, the first time in mid-April, the second about two weeks later, and if it is not an off year and the pecans are setting, set out the eggs a third time after another two weeks. About one package (5,000 wasps) should be used to every three or four trees, unless the trees are widely separated, in which case you should use one package per tree.

Fall webworms [color] can strip and even kill a tree. Check for them after each rainy spell. Twigs bearing clusters of these small, pale green to yellow caterpillars should be pruned and burned. The worm can be identified by a dark stripe running down the back paralleled on either side by a yellow stripe. If clusters of their tiny greenish eggs are noticed on the underside of leaves, pick the leaves and burn them. Clean up debris around trees.

Diseases

Crown gall [color] is a bacterial disease of pecan trees characterized by the presence of wartlike growths on the roots or at the base of the trunk. The galls range from pea-size to several inches in diameter. Trees fail to grow properly and may eventually die.

Once a tree becomes diseased, there is no effective control, although some trees can be saved by removing the large exposed galls. Avoid making plantings in soil where diseased plants have grown. Inspect planting stock carefully and reject plants that have suspicious bumps or swellings near the crown or graft union.

Pecan **dieback** often occurs in areas having hard-pan layers, caliche soils, high salt, or poor drainage. When root growth is restricted to a small planting hole, normal tree growth cannot be expected; trees may make adequate growth for a few years and then began dying back from the tips in later years.

Avoid planting pecan trees in heavy soils with poor drainage. A caliche or hard-pan layer can be detected by digging a hole five to six feet deep; if you don't see such a layer, there should be no problem. Dieback sometimes occurs because of a lack of water during winter months, particularly in light, sandy soils, and can in this case be remedied by regular deep waterings.

Root rot sometimes affects pecan trees in the Southwest. The first symptom is a sudden wilting and drying of foliage. An examination of the roots reveals the rot.

Avoid planting trees on land where other plants have shown symptoms of this fungus disease. Trees can often be saved if half or more of the top growth is pruned when symptoms first appear. Cover the ground with two inches of manure and then water to a depth of three feet or more. Continue to make sure the trees get adequate water.

The symptoms of **sun scald** are dead or cankerous areas on the trunk or upper surfaces of large branches. The unshaded trunks of young trees are especially subject to sun scald. Protect them by wrapping with burlap strips, kraft paper, or aluminum foil. Avoid excess pruning of lower branches of young trees.

Winter injury causes bark to appear sunken and cracked where it meets the growing tissue. Healthy trees in a dormant condition can withstand low temperatures, but if the tree makes excessive growth late into fall, proper hardening of tissues does not take place.

Plants overfed with a high-nitrogen fertilizer, and those receiving heavy early-fall waterings, are most likely to become injured. During September, reduce or halt irrigations until the trees become dormant, at which time they can be watered again to provide a favorable condition for the roots over the winter. Fertilizer applications should be made in winter or early spring; do not use high-nitrogen fertilizers.

Zinc deficiency, causing a condition called rosette, occurs most often in light sandy soils, and also in heavier alkaline soils. Symptoms appear the second or third year after new trees are planted. The first symptom is the appearance of small, narrow leaves that are yellow and mottled. Reddish brown areas or perforations often appear between the veins of older leaves. An excess of small branches form, giving the foliage a rosetted appearance. In the final stages, the shoots die back from the tips. Seriously affected trees rarely bear nuts, and those that do form are small and poorly filled.

To correct this deficiency, see the control for little leaf under APRICOT.

Peony

Insects

Ants on peonies do not signal trouble—they are feeding on the sweet secretion of the flower buds and do no harm.

At least four species of **flower thrips** cause peony and rose buds to turn brown. Adults are typically slender, winged, lemon-yellow to brown, and very active. Larvae are wingless, and lemon-yellow to orange. Thrips can be observed by shaking infested flowers over a sheet of paper. You'll find that they prefer certain colors of flower to others. Heavy infestations are likely to occur on other plants as well, such as Japanese iris, day lily, garden lily, carnation, gladiolus, and rose.

Flower Thrip

Peak activity of this pest occurs in May and June near Washington, D.C., and later in the North and sooner in the South. Late-spring and early-summer flowers can be protected by coarse cloth suspended on a frame. During this time, some growers cut peony and roses in the tight bud stage and bring them indoors to open. Affected buds should be snipped off and destroyed. Later in the season, flower thrips get much competition from their natural enemies, and usually do not cause serious trouble.

Rose chafers feed upon and dirty white flowers; see ROSE.

Rose Chafer

Diseases

Many flower growers run into **botrytis blight.** Flowers are blasted, buds turn dark, and young shoots may be rotted at the base. Snip off all tops at ground level, burn all old stalks in fall, and remove mulch early in spring. If the case is particularly severe, it sometimes helps to replace the top two inches of soil with new soil. These control measures will discourage other diseases as well.

Botrytis Blight

Pepper

Insects

In addition to the remedies discussed below, planting well-known mints and monarda (bee balm, bergamot, and Oswego tea) nearby will help keep many pests away.

Four species of **aphid** are known to infest pepper plants; for control, see APHID.

Young peppers may be protected from the fat, smooth **cutworm** by setting a cardboard collar deep in the soil around each plant. If other controls are needed, see CUTWORM.

Peppers are one of more than 200 crops attacked by the **European corn borer.** This is a flesh-colored caterpillar that grows to one inch in length and has brown spots and a dark brown head. The worm bores into stems, branches of large plants, and fruits, causing the affected peppers to drop. These injuries render

European Corn Borer

plants vulnerable to wilt. Chances of corn borer damage are much greater if corn and pepper are planted adjacent to each other. For control, see CORN.

Pepper maggots infest fruits of pepper plants, causing them to decay or drop. The eggs are deposited in the wall or interior cavity of the fruit, and after hatching the larvae feed inside the core before leaving near the stem and heading for the ground to pupate. *The Gardener's Bug Book* describes the maggots as resembling "sharp-pointed pegs," at first translucent white, and turning yellow as they feed.

You can discourage the adult (a yellow fly with three brown bands across both wings) from depositing its eggs by sprinkling some talc on the fruit. This should be done during the egg-laying period in July and August. If the fly has already gotten to the peppers, remove and destroy those that are damaged.

The **pepper weevil** is a brown or black snout beetle, ⅛ inch long with a brasslike luster. It feeds on foliage, blossom buds, and tender pods. The larval form, a ¼-inch-long white worm with a pale brown head, feeds within buds and pods. Weevil feeding results in misshapen and discolored large pods; in serious cases, buds and pods may drop off plants. They are a pest from Florida and Georgia west to California.

Thorough clean-ups after harvest and rotenone dust in emergencies should handle this weevil.

Potato Flea Beetles

The tiny (¹⁄₁₆-inch-long), black **potato flea beetle** is so-named because it jumps like a flea when disturbed. Another species, the striped flea beetle, is identified by a crooked yellow stripe on each wing cover. See POTATO for means of controlling these pests.

The **serpentine leaf miner** gets its name from the long, winding, white mines it makes in upper leaves. The work of these yellow maggots opens the door to diseases. Natural parasites do much to control miners; pick off any leaves that show mines.

Tomato Hornworm

Two nearly identical twins, the **tomato hornworm** and the **tobacco hornworm,** eat pepper foliage and an occasional fruit. They are light to dark green with white stripes, and can grow to an impressive four inches long. The former has a black horn at its back end, while the latter's horn is red. Both species are often found in the same gardens. Handpicking is a reliable method of control, for the size of a hornworm makes it easy to locate. For other controls, see TOMATO.

Diseases

On either green or ripe pepper fruit, **anthracnose** shows as dark, circular sunken spots that vary in size to more than an inch in diameter. Within these areas are black dots that contain the spores of the fungus. After rain or heavy dew, pinkish masses of spores exude from these dots. Infected fruit may be completely rotted, and either fall from the plants or hang on as withered mummies. On stems and leaves the symptoms are usually so slight that the plant does not appear diseased until fruit develop. Diseased fruit serve as sources of spores that wash and splash around to other fruit; the disease also infects and survives on stems and leaves throughout the season. Areas most likely to have trouble with this disease are the central, southern, and Atlantic coast states.

To control this disease, use clean seed and practice crop rotation on a three-year basis. Avoid touching the plants while they are wet, and keep the pepper and bean plantings separate in the garden, since both vegetables are susceptible to anthracnose.

Bacterial spot [color] occurs in all but semiarid regions. Young leaves develop small yellow green spots; older leaves have larger spots ($\frac{1}{8}$ to $\frac{1}{4}$ inch in diameter) and dead, straw-colored centers with dark margins. The older leaves turn yellow and drop.

Since the bacteria live in the soil, plant seed in new seedbed soil in order to reduce chances of transferring the disease. Generally, soil that has not been grown to peppers or tomatoes for the past three years is satisfactory. See RESISTANT VARIETIES.

Blossom-end rot is a physiological disease that causes light-colored, sunken, water-soaked spots near the blossom end of fruit. The spots enlarge, and a third of the fruit may become dark and shriveled. Fungi can be observed growing over the affected areas.

To prevent blossom-end rot, avoid the excessive use of nitrogenous fertilizer and use ample amounts of ground phosphate rock and ground limestone. Be certain to maintain even soil moisture at all times.

Cercospora leaf spot is a fungal disease that causes water-soaked spots on leaves and stems. As these spots enlarge, they turn white in the center and develop dark margins. Infected leaves often drop, and plants are occasionally seriously damaged. Most harm is done in southeastern and Gulf states. For control measures, see bacterial leaf spot, above.

Mosaic on pepper plants may be caused by any one of several viruses, such as tomato mosaic or cucumber mosaic. The virus overwinters in wild perennial host plants. Peppers set early in the season become severely stunted and develop mottled green and yellow leaves that are often curled; usually, few fruit set. Plants that become infected about blossom time may manifest a slight mottling of terminal leaves, and the fruit are often bumpy and bitter to the taste.

All wild, solanaceous perennials (members of the nightshade family) and wild cucumbers should be eradicated from the garden area, as they serve as host plants. Sunflowers are sometimes grown as a barrier crop to block the pathogen. Try to control aphids, which serve as vectors (see APHID). Do not plant peppers next to tomatoes, cucumbers, tobacco, alfalfa, or clover, and pull up and destroy any plants that show the described symptoms. To prevent mosaic from spreading, spray plants with dry or fresh milk from 24 to 48 hours before transplanting them. The tobacco mosaic virus is often present in manufactured tobacco, and smokers may carry it on their hands; to avoid spreading infection, smokers should wash their hands thoroughly before handling pepper plants. A number of mosaic-resistant varieties are available, including Bellringer, Keystone Resistant Giant, and Yolo Wonder.

Petunia

Insects

The invisibly small **tomato russet mite** causes bronzing or russeting of stem and leaf surfaces. Injury appears suddenly, as mites multiply with great facility. These mites are found throughout the year in California and southern states and are carried to other states on host plants (including tomato and related plants). They are vectors of mosaic. See SPIDER MITES for controls.

Other pests of petunia include the potato flea beetle (shot holes in leaves; see POTATO), tomato hornworm (TOMATO), LYGUS BUGS, MEALYBUGS, six-spotted leafhopper (ASTER), spotted cucumber beetle (CUCUMBER), and yellow woolybear caterpillar (see imported cabbageworm under CABBAGE).

Diseases

Petunia is susceptible to a number of **viruses** that also plague tomato and potato. Symptoms include green mottled areas, crinkled leaves, dwarfed and cupped leaves, and witches' broom effects. Viruses can be spread by mechanical contact, so rogue infected plants and control insects that might serve as vectors. Place petunias at some distance from other solanaceous plants such as tomato, flowering tobacco, potatoes, eggplants, and peppers.

Phlox

Insects

The orange, ¼-inch-long **phlox plant bug** and bright red nymphs feed on the upper side of young leaves of perennial phlox. This leads to yellow, stippled areas, stunted growth, and deformed blossom heads. Seriously affected plants may die. The phlox plant bug chiefly occurs in northern states, wherever phlox is grown locally.

Clean up old phlox stems after frost in fall, and burn them to destroy overwintering eggs.

The most serious animal pest of phlox is the **two-spotted mite.** It infests the underside of leaves, making them turn light yellow, and plants take on a generally unthrifty appearance. Webs may be formed on either side of leaves. See SPIDER MITES.

Occasional pests worth a mention are blister beetles (see ASTER), corn earworm (CHRYSANTHEMUM), flea beetles (POTATO), four-lined plant bug (CHRYSANTHEMUM), NEMATODES, six-spotted leafhopper (ASTER), SPIDER MITES, stalk borer (DAHLIA, ZINNIA), and WIREWORMS.

Two-Spotted
Spider Mite

Diseases

The use of resistant varieties still help to control **powdery mildew,** which appears as a white growth on leaves and stems. Shaded plants with little air circulating about them are especially apt to be damaged.

Pine

Insects

The **European pine shoot moths,** as small larvae or caterpillars, hollow out and kill the tips of new shoots and buds. Look for short dead needles near the apex of the new shoots, with partially developed or hollowed-out buds. Young pines up to 12 feet are most seriously affected and may become stunted and bushy from heavy infestation.

Since the insects winter as pupae in the injured tips, cut off the infested tips and destroy the overwintering pupae before growth starts in spring. In the northern Great Plains and the West, this should be done as soon as the dying needles become evident and before the larvae have left them to pupate in the ground.

The Lake States Forest Experiment Station has found that pruning is an answer in controlling the European pine shoot moth. Snow-depth pruning promotes the insect's winter mortality. In young plantations, many infested tips on low branches may be covered by snow, insulating the overwintering larvae from killing winter temperatures. Pruning off the branches likely to be covered by snow removes this refuge, increasing the insect's winter mortality and reversing upward population trends.

Pine shoot moths have their share of natural enemies, including several spiders. Lester Swann reports in *Beneficial Insects* that, of the many imported parasites that have been released, four species have become established in Canada and three in this country. The number-one imported helper is *Orgilus obscurator,* a braconid wasp.

In Christmas tree plantations, infestations can be controlled by delaying summer pruning until the larvae are either on the twigs or inside the buds. The clippings then should be burned.

Matsucoccus scales live on the bark of pine trees and are very inconspicuous until trees become heavily infested. Severe infestations cause the needles to turn yellow, and cottony masses appear on the underside of branches, especially at branch axils. Pitch pine and red pine are susceptible to these insects, but white pine is not.

As the crawling stage of the scale appears on new growth, spray with lime sulfur if necessary.

The **pales weevil** [color] is a weevil or snout beetle that has a reputation for gnawing the bark from the trunk and twigs of younger seedling pines and from the lower branches of older trees. Young trees are particularly endangered if they have been planted where pine trees have recently been cut.

It is safer to burn the slash and wait two years before planting young trees on the lumbered land. Thinning young pine stands instead of clean-cutting may reduce the hazard of damage. Freshly sawed pine lumber should not be stored near young pine stands because it attracts weevils to the trees.

A variety of **pine beetles** attack all sizes of pines and are especially dangerous following prolonged drought. The adult beetle is short-legged, stout, and about ⅛ inch long; the young beetle is soft and yellow in color, but soon hardens and darkens to a dull, dark brown color. Beetles of overwintering broods emerge and attack trees in spring—about the time the dogwood is in full bloom—although they may be active during prolonged warm periods in winter. They usually attack the mid-trunk first and then work both upward and downward.

The beetles are generally attracted to weakened trees. They bore through the outer bark and construct S-shaped crisscrossing tunnels throughout the inner bark. This boring girdles the tree, and introduces a blue strain fungus that may hasten death. The earliest signs of infestation are numerous white, yellow, or red brown pitch tubes (about as large as a wad of gum) scattered over the outer bark of the tree. Trees show yellowish green foliage from 10 to 14 days after attack. New broods often leave the trees when the foliage is only slightly faded or yellow. When the crown of a tree turns red, the beetles have usually left, except during the winter months. It is therefore necessary to locate red-crowned trees and check for the presence of beetles. If trees are infested, they should be removed before the weather warms up and the beetles emerge to attack other trees.

Keeping pine stands properly thinned and removing damaged, old, or unhealthy trees will help keep beetle damage to a minimum. Trees that are cut can in most cases be sold as sawlogs or pulpwood. Slabs cut from infested trees and bark knocked off in felling trees should be destroyed, preferably by burning.

One of the most important measures for successful control is to make a check of the area. Infested areas should be checked during the summer months for additional infested trees that might have been left. It's important that landowners check the condition of their pine trees for possible beetle attacks. Infested trees can be spotted during winter by the color of their needles. Groups of red and yellowish topped pines are the best indicators of beetle attack. Prompt removal of infested trees helps reduce future population of beetles, and lessens the probability of further attacks of epidemic proportions.

Pine needle scale may become so abundant on the needles that the entire tree takes on a whitened appearance. The scales weaken trees by sucking plant juices and make them more subject to attack from other insects, including borers and bark beetles. Pine needle scales are usually white and elongate, the females averaging ⅛ inch in length and tapering at one end. The males

Pine Leaf Scale

are narrow and even smaller. The reddish purple eggs overwinter under the shells, and broods hatch in May and July.

Apply a dormant-oil spray, mixed 1 part oil to 15 parts water. If infestations are confined to a branch or two, you should be able to get by with a bit of pruning. Woodpeckers have proven to be an effective natural foe of such beetles. The birds can be lured to plantings of pine with suet and houses built to the proper design.

There are several species of **pine sawflies,** the larvae of which devour the needles and sometimes defoliate trees. The larvae are so tiny that it may take several hundred just to demolish one twig, and they are rarely seen until after the damage is done. See photo of red-headed sawfly [color].

Control of the insect often is accomplished naturally by natural enemies. You can help by raking up plant debris from under the trees, as this area is home to sawfly pupae. Should an infestation become serious, you may need to turn to rotenone.

The **white pine weevil** is a notorious troublemaker in pine trees. It is brownish and mottled with light and dark scales. Although preferring white pine, the weevil also damages jack, red, and Scotch pine, as well as Norway spruce. Luckily, red pine, white spruce, balsam fir, and Douglas fir are virtually immune to this weevil. Usually, the first evidence of damage is tiny drops of resin on the bark, a sign of feeding or egg laying. The feeding larvae usually girdle the terminal, which then withers, bends over, and dies.

The Agricultural Experiment Station of the University of Maine notes that although it rarely kills young trees, the insect deforms and stunts them to produce forked and crooked trunks. Because the weevil attacks the leader or terminal shoot, height growth is retarded. The trees are usually first attacked at a height of three to four feet, and annually thereafter until they reach 25 feet. After the tree reaches a height of 30 feet or so, weevil attacks become less important. These insects invariably seek the tallest, most vigorous trees for feeding and egg laying.

The adult weevil overwinters in litter on the ground and crawls up the tree in the warm days of early spring. They begin to feed on wood tissues or buds, then mate. The female lays from 50 to 150 eggs in holes in the terminal. Both egg laying and feeding cause holes that exude drops of pitch. Upon hatching, yellow grubs group together in bands, and the wilted, bent, infested terminals are easily spotted at this time. The grubs move downward as they mature, emerging as adult beetles in mid-summer. They then cut their way to the outside through the bark and continue feeding on the bud and bark tissue until the onset of cold weather.

Remove and burn tips well below the dead part to prevent emergence of the beetles. The Canadian Department of Forestry has conducted tests that indicate that trees planted in shaded areas are not as attractive to weevils as those in full sun. If you can select a shady site for your pine planting, you will have less trouble from the white pine weevil. Also, varieties having a thicker bark and wider trunk diameter are less susceptible to attack.

Diseases

Pine **dieback** causes stunted tip growth for several years. The needles on the affected branches are short and turn brown prematurely, usually showing small black fruiting bodies at or below the sheath. Control by pruning infected twigs.

Dieback

Needle rust [color] is caused by a fungus that attacks the needles of two- and three-needled pines. Red pine is particularly susceptible. The disease develops in spring as small, cream-colored, baglike pustules on needles. These pustules rupture and orange spores are blown to infect goldenrod and asters. The rust overwinters, and can live indefinitely, in the crowns of these alternate hosts. During summer and autumn, spores from golden-rod and asters in turn infect needles of the pines. This disease may cause needle drop and much damage to older trees. If it is necessary to control the disease near valuable pine plantings, destroy goldenrod and asters in the nearby area.

Needle Rust

White pine blister rust is perhaps the most destructive disease of pines. This is a fungus disease that was brought into this country from Europe on pines that were planted in the north-eastern states early in the century. The disease is now well established in our native white pine forests.

Blister rust is one of those plant diseases that must have an alternate native host plant on which to complete its life cycle—it can't spread directly from tree to tree. In spring, wind-borne spores carry the fungus from diseased pines to the alternate hosts, currant and gooseberry.

The blister rust kills white pines, regardless of size, although the smaller trees die more quickly. Large ones may continue to live 20 years or more after infection. The fungus enters trees through the needles and grows into the bark, where it causes lesions known as cankers. Branches and stems are girdled by these cankers. New infections may occur each year as long as diseased alternate hosts remain nearby, and the trees are gradually killed.

Control by removing gooseberry and currant within 900 feet of white pines and then keeping the area free of such plants.

Pineapple

Insects

The primary insect pest of pineapples is the **pineapple mealybug.** Besides pineapple, this insect infests nutgrass, panic grass, Spanish needle, caladium, avocado, citrus, mulberry, royal palm, hibiscus, mangrove, sugarcane, ferns, and some air plants. Pineapple mealybugs are fleshy, wingless, white or gray insects that are covered with a mealy white, waxy excretion. Often the waxy filaments make a ragged fringe around the body. Adult females may reach a length of $\frac{1}{6}$ inch. They give birth to young that are much smaller but resemble the mother. Large numbers of mealybugs may be found on pineapple leaf bases or stems, near or just below the ground level. They suck the plant juices and produce a type of wilt. Mealybug feeding, in fact, is considered to be the cause of pineapple wilt disease. Wilted plants are stunted and have leaves of red or reddish yellow with light green spots, and show withered, dead, and dying leaf tips. Such plants are unproductive. Sooty mold grows on the liquid excretions of mealybugs and the unsightly presence of this mold on the fruit reduces the market value.

Fire ants feed on the sweet honeydew excreted by pineapple mealybugs and protect the pest colonies. The ants often carry individual mealybugs from wilted plants to healthy, succulent plants, and are thus an important means of spreading both mealybugs and the resultant wilt. Other sources of mealybug infestations are infested grasses or other host plants in fields prepared for new plantings, and infested planting stock used to set the beds.

Control of this mealybug has been made possible biologically by an imported parasite, *Hambletonia pseudococcina*. This tiny wasp stings mealybugs and lays its eggs in them. The progeny develop in the bodies of the mealybugs. Although this parasite is very useful in the control of the mealybug, its effect can be nullified by the use of insecticides. The pineapple farmer should cultivate or disk the soil for several weeks before planting to kill out all grass and weeds that might be host to the pests. They can be swept into a jar containing alcohol. A water spray will knock mealybugs from infested plants. In extreme infestations, a dormant-oil spray may be necessary. In small plantings, you might scatter crushed bone meal around the plants to ward off the ants. See MEALYBUGS.

Mites and red spiders may also bother pineapples. See FIG for control. If red scale is troublesome, follow the methods for control of scales under OLIVE.

Plum

Insects

For an effective spray program, see FRUIT TREES.

A number of species of **aphid** are known to infest plum trees from time to time. See PEACH for control measures.

The **apple maggot** is occasionally found in plums. The Connecticut Agricultural Experiment Station suggests that the best means of control may be to control the pest on nearby apples. See APPLE.

The **European red mite** is sometimes found on plums interplanted with apple trees. See APPLE.

The **plum curculio** [color] is a brown snout beetle, mottled with gray, and distinguished by four humps on its back. It reaches a length of about ¼ inch. Hibernating in woodlands, the beetle appears in the orchard about the time the trees blossom. It feeds on fruit as soon as they reach a diameter of ¼ inch, leaving crescent-shaped cuts in the skin. An egg is laid under each crescent and the resulting grubs feed within the fruit, which usually drops and decays. The grubs leave the drops and pupate in the ground, to emerge as adults about one month later. The adults feed on fruit for a while, and then head to the woods to spend the winter.

Plum/Plum Curculio

As the grubs stay in the drops for a while before burrowing in the ground, you can interrupt their life cycle by gathering up drops daily. Either bury the fruit in a deep hole or in the warm depths of the compost pile. You can take advantage of the curculio's habit of playing possum when frightened by knocking branches with a padded board or pole. They'll fold up their legs and drop to a sheet or tarp on the ground. Chickens, geese, or ducks will help pick them up.

The **San José scale** infests plum, especially the Japanese plum; see APPLE.

The **shot-hole borer** is a bark beetle that occasionally infests plum trees; see PEACH.

Diseases

Bacterial spot of plum is caused by the same organism that attacks peach but the symptoms are likely to be quite different. Infected areas on leaves soon fall out to give a pronounced shot-hole effect. On the fruit, infection shows as purplish black, sunken spots on the green fruit. On a few cultivars, small pitlike spots occur. See PEACH. While there are a number of peach varieties that enjoy some resistance, plums do not fare so well. Some of the very susceptible plum varieties are Abundance, Formosa, Satsuna, and Wickson. Bradsha and President are very resistant, according to the Penn State University College of Agriculture.

Black knot [color] is seen as conspicuous black elongated galls on the twigs and branches. The color is due to a layer of black spore-bearing receptacles on the surface of the gall. Spores from these receptacles are washed onto the new twig growth early in the season, causing new infections that will not be apparent for one or two years. The disease is not harmful to the tree until a gall completely encircles the branch, with consequent girdling and death of the branch beyond the gall. Some of the Connecticut Agriculture Experiment Station's early work on the control of black knot showed that liquid lime sulfur prevented the production of spores on the galls but it was not definitely shown that control resulted. Recent work elsewhere has shown that liquid lime sulfur sprays at the dormant, full-bloom, and shuck-fall periods give satisfactory control. If you have only a few trees, it is probably more satisfactory to cut off and burn the knots, making sure to cut several inches behind the knot to insure against leaving any infected tissue. All wounds should be covered with grafting wax and the knotted tissue removed from the orchard and burned. An additional inspection should be made in April and all newly formed knots removed. Wild plum and cherry trees in the immediate area should be destroyed if they are knotted because they serve as a source of spores for new infections. Plums vary greatly in their resistance to black knot. Among the most susceptible are Blufre, Damson, Shropshire, and Stanley. President is quite resistant.

Plum trees are all susceptible to **heart rot,** a rather general term applied to results of wood-decaying organisms which find entrance to the tree through wounds, such as long stubs left in pruning, bad crotches, or pockets resulting from improperly formed tree tops. When pruning a plum, be very careful to cut all the limbs as short as possible. Stubs left too long to heal over permit the entry of bacteria to the heart wood, and heart rot results.

For other diseases of plum, see PEACH.

Poinsettia

Insects

Kerosene is lethal to the **mealybug.** Dip a small stick wrapped with cotton in alcohol, and touch it to a pest for just an instant. See MEALYBUGS for other controls.

Root aphids cause plants to become weak and stunted, and plants may die in severe cases. You can make it hard for these pests to get to roots by packing the dirt firmly around the plant.

Diseases

Poinsettia scab is especially troublesome on double-red varieties, and is most prevalent in summer. It appears as conspicuous, raised lesions or cankers on the stem or cane. The lesions are usually circular, but in advanced stages they combine to form large, irregular areas. In severe cases, the plant will lose its leaves when the stem is girdled by cankers. Scab infected branches should be pruned and burned as soon as they are noted.

Sometimes plants are attacked by fungi causing both **root** and **stem rot.** Stem rot starts at the ground line and is the most prevalent and troublesome.

Once this disease becomes evident, little can be done to save the plants, so rogue any that are affected. Cuttings taken at the first sign of wilting should be made from the stems. Good soil, plenty of water, good drainage, and plenty of sunshine aid poinsettias in resisting this and other diseases. As an added precaution, you can grow poinsettias in soil where only grasses have grown for five years.

Other diseases, including fungal black root rot, bacterial stem canker, and leaf spot, can be prevented by using cuttings from healthy mother plants and by setting them into sterilized media.

Poplar (Tulip Tree)

Insects

The small **European shot-hole borer** is often a concern to home owners who plant poplars on their property. The adult female is dark brown to black, about $\frac{1}{5}$ inch long; the male is more or less oval and is even smaller. Winter is spent as an adult in wooden tunnels made in the host. Eggs are laid in late spring.

The adult beetles make their entrance holes about the bud scars or some other roughened place. After burrowing into the wood for about $\frac{1}{4}$ inch, they make branched tunnels. At the end of each tunnel they deposit eggs. The larvae do not eat wood themselves but feed on fungus growths that the adults introduce at the time of egg deposition. The blackening of the so-called shot holes is due to fungus discoloration. The tunnels in the wood weaken the tree, causing considerable wind breakage. These tunnels also are excellent places for pathogenic fungi to enter.

It is fairly certain that only trees weakened by drought, winter injury, transplanting, mechanical injuries, and poor growing conditions are attacked. The only means of control is to keep trees in a thrifty growing condition. Prune out and destroy any affected plant parts early in spring.

The large, conspicuous caterpillar of the **polyphemus moth** is occasionally found on poplar. You may actually enjoy the presence of this insect, as it is very beautiful both as a moth and larva. It is seldom of economic importance.

The moths have a wingspread of four to five inches. The wings are pale brown to red with a large pale spot margined with black on each wing. The larvae are about three inches long when fully grown, pale green in color, and have a light yellow oblique line on the side of each abdominal segment. The larvae also are marked by numerous orange and reddish spots on the sides. Hibernation takes place in leaf-covered cocoons attached to the limb of the host. The moths emerge in spring. Defoliation by this insect is not serious, as it seldom occurs in large numbers.

The best control method is by far the easiest. Wait until winter has forced the moth into cocoon hibernation and then handpick and burn the oval, $1\frac{1}{2}$-inch-long cocoons.

The larval **poplar borer** bores into the trunk and branches of poplar, causing blackened and swollen scars. Eggs are laid in slits in the bark during July and August, and the young borers tunnel into the inner bark and sapwood and later work deeper into the wood. They overwinter in galleries. The full-grown grub measures about two inches long. The adult, an ash-gray, yellow-spotted beetle, is 1¼ inches long. Control these pests by injecting nicotine sulfate into their burrows, as described for the locust borer under LOCUST.

The **poplar-and-willow borer** infests and destroys pussy willows and several types of poplars. The adults emerge in mid-summer and lay their eggs in punctures in the bark. The larva is about ½ inch long, white, and legless. The adult is a ⅓-inch-long beetle, colored black with partly white wing covers.

Poplar and Willow Borer Adult

The infested parts of the trees should be cut and burned before the beetles emerge. An oil emulsion may be sprayed or brushed on the infested parts in early spring to kill the larvae.

The **poplar leafhopper** is sometimes abundant on poplars. These tiny insects suck the juices of the plant, thereby weakening it. A pyrethrum spray is effective.

Two types of **scale** are particular pests of poplar trees. One type also infests magnolias; see MAGNOLIA for description and control. The other is the cottony maple scale (see MAPLE).

Diseases

Cytospora canker results from a fungus entering the tree through wounds or weakened twigs. Twigs are killed back to larger branches on the trunk and brownish, circular cankers with sunken bark are formed. During moist weather, yellow to reddish threads of the fungus spores appear from fruiting bodies on diseased bark. Spores are spread to healthy trees by rain, wind, insects, and birds. Lombardy and Simon poplars are susceptible.

Control by keeping trees growing vigorously through the use of organic fertilizer and continued watering. Prune affected limbs and cut out cankers, disinfecting cut surfaces by swabbing with tree paint.

Dothichiza canker is a disease destructive to Simon and Lombardy poplars. Gray to brown irregular spots are formed on leaves and the fungus grows down through the leaf stem to form oval to elongate sunken cankers on twigs. Cankers may appear on larger branches and trunks. Large trees often survive for several years, but they are disfigured by many dead twigs and branches that result from girdling by cankers. All infected trees should be removed and destroyed. Avoid wounds and pruning if at all possible. A dormant spray of lime sulfur has proved an effective control measure.

Leaf rust is a fungus disease that produces yellowish orange pustules on lower leaf surfaces. Hemlock is an alternate host, and poplars should be grown at least 100 yards from these trees.

Leaf spot appears on tulip trees as large, brown, irregular blotches with dark brown borders. To control, compost infected leaves.

Leaf yellowing may occur during hot, dry periods in midsummer. Leaves of recently transplanted or weakened tulip trees may turn yellow and drop prematurely. Small, angular brownish specks often appear between the veins of affected leaves. The yellowing and scorch result when roots fail to supply enough moisture to replace that lost during hot, dry periods. Control by supplying water during dry periods.

Poppy

Insects

Poppies are vulnerable to APHIDS, corn earworm (see CHRYSANTHEMUM), four-lined plant bug (CHRYSANTHE-MUM), LYGUS BUGS, MEALYBUGS, rose chafer (ROSE), and six-spotted leafhopper (ASTER).

Diseases

Bacterial blight is a fairly widespread disease. Infection first shows as water-soaked areas that soon become black and surrounded by a translucent ring. Bacterial exudate may be found on the spots. Plants die when stems are girdled. Rogue infected plants and remember that it is best to plant clean seed in areas that have not hosted this disease.

Potato (See also Sweet Potato)

Insects

As a general rule, both above- and below-ground pests will find potatoes a lot less attractive if onions are growing nearby. The Irish potato is attacked by dozens of insects: below, you will find those that are most likely to cause trouble. Although a particular species may not be described exactly, you should be able to find a similar pest that has similar controls. As an example, the more than two dozen beetles known to attack various parts of the potato plant have in common several reliable controls.

The feeding of **aphids** causes potato foliage to curl and vines to turn brown, and growth is consequently retarded. In cases of severe infestation, plants may die. The potato aphid is pink and green, and usually overwinters on roses. The buckthorn aphid, most important in the Northeast, comes in yellow, green, or black, and overwinters on buckthorn. The green peach aphid is yellow green with three dark lines on its back, and overwinters on peach trees; it is a vector of leaf roll of potatoes (see virus, below). These three species live on their hosts for two or three generations before migrating to potatoes or other herbaceous plants.

Potato/Potato Aphid Damage

Of the several means of controlling aphids, spraying plants with a strong stream of water from a garden hose is particularly effective, especially if done early in the growing season. See APHID and RESISTANT VARIETIES.

Several **blister beetles** attack the potato; the black blister beetle, also known as the old-fashioned potato bug, Yankee bug, and just plain "blister beetle," is representative of the various species. It is a fairly long (up to ¾-inch) and slender beetle, with soft, flexible wing covers. The entire body is black or dark gray, and the covers may be marked with white stripes on the margins. Swarms or colonies of blister beetles may be seen feeding on potato foliage. For a description of habits and control measures, see BEET.

Both the adult and larval form of the **Colorado potato beetle** [color] may defoliate potatoes. They are particularly harmful to home gardeners with small plantings, and are so common that they are often simply called potato bugs. The adult is a yellow beetle with a broad, convex back, and averages ⅜ inch in length. Running down both wing covers are fine black lines, and the thorax is decorated with black spots. The larval form is a hump-backed, dark red grub with two rows of black spots on each side and a black head; the last larval stage is somewhat lighter. This beetle is a pest in all continental states except California and Nevada; the eastern states are particularly vulnerable.

Potato/Colorado Potato Beetle

One of the easiest and most effective means of dodging the Colorado potato beetle is to grow potatoes on top of the ground. Gardeners without much cultivating equipment and those plagued by summer drought will especially benefit from this method. First, drop seed on sod or on a three-foot layer of leaves from the previous fall. (The leaves pack down over the winter and earthworms have a chance to work on them.) Next, cover the garden area with a three-inch layer of straw and drop a cupful of bone meal over each seed. Then add more straw until the entire garden is covered by a 10- or 12-inch layer. Make sure that this covering is uniform, as skins of growing potatoes will turn green if exposed to light. The vines eventually work up through the straw, leaving the bugs behind, and you will begin to notice bulges in the mulch— these are the tubers, growing just beneath their protective cap. Harvesting is easy, and the potatoes are clean and relatively free from insect and scab injury.

A biologist, William J. Yurkiewicz, has found a way to foil the beetle by covering the ground between conventionally planted potatoes. He lays down a one-inch thickness of newspaper mulch and a three-inch blanket of damp, rich compost. For the next six to eight weeks, compost is added wherever soil or newspaper starts to show through. He adds anything available: grass clippings, garden weeds, and pea and bean hulls. Yurkiewicz reports 40 percent fewer larvae than on untreated plants, and the yield from the mulched and composted area was about 25 percent greater. He theorizes that the healthy, treated plants were more readily able to synthesize repellents to reduce the beetle infestation, and that the compost and mulch harbored microorganisms that attacked the pests.

It has been found at the Rodale Experimental Farm that a one-foot layer of hay or straw mulch (preferably the former) will keep the new, adult potato bugs from climbing from the soil to the stems. An Arkansas grower, Mrs. Paul W. Meyer, has noticed the same benefits when using shavings from a hardwood handle mill. At the end of the season, the mulch should be plowed under, thereby enriching the soil with valuable organic matter and giving it better structure.

In addition to deciding what cultural methods to employ, consider interplanting potatoes with one or more of these beetle repellents: flax, horseradish, garlic, marigolds, eggplant, and green or bush (snap) beans. A Washington State gardener, James D. Bowen, M.D., describes the advantages of letting one weed go unmolested in the garden—nightshade. "Hordes of potato bugs on my new garden eagerly sought out the nightshade plants and gorged themselves to death. Some were lying dead in a pile under the nightshade plants. Both adults and larvae had been destroyed by their obsession for nightshade." Dr. Bowen says that this weed has helped commercial growers produce excellent crops of unsprayed potatoes.

When the potato beetle strikes, handpicking of the adults and crushing of the yellow eggs (found on the underside of leaves) work well. A clever method devised by gardeners makes use of the beetle's gluttony. The tops of wet potato plants are dusted with wheat bran which, when eaten, causes the beetle to bloat up and rupture. Other gardeners put their faith in a spray made from the extracts of common basil or sweet basil. A simple trap may be made by folding a colored plastic sheet twice, and placing it under the plants every three days or so. Shake off the collected insects into a bucket of water. Lastly, you can take confidence in knowing that toads eat a good number of these pests, and that ladybugs can be purchased and introduced to the garden to keep the beetle population low.

Natural enemies finish off a good share of the beetles. A bacterial disease known as potato-beetle septicemia causes the pest to slow down, cease feeding, and turn to a brownish gray and finally to nearly black. A fungus, *Beauveria bassiana,* hits a number of well-known pests, the Colorado potato beetle among them. Nematodes attack adults hibernating in the soil. See RESISTANT VARIETIES.

Cutworm

New growth and young tubers provide meals for several species of **cutworm.** These soft-bodied, smooth caterpillars are familiar to most gardeners; they grow up to 1¼ inches long, may be brown, gray, or black, and have the habit of curling up tightly when disturbed. See TOMATO for further control methods.

European Corn Borer

The larva of the **European corn borer** tunnels into potato stalks, and these openings enable disease to infect the plants. This is a flesh-colored caterpillar that grows up to an inch long and is distinguished by brown spots and a brown head. A number of applicable controls for the borer are discussed under CORN.

Several species of **flea beetle** nibble on potato foliage from the underside, leaving behind a shot-hole pattern. Color and pattern vary, but all are very small and jump around like fleas when disturbed. Great numbers of them may infest a single plant.

Flea Beetle

Because flea beetle eggs are deposited in the soil, your control program should include frequent cultivation. Keep the garden area free from trash in order to discourage these insects from settling near your plot for the winter. Weeds should be cleared out as well, as they provide food for both adults and larvae. By planting seed thickly and thinning after the danger of infestation is past (flea beetle damage is greatest early in the growing season), you should be able to grow full rows of vege-

Potato/Flea Beetles

tables—this is because these insects shy away from shade. Some gardeners get good results by interplanting potatoes and other susceptible crops near shade-giving crops. Wood ashes repel flea beetles, and can be used in two ways: either place a mixture of equal parts of ashes and agricultural lime in small containers around the plants, or simply sprinkle a spoonful of ashes on each plant two or three times a week. You should get excellent results with a spray made from garlic. Bulbs or whole garlic plants are minced in an electric blender with a cup of water, and the resulting brew is strained, diluted, and sprayed on the vines. Within half an hour, the flea beetles should be on their way.

The **garden symphilid,** also known as the garden centipede, is a white, fragile insect that grows up to ⅜ inch long. It is not actually a centipede, but is quite similar in appearance. Adults have 12 pairs of legs, while the young have fewer. This pest travels rapidly through tiny cracks in the soil, constantly waving its antennae, and is rarely seen above ground. It feeds on rootlets and root hairs, and its presence may first be made known by stunted growth. For methods of control, see GARDEN SYMPHI-LID.

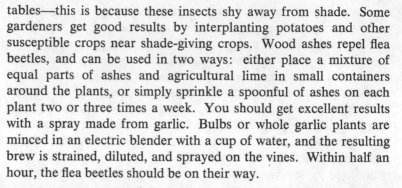

Grasshopper

Many species of **grasshopper** feed on potato plants, and large infestations may destroy complete plantings. Both adults and nymphs cause trouble, and they may be brown, gray, black, or yellow. Grasshoppers do their worst in the central and northwestern states. See GRASSHOPPER.

The **nematode** is a tiny creature that lives in the soil, feeding on the below-ground parts of plants; some are so miniscule as to be invisible to the gardener's eye. Symptoms of nematode damage are poor growth, yellowing of foliage, and wilting followed by recovery as a hot day turns into a cool evening. These worms also cause root-knot (or nematode gall). See below for a discussion of the symptoms of and controls for root-knot.

Potato Leafhopper

The **potato leafhopper** (called the bean jassid in the South) is a small, wedge-shaped, green leafhopper; the corresponding western species is the western potato leafhopper. Look for white spots on its head and thorax. The adults grow up to ⅛ inch long, and will fly away rapidly if disturbed. The nymphs resemble the adults, but are smaller and have the unusual habit of crawling sideways like crabs. Leafhoppers, both mature and immature, cause a blightlike condition known as hopperburn in which the tips and sides of the potato leaves curl upward, turn yellow or brown, and become brittle. As a result, the food-making capacity of the plant is impaired and yields are lower.

Because the leafhopper seems to prefer open areas, it may help to plant potatoes in a sheltered area. If this is not practical, you can keep away the egg-laying adults with canopies of cheesecloth, muslin, or plastic netting. The crucial period for this protection is about one month, beginning when the plants are a few inches high. During this time, the beetles attempt to lay their eggs in main veins or in petioles on the underside of leaves. A research team at Purdue University found that 15-watt blacklight fluorescent lamps can be used to attract potato leafhoppers to a trap. Sequoia is a variety resistant to both the leafhopper and the potato flea beetle; it is, however, quite susceptible to aphid damage. See RESISTANT VARIETIES.

The tiny **potato psyllid** (also known as the tomato psyllid) grows to no more than $\frac{1}{10}$ inch long. The newly hatched insect is green, but within two or three days it turns black with white markings, giving it a grayish appearance. Psyllids are occasionally called jumping plant lice because of their resemblance to species of plant lice (aphids). Your real enemy is the nymphal form, which is pale green, flat, scalelike, and has a fringe of tiny hairs. As it feeds, the nymph injects a substance, perhaps a virus, that disturbs proper plant growth. Short sprouts appear from the eyes of undersized and immature tubers, and new tubers may form on the sprouts. Eventually a chain of several deformed tubers may occur on one stolon, none of which is of marketable size. Leaves may be discolored yellow or reddish, or turn brown and die. These conditions are known collectively as psyllid yellows. Early crops are usually more susceptible to severe injury.

Chances of a psyllid infestation are lowered by eliminating winter hosts, especially matrimony vine (lycium). Clear the garden of any discarded sprouting potatoes. Parasites and predators have some effect on keeping the psyllid in check; both larval and adult ladybugs prey on psyllid nymphs.

The **potato tuberworm** is a pinkish white worm with a brown head that grows up to $\frac{1}{2}$ inch long. It tunnels in the stems, leaves, and tubers of potatoes, causing shoots to wilt and die. Local infestations of this pest are found in the South and west to California. Growers outside this area may find an occasional tuberworm at work, but control should not be necessary.

Potato Tuberworm

Discourage the tuberworm by keeping the garden clear of weeds and culls, and by making sure that potato plants are deeply hilled with soil. The tuber moth may lay its eggs in the eyes of potato tubers, and newly dug potatoes should therefore not be left exposed late in the day or overnight. You can interrupt this pest's life cycle by clipping off and destroying any affected vines.

Several species of **white-fringed beetle** attack the roots of potatoes, and may be found throughout the southeastern United States; infestations are localized. The adults are dark gray snout beetles, ½ inch long, and decorated with a light band along each side. They are covered with short hairs, and are unable to fly because the wing covers are fused together. They are not picky eaters, nibbling on almost anything in their path, but it is the yellowish white, fleshy larvae that cause growers the most concern. The worms eat roots and tubers, causing plants to yellow, wilt, and die.

If white-fringed beetles have invaded your area, deep cultivation in the early spring may keep the adults from appearing in May. The larvae overwinter in the soil, usually not lower than nine inches.

White grubs may devour the roots and tubers of potatoes. They are white to pale yellow, have hard, brown heads, and measure up to 1½ inches in length. The adult form is the familiar dark brown May beetle, or June bug, which may also damage potatoes by feeding on foliage. For control measures, see JAPANESE BEETLE.

Wireworm

Many species of **wireworm** attack vegetables throughout the United States, and potatoes are one of the most vulnerable crops. The worms are wirelike and white at first, turning brown as they grow to their full length of ½ to ¾ inch. Potatoes are damaged when wireworms feed on tubers; the appearance is marred and this means that parts of the potato have to be cut away before cooking. On a large scale, lots containing badly damaged tubers either are downgraded and sold at reduced prices or are made eligible for top grades by discarding a number of the damaged tubers. Most injury occurs as the potatoes approach maturity. Generally, the earlier the injury, the deeper the holes will be at harvest. The adult wireworm is a ¼-inch-long click beetle. When placed on its back, the beetle flips to its feet with a sharp click. They are also known as skipjacks. Millipedes are sometimes confused with wireworms; while millipedes have many pairs of legs over the length of their bodies, wireworms have but three pairs of legs positioned well forward. Also, millipedes characteristically curl up into a loose spiral position when disturbed, and wireworms do not.

If wireworms are a problem, you may benefit from learning to identify a few of the more important species, as controls vary. The eastern field wireworm confronts gardeners and farmers in the East, especially attacking potatoes that have been continuously planted on light, sandy soil. Continued cultivation seems to *encourage* this pest. If you discover that a field is infested after plant growth has begun, harvesting should be as early as possible to avoid further damage. According to the Connecticut Agricultural Experiment Station, two species are apt to damage crops that follow sod. The wheat wireworm is found in the eastern and central states, is yellowish brown as a beetle and bright yellow as a larva, and has two eyelike spots on the ninth, or posterior, body segment. It most often occurs in heavy loam soil that retains moisture. The corn wireworm (also known as the community wireworm) is restricted to the eastern half of the continent, also occurs in heavy soil, is reddish brown as an adult, and the larva may be distinguished from that of the wheat wireworm by a reddish brown rear segment. Both wheat and corn wireworm populations will *decrease* with continued cultivation. See WIREWORM.

Diseases

You can help to keep potatoes free from disease by rotating annually in loamy, well-drained soil. Potatoes do poorly in an alkaline medium, and need an acidic soil with a pH factor of between 5 and 6.5. Don't plant where wood ashes or lime have been scattered, as these will make the soil too acidic.

The first symptoms of **blackleg** are the rolling of the upper leaves of one or more shoots and the gradual fading of the foliage to yellow green. Plants eventually turn a distinct yellow color, and gradually die as the bases of stems are rotted away by the causal bacteria. Presence of blackleg is easily confirmed in the field by pulling affected stems; they will snap off with little resistance. Stems at the soil line become slimy and black, and tubers are decayed. Blackleg is favored by abnormally rainy seasons.

Black Leg

To control this disease, plant only tubers from disease-free fields, use sound seed that has healed well after cutting, and provide well-drained soil. Cut seed can be healed by keeping them at 60° to 70°F. and approximately 85 percent relative humidity, with adequate ventilation, for about a week.

Common scab is known to exist in every potato-growing section of the United States. It is caused by a fungus that develops readily in soil having slightly less than the optimum amount of moisture for growing potatoes. If the soil is of such a texture that there is abundant aeration, scab may spread quickly even though the soil is wet. The scabs vary from a minor russeting of the tuber skin to very rough, corky areas that may be raised or pitted. The spots may be single, or several may join together to cover large areas. Scab is particularly severe in neutral or alkaline soils, causing little damage in an acid soil with a pH of 5.2 or less, and it is usually worse in dry than in moist soil.

Common scab of potato can be successfully controlled with green manuring. You should avoid using lime, wood ashes, or fresh barnyard manure on infested soil, as these will increase the alkalinity. If liming is unavoidable, it should be done in fall after harvest, and the amount of lime should be determined by soil analysis. Farmers have found that if soybeans are grown on infested soil and then turned under, two desirable things take place: the soil becomes more acidic, and beneficial bacterium and fungi that compete with scab are encouraged by the rapidly decaying organic matter. (It is thought that good, organically fertilized soil may enable these beneficial organisms to discharge antibiotics which overcome scab and other diseases.) Rotations with nonsusceptible crops such as rye, alfalfa, and soybeans may reduce the incidence of scab, but the length of time between potato crops is just as important as the crop selected for the interim period: you should wait from three to five years before again planting potatoes.

The best way to avoid problems with common scab is the use of resistant varieties; although no variety is truly immune to attack, the following should do well for you: Cayuga, Cherokee, Early Gem, Menominee, Ontario, and Seneca are recommended by the USDA, and the Canada Department of Agriculture suggests Cinook, Huron, Avon, Sable, Cariboo, Cherokee, Norland, and Netted Gem.

Early blight, also known as leaf spot, causes brown spots on leaves which, as they enlarge, develop concentric rings with a targetlike effect. When the spots are numerous, they can kill the leaves and thereby serve to reduce the yield of potatoes. The fungus later spreads to tubers, causing shallow decay in the form of small, shallow, roughly circular lesions that are surrounded by slightly puckered skin. These lesions may afford an entrance for saprophytic molds that complete the rotting of the tuber. Early blight fungus spreads rapidly in warm spells.

Since the fungus may be present in tubers, be sure to plant clean tubers. Early blight may also be present in the soil, and the

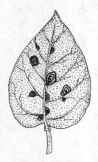

Early Blight

use of well-composted humus in the potato patch will help to insure plants against infection.

Large, overgrown potatoes are apt to have an **environmental condition** known as hollow-heart; this is not a disease, but the result of the tuber having grown too large, too fast. Another defect not caused by a pathogen is blackheart, brought about by insufficient oxygen in the center of the tuber as a result of too much heat in storage. Erratic growing conditions may cause strangely shaped tubers and growth cracks; jelly-end rot may appear at the tips of off-shape tubers. Enlarged lenticels (pores) are caused by excessive soil moisture before harvest.

Speckle leaf is a recently recognized environmental disease that leads to early-maturing Irish potatoes having extremely small tubers. Leaflets develop sunken areas on the underside, eventually showing on the upper surface as a dark speckling. R. E. Baldwin of the Virginia Truck and Ornamental Research Station reports that the cause of this disease is excessive ozone in the atmosphere. The best way to get around the trouble is to select varieties that appear to be tolerant. Another important consideration, says Baldwin, is the vigor of the plant. "A vigorously growing plant will be able to withstand a greater stress than a weak one. Therefore, it is important that satisfactory soil pH and high fertility be maintained."

Late blight is so called because it attacks plants after the blossoming stage. This fungal disease is most common in the northcentral, northeastern, and Atlantic states. Look for purplish or brownish black areas on the blade of the leaflet or the leaf stalk, flower pedicel, or stem. Usually the lower leaves are the first to be affected. The diseased areas have a water-soaked zone about their margin, indicating the location of the advancing fungus. The recently invaded area becomes lighter colored than the normal green of the leaf, appearing as a light-colored halo about the blackened area, and in turn it blackens and dies. Under favorable warm and moist conditions, the disease spreads rapidly, with the result that all the plants in the field may be killed within a few days. The diseased and decaying tissues give off a characteristic odor that becomes very pronounced in fields that are severely attacked.

Late Blight

The spores of late blight begin to multiply on the underside of infected leaves. Then they are blown by the wind or splashed by the rain to infect nearby plants. Winds can carry late blight spores several miles. The spores can also be moved from one field to another by running water in small streams or drainage ditches.

Cool, moist nights encourage blight spores to form and germinate, which means that blight infection will build up rapidly. To get started, late blight needs a period of at least ten hours of temperatures below 70°F. and humidity about 91 percent. But a warm, humid period followed by a drop to about 60° is very apt to start an attack. Once late blight has gained a foothold, warmer day temperatures will make it grow rapidly on potato and tomato plants.

If late blight has been particularly prevalent in the field late in the season, it is much better to delay digging the potatoes until two weeks after the potato tops are dead, preferably until after a frost has killed the vines. This delay is necessary to allow the numerous spores on the old dead plants and on the surface of the soil to die before the potatoes are dug. Without this two weeks' delay, a large number of the potatoes will become infected by the living spores with which they come in contact during the digging process. The Canadian Department of Agriculture says that tops may also be removed by hand, two weeks before harvesting.

Make sure that potato dumps or cull piles do not begin to sprout. This is very important, because blight can't start in your crop unless there is an infection present and unless conditions are favorable. Don't feel safe in dumping cull potatoes in a nearby field, for wind and water can carry spores a great distance. The disease may be rendered harmless by baking the potatoes—place the tubers in thin layers in combustible material and set the pile on fire. If it is absolutely necessary to dump potatoes on top of the ground, spread them in a thin layer so that all the tubers will freeze solid. Remember that any volunteer potato plant may be a source of infection. Late blight can be carried in the seed you plant, so don't use seed potatoes known to be infected from late blight or those that come from fields where there was late blight infection last year. If possible, see that potatoes go into storage dry and free from dirt. Clean out and disinfect the storage cellars. They should be ventilated so that there will be no condensation of moisture on the tubers or on the ceiling to drop on tubers in bins below; it's best to introduce air into cellars near the floor. Keep the cellar roof in good repair.

There are several good blight-resistant varieties available. If late blight is a problem, try one of the following: Ona, Sebago, Kennebec, Saco, Pungo, or Essex.

The most characteristic symptom of **leak** is the extremely watery nature of the affected tissues. The water is usually held by the disintegrated tissues, but when pressure is applied a yellowish to brown liquid is given off readily. Another characteristic symptom is the granular nature of the affected tissues.

Externally, the affected tissues appear turgid and may show discoloration ranging from a metallic gray (in the red varieties) to brown shades (in the white and dark-skinned varieties). Internally, the affected tissues are at first a creamy color. Later they turn to slightly reddish, tan, brown, and finally inky black. The diseased areas are generally sharply set off from the healthy areas, yet rarely is there a discernible fungus growth, either internally or externally.

Tubers become contaminated in the field, where the organisms live as soil fungi. Infection takes place in hot weather and apparently gains access to the plant only through the wounds, although these need not be visible. Leak frequently is found in tubers affected with sunburn or sunscald, especially when these occur in tubers allowed to lie in or on hot soils after being dug. In potato crops that are harvested and moved during extremely hot weather, leak may be serious, but careful handling of the crop can eliminate this possibility.

Control involves keeping tubers as cool and dry as possible during harvesting and loading, as well as in the early stages of transit and storage. Be certain to avoid injury to the skin.

Several viruses are responsible for **mosaic** in potatoes, a disease that causes a mottled, light and dark green pattern on curled or crinkled leaves. Brown specks may appear on the tubers and the plants often become yellow, droop, and die prematurely. In northern regions, hot and dry weather may subdue these symptoms and make the disease hard to detect. Nevertheless, these plants or their progeny will show the mottled symptoms if again placed under conditions favorable for development of the disease.

To keep mosaic in check, be certain to plant clean tubers and to use seed that is certified disease-free. The following varieties have been found not to contract the disease in the field, and although some of them have become infected through grafting, they are resistant for all practical purposes: Ona, Penobscot, Cherokee, Chippewa, Katahdin, Kennebec, Pungo, Saco, Sebago, Houma, and Earlaine.

Rhizoctonia, or black scurf, is a fungal disease that first makes its presence known by dark brown cankers that "burn off" tender young sprouts. These cankers may also girdle the sprouts below their growing tips. Once growth is arrested in this manner, new sprouts appear below the dead areas, and these too may be killed; this process forms a rosette of branching sprouts. A later symptom is brown, sunken dead areas on mature stalks near the soil line. These cankers interfere with the distribution of nutrients in the plant, causing leaves to wilt and impairing development of tubers. In warm, moist conditions, a grayish white collar of fungus growth may form on the stem just above the soil line. Hard, black bodies (black scurf) are evident on the tubers, especially after they have been washed. These structures, called sclerotia, are the resting bodies of the fungus. Rhizoctonia may also cause the tuber skin to be roughened in a criss-cross pattern, a condition often referred to as russet scab. Both scurf and russeting reduce the value of tubers as table stock.

The New York State College of Agriculture has come up with several ways in which you can minimize the danger of rhizoctonia. First, plant clean certified seed that is as free as possible from sclerotia. If possible, grow potatoes once in every three to five years, rotating with corn and cereal grains, as these crops aren't susceptible to the same strain of fungus. The college points out that this practice will not eradicate the fungus since it can live almost indefinitely in the soil, but the fungus population will be reduced. If conditions are wet and cold, growers are advised to either plant shallow or plant deep and cover with a thin layer of soil. The rationale behind this is that rapid initial growth of the sprouts is encouraged, giving them a good head start on the disease. Finally, avoid planting in heavy, poorly drained soils, and delay planting until warm weather, if possible.

Ring rot, or bacterial ring rot, is an extremely infectious disease caused by a bacteria that overwinters in slightly affected tubers. The disease cannot be detected in many of these tubers, and yet they contain sufficient bacteria to contaminate the knife and planter, and these then inoculate healthy sets. Symptoms on plants do not become evident until late in the growing season, and some plants can be generally affected and show no visible signs above ground; in other cases one or more stems in a hill may wilt and become stunted, while the remainder of the plant stays healthy. When affected plants are dug up you can usually find all gradations of the disease, from healthy to completely decayed tubers. The decay begins in the vascular ring, which is located about ⅛ inch beneath the skin of the tuber. If the tuber is squeezed by hand, a yellowish white ooze may appear in cheesy ribbons. The interior of the tuber eventually rots, leaving a shell of firm tissue.

Ring Rot

You can prevent bacterial ring rot by the exclusive use of disease-free stock. This disease increases very rapidly, and experiments have shown that a crop having a mere trace of the disease may lose from 10 to 30 percent the next year. Because cutting and handling freshly dug seed potatoes can serve to spread the disease, the use of whole tubers is good practice. Store seed tubers in clean sacks, and containers and implements should be thoroughly disinfected if ring rot has previously been a problem.

Root-knot, or nematode gall, is a condition in which galls are produced on tubers and roots by the parasitic action of nematodes (eelworms). The galls vary in size and are more or less round, but they frequently run together to give the tuber a grotesque, knobby appearance. Nematodes are transmitted from field to field by running water, in soil clinging to implements, and on the hoofs of animals and the feet of people.

No potatoes from a field known to be infested should ever be used for seed. A mere visual inspection of tubers may lead you to believe that they are healthy, but light infection can go unnoticed. For a number of control measures, see NEMATODE.

Stem decay, caused by bacteria and fungi, affects damaged, above-ground stems, especially in wet weather. The shoot above the decay wilts and dies. Since the disease organisms gain access through insect and machine injuries, infection is reduced as pest populations decline. Be sure not to give plants more water than they need.

Verticillium wilt is evident late in the season, when the older, lower leaves become yellow and die. There may be some curling and rolling of the leaflets and instances of tip-burning. Affected vines die prematurely, but the denuded stalk remains upright, looking like a pole with a flag of wilted upper leaves. The disease works its way up from the base until there is often only a small cluster of leaves at the top. The inside of the stem is invariably discolored a yellow or brown, from the base well up into the top of the plant. The tubers often show a "pink eye" discoloration. A somewhat similar disease, fusarium wilt, produces a burning, bronzing, and slight yellowing of upper leaflets, and leaves eventually wilt and die. Stems of affected plants show a brownish flecking when cut longitudinally.

Verticillium Wilt

Wilt is best controlled by seed selection and an extended (four-year) crop rotation, as the disease carries over from one crop to another in seed potatoes and in the soil. The seed plot offers a good chance for roguing out affected seedlings before they can do much harm. To be safe, also take out and destroy the plants adjacent to the sick ones. Varieties resistant to wilt include Pontiac, Ona, Shoshoni, Katahdin, and Green Mountain.

Potatoes may be injured by a number of **viruses.** Symptoms include mosaic or leaf distortion and mottling, leaf roll, yellow and purple top, and "spindle tubers." In the field, viruses are usually carried about by insects, especially aphids and leafhoppers. Use clean seed, and keep these two pests from getting an early start in the garden. Walter Carter suggests in *Insects in Relation to Plant Disease* that early harvest of seed potatoes in Maine substantially reduces leaf roll, mosaic, and spindle-tuber infection.

Praying Mantis

There are about 20 species of praying mantises [color] now established in this country, some having been brought over from Europe and China, and all play a similar biological role as destroyers of other insects. Mantises are also cannibalistic. The female often devours the male after mating, and newly hatched youngsters may feed on their siblings.

Praying Mantis

The eggs are laid in large foamlike, straw-colored masses in fall. In May and June little mantises hatch out, resembling their parents except for the absence of wings. They grow slowly, reaching maturity sometime in August. In the northern states, mantises only live a single summer, the onset of cold weather marking the end of their lives. In the deep South they may enter a quiet interval, known as diapause, during extremely dry weather.

You should have little trouble introducing praying mantises to the garden, but there's no guarantee that they will stay put. Enough hatch from a single egg case, however (anywhere from 100 to 300 or more), that several cases stocked in strategic spots around the yard will provide enough for both you and the neighbors as well. Insects, like all animals, have a tendency to go where food is plentiful. If your garden develops a sudden outbreak of pests late in the season, the local mantises will usually be back to feed on them.

The first food of the newly hatched, wingless predators is probably aphids and other small, slow-moving prey. As they molt and grow, mantises can handle larger food, up to an occasional salamander, shrew, or even a small toad or frog. No matter what the victim, the praying mantis always begins its meal in the same way—by biting into the back of the neck, apparently to sever the main nerves and render the animal helpless.

There are several commercial sources of praying mantis egg cases in the United States; see Appendix 1. But anyone with an observant eye should be able to gather an ample supply of egg cases from late fall into early spring. Look for them wherever plants grow in clumps a few feet high. Goldenrod clusters, hedgerows between fields, and roadside borders may all yield egg cases for your garden. When gathering your own cases, leave them attached to a section of twig. They can then either be stored in the refrigerator or, better yet, immediately placed in the garden area.

Place the egg cases off the ground so that they aren't soaked by spring rains or gnawed upon by hungry field mice. Lash the egg-bearing sticks to plant branches or to three-foot sticks set firmly in the ground. If you store the cases over winter, keep them cold. More than one schoolchild has found that a dormant egg case can fill a warm bedroom full of tiny mantises. So, keep them in the refrigerator or outdoors. They're very winter hardy, able to stand sub-freezing temperatures. How many cases are needed for adequate protection? A general rule is one egg case for each major shrub or tree, and four cases per quarter-acre without shrubbery. It should be noted that egg cases can be sent by mail only during the dormant period—approximately November 1 to May 15. Since the mantis is recognized as a beneficial insect, there are no restrictions on its eggs being sent through the mails and it is exempt from insect control laws.

Primrose

Insects

The feeding of **foliar nematodes** causes stunting of both crown and buds, and leaves are curled and distorted. Rogue diseased plants and change the surrounding soil.

You may also encounter APHIDS, flea beetles (see POTATO), the fuller rose beetle (ROSE), MEALYBUGS, SPIDER MITES, and WHITE FLIES.

Diseases

Several of the most common diseases of primrose can be prevented or reduced by picking and destroying sickly leaves and by a thorough clean-up in spring.

Privet

Insects

The **privet mite** causes privet leaves to yellow or fade. The mites feed on the underside of leaves, sucking plant juices and causing the foliage to drop in severe cases. The orange or red mites are nearly too small to be seen with the naked eye, being only $\frac{1}{100}$ inch long. In serious cases, control by spraying with lime sulfur. Care must be taken to cover the underside of leaves.

The most serious insect pest of this shrub is the **privet thrip.** Infested foliage may be small and puckered. The leaves become yellowish or grayish, and seriously injured foliage may fall to the ground in late summer. As the plants produce new foliage the thrips abandon the older ruined leaves for newer ones at the top and side. Thus, each successive generation of the pest injures new foliage as it is produced. The winged adults are flat, elongate, and about $\frac{1}{16}$ inch long. They are yellow to blackish with gray markings. Nymphs are translucent, becoming light green to yellowish white as they mature. Eggs are typically deposited on the lower surface of leaves, with a few on the upper sides. There are three generations a year in northern states. Adults overwinter in leaf litter under privet plants, under tree bark, and in moss.

Spray the bush thoroughly with a harsh soap solution. The thrips will soon seek out a more amiable environment. It is also a good idea to remove any crumpled or unhealthy leaves to the compost heap. See THRIPS.

Many pests of privet shrubs are also common to LILAC, such as the lilac borer, lilac leaf miner, and San José scale. See also APHID, MEALYBUGS, and SPIDER MITES.

Diseases

Anthracnose (also canker or twig blight) is a fungus disease that causes leaves to dry out and cling to the stem. The twigs may become blighted, and cankers dotted with pinkish fruiting bodies are formed at the base of the main stems. Often the bark and wood of diseased portions become brown and split. When the stems become completely girdled, the affected plants die.

Plant resistant varieties. Possible choices are Amur, Ibota, Regal, and California privet. European and Lodenese privet are susceptible. Once the disease hits, it is best to cut out and burn or compost all diseased branches.

Galls are probably the result of a fungus. Nodular galls measure up to six inches long and 1½ inches in diameter. It is best to destroy the entire stem on which they occur, pruning back until arriving at healthy wood. If you use plenty of properly composted humus around privets, the plant should have enough strength to produce new shoots and remain healthy. Once gall disease is allowed to go too far, plants will have to be removed from the garden.

Prune

Insects

Various **scale** insects infest prunes, including olive scale, San José scale, brown apricot scale, and the Italian pear scale. These are minute, gray, disc-shaped insects that settle on the bark and limbs of trees in great numbers. The olive scale (see OLIVE), Italian pear scale, and San José scale (see APPLE) are described as armored because they construct a shell and live under it. The brown apricot scale is unarmored and is therefore easier to control.

A five-percent dormant-oil spray, applied when trees are fully dormant and after the first heavy rains, will kill armored species. Unarmored scale is controlled with a four-percent spray.

The **shot-hole borer** is a small (about $\frac{3}{32}$-inch-long) brown or black beetle that deposits its eggs under the bark. These hatch into white grubs that mine the sapwood and, in severe cases, reduce it to a powder. In numbers, borers cause a trunk to look as though it had been hit at close range by a shot gun blast. For control of this borer and the peach tree and twig borers, see PEACH.

The **western flat-headed borer** attacks sunburned or otherwise injured areas of trunks and larger limbs, tunneling into the inner bark and sapwood, and sometimes girdling limbs. The larvae are white grubs with flattened bodies greatly enlarged at the front end. Control is a matter of pruning to reduce sunburn and keeping trees healthy and vigorous.

Diseases

Crown gall is the name given to rough growths that develop on the roots and crowns of prune trees as a result of a bacterial parasite. It may be necessary to uncover the crown and perhaps some of the roots of affected trees to observe the galls. They will appear as ugly circular growths around several of the roots. Check nursery trees for galls before buying them. It's best to refuse an entire lot of trees if even one appears to be affected. Galls under four inches in diameter should be generously coated with a tree surgeon's solution. If larger than four inches, galls should be removed by chiseling or knocking and then painted with the solution. It may be necessary to cover the treated area with soil to prevent sunburn or freezing injury. The choice of a resistant rootstock will help to avoid the disease also. Marianna 2623, Marianna 2624, and Myrobalan 29 have shown a creditable amount of resistance to crown gall.

On Italian prunes, **cytospora canker** has been responsible for wiping out whole orchards. Fruit in Idaho is especially hard-hit. Look for yellowed or brown dead leaves, accompanied by gummy cankers or elongated necrotic streaks in the bark. All suspicious wood should be cut out and removed from the orchard for burning.

Diamond canker is a virus disease that attacks French prunes almost exclusively. The symptoms of this disease are roughly shaped cankers produced by thickened corky tissue. These out-growths tend to form at the bases of the lateral branches at pruning wounds and at the margin of areas killed by the canker organism. Rough areas where the outer bark becomes cracked and loosened are sometimes found on the youngest twigs of affected trees, and these areas develop into typical diamond cankers as the twigs grow older.

Trees seldom die from the effects of diamond canker, but they remain stunted and gradually succumb to wood rots and insect borers. In the early stages, diseased trees often produce greater quantities of large-sized fruit than trees that are not affected. But the disease takes its toll in time, and cankered trees should be replaced with resistant varieties.

Pumpkin

When pumpkin fruit first appears, be sure to set protective layers of plastic, cloth, or paper under each to prevent insect attacks and soil damage. Some growers place summer pumpkins between rows of corn to shade them from the direct rays of the sun; plants can also be set to good advantage near bushes or trees.

The *Vegetable Growers News* suggests that pumpkins and all of the winter squash varieties store best when harvested at full maturity before frost and when cured before being placed in storage. To cure the rind, clean it of any clinging debris and place the pumpkin in a warm, dry environment for three to seven days.

This will dry and harden the rind, making it more resistant to decay.

Several kinds of **aphids,** such as the melon, squash, and potato aphids, may damage pumpkin foliage; see APHID.

The **squash borer** may injure pumpkins, but as this crop is usually planted late it is better off than squash; see SQUASH.

Dark brown, hard-shelled **squash bugs** are often mistaken for stink bugs, as they put off a vile odor when stepped on. As the bugs suck sap from leaves, they apparently inject a toxic substance that causes wilting, especially at midday. It helps to water all along the stalk, since this causes them to crawl out into view so that they can be handpicked. Keep an eye out for their brick-red eggs, laid between vines on the underside of leaves; scrape them from the leaf into a container for disposal. See SQUASH.

Squash Bug and Nymph

Other pests include the melonworm (see MELON) and the striped cucumber beetle (CUCUMBER).

Quince (Flowering)

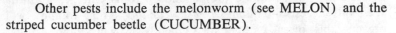

Insects

Dormant-oil sprays give the most satisfactory control of **scale,** although there may be beneficial insects that will handle the scale if left alone.

Diseases

Amylovora may severely blight quince flowers. Since this bacterium is the same one that causes fire blight, it is a good idea to seek out and destroy any diseased and neglected pear, quince, or apple trees that may harbor this dread disease. Prune back the branches of quince until healthy wood is uncovered, and break out any blighted fruit spurs. A dormant-oil spray has been found effective in the prevention of this disease.

Radish

Insects

The only insects likely to cause much trouble in the radish rows are several species of **root maggots.** All concerned are yellowish white, legless, and measure from ¼ to ½ inch long. Seed-corn and cabbage maggots are particularly common. They tunnel into the roots, making them unsalable and less than appetizing. Because maggots are so fond of this crop, radishes are often planted as a trap crop to protect other vegetables. The maggot-infested roots are removed from the soil before they can complete their life cycles.

But if it's the radishes you're after, protect them by spading in generous amounts of hardwood ashes. Ideally, radishes should not be planted in soil that has hosted a member of the cabbage family for at least three years. In planning your garden for next year, try interplanting radishes with cucumbers, as radishes repel the cucumber beetle.

For other pests, see CABBAGE.

Diseases

Radishes are little troubled by diseases. **Black root** appears as blackened areas where the secondary roots emerge. Cynthia Westcott suggests in *Plant Disease Handbook* that rotation will prevent this disease. She recommends growing globe rather than long varieties if black root has been a problem.

The variety Red Prince is resistant to **fusarium wilt.**

Raspberry

Insects

The **raspberry cane borer** is one of the worst pests of raspberries, causing weak canes that often die before fruiting. The adult borer, a long-horned, black-and-yellow beetle, makes two rows of punctures about an inch apart on the cane, causing it to wilt. An egg is laid between the two rows which later hatches into a small worm that burrows toward the base of the cane.

Cut the cane a few inches below the puncture marks. If the plant is vigorous and healthy, it will survive this pruning and put out new growth.

The **raspberry cane maggot,** a northern insect from the East to the West Coast, will cause the tips of the canes to wilt, often with a purplish discoloration. Sometimes the tips look as if they were cut, and there may be galls on the canes. The adult insect appears in late April, lays its eggs, and the maggot that does the damage reaches maturity in late June or early July. These white, ⅓-inch-long maggots tunnel into the canes, eventually emerging as adult flies ready to deposit their eggs in canes and young shoots for another cycle.

Prune back and destroy infested canes in May to keep the cane maggot under control. Make the cut several inches below the infested part.

The **raspberry fruitworm** is a light brown beetle, ⅛ to ⅙ inch long, that feeds on buds, blossoms, and new leaves. Eggs laid on blossoms and young fruit will hatch into grubs that bore into the fruit, causing it to dry up. Later they drop to the ground and overwinter in the soil. To prevent this pupation, cultivate the soil thoroughly in late summer.

The **raspberry root borer,** also called the raspberry crown borer, does its work in the base of the canes and crown. The round, rust-colored eggs, about the size of a mustard seed, are laid on the underside of leaves late in the growing season. The larvae hibernate during winter and in spring begin to bore into the crown or canes, weakening the plant through partial or complete girdling. The adult moth has a black body with four yellow stripes and transparent wings. This pest prefers red raspberries to black. It is hard to spot once in the crown, but the cane will produce poorly and the plant may become stunted. The best control for this borer is to cut and destroy the affected canes at or below the soil line.

The **raspberry sawfly** is much like the blackberry sawfly, except for the coloring: larvae are pale green and spiny and adult flies are black with yellow and red markings. For symptoms and control, see BLACKBERRY.

Spider mites such as the two-spotted mite are common pests of raspberries. They gather on the underside of leaves and are so minute that they are scarcely visible until there are large numbers of them and much damage is done. Leaves will be pale or undersized. The use of chemical sprays has killed off many of the spider mite's natural predators, while the mites themselves quickly become resistant to new chemicals.

Two-Spotted
Spider Mite

Spider mites will seldom be a problem with well-watered plants. Some gardeners use a hard spray of water to knock the mites off. You may need to use an angular or curved nozzle to spray the underside of leaves. For further information, see SPIDER MITES.

The red-necked cane borer, rose scale, and the tree cricket are pests of raspberries as well as blackberries; see BLACKBERRY. Raspberries will sometimes be troubled by APHIDS, European corn borers (CORN), and JAPANESE BEETLES.

Diseases

Raspberries are more susceptible to virus diseases than any other berry in the United States. The chief ones are leaf curl, mosaic, and streak. Other viruses may cause plants to decline in vigor and production, but have no other symptom.

Viruses are often spread from plant to plant by feeding aphids. Once infected, all parts of the plant will be diseased, usually beyond recovery. Since viruses are not curable except by a heat treatment that must be done in a laboratory, concentrate on prevention. Be sure to buy high-quality, certified virus-free plants, and choose disease-resistant varieties. Because aphids may be blown in the wind, you should plant your berries 500 or even 1,000 feet away from wild raspberries or old domestic plants that may be infected. Blackberry plants and other brambles sometimes harbor diseases that infect raspberries, so it is best to keep them separate.

There are other preventive measures that should be followed as a matter of course: check plants regularly for virus symptoms; keep the berry patch free of weeds; remove all old canes after harvest; destroy the entire plant which shows evidence of disease; and provide a healthy soil by working in plenty of organic matter and by keeping the plants well-mulched.

Of the fungus and bacterial diseases, **anthracnose** is the most prevalent. The BLACKBERRY section describes the symptoms and control of the disease for black raspberries. On red raspberries, the lesions are very small and inconspicuous. During late summer the fungus produces an extensive grayish white growth on the shoots of the current season. This is known as the gray-bark phase of the disease. Pinpoint-sized black dots, the fruiting bodies of the fungus, appear on these areas of the canes. For control, see BLACKBERRY.

Botrytis fruit rot may be a danger to ripening bramble berries, especially during a wet spell of several days. Bruised or overripe fruit are most susceptible to this fungus, which may cause a grayish mold on the berries. The fungi causing this rot are airborne and the spores are easily spread.

Control by continuous picking to prevent accumulation of overripe berries on the plants. Handle the fruit gently to avoid squeezing or crushing it. Give the containers of picked fruit good ventilation to allow drying.

Cane blight may affect any bramble fruit plants, particularly weak plants or those with insect injury, broken stems, or injury from pruning. The fungus enters through the wounds and advances rapidly through the bark and cambium tissues. Spores on the infected areas are spread by splashing rain and air currents. Infection is not apparent until late in the season, when brownish purple discolorations appear on the cut or broken part of the cane and move down the cane or encircle it. Eventually, all lateral branches in that area will show discoloration and may wilt and die. Dead infected canes may keep on producing spores and remain a source of infection for two years or more.

Cane blight is more common on black raspberries than red. Vigorous plants are less susceptible. Controlling insects will help prevent the plant injuries that lead to cane blight. Remove and burn all dead canes, prunings, and stubs.

Cane gall affects black raspberries, and only rarely the red ones. It is much like crown gall (see BLACKBERRY) except that the galls are found on the fruiting canes rather than the crowns. The galls change from white to light brown; late in the season they disintegrate and the cane may split. Roots and new shoots are not infected. The bacteria that cause cane gall infect the plant through wounds. See the discussion of crown gall under BLACKBERRY.

Mild streak affects the black raspberry, but not the red. This virus disease is hard to detect. Faint purplish streaks appear on the lower part of new canes in summer, the leaves appear slightly hooked or twisted, and mottling may develop in lower leaves. The plants remain vigorous and produce well, although the fruits are seedy, crumbly, and of poor quality. Be sure your planting stock is known to be free of mild streak, and see to it that no wild blackberries or wild raspberries are growing near your cultivated plants.

A similar disease, severe streak, is less common but far more noticeable. The symptoms are generally the same as those of mild streak, except much more pronounced: leaves will be severely hooked, and vertical streaks are dark blue and very definite. Severe streak is controlled by rooting out all infected plants and removing any wild blackberries in the vicinity.

Mosaic is probably the most common and most damaging of the raspberry virus diseases. With some strains of mosaic there are no distinguishing symptoms, but the infected plants will be weaker, produce fewer canes and fewer berries. Some strains of mosaic will be evident from short canes and yellowish, mottled foliage. Fruit from infected plants may be dry, seedy, flavorless, and crumbly. One symptom of mosaic diseases on red raspberries is the presence of large green blisters on the foliage in late spring, with yellowish tissue around them. The tips of infected black and purple raspberry canes may bend over, turn black, and die. Leaves become mottled and plants are stunted.

Dig out and burn all infected plants, including the roots, within three feet of the infected plant. Isolate new plantings well away from virus disease sources such as wild brambles or old infected plantings. Some varieties of red raspberries are mosaic-resistant; purple and black raspberries are susceptible. Remember that mosaic is not evident at planting time, so inspect your plants regularly.

Mosaic may be mistaken for other conditions. Late spring frosts, for example, sometimes produce a mottling on the leaves of older canes that resembles mosaic, but the young canes produced in early summer will be normal. Powdery mildew (see below) is sometimes mistaken for mosaic, as are the symptoms of a spider mite infestation (see above).

Orange rust is a disease of black raspberries only; both wild and cultivated plants are susceptible. See BLACKBERRY for symptoms and control.

Although **powdery mildew** may occur on all bramble fruits, it is usually not a serious problem on any but red raspberries. The first symptom is a dwarfing and twisting of tip leaves in early summer, followed by a white powdery fungus growth on the underside of leaves. Affected parts are yellowed and stunted. This fungus disease is spread by spores, which germinate best in warm temperatures when the humidity is very high. Latham is especially vulnerable.

Treatment is seldom necessary unless the mildew becomes severe, in which case you can spray or dust with sulfur. If plants are kept thinned out to let in sun and air, there will be less chance of powdery mildew developing.

There are two strains of **raspberry leaf curl virus,** one affecting black raspberries and the other red raspberries. The disease is first evident on the tips of canes, where the new leaves of red raspberries will curl downward; those of black raspberries will arch upwards. The next season, all the leaves will be stunted and curled and the shoots will be abnormally short. The affected shoots will be pale and yellowish green when they first appear above ground, and later will darken. In late summer the leaves turn from pale green to reddish brown. The fruit of affected canes is small, dry, seedy, and unpleasant-tasting. Infected plants never recover.

Destroy all diseased plants, and make new plantings from disease-free stock. Keep healthy raspberries away from diseased plants, and do not plant red raspberries near black raspberries, even when both are disease-free. Wild bramble fruit bushes should be eliminated from the vicinity of cultivated raspberries.

Spur blight is a fairly common disease of red raspberries, and less of a problem with black ones. It is seldom serious. Spur blight is first evident in late spring as discolored brown or purplish areas on the shoot at the spur (the point of leaf attachment). Usually the buds near ground level are affected more than those higher up on the canes. The spots enlarge, and by late summer the bark in these areas splits and small, black, spore-producing growths appear. The following season, growth from buds in the affected areas will be weak, the leaves stunted, and fruit production severely reduced. Plants with spur blight are especially vulnerable to winter injury from low temperatures.

As this fungus is spread by splashing rain and nurtured by moisture on the plants, careful sanitation will help control it, especially eliminating weeds and thinning plants to let air circulate and dry the foliage. Always remove and destroy old canes after harvest. Another way to eliminate spur blight is to plant the fall-bearing variety Durham, because its canes may all be cut back to the ground to eliminate the source of this disease without sacrificing a crop.

Verticillium wilt, also known as bluestripe or bluestem, affects many kinds of plants, including raspberries (particularly black raspberries), potatoes, tomatoes, peppers, eggplants, stone fruits, and such weeds as horsenettle or nightshade. On black raspberries, the lower leaves develop an off-green or yellowish bronze tinge in June or early July. Leaves curl upward, become yellow, and then brown and fall off. The disease progresses up the plant. Canes show blue or purple streaks, beginning at the soil line and moving up the cane. Often the canes die before the fruits mature, and eventually the entire plant dies.

On the red raspberry, which is generally more resistant, verticillium wilt is evident later in summer, and the discolored leaves curl downward. The cane discoloration is often missing or hard to distinguish from the plant's normal red or bronze color.

The verticillium fungus lives in the soil and enters the plant through injured tissue, e.g. roots damaged by frost, transplanting, or nematodes. Once present in a planting it will be spread by soil cultivation or flowing water. Often the fungus will be borne in the soil if the crops mentioned above have been grown previously. Verticillium wilt is most likely in heavy, poorly drained soils, and is at its worst during cool seasons. For these reasons, do not plant raspberries where wilt-susceptible plants have grown. Avoid heavy soils, and be sure the drainage is good. Your planting stock should come from a nursery that practices good verticillium wilt control.

Winterkill hits the green, immature wood of raspberry canes. Fertilizer should be applied in late winter or very early spring so that growth will slow down and harden before frost. You can provide winter protection in severe climates by bending the canes to the ground and covering at least a third of their length with soil before the ground freezes. The bent canes will form a snow trap, and the drifts that cover the canes will protect them from fluctuating temperatures and drying winds. When snow melts in spring, the canes can be raised and tied to their supports, and winterkilled portions can be removed with the spring pruning.

Wildlife

To keep the **birds** from your raspberries, you will need an enclosure or netting. See BLUEBERRY for details.

If **rabbits** are a problem to your raspberries, keep them out with a four- or five-foot-high fence of chicken wire.

Red Cedar, see Juniper

Resistant Varieties

SOME INSECT-RESISTANT VARIETIES FOR YOUR GARDEN

These lists have been compiled mainly from *Organic Gardening and Farming* and from work done by Dr. Charles H. Brett and associates at the North Carolina Agricultural Experiment Station at North Carolina State University, Raleigh. As explained in this chapter, both varieties and the bugs that eat them are very subject to change. A pea aphid in Quebec is not the same as a pea aphid in Kansas, and resistant varieties may not work in some areas. Most lists are arranged from most resistant to least resistant (most susceptible); those few that aren't arranged in such order, because their relative resistance hasn't been determined, are marked (*).

ALFALFA
Alfalfa aphid.
- Resistant: Cody, Lahontan, and Zia.
- Susceptible: Buffalo.

BARLEY
Greenbug.
- Resistant: Omugi, Dictoo, and Will.
- Susceptible: Rogers and Reno.

BEANS
Mexican bean beetle.
- Resistant: Wade, Logan, and Black Valentine.
- Susceptible: State, Bountiful, and Dwarf Horticultural.

BROCCOLI
Diamondback moth.
- Moderately resistant: Coastal, Italian Green Sprouting, and Atlantic.
- Susceptible: De Cicco.

Harlequin bug.
- Resistant: Grande, Atlantic, and Coastal.
- Moderately resistant: Gem.

Striped flea beetle.
- Resistant: De Cicco, Coastal, Italian Green Sprouting, and Atlantic.
- Moderately resistant: Gem.

CABBAGE
Cabbage looper and imported cabbageworm.
- Resistant: Mammoth Red Rock, Savoy Chieftain, and Savoy Perfection Drumhead.
- Moderately resistant: Special Red Rock, Penn State Ball Head, Early Flat Dutch, Badger Ball Head, Wisconsin Hollander, Red Acre, Danish Ball Head, Charleston Wakefield, Premium Late Flat Dutch, Glory of Enkhuizen, Globe, All Seasons, Midseason Market, Bugner, Succession, Early Round Dutch, Stein's Early Flat Dutch, Badger Market, Large Late Flat Dutch, Jersey Wakefield, Marion Market, Wisconsin Ball Head, Large Charleston Wakefield, Early Glory, Green Acre, Round Dutch, Resistant Detroit, and Wisconsin All Season.
- Susceptible: Golden Acre, Elite, Copenhagen Market 86, and Stein's Flat Dutch.

Diamondback moth.
- Resistant: Michihli Chinese and Mammoth Red Rock.
- Moderately resistant: Stein's Early Flat Dutch, Savoy Perfection Drumhead, Early Jersey Wakefield, and Ferry's Round Dutch.
- Susceptible: Copenhagen Market 86.

Harlequin bug.
- Resistant: Copenhagen Market 86, Headstart, Savoy Perfection Drumhead, Stein's Flat Dutch, Early Jersey Wakefield.
- Susceptible: Michihli Chinese.

Mexican bean beetle.
- Resistant: Copenhagen Market 86, Early Jersey Wakefield.
- Susceptible: Michihli Chinese.

Striped flea beetle.
- Resistant: Stein's Early Flat Dutch, Mammoth Red Rock, Savoy Perfection Drumhead, Early Jersey Wakefield, Copenhagen Market 86, and Ferry's Round Dutch.
- Moderately resistant to susceptible: Michihli Chinese.
- Susceptible (Canada): North Star and Northern Belle.

CANTALOUPE

Mexican bean beetle. Cantaloupe is generally resistant to this pest, but serious damage was done to **Rocky Ford Earliest** during an infestation.

Spotted cucumber beetle.
- Resistant (foliage): Edisto 47, Edisto, and Harper Hybrid.
- Susceptible (seedlings): Edisto, Edisto 47, Harper Hybrid, and Honey Dew.

  Susceptible (foliage): Honey Dew.

CAULIFLOWER

Diamondback moth.
- Moderately resistant: Snowball A.

Harlequin bug.
- Resistant: Early Snowball X and Snowball Y.

Striped flea beetle.
- Resistant: Snowball A and Early Snowball X.

COLLARD

Diamondback moth.
- Resistant: Green Glaze.
- Moderately resistant: Morris Heading, Vates, and Georgia Southern.

Harlequin bug.
- Resistant: Vates, Morris Improved Heading, and Green Glaze.
- Moderately resistant: Georgia LS and Georgia.

Mexican bean beetle.
- Resistant: Georgia LS, Green Glaze, and Vates.

Striped flea beetle.
- Resistant: Vates, Georgia, and Georgia LS.
- Moderately resistant: Morris Heading.
- Susceptible: Green Glaze.

SWEET CORN

Corn earworm. Any corn with long, tight husks physically helps to prevent ear penetration by earworms.
- Resistant: Dixie 18 (field corn), Calumet, Country Gentleman, Staygold, Victory Golden, Golden Security, Silver Cross Bantam, and Silvergent.
- Susceptible: Ioana, Aristogold Bantam Evergreen, Seneca Chief, Spancross, North Star, and Evertender.

Fall armyworm. Late sweet corn crops and second crops are especially vulnerable. Resistance depends on the planting time and tolerance of a variety. The varieties are arranged by survival rates, from best to worst.
- Resistant: Golden Market, Long Chief, Golden Security, Evertender, Marcross, Golden Regent, Silver Cross Bantam, Calumet, Victory Golden, Golden Sensation, Spancross, Golden Cross Bantam, Aristogold Bantam Evergreen, Golden Beauty, Triplegold, Deep Gold, and Ioana.

Sap beetles. As with the corn earworm, any corn with long, tight husks physically helps to discourage the sap beetle.
- Resistant*: Country Gentleman, Deligold, Gold Pack, Golden Security, Harris Gold Cup, Tender Joy, Trucker's Favorite, Stowell's Evergreen, and Victory Golden.
- Moderately resistant*: Atlas, Duet, Eastern Market, Gold Strike, Golden Grain, Golden Security, Marcross, Merit, Midway, Royal Crest, Silver Queen, Spring Gold, Stowell's Evergreen, Tendercrisp, Wintergreen, and Victory Golden.
- Susceptible* (In many cases, sap beetles gained access to these varieties by way of entrances previously made by corn earworms): Aristogold Bantam Evergreen, Calumet, Carmelcross, Corona, Deep Gold, Floriglade, Gold Mine, Golden Beauty, Golden Fancy, Ioana, Merit, Northern Belle, Seneca Chief, Seneca Explorer, Silvergent, Sixty Pak, Spancross, Spring Bounty, Titian, Vanguard, and White Silk Tendermost.

CUCUMBERS

Mexican bean beetle. While not normally a serious pest of cucumbers, this beetle severely damaged these varieties in an outbreak: Arkansas Hybrid No. 4, Colorado, Crispy,

Hokus, Marketer, NK804, Nappa 63, Piccadilly, Pico, Pixie, and Triumph.

Pickleworm.
- Resistant: Arkansas Hybrid No. 4, Cubit, Gemini, Nappa 61, Nappa 63, Pixie, Princess, Spartan Dawn, Stono, Ashley, Colorado, Hokus, Long Ashley, Model, Piccadilly, Packer, and Table Green.

Spotted cucumber beetle.
- Resistant (seedlings): Ashley, Chipper, Crispy, Explorer, Frontier, Gemini, Jet, Princess, Spartan Dawn, and White Wonder.
 Resistant (foliage): Ashley, Cherokee, Chipper, Gemini, High Mark II, Ohio MR 17, Poinsett, Stono (Stono is reported resistant to both striped and spotted cucumber beetles, and Fletcher and Niagra are moderately resistant to the two pests.), and Southern Cross.
- Moderately resistant (seedlings): Cubit, High Mark II, Hokus, Nappa 63, Pixie, Poinsett, and SMR 58.
 Moderately resistant (foliage): Colorado, Crispy, Explorer, Frontier, Long Ashley, Nappa 61, Pixie, and Table Green.
- Susceptible (seedlings): Cherokee, Coolgreen, Model, Nappa 61, Packer, Pioneer, Southern Cross, and Table Green.
 Susceptible (foliage): Coolgreen, Cubit, Hokus, Jet, Model, Nappa 63, Packer, Pioneer, Spartan Dawn, and SMR 58.

KALE

Diamondback moth.
- Resistant: Vates (protected by antibiosis, as a result of compact cell structure within the leaf).
- Susceptible: Early Siberian and Dwarf Siberian (has loosely arranged cells that are apparently easy for the larvae to mine).

Harlequin bug.
- Resistant: Vale.
- Susceptible: Dwarf Siberian.

Mexican bean beetle.
- Resistant: Dwarf Siberian.

Striped flea beetle.
- Resistant: Vates, Dwarf Siberian, Dwarf Green Curled Scotch, and Early Siberian.

MUSKMELON

Striped and spotted cucumber beetle.
- Resistant: Hearts of Gold.
- Susceptible: Smith Perfect and Crenshaw.

MUSTARD

Diamondback moth.
- Resistant: Southern Giant Curled.
- Moderately resistant: Florida Broadleaf.

Harlequin bug.
- Moderately resistant: Old Fashion.
- Susceptible: Southern Giant Curled, Green Wave, and Florida Broadleaf.

Mexican bean beetle.
- Resistant: Green Wave.
- Susceptible: Southern Giant Curled.

Striped flea beetle.
- Resistant: Florida Broadleaf.
- Moderately resistant: Southern Giant Curled and Green Wave.

POTATO

Aphids.
- Resistant: British Queen, DeSota, Early Pinkeye, Houma, Irish Daisy, and LaSalle.
- Tolerant: Red Warba, Triumph, President, Peach Blow, and Early Rose.
- Susceptible: Katahdin, Irish Cobbler, Idaho Russet, Sebago, and Sequoia.

Colorado potato beetle.
- Resistant: Sequoia and Katahdin.
- Susceptible: Fundy, Plymouth, and Catoosa.

Potato leafhopper.
- Resistant: Delus.
- Moderately resistant: Sebago, Pungo, and Plymouth.
- Susceptible: Cobbler.

PUMPKINS

Serpentine leaf miner (only four varieties were tested).
- Resistant: Mammoth Chili and Small Sugar.
- Susceptible: King of the Mammoth and Green Striped Cushaw.

Spotted cucumber beetle.
- Resistant (foliage): King of the Mammoth, Mammoth Chili, and Dickinson Field.
- Susceptible (seedlings): Green Striped Cushaw, King of the Mammoth, Mammoth Chili, and Small Sugar.
  Susceptible (foliage): Connecticut Field, Green Striped Cushaw, and Small Sugar.

RADISH
Cabbage webworm.
- Resistant: Cherry Belle.
- Moderately resistant: Globemaster.
- Susceptible: White Icicle, Red Devil, and Champion.
Diamondback moth.
- Resistant: Cherry Belle, White Icicle, Globemaster, and Champion.
Harlequin bug.
- Resistant: Red Devil, White Icicle, Globemaster, Cherry Belle, Champion, and Red Prince.
- Moderately resistant: Crimson Sweet.
Mexican bean beetle.
- Susceptible: Sparkler, Champion, and White Icicle.
Striped flea beetle.
- Moderately resistant: Champion and Sparkler.
- Susceptible: Globemaster, Cherry Belle, and White Icicle.

RUTABAGA
Diamondback moth.
- Moderately resistant: American Purple Top.
Harlequin bug.
- Susceptible: American Purple Top.
Striped flea beetle.
- Resistant: American Purple Top.

SORGHUM
Chinch bug.
- Resistant: Atlas.
- Susceptible: Milo.
Corn leaf aphid.
- Resistant: Sudan.
- Susceptible: White Martin.

SQUASH
Mexican bean beetle. Although this beetle is not normally a serious pest of squash, White Bush Scallop was damaged severely in an outbreak.

Pickleworm.
- Resistant: Summer Crookneck, Butternut 23, Buttercup, Boston Marrow, Blue Hubbard, and Green Hubbard. (Butternut 23 is also resistant to the squash vine borer.)
- Moderately resistant: Early Prolific Straightneck, Early Yellow Summer Crookneck, and White Bush Scallop.
- Susceptible: Black Beauty, U Conn, Marine Black Zucchini, Seneca Zucchini, Cozella Hybrid, Long Cocozelle, Ben-

ning's Green Tint Scallop, Short Cocozelle, Zucchini, Caserta, Black Zucchini, and Cozini.

Serpentine leaf miner.
- Resistant: Butternut 23 and Cozella.
- Moderately resistant: Blue Hubbard, Zucchini, Benning's Green Tint Scallop, Summer Straightneck, Boston Marrow, Buttercup, and Pink Banana.
- Susceptible: Seneca Prolific, Green Hubbard, Seneca Zucchini, Summer Crookneck, Black Zucchini, Cozini, and Long Cozella.

Spotted cucumber beetle. These beetles are attracted to the odor of the germinating seeds of some varieties, and often dig through the soil to eat seedlings even before they've grown to the surface. Mature varieties with flowers having a strong, sweet smell attract these beetles in greater numbers than do other varieties.
- Resistant (seedlings): Blue Hubbard, Green Hubbard, Long Cozella, Seneca Prolific, Summer Crookneck, and Summer Straightneck.
  Resistant (foliage): Black Zucchini, Benning's Green Tint Scallop, and Blue Hubbard. (Royal Acorn and Early Golden Bush Scallop were found to be resistant to both the striped and spotted cucumber beetles.)
- Moderately resistant (seedlings): Boston Marrow, Buttercup, and Pink Banana.
  Moderately resistant (foliage): Green Hubbard, Pink Banana, Seneca Zucchini, Summer Crookneck, and Summer Straightneck.
- Susceptible (seedlings): Benning's Green Tint Scallop, Black Zucchini, Cozella, Cozini, Seneca Zucchini, and Zucchini.
  Susceptible (foliage): Boston Marrow, Buttercup, Cozella, Cozini, Long Cocozelle, Seneca Prolific, and Zucchini.

Squash bug.
- Resistant: Butternut, Table Queen, Royal Acorn, Sweet Cheese, Early Golden Bush Scallop, Early Summer Crookneck, Early Prolific Straightneck, and Improved Green Hubbard.
- Susceptible: Striped Green Cushaw, Pink Banana, and Black Zucchini.

Striped cucumber beetle.
- Resistant: Early Prolific Straightneck, U Conn, Long Cocozelle, White Bush Scallop, Benning's Green Tint Scallop, Early Yellow Summer Crookneck, Cozella Hybrid, Marine

Black Zucchini, Butternut 23, Short Cocozelle, Summer Crookneck, and Zucchini. (Royal Acorn and Early Golden Bush Scallop were found to be resistant to both the striped and spotted cucumber beetles.)
- Susceptible: Black Zucchini, Cozini, Caserta, and Black Beauty.

SWEET POTATO

Southern potato wireworm.
- Resistant: Nugget and All Gold.
- Moderately resistant: Porto Rico, Centennial, Georgia Red, and Gold Rush.

Sweet potato flea beetle.
- Resistant: Jewel.
- Moderately resistant: Centennial, All Gold, Georgia Red, Porto Rico, and Gem.
- Susceptible: Nugget, Red Jewel, Georgia 41, Nemagold, and Jullian.

TOMATO

Two-spotted mite.
- Resistant: Campbell 135.
- Moderately resistant: Campbell 146.
- Susceptible: Homestead 24.

TURNIP

Diamondback moth.
- Resistant: Seven Top and Purple Top White Globe.

Harlequin bug.
- Susceptible: Amber Globe, Purple Top White Globe, and White Egg.

Mexican bean beetle.
- Susceptible: Amber Globe and Purple Top White Globe.

Striped flea beetle.
- Moderately resistant: Seven Top.
- Susceptible: Purple Top White Globe and Amber Globe.

WATERMELONS

Spotted cucumber beetle.
- Resistant (foliage): Crimson Sweet and Sweet Princess.
- Susceptible (seedlings): Blue Ribbon, Charleston Gray, Crimson Sweet, Sugar Baby, and Sweet Princess.

  Susceptible (foliage): Charleston Gray, Blue Ribbon, and Sugar Baby.

WHEAT

Hessian fly.
- Resistant: Ottawa, Ponca, Pawnee, Big Club 43, Dual, Rus-

sell, Todd, Dawson, Honor, Illino Chief, Fulhard, Red Rock, and Michigan Wonder.
- Moderately Resistant: Blackhull, Superhard, Early Blackhull, Harvest Queen, Red Winter, and Fulcaster.
- Susceptible: Tenmarq, Bison, Turkey, Kharkoff, Kanred, Oro, Cheyenne, Minturki, and Zimmermann.

Wheat stem sawfly.
- Resistant (Solid-stem varieties of wheat are more resistant than hollow stem varieties): Rescue and Chinook.

A SAMPLING OF THE MANY AVAILABLE DISEASE-RESISTANT VARIETIES

The information in this table was supplied by several state experiment stations and the USDA. These varieties aren't universally effective—they work best in certain locales, and even the most formidable lose their resistance in time. Check with your experiment station for updated information. Please note that the following lists of varieties are **not** ordered by comparative degree of resistance.

CROP	DISEASE	VARIETY
APPLE	Alternaria cork rot	Delicious, Rome Beauty, Winesap, and Stayman Winesap.
	Apple blotch	Grimes Golden, Jonathan, Stayman Winesap, and Winesap.
	Bitter rot	Delicious, Rome Beauty, Stayman Winesap, Winesap, York Imperial, and Yellow Transparent.
	Black pox	Transparent, York Imperial, and Gano.
	Cedar apple rust	Baldwin, Delicious, Rhode Island, Northwestern Greening, Franklin, Melrose, Red Astrachan, Stayman, Transparent, Golden Delicious, Winesap, Grimes Golden, and Duchess.
	Collar rot	Delicious, Winesap, and Wealthy. Moderately resistant varieties include Jonathan, Golden Delicious, McIntosh, and Rome Beauty.

CROP	DISEASE	VARIETY
		A susceptible variety can be grafted on to a resistant one, with good results; Grimes Golden on a Delicious trunk is standard practice. Also, Malling IX and VII rootstocks are resistant.
	Fire blight	Baldwin, Ben Davis, Delicious, Duchess, McIntosh, Northern Spy, Prima, Stayman, and Winter Banana.
	Mildew	Prima.
	Quince rust	Jonathan, Rome, Ben Davis, and Wealthy.
	Scab	Prima.
	Scar skin	Golden Delicious (tolerant).
ASPARAGUS	Asparagus rust	Supplanting the older Mary and Martha Washington are Waltham Washington, Seneca Washington, and California 500.
BEAN	Bacterial blight and wilt	Tendergreen (some types).
	Common mosaic	Robust, Great Northern, U.S. No. 5, Refugee, Idaho Refugee, and Wisconsin Refugee.
	Powdery mildew	Contender.
	Rust	Tendergreen (some types), Harvester, and Cherokee Wax (yellow).
DRY BEAN	Bean halo blight	Many, including Pinto, Great Northern, Red Mexican, and Michelite.
LIMA BEAN	Downy mildew	Thaxter.
SOYBEAN	Bacterial blight	Flambeau and Hawkeye.
BEET	Boron deficiency	Detroit Dark Red.
BLACK-BERRY	Orange rust	Eldorado, Orange Evergreen, Russell, Snyder, and Ebony King.
	Yellow rust, cane rust	Nanticoke, Austin Thornless, Boysen Brainerd, Burbank Thornless, and Jersey Black, as well as most European varieties.
BLUEBERRY	Blueberry canker	Weymouth, June, and Rancocas.

CROP	DISEASE	VARIETY
	Mildew	Stanley, Rancocas, Harding, and Katherine.
CABBAGE	Yellows and fusarium wilt	Many, including Jersey Queen, Marion Market, Wisconsin Golden Acre, Resistant Detroit, Charleston Wakefield, Globe, Wisconsin All Season, Wisconsin Hollander, some strains of Jersey Wakefield, Market Topper, Market Prize, Greenback, King Cole, Resistant Danish, Vanguard II, Savoy King, Red Danish, Red Ball, and Red Head.
CANTA-LOUPE	Downy mildew	Texas Resistant No. 1 and Georgia 47 (also resistant to aphids).
CAULI-FLOWER	Yellows	Early Snowball.
CELERY	Fusarium wilt, yellows	Grow green petiole varieties or somewhat resistant Michigan Golden, Cornell 19, Tall Golden Plume, Golden Pascal, and Emerson Pascal.
SWEET CORN	Bacterial wilt	Many, including Golden Cross Bantam, Golden Beauty, F-M Cross, Carmelcross, Ioana, Marcross, Seneca Chief, N.K. 199, Iochief, and two white varieties, Silver Queen and Country Gent.
	Helminthosporium smut	Gold Cup and Silver Queen (white). Golden Cross Bantam and Country Gent (white).
CUCUMBER	Downy mildew	Burpee Hybrid, M&M Hybrid, Saticoy, Salty, and Poinsett (also resistant to anthracnose and leaf spot).
	Mosaic	Spartan Dawn, SMR, and Salty.
	Scab	Maine No. 2, Wisconsin SR 10 and SR 6, Highmoor, and Salty.
RED CURRANT	White pine blister beetle	Viking and Red Dutch.

CROP	DISEASE	VARIETY
DEWBERRY	Orange rust	Leucretia.
EGGPLANT	Phomopsis blight	Florida Market and Florida Beauty.
GRAPE	Anthracnose	Concord, Delaware, Moore Early, and Niagra.
DUTCH IRIS	Iris rust	Early Blue, Gold and Silver, Golden West, Imperator, Lemon Queen, and Texas Gold.
LETTUCE	Downy mildew	There are many strains of this disease, so consult your extension service.
	"Multiple resistance"	Grand Rapids and Salad Bowl.
	Tipburn	Slobolt, Summer Bibb, and Ruby.
MIMOSA	Mimosa wilt	Charlotte and Tryon.
MUSK-MELON	Alternaria blight	Harper Hybrid.
	Fusarium wilt	Gold Star, Harvest Queen, Samson, Chaca, and Supermarket.
	Mosaic	Harper Hybrid.
	Powdery mildew	Samson, Supermarket, and Chaca.
MUSTARD	Turnip anthracnose	Southern Giant Curled.
ONION	Fusarium rot	Early Yellow Globe and Southport Red Globe.
	Pink root	Nebuka (Welsh onion), Beltsville Bunching, and Brown Beauty; (in Arizona, Granex bears best).
	Smudge	Early Yellow Globe, Downings Yellow Globe, and Southport Red Globe.
	Smut	Evergreen (bunching).
PARSLEY	Septoria blight	Paramount.
PARSNIP	Root canker	Model.
PEA	Fusarium wilt	Wisconsin Early Sweet, Little Marvel, Thomas Laxton (all early varieties), and Frosty, Pride, Early Perfection, Sparkle, Wando, and Green Arrow (all medium to late varieties).
PEAR	Fire blight	Old Home, Orient, and Kieffer.

CROP	DISEASE	VARIETY
	Leaf blight and fruit spot	Kieffer shows some resistance.
	Leaf spot	Kieffer, Flemish Beauty, Duchess, and Winter Nellis are moderately resistant.
	Pear scab	Bartlett.
PECAN	Zinc deficiency	Money-maker.
PEPPER	Bacterial leaf spot	Sunnybrook (sweet salad variety), and two hot varieties, Long Red Cayenne and Red Chili.
	Mosaic	Sweet stuffing varieties; Bellringer, Keystone Resistant Giant, and Yolo Wonder.
PLUM	Armillaria root rot	Myrobolan 29 and Mariana 2624.
POTATO	Common scab	Menonimee, Ontario, Cayuga, Seneca, Superior, Haig, Pungo, and Norchip.
	Late blight	Kennebec, Essex, Pungo, and Cherokee are resistant or tolerant to some strains.
	Leaf roll	Katahdin.
	Potato crinkle, mild mosaic	Katahdin, Chippewa, Houma, and Sebago.
	Southern bacterial wilt (also known as brown rot, bacterial ring disease, and slime disease)	Northern seed varieties, and Sebago and Katahdin.
RADISH	Fusarium wilt	Red Prince.
ROSE (Grafted)	Black mold	Ragged Robin.
SHALLOT	Pink root	Evergreen.
SPINACH	Downy mildew	Califlay and Texas Early Hybrid 7.
SQUASH	Bacterial wilt	Table Queen (acorn), Butternut, and Buttercup.
STRAW-BERRY	Hop mildew	Sparkle, Puget Beauty, Siletz, and India.
	Leaf scorch	Catskill, Midland, Fairfax, Howard 17, Blakemore, and Wouthland.
	Red stele disease	Aberdeen, Stelemaster, Redchief, Darrow, and Guardian.

CROP	DISEASE	VARIETY
SWEET POTATO	Black rot	Allgold.
	Internal cork	Allgold, Centennial, and Nemagold.
	Root-knot	Nemagold.
	Soil rot	Allgold.
	White rust	Goldrush.
	Wilt	Allgold, Centennial, Goldrush, and Nemagold.
TOMATO	Blossom drop	Summerset, Hotset, Summer Prolific, and Porter.
	Curly top	Owyhee and Payette.
	Early blight	Varieties that do not bear heavily are somewhat more resistant: Manalucie, Southland, Floradel, and Manahill.
	Fusarium wilt	Heinz 1350, Heinz 1370, Campbell 1327, Jet Star, Better Boy, Supersonic, Burpee VF, Small Fry, Springset, Fantastic, Manapal, Manalucie, Roma VF, Rutgers, Kokoma, Marion, Porter, and Homestead.
	Gray spot	Manahill, Manalucie, and a number of Hawaiian varieties.
	Graywall	Manalucie, Tropi-red, Tropigrow, Indian River, Ohio WR Seven, and Strain A Globe.
	Late blight	New Hampshire, Surecrop, New Yorker, Nova (a paste tomato), West Virginia, and Rockingham.
	Leaf mold	Tuckcross 520, Ohio Hybrid O, Manalucie, Manapal, Vantage, Veegan, Vinequeen, Waltham. This fungus has mutated into new forms, and the older resistant varieties may no longer work well. Keep an eye out for new varieties.
	Mosaic virus	Moto-red, Ohio M-R9, Ohio M-R12, and Vendor.
	Nailhead spot	Marglobe, Pritchard, Glovel, and Break O'Day.

CROP	DISEASE	VARIETY
	Root-knot	Better Boy.
	Spotted wilt	Pearl Harbor.
	Verticillium wilt	Galaxy, Supersonic, New Yorker, Jet Star, Tom Tom, Roma VF, Heinz 1350, Campbell 1327, Better Boy, Burpee VF, Springset, Small Fry, and Loran Blood.
WATER-MELON	Fusarium wilt	Charleston Gray, Crimson Sweet, Sweet Princess, Improved Kleckly Sweet, and Klondike.
	Melon anthracnose	Charleston Gray, Congo, Fairfax, Black Kleckly, Crimson Sweet, Sweet Princess, and two seedless varieties, Tri-X313 and Triple Sweet.

Rhododendron

Insects

The **pitted ambrosia beetle** is a stout black beetle, about ⅛ inch long. The small whitish larvae make horizontal galleries in the wood at the base stems, causing plants to wilt or break off at ground level. Rhododendrons growing in the shade and those that are well-mulched are most susceptible to attack.

Cut out and burn affected stems. Pull the mulch away from plant bases and remove any excess mulch. It helps to select a sunny planting site at the beginning of the season.

As larvae, yellowish white **rhododendron borers** bore in stems and larger branches of rhododendron plants, causing them to wilt or break off. As they get larger, these larvae bore into the woody part of plants, pushing out fine sawdust as they go. Rhododendron borers overwinter as partly grown larvae in their stem burrows. Adults emerge in June, and eggs are laid on leaves, new twigs, or the rough bark of the main stem. The adult moths are small and black with three yellow stripes on the abdomen.

Prune and burn affected stems. Paint wounds with tree paint or paraffin. In June, crush any eggs that you can find. For other controls, see the suggestions for peach tree borers under PEACH.

The **rhododendron lacebug** is one of the most common pests attacking this plant. When adults and nymphs suck sap from the underside of leaves, the top surface takes on a mottled appearance much as if it had been sprinkled with white pepper. These pale areas show where chlorophyll has been destroyed as the result of feeding. The bottom is spotted with brown excrement that looks much like dots of varnish. The injury is prominent when plants are grown in full sun, and the shrubs take on a yellow cast, says Cynthia Westcott in *The Gardener's Bug Book*. Adult lacebugs are ⅛-inch-long flies, flattened and dark brown or black. They have lacy wings folded over the back to lend a squarish appearance to the insect. The nymphs are dark, spiny, and move with a strange sideways motion, observes Ms. Westcott.

If you see the characteristic mottling, draw the affected leaves between thumb and forefinger to squeeze the bugs to death.

The larva of the **rhododendron tip midge** is a whitish maggot that prevents the normal growth of plants by rolling young leaves. Remove damaged leaves as soon as possible. It is best not to use sprays, as they would likely discourage the midge's important natural enemies. One gardener who used rotenone on this pest was greeted by a serious resurgence two weeks later.

Diseases

Many rhododendron troubles that appear to be diseases are caused by environmental factors. So, before pruning or roguing, wait a while to test your conclusions—your plants might very well grow out of whatever ails them. Brown spots around the edges of leaves can be the result of summer drought. Scorching during winter months causes regularly spaced yellow or brown spots on either side of the midvein. Glazed ice on rolled leaves may act as a focusing agent for the sun's rays if the ice has not fallen by the time the sun comes out. Unlike the progressive effects of nutritional troubles, the spots caused by ice injury remain static, with sharply defined edges.

Azalea **bud** and **twig blight** is first known by the dwarfing of flower buds, followed by their browning and death in late summer or early fall. Fruiting bodies on buds resemble tiny pins stuck into the plant. Pick and burn infected plant parts either in late fall or early spring. Remove seed pods as soon as flowers have withered.

Chlorosis (or yellowing of leaves) while veins remain green can progress to the point that leaves become very pale and turn brown at the tips. This condition is usually caused by a deficiency of iron, which results from a number of factors: 1) destroying feeding roots by tillage or cultivation; 2) injuring roots by allowing soil to dry out; 3) sandy soil, with insufficient organic matter; 4) an overabundance of hard coal ash in the soil; 5) poor soil drainage; and 6) alkaline conditions, caused by too much lime in the soil or by setting plants near cement walls.

The permanent solution to chlorosis lies in improving the condition of the soil. Use plenty of organic matter, including an ample mulch. Chlorosis is also tied with winter injury. When loss of water from the leaf surface is greater than the water the roots can absorb, a yellowing of the interveinal areas may result, leaving the tissue immediately adjacent to the veins a normal green. Root injuries (possibly caused by mice feeding underground) may also be responsible for chlorosis. Other possible causes include soil that is not acid enough, receiving water from a building's downspout, or adding too much fertilizer, lime, or phosphate.

Leaf curl causes shoot leaves to become swollen and curled, and forms an irregular gall that is first pinkish and later becomes white when spore formation occurs. These swellings are known as pinkster apples, swamp apples, or honeysuckle apples. The disease may be reduced by handpicking and destroying all galls.

Leaf spots may be on the tips, along the margins, or in the middle of the leaf blade. They are usually silvery gray above and brown beneath, but sometimes they are brown above and show concentric rings caused by the advancing growth of the fungus. Spots caused by disease are easily distinguished from those caused by unfavorable environmental conditions—look for the tiny black fruiting pustules of the fungus imbedded in the upper surface of the discolored tissues. They are easily seen with a magnifying glass. The environmental spots are caused by winter injury (see below) and ice injury (see above).

In small plantings, pick off and burn badly spotted leaf areas. It is important to note that leaf spot is a secondary effect of the bush being in poor condition from some other cause.

Rhododendron dieback is a fungus malady causing terminal buds or leaves to brown and hang limp in winter. Twigs are cankered, and leaves and flower clusters of shaded plants become brown and wilted. High humidity favors this disease.

Select sunny planting sites with good air circulation. Rhododendrons should not be planted near lilacs, which share the disease. Cut off browned or cankered branches well below the infected area. Remove severely affected plants from the garden.

Death of terminal twigs may result from a disease known as **twig canker.** If no borers are found in the wilting or dead twig, scrape the bark with a sharp knife to see if a small reddish brown canker lies just beneath the bark. To eradicate canker disease, remove all affected tips, making sure that the cut is about two inches below the canker area.

If entire branches die and no insects can be found, the bark should be scraped from the branch at the soil line and the inner wood inspected for reddish streaks. These streaks indicate **wilt.** Wilt is caused when the fungus enters the young roots and works its way up to the crown. At first, single branches yellow and wilt; later, the entire plant may become affected. The disease is most destructive in cool locations in the seedbed or nursery, and where the soil is not acid enough for good growth. The pathogens can enter the injured roots of newly transplanted seedlings or through growth cracks that often occur during the second year of the seedlings' growth.

Do not plant rhododendrons in soil known to have harbored this disease. In the nursery, rotate frames. Use light soils in drainage beds and avoid overwatering. Adjust soil acidity to a pH of 4 or 4.5.

Winter injury can effect browning on the margins and tips of leaves, caused when the loss of water from the leaf surface is greater than the ability of the roots to absorb water (also see chlorosis, above). Rhododendron leaves normally remain green in winter, and curl and hang down in very cold weather (see also ice injury, above). March winds may aggravate injury to plants in an exposed location. Discourage late growth and protect roots with a good mulch to minimize damage; if possible, drape cloth over plant tops when necessary.

Cold winter weather can kill flower buds also, especially of those rhododendrons that are not adapted to the local climate. Such plants are particularly susceptible because of late fall development which occurs in a prolonged growing season (sometimes created by a dry summer period followed by a rain). If flower bud scales become separated and even a flower or two appear, water can enter these buds during the winter to freeze and kill them.

Rhubarb

Insects

The **rhubarb curculio** has a reputation as the most trouble-some of rhubarb pests. This is a large (¾-inch-long) snout beetle that looks as though dusted with yellow powder. If the powder is rubbed off, the insect can be seen to be grayish brown beneath. It bores into stalks, crowns, and roots and punctures the stems. Curculios are distributed from New England to Idaho, and south to Florida and Louisiana.

Rhubarb Curculio

The beetle is easily seen and handpicking is an efficient control. It deposits its eggs in certain species of dock plants, particularly curly dock, and all wild dock should be dug out and destroyed in July while the eggs lay unhatched on the leaves.

Other pests include the European corn borer, which some-times tunnels in the stalks (see CORN), stalk borer (TOMATO), and the yellow woolybear caterpillar (see imported cabbageworm under CABBAGE).

Diseases

Anthracnose of rhubarb (known also as stalk rot) is char-acterized by watery soft areas on stalks. Eventually, leaves wilt and die. Once this malady has struck, there is little you can do to control it, but you can get a good start on next year's crop by cleaning up rhubarb debris after harvest.

Crown rot causes rotting of the crown and main roots of rhubarb plants by water mold fungi. Plants usually have yellowed leaves that subsequently collapse and leave the plant wilted. In-fected crowns are soft and water-soaked. Apparently–healthy petioles collected from diseased plants frequently decay after packing. Dig up and burn affected plants.

Leaf spot is seen as small, circular, brown spots scattered over leaf surfaces; a fungus is responsible. While common in some areas, the disease doesn't do enough harm to require control.

Verticillium wilt is caused by a soil-borne fungus and is capable of infecting many other kinds of plants. Symptoms in-clude wilting and pronounced yellowing, and marginal and inter-veinal dying of basal leaves. Early in the season, yellowing frequently occurs without wilting and is often confused with nutri-tional disorders. Heavy losses have occurred in some fields. The disease is usually widely distributed in coastal areas devoted to rhubarb production, particularly where other susceptible host plants, such as strawberries, tomatoes, and peppers, have been grown.

A wise precaution is to plant rhubarb on land that has not been used for growing other susceptible crops. Do not use planting stock from fields showing symptoms of the disease.

Rose

For gardeners who take pride in growing first-quality roses without resorting to poisons, garden sanitation is an important precaution. Remove garden trash and mulches from rose beds each spring, and let the sun dry the soil for at least a month. This drying process kills many spores and fungi that overwinter in the mulch or soil. It is good practice to assume that leaves that wilt or fall during the growing season are affected by a disease or insect pest; remove these leaves to the compost pile as soon as possible. When selecting plants, look for varieties with inbred resistance to the more important diseases.

Roses are the focus of more poisonous sprays and dusts than any other flower, but garden sanitation, resistant varieties, and the following suggestions—along with a good dose of common sense —will get your plants safely through the season.

Insects

You are likely to find tiny **aphids** [color], the green rose aphid and green and pink potato aphids being most common, clustered about the tips of young growing shoots. Roses are as popular with aphids as they are with humans, and you may see other species as well, in various hues and stages of hairiness.

The easiest control is to wipe the pests off by hand. Aphids prefer new growth, so you'll know where to look for them. This won't kill all of them, and because they reproduce prolifically, you can expect them to return in numbers before long. Other gardeners get along with just a forcible spray from the garden hose (this works against mildew, as well). But even these simple controls may be unnecessary if a good balance of insect life is at work in the garden. Aphid lions and the larvae of ladybugs will eat great numbers of aphids if given a chance. So before you influence the insect world with your thumb or a flood, let nature take its course for a time. Many gardeners have proved to themselves that interplanting chives with roses will keep aphids at a distance. As the chives develop, the clumps can be separated and spread to new spots.

Several species of **bees** damage roses occasionally. The female leaf-cutter bee cuts neat circles from the margins of leaves. She then stores the bits of leaf as food for her young, either in the excavated stems of dahlia or in tunnels in wood. The bees also stash away aphids and other insects, and thus rate as beneficials. Cynthia Westcott, who recommends an array of insecticides in *The Gardener's Bug Book,* is moved to write: "Although rose foliage all over the country may be disfigured somewhat by these bees, one should not begrudge a few leaf portions required by this primarily beneficial insect. It is better to admire the perfection of its tailoring."

Carpenter bees (known also as leaf-cutter bees) deserve less compassion, however, as they bore out the pith of rose canes to cause wilting. Control by pruning canes below the infested section in spring, or whenever wilted canes are noticed. To keep the bees from entering cut canes, insert a flat-headed tack in the end or plug the hole with grafting wax, putty, or paraffin; you might also paint the end with shellac or tree-wound paint.

The **buffalo treehopper** may sound like an improbable bit of Wild West exotica, but is actually a tiny ($\frac{1}{4}$-inch-long) insect distinguished by a pair of short horns on its head. Viewed from above, the treehopper appears triangular and is pointed at the rear. When females lay their eggs they cut curved slits in the bark of rose twigs, and these wounds make entrance for rose canker and other diseases.

Buffalo Treehopper Damage

To control this pest, remove weeds and grass from the immediate area, if possible. Alfalfa and sweet clover are especially favorable to treehoppers. Planting roses near other susceptible hosts may aggravate trouble; these include fruit trees and elm, cottonwood, and locust. The eggs within the twigs can be killed with a light dormant-oil spray applied before spring.

If you find holes in canes, especially while pruning in spring or fall, suspect the **carpenter ant.** Discard as much of the cane as has been hollowed out—tunnels sometimes go all the way down to the roots.

Flower thrips attack rose buds and cause discoloration of the petals. Their feeding usually results in deformity or failure of the flowers to mature. Adult thrips are extremely active, slender, and brownish yellow in color, with feathery wings. The young are lemon-yellow. Thrips breed in grass and weeds neigh-

Flower Thrip

boring the garden. Because a new generation can come along every two weeks, especially if the weather is hot and dry, populations tend to build up quickly. Light-colored and many-petalled flowers seem to be the most attractive to thrips.

It is sometimes practicable to remove the outer petals as the rose is just opening and to crush the offending thrips by hand. The rose should then open normally. Cut off and burn seriously affected flowers.

The gray brown **fuller rose beetle** eats ragged areas from the margins of many outdoor plants, including azalea, begonia, camelia, canna, carnation, chrysanthemum, gardenia, geranium, and primrose. This nocturnal pest has a cream-colored strip on each side, and is about ⅓ inch long. The yellowish, brown-headed larvae work underground, feeding on roots and girdling stems to cause the yellowing or death of plants. This rose beetle is distributed in the South and in California, and is considered a serious greenhouse pest in the North, where they are most abundant in December.

The beetle hides on twigs or foliage during the day, and can be handpicked. You might try placing a stick barrier on stalks to keep this wingless pest from crawling to the flowers.

The hairy, lemon-yellow **goldsmith beetle** is a large (one-inch-long) cousin of the June bug. The larvae resemble grubs and attack the roots of rose, chrysanthemum, canna, and other ornamentals. They are common in the eastern states and the Southwest. For control of the larvae, see the discussion of milky spore disease under JAPANESE BEETLE.

Japanese beetles need little introduction. Roses are just one of the hundreds of plants that these pests dine on. Many gardeners patrol the garden in early morning or evening to handpick them; at these times of day, the beetles are less inclined to fly and can be dropped into a can of water topped with kerosene. See JAPANESE BEETLE for a number of controls that will handle this and most any other beetle found on roses.

Leaf rollers are caterpillars that gorge themselves on foliage and then pupate within the protection of rolled leaves. There are several species of occasional importance. Now that DDT is no longer around to kill the parasites of these worms, rose growers should have a lot less trouble with leaf rollers. If the sensation isn't too unpleasant, pinch the worms while in their rolled hideouts.

Two-Spotted
Spider Mite

Two-spotted **red spider mites** appear as tiny dots on the

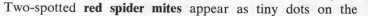

underside of foliage. Leaves become discolored in a stippled pattern, and you may see tiny webs strung across the leaf surface or on new growth. As the injury progresses, leaves brown, curl, and drop off. Mites overwinter on perennials and weeds, and become abundant in hot, dry weather.

Frequent hosings will wash mites off foliage. Clean up trash and weeds from the garden before the growing season. See SPIDER MITES.

A frequent and often unrecognized cause of poor growth is the **root-knot nematode.** Stunting, yellowing, and premature death may be attributable to other causes as well, so it is necessary to examine the roots for the characteristic swellings—knots of between ¼ and ⅛ inch in diameter, and ½ inch or more in length. In some infestations, the roots decay and fibrous roots are scarce. Roots often look like a string of beads. A magnifying glass will enable you to see the tiny worms within a bisected knot.

Examine the roots of barefooted roses before planting, and discard any having root knots. If roses are growing in pots, infestation can usually be detected by examining the roots on the surface of the ball of soil after the container is removed. Once serious damage has occurred, remove the plant and replace the soil before planting other susceptible plants. You can extend the useful life of slightly injured plants by enriching the surrounding soil with organic matter. Resistant varieties are available. See NEMATODE for other controls.

The **rose chafer** [color] (known also as the **rose bug** or **rose beetle**) is a tannish, long-legged beetle that measures ¼ inch in length. It skeletonizes foliage, and damages flowers (especially white ones) by feeding on the petals and soiling them with excrement. The creamy white, brown-headed larvae feed on the roots of grasses and weeds. Rose chafers are most common in the northeastern states, are troublesome as far west as Colorado, and breed most abundantly in sandy waste and lawns. Adults appear suddenly, damage plants for from four to six weeks, and then suddenly disappear.

Rose Chafer

Handpicking is the first line of defense against the chafer. An effective barrier can be made of cheesecloth or mosquito netting, either as a canopy or fence. The beetles can fly, but will seldom make it over a barrier. Suburban gardeners are rarely troubled much by this insect, but growers whose roses are near fallow fields shouldn't be surprised to see chafers stalking about. The USDA suggests that growing cultivated crops in wasteland breeding areas will reduce infestation. Cynthia Westcott warns that rose chafers are poisonous to chickens.

The **rose curculio** is a peculiar-looking beetle—it's colored red and carries a long, black snout. Adults eat holes in the buds of wild and garden roses, and the buds often fail to open as a result. White larvae feed on seeds and flowers. This pest is found throughout the United States, and is most common in northern, colder regions; North Dakota sees particularly severe infestations.

Handpicking works well enough in most cases. Collect and burn dried buds before larvae have a chance to complete their development and pupate in the soil. To control the larvae in the soil, see JAPANESE BEETLE.

Rose galls on stems are caused when any of a few species of tiny four-winged wasps lay their eggs. If a gall is cut open, larvae may be seen living in the plant cells. One variety, mossy rose gall, is fibrous mass of green to purple filaments on the stem. Another, rose root gall, is a conspicuous, rounded swelling at the base of the plant or below ground, reaching one or two inches in diameter. In either case, cutting open the growth will distinguish it from crown gall infection, which is caused by bacteria. Cut and burn infested galls as you find them.

The **rose leaf beetle** is a small, oval, metallic insect that appears late in spring to bore into buds and partially opened flowers. When abundant, the beetles also may eat shot-holes in flowers at any stage of development. Larvae sometimes damage the roots of roses. The beetles can be handpicked or jarred from plants into a bucket of water topped with kerosene. Should an infestation get out of hand, you may have to fall back on a high-powered botanical such as pyrethrum.

A white, peppered effect on the top surface of leaves could be evidence that **rose leafhoppers** are feeding on the underside. Both adults and nymphs suck sap, causing severely infested leaves to drop prematurely. These pests hop about nervously when disturbed. They are narrow in shape and colored yellow white. A second generation appears in fall, and is more damaging than the first.

Leafhoppers are too small and too energetic for the hands of most gardeners, so you had best resort to botanical sprays to repel them from valued plants.

The tiny yellow brown **rose midge** brings trouble when it lands on roses and deposits its yellow eggs on the tender growth near flower buds. These eggs hatch in just two days, and the larvae start feeding at the base of flower beds or leaf stems, causing them to become distorted; the plant parts later turn brown and die. Twenty or 30 white maggots may be at work inside a single bud. Within a week, the larvae mature and build small white cocoons on the soil, and just one week later a new generation of midges flies out into the world. In greenhouses, most injury occurs between May and November, and midges are seldom seen during the winter. They can be controlled by mixing tobacco dust with the greenhouse soil. Cut off and destroy all infested buds.

Snow-white **rose scale** often thickly infests older canes. They feed on plant juices, resulting in weakened plant growth or even death. Remove and destroy infested canes. It helps to prune nearby berry canes of infested sections. During the dormant season, spray with a white-oil emulsion.

Rose/Rose Scale

Spiral mines that travel around canes are the work of **rose stem girdler** larvae. Stems swell up, split, and often die. Rugosa and hugonis roses are especially attractive to this pest. The metallic green, ¼-inch-long adult beetles appear in June and July, and place eggs under the bark of rose and raspberry stems. Clip off and burn the infested parts in winter or early spring.

Several types of **slugs** feed on rose leaves. Both wild and cultivated roses are susceptible. Most damage occurs in the early spring on new foliage, but one species, the greenish white, bristly rose slug, continues to breed and eat all summer.

A strong jet of water will put most rose slugs out of commission, but if they keep coming back for more, try a spray of garlic or even stronger stuff. It's important to control these pests as early in the season as possible, as it doesn't take them long to make a shambles of a rose garden.

Two species of **stem borer** larvae chew their way downward into the pith of stems until they reach the crowns, a journey that may take them one or two seasons. Branches are weakened and are likely to die. Both species are yellowish white worms with brown heads, growing to ⅗ inch in length. While they spend most of this stage hidden from sight, keep an eye out for the adults —one, the rose stem sawfly, is a waspish insect with transparent wings, appearing in the garden in early summer; the other, the adult raspberry cane borer, is a slender beetle, striped black and yellow, and measuring about ½ inch.

Cut off rose canes a good six inches below the lowest point of injury, and either burn them or slit the stem and pluck out the borer (there is only one per cane). If possible, control borers on other hosts in the area, including blackberry, raspberry, and occasionally azalea.

One pest that shouldn't be handpicked, not without gloves at any rate, is the **stinging rose caterpillar,** a sluglike beast marked with red, white, and violet stripes. It measures up to ¾ inch long and bears seven pairs of large, spine-bearing tufts that can give a burning sensation for several hours. These caterpillars are usually found on the underside of leaves. Since the overwintering cocoons are in plant refuse, a thorough fall cleanup will prove effective in preventing trouble.

Other pests of occasional importance are the celery leaf tier (see CELERY), corn earworm (CHRYSANTHEMUM), EAR-WIGS, four-lined plant bug (CHRYSANTHEMUM), GARDEN SYMPHILID, harlequin bug (CABBAGE), WHITE FLY, LYGUS BUGS, potato leafhopper (POTATO), and spotted cucumber beetle (CUCUMBER).

Diseases

The four most common diseases damaging roses are black spot, powdery mildew, brown canker and other cane diseases, and rust.

Black Spot

Black spot [color] may appear from the first flush of growth in spring to leaf drop in fall. Symptoms appear as coal-black lesions on both the upper and lower surfaces of leaves. Black spot can readily be distinguished from other leaf spots by the darker color and fringed or feathery margin surrounding the spot. Heavily diseased leaves tend to turn yellow and drop prematurely. When excessive premature defoliation occurs, the plant forms a new set of leaves, which causes a considerable drain on the food reserves in the roots. This results in a weakened plant with poorly matured wood. Such plants are especially subject to winter injury.

A few days after the spots first appear, little black pimples show up in the spots; this signals that the spores are about to be discharged, and that you had better act fast. Spores are carried by air currents, as well as on tools, insects, and the gardener's hands and clothing. Those that land on rose leaves will germinate and produce an infection, providing the environmental conditions are favorable. Free moisture on the leaves from rainfall, dew, or excessive sprinkling will favor the development of black spot. With this moisture and favorable temperatures, the spots will appear in a week or ten days and then produce new spores to continue the disease cycle. Black spot is indirectly responsible for a pale flower color; this is because diseased leaves and defoliated plants manufacture less of the sugars that help to intensify flower color.

All kinds of roses are susceptible to black spot in some degree. The disease does its worst when highly susceptible plants are grown together, and it is best to buffer these varieties with roses that enjoy a tolerance to black spot. Keep in mind that a tolerant variety isn't safe from all of the many strains of black spot fungus, and therefore will do better in some areas than in others.

As virulent and persistent as black spot may be, there are several preventative measures that, when used together, should get your roses through the season. A control program begins in fall with the gathering and disposal of fallen leaves. In spring, after the danger of frost is past, remove the mulch and rake the ground thoroughly. Then, let the garden plot lie exposed to the sun's rays. When the first shoots appear, apply new mulch in generous amounts. Infected leaves and twigs should be removed from plants as they likely harbor overwintering fungus, but do so only if they are completely dry. Prune sickly canes freely. If worse comes to worse, you may have to rely on a dusting of finely ground sulfur to save your plants. The sulfur may burn leaves if applied in very hot weather.

A special value of mulch becomes clear when plants are watered. The consistency of this ground cover keeps water drops and rain drops from splashing on leaves, and dry leaves won't support the fungus. Some gardeners push a hose nozzle right into the mulch to make sure the leaves stay dry. At any rate, never sprinkle roses from overhead, especially in the evening when the foliage cannot dry before nightfall.

Although you're not likely to come across **brand canker,** it is a serious disease and deserves mention here. It is first known by dark red cankers with red or purplish margins that appear on stems. After a time the center of the spots becomes light brown, and navy green spores may be seen. Cankers can girdle stems and kill them.

The disease develops during the winter, when it is sheltered from the elements by the heavy protective covering that many growers put around the base of their plants. It is better to use a light winter mulch and to avoid piling dirt up around the canes. Or, if canker has been a problem and winters are not too severe, omit the mulch entirely.

Common canker (stem canker) occurs in wounds on canes and in the cut ends of pruned canes, especially if the cut is not made close to a bud. Canes should be inspected in spring, and damaged tissue cut back. Prompt pruning is the best control. The danger of a canker infection is reduced by proper pruning—make clean cuts just above a bud. Such cuts heal quickly, while ragged cuts and those made too far from a bud heal slowly and are thus prime targets for infection. Disinfect shears and other cutting tools after using them on cankered plants.

Crown Gall

Irregular or spherical galls on roots, crowns, or canes are symptoms of **crown gall.** While the organism causing the disease does not kill the tissue, it does stimulate abnormal growth. Control is largely a matter of prevention. Buy disease-free plants, and plant in uninfested soil. The causal bacteria can be kept out by avoiding wounds. Remove and destroy affected plant parts as soon as possible.

Downy mildew appears as irregular brown spots on the underside of leaves of greenhouse roses. Plants grown out-of-doors are rarely affected. Keep the humidity in the greenhouse below 85 percent, and keep daytime temperatures high. Many of the newer rose varieties are resistant to mildew; check with the nursery or consult recent catalogs.

Rust

Leaf rust is an important fungus disease that produces bright orange pustules on the underside of leaves and pale yellow spots on top. Pustules eventually become brick-red, and wilting and defoliation follow. Pick off and destroy affected leaves as soon as they are spotted. Because leaves must be wet for four hours in order to become infected, careful watering and a loose mulch will go a long way toward preventing trouble. Rake up all leaves from the ground in fall or early spring. Periodic dustings of sulfur have been found effective, but you should not fall back on this unless preventative measures have failed you first.

Three **physiological diseases** are worthy of note. These are not caused by disease pathogens, but result from problems with the plant's environment.

• *Chlorosis* can be induced by an excess of lime in the soil; leaf blades of affected plants become uniformly yellow. Ms. Westcott suggests that chlorosis may also be induced by a deficiency of iron (upper leaves are yellow with green veins), nitrogen (lower leaves are paled), or potassium (leaves turn gray and stems are weakened).

• *Leaf scorch* can be traced to deficiencies of potash or, in the greenhouse, of boron or calcium.

• Another greenhouse disease, *mercury toxicity,* occurs when paint containing mercury is used on sashes. The solutions for these physiological diseases lie in identifying them and eliminating the cause.

Powdery mildew ranks as one of the most serious of rose diseases. It causes a white or grayish, powdery coating on the surface of leaves, stems, buds, fruit, or other plant parts. Leaves and young shoots are most often affected. This visible coating consists of an intertwined network of threads and chains of egg-shaped summer spores that are easily detached and carried away by the wind. Such spores are produced throughout the growing season and new generations can occur every four days, providing that conditions are just right. In fall, black dormant resting bodies may be seen in the felty growth. These structures, along with infections in buds, serve to carry the fungus through the winter.

Unlike most fungi, spores of powdery mildew do not germinate readily in wet conditions. Frequent syringing and hosing therefore reduce the amount of mildew, but may encourage the spread of black spot at the same time. Powdery mildew is also somewhat special in that it feeds on the surface cells of plants, not inside them, and thus is one of the few rose diseases that can be cured. The plants are affected very gradually, and the powdery coating is therefore the first visible symptom. Other symptoms include: stunting and distortion of leaves, buds, growing tips, and fruit; distortion and stunting of leaves and buds; death of invaded surface tissues; a general decline in plant growth; yellowing of leaves; and premature leaf fall.

Rose varieties vary greatly in their susceptibility to powdery mildew. Hybrid teas, many red roses, and floribundas are usually considered susceptible, while shiny-leaved climbers, Welch multiflora, and Rugosa types get by without much damage. "Garden planting avoids a lot of mildew trouble," writes Ms. Westcott in *Plant Disease Handbook.* "Keep the plants well spaced, in beds away from buildings, and not surrounded by tall hedges or walls."

A common virus disease on the West Coast is **rose mosaic.** The symptoms include chlorotic spots that are most numerous at or near the midribs of leaflets. Ring, oak-leaf, and watermark patterns are also seen in some cases. Plants are often dwarfed, and buds are bleached. Although this disease is primarily of concern to West Coast growers, greenhouse roses and those shipped from the West are also vulnerable. Heat-treated rootstocks are free of disease. Any plant found to be affected should promptly be discarded.

Another virus disease, **rose streak,** affects roses grown in the East. Symptoms include brown rings on leaves, brown and yellowish vein banding, and necrotic lesions on canes above the buds. Streak is usually transmitted by grafting.

Rose Of Sharon, see Hibiscus

Rutabaga, see Turnip, Cabbage, and Broccoli

Scale

Although inconspicuous individually, infestations of scale may encrust whole branches of trees. In great numbers, they cause host plants to become stunted and chlorotic by sucking sap. The honeydew they produce frequently supports the growth of dark sooty molds that can interfere with photosynthesis. Ants are attracted to honeydew, and carry scales from plant to plant as they do with aphids.

Scales are curiously simple organisms in the last stage of their life. After a brief mobile period, the female settles down permanently for a life of egg-laying. Her legs drop off, almost all of her internal organs disappear, and she produces eggs—typically over a thousand—until there is little left of her.

The first nymphal stage is a pale, flat, six-legged creature with prominent eye-spots. After a moult, the males become elongate and the females circular. In the third stage the female builds a curved shell within which the eggs are laid. Adult male scales have a single, puny set of wings, capable of propelling them only a few feet at a time. This stage never eats, having no digestive system. They live to copulate, and usually die on top of the female after doing so. Fertilized females produce both males and females, while those that aren't give birth to females alone.

San José Scale

Scales may be efficiently controlled by smothering them with a "superior" or "supreme" type of dormant-oil spray. Timing depends on the crop, but sprays should generally be applied before the buds break open. Scales can also be scraped from trees, or killed by brushing turpentine or soapy water over them. A spray of glue dissolved in water is effective. See entries for each fruit for other control methods.

Scales have proven very good subjects for biological control. A chalcid wasp, *Comperiella bifasciata,* was imported from the Far East early in the century and now offers economic control of yellow scale if there is not too much interference from ants. Another citrus pest, Florida red scale, is parasitized by a variety of chalcid wasps. In California, the chalcid *Aphytus luteolus* keeps down soft scale. The damage of the purple scale to the citrus industry has been kept at very low levels by colonizations of *A. lepidosaphes,* imported from China and Formosa in the twenties. Growers can integrate the more traditional controls with this chalcid's help by spraying strips rather than a whole orchard at one shot; the beneficials can then retreat to unsprayed sections to continue their work. Swann says in *Beneficial Insects* that growers had success with "a twelve-month alternate strip treatment," whereby every other pair of rows was treated each year. Pest control costs were halved, and the results were equal to or better than those made with conventional chemical control. Success has also been scored against the olive scale with a chalcid import from Persia, the nigra and black scale with a chalcid from South Africa, and the California red scale with four species. A parasitic fly and a ladybug species take care of cottony cushion scale. Ladybugs also help out in the control of a few of the above-named species.

Serviceberry

Insects

There are not too many insects that trouble the serviceberry. Among the more common ones are oystershell scale (see LILAC), lesser peach borer (PEACH), and shothole borer (peach tree borer under PEACH).

Diseases

Rust infects leaves, causing brownish orange spots of up to ¼ inch in diameter. In wet springs, light-colored spore horns are formed on the fruit and on leaf spots. Spores from these horns infect nearby red cedars, the alternate host of the rust fungus. The fact that the rust must infect the red cedar to complete its life cycle suggests that serviceberry not be planted within 500 yards of cedars or junipers.

Witches' broom (or black mildew) is a fungus disease that causes a stimulation of the growing point of a plant, giving rise to many new shoots with a broomlike appearance. There is usually a heavy coating of black mold on the underside of leaves. The best control is to prune and burn affected leaves and twigs.

Slugs And Snails

Snail

Slugs are not merely snails without houses, but make up a closely related family under the phylum Mollusca. They have a mantle, or internal shield, that corresponds to the snail's shell. When contracted, slugs draw their head and tentacles (eye stalks) below the mantle. Both slugs and snails have soft bodies and exude a slimy mucus. A silvery trail of mucus shows where these mollusks have traveled on their nocturnal forages.

These are pests of both garden and greenhouse. To keep them from the greenhouse, surround it with a border free from grass and weeds. Store pots and boxes away from weeds and plant debris.

Dry, cold weather and daylight send slugs and snails under boards, cabbage leaves, or pieces of potato and other garden debris. These shelters can be set out as traps in otherwise clean gardens. Dispose of the hiding creatures by handpicking or sprinking a bit of salt.

Hussey, Read, and Hesling explain in *The Pests of Protected Cultivation* that such irritations cause slugs to produce great quantities of slime, and they destroy themselves through desiccation.

These soft creatures are repelled by a mulch of oak leaves, tobacco stem meal, and wormwood tea as a soil drench. Hellebore has long been used to keep slugs from grape vines. Quassia, another plant-based insecticide, is also potent. Possibly the best way to be rid of slugs and snails is to set out saucers or jar lids full of stale beer. The fermented liquid draws them from far and wide, and they drown in their drink. If it appears that they are taking a sip and then leaving, mix in a bit of pastry flour to make a sticky mixture.

Larvae of the lightning bug are able to climb up a snails' back and sink their sicklelike jaws into the victim's head. Garter snakes, grass snakes, box turtles, and salamanders also have a penchant for escargot.

Snapdragon

Several species of shield-shaped **stink bugs** spoil snapdragons by sucking sap. They are also found on columbine, sunflower, verbascum, lupine, and other flowering plants. If you can't identify these pests by their shape, the odor they put off should clue you in. Stink bug populations will stay down if you carefully weed the garden area.

Stink Bug

Other pests include APHIDS, cabbage looper (see CABBAGE), corn earworm (CHRYSANTHEMUM), four-lined plant bug (CHRYSANTHEMUM), GARDEN SYMPHILID, LYGUS BUGS, NEMATODES, SLUGS AND SNAILS, and SPIDER MITES.

Soybean

Insects

Soybeans are generally not susceptible to a large number of insect pests. They may be bothered by the **Japanese beetle,** but this once-troublesome insect can be controlled by the use of milky spore disease. These beetles do not bother soybeans much early in the season, but by August they flock in ceaseless hordes and, if unchecked, will defoliate the plants very rapidly. See JAPANESE BEETLE.

Japanese Beetle

The **velvetbean caterpillar** [color] is frequently a pest in the southeastern states, where it attacks soybeans as well as velvetbeans, peanuts, kudzu, alfalfa, and horsebeans. The insect is a tropical species that does not survive the winter in the continental United States, except perhaps in the southern tip of Florida. The moths fly into this country sometime in June or July and may produce as many as three to four generations during a season. The insect does not usually become very abundant until late summer or early fall. However, a heavy infestation may completely strip the plants in a field within a few days. The small white, roundish eggs are laid singly on leaves and hatch within three to five days. The caterpillars feed for about three weeks. They are very active and will spring wriggling into the air when disturbed, at the same time spitting a brownish liquid. After completing feeding, the caterpillars enter the soil to pupate at a depth of $\frac{1}{4}$ to 2 inches. The adult moths emerge about ten days later.

Handpicking is an effective control method because the

caterpillars rarely become abundant, thanks in part to naturally occurring egg parasites and a fungus. Should the caterpillar population threaten to get out of hand, you can turn to the bacterium *Bacillus thuringiensis,* available commercially.

Diseases

While commercial growers are confronted by many potentially significant diseases, the gardener who sows a few plants for the edible beans should have little or no trouble.

Bacterial blight is a disease that causes leaves to assume small angular brown or black spots. Cool, rainy weather favors this disease. Leaf tissue that is affected may drop out, giving the leaves a ragged appearance.

Reduce damage by crop rotation, deep plowing, avoiding overwatering, and the planting of seed from disease-free fields. Commercial varieties that have displayed some resistance include Hawkeye and Bethel.

Bacterial pustule is a warm-weather disease that usually appears in July. First symptoms are small, yellow green spots with reddish brown centers. The spots are most conspicuous on the upper surface of the leaf. The central portion of the spots is slightly raised, developing into a small pustule, especially on the underside of the leaf. In the later stages the pustules rupture and dry. The disease-producing bacteria overwinter on diseased leaves.

Plant only from seed that is known to be free from bacterial pustule. Rotation of crops is a sound cultural practice. The variety CNS is highly resistant, and Ogden is somewhat resistant.

Brown spot is a fungus that is generally one of the first diseases to appear on the leaves of young plants. When this disease strikes, the lower leaves become infected first, turning yellow and falling off. The fungus can be carried through the winter on diseased stems and leaves of plants. If you are growing your soybean crop in two successive years, be certain to plow the stubble deeply so that the stems and leaves are buried deep.

Downy mildew [color] is a widespread fungus disease that causes small, pale green spots to appear on the upper surface of the leaves. They soon enlarge, grow together, and become brown as the leaf dies. Grayish tufts of moldy growth appear on the lower surface of the leaf. Because this fungus overwinters on diseased foliage and seed, crop rotation and disease-free seed will prevent trouble. Although few varieties are resistant to downy mildew, Harosoy, Lindarin, Kent, Lincoln, and Clark are less susceptible than others.

Weeds left in fields until harvest time have been found to reduce yields as much as 17 percent. Proper seed bed preparation is the best method of controlling weeds. By working the soil to start the weeds growing, then working the surface to kill the weeds that have come up, you can be rid of them before planting time. Although the soil may have to be worked a number of times, it is necessary if a high–yielding crop is expected. Soybeans are particularly vulnerable to weeds because the crop grows very slowly during the early stages of life, allowing the weeds to outgrow them and offer severe competition for water, nutrients, and light.

Spearmint

This is one plant that generally takes care of itself. Occasionally disease or insects (particularly the four-lined plant bug and garden flea hopper) may injure a few plants, but mint grows so prolifically that only commercial growers should have reason for concern.

Spider Mites

Mites are members of the anthropodan class Arachnida, along with ticks, scorpions, and spiders. This should suggest to you that they have four pairs of legs, unlike other pests of the garden and orchard. The mites' relations also suggest their habit of spinning webs—not very large or dramatic ones, as they are used only for protection. The webs do not physically damage plants, but interfere with the looks of flowers.

Red Spider Mite

Mite populations are very sensitive to changes in the habitat. Nutritional sprays of copper and zinc, for example, increase the numbers of the citrus red mite, while the citrus rust mite is favored by copper. On apple trees, populations of the European red mite and two-spotted spider mite increase if trees are fed nitrogen-rich fertilizer. This is bad news for orchardists, as mites can lower the chlorophyll content of leaves by as much as 35 percent, reports J. G. Rodriguez in *Biological and Chemical Control of Plant and Animal Pests* (American Association for the Advancement of Science, 1960).

Tests in Nova Scotia apple orchards that had never been sprayed demonstrated that a balance exists between populations of the European red mite and those of its predators, and that some chemicals will upset the balance and lead to trouble. The best control of orchard mites is obtained with light- to medium-weight petroleum oils. Too much of even this non-toxic spray can damage trees by blocking light from leaves and inhibiting photosynthesis. The sprays also may act to shock trees and make their leaves fall if applied in dry, hot (over 90°F.), or unusually cool weather, state De Ong, Bishop, and Bishop in *Insect, Disease, and Weed Control*.

Heavy infestations cause a lightening or yellowing of leaves. In woody plants, defoliation follows the characteristic yellowing or fading, whereas herbaceous plants soon wilt and die.

Adult mites hibernate during the winter and begin laying eggs in the warm weather of spring and summer. Eggs are laid on the leaves of plants and hatch in three to five days. The young mites, quite similar to the adults in appearance, require about ten days to mature in hot, dry weather. The webs afford protection from wind and rain. Several generations are produced out-of-doors in the summer. In greenhouses or on house plants the mites will live and breed the year round.

• **Control measures.**   Red spider mite infestations are favored by warm, dry weather. Wet weather slows reproduction and favors the development of their natural enemies. Frequent high-pressure syringing with cold water will tend to reduce infestations.

One interesting control method that protects orchards from the red spider was developed by Dr. G. Edward Marshall of Purdue University. Dr. Marshall used a mixture of 20 pounds of cheap wheat flour and two quarts of buttermilk. The flour was mixed to a fairly thick slurry by the use of a high-pressure gun, and the two quarts of buttermilk were added as the slurry was almost complete. This combination was added to 100 gallons of water for application. As you might guess, the flour and buttermilk make a very sticky soup, and that's just the quality Dr. Marshall was after. Unlike an oil cover which would form too continuous a film and reduce transpiration, the flour-buttermilk spray safely destroys the mites by sticking them to the leaf's surface. Their mouths become stuck in the gluelike mixture and they suffocate with their hind ends up in the air. Some of the sprayed mites appear to have exploded after the spray dries. Rock phosphate or ground limestone can also be mixed with a liquid that helps the powder adhere to the leaf surface. Use the spray mixture after the leaves have had a chance to mature and as soon as the mite population is up to about three mites per leaf. Thorough applica-

Two-Spotted Spider Mite

tion is needed, but you are not endangering yourself by standing right under the tree. Three thousand pounds of flour and 15 gallons of buttermilk will be needed for every ten acres of bearing orchard.

Probably at least two sprays will be needed where mites have been a problem but you may find that some orchard plots don't need any sprays. Natural control such as ladybugs, lacewings, and predacious mites just might do the job for you. Of the mite's natural predators, the ladybug is the best known. They are credited with controlling the citrus red mite in unsprayed California orchards. Powdery lacewings are of importance in controlling red spider mites in English orchards, says Lester A. Swann in his very informative book, *Beneficial Insects*. Other beneficials include damsel bugs and dance flies.

A final control: Swann says that rotating oats, buckwheat, corn, or sorghum with wheat will break up the life cycle of the winter grain mite.

• **Beneficial mites.**   Not all mites are pests, and some rate as important predators. Two predatory mites will control the cyclamen mite, the number-one enemy of strawberries in California, according to a publication of that state's agricultural experiment station. But the good mites can only do their work if unhindered by pesticides. Another strawberry pest, the two-spotted mite, is heavily preyed upon by a third beneficial species, fortunately one that has a bit more resistance to some pesticides. Heavy infestations of purple scale are reduced by a mite that suffers from poor powers of locomotion—when the scales are few and far between, it has trouble locating a meal. Swann tells of an interesting way in which the mite has gotten around the problem— it hitches rides on ladybugs, hopping off when it happens by a scale host.

Growers in the Midwest are grateful to the grasshopper mite, an important predator of grasshoppers. In its larval stage it is parasitic on grasshopper larvae and adults, and as a nymph and adult it becomes a predator of the eggs. The habits of the grasshopper mite are detailed in a publication of the agricultural experiment station at South Dakota State College. The station notes that the larval mites have little direct effect upon the health of the infested grasshoppers, except to weaken them somewhat. However, when an adult grasshopper becomes heavily infested, the mites may be unable to fold their wings or fly properly. Each grasshopper mite nymph and adult drains a few eggs, some of which will not recover. The mites have been so abundant in some years that they actually controlled severe outbreaks of grasshoppers.

Spinach

Insects

Among the **aphids** that infest this crop, the yellow green spinach aphid (also known as the green peach aphid) is particularly voracious. See APHID for control measures.

The **beet webworm** sometimes injures spinach; see BEET.

The **spinach flea beetle** is one of several flea beetles that eat spinach. This is a $\frac{1}{5}$-inch-long insect with greenish black wing covers and a yellow thorax. It hibernates as a beetle, and appears in the field in early spring to deposit clusters of orange eggs on the ground at the base of the plant. The short, dirty gray to purplish larvae feed on the underside of the leaves. When disturbed, they drop to the ground and remain hidden until they perceive that danger is past. Pupation takes place underground, near the surface.

Control weeds in and around the garden area. Flea beetles avoid shaded areas, and you might plant spinach near houses or taller plants. Should infestation become a great problem, try garlic and, as a last resort, rotenone.

Spinach/Spinach Leaf Miner Damages

The **spinach leaf miner** is likely the most destructive pest of spinach; it also infests beets, chard, and the common weed known as lamb's-quarters. As a larva, it is a slender insect that mines its way into the veins of the leaves to cause a blotchy appearance. The plant is stunted and is usually unfit for use. Destroy affected leaves, since the miners are usually within, and burn or compost them. Keep down weeds in the area, especially lamb's-quarters.

Diseases

Yellowed and curled leaves, stunted plants, and reduced yields are indicative of **blight** (or yellows), a disease caused by the cucumber mosaic virus and spread by aphids. Grow blight-resistant varieties, such as 56 and 612. Remove and destroy perennial weeds. See APHID for methods of controlling this vector.

Wet weather often brings **damping-off** with it. If you are growing spinach from seed, plant enough so that you can fill in the gaps with extra plants.

A drawback to the preference of spinach for cool, moist days is susceptibility to **downy mildew** (chard blue mold), the most destructive disease of the crop. Affected plants show yellow leaf spots, with a fuzzy purple growth on the underside. These spots may quickly run together, killing leaves or the entire plant. The causal fungus is soil- and seed-borne, and is favored by wet, cool weather. In *Plant Disease Handbook,* Dr. Westcott says that the initial infection requires humidity above 85 percent and a mean temperature between 45° and 65°F. for a period of one week.

Prevent this disease by using clean seed, planting on fertile, well-drained soil, and using a three-year rotation. Do not crowd plants, and water on sunny mornings. Once the disease strikes, do not plant winter spinach, as it may carry over downy mildew from one growing season to the next. Resistant varieties include Dixie Market and Dixie Savoy (savoy); resistant hybrids include 7 (semisavoy), and 424 and 425 (smooth leaf). New varieties will likely be introduced as time goes on; check with your extension agent.

When **fusarium wilt** hits, the plant will generally turn yellow and the lower leaves lose their firmness and wilt. Look for a brown discoloration of the water channels. Virginia and Texas report the most severe damage. Although crop rotation reduces this disease, resistant strains offer the best answer.

Spirea

The foliage and flower buds of spirea are occasionally fed upon by the **oblique-banded leaf roller.** This caterpillar conceals itself by rolling the leaf on which it is feeding. It also ties the terminal leaves together, thus marring the plant and interfering with its normal growth. The roller is yellowish to pale green and ¾ inch long when mature. There are two generations annually, one in spring and the other in late summer.

If the infestation is light you can pinch off and destroy affected parts. Should stronger measures be necessary, dust the plants with a mixture of equal parts tobacco dust and pyrethrum powder, or a spray of pyrethrum and rotenone. Both dust and spray should be made in two applications half an hour apart; the first drives the caterpillars from their hiding places, while the second one kills them.

Spruce

Insects

Spruce/Spruce Aphid Gall

The best control for **aphids** is a dormant-oil spray applied in early spring to kill overwintering adults. Use a miscible oil mixed 1 part in 25 parts of water. Oil removes the bloom from blue spruces, however. A subsequent spray of nicotine sulfate, applied soon after the new growth begins in later spring, will control the young gall aphids before the pineapplelike galls are formed. When only a few galls occur, they may be cut off and destroyed before the insects emerge.

The **eastern spruce beetle** is a small bark beetle that emerges in June and July from small round holes resembling shot holes. Weak trees are particularly vulnerable, and the beetle prefers trees a foot or more in diameter. Its presence is made evident by an exuding gum mixed with sawdust on the trunk. The females lay their eggs in early summer and the larvae tunnel under the bark, hibernating in burrows in a partly grown condition and completing their development the following spring.

Infested trees should be cut and the bark removed before the middle of May to prevent the beetles from reaching maturity. See also the discussion of bark beetles under PINE.

The **spruce bud scale** is especially injurious to Norway spruce. The reddish brown adult scale, which is globular and ⅛ inch in diameter, closely resembles the new buds of trees. These insects pass the winter in an immature condition at the base of the terminal buds. Eggs hatch during early June and the young attack the new growth. A dormant-oil spray will control the scales as they overwinter.

Spruce trees are occasionally infested by the **spruce epizeuxis,** the larval form webbing together and feeding upon the needles. Larvae are brown and covered with wartlike protuberances, and resemble the spruce budworm (see FIR). The moths are a brownish gray, with a wingspread of less than an inch and narrow wavy bands marking the wings. They appear in the first half of summer. Control by removing and burning the dried needle masses in which larvae overwinter.

The **spruce mite** is reported to occur on spruce, pine, hemlock, and arborvitae. At times infestation may be extremely heavy. The mites are dull green to nearly black with a pale stripe on the back. The eggs are brownish and more or less flattened and it is in this stage that winter is passed. The mite spins webs and causes a graying or browning of the needles.

Dormant-oil sprays usually give good control of the eggs if applied thoroughly. See ARBORVITAE and SPIDER MITES.

If dark brown moths are flying about your spruce trees, you may be in for a visit from the **spruce needle miner.** The moths lay their eggs early in summer and the resultant larvae bore into the base of the needles. Often the heaviest infestation is on the lower branches, where many of the needles may be destroyed.

Control by washing the tree with a strong spray from the garden hose. Clean up and burn any trash that falls to the ground.

Other insect pests of spruce trees are APHID, gypsy moth (see TREES: INSECTS), spruce budworm (FIR), and the white pine weevil (PINE).

Diseases

Cytospora canker is a fungus disease that attacks the Norway and Colorado spruce, causing death first of the lower branches and then of branches higher on the tree. Cankers produced on affected branches are inconspicuous. They may be covered by quantities of resin which often drips to the lower branches. During rainy weather, threadlike, yellowish, gelatinous spore masses ooze from fruiting bodies on the cankers. These spores are spread by rain, wind, or pruning tools to other spruces where they enter through wounds.

Control involves pruning all diseased branches back to the trunk or nearest healthy lateral branch. Be careful to prune only when the trees are dry. It is beneficial to fertilize the trees to stimulate vigorous growth. Avoid nicking bark when mowing the lawn.

Unusually heavy **needle drop,** if not caused by spider mites, may be due to wet or poorly drained soils or to an unusually dry summer.

For gray mold blight, see FIR. For cankers, rusts, and witches' broom, see TREES: DISEASES.

Squash (and Pumpkin)

Insects

Several species of **aphid** infest squash; see APHID.

The **garden springtail** feeds upon young squash plants; see BEET.

Pickleworms feed on the flowers and leaf buds of squash and tunnel within flowers, terminal buds, vines, and fruits. They are one inch long, yellowish white (with numerous spots on the young worms), and brown-headed. The worms are active in winters in Florida and Texas, and spread as far north as Connecticut, Illinois, Iowa, and Kansas late in the season.

You can often get by this pest by planting very early; late plantings may be destroyed. Some growers use squash as a trap crop to protect melons, but the squash vines should be removed and burned before the larvae are fully grown. An early-fall cultivation will take care of underground pupae. Clean up the squash patch thoroughly immediately following harvest. See RESISTANT VARIETIES.

Squash Bug

Squash bugs are dingy brownish black insects, about ⅝ inch long, that have a very disagreeable odor when crushed. The young bugs have this same odor. When newly hatched, they have reddish heads and legs and green bodies. Later they become darker, the head and legs turning black and the bodies light to dark gray. In a more mature stage, they are brownish black. The shiny brick-red eggs are found on the leaves. They are about ¹⁄₁₆ inch long and are laid in clusters. The young bugs remain in clusters after hatching.

The squash bug feeds by inserting its needlelike mouth parts into the plant tissue and withdrawing the sap. Vine crops are easily killed by these bugs during the early part of the growing season. Older plants often have one or more runners damaged. The leaves on these damaged runners wilt, become crisp and dark brown, and later die.

The squash bug can be repelled from squash and other susceptible plants by growing radishes, nasturtiums, or marigolds nearby. Garden sanitation is important, as it has been discovered that the squash bug likes moist protected areas and often hibernates under piles of boards or in garden trash. Rotate crops to be certain that sweet potatoes do not follow sweet potatoes. Try to plant the new crop as far away as possible from the crop of the previous year. Pick eggs and insects off plants. See RESISTANT VARIETIES.

Squash Borer

The larval form of the **squash vine borer** is a one-inch-long worm, colored white with a brown head and small brown legs. They make their presence known by wilted runners and vines, and deposits of yellow, sawdustlike frass near the base of the stems. When mature, the larvae leave the plant and descend into the soil, where they spin a cocoon and remain until the following spring. There are two generations in the South, and usually but one in northern states.

Keep a look out for a sudden wilt of plant parts, as you can control borers by slitting affected stems and then killing the worm within. A delayed planting of summer squash may miss the feeding larvae. Earlier varieties can work too, as the borer doesn't lay its eggs until July, by which time the plants are large enough to withstand attacks. Baby blue and butternut squash are both somewhat resistant; winter squash varieties such as Hubbard are most severely injured. Encourage the vines to root at the joints from which the leaves grow by covering the joints with damp soil or decaying mulch. Clean up and dispose of vines after harvest.

Other pests of note include spotted and striped cucumber beetles (see CUCUMBER and RESISTANT VARIETIES), yellow woolybear caterpillar (see imported cabbageworm under CABBAGE), corn earworm (CORN), beet leafhopper (BEET), onion thrips (ONION), WHITE FLIES, and MEXICAN BEAN BEETLE.

Tall cover crops can in some cases protect an undergrown crop from insect vectors of disease. R. E. F. Matthews says in *Plant Virology* that cucurbits have successfully been interplanted with maize.

Diseases

Bacterial wilt is a disease spread by striped or spotted cucumber beetles. The bacteria are carried in the digestive tract, and as the beetles feed their droppings spread the pathogen in the feeding wounds. Usually a single leaf gradually wilts and dies, followed by a vine and then the whole plant. Plants are often stunted.

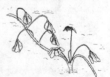

Bacterial Wilt

If a plant is suspected of bacterial wilt, cut across a stem and squeeze it to press out some of the plant juice. Touch the juice to your finger and slowly move your finger away. Juice from a diseased plant will be sticky and stringy. Once a plant has bacterial wilt, there is no cure. Control the cucumber beetles (see CUCUMBER) and remove and destroy wilted plants early in the season. Acorn and butternut squashes are resistant.

Mosaic virus is most common on straightneck and crookneck summer squash. Plants develop yellow spots on the leaves and sometimes on the fruit. The plants become stunted and the yields are reduced. There are two species of virus: cucumber mosaic is carried by aphids; squash mosaic is spread on seeds and by the cucumber beetle, and is most common in the Southwest.

There is no cure for mosaic once the plants have been affected. Do not allow perennial weeds such as milkweed, wild cucumber, and catnip to grow near squash or pumpkin fields, as insects feed on the weeds and carry the virus to healthy crops. See APHID and cucumber beetle under CUCUMBER for methods of controlling these vectors.

Strawberry

Insects

Two types of **aphids** do harm to strawberry plants: the leaf aphid and the strawberry root aphid. Leaf aphids transfer virus diseases from old or infected plants, which should be rogued out. The strawberry root aphids, which suck juice from the plant, are distributed below ground by the cornfield ant. Frequent soil cultivation will help control the ant and thus the aphid.

Cyclamen Mite

Both the cyclamen **mite** (also called the strawberry crown mite) and the spider mite may cause trouble. The cyclamen mite, invisible to the naked eye, feeds on buds and leaves to cause distorted or blotched blooms, curled-up purplish foliage, and no fruit. It is a cool-weather mite, seldom active in the heat of summer.

The cyclamen mite is usually kept under control by its natural predators, unless these have been destroyed by insecticides. Buy healthy certified strawberry plants, and avoid touching clean plants after handling those that may be infested. For control of the spider mite, see SPIDER MITES.

Nematodes are nearly invisible worms that live in the soil. There are several varieties, notably the root-knot nematode in the North, the sting nematode in the South, and the root-lesion nematode in both areas. Nematodes cause swellings or galls on the roots and weaken the plants, causing a much lower fruit yield. Flourishing in sandy soil rather than in clay, they are rarely troublesome in fertile soil rich in organic matter.

Marigolds tend to repel nematodes, and frequent but shallow cultivation will prevent damage to the roots. Keep plenty of organic matter in your soil and nematodes should be no problem; see NEMATODE.

In the Pacific Coast area, the **omnivorous leaf tier** may cause problems. Since the larvae overwinter in the crevices of rough-barked trees, the best preventive is not to plant strawberries near such trees.

Root weevils produce larvae that feed on the roots and crowns of strawberry plants. The adult strawberry weevil is a

¼-inch-long, reddish brown, black-snouted beetle that almost completely severs the unopened buds, leaving them hanging. You may first notice the weevil's presence by small holes in the petals of the blossoms. Plants are stunted, leaves bunched together, and roots and crown eaten away. The female weevil leaves eggs inside the unopened bud before crawling into the stem, girdling it and nearly severing it. The weevils emerge from the soil in early June and lay eggs throughout summer. A new beetle develops inside the bud, emerging in July after the fruit has been harvested. Larvae feed on roots until cold weather, when they move down deeper into the soil.

Strawberry Weevil

Since there is only one generation a year, control the root weevil by destroying any stems hanging by a thread and those which have already fallen, for they are the ones containing eggs. Often trash, wild brambles, hedgerows, and similar foliage are hibernating places for the adult weevils, and if it is practical, such shelter should be eliminated.

Garden **slugs,** which are often present in mulch, may become a problem for strawberries. While slugs usually feed on dead vegetation and help to break down organic matter, they sometimes develop a taste for strawberries. The mollusks do most of their damage on the bottom of berries that grow close to the soil or damp mulch, as they dislike dry surfaces.

If slugs are causing much damage to your berry plants, control them by placing large pieces of shingle between the fruit clusters. The slugs will crawl under them, and in the morning you can uncover the pests and sprinkle salt on them, whereupon they will melt before your eyes. See SLUGS AND SNAILS.

The **strawberry crown borer** is a grub that bores into the main root of the plant, weakening or even killing it. The adult is a brown beetle, ⅕ inch long, with reddish patches on the wings. The adults feed on stems and leaves, but it is the grubs that do the chief damage. Crown borers pass the winter under leaves or just under the surface of the soil. In late March they become active and lay their eggs in the crowns. Since eggs are laid from March to August, the grubs can do their damage all summer.

Strawberry Crown Borer

Injury to strawberries can be avoided by taking advantage of the two weak points in the insect's habits. First, the adult beetles cannot fly. Second, they do not begin to lay eggs until the last of March. If new beds are some distance from old beds, preferably 300 yards away, adult crown borers will not migrate to spread trouble. To avoid setting infested plants, dig them in February or early March before the eggs have been laid. Since

crown borers are harbored by wild strawberry plants and cinquefoil, be certain to destroy any that are in the neighborhood before
starting a strawberry bed. The only remedy for serious infestations is to plow the plants under after harvest and set another bed
on a new site. To be completely sure that the new bed will be free
from infestation, use disease-free plants and situate the new bed
as far away from the other bed as possible—at least 300 yards.
Strawberries can repel the onslaughts of the crown borer if they
are strong and vigorous, so see to it that the soil is bolstered with
compost.

The **strawberry crown mite,** a $\frac{1}{4}$-inch-long, reddish larva,
burrows into the crowns of plants to cause stunting and a general
weakening of the plant. Eggs are laid about the crown. Control
through sanitary measures and crop rotation.

The mark of the **strawberry leaf roller** is the folded, webbed
leaves within which the larvae feed. In spring, the larvae pupate
and become inconspicuous reddish brown moths with a wing-
spread of $\frac{1}{2}$ inch. Eggs are laid on the underside of leaves, and as
soon as the larvae hatch they feed on the leaves, folding them
together for protection. Plants are weakened, leaves turn brown,
and fruits are deformed. The rolled leaves protect these pests from
most insecticides, which only serve to kill the leaf roller's natural
predators. The full-grown larvae are $\frac{1}{2}$ inch long and colored
yellowish green or greenish brown. There are two generations, the
second of which feeds from August to cold weather; the larvae
then pass the winter in their folded leaves.

Natural parasites usually prevent serious infestations of this
pest. Rotenone has been found effective when applied to the
underside of leaves, but hold off with this powerful botanical as
long as feasible.

The **strawberry white fly** occasionally puts in an appearance.
Eggs are laid on the underside of leaves, and the nymphs remain
to suck the sap. The adult white flies are about $\frac{1}{16}$ inch long and
covered with a grayish powder. Infestations are usually in patches,
not in a whole field. If control is necessary, spray the underside
of leaves with rotenone.

White grubs and **wireworms** seldom cause serious damage,
and are usually not a problem if you avoid planting berries on
land that was recently sodded.

Diseases

Several precautions of strawberry culture, if carefully followed, will prevent many ailments. When making a new bed,

plant the crop on soil that has not been used for strawberries for many years, and as far as possible from any old, infected beds. Plant in well-drained soil that is enriched with plenty of manure, compost, or other humus-rich organic matter.

Prevent crowding of runners; if necessary, thin them out several times through the summer. Pull all weak or diseased plants promptly. Your plants should go into the winter thinned and pruned and ready for spring. Mulches will protect plants from winter injury. Coarse hay, dried alfalfa, and sweet clover are excellent choices: they don't pack down, are free of weed seeds, and allow the berry plants to be uncovered gradually. Use clean tools to lessen the chance of spreading infection and avoid working with plants when they are wet.

You will have fewer problems if you buy inspected, disease-free stock from reputable nurseries. Because of the virus control program in this country, most plants are now certified as virtually virus-free. This does not, of course, guarantee one-hundred percent protection, but it is decidedly safer to buy registered plants than unregistered.

Buy varieties that grow well in your area and those resistant to diseases prevalent in your area. A healthy, vigorous plant is much less vulnerable to disease. Rotate your berry patch regularly to avoid insect or disease buildup; a one- or two-year rotation is best. Plow under old fields soon after harvest and control wild strawberries nearby, as these likely are sources of virus.

Black root rot is a disease caused by a number of different fungi that are common in most soils. Healthy roots are white or clear while young, and with age they become brownish or darker on the surface and have a yellowish living core. The roots of affected plants are black throughout, with few if any healthy laterals. Plants have reduced vigor and may die. Feeder roots are quickly killed, and the darkened patches on the main root give way to the blackening that gives this disease its name. Winter injury, poor drainage, and acid or alkaline soil all favor attack by the root rot fungi. Plants affected with other organisms, such as red stele, verticillium wilt, or nematodes, are usually also attacked by root rot fungi. Black root rot fungi are present in most soils and can be introduced with contaminated soil or plants.

Be sure your plants have clear white roots, and plant them in soil that is well-drained to a depth of at least two feet. Soil should be neither too acid nor too alkaline—a pH of 5.5 to 6.5 is best for strawberries. The use of mulch will help prevent injury to roots.

Fruit rot [color], of which there are several types, causes trouble on ripening or picked fruit. Gray mold, caused by the botrytis fungus, affects blossoms and green and ripe fruits. Infection often starts in frost-injured blossoms or in berries near the ground. Any injury to blossom or fruit will allow the fungus to enter, spreading a light brown, soft rot. Gray mold disease is favored by rainy weather and moist conditions, and thinning plants will help you to keep infection to a minimum.

Other fruit rots include hard rot, which attacks berries that touch the soil and causes a hard brown area on them, and leather rot, a discoloration and leathery texture on berries that touch the soil, either directly or through splashing. Both these minor rots are controlled by thinning plants and laying down a mulch to keep berries off the soil.

Although foliage diseases are widespread, they seldom cause severe losses. **Leaf blight** leads to large, red to brown spots surrounded by a purplish margin, and is most destructive to weak or slow-growing plants. Some varieties are more susceptible, as are older plants. **Leaf scorch** causes small, dark purplish spots on leaves and sometimes on fruit stalks. Usually it occurs during wet spring months, or occasionally in autumn. In severe cases, plants may die. See RESISTANT VARIETIES. **Leaf spot** [color] is similar in appearance to leaf scorch, but the purple spots have graying or white centers. This fungus disease attacks early in the season, especially where growth is very succulent or where heavy nitrogenous fertilizer has been used. Leaves become resistant as they mature. The leaf spot fungus sometimes attacks fruit and causes black seed, affecting the berry with one or two black spots.

Control for all the above foliage diseases is the same. Choose resistant varieties, and plant in well-drained soil in an unshaded area. Keep weeds down and avoid overgrowth. Rotate or renew plantings often.

Leaf variegation, also known as June or spring yellows, is a condition in some varieties of strawberry that is due to a hereditary factor. As the names imply, a mottling of the leaves is the chief symptom. Yellowing is severe in cool spring weather, but later disappears. Blakemore, Premier, and the everbearing varieties seem especially susceptible to this trait. The condition is not infectious. The only method of control is to plant stock that is free of the inherent weakness of leaf variegation.

Another of the foliar diseases is **powdery mildew.** It causes an upward curling of leaf margins, and a white powdery fungus may be visible on the upper leaf surface. It usually develops in spring or fall under overly moist conditions.

Choose resistant varieties, and plant in well-drained soil in an unshaded area. Keep weeds down, avoid overgrowth, and rotate or renew plantings often.

One of the strawberry plant's greatest enemies is the root disease **red stele,** a destructive fungus disease that causes plants to become severely stunted and to wilt, often just before the fruit becomes ripe. The plants have a dull bluish green color, and the small white feeder roots are lost, leaving long, rattaillike main roots that are often discolored at the tip. Some or all of the roots will show a reddish color when split, showing either near the tip or extending through the entire root. The red color is rarely seen during summer, but in spring and late autumn as a rule. The rotted roots prevent water from reaching the plant, and severely affected plants may die. Others may appear to recover in warm summer weather, but will develop symptoms again when cool, wet fall weather arrives and again the following spring. Because the fungus develops at cool temperatures with plenty of moisture, it is especially dangerous in spring. Red stele is extremely infectious. It can survive many years in the soil, and may be spread by soil adhering to cultivating and farm equipment, by water running off from affected fields, or by transplanting diseased plants.

If you know of red stele in the neighborhood, you might seriously question planting any strawberries. Control of red stele is difficult, but fortunately there are resistant varieties. Any plant with the symptoms should be dug up for inspection of the roots. Correct faulty drainage in the strawberry bed. Inspect plants carefully before putting them in the ground; if you spot the rat's tail or branchless root, you may have a case of red stele. Cut into the suspicious-looking roots to check for the reddish center. See RESISTANT VARIETIES.

Rhizopus rot or **leak** attacks berries after harvest, causing juice to run from the berries. It will destroy the fruit very rapidly, causing a whitish mold and brown color. It is spread through bruised or wounded berries and can also be spread by direct contact. This rot is most active at warm temperatures. Control by handling fruit carefully and keeping it at a cool 40° to 45°F.

Verticillium wilt is another fungus disease that is most active in cool, humid weather. Symptoms often appear just as the plant is about to ripen. Leaves wilt and dry at the margins and between the veins. New growth is retarded, giving the plant a stunted appearance. New roots growing from the crown are shortened and usually have blackened tips. Black streaks may appear on leaf stalks and runners. Severely affected plants sometimes suddenly collapse and die, while slightly affected ones often recover and produce normally the following year. (In the West, however, affected plants do not usually recover.) The disease may spare the rooted runners from a diseased mother plant.

The verticillium wilt fungus can survive many years in the soil. There are no strawberry varieties completely resistant to it, but some are better off than others. Varieties that are somewhat resistant are Blakemore, Catskill, Guardian, Marshall, Redchief, Salinas, Robinson, Siletz, Sunrise, Surecrop, and Vermilion. Varieties most susceptible to verticillium wilt are Daybreak, Dixieland, Earlidawn, Jerseybelle, Klondike, Lassen, Molalla, Northwest, Raritan, Shasta, and Vesper.

Avoid rotating your strawberry plantings with crops such as tomatoes, peppers, eggplant, or potatoes, as they may have left the fungus in the soil. The USDA advises that you not plant strawberries where cotton, okra, melons, mint, apricots, almonds, pecans, cherries, avocadoes, roses, or cane fruit grew at anytime in the previous ten years.

Any one of several **virus diseases** may affect the yield of your strawberry plants. Some virus diseases do not show any clear-cut symptoms, but are responsible for a less vigorous or even stunted plant with fewer runners. Two virus diseases, aster yellows and leaf roll, will cause leaves to be twisted, rolled, or cupped downward. Multiplier disease results in spindly plants that have many crowns, few short runners, if any, and leaves $\frac{1}{3}$ to $\frac{1}{2}$ of normal size.

For control, plant virus-free stock, such as the flavorful new strain of Suwanee developed by plant pathologists in Beltsville, Maryland. Follow the precautionary measures described in the introduction to this section.

Weeds, if not controlled by cultivation, will compete with the strawberries for soil nutrients, and you'll end up with less of a crop. Hoeing or hand weeding is necessary in small gardens. When a cultivator is used in large commercial beds, it should be operated in the same direction each time, for going in different directions will often pull out runners that have been dragged into position at the edge of the row.

Wildlife

Birds are fond of strawberries, and you may need to set up wire cages or plastic netting stretched over a frame.

Mice sometimes take up their winter quarters in a mulched strawberry bed, and may do damage by rooting around among the stems. In order to avoid this, thin out the plants in early fall before the mice begin to make their winter nests, and do not spread the winter mulch too early. By the time the top of the ground has a frosty crust, mice will have made their winter homes elsewhere and the winter protection may be safely spread on the strawberries.

Sweet Potato

Insects

Root-knot nematodes are small soil pests that attack the roots of many plants, including sweet potatoes. These nematodes produce small galls or swellings on the fine feeder roots, but they can also enter the storage roots and feed in the tissues beneath the skin without causing the common galls found on root crops. Symptoms include decayed areas under the skin, surface blemishes and pitting, deformed roots, poor color, and sometimes severe surface cracking. The vines of infested plants are usually stunted and yellowish, the leaves may show brown dead spots, and the plants may be killed in severe cases.

Whenever possible, plant sweet potatoes in soil that is free of this pest. Nematodes are found not only in the soil but also on the roots of plants, and it is important to obtain nematode-free plants for transplanting into the field. The sources of infestation for plants are infested seed stock and plant-bed soils. You can use vine cuttings in clean soil as a sure way of getting clean seed.

Yellow Jersey, Heartogold, and Nemagold have been found resistant to the common root-knot nematode. In the Nemagold variety, the nematodes enter the roots but fail to develop and usually die. See NEMATODE.

The **sweet potato weevil** is about ¼ inch long and resembles a large ant. The head, snout, and wing covers are a dark blue, and the prothorax and legs are a reddish orange. It has well-developed wings and is capable of limited flight. The eggs are yellowish white while the larvae are white, legless, and about ⅜ inch long. The pupa is white and somewhat shorter.

The adult places its eggs in small cavities that it punctures

Sweet Potato Weevil

either into the stem of the plant near the ground or directly into the sweet potato. The eggs hatch in about a week, and the grubs then feed in the vine or potato for about two or three weeks. The pupa is formed within the stem. The adult may live for several months, the time varying depending on the weather and the conditions under which the potatoes are stored. In a year, six to eight generations may be produced. The adult weevils damage sweet potato plants by feeding on leaves, vines, and roots and by pitting the potatoes with feeding and egg deposition cavities. However, it is the larvae that cause the gravest damage by their feeding and tunneling through vines and potatoes.

In areas of commercial production where weevil infestation is light, non-planting zones can be established. The weevil is wiped out by depriving it of its food for about a year; no sweet potatoes are grown, bedded, or stored within a zone extending at least ½ mile from the point of infestation. The procedure has resulted in eradication of the weevil from single farms and on a community level. Potatoes still in the ground when infestation is discovered should be removed from the premises at harvest time and disposed of in such a way as to prevent infestation of other properties. Before the potatoes are plowed out, vines should be cut off at the surface of the ground and burned when dry. Destroy all potato roots, crowns, small sweet potatoes, and scraps in the field by cultivating and by grazing livestock in the field after harvest. The old potato fields should be plowed at least twice during the winter in order to expose any roots or potatoes missed. After the waiting period is up, plant new plantings in the zones that have been out of production.

In areas generally infested with weevils and in places where the extent of commercial production does not warrant the establishment of non-planting zones, effective control can be maintained by the recommended cultural and sanitary practices. Use state-certified seed sweet potatoes and be certain to destroy plants and tubers in seedbeds as soon as you have produced enough plants. Rotate crops and try to plant the new crop as far away as possible from the crop of the previous year. See RESISTANT VARIETIES.

Diseases

Black rot is a fungus disease that causes potatoes to rot both in the field and in storage. It can also attack the underground stem of the growing plants, causing dark decayed spots and sometimes resulting in death of the plant. On the potatoes themselves this rot is characterized by dark, slightly sunken corky areas on the surface. Spots are usually circular, with the diseased areas sharply defined from the healthy areas. As decay develops the spots penetrate into the flesh of the potato. Decayed tissue often takes on a greenish tinge when cut open. A bitter taste is associated with this rot. All potatoes showing visible signs are culls, and black rot can sometimes cause serious cullage in the fields and after storage.

Plants can become infected in the seedbed from diseased seed roots or from infected soil. The disease is carried on seed potatoes in both active and spore form and can live in the fields or plantbed soil for a year or longer. Sweet potatoes that are washed before packing may be infected by spores in the wash water. Black rot that develops in transit may make the whole lot unsalable when it reaches the market. Varieties enjoying considerable resistance are available; Yellow Jersey, on the other hand, is especially susceptible.

Discard seed potatoes with black rot, practice a three-to-four-year crop rotation, and cure quickly with high temperatures and humidity. One easy way to control black rot is to cut the sprouts above the seedbed soil line instead of pulling them. Since black rot occurs only on the underground stem, only the healthy part is planted. Sprout cuttings live and yield as well as field sprouts.

Dry rot causes sweet potatoes to mummify in storage. Cool storage discourages this fungus, as the ideal range of temperatures for the pathogen is 75° to 90°F.

Scurf [color] is a fungus disease that lives on the outermost layers of cells on the potatoes and causes superficial round, brownish black spots. Individual infections are relatively small, but they may be numerous enough on a root to cause almost complete discoloration of the surface. While eating quality is not harmed, the poor appearance of the diseased potatoes greatly reduces market acceptability. Although this disease is not caused by moisture, moist conditions favor its growth. It develops on potatoes in the field and in storage when the spores are carried in from the field. The disease or its spores can live over for a season in hotbed sites or in the field as well as on the potatoes.

Use healthy sprouts only. They should be bedded in sand that has not previously hosted sweet potatoes.

Soft rot [color] is a storage disease characterized by a rapid, soft, watery rot and a whiskery growth. Nancy Hall and Southern Queen offer some resistance to this disease. Sweet potatoes should be cured for 10 to 14 days at a humid 80° to 85°F., followed by storage at 55°F.

Stem rot or **wilt** [color] is caused by a fungus of the fusarium group and lives within the roots and stem of the plant. Sweet potato plants may become infected from infected seed roots or infected soil in the field or in the seedbed. Aside from the direct infection of plants produced on infected seed roots, the principal entrance of the fungus appears to be made through wounds incured during pulling or transplanting. Considerable spread may take place when the plants are dipped or soaked in basins or sumps while being held before setting in the field. Infection in the field may occur when the stem or roots are injured by insects, tillage tools, or wind.

Young plants infected in the seedbed often die after transplanting. Surviving plants first show a few bright yellow leaves around the crown, then dwarfed leaves and crown, and later badly rotted stems. Although they may survive throughout the season, the potatoes are usually small and yields are poor.

The stem-rot fungus lives in the potatoes through the storage season without causing external symptoms. Spores of the disease picked up in the field during harvest may adhere to the roots during storage.

Southern Queen, Yellow Stransburg, and Triumph are quite resistant; among highly susceptible varieties are Big Stem Jersey, Little Stem Jersey, Maryland Golden, and Nancy Hall. Be certain to use plants with clean white roots and to remove and destroy diseased plants. It is not a good idea to plant sweet potatoes in the same soil every year.

Swiss Chard, see Chard

Sycamore

Insects

Sycamore Lacebug

The **sycamore lace bug** is very common on the underside of leaves. The upper surface will show a white-peppered spotting which indicates where the bug has sucked sap. The adult bugs hibernate under the edges of the bark and emerge soon after the leaves unfold to lay their eggs. A spray of nicotine sulfate and soap twice in spring will control the lace bug on sycamores.

Other insects that may trouble sycamores are APHIDS, terrapin scale (see MAPLE), and the white-marked tussock moth (HORSECHESTNUT).

Diseases

For description and control of **anthracnose,** see TREES: DISEASES.

Tangerine, see Citrus

Tent Caterpillars

The larvae of several moths and butterflies are collectively referred to as tent caterpillars. The name is especially applied to *Malacosoma americana,* known as the eastern tent caterpillar [color] and sometimes as the apple tent caterpillar. Tent caterpillars multiply rapidly and can defoliate many deciduous trees and shrubs over a wide area in a short time. Wild cherry trees and apple trees are most often attacked; peach, pear, plum, rose, hawthorn, and various shade and forest trees are occasionally infested. In spring, the pests' unsightly nests, or tents, are conspicuous on susceptible trees by the roadside or in neglected orchards. These caterpillars are abundant and troublesome for several years in a row. They often eat all the leaves on a tree, weakening the tree but seldom killing it. Once the caterpillars mature, in early summer, they cause no further feeding damage.

Tent Caterpillar

• **Life cycle.** One generation of the eastern tent caterpillar develops in a year. Larvae are present in late spring, cocoons and moths in early summer, and eggs for the remainder of the time.

The larvae, or caterpillars, hatch in spring from egg masses about the time the first leaves are opening. The young caterpillars keep together and spin threads of silken web. After feeding for about two days, they begin to weave their tent in a nearby tree crotch, sometimes joining with caterpillars from other egg masses. As the caterpillars grow, they enlarge the tent until it consists of several layers. In good weather they leave the tent several times a day in search of food, stringing silk after them, while bad weather sends them between the layers of the tent. When they finish feeding on a tree, the caterpillars leave the nest and search for food. Upon reaching maturity they spin cocoons on tree bark, fences, brush, weeds, or buildings, or among dead leaves and debris on the ground. When full grown, about six weeks after hatching, the caterpillar is almost two inches long and sparsely hairy. It is black, has white and blue markings, and shows a white stripe along the middle of its back.

The pupal cocoon is about one inch long and white or yellowish white. In early summer, reddish brown moths emerge, and the females deposit masses of eggs in bands around twigs. The eggs are covered with a foamy secretion that dries to a firm brown covering that looks like an enlargement of the twig. An egg mass usually contains about 200 eggs.

• Control methods.   You can control the eastern tent caterpillar by hand if you have only a few infested trees. Since many insects are concentrated in a few groups, they can be easily destroyed. Take action when you first see the nests before the larvae start to feed. Tear the nests out by hand or with a brush or pole, and either crush any surviving caterpillars on the ground or burn them with a torch made from oily rags tied to a pole. If you elect the latter method, be careful that the tree is not singed and that the fire does not get out of hand. In winter, you can destroy the egg masses by cutting off the infested twigs and burning them. Remove wild cherry trees growing in the vicinity of orchards, if possible.

• Natural enemies.   Soon after the female moth lays her eggs, they are apt to be attacked by a minute wasplike insect known as *Tetrastichus*. This parasite measures only $\frac{1}{16}$ inch in length and is shiny dark green with red eyes and iridescent wings. It lays one egg in each tent caterpillar egg and the tiny white grub that soon hatches proceeds to devour the egg of the pest. When the grub is full grown, it entirely fills the hard caterpillar egg shell and spends the winter in this snug retreat.

The star insect enemy of a western species, the Rocky Mountain tent caterpillar, is a digger wasp labeled *Podalonia occidentalis*. This insect is somewhat less than an inch in length and is entirely black with the exception of the abdomen, which is gleaming red orange with a black tip. Although the adult female parasite feeds entirely upon the nectar of wild flowers, her young are carnivorous and must have living flesh for food. To provide this, the wasp paralyzes the caterpillars with an anesthetic that she injects into the central nervous system. The wasp then drags the caterpillar to an underground burrow which she has previously prepared, lays an egg on the skin of the pest, covers up the entrance to the chamber, and hurries off to seek a new victim. The parasite grub soon hatches and drills into the body of the slumbering caterpillar and proceeds to feed. It first devours the non-vital tissues so that it may continue to have fresh food to eat. It keeps from fouling its food supply by delaying the evacuation of waste products until it reaches full size and emerges from the host carcass. The grub then constructs a tough, parchment-like cocoon about itself and remains underground until the following spring when it transforms into an adult wasp.

Full-grown caterpillars that have escaped the digger wasps are often attacked by an important parasite that you might mistake for the common housefly. It is, however, twice the size of the latter. Known as *Sarcophaga aldrichi,* its light gray thorax bears three longitudinal black stripes and the abdomen is divided into alternating light and dark squares. These extremely beneficial flies insert their living maggots beneath the skin of caterpillars. The pests usually live long enough to spin their cocoons and transform to pupae before succumbing. When the maggots reach full growth, they emerge from the caterpillar cocoon and drop to the ground. Digging quickly beneath the surface to escape natural enemies, their outer skin hardens into a dark brown, seedlike shell inside of which they transform to pupae. With the advent of spring, the pupae change to flies and emerge from the soil.

A commercially available pathogen, *Bacillus thuringiensis,* is a very effective control. Baltimore orioles have been known to clean up entire infestations, and the birds' hanging saclike nests are a sign that your trees are insured against tent caterpillar trouble.

• **Similar pests.**   The forest tent caterpillar (*Malacosoma disstria*) and the fall webworm (*Hyphantria cunea*) are sometimes mistaken for the eastern tent caterpillar. The forest tent caterpillar may be distinguished from the eastern tent caterpillar by a row of creamy white spots along its back, instead of a stripe. The caterpillars are found more often on forest trees than on fruit trees. They differ from other species in that they do not form webs.

The fall webworm makes a nest resembling that of the eastern tent caterpillar, but it is located at the tip of a branch instead of at the crotch. In addition, the fall webworm is smaller and hairier, and is present from midsummer to autumn. It feeds on many kinds of trees, including most of those attacked by the eastern tent caterpillar.

These insects may be controlled with the same spray materials used on the eastern tent caterpillar. For more information, consult your county agricultural agent, state agricultural experiment station, or state agricultural college.

Thrips

Thrip

Thrips are small, slender insects that damage plants by sucking their juices, stinging them, and rasping at fruit and leaves to cause scars.

Infested flowers and buds should be promptly removed to avoid infesting plantings. Trevor Lewis's book, *Thrips, Their Biology, Ecology, and Economic Importance,* suggests a number of other controls that should control this pest. Prevention is the first step: "Appropriate cultural methods coupled with clean management of farms and orchards," says Lewis, "can sometimes completely prevent damage by thrips and thrip-borne diseases, and often decrease it." Plants under water stress are particularly susceptible to trouble, and seeing to it that plants are properly watered or irrigated in hot seasons, especially in dry areas, should decrease losses. On a large scale, growers can get around thrips by not growing susceptible crops in consecutive years; a three-year crop rotation, e.g. red clover or potatoes, oats, and then flax, will help.

As many thrips have a wide range of hosts that includes many weeds, they can often survive in the garden area even if no susceptible crops are grown. So, control of weeds and volunteer plants may be well worth your while for controlling this pest alone, especially if tomato spotted wilt virus has been a problem for you. The area of clean culture should extend for some distance; thrips are weak fliers, but they can beat the air hard enough so that the wind will blow them a good ways. In still air, the smaller species can manage a speed of 10 centimeters a second, while larger thrips can hit 50 centimeters a second. But the wind usually blows them wherever it will. Thrips stick to the ground when stiffened by the cold, and won't take off if the temperature is below 64° to 69°F.

Aluminum mulches are effective in keeping thrips off low-growing crops. The pests will avoid rose blossoms if you place foil-wrapped boards around the plant base so that they extend a foot or two beyond the canopy. When the shiny boards were placed in position several weeks before flowering, reports Lewis, this method proved superior to certain insecticides applied to the soil. As is true of aphids, the thrips apparently lose track of what's up and what's down.

Thrips are vulnerable to oil-and-water and tobacco sprays. Rotenone works too, and you might try making a repellent spray of common field larkspur. See also gladiolus thrips under GLADIOLUS.

Tomato

In planning the tomato patch, pay particular attention to recent resistant varieties; the old standards are gradually being replaced by new and better-yielding varieties.

Many growers start their tomatoes indoors. For a sterile potting medium, heat three to five inches of moist soil in the oven at 350° to 400°F. for one hour. Plants should be thinned so that they are two to three inches apart by the time they reach a height of one inch; transplant the extras to flats or peat pots. If plants are left unthinned, they will become spindly and more subject to disease. Tomato plants grown in protected places tend to become somewhat weak and spindly, and a few days exposure to the outdoor environment while they are still in the containers will help them survive transplanting. Transplant when conditions are at their best—soon after a rain, when cloudy, or in late afternoon. A cardboard band or tin can inserted into the soil around each plant will ward off cutworms.

While animal manures are excellent fertilizer, an overdose often results in excessive vine growth and poor fruit-set. Add lime, if necessary, to bring the pH up to between 6.0 and 6.8. Finally, a mulch of straw, leaves, dried lawn clippings, or plastic will serve to keep down weeds. To conserve space and keep fruit off the ground, it's good practice to stake plants. You can encourage plants to produce larger fruit by removing side branches as they emerge. Leave two or three main stems to each plant.

Large-scale plantings should be rotated so that tomatoes are grown once every three years. It is not a good idea to grow tomatoes in rotation with potatoes, eggplant, okra, or peppers, as these crops are susceptible to many of the diseases that hit tomatoes. Keep out of the field when the plants are wet to avoid spreading such diseases as gray leaf spot, early blight, late blight, and septoria leaf spot. If you are a smoker, be aware that tobacco often carries a virus that can easily pass to tomatoes; wash your hands thoroughly before working with the plants. Dr. Carl D. Clayberg, geneticist at the Connecticut Agricultural Experiment Station, says that 40 percent of cigarette tobacco is infected with tobacco mosaic virus—one of the most serious diseases affecting tomatoes. So, here's another good reason for dropping the habit.

While you're setting out the tomatoes, why not sow some marigolds, borage, or opal basil around and through the rows? These pungent plants will repel the tomato hornworm through the season.

Resistant varieties offer protection from many of the more important diseases, and the *New York Times* recently reported that researchers are working with a wild South American relative of the tomato that is resistant to the flea beetle, white fly, Colorado potato beetle, and aphids. It is hoped that the wild species will introduce its resistant quality—namely, a hairy exterior—to economically important tomato and potato crops.

At the season's end, all old tomato vines should be plowed under, as some of the fungi that cause disease live from year to year on the plant refuse.

Insects

Potato/Colorado Potato Beetle

Both larval and adult **Colorado potato beetles** feed on tomato foliage and may strip plants if they occur in numbers. The oval, hard-shelled adult is about ⅜ inch long, with alternating black and yellow stripes on the wing covers. The full-grown young are sluggish, soft-bodied, humpbacked grubs, colored red with two rows of black spots on each side of the body. See POTATO for controls.

Cutworm

Several species of **cutworms** have earned reputations as primary tomato pests. Although they vary considerably in habits and appearance, they are usually gray to brown or black in color and measure from one to 1½ inches long when fully grown.

Cutworms are ordinarily most troublesome in spring, doing their damage in the hotbed or in the field and garden soon after transplanting. They may cut the plants off near the ground level, feed on the foliage or fruit, or destroy the roots. The cutting off of the young plants is the most noticeable injury.

Clean cultivation of the crops that precede tomatoes is of considerable importance in cutworm control. Sod or weedy ground on which tomatoes are to be grown the following year should be plowed under in late summer or early fall and kept clean in order to prevent the cutworm from laying its eggs. In a small garden, cutworms can be collected by hand. Young tomatoes are usually protected by pressing tin, tarpaper, or cardboard cylinders into the soil around the plants, or by wrapping the stems with four-inch collars of paper at transplanting time. Cutworms have been found vulnerable to *Bacillus thuringiensis*.

The **European corn borer** occasionally moves into tomato rows if early corn is planted nearby. The borers migrate from the dying corn to find a new source of food. See CORN.

European Corn Borer

Many species of **flea beetle** attack plants, especially young transplants. Leaves look as though shot full of holes. These insects are about $\frac{1}{16}$ inch long, and jump about when disturbed. A garlic spray should repel them. For other control measures, see potato flea beetle under POTATO.

The **greenhouse white fly** commonly infests tomato under glass and is often carried into the field where it may persist on the plants. The tiny mothlike adult has a mealy appearance due to small particles of wax that it secretes. It lays groups of eggs on the underside of leaves, which hatch into small oval larvae that suck sap. Spraying a solution of nicotine sulfate and soap at the underside of leaves is a sure means of control, either in the greenhouse or out. See WHITE FLY.

Potato/Flea Beetles

Whitefly

The **stalk borer** is a slender insect that grows up to $1\frac{1}{4}$ inches long. When young it is creamy white with a dark purple band around the body and several brown or purple stripes running lengthwise. The full-grown borer is creamy white to light purple, and is without the stripes. The stalk borer eats a tunnel in the stem of the plant, causing it to wither and die. This tunnel has an opening up to $\frac{1}{4}$ inch in diameter at its lowest end, and is a telltale sign of trouble within. To locate the borer, simply split the stems lengthwise above the opening to the tunnel. The plant may be saved by puncturing the insect and then binding up the split stem. Give the plant liberal doses of water for several days.

The **tomato fruitworm** [color], also known as the corn earworm and bollworm, comes in green, brown, or pink, has light stripes along its sides and back, and reaches a length of $1\frac{3}{4}$ inches. It eats holes in fruits and buds.

In the southern states and California, the fruitworm is an annual pest. In the extreme South the moths may emerge from their pupal cells as early as January, although most of them appear later in spring. Soon after she emerges, the female moth begins to lay single eggs, no larger than a pinhead, on the leaves. As the larva hatches it crawls over the leaves, feeding sparingly until it finds the fruit. Arriving at a tomato, it cuts a hole and burrows inside, usually at the stem end. A worm may feed until fully grown upon a single tomato, or it may move from one tomato to another, injuring several as it completes its growth. The mature worm leaves the fruit and enters the soil, where it transforms into the pupal or resting stage. There may be two or more broods in a single season.

In home gardens having a few plants, the fruitworms may be picked by hand. Garlic and onion sprays should reduce the number of feeding pests. Rotenone has been used successfully as both a dust and a spray.

The tachnid fly *Lydella stabulans grisescens* was imported to parasitize the fruitworm, and is now well established in Massachusetts, Connecticut, Rhode Island, and the Middle Atlantic states; from 16 to 45 percent of the pests are taken care of, according to Lester A. Swann in *Beneficial Insects*. *Lydella* has also caught on in Illinois, Indiana, Iowa, Kentucky, and southwestern Ohio, and that region sees a range of from 45 to 75 percent parasitization. In a trial at Purdue University, Deay and Hartsock protected a vegetable plot from the fruitworm moth and other winged pests by a trap equipped with three 15-watt blacklight fluorescent lamps. Fruitworm larvae are susceptible to a nuclear polyhedrosis virus; although this virus is not yet commercially available, you should be able to mix up your own viral spray without too much trouble. See the controls for corn earworm under CORN.

The **tomato hornworm** is one of the most important and certainly the largest of tomato pests. This green worm, distinguished by a series of white diagonal bars along each side and a prominent horn at the back end, reaches a length of four inches—big enough to make handpicking an ordeal for the squeamish. The greenish eggs are deposited singly on the underside of leaves and hatch in from three to eight days. Larvae feed on leaves and sometimes the fruit, reaching full size after three or four weeks of steady eating. Winters are spent as a hard-shelled pupae, three or four inches below the ground. Moths appear in May or June; these are variously known as sphinx, hummingbird, or hawk moths, have a wingspan of four or five inches, and fly on long, narrow gray wings. They fly at twilight and poise in the air to sip nectar from deep-throated flowers in the manner of a hummingbird. While northern growers have but one generation to contend with, there may be two or more in the South.

Tomato Hornworm

The **tobacco hornworm** [color] is nearly identical to the tomato species, and can be quickly distinguished by the color of the horn—red on the former worm, and green and black on the latter.

Because they're so easy to see, hornworms are most often controlled in small plantings by handpicking. This task becomes even easier if dill is interplanted as a trap crop, as the fat pests are impossible to miss on the spindly herb stalks. If you spot a worm carrying about white pupae, or cocoon-spinning grubs, let it be— the pest is the victim of a parasitic brachonid wasp, and should be left to nurture a new brood of beneficials. Some gardeners have success with sprinkling hot pepper on plants. The moth can be plucked out of the hornworm life cycle by drawing them to a blacklight trap of the sort used to control the tomato fruitworm, above.

Hornworms are particularly vulnerable to biological controls. A spray of the commercially available *Bacillus thuringiensis* bacterium is effective; see BACILLUS THURINGIENSIS for more information. Trichogramma wasps parasitize eggs, and are available through the mails as eggs. Lester A. Swann reports in *Beneficial Insects* that southern tobacco growers have taken full advantage of a naturally occurring wasp predator, *Polistes exclamans,* by setting up inexpensive shelters or nesting boxes to save the wasps from other predators; locally, the hornworm was removed from pest status. The males and young queens arrive in late summer. Males and the queens die with the approach of winter, leaving young queens to find shelter in cracks and crevices and under the bark of trees—or, in the shelters provided by growers. *Bacillus thuringiensis* is not harmful to this wasp.

Swann reports that 370 blacklight traps were used in a 113-square-mile area in North Carolina and took care of an estimated 50 to 60 percent of the tobacco hornworm moths in the area. If the above measures have failed, rotenone will kill young caterpillars, according to the Connecticut Agricultural Experimentation Station.

Diseases

Anthracnose [color] is a fungus disease that primarily affects ripe fruit and causes a slight sunken spot rot. Because the symptoms are not prominent until the fruit ripens, many growers do not become concerned about this disease until it's too late to prevent infection. The earliest symptoms are circular sunken spots in the skin, which look as though they had been made with a match head or eraser. On ripe fruits these spots enlarge rapidly and the central portion may appear to be dark because of black fungus structures just under the skin. Soon the entire fruit rots as other organisms enter and break down the tissues. Sunken, circular, dime-sized spots with black specks in them are typical of this disease. When August temperatures are high and heavy rains or dews occur, be on the lookout for anthracnose. The fungus over-winters both in diseased vines and on and in the seeds. Long rotations and hot water seed treatment (122°F. for 25 minutes) facilitate control.

Bacterial canker is a destructive tomato disease caused by a seed-borne bacterium. In recent years, losses from this disease have been slight, principally because of the increased use of certi-fied seed by southern plant growers. However, growers who save their own seed and ignore control measures can still expect to suffer losses from canker if the weather conditions are favorable. The disease is occasionally found in the greenhouse as well as the field, and attacks plants at any stage of growth. Seedlings may be rapidly destroyed or may produce plants that remain stunted and valueless. Occasionally there will be no evidence of the disease until some time after transplanting. On older plants the first symp-tom is wilting of the margins on leaflets of the lower leaves. This wilting usually appears first on only one side of the leaf. As the margins become dry, the leaves curl upward, turn brown, wither, and die. The petioles remain attached to the stem, a characteristic that distinguishes this disease from fusarium and verticillium wilts. The plant itself often shows a one-sided development of the disease, causing it to lie over in a characteristic fashion. On larger plants, a single shoot may be killed early while the remainder of the plant appears normal. Eventually, however, the entire plant is affected as the dying continues up the stem and much of the foliage is destroyed. As the decay progresses, the pith becomes yellow and mealy in appearance and cavities form within the stem. Later, the destruction of the tissues extends to the outer surface of the stem, forming the open cankers that give the disease its name. Diseased plants may die early, but they often survive until harvest.

Often the fruit is infected on the surface, where the symptoms appear first as small, raised, snowy white dots, $\frac{1}{8}$ to $\frac{1}{4}$ inch in diameter. The centers of those spots later break open and become brown and roughened. The white color persists as a halo about the margin and produces a bird's-eye typical of the disease. These spots are caused by rain washing the bacteria from open cankers to the fruit and do not extend deeply into the flesh. When the plants are severely diseased, however, the fruit may also be in-ternally affected. If this occurs when the fruit is small, it is stunted and deformed. Internally infected fruits show no external evi-dence of the disease, but small cavities may be found in portions of the fruit.

Never save seed from fields known to have bacterial canker. If you buy seed, it is worthwhile to buy certified seed; such seed is usually canker free. If it is necessary to use seed that is of unknown origin, it can be put in a loosely woven bag and soaked for 25 minutes in water at 122°F. This treatment will eliminate most internal and external disease organisms that are seed-borne. It is very important that the water does not get any hotter than the recommended temperature, as the seed is easily damaged by heat. The bacteria are also sensitive to acid conditions, and a cloth bag of seeds can be soaked for 24 hours in a mixture of one ounce pure acetic acid in one gallon of water. This amount of acid and water will treat about one pound of seed. Use only ¾ ounce of acid if seeds are already dried. Diseased seed can also be rendered safe if it is fermented in the crushed pulp of the fruit for 96 hours. Keep the temperature at 70°F. and stir the stuff twice a day. In addition, it may be helpful to either sterilize the seedbed soil or else replace it if it is not known to be free from disease.

If you have soil that is known to be infected with canker, you should grow another crop for at least three years before planting tomatoes again. In small gardens where three-year rotations are not practical, it's important to pull up and destroy tomato vines after harvest. All tools used either in the greenhouse or field should be disinfected in household bleach mixed one part to ten of water; effective disinfection requires that all surfaces be clean before treatment, notes the Cooperative Extension Service of Ohio State University.

Rainy seasons favor the growth and spread of **bacterial spot** [color], a disease that first shows up as small, dark, greasy-looking spots on leaflets. Soon there may be blossom drop and small, water-soaked spots, slightly raised and rapidly enlarging from ⅛ to ¼ inch on young green fruit. These spots have whitish halos at first, but later disappear and the centers become rough, light brown, and sunken.

Especially in the South, buy only certified seedlings if possible. Pasteurize the soil in which you will start seedlings, and avoid areas of the garden that have previously carried the disease.

Bacterial wilt [color] is most common on tomatoes in the southern states, but is occasionally found in other tomato-growing areas. Symptoms include a rather rapid wilting and death of the entire plant without any yellowing or spotting of the leaves. If a stem of a wilted plant is cut across near the ground line, the pith shows a darkened, water-soaked appearance, and a slimy gray exudate shows when the stem is pressed. In later stages of the disease there is also a brown decay of the pith, and cavities may be formed in the stem. Bacterial wilt does not cause spotting of the fruit.

The causal bacteria live in the soil and infect the plant through the roots or stem. Pathogens are most common in low, moist soils and are most active at temperatures above 75°F. The bacteria occur both in newly cleared land and land that has previously grown susceptible crops. Fields frequently are first infected as a result of planting infected seedlings. The bacteria may also be carried by drainage water from an adjacent field.

If the disease occurs, tomatoes and susceptible crops such as tobacco, potato, eggplant, and pepper should not be grown on or near infested soil for a period of four or five years. Instead, try grains, legumes, or corn. If a few wilted plants are noticed in the field, they should be removed at once and destroyed to prevent further spread of this disease. Resistant varieties include Venus and Saturn.

Blossom drop describes a condition in which tomato plants fail to set a normal crop of fruit because of the dropping of blossoms about the time the flowers are fully developed. This disease comes about as the result of environmental factors and is not the product of a pathogen; it usually strikes when soil moisture is low and the plants are dried by hot winds. Other possible causes include sudden periods of cold weather, heavy rains, an overdose of nitrogenous fertilizer, and the influence of parasitic bacteria or fungi, such as those causing early blight, septoria leaf spot, and bacterial spot.

Because large-fruited varieties of the Ponderosa type are very susceptible, they should not be grown in areas with hot and dry summers. Instead, select a variety that can handle such a climate: Summerset, Hotset, Summer Prolific, and Porter should succeed. Although the reason is not clear, fruit set can sometimes be increased by shaking the plant or hitting the top of the stake in the middle of a warm sunny day.

Blossom End Rot

Gardeners often experience disappointment when they reach for that first tomato and find that the bottom half is rotten. This trouble is known as **blossom-end rot,** a nonparasitic disease of tomatoes that causes damage in both the field and the greenhouse. Like other nonparasitic diseases, it is not limited to any particular region and occurs wherever conditions are favorable. Control depends entirely upon avoiding these conditions.

The first evidence of injury is a brown discoloration of the tissues near the bottom end of the fruit. These spots enlarge and darken until they cover ⅓ to ½ of the fruit. As the spots increase in size, the tissues become shrunken and affected surfaces become sunken, black, and leathery. Soft rotting of the fruit may occur if secondary fungi or bacteria invade the spots.

Blossom-end rot is most apt to occur when the plants have been grown under favorable conditions during the early part of the season and are then subjected to a long period of drought at the time the fruit is in an early stage of development. Breakdown and shrinkage apparently occur when cells at the blossom end fail to receive sufficient water to support their growth. Blossom-end rot also occurs after periods of considerable rainfall, possibly because the soil becomes so nearly saturated with moisture that many small rootlets are killed by lack of aeration or destroyed by certain fungi that are particularly active in moist soils, and the root system is damaged and cannot supply fruit with sufficient moisture.

In the greenhouse, this disease can largely be prevented by maintaining a uniform supply of moisture. In dry weather, field plants should only be cultivated as necessary to avoid drying out the soil. Take care not to hoe or cultivate closer than one foot from the plants so that the roots aren't pruned. Water evenly and only as needed. Overdoses of nitrogenous fertilizer are suspected to aggravate this disease by blocking the plant's uptake of calcium. Check to see if the soil has sufficient calcium by testing in fall or very early in spring. If you find a deficiency, add finely ground limestone before setting out plants. To raise the pH value of the soil by one unit, use about ½ pound of limestone to each ten square feet.

The Cooperative Extension Service at Ohio State University suggests that other factors hindering a plant's uptake of calcium and water might include parasitic fungi, nematodes, and a lack of aeration resulting from soil compaction. Generally the disease is more serious on staked plants than on prostrate or bushy ones. Tomatoes planted unusually early in cold soils are likely to develop this rot on their first fruits. Certain varieties are less vulnerable to blossom-end rot than others; check with your state extension agent.

Mulching the soil around the plants with sawdust, peat moss, grass clippings, or even tin foil will prevent the loss of moisture and cut down on the amount of blossom-end rot.

Botrytis fruit rot (gray mold) may be an important disease of greenhouse tomatoes in periods of cool temperatures and high humidity. Tremendous numbers of fungus spores are loosened whenever infected plants are jarred, and travel in air currents to infect other plants. The disease first shows as small water-soaked spots that enlarge rapidly, sometimes involving the entire fruit. Diseased areas are covered by a gray powdery growth. Control by raising the temperature and reducing the humidity in the greenhouse.

Buckeye rot is a fungus disease that frequently hits greenhouse tomatoes when the soil is not mulched. Apparently, the pathogen is splashed from the soil onto young developing fruits during watering. This disease causes large, dark brown lesions on the fruit that tend to become soft; look for distinct rings. Affected fruit breaks down quite easily. Mulch plants to prevent water from splashing. It also helps to sterilize greenhouse soil.

Cloudy spot describes the marks left by the feeding of stink bugs. White, spongy cells can be seen beneath the site of injury. A garlic spray should keep these pests from puncturing fruit.

A **cracking** of the surface at the stem end of the fruit occurs during periods of rapid growth brought on by abundant moisture and high temperatures. Cracks may radiate from the stem or extend longitudinally around the shoulders of the fruit. They vary in depth, but often extend deep into the flesh. Where they develop slowly, the surface tissue heals and becomes fairly firm, but it is likely to rupture in handling. These cracks not only blemish the fruit but also are points of invasion by early blight and other rots of the fruit. Little can be done to control this trouble except to try to provide an even supply of moisture, thus preventing alternate periods of slow and rapid growth. Since the tendency to crack increases with ripeness, loss can be reduced in part by picking the fruit before it reaches full color.

Use such resistant varieties as Campbell's 17 and 29 and H1350, H1409, H1370, and H6201. Paste tomatoes Roma, Chico, and Parker are all markedly resistant to cracking. Homestead 24, Manalucie, Marion, Manapal, Indian River, Floradel, Floralou, and Pearson Improved are listed as relatively free from trouble.

Curly top, or western yellow blight, is caused by the same virus as curly top of sugar beets. It appears to be carried by a single insect species, the beet leafhopper, a migratory insect that has breeding grounds in weedy abandoned lands and sagebrush areas west of the Rocky Mountains. In those sections where great numbers of the leafhoppers appear each year, it is almost impossible to grow profitable crops of tomatoes, beans, spinach, and other susceptible crops. Although the tomato is susceptible to curly top infection at any stage of growth, the susceptibility decreases markedly as the plants grow older. Infected seedlings soon show a yellowing of the foliage accompanied by curling and twisting of the leaves. Such plants ordinarily die within a short time.

On well-established plants in the field, the first symptoms consist of a pronounced upward rolling and twisting of the leaflets that exposes their undersurface. The foliage becomes stiff and leathery and the entire plant assumes a dull, yellowed appearance. The branches and stems are abnormally erect, and the petioles of the leaves curl downward. There often is some purpling of the veins of the leaflets, and the entire plant is usually very stunted. Many of the roots and rootlets are killed. Very few, if any, fruits are produced after infection, and those that are already set turn red prematurely. All standard varieties of tomatoes are severely injured by curly top, but early varieties appear to be killed more quickly than those that set their fruits later in the season. Owyhee and Payette show resistance.

Leafhoppers become carriers of the curly top virus by feeding on infected wild or cultivated host plants. See the discussion of curly top under BEET.

Tomatoes are more likely to be injured if grown near sugar beets or other favorable hosts. Local experience should suggest a time for planting to avoid the period of leafhopper migration. Because leafhoppers prefer to feed on plants in the open, shading plants with muslin will offer considerable control, and it helps to set plants as close as six inches apart. As a rule the infection is reduced whenever plants are grown in partly shaded areas. Because of the extra labor and material involved, these methods are suited to home gardens rather than commercial plantings.

Damping-off describes the wilt that attacks tomato seedlings at the soil line and kills them. Usually the roots are killed and the affected plants are water-soaked and appear shriveled. The disease typically occurs in small patches scattered through the seed beds. Seedlings grow out of their susceptibility after about two weeks; by this time, the stem is hard and sturdy enough to stave off trouble.

Pasteurize soil, and provide well-drained soil seedbeds. Coolness and sunlight discourage this disease.

A variety of nutrient **deficiencies** may be signalled by plant symptoms. A nitrogen deficiency leads to a very slow growth of plants, followed by a progressive paling of the leaves that starts at the tip and at the top of the plant. Leaves are small and thin, and you may notice some purple veins. Eventually the stems become stunted, brown, and die. Flower buds yellow and drop off. Apply compost immediately and supplement it with blood meal, cottonseed meal, hoof and horn meal, or other materials rich in nitrogen.

If, on the other hand, your plants grow an abundance of bright, light green leaves, and there are few blossoms and fruit, suspect an *excess* of nitrogen. The cure for this is to cut down on fertilization. You can also increase the supply of bone meal and granite dust to bring phosphorus and potassium up to be in correct ratio to the nitrogen content. This trouble is most likely to appear during the seedling period, but it can also affect plants in the garden or field if the soil is overnourished with nitrogen.

A phosphorus deficiency contributes to slow growth, and plants are tinged purple. Leaves are unnaturally small and seem to be rather fibrous. A phosphorus deficiency will also delay the setting of fruit. A good supply of bone meal applied from the time that you put the tomato plants in the ground, will help prevent this problem. Once plants are set, you can still side-dress with bone meal.

A calcium deficiency retards growth and causes stems to get thick and woody. Upper leaves appear yellow (as contrasted to the yellowing of leaves in the lower plant as in nitrogen, phosphorus, or potassium deficiencies). Plants seem weak and flabby, fruit is prone to blossom-end rot, and terminal buds will probably die. Use any good grade of lime preferably dolomitic limestone, to counteract this deficiency.

Limestone can also remedy a magnesium deficiency. Tomatoes deficient in this nutrient have brittle leaves that curl up and turn yellow. The yellowing appears in the leaves rather than the stems, in the areas farthest away from the veins. Use dolomitic limestone, or put a handful of Epsom salts in the hole before you set the plant.

A boron deficiency causes blackened areas at the growing tip of the stunted stem. The terminal shoots will curl, then turn yellow and die. In severe cases, fruit may darken and dry out in certain areas, and the whole plant will have an abnormally bushy appearance. A little borax will save the day.

Iron deficiency produces spotted, colorless areas on young leaves and on the upper parts of plants. New shoots may die if the deficiency is severe. Apply plenty of manure, sludge if you can get it, and dried blood to correct the trouble.

Tomatoes deficient in copper show stunted shoot growth

and very poor root development, which will make the whole plant undersized and sickly. The foliage turns bluish green and the leaves curl. Few or no flowers form, and leaves get flabby. Use plenty of manure as a deterrent.

Use manure also for a zinc deficiency, which is identified by very long, narrow leaves that are colored yellow and mottled with dead areas.

Manganese deficiency shows up as very slow growth and very light green foliage, with dead areas in the center of the yellow areas. There are few blossoms and no fruit. Manure is a good cure.

Early blight [color] is one of the most common tomato diseases in home gardens. It is primarily a foliage blight but also may cause fruit rot around the stem end of the fruits in late fall. Early blight is characterized by irregular brown spots with concentric rings in a target pattern on the lower leaves. These spots soon enlarge to ¼ to ½ inch in diameter, run together, and cause the leaf to turn brown and usually to drop off the plant. Robbing the plant of its leaves serves to decrease the size of fruit and expose it to sunscald. If weather conditions are favorable, this blight will move up the plant until all leaves on the lower half have fallen. Spotting and girdling of the stems also may occur.

The early blight fungus overwinters in old tomato debris and on weeds such as Jimson, horsenettle, ground cherry, and nightshade. Seeds or transplants also may carry the fungus. A three-year rotation should help prevent trouble; do not alternate tomatoes with members of the potato family. Infected plant waste should be turned under immediately following harvest. Plant resistant varieties, such as Manalucie, Southland, Floradel, and Manahill. If you're growing tomatoes from seed, be sure that they come from healthy plants.

Fusarium wilt [color] is one of the most prevalent and damaging diseases of tomatoes. The fungus causes trouble by growing in the food and water channels of the plant. It is found in the greenhouse as well as the field and can live for long periods in the soil. This organism generally does not cause damage unless the soil and air temperatures are rather high during much of the season. Susceptible varieties are either killed or damaged so badly that they produce little fruit. Once fields become infested they are no longer suitable for growing tomatoes.

Many growers know this wilt disease as yellows because of the characteristic color of infected plants. The first symptom is a slight yellowing of a single leaf or a slight wilting and drooping of the lower leaves. A distinct brown discoloration of the water and food channels can be seen in a cross section of a stem close to the base of the plant. This discoloration often extends upward for some distance and is particularly evident in the petioles of wilted leaves at the point where they join the stem.

The fusarium wilt fungus enters through the roots and passes upward into the stem, where toxic substances that cause the wilting and death are produced. In severely affected plants the fungus may pass into the fruit and seed. However, infection from internally infected seed is rare, as fruit usually decays and drops.

To control fusarium wilt, grow seedlings in clean soil; wilt-free fields may become contaminated by the use of infected transplants. Seedlings should not be located on old garden soil or on land where wilt is known to have occurred. If you intend to purchase the plants, be certain that the grower's fields are free from wilt. Tomatoes should not be grown on the same land more than once in four years if possible; a slight wilt infestation soon can be greatly increased by growing tomatoes repeatedly in the same place. Pull up and destroy affected tomato plants at the end of the season. Certified seed is less likely to carry the wilt fungus than uncertified seed. If you use home-saved seed, be sure that it comes from plants completely free from wilt. A number of varieties show resistance to wilt. Susceptibility varies with time and location, so consult with the local agricultural agent. Regardless of variety, nematode injury renders tomatoes especially vulnerable to wilt; see NEMATODE and RESISTANT VARIETIES.

Ghost spot is caused by the same fungus responsible for gray mold. Look for small whitish rings, measuring ⅛ to ¼ inch in diameter, on young green tomatoes. The spots do not extend far into the fruit, and so do not greatly affect marketability. High temperatures and low humidity discourage the disease. Avoid planting where gray mold has been, especially in damp locations. In the greenhouse, lower the humidity, raise temperatures, and improve ventilation.

Gardeners in the southeastern states are apt to be visited by **gray leaf spot** [color] fungus on tomatoes, peppers, eggplant, ground cherries, and other related plants. It can be distinguished from other fungi diseases that thrive in warm, moist weather by the appearance of dark brown spots on the undersurface of older leaves. These leaves eventually yellow, wither, and drop. Serious infestations will kill all but a few tip leaves, and few fruit will appear.

Because this fungus is carried over from season to season on the remains of diseased plants in the soil, use a three- or four-year rotation. See RESISTANT VARIETIES.

Gray mold first appears as a heavy gray growth on dead leaves or stems at the base of the plant. The gray spots then travel to growing leaves, tan markings appear on stems, and gray or yellowish soft spots show up on fruit. If this mold appears in the greenhouse or hot bed in spring, raise the temperature and lower the humidity to discourage growth of the fungus.

Late blight is a fungus disease that causes severe defoliation and destructive rots of fruit. The first symptoms of the disease are irregular, greenish black, water-soaked patches on the older leaves. These spots enlarge rapidly and in moist weather may show a white, downy growth of the fungus on their surfaces. In moderately warm, wet weather, the spread of infection is so rapid that plants look as though they had been frosted. Fruits may be attacked at any stage in their development. Affected areas on the fruit are usually large, dark colored, firm, and have a rough surface. The disease is favored by rainy, foggy weather with temperatures of 40° to 60°F. at night and 70° to 80°F. in the day. It is checked when the weather turns hot and dry. With favorable weather conditions, late blight may be spread to tomatoes from diseased potato vines, be brought into the area on infected transplants, or blow in from other regions. This disease is particularly important east of the Mississippi.

In the greenhouse, late blight can be controlled by lowering the relative humidity in the house. Although this will quickly check the enlargement of lesions, it will not kill the fungus, and the growth of the fungus will be resumed as soon as cool humid conditions recur. The best way to reduce relative humidity is to raise the temperature inside the house and provide ample ventilation. Keeping night temperatures to 65°F. or above usually holds the relative humidity sufficiently low to avoid further development of the disease. In the field, control begins with destruction of infected plants and tubers; it is believed that blight cannot live on in soil alone. In the South, be sure to get certified plants from nurseries that grow tomatoes far from potatoes. If you buy seedlings in the North, check they are not from a greenhouse that suffers from blight. See RESISTANT VARIETIES.

Leaf mold [color] is principally a greenhouse trouble, although on occasion it may develop in the garden or field. All aboveground parts are affected, particularly the leaves. The first symptoms usually appear on the surfaces of the older leaves in the form of diffuse whitish spots that rapidly enlarge and become yellow. Under humid conditions, the lower surface of these patches becomes covered with a velvety, olive-brown coating of the causal fungus. When conditions favor the development of the disease in the greenhouse, much of the foliage is killed and the crop is greatly reduced. Although fruit infection is rare, the fruit stems and blossoms may also be affected.

The fungus spores are produced in great numbers on the under surface of the leaves and are spread by air currents, watering, and contact with the plants. The spores are tough and may survive around the greenhouse for several months after the plants have been removed. Occasionally the spores may also be carried on the seed.

The disease can be controlled to a considerable degree if adequate ventilation is provided during fall and spring months. During the warmer spring and fall months, the ventilators should be handled so as to provide maximum ventilation and sufficient heat at temperatures of at least 60° to 65°F. If heat is provided at night, the relative humidity will be kept down. The disease will usually not be severe if the relative humidity is kept below 90 percent. Resistant varieties are available, but the fungus mutates into new forms and older varieties may lose their resistance. See RESISTANT VARIETIES.

Leaf roll is a nonparasitic disease that generally follows periods of wet weather and is likely to occur on plants in poorly drained soils. It has also been observed after close cultivation and extremely close pruning. Overwatering and deep cultivation may also cause this disease.

The rolling generally starts on the lower leaves and proceeds upward until, in some instances, almost all the leaves are affected. In severe cases, the rolled leaves are somewhat thickened and tend to rattle when the plant is shaken. Ordinarily, affected plants bear a normal or nearly normal crop of fruit, but plants may lose ⅓ to ½ of their leaves with a corresponding loss in fruit quality and yield. This defoliation is most severe on staked plants.

The conditions that cause the plants to lose their leaves are not fully understood. One theory is that heavy rains that whip and riddle older rolled leaves may be partly responsible. Or, it could be that aphids cause the trouble. Perhaps the best explanation is that loss of leaves is caused by an accumulation of carbohydrates in the plant. Heavy pruning and the removal of suckers is thought to restrict plant growth and increase carbohydrates in the lower leaves.

This condition is not particularly damaging and plants recover with more favorable weather. To lessen damage from leaf roll, choose well-drained areas for tomatoes, particularly if you are growing them in the garden. Do not cultivate deeply near the plants, and avoid extremely close pruning.

Mosaic diseases are common tomato troubles. Four of the most widespread are common mosaic, tobacco mosaic, aucuba mosaic, and cucumber mosaic.

• The most characteristic symptom of *common mosaic* is mottled areas of light and dark green in the leaves. The dark green areas usually appear somewhat raised and puckered. Young leaves at the tips of growing branches tend to be bunched and to unfold unevenly. Plants affected in the early stages of growth usually have a yellowish cast and stunted growth. Ordinarily the fruit does not show any marked disfiguration. Both number and size of fruit are reduced, however, resulting in lower yields. If infection occurs before or during transplanting to the field, the yields may be reduced by as much as 50 percent. The common mosaic virus is so extremely infectious that a person can transmit it by merely touching a healthy tomato plant after having handled an infected one. Transplanting, cultivating, weeding, and attacks by insects are other ways of transmitting the virus. Greenhouse infections are correlated with hand operations such as pruning and tying the plant. Since the virus will live for several years in dried leaves and stems, it may be spread to growing plants from the remains of the previous crop. Certain ornamental plants and perennial weeds such as zinnia, snapdragon, phlox, petunia, ground cherry, and horsenettle are infected by the virus and may serve as sources of early infection in the field, seedbed, and greenhouse.

• *Tobacco mosaic* is the most common and most serious virus disease of greenhouse tomatoes. According to the Cooperative Extension Service at Ohio State University, the almost universal prevalence of the disease may be due to its highly infectious nature. The symptoms of tobacco mosaic are so varied that it is often difficult to see any difference between healthy and infected plants.

The most common symptom observed in young plants is malformation of the leaflets. On older plants very little malformation is present, and mottling is the distinguishing symptom. Leaflets may tend to be long and stringy or they may only show a strong tendency to be pointed. Generally, the young leaflets point straight up and the plants exhibit a slightly grayish appearance.

Mosaic-infected plants wilt much more severely in a bright period following a cloudy period. In older plants the main symptom of the disease is mottling of the leaves. When looking for diseased plants, work with the light to your back so that the plants are shaded, as the deformation and mottling will be much easier to see.

In all probability, the greatest spread is brought about by handling. It has been shown at the Ohio Agricultural Research and Development Center that a worker with virus on his hands, working with healthy tomato plants, can bring about infection as far away as the 80th plant. All 80 plants will not be infected, but a large percentage of the first plants the worker touches will become infected; the amount of infection decreases until only an occasional plant contracts the disease.

Although the virus may remain in a living form in the soil for several months, the amount of spread through soil is greatly reduced if a period of 20 days elapses between the removal of an old diseased crop and the planting of a healthy crop.

Control of tobacco mosaic is very difficult. Constantly inspect and rogue diseased plants. Remove one plant on either side of the diseased one, as it is almost impossible to remove a diseased plant and not contaminate healthy adjacent ones.

Tobacco mosaic virus problems may be reduced if the root system of susceptible plants is not allowed to grow below the disinfested soil; proper watering will keep the new root system confined to the top soil layer and prevent contact with old root tissue that may harbor the virus at levels below the disinfested zone. Resistant varieties are available, and new ones continue to be developed. A strain of tobacco mosaic can be passed on to tomatoes by smokers or tobacco chewers. Should you entertain either habit, wash your hands thoroughly before entering the tomato patch or greenhouse.

• *Aucuba mosaic* causes a striking yellow mottling of the leaves and sometimes yellowing and bleaching of the upper parts of stems and branches. The fruit may be mottled—light and dark green when immature, and yellow and red when ripe—and is generally unacceptable for marketing. The aucuba mosaic virus is introduced and spread among tomato plants in much the same way as common mosaic except that the aucuba virus is not quite so easily transmitted by contact.

• Tomato plants affected with *cucumber mosaic* are stunted, yellowed, and bushy. Although leaves may show a mottling suggestive of common mosaic, the most pronounced symptom is a shoestring appearance of the leaves. Sometimes the leaves are so distorted that very little remains of the leaf blade but the midrib.

Severely affected plants produce but few fruit, and these are usually smaller than the fruit from healthy plants.

This virus overwinters in certain perennial weeds such as pokeweed, catnip, and milkweed. At least five species of aphids as well as striped and spotted cucumber beetles are capable of transmitting this disease. However, cucumber mosaic is not transmitted in tomato seed, is not easily transmitted by rubbing and handling the plants, and does not persist in the soil or on the hands of those working with affected plants. This low infectivity means that you needn't remove adjoining plants when roguing diseased tomatoes.

To control mosaic diseases, be certain to eradicate all perennial weeds from the seedbed, greenhouse, and surrounding areas. It is especially important to get rid of ground cherry, horseweed, milkweed, catnip, and pokeweed. If you have been using tobacco in any form, wash your hands in soap and water to inactivate any viruses. Sanitation is improved if you dip your hands in milk often enough to keep them wet. Seedlings suspected of infection should be sprayed with milk at least twice.

In the field or garden, do not grow tomatoes next to such crops as potatoes, cucumber, tobacco, and related plants, as they are likely to carry viruses. If possible, tomato plants should not be grown in seedbeds or sections of greenhouses used for flower production. Do not plant cucumbers and melons next to the greenhouses in which a fall or spring crop of tomatoes is to be grown; otherwise, virus-bearing aphids and cucumber beetles may move into the greenhouses as the cucumbers and melons mature. Aphid control is important in preventing the spread of mosaic diseases once a few plants in the garden are infected (see APHID). Rogue out all early infected plants and burn them. When pruning, pinch off blossoms without touching any other part of the plant; do not use a knife.

Psyllid yellows is a disease caused by the feeding of the tomato (or potato) psyllid. The damage is principally due to a toxic substance that is released into the plant as the insect feeds. Look for a thickening of the older leaves and an upward rolling at their base as they turn yellow and develop purplish veins and margins. Younger leaves may curl and plants are sometimes dwarfed. The stems and petioles seem unusually slender, and plants take on a spindly appearance. If the disease hits young plants, they will produce little or no fruit; if the disease happens later, tomatoes that are already set will likely be yellowish red, quite soft, and of poor quality.

Psyllids cause trouble in the nymph stage; they are flat and look something like fringed scales, and change in color from yellow to orange to green. To control them, clear the area of weed hosts, including Chinese lantern and ground cherry. A garlic spray may keep psyllids from feeding.

Root-knot is caused by tiny parasitic worms known as nematodes; see NEMATODE. Better Boy is a resistant variety.

Septoria leaf spot or **septoria blight** is one of the most damaging of tomato diseases and often causes severe losses in the Atlantic and Central states. It also occurs frequently as far south as Arkansas, Tennessee, and North Carolina. The disease is most severe during rainy seasons and in fields where plants are crowded and are bearing a heavy fruit load.

As a rule, the disease is slow in getting started and is not much in evidence before early or middle July and not before the plants have begun to set fruits. The first infection is ordinarily found on the older leaves near the ground; look for small, water-soaked spots scattered thickly over the leaf. These spots soon become roughly circular and have gray centers surrounded by darker margins. Later, the centers show tiny dark specks in which the spores of the fungus are produced. The spots are more numerous and smaller than those of early blight, usually measuring $\frac{1}{16}$ to $\frac{1}{8}$ inch in diameter. If they are numerous, the leaflet usually dies and drops from the plant. When conditions favor infection, there is a progressive loss of foliage until only a few leaves are left at the top of the stem so that the fruit is exposed to sunscald. The fruit is rarely affected, but there may be spotting of the stem and blossoms.

It has been found that this leaf spot fungus will not live over on the remains of plants buried deeply in the soil. If all the vines are covered, deep cultivation or plowing in fall or spring will do much to prevent infection. The plants in small gardens may be collected in fall and burned. Clean cultivation, control of weeds, and rotations will help to free growing areas of the fungus. Stay. out of the tomato patch when plants are wet, as the fungus is easily transmitted by brushing against them.

Soil rot fungus [color] is the same pathogen responsible for damping-off of seedlings. The first symptom is a slightly sunken brown spot on the fruit, outlined with concentric markings. The spot enlarges and may break open, unlike the somewhat similar condition known as buckeye rot. Infections occur when plants touch the ground or are splashed by rainwater, and a good mulch should help here. Avoid setting tomatoes in poorly drained soil, and use varieties that can be staked.

Spotted wilt first appears on young plants as numerous small, dark, circular dead spots on younger leaves. Spots may turn bronzy before becoming dark and withered. The tips of stems are darkly streaked and often wither. If young plants are able to survive, the new growth is very dwarfed and the leaflets appear distorted. On older plants the growing tips are somewhat damaged and the foliage has a yellow tinge to it. The fruit has many spots with concentric, circular markings.

Control involves eliminating weed hosts and keeping the tomato patch isolated from such vulnerable vegetables as lettuce, celery, spinach, peppers, and potatoes. Infected seedlings can be removed to stop an infestation and can be replaced with healthy plants, as the disease is not soil-borne. Varieties developed in Hawaii are considered resistant to spotted wilt virus, and include Pearl Harbor, Anahu, and Kalohi.

Sunscald can occur whenever green tomatoes are exposed to the sun, but is most frequent in hot, dry weather. This injury is common on plants that have suffered a premature loss of their foliage from leaf spot diseases, such as early blight or septoria leaf spot, and is a major cause of loss from these diseases. Fruit of plants suffering from verticillium or fusarium wilt also are likely to suffer from sunscald as a result of the loss of the lower foliage.

Varieties resistant to graywall, leaf mold, nailhead spot, and verticillium wilt are listed under RESISTANT VARIETIES.

Trees

For the sake of convenience, many of the troubles that trees have in common are dealt with in this entry. You'll find these troubles arranged as follows:

Trees: General Care

A tree is unique among all living organisms. It lives longer and grows taller and larger than any other organism of land or sea.

Yet a tree, like a human being, can be hurt and can die from its wound. When a tree is wounded, a chemical reaction takes place to protect the wound and compartmentalize it. If the tree is healthy it will heal, for wound healing is the rule in nature. But often the wound provides an entry for bacteria, fungi, and viruses.

A tree wound might be caused by a bird, animal, or insect; by fire or storm damage; by heavy mechanical equipment; by a nail; or by a branch breaking off to leave a poorly healed stub. Any part of the tree is susceptible—roots, trunk, branches, and bark. The Forest Service of the USDA urges everyone to become aware of the problem of tree wounds. The better we are at detecting tree troubles, the better we can prevent and control decay, the major cause of damage to trees. First, greater care must be taken to prevent wounds. Too many people take trees for granted, assuming that they will continue to grow no matter what is done to them. Small wounds may not seem serious, but an accumulation of them may add up to serious trouble.

Second, help the tree help itself after wounding. Remove the obviously injured bark and wood as well as dead and dying branches. Shape the wound like an ellipse if possible. Fertilize and water properly, and remove less valuable trees or shrubs that may be crowding the injured tree.

Third, if the tree becomes too unsightly or too dangerous because of the threat of falling limbs, remove it. A professional arborist can help make the decision as to when this is necessary.

Fourth, when planting new trees, plan ahead to avoid likely accidents to trees. For example, trees should be planted away from driveways, curbs, and walkways.

• **Planting.**   The time of transplanting is a precarious one for trees, and extra care must be given them to help them become established. The Department of Plant Pathology of the University of Massachusetts suggests the following plans of insuring the survival and health of new trees.

The best time of year for planting, usually early spring or late fall, varies with species and location. Check with your local nursery for this information. Planting holes should be wide and deep enough to accommodate bare-rooted trees without any cramping of the roots. For balled-root stock, make the holes at least a foot wider than the diameter of the ball. Untie and roll back burlap wraps from the trunk after planting. Plastic burlap and plastic bag wraps will not decompose in the soil and should be completely removed. Fill the hole with topsoil and cover to the depth that the tree was growing in the nursery—that is, the depth at which it grows naturally, but no deeper. Add water immediately after planting and continue to water periodically for two seasons. Evergreens require more water than deciduous trees and shrubs. Water heavily near the roots about once a week for several hours unless there is enough rain to saturate the soil. Begin to water seven to ten days after the last rain, and continue through the growing season and well into fall. The soil should be saturated but not waterlogged.

When planting trees three feet or over additional precautions may be advisable. To help support the trees until the roots become firmly established, hose-wrapped guy wires can be connected from the tree to supporting poles. These supports should be left in place for one to two years, when they must be removed to prevent them from girdling the trunk. Damage from sunscald and minor wounds can be prevented by wrapping bare trunks with burlap, creped kraft paper, or a couple thicknesses of aluminum foil.

Wire mesh supported by stakes around the tree, several inches from the trunk, will help prevent animal damage. It should be a heavy enough gauge to repel larger animals, but a fine enough mesh to keep small rodents from getting to the bark. The aluminum mesh sold to protect gutters from leaves seems to work well. Anything tied around the tree trunk or around a branch should be loosened each year and removed as soon as possible.

• **Mulching and fertilizing.**   Tree leaves are a natural mulch, and the leaves that fall from healthy trees and shrubs should be put back into the soil below. In time, the layer of leaves weathers down to rich, black, humusy soil. This method of mulching provides both aeration for absorbing moisture and necessary minerals for the root system. Trees thrive on it. If the leaves are thought to carry insect eggs or disease spores, however, it is advisable to rake them and add them to the compost heap. If the compost is properly made so that it is heated to 130° to 140°F., pests on the leaves will be killed. Then in spring, when it is needed for plant growth, return the fully rotted compost to your trees.

Although mulch is important in preserving soil moisture, there are times when it is wise to rake off all the old mulch and let the sun shine on the soil for a while. This is especially true where trees or shrubs are prone to mildew or fungus diseases fostered by dampness. If you garden in a damp climate, give your soil a sun bath each spring. Remove all the old mulch and let the sun kill off the disease spores in the top layer. After a few weeks of baking, mulch again with fresh material.

To make sure your trees get all the nutrients they need, apply a mixture of balanced minerals and fertilizers. A mixture recommended by the Rodale Organic Experimental Farm is equal quantities (by weight) of: 1) cottonseed meal or dried blood; 2) phosphate rock or bone meal; 3) wood ashes, granite dust, or greensand; and 4) dolomitic limestone. For small trees set in open soil, these nutrients may be spread and filled into the earth. But the most practical way to fertilize large trees or those whose roots are covered with sod is to punch 18-inch-deep holes in the soil with a pipe or crowbar, slanting them in toward the trunk. These holes should be two inches apart, covering the entire area beneath the crown out to the dripline. Full each hole with six to eight ounces of the fertilizer mix and then cap it with peat moss or topsoil.

• Pruning.

Pruning of trees and shrubs adds to their health and their good looks, helping nature to grow the plant in the most attractive and productive form. By insuring adequate sunlight and air circulation, and by removing weak or crowded growth, you will strengthen your plant's resistance to infection and insects. Dark, overly damp growth often makes a favorable breeding environment for trouble.

Three types of pruning contribute to the appearance and health of trees and shrubs. *Basic* pruning gives plants a structure that prevents weakness, intemperate growth, and deformity. This would include pruning to balance top and roots after planting, training the young plant, and general control of its size and shape. If a tree grows where machinery must pass, prune to allow plenty of room, as bruised or broken-off branches are unsightly and unhealthy.

Maintenance includes regular pruning to maintain an optimum balance between old and new wood, foliage, and the flowering and fruiting parts of the plant. Maintenance pruning also means prompt removal of all dead, diseased, or injured parts that would allow rot and disease organisms to enter the plant. Suckers and watersprouts are other energy-stealers that must be pruned out.

Renewal is a type of pruning that many gardeners hesitate to try, though it is often simple. This pruning aims at the rejuvenation of old trees or shrubs, which in most cases is accomplished by thinning out the older growths and heading back the larger of the young branches to force development of strong, healthy new growth. Such an operation should be done gradually over several years, not all at once.

Most pruning can be done any time, although maples and birches "bleed" heavily in spring and thus should be trimmed in summer. Those evergreens that are pruned to induce bushiness or extra foliage, such as white pines, Norway spruce, and Colorado blue spruce, should be pruned back to a lateral bud in spring. Summer is a good time to observe which branches are diseased or dying; these can be pruned in late fall.

All broken, dead, or diseased wood is cut out to prevent the spread of decay. Live stems are often removed to improve air circulation, to admit more light, or to push the remaining part of the crown to more foliage. Restrict your cutting when possible to small branches, as heavy pruning can lead to shock from loss of food manufacture and may bring on sun scald.

Start at the top and work your way down looking for misshapen, diseased or obstructing branches as you go. Weak growths and crotches should also be removed to prevent splitting. If you must remove a larger branch, make a preliminary undercut so you don't strip the bark when the branch snaps off. Coat all wounds and cuts with a wound dressing—they're usually tar derivatives, available at most garden and farm supply stores.

Don't neglect wounds that expose the wood beneath the bark, as they have killed off many a good tree. Such openings are invitations to bacteria, fungi, and many insects that normally leave healthy trees alone. The tree itself will put forth a normal callus growth to close the opening; you can help by carefully trimming and paring off loose, rough or protruding bits of torn wood. When you cut a branch, don't leave a stub that will interfere with the normal growth of a protective callus. Ornamental shade trees such as dogwood, Japanese weeping cherry, and flowering crab apple easily become malformed from improper care of wounds.

If the wound is large, shape it into an ellipse by careful paring and trimming to encourage and promote healing. Cut the bark down to solid, sound wood, removing all bruised tissues as you work the incision into an egg shape. Alow it to dry and then apply the wound dressing over the entire surface. Repeated applications may be necessary once a year until the callus has covered the wound.

• **Restoration of old trees.**   If you acquire land with old trees on it, they are likely to need some attention. The first step is a survey of the old trees to estimate what kind and how much repair they will need. A professional arborist, either public or private, should be called in for advice. Often the most picturesque old trees are imperfect ones that take their unique character from a gerontic deformity, scar, or irregular growth pattern, and it would be folly to try to change the very quirks that make them interesting.

Safety is the first concern, says John Stuart Martin in *The Home Owner's Tree Book*. While you may be able to spot a heavy branch hanging perilously over the house, walk, or driveway, less obvious are defects such as a faulty crotch, cavity, or imbalanced tree that could become dangerous in high winds or snowstorms. Once the old trees have been made safe, the next step is to renew their vigor. You will need to dig a few test holes to determine the soil strata and the levels at which the trees' roots run. If the root systems are predominantly shallow, spiking the turf as described above may be the best way for fertilizer to reach them. If they are deeply rooted, the food insertions will have to be close together, shallower, and far beyond the branch spread. Root systems of trees reach out much further than you might think —as far as twice the reach of the crowns.

Sometimes a steadily declining old tree will suddenly burst into exaggerated bloom or fruit bearing, and then die in a year or two. This is a natural phenomenon for some trees, but a program of feeding, pruning, and root doctoring is not likely to cause such quick, dramatic results; instead, leaf color, annual growth, and revived vigor will be gradual.

Trees: Environmental Problems

A well-fed, vigorous tree, planted in the proper climate and surroundings, is not often seriously troubled by pests or diseases. However, a tree never exists in isolation, and a great variety of environmental factors that you may have taken for granted can make all the difference between healthy and sickly trees.

In urban and suburban areas, parks and recreation places, or wherever there are numbers of people, trees may be directly or indirectly harmed by human activities. People-Pressure Diseases (PPD) is a term coined by Dr. Alex Shigo, plant pathologist of the USDA's Northeast Forest Experiment Station in Durham, New Hampshire. Common symptoms of PPD are small and discolored leaves, premature fall coloration and loss of leaves, reduced twig growth, dying twigs in the upper crown, and the decline of parts or all of the tree.

PPD may denote air pollution, building and road construction, improper use of home and garden equipment, deicing salt on highways, soil compaction, improper pruning and planting, use of agricultural chemicals, flooding, smothering, improper wound treatment, or any combination of these.

Plant a Tree, by Michael A. Weiner, is a good source of environmental precautions, some of which follow.

It is a mistake to assume that **air pollution** only damages trees in and around large cities—air pollutants occur also in rural areas. There are two main classes of gaseous air pollutants, point sources and oxidants. Point source pollutants come from a smoke stack or burning area. The most common pollutants from a point source are sulfur dioxide (SO_2) and fluorides. SO_2 comes mostly from burning coal and oil for the generation of electricity. However, SO_2 can also be produced by smelting sulfur-containing ores or manufacturing sulfur products. Fluorides are produced by reduction of aluminum ore, manufacture of phosphate fertilizer, and most stone processing operations. Other less common pollutants of this class are ethylene, hydrogen chloride, and ammonia.

Oxidants are formed in large regions of the atmosphere from chemical reactions powered by sunlight. Ozone and PAN (peroxy acetyl nitrate) are produced mostly from industrial and auto emissions. Low concentrations of ozone also occur naturally in the atmosphere. The oxidants are common components of smog.

Individually, you can help to minimize pollution in such ways as keeping automobiles tuned up and not burning trash. However, the most serious forms of air pollution are difficult to prevent without a community effort. Many towns now have conservation commissions that can be contacted for local support to abate air pollution.

Construction of buildings, roads, and ditches is one of the main sources of man-caused damage to trees. The traffic of heavy equipment may damage tree roots through the effects of soil compaction. Diseases may enter the wounds caused by construction equipment. Trees are hurt when the ground is covered with soil fill or by asphalt or concrete. Even the addition of a few inches of soil will change the amount of water and oxygen available to the roots. Feeding roots are very sensitive to changes in the water level, and if they cannot reach their normal water supply, trouble will result. Carbon dioxide and other gases may build up in the filled soil to produce a toxic effect. Growth slows down, foliage may become discolored, and the trees decline and often die within a few years. USDA plant pathologist Dr. G. J. Bart calls this malady "bulldozer wilt."

Constructing a small well around the trunk of an established tree, as is done in many construction areas, will prevent smothering of trunk tissues but not of the roots. If possible, avoid adding excessive soil or impervious materials within the drip line (the entire area under the branches) of the tree. A retaining wall outside this area should prevent a builder from dumping indiscriminate fill over the roots.

Another possibility is to check with an arborist about the value of trees on the lot where you intend to build. Consider whether in the long run it might be more economical to remove undesirable species of trees and those with low vigor before beginning to build.

Trees will show the effects of **drought** the following summer, especially if they were not watered during the dry period. If the leaves are scorched or drop off from lack of water, the tree will not be able to store its normal supply of food. So keep your trees well watered in dry times.

Electric currents from service wires may make rough wounds where wires come in contact with trees. Entire limbs or trees may die. Wet weather helps to cause the short circuiting of current that causes high temperatures to reach lethal levels in tender tree tissue. Be sure that wires close to the trees are thoroughly insulated. Wires may also cause mechanical injury by chafing, so keep them away from trees or limbs either by choice of location or by judiciously pruning the branches nearby.

Flooding and changes in normal drainage patterns, especially during the growing season, may kill tree roots by depriving them of oxygen. Low-lying areas subject to flooding are poor sites for some species, including the eastern white pine, hemlock, paper birch, red cedar, red pine, white spruce, and sugar maple, all of which will decline and eventually die if flooded. Trees that tolerate occasional flooding and can be planted in damp sites are ash, black gum, cottonwood, elm, overcup oak, red maple, river birch, silver maple, sweetgum, sycamore, white cedar, and willows.

Frost and unseasonably cold weather may kill parts of trees in autumn and new growth in spring. To harden your trees against such damage, do not stimulate them to grow late in the season, as new growth cannot stand up to the winter cold. Plant native trees or those known to be hardy. Valuable and small exotic trees that may be especially frost-susceptible should be protected with shelters in the winter. **Frost cracks** appear as longitudinal splits in the tree trunk that tend to form successive layers of callus until a large, so-called frost rib protrudes from the trunk. These cracks are often a result of ice formation and sudden changes in winter temperature. They occur particularly in early winter, after autumn rainfall has caused a spurt of late growth of immature bark and sapwood. You can help prevent frost cracks by making sure your trees have proper drainage so that excess moisture doesn't collect about the base. Dead bark can be cut away from the edges, and a disinfectant and a wound dressing applied. See winter injury, below.

Illuminating **gas** from a leaking or broken gas main can cause yellowing foliage, slow growth, or even the death of the tree. You may see blue or brown streaks in the wood of roots and trunk. Breaks in the main some distance down the street may miss other trees in the neighborhood and nevertheless hit yours because of some quality of the subsoil layers. The utility company will respond immediately to a call for detection of gas leakage, but here's how to make the test yourself. In the lawn area between the tree and the suspected gas leakage, dig a hole large enough to accommodate a half-bushel basket. In this hole, place a potted tomato plant. Then cover the hole with boards, some paper or burlap, and finally a small amount of the soil. Thus the tomato plant is in the same atmosphere as that in which the tree roots have been growing. After 24 to 36 hours remove the plant and examine it. If all the branches and leaves bend down sharply and firmly from the main stem (not just presenting the wilted appearance of a plant needing water), gas is present in the soil.

Once the gas leak is repaired, you can help your tree back to health by digging a trench on the side of the leak or all around the tree and then aerating the soil thoroughly by compressed air. Next, water heavily. This process should also be followed when replacing dead trees with new trees.

Lightning strikes trees and roots to cause a wilting of foliage and possibly trunk abrasions. The lightning may burn a complete ring around the cambium layer of the lower trunk, in which case the whole tree will die. Sometimes a tree whose cambium has been destroyed from top to bottom will remain green through the rest of the season and even put out new leaves the following spring, only to die later that year. The tree can be helped to recover from its wound by fertilizing and watering. Lightning rods may help prevent trouble.

You may observe **mosses** and grayish green growth lichens on the trunks of trees and bases of shrubs, especially those growing in damp areas. Lichens, made up of certain fungi and algae, take the form of crusts, leaves, or cushions. Mosses usually have leafy, erect, or creeping stems that develop from a heavily branched green structure; the plants develop in dense clusters or cushions. Dr. R. E. Partyka, plant pathologist of Ohio State University, says that mosses and lichen are no cause for alarm as they seldom affect the growth of the tree or shrub, and it is not necessary to remove them.

If **pesticides** or herbicides have been used nearby, your trees may suffer. A neighboring building may have been treated for termites, for example. Many of the materials used by exterminators for this purpose are extremely toxic to plants. If poisonous gas is employed, the vapors may find their way to your property. Some trees show such poisoning by a browning of the midveins of the leaves; on others, the whole leaf turns brown. The injury will show in one month if the tree is in leaf, but not until the following spring if the leaves have fallen.

Even if you have not sprayed your trees, your neighbors or highway department may have. If you are lucky, only this year's crop of leaves will be damaged, but you may lose the tree. In this case, find out where the spray materials came from and what your rights in the matter are under state law.

Factory **pollution,** in the form of gases, dusts, or smoke, may cause discoloration, mottling, or browning of foliage, especially on evergreens. Some gases contain arsenic and forms of sulfur that are poisonous to leaves while dusts may simply smother the foliage. In general, hardwoods are the most resistant to noxious fumes.

Other domestic poisons can affect your trees. Strong detergents or chemicals poured into nearby sewage may kill a tree whose roots are in the drainage field. Oil from a nearby oil-burner intake pipe may soak the root area. Soaps, oils, and salts that leak from nearby auto service stations, laundries, tennis courts, or refuse dumps may all suffocate or poison tree roots. See the discussion of salt injury, below.

Roadside trees are sometimes menaced as much by **salt** as by weedkillers. When streets and highways are salted during winter snow and ice storms, adjacent trees are attacked through their roots and irrigation systems. Evergreens can be killed by salty slush splashed on their limbs by passing cars. Sodium chloride (common table salt) and calcium chloride, another deicer, are both toxic to plants.

The University of Massachusetts Plant Pathology Department recommends planting salt-tolerant trees such as Austrian pine, birches, black cherry, black locust, big tooth aspen, Japanese black pine, pitch pine, quaking aspen, red cedar, red oak, white ash, white oak, white spruce, and yews. Trees that do not tolerate salt well are American elm, basswood, eastern white pine, hemlock, ironwood, red maple, red pine, shagbark hickory, speckled alder, and sugar maple.

Shade and lack of sunlight often result in spindly growth and the death of the lower limbs or inner twigs. Light-loving trees may do very poorly under the heavy shade of larger trees. When transplanting, it is important to keep trees, especially evergreens, well spaced. Plant shade-tolerant trees in areas shaded by larger trees, and prune out the inner limbs of such heavy shade trees as the Norway maple.

Poor foliage and twig growth, lichen on the bark, and general weakening of the tree are occasionally due to **starvation,** which in turn may be caused by planting in poor soil, exhaustion of soil food, lack of water, extensive paving, packing of surface soil, or a combination of these. The remedy is to fertilize and water properly, to leave space between pavement and trees, and to aerate or cultivate the soil in the root area.

High-intensity sodium **street lights** in your neighborhood may do indirect damage to trees by causing them to grow faster and keeping them growing longer into autumn than normal. This increases trees' vulnerability to air pollution and to frost damage, particularly in the case of young trees. London plane trees are particularly susceptible. Combat such damage by planting dormant trees in fall, by choosing more resistant trees such as ginkgo, or by getting rid of such lights, if possible.

Sun scald affects the bark tissues, and you will see dry, cracking, or curling bark on limbs and trunks that had been smooth. When bark accustomed to shade or protection is suddenly exposed to drying and heat from sun or wind, as in the case of thinning out or planting young trees in open areas, sun scald is apt to result. Young trees can be protected on the south exposure by setting up a vertical board or by winding the trunk with burlap or wrapping tape.

Sun scorch, in times of high temperature or drought, will cause injured or diseased roots and keep parts or all of the tree from receiving adequate moisture. The visible symptoms of sun scorch will be the yellowing, browning, and withering of leaves on one side or the whole tree. The condition starts on leaf tips and edges. Avoid disturbing the roots, if possible, but if they already have been disturbed, prune the tree to balance the reduced root system. Keep your trees well watered in dry spells, and conserve soil moisture with mulch.

The process of **transplanting** may cause somewhat of a shock to trees, and you should expect a recovery period before they again grow well and flourish. Proper pruning at transplanting time helps minimize the shock.

If soluble salts from dog **urine** enter the soil, tree roots may be killed. A metal collar on the trunk protects only the bark, not the roots, and the entire planting area may have to be screened off from dogs.

In addition to frost damage, your trees may suffer **winter injury** or drying. The usual symptoms in late winter and spring are the browning and withering of foliage and twigs. This is a common condition on evergreens. It is caused by dry winds that remove moisture while the roots and soil water are still frozen. Sun reflection from buildings and pavement may also cause drying.

You can help prevent such winter injury by mulching about the base in early fall and watering thoroughly. Burlap screens or wax emulsions also give some protection.

Trees: Insects

If you were to prepare a list of the insects that are found on trees and shrubs throughout the country, it would run to several pages. Most of them are harmless, many are helpful, and all but a few of the remainder are kept under control by their natural enemies—birds, diseases, and insect predators and parasites.

Most insect attacks are not fatal to trees, and it is not necessary to resort to chemical insecticides. Michael A. Weiner suggests in *Plant a Tree* that you try to live with the bugs. If you find this impossible, try water sprays, organic fertilizers, and a pruning of the infested branches. If the pest persists, find out if a biological control agent—*Bacillus thuringiensis,* ladybugs, or trichogramma wasps—can be of any help. As a last resort, turn to an organic pesticide, such as an oil spray or a recipe suggested in Chapter 10, "Repellents and Poisons."

• **Chewers and foliage-feeders.**   There are five main groups of insects that damage trees. The first group consists of chewers or foliage feeders, including the various caterpillars, sawfly larvae, beetles and their grubs, and leaf miners (which split the leaf apart and mine out the tissues). These insects devour foliage, and some, such as the gypsy moth, can deforest whole areas of woodlands.

There are two generations of **cankerworms** (or inchworms), one in spring and one in fall. Full-grown cankerworms are about an inch long, pale yellow, green, brown, or black, with several light-colored stripes running lengthwise down the body. See APPLE for their life cycles and controls.

Luckily, the **gypsy moth's** natural enemies, including birds, tachinid flies, and certain species of beetles and wasps, will help even a heavily defoliated area recover naturally.

Gypsy Moth

Tent caterpillars like to pupate in wood piles and under old baskets and boxes, so clean up these areas. You can remove the egg bands of tent caterpillars by hand or scrape them off with a dull knife. This egg band is a ringlike mass that has the appearance of brownish black, glossy caviar. Toward spring, the gloss dulls and the bands are harder to spot. Once they've hatched, you can prune out each individual nest and destroy all the worms. In cleaning out the egg masses, be sure you don't destroy praying mantis cocoons, which are silvery or tan, papery, spindle-shaped, and spun around the branches of shrubs and low trees.

Large numbers of tent caterpillar moths and moths of many other species may be captured in blacklight traps. Burning tent caterpillars is not recommended both because of the fire hazard and the fact that many caterpillars fall to the ground unburned and escape. See also TENT CATERPILLAR.

Tent Caterpillar

• **Gnawers or wood-feeders.** In the second group of tree-damaging insects are the gnawers or wood-feeders, such as: bark beetles and borers that eat small holes in trunks and limbs, forcing out the sap; carpenter ants that honeycomb the interior wood of trees; and the oak twig pruning beetle, whose presence is made known by numerous twigs of oak lying on the ground with the pith eaten out and grubs inside.

The **carpenterworm** often makes large galleries in the trunks and larger branches of locust, ash, oak, and maple. Large unsightly scars are evident wherever this insect occurs. Fortunately, the carpenterworm is usually not in sufficient abundance to cause serious injury. The females deposit their eggs in the vicinity of wounds. The young larvae first feed on the inner bark, then burrow in the wood. The mature larvae are about 2½ inches long and pinkish with brown heads. The adult moths are gray with brown or black markings, have a wingspread of about three inches, and are thought to live about three years.

Removal and destruction of infested branches helps reduce damage. Avoid damaging or wounding the tree when working around it. All wounds should be dressed and painted to keep the moths from laying eggs in the tree. A light trap may be effective against the adult moths. It is best to use it in early summer when the moths emerge.

Flat-head borers are among the worst enemies of deciduous trees and shrubs. Damage is especially severe to young, newly transplanted trees. The larvae burrow underneath the bark, girdling the tree. Adult borers are beetles with a metallic sheen that emerge in early summer and lay eggs in bark wounds. When the borers hatch, they eat through the bark to the cambium layer, and their holes diminish the value of the lumber when the trees are cut; hence, they are a serious problem on commercial plantations. See flat-headed apple tree borer under APPLE.

A group of insects called **twig girdlers** gnaws through the bark of twigs or branches, breaking the central part of the stem. You may see branches hanging from the trees in late summer, fall, or winter. Or, the larvae may cut the twig from within, hollowing out the center and then cutting the edge off cleanly and leaving the bark irregularly broken. Whatever you can do to encourage bug-eating birds, especially fall tree-dwellers, will keep these girdlers and borers from doing too much damage (see Chapter 12, "The Good and Bad of Wildlife in the Garden"). But in making your diagnosis, remember that playful squirrels can also be the cause of fallen twigs.

• Suckers or sap-feeders.   The third group of insects are the suckers or sap-feeders, such as aphids (plant lice), mealybugs, and scale insects. These feed by piercing the tissues and sucking out the juices, causing slowing of growth and death of twigs or limbs. When you notice raised scalelike material or white woolly or cottony masses on trunks, twigs, or buds, it means these insects are present. You may see winged or wingless insects cluster on the foliage, giving off shiny or dark-colored secretions onto the leaves and twigs below.

Aphids are small, soft-bodied sucking insects that attack most trees and shrubs. On otherwise healthy trees, they are primarily a nuisance. They excrete a honeydew which attracts ants and flies, provides a substrata on which mold grows, and causes spots on automobiles and outdoor furniture. On injured trees or trees subject to a stressful environment, aphids may cause more severe injury. An important natural enemy of aphids is the ladybug, which normally keeps them in check. When plants are starved or become thirsty, aphids may multiply to the point that ladybugs and other beneficials can no longer control them. If an aphid-ridden plant is treated for nutritional deficiency and thoroughly watered, the aphid population should decline. An old-time formula for controlling aphids on trees is made of two gallons of kerosene, ½ pound of hard soap, and one gallon of water. Heat the solution of soap and add it boiling hot to the kerosene. Churn the mixture by means of a force pump and spray nozzle for five to ten minutes. The emulsion forms a cream that thickens on cooling and should adhere without oiliness to the surface of glass. Before using, dilute one part of the emulsion with nine parts of cold water. This formula gives three gallons of emulsion and makes, when diluted, thirty gallons of wash. Also see APHID.

Lace bugs, whose wings show a gossamer lacy pattern under magnification, are seen on sycamore, basswood, hawthorn, cherry, white oak, and many broad-leaved evergreens. These small, flat insects, about ⅛ inch long, suck juices from the leaves, causing whitish or yellowish spots. Their molasseslike drops of excrement can be seen on the underside of leaves. Lace bugs seldom cause serious injury to deciduous trees, but leaves may drop from evergreens, causing dieback of twigs and small branches. If necessary, control by spraying or dusting the foliage with nicotine or pyrethrum.

Most **scale** insects are so small that they are not easily seen in their early stages of development. Some types of scales secrete a honeydew on which an unsightly black covering of sooty fungus soon develops on foliage, twigs, and branches. The fungus blocks the light needed by chlorophyll, and growth may be stunted and branches killed.

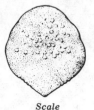

Scale

Scale can be controlled by a miscible petroleum oil spray applied when plants are dormant. The Agricultural Experiment Station of the University of Rhode Island cautions that many trees and shrubs will not tolerate petroleum oils, including various species of beech and maple, hickory, mountain ash, red and black oak, walnut, butternut, and taxus or yew. Those plants relatively tolerant to oils include elm, boxelder, apple, dogwood, linden, pin oak, burr oak, white oak, and post oak.

• **Gall insects.** The fourth type covers those that form galls. Galls are swellings produced by the tree when insects feed on and stimulate local areas of the tree. You may see them on buds, leaves, twigs, and branches. There is little you can do to control the responsible insects.

• **Nematodes.**   The fifth type of pests is nematodes, (small wireworms), some almost microscopic, that parasitize the roots of trees and shrubs. See NEMATODE.

Trees: Animal Pests

Birds like to raid fruit trees, often landing first on a branch for a look and then hopping to the fruit. Tree Tanglefoot, a commercial preparation that is smeared on branches where the birds alight, seems to repel them without harming them. It can be applied by using a long pole with a dauber of cloth wired to one end.

Sapsuckers leave numerous shallow holes in tree bark, whereas woodpeckers make small, deep, roughly rectangular holes. An application of lime sulfur on the trunk helps repel these birds. To help the tree recover from the wounds left by these birds, apply tree paint to the wounded areas.

Young trees are frequently set on by **rabbits** and **field mice.** Rabbits chew the tender bark and sometimes the lower branches, and completely girdled trees usually will die. One method of protection is to surround the trunks with a cylinder of ¼-inch hardware mesh, extending from slightly beneath the soil line up to the lower branches. Or, strips of aluminum foil can be wrapped around the trunks and lower branches (this also protects against sun scald). Even magazines can be wrapped around the base of the trunk. The magazine barrier should reach at least 12 inches high and be tied securely in two or three places with strong cord.

Meadow mice will nest in the mulch at the base of trees and feed on the bark; to reduce the possibility of such damage, pull the mulch at least two feet away from the trunks.

Trees: Diseases

Trees are susceptible to various kinds of diseases: wilts, rusts, cankers, mildews, root rots, and wood decay. Many of these can be avoided by taking care not to injure the tree, or by dressing the wounds it does receive. Once disease begins, pruning and burning the affected branches will often halt its spread. Pruning tools should be disinfected afterwards to prevent spreading the disease-causing fungus or bacteria. If only the leaves are affected, rake and burn them when they fall.

Nature has her own method of preventing and curing tree diseases. Doctor John E. Bier, Professor of Forest Pathology at the University of British Columbia, Canada, has been working to see if man can use that method, too. Dr. Bier has found that the bark and leaves of a healthy tree are covered with and penetrated by colonies of harmless fungi—bacteria and yeasts (saprophytes) that have the power of preventing the growth of pathogenic fungi, or of stopping that growth once it has started. Dr. Bier makes a saprophyte solution by soaking shredded bark from healthy trees in water. He finds that tree cuttings dipped for one hour in this solution and then kept well supplied with water are completely resistant to inoculation with canker. Drops of the solution applied daily to cankers on infected cuttings will arrest the disease. This natural method of disease control has important advantages over present poison-spray techniques. Toxic sprays may kill pathogens, but they also kill the beneficial saprophytes.

Dr. Bier scrapes healthy bark off a tree branch and shreds it in an electric blender. Healthy leaves may be used instead if bark is not available. He soaks one gram of the bark in 75 cc. of water. Using roughly the same proportions, you can put ¼ ounce shredded bark in one pint of water. Keep the solution in a warm room for five days. It must be well aerated; in the lab, this is done by standing containers on a mechanical rocker, but at home, you can aerate your culture by simply pouring it back and forth between two jars several times a day.

After five days, pass the solution through a strainer to remove the bits of bark. You might try out the brew in any of several ways. For one, stand the base ends of cuttings in solution for an hour before setting in rooting medium; use the solution for watering; or paint the solution for several days running on cankered spots of fruit trees or rose bushes. Try spraying new foliage and shoots of trees and vegetables with the solution to test for control of insect damage. Finally, try the solution as a stimulant for your compost pile. In each case, you can conduct control experiments by using plain water to observe what difference the solution makes.

• **Decay.**   Before decay begins in a tree's wood, a series of events takes place, according to Dr. Alex L. Shigo of the USDA Forest Service. The first is some injury, whether from fire, birds, animals, breaking branches, lightning, or jarring from mechanical equipment. The tree reacts to its injury: chemical changes take place in the wood and the wood discolors, either darkening or bleaching lighter. Next, bacteria and certain non-decay fungi become active; a growth ring forms, the cells of which act as a barrier and help seal off the injury. The wood discolors further; decay fungi infect, and decay begins. The process is irreversible and cannot be short cut. Decay begins only after the other events in the sequence, after the wood has become discolored. Of course, the process may stop at any stage: an injury to a tree does not inevitably mean decay. The tree often heals its wounds, or other microorganisms may come into play that compete with the decay-causing fungi.

In northern hardwood trees, the discoloration and decay take a definite pattern, forming a column in the tree related to the location of the injury. This column spreads up and down inside the tree, but seldom spreads outward. Because the tree will grow healthy new wood around the defect, the column of discoloration and decay is no larger in diameter than the tree was at the time it was injured. If there have been repeated injuries, as is often the case with forest trees, several columns may be present in various stages of development at the same time and place. These multiple columns can sometimes be seen on the ends of logs, where they take on a concentric pattern or a cloudlike pattern.

The defects that form in a tree under cankers produce a somewhat different pattern. A canker (a dead area in the bark) tends to form a localized defect rather than a column of discoloration and decay. When a canker develops about a wound, the defect usually does not spread around the entire stem, but lies immediately beneath the canker.

Of northern hardwoods, red maple and yellow birch are highly susceptible to this decay process, and sugar maple ranks as the most resistant.

Prevention of decay is not entirely possible, since trees are subject to injury from many different sources. All decay is not serious—some wounds that look very bad actually do little damage to the wood.

In estimating the extent of decay, remember that a process is involved; time is important. If the wound was recent, this process will not be far advanced. Many poorly healed branch stubs usually indicate a good-sized central column of moist wood and decay. Multiple wounds on a tree frequently result in severe defect. A dark surface on a wound indicates more defect than a smooth one. Healed wounds and vigorous calluses are good signs that the decay is limited.

Some common diseases of trees follow.

Anthracnose is a fungus disease most evident as spotted, blotched, distorted leaves that often fall prematurely. On twigs and branches, the effect of anthracnose is usually disfigurement. Buds and small twigs may be blighted early in the season, appearing to be frost-injured. Cankers (dead areas in the bark) often form at the juncture of buds and twigs. Anthracnose fungi overwinter in leaves on the ground or are carried over to the next year in infected buds and twigs. The spores develop under cool, moist conditions.

Gather and destroy the diseased leaves when they fall, or compost them under several inches of soil. Prune out infected twigs and branches. When planting new trees or shrubs, consider using anthracnose-resistant species. The London plane is more resistant than the American sycamore, and black oaks are much more resistant than white oaks.

Leaves of ash, beech, dogwood, elm, horsechestnut, linden, maple, and oak are often affected by **leaf scorch,** a noninfectious disease that causes a browning between veins or along margins of the leaves. Scorch usually develops during July or August and is especially severe following periods of drying winds and high temperatures, when the roots are unable to supply enough water to the tree to keep up with the large amount of water lost through the leaves. The condition may also result from, or be made worse by, shallow soils, roots that girdle the crown of the tree, a diseased root system, drought, and other diseases that weaken the tree. Fir, pine and spruce often show leaf scorch as a brown discoloration of the needle tips. The more severe the scorch, the farther down the needle the browning is found. Scorch on needles may result either from hot, dry weather or from high winds during cold weather.

Trees should be fertilized to prevent new growth from becoming easily susceptible. Watering is very helpful, particularly to those trees that have been recently planted. Apply water to the ground around the trees, not to the limbs or foliage.

The group of **leaf spot** diseases is characterized by yellow, brown, or black dead blotches in leaves. Heavily infected leaves may turn yellow or brown and fall prematurely. The leaf spots of deciduous trees and shrubs are caused by fungi that overwinter in dead leaves on the ground. Under the warmer, moist conditions of spring, the spores germinate and the fungus grows into the leaf. Some leaf spot fungi produce summer spores that splash about in rainy weather and intensify the disease. On conifers and broad-leaved evergreens, the fungi pass the year on the host plant. All leaf spot diseases caused by fungi are favored by cool, moist weather, especially early in the growing season as new leaves are developing.

To prevent leaf spot, gather and compost fallen leaves in autumn. If only a few leaves are infected, they may be removed by hand. A strong stream of water often helps remove dead foliage from dense evergreen shrubs such as boxwood or arborvitae. For evergreens, spacing the plants well and keeping down weeds and grass under the lower branches provides better ventilation and reduces the moist conditions that favor infection.

Mistletoe is a parasite of trees found in many areas of the country, particularly the East and West Coasts, and all across the South. The pale, waxy berries are carried by birds and dropped into bark crevices, where they germinate. Their rootlets attach themselves onto the host tree, and the parasite takes its nourishment from the tree's sap veins; it cannot live in soil. Where mistletoe fastens on, grotesque swellings ensue, and the tree may eventually die.

Nectaria canker attacks birch, elm, linden, black walnut, and other hardwoods in the Northeast. Water-soaked areas, darker in color than the adjacent healthy bark, are formed on the trunk and large limbs. The edge of the diseased areas cracks, and callus tissue that forms under the cracked bark becomes infected and dies. The annual repetition of this process forms concentric circles of dead callus tissue. When a canker completely girdles the trunk or branch, the portion above the canker dies.

Where the cankers are not too large, it is important to cut out the diseased areas and treat the wounds with a wound dressing.

Needle rust is a fungus that attacks needles of two- and three-needled pines. Red pine is very susceptible. The disease develops in spring as small cream-colored, baglike pustules on needles. The pustules rupture and orange spores are blown to infect goldenrod and asters. The rust overwinters and can live indefinitely in the crowns of these alternate hosts. During summer and autumn, spores from goldenrod and asters infect needles of the pines. This disease may cause needle drop and stunt young pines, but it seldom causes much damage on older trees.

Control by destroying goldenrod and asters near valuable pine plantings or nurseries.

Fungi of the **powdery mildew** group infect the leaves of various trees, producing powdery patches of white or gray on leaf surfaces. Tiny black fruiting bodies of the powdery mildew fungus are often found on the white patches. Trees commonly affected with powdery mildew in the Northeast are catalpa, dogwood, horsechestnut, linden, magnolia, and sycamore.

In most cases mildew is more unsightly than harmful. Sanitary measures, as described above, are usually sufficient to control the trouble.

Rust fungi found on junipers in the Northeast cause reddish brown round galls up to 1½ inches in diameter on the twigs, or slight swellings on the branches or trunks. During rainy weather in the spring, sticky orange spore masses or horns protrude from the galls or swellings. The spores are carried by wind to leaves or fruits of nearby alternate host plants, such as apple, pear, ornamental crab, hawthorn, shadbush, quince, mountain ash, or chokeberry. These alternate hosts are needed for completion of the life cycle of rust fungi, since spores produced on junipers are unable to reinfect junipers. If the alternate hosts are removed, rust fungi cannot survive. Handpicking galls in spring before spore horns appear will give good control of rust.

Shoestring root rot (also known as mushroom or armillaria root rot) infects many trees, including birch, black locust, chestnut, maple, mountain ash, sycamore, poplar, oak, pine, spruce, larch, and yew. Affected trees show a decline in vigor of all or part of the top of the tree. Foliage becomes scant, withers, turns yellow, and drops prematurely. Fan-shaped white fungus growths are found between bark and wood close to and below the ground line. Rootlike dark brown or black "shoestrings" of the causal fungus grow beneath bark and in soil near affected roots. These strands are rather brittle, and they fuse or grow together where they cross. When one of them is opened, the inside appears to be a mass of white compressed cotton. The strands may cause infection of roots of nearby trees, especially if these trees are in poor vigor. In late fall, clusters of honey-colored mushrooms are often found growing around the base of affected trees. Prevent trouble by avoiding injuries to the roots of healthy trees.

Sooty mold fungi grow as saprophytes on honeydew secretions of such insects as aphids and scales. The heavy sooty growth covers needles of various evergreens and leaves of elm, linden, magnolia, maple, and tulip tree. Although the heavy coating of mold on leaves is unsightly, it does not often interfere seriously with food manufacture in the leaf.

Control the insects responsible for secreting the honeydew on which the mold exists. Aphids are usually at the root of the trouble. Ladybugs can be depended upon to keep their numbers down; you can help by applying a sticky band around the trunk to keep aphid-carrying ants on the ground.

Spanish moss is not a true parasite, but an air plant, as are lichens and orchids. The hanging, grayish strips of this moss are common in the South. Though it does not suck the tree's juices like mistletoe, this plant may smother the tree to death if it runs rampant.

Verticillium wilt is a fungus disease that attacks many trees, causing a wilting and yellowing of foliage that is followed by premature defoliation. One limb or the entire tree may be affected. Some trees wilt and die suddenly, while others gradually fade over a period of years. Yellowish brown streaks are present in the outer rings of the wood of infected branches.

Prune all dead branches and fertilize affected trees to stimulate vigorous growth. Remove badly infected trees, together with as many roots as possible. Do not replant ailanthus or other wilt-susceptible trees in the same location: black locust, catalpa, elm, Kentucky coffee tree, linden, maple, redbud, smoke tree, tulip tree, and yellowwood.

A powdery mildew fungus and gall mites are usually associated with broomlike growths on branches known as **witches' broom.** Several hundred galls may be found on a single tree, causing an unsightly appearance in winter. Affected branches are weakened and break easily during wind storms, and the broken wood is exposed to wood-decaying fungi. Affected buds are larger and more open and hairy than normal. Mites may be found inside the buds along with small black fruiting bodies of the mildew. Threadlike strands of mildew are found on the outside of the bud. Branches that develop from these buds are dwarfed and clustered, giving the witches' broom effect. There is no practical control for this disease. If the brooms are unsightly, prune them off.

Trees: Biological Controls

Insect viruses, bacterial diseases, sex attractants, hormones, predators, parasites, and plant culture techniques are all getting increased attention from scientists today. More than half the insect research budget of the USDA now goes to finding biological and other nonchemical control methods.

While most pathogens are still in the testing stage, you can buy an important biological control for the gypsy moth, tent caterpillar, and the inchworm or cankerworm—*Bacillus thuringiensis* (BT). This is a bacterial disease marketed under the brand names Thuricide, Biotrol, and Dipel. It is harmless to humans, animals, and non-leaf eating insects.

BT is mixed with water as directed on the package or bottle and sprayed on as soon as the caterpillars emerge in spring. Sticking agents are often added to the spraying solution to increase its weathering ability. The tent caterpillar is the first victim to emerge, coming out of the egg stage as soon as the buds break open on apple and wild cherry trees. The inchworm follows shortly thereafter and by the end of May the gypsy moth caterpillars have all emerged. It is extremely important to spray as soon as the insects appear because they are much easier to kill at that time. Early spraying should be followed by other applications because of the new leaf growth that has no insecticide on it. Should a rain follow spraying, it would be advisable to spray again when the leaves dry. See BACILLUS THURINGIENSIS.

A two-year experiment at Daytona Beach Community College in Florida, aimed at minimizing the use of hazardous insecticides, has proved highly successful. When chemical poisons were discontinued, the natural predators of white flies and aphids, such as ladybugs, lacewings, and aphid lions, increased to the point where they virtually annihilated these pests. The few remaining aphids were easily controlled with nicotine sulfate and soap.

The city of Berkeley, with the help of University of California scientists, recently discontinued using poisonous insecticides on its 35,000 street trees of some 123 different species. University entomologists began research to find out which insects caused the most troubles on which trees. Two groups of insects, oakworms and aphids, were found to be the chief pests. Though leafhoppers were present in great numbers, they were not harming trees or the property beneath them, so the spraying program was simply discontinued. To control oakworms, a program of spraying trees with BT was started. Aphids were removed from some trees by washing them with a high-pressure stream of plain water. On other trees, aphid infestations were controlled by the introduction of aphid parasites imported from Europe.

Trees: Woodlot Management

The management of a woodlot is closely related to its purpose. If you are raising a crop of hardwood trees for commercial lumber or a plantation of evergreens for Christmas tree sales, the management, care, and planning will be different than if your woods provides mainly enjoyment, recreation, a haven for birds and wildlife, or an aesthetic backdrop.

It is a good idea to get in touch with your state forester or extension forester, as well as your state's soil conservation service. You will probably want to know the principal species of trees in your plantation, their value, the conditions favorable to their growth and vigor, and what are likely to be their chief enemies in your locale. (See the discussions of the pests and diseases of each major tree species, under separate entries.)

On any woodlands or tree plantation, there is a possibility of fire. Discuss preventative measures with your local fire warden. It may be wise to establish fire lanes along the boundaries of your woods to give a firefighting crew a place to fight a fire. An abundant supply of water in the area will help firefighters, and you should always keep portable fire pumps handy, as well as any other hand tools the fire warden might recommend.

Every plantation is susceptible to insects and diseases. Your state agriculture or forest extension service will have information on the chief pests in your area, and measures to control them. A mixed plantation resists disease and insects better than pure stands. The American Forestry Association warns against trying to reorganize nature too severely. If you have a plantation of needle-leaved trees, for example, and a native broad-leaved species begins to grow in an opening, it should be welcomed. Foresters know now that forest soils in certain areas of Europe deteriorated seriously after many years of raising tree crops of only needle-leaved species. The pulp and lumber industries have developed the technology to get rid of unwanted species in order to produce pure stands of pine. Their methods—clear cutting, so-called "controlled burning," and chemical spraying—are cheap and efficient. But in the long run, soil exhaustion may be the price to pay for the process, and it is a high price. Rotation of crops is a standard practice in agriculture to preserve soil fertility, and a similar method is called for in silviculture.

Your plantation may benefit from thinning to provide adequate growing space for more valuable species. First, you should survey the plantation to determine which trees are the most valuable. If deformed, insect-damaged, or severely diseased trees are competing with the valuable trees for space, sun, and nutrients, they likely should be removed. The purpose of thinning is to concentrate the growth of the stand on fewer, better formed, and more vigorous trees, and to keep the trees in balance with the capacity of the site. Young stands of trees respond very well to a thinning, and may grow as much as 40 to 60 percent larger as a result.

Unwanted trees may be eliminated by girdling or by felling. The latter method is more hazardous, for even careful felling may cause serious damage to crowns of standing trees. But, it is faster. Girdling involves the complete severing of the cambium layer. A girdled tree will die slowly and tends to come down in pieces, thereby doing less damage to the residual stand. Girdling can be accomplished with an ax, a chain saw, a power girdler, or by strip-peeling a band of bark two to four inches wide completely around the trunk. A big disadvantage to girdling is that the slowly dying trees are apt to harbor various insects that may then attack sound trees.

Animals, both domestic and wild, are potential trouble-makers. Livestock can break or trample young trees, shred the bark, or compact the soil. An electric fence will keep them out of your plantation.

Rabbits may bite off tree seedlings; in some areas of the country, deer are so numerous that they are a serious threat to a plantation; porcupines will feed on the needles and gnaw the bark of most northern hardwoods (they seem to be particularly fond of larches). See Chapter 12, "The Good and Bad of Wildlife in the Garden."

Tulip

Insects

Tulips avoid the summer rush of insects, being spring bloomers. This is not to say that tulips are entirely untroubled, however. A number of **aphids,** the grayish tulip bulb and green tulip leaf aphids in particular, impair growth by sucking plant juices. The tulip bulb aphid is found in most northern and western states, and causes damage by robbing the juices from exposed leaves on growing plants to cause severe distortion, stunting, and sometimes death of the plant. They build up dense colonies on stored bulbs, especially those with cracked outer scales, and may also pick on iris bulbs. The tulip leaf aphid is somewhat smaller, and occurs in clusters on leaves and shoots, causing leaves and flowers to fail to open. Again, iris are vulnerable, too. This aphid winters between crops on dormant bulbs. For controls, see APHID.

Aphid

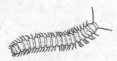

Millipede

Millipedes frequently attack bulbs in tulip beds, especially in old beds in which the bulbs are not reset each year. The holes they eat into the bulbs are often followed by decay, and good numbers of bulbs may be destroyed. When abundant, these pests also injure bulbs and roots of other plants, strawberries in particular. If you have run into millipede trouble, dig up tulip bulbs after they have flowered, and keep them cool and dry until fall planting. See MILLIPEDES.

Other tulip pests include SPIDER MITES and WIRE-WORMS.

Diseases

Breaking is a viral disease that causes variegated flowers with stripes or streaks of color. Leaves are distinctly mottled, and the size and production of bulbils (aerial bulbs) are reduced. In normal flowers the color is uniform, except at the base of the flower.

Aphids can transmit this disease, and some gardeners will want to separate parrot and bicolored tulips from solid-color plants; white flowers usually aren't changed. Other growers actually enjoy the exotic color variations wrought by this virus. At any rate, foliage and plant health is not frequently damaged.

Tulip Fire

Tulip fire (botrytis blight [color]), is a common disease that is especially damaging in springs that pour forth more than their share of rain. Spotting and collapse of stems, leaves, and flowers are usually accompanied by the brownish gray mold of the fruiting stage. Tiny black sclerotia carry the fungus to the soil to infest plants the following spring. The disease may be spread by windblown spores from infected plants.

Once plants are infected, they should be pulled and burned. The disease is most serious when tulips are grown in the same area year after year. Tulip fire will have a hard time catching up with the flowers if the tulip bed is moved each year. Stems should be removed from bulbs right after they are dug up, and any diseased bulbs must be stored during the summer in a cool, dry place if they are to be of any value. Remove husks from bulbs just before they are planted, and any bulbs that look sick at this time should be discarded.

Once plants are up, remove and destroy infected leaves, buds, and blossoms, and burn plant refuse at the season's end.

Wildlife

The nibbling of mice, squirrels, chipmunks, rabbits, and moles may cause more trouble than insects and diseases combined.

Many gardeners therefore grow their tulips inside protective wire baskets.

Tulip Tree, See Poplar

Turnip

Turnips have no pests that are unique to them, but share many with cole crops such as broccoli, cabbage, horseradish, and kale. Insects you're likely to run into on turnip include aphids, cabbage maggots (tunnel into the underground stems and roots of early plants to cause wilt and stunting), harlequin bug, cabbage looper, yellow woolybear caterpillar, cabbage curculio, and serpentine leaf miner; see CABBAGE. Diseases, too, are very similar to those affecting CABBAGE. Also see RESISTANT VARIETIES.

Verbena

Insects

The **verbena budworm** bores within the new shoots of verbena, causing them to wilt. This pest is a greenish yellow worm with a black head, growing to a little less than ½ inch when mature. The adult is a purplish brown moth with a wingspread of ½ inch. Ordinary infestations can be controlled by handpicking or clipping and then burning the infested tips. Growers outside the eastern states should have little trouble.

The small, **yellow verbena leaf miner** feeds between leaf surfaces, making mines that appear as blisters or blotches. This pest is found throughout the United States, wherever verbena is grown. Handpick infested leaves.

The **yellow woolybear caterpillar** is indeed wooly and yellow. Verbena is one of many plants that feed this common garden pest. Because of its sloth and size—it grows to a length of two inches— handpicking is the recommended control.

Diseases

Powdery mildew is apt to seriously injure greenhouse verbena. It appears as white moldy patches on leaves and young shoots late in the season. See ZINNIA.

Viburnum

The snowball **aphid** causes young leaves to become severely curled, deformed, and discolored with a sooty mold that develops on aphid honeydew. The aphid varies in color from gray to dark green. It attacks new growth early in the season, and in June moves on to other plants. For control, see APHID.

Violet

Insects

Deep red **aphids** occasionally infest violet leaves. See APHID.

The **violet gall midge** is a small two-winged fly that lays its white eggs in the curled margins of unfolded new leaves. The larvae that hatch remain in the curled margins, causing further curling, distortion, and twisting of leaves. There are likely several generations in greenhouses each year. Clean up leaves as they drop.

If leaves are skeletonized or eaten through overnight, suspect the larvae of the **violet sawfly.** These half-inch-long worms are either colored olive-green or blue black, and are marked with whitish tubercules. They hide under the lower leaves or in the soil during the day. The adult is a black, four-winged fly that measures ⅝ inch in length. It lays its eggs in blisterlike incisions in leaves. There is only one brood in the North, and overlapping generations in the South.

Nocturnal handpicking raids may do for the energetic, but other gardeners will have to rely on daily inspections of lower leaves and botanical sprays on foliage.

Keep an eye out for the cyclamen mite (see AZALEA, DELPHINIUM), flea beetles (POTATO), celery leaf tier (CELERY), MEALYBUGS, red-banded leaf roller (ROSE), SLUGS AND SNAILS, SPIDER MITES, and yellow woolybear caterpillar (see controls for imported cabbageworm under CABBAGE).

Diseases

For diseases of violet, see PANSY.

Walnut

Insects

The worst insect pest of black walnuts is the **walnut caterpillar.** If you see a black walnut tree partially stripped of leaves during midsummer, it likely is the work of this worm. There is one generation in the North, and two in the South. Like many insects, their population goes in cycles; they may be bad for a year or two and nearly disappear for several seasons. Their habit of congregating at the base of branches each night makes them easy to eradicate on small trees. Just rub them out during late evening with a rolled-up burlap bag. If you don't mind climbing a ladder, you can get to pests on larger trees.

The **walnut husk fly** can be a serious pest of walnut trees. It overwinters in the soil under the trees in small hard, brown cases. Adults emerge in late summer, usually August, and spend two or three weeks on the foliage before they mate and begin to lay eggs. Adult flies are about the size of a housefly and are colored brown with a yellow semicircle on the back. The female penetrates the husk of the nut to lay her eggs. The hatching larvae feed on the husk and then tunnel to the outside of the nut and drop to the ground.

The chief injury to the walnut is caused by the feeding larvae, which release a dark liquid stain over the shells and sometimes the kernels. Otherwise, the nut is not harmed. Worms may be destroyed by dropping the infested nuts into a pail of water; after being drowned, the maggots can easily be removed along with the husk.

Diseases

For **anthracnose,** see TREES: DISEASES.

Blackline of walnuts is a disorder of grafted walnut trees. According to the Cooperative Extension Service of Oregon State University, it rarely develops in trees less than ten years of age and is most common in 15 to 25 year old trees. The first symptoms are weak growth, sparse foliage, and yellowing and premature dropping of leaves from certain branches. The death of the affected branches follows. Finally the entire tree top dies. This disease is caused by the failure of the newly formed wood (xylem) of the walnut top to unite with the wood of the black walnut rootstock at the graft union. A dark brown or black layer of corklike tissue forms between the xylem of the rootstock and the scion. At first this layer is very narrow, but later it may become as wide as $\frac{1}{4}$ inch.

After blackline becomes well established, decay of the bark frequently occurs beneath the graft union. Affected trees usually die within four to six years after symptoms are first noted, although some trees live longer. The exact cause of blackline is not known, but trees lacking in vigor appear to be especially susceptible to the disease.

Once infected, a tree cannot be cured. The only known preventive measure is to plant Persian walnut varieties that have been grafted on Persian walnut rootstocks. The more vigorous types of Persian seedlings, such as Manregian, should be used for the rootstocks.

Watermelon

Insects

Melon Aphid

The melon **aphid** generally makes its appearance in the field late in summer and soon becomes abundant on the underside of the leaves. Leaves curl, the vine becomes too stunted to produce a crop, and plants may wilt and die. The small, dark green insect may attract other insects such as wasps or flies to the melons with the honeydew it produces. Eliminate as many weeds as possible from the growing area, especially live-forever in northern states, to deprive these pests of overwintering sites. Plants grown in rich soil fare better against aphids. Ladybugs consume great numbers of aphids and can be purchased if the naturally occurring population is low.

Cucumber beetles attack vines, especially those of young plants. As with cantaloupes, much of the damage can be prevented by covering the vines with plastic hotcaps or netting until they have developed half-a-dozen leaves.

Lester L. Detweiler of Wattsville, Virginia, suggests that if watermelons, cantaloupes, or cucumbers are bothered by the spotted or striped cucumber beetle, you might try dropping a few radish seeds in each hill. The radishes will repel the beetles and offer fine eating in their own right. See CUCUMBER for more information on cucumber beetles.

The **melon fly** female lays eggs in the stems of the vines and in young fruit. After the eggs hatch, the developing larvae feed on the surrounding plant tissue and usually kill the vine or spoil the fruit. The melon fly rests on castor bean, cocklebur, and Jimson weed in preference to crop plants. Under dry conditions or in areas where weeds have dried, and in areas where there are no broad-leaved weeds, a corn border will help attract flies away from the melons. Infested fruit should be removed and destroyed, and nearby tomato and cucurbit crops should be plowed under as soon as harvesting is completed. If you haven't too many plants, you can protect fruit by stapling paper bags around them. These bags may be left on until the fruit is ready for harvest.

Diseases

Anthracnose [color] is a common disease of cucumbers, muskmelons, and watermelons. Leaves, fruits, and stems of infected plants show water-soaked areas, followed by the death of the plant. Crop rotation helps somewhat. Resistant varieties, such as Charleston Gray, Crimson Sweet, Sweet Princess, Improved Kleckly Sweet, and Klondike, will get you by this disease. For other prevention methods, see CUCUMBER.

Watermelon/ Anthracnose

Fusarium wilt [color] is probably the most serious disease of watermelon. It is caused by a fungus that lives in the soil and penetrates the roots. Symptoms are a brown discoloration of the stems, followed by a wilting of the branches and death of the plant. Planting wilt-resistant seed and long rotations with other vegetables are the best methods of controlling this disease. Resistant varieties include Charleston Gray, Congo, Fairfax, Black Kleckly, Crimson Sweet, Sweet Princess, and two seedless varieties, Tri-X313 and Triple Sweet.

Mosaic is a virus disease transmitted by aphids that causes mottling of the leaves, stunting of the plants, and misshapen fruits. Good control of aphids and eradication of other cucurbit plants from the vicinity may help to check the spread of this disease. See also APHID and CUCUMBER.

For other diseases of watermelons, see CUCUMBER and CANTALOUPE.

White Fly

The various species of white fly [color] are among the most universal pests of both greenhouse and garden. The adults are about $\frac{1}{16}$ inch long and fly on white powdery wings. They feed and lay their eggs on the underside of young leaves. Eggs are pale yellow at first, turn gray in five days to a week, and then hatch into tiny white "crawlers," or nymphs, that move around on the leaves for a few days before settling down in one place to feed. The nymphs develop fully in two weeks at normal greenhouse temperatures. The pupae are slightly larger and thicker than the nymphs. Adults appear in about ten days, and the entire life cycle takes about a month.

In cold regions (like Canada) the insects can survive the

Whitefly Nymph

winter only indoors or in greenhouses. In spring, the adults leave through doors and ventilators or on vegetable transplants, and are soon established on garden or field crops and weeds. R. J. McClanahan of the Research Station in Harrow, Ontario, writes in a bulletin that "the critical time in the annual cycle is in fall, when white flies enter the greenhouse. They may fly in, or be taken inside on ornamental plants such as geraniums or chrysanthemums. A few weeds left in a supposedly empty greenhouse may support the white flies through the winter." McClanahan also states that adults cannot survive for more than a week without food plants.

• Biological control.

There is an effective biological control for the pesty fly in homes, gardens and greenhouses. It's a small parasite known as *Encarsia formosa,* which is sure death to white flies. The parasite occurs naturally in Canada, United States, and England. Mass rearing of this helpful insect started in England way back in 1926, and in Canada in 1928. Thousands of the tiny wasps were released to greenhouse operators, but were not widely used from 1945 to 1969 because they cannot survive where growers spray with DDT or use a fumigant.

Whitefly Parasite (Encarsia)

Don Moore, Manager of the Ontario (Canada) Greenhouse Vegetable Producers Marketing Board, says, "Our Association has contracted one of our growers to raise the parasites and they are made available free to any grower of greenhouse vegetables in Ontario." For orders outside of Ontario, there is a charge.

The adult parasite is about $\frac{1}{40}$ inch long, and all (except one or two in 1,000) are females who produce without mating. The female searches for white fly nymphs and pupae on the leaves, and lays an egg in each white fly nymph. The egg hatches into a larva inside the white fly, causing the pest to turn black and appear like specks of black pepper on the leaf undersurface. Inside each black speck is a parasite adult which emerges by cutting a round hole in the top of the white fly. Inside the home or greenhouse, it takes about 20 days for the parasite to complete its life cycle.

It's rare to get 100 percent control—usually about 80 to 90 percent is more like it—but the surviving white flies are not numerous enough to harm your plants. Actually, you need some white flies to keep the parasites alive, since they eat nothing else. They are absolutely harmless to plants, and do not bite, sting, or otherwise bother people. In fact, you have to look closely even to see them. Many commercial greenhouse operators have their own parasite production center, so perhaps your florist has the white fly parasite. If he sprays or fumigates, though, it will kill the parasite, and you won't get the extra bonus when you buy a plant from him. For information on ordering the parasites, write to Greenhouse Bio-Controls, 61 Horwath St., Kingsville, Ontario, Canada. Residents of the United States must first obtain an "Importation Authorized" label for shipment of *"Trialeurodes vaporariorum* parasitized with *Encarsia formosa";* write: Mr. J. E. Lipes, Technical Service Staff, PP&Q APHIS USDA, Federal Center Building, Hyattsville, MD 20782. The label must be sent with your order for white flies.

Another species of the pest, the citrus white fly, is vulnerable to fungus diseases. Growers can take advantage of one of the naturally occurring diseases, known as red aschersonia, by making an inoculative spray. The first step is to find infected white flies. They become swollen and secrete more than the normal amount of honeydew, according to Lester A. Swann in *Beneficial Insects*. After the pest dies, fungal strands extend through the body to make a fringe and red spore-bearing pustules develop. To cultivate the disease, sterilized slices of sweet potato are inoculated with the fungus and placed in pint jars for 30 to 40 days. Water is added to the jar, the jar is shaken, and the contents are filtered and sprayed. In moist periods of June and July, just one pint of the preparation proved sufficient for controlling citrus white flies in an acre of orchard. A second fungus, known as yellow aschersonia, causes similar effects as the red variety, except for the color of the pustules. A spray can be prepared by the same method.

White flies are prey for lacewings and ladybugs. Populations of these beneficials can be supplemented by commercially available reinforcements.

• **Conventional controls.**   White flies are put off by anything with nicotine in it, and tobacco dust and tobacco tea have long been used to keep them from plants. The tea can be thickened with a bit of soap or white flour to make it stick better to the underside of leaves. Sprays made from ryania should also do the trick. Oil sprays suffocate adults, nymphs, and eggs. Beatrice Trum Hunter suggests in *Gardening Without Poisons* that tomatoes won't be bothered by white flies unless they suffer from deficiencies of magnesium and phosphorus.

Willow

Insects

The **leopard moth** lays its eggs in bark openings, and the larvae bore into the twigs and limbs of the tree, causing them to wilt. The borers are yellow or pinkish with brown or black hairs. When infestation is heavy, many of the limbs wilt, hang down, and even die. Sawdust may protrude from the holes in the bark.

Control procedures involve cutting and pruning all infested branches. If this is done at the first sign of trouble, the larvae may be caught inside the pruned branches. On lightly infested or large branches, probe into the holes with a wire to kill any borers that may be present. Heavily infested trees may have to be destroyed. Keep trees in such a vigorous state that the borers will have to go elsewhere.

The **willowshoot sawfly** is a ½-inch-long, wasplike insect that appears in early spring to lay eggs in the new shoots of willow, girdling the stem below the eggs in the process. The larvae bore in the shoots, sometimes tunneling them for two feet. They reach maturity in November. Cut and burn the wilted shoots.

Many of the pests of poplar also trouble willows; see POPLAR. Other pests include APHIDS, gypsy moth (see TREES: INSECTS), and oystershell scale (LILAC).

Diseases

Two types of fungus cause a **blight** that blackens and shrivels willow leaves and produces black lesions on branches. Repeated infections will cause the tree to die. Control the disease by pruning and burning infected wood in early spring.

The small black sunken **cankers** that appear on twigs, branches, and trunk may kill the tree within a few years. No control is known, but vigorous trees apparently resist this infection better than those weakened by blight (see above) or winter injury (below).

Crown gall is caused by a bacterium that invades roots, trunk, or branches of the willow, stimulating cell growth to cause tumor-like swellings that grow to the size of a pea or larger. Galls on the trunk sometimes grow to one or two feet in diameter. Growth of the tree is sometimes retarded. Leaves turn yellow and branches or roots may die.

Infected young trees and nursery stock should be removed and burned. Do not replant the area with willow, poplar, chestnut, sycamore, maple, walnut, or fruit trees. Older trees may survive an attack of this disease without being greatly injured. Make every effort to avoid wounding the stems and roots of healthy trees, since infection occurs through such openings in the bark.

Various stages of **rust** appear as orange and red blisters on the underside of leaves. The alternate hosts of these different rusts are balsam fir, larch, currants, and gooseberries. Control is usually unnecessary, but in nurseries the rust-infected parts of the trees should be promptly pruned and destroyed.

Tar spot is a fungus infection that causes thick black raised spots to appear on leaves. Raking and burning fallen leaves gives sufficient control, as the fungus overwinters on them.

Winter injury describes the effects of alternate freezing and thawing of the bark on the south or southwest side of the tree during late winter. Symptoms include long vertical cracks, which may later be invaded by disease organisms.

Leaning a wide board against the tree on the exposed side will prevent the sun's rays from warming the bark; heat on the bark is a danger when contrasted with freezing temperatures at night. Painting the trunk white will accomplish the same result.

Wireworms

Wireworms [color] are the larvae of a family of beetles commonly called click beetles or skipjacks. The larvae are slender, jointed, unusually hard-shelled worms. They range in color from light to dark brown, and grow up to a length of 1½ inches. These chewing insects feed entirely underground, attacking germinating seeds and the roots, underground stems, and tubers of growing plants. Potatoes, beets, beans, cabbage, carrots, corn, lettuce, onions, and turnips are among the crops subject to injury. Damage is most likely to occur on poorly drained soil and on land that has recently been grass sod. Because they operate out of sight, wireworms are not suspected of much of the trouble they cause.

Wireworm

Millipedes are often confused with this pest, but the former have many pairs of slender legs located on the segments from front to back, while wireworms have but three pairs of legs positioned well forward. Millipedes, or thousand leggers as they are often called, characteristically curl up into a loose spiral position when disturbed; wireworms do not.

The wheat wireworm is somewhat typical of the several important species. It takes usually three years to complete the cycle from egg to adult. Eggs are laid in June or July and hatch into tiny worms that eat their way through two growing seasons. In August of the third summer, they enter their pupal cells and transform into beetles, which emerge from the soil the following year. Click beetles flip up into the air with a clicking sound when placed on their backs. They vary in color from light tan to dark brown, and are incapable of sustained flight.

• **Control.**   If sod land must be used for the garden, thoroughly plow or stir it once a week for four to six weeks in the preceding fall. This aerates the soil, exposes the insects to weather and natural enemies, and crushes many others. Hardpan can be broken up by trenching—that is, digging a deep trench and throwing the soil over the surface. The trench is then filled by digging a second, parallel trench.

On a large scale, it is best to select crops known not to be favored by wireworms. A Maine Agricultural Experiment Station Bulletin says that this is especially important when the crops chosen are cultivated annuals, because cultivation of the soil at regular intervals makes conditions unfavorable to the egg-laying adults. Just as in the garden, cultivation exposes all stages of the pest to weather and enemies. Tests in Maine have shown that thorough cultivation is effective in controlling most species of wireworm, although fields hosting witchgrass are likely to continue to support wireworm infestations. The Maine Experiment Station notes it is best to cultivate when temperatures are sufficiently low to slow up the exposed wireworms, as they are then easy prey to natural enemies.

You can keep wireworms to a minimum by growing annual green manure crops. Clover is a good choice, but hay mixtures including timothy or red top will support a pest population. Oats, wheat, barley, and rye are seldom seriously injured by wireworms. In the Northwest, farmers may avoid damage by growing alfalfa for at least three years, then one year of potatoes, and finally one or two years of a suitable vegetable crop such as corn, beans, peas, or sugar beets.

Potatoes are attractive to wireworms and can be used as a simple trap. Cut a potato in half, cut out the eyes to prevent it from growing, and run a stick through the middle. Bury the spud about one inch under so that the stick stands vertically as a handle, and pull the traps out after a day or two. Some potatoes have yielded as many as 15 to 20 pests.

Yellow Poplar, see Poplar

Yew

Insects

The **black vine weevil** (or taxus weevil) feeds on a variety of plants, but does the most damage to yew. The adult weevils feed on the foliage and buds of the plant during the night, hiding by day either in dense foliage or in debris on the ground beneath. Injury by the adult is negligible; the larvae cause the chief damage by feeding on the roots. Leaves of root-damaged plants turn yellow and eventually wither. Severely injured plants become stunted or die.

The adult is an oblong brownish black insect measuring ⅓ inch long. It does not fly, but walks from place to place. The weevil deposits its tiny white eggs in the soil during summer months. The larva is white with a yellowish head, and is approximately ½ inch long when fully developed. It overwinters in the soil, pupates the following spring, after a short period of feeding.

The adults emerge from the pupae in June, and it is best to anticipate them by placing bands of something sticky, such as the commercially available Tanglefoot or Stikem, around the trunks. The weevils will be trapped as they try to walk to the foliage above.

Several sucking insects, namely **mealybugs** and **scales,** occasionally attack the yew. See MEALYBUG. Scale insects are brown and inconspicuous; they attach themselves to the foliage and remain there the rest of their lives. Control them with a dormant-oil spray in late winter or early spring.

Mealybug

Diseases

Most diseases of yew trees stem from unfavorable environmental factors, according to the Cooperative Extension Service of Rutgers University.

Scale

Too much water around yew roots may cause **wet feet.** Affected plants grow poorly or even die. Such yews are most often found in poorly drained soils, at corners of buildings near rainspouts, or in areas that have been overwatered. When these conditions are corrected, the plant will regain its healthy condition.

A general **yellowing** of the plant may be the result of placing yews with acid-loving plants such as laurel, rhododendron, or azalea. Yews thrive in a sweet or neutral soil with a pH of 6.0 to 6.5, whereas heath-type plants grow better in an acid soil (pH of 4.5 to 5.5), and it is best to keep these two types of plants separate. If this is impossible, ground limestone may be added around the base of yews; apply three pounds of limestone per 100 square feet of soil area around the yews, and repeat every third year.

Zinnia

Insects

If zinnias wilt without an apparent cause, look to the **stalk borer.** The young borer is creamy white with a dark purple band around its body and several brown or purple stripes running the length of its body. The full-grown larva is creamy white to light purple, and has no stripes. When young borers hatch in the spring from eggs on grass and weeds, they first feed on the leaves of the nearest plants and then gradually work their way to larger, stemmed plants.

Remove and destroy nearby weeds, leaving a clean area around the zinnia bed. Infested plants can sometimes be saved by slitting stems, destroying the borer within, then binding the stems and keeping plants watered. If it is necessary to pull a badly damaged plant, pinch the stem to kill the offending borer. If affected stems are cut off below the boring, the plant may develop side shoots that will later flower.

Other bugs to look out for are APHIDS, blister beetles (see ASTER), cyclamen mite (AZALEA, DELPHINIUM), European corn borer (CORN), flea beetles (POTATO), flower thrips (PEONY, ROSE), four-lined plant bug (CHRYSANTHEMUM), JAPANESE BEETLE, MEALYBUGS, red-banded leaf roller (ROSE), SPIDER MITES, spotted cucumber beetle (CUCUMBER), and WHITE FLIES.

Diseases

Leaf spot is a fungus disease characterized by irregular black spots on the foliage. It seldom causes much damage, but is sometimes a problem following rainy periods. Zinnias grown in confined areas such as cold frames, greenhouses, and cloth enclosures are more commonly affected than those grown in open fields or gardens. If you have had trouble with leaf spot, do not grow zinnias in the same soil year after year. Remove any infected flowerheads promptly.

Mildew is generally the most serious obstacle to zinnia growers. The first noticeable symptom is a powdery white growth on leaves. Under favorable weather conditions, the mildew grows rapidly and may soon cover all leaves, stems and buds. The plants often live until frost, producing dwarfed, distorted leaves and flowers. The disease is most severe in late summer during cool, damp, cloudy weather, and plants grown in shady and confined areas are most susceptible.

It is best to water on cloudy days or in late evenings, since this produces the best growth; frequent, light watering causes shallow root formation. The water should be applied directly to the soil to keep the foliage dry, as wet foliage is a prime cause of mildew. Plan your garden so that zinnias are not in the shade or sheltered, but out in the open so that they may benefit from sun and good air circulation.

Zucchini, see Squash

Appendix 1
Where To Find Commercial
Products

As more and more gardeners and orchardists abandon chemical pesticides, an increasing number of plant protection products have hit the market—botanical powders and spray bases, insect predators and parasites, insect diseases, nets, exploding scares, and so on. Your local garden supply center may stock some, and many of those products you can't find are available through the mails. A handy list of manufacturers and suppliers has been compiled by *Organic Gardening and Farming* Reader Service personnel. You can get a copy by writing OGF Reader Service at 33 East Minor Street, Emmaus, Pennsylvania 18049.

Appendix 2
Insecticidal Plants For
Home Experimenting

Insecticides from Plants, a review of the literature from 1941 through 1953, lists a number of plants that have been found to have insecticidal powers. The information was compiled by Martin Jacobson of the Entomology Research Division, Agricultural Research Service, and the book is published by the USDA. To encourage experimentation on your part, we are listing here some domestic plants and their applications. The studies reported were concerned only with a limited number of insects, and therefore it is likely that pests other than those named will be affected by these botanical preparations.

American plum (*Prunus americana*)
Leaves and flowers toxic to insects.

American wisteria (*Wisteria frutescens*)
Acetone extract of seeds somewhat toxic to codling moth larvae.

Balsamroot (*Balsomorhiza sagittata*)
Powder of stems and leaves somewhat toxic to pea aphids. Seeds are edible for humans, and can be roasted, ground, and mixed with flour to make a flavorful bread, says Nelson Coon.

Bear hops (*Humulus lupulus*)
Powdered leaves toxic to southern armyworms and melonworms.

Black Indian hemp (*Apocynum cannabinum*)
Extract of twigs and stems controls codling moth larvae.

Black walnut (*Juglans nigra*)
Odor of leaves repellent to insects.

Buffalo gourd (*Cucurbita foetidissima*)
Powdered root somewhat toxic to cucumber beetles; mix a little water with powder for hand soap.

California buckeye (*Aesculus californica*)
Flours made with meat hulls of nuts toxic to larvae and adults of Mexican bean beetle; parts of plant toxic to humans.

Canadian fleabane (*Erigeron canadensis*)
Can be ground up to make melonworm repellent.

Chinaberry (*Melia azedarach*)
Shade tree, repellent to grasshoppers and locusts. A repellent tea can be made with live or dried leaves. Powdered fruit slightly toxic to European corn borer larvae.

Chinese wingnut (*Pterocarya stenoptera*)	Powdered leaves fairly toxic to Mexican bean beetle larvae. An ornamental tree.
Chinese wisteria (*Wisteria sinensis*)	Acetone extract of seeds somewhat toxic to codling moth larvae.
Common oleander (*Nerium oleander*)	Effective against codling moth.
Cucumber, cantaloupe, and pumpkin	Acetone extract of seeds (and aqueous extract of pumpkin seeds) toxic to mosquito larvae and might be lethal to other pests.
Dwarf or red buckeye (*Aesculus pavia*)	Flowers attract and kill Japanese beetles.
False indigo (*Amorpha fruticosa*)	Acetone extract of flowers repellent to chinch bugs and striped cucumber beetles. Powdered mature pods with seeds moderately toxic to Mexican bean beetle larvae. A sugar derivative, amorpha, effective as dust against chinch bugs, cotton aphids, squash bugs, tarnished plant bugs, potato leafhoppers, blister beetles, and spotted cucumber beetles. The fruit is more insecticidal than roots.
Japaca, yellow oleander (*Thevetia peruviana*)	All parts, except leaves and fruit pulp, used to make cold water extraction effective against a number of pests, especially aphids.
Larkspur (*Delphinium* sp.)	Powdered roots toxic to bean leaf rollers, cross-striped cabbageworms, cabbage loopers and melonworms.
Manroot, wild cucumber (*Echinocystis fabacea*)	Powdered root toxic to European corn borer larvae.
Mescal or coral bean (*Sophora secundiflora*)	Powdered seeds of this flowering shrub toxic to armyworms.
Nutmeg (*Myristica fragrans*)	Oil has toxic properties.
Osage orange (*Maclura pomifera*)	Roots, wood, and bark repel insects.
Pawpaw (*Asimina triloba*)	Powdered aerial portion has some effect on mealyworms.

Peach (*Prunus persica*)   Leaves and flowers toxic to insects.

Pine (various species)   Pine tar oil improved performance of standard codling moth baits.

Prairie zinnia (*Zinnia grandiflora*)   Slightly toxic to celery leaf tiers.

Rayless chamomile (*M. matricarioides*)   Powdered heads fairly toxic to diamondback moths.

Scentless false chamomile, mayweed (*Matricaria indora* or *M. chamimile*)   Flower heads as effective as commercial pyrethrum in controlling face flies; may well have applications in the garden.

Sesame (*Sesamum indicum*)   An effective synergist for pyrethrins.

Soap plant, soap root (*Chlorogalum pomeridianum*)   Grows from California north to Oregon. Powdered bulbs toxic to armyworms and melonworms.

Sour sop (*Annona muricata*)   Powdered seeds toxic to armyworms and pea aphids.

Spanish dagger (*Yucca shidigera*)   Powdered leaves toxic to melonworms, bean leaf rollers, and celery leaf tiers.

Spindle tree (*Euonymus europaeus*)   Fruit has paralyzing action on aphids.

Sugar apple   Seeds and roots extracted with ether, converted to resinous substance to make contact poison for aphids. Toxic and repellent to diamondback moth larvae. Hot-pressed and heat-extracted oils of seeds highly toxic contact poisonous to several pests.

Sweet flag, calamus (*Acorus calamus*)   Alkaloid root works as contact poison to insects, even though it is edible to humans. Grows commonly in swamps and along brooks.

Tung-oil tree (*Aleurites fordii*)   Tung-oil soap somewhat toxic to sugarcane wooly aphids.

Turkey mullein (*Eremocarpus setigerus*)   Used by American Indians as fish poison; toxic to cross-striped cabbageworms.

Wood fern, shield fern (*Dryopteris felix-mas*)

Powdered rhizome toxic to army-worms.

Wormseed, Jerusalem tea (*Chenopodium ambrosioides*)

Some parts toxic as extracts or dusts on several species of leaf-eating larvae.

Yellow azalea (*Rhododendron molle*)

Dried and pulverized flowers work as contact and stomach poison. Powdered flowers can be sprayed to control certain species of lepidopterous larvae. Roots and leaves not insecticidal.

Bibliography

Burges, H. D., and N. W. Hussey, eds. **Microbial Control of Insects and Mites** (New York: Academic Press, 1971). Although this is a technical record of research, several chapters detail the workings of two insect pathogens you can buy, *Bacillus thuringiensis* and milky spore disease.

Carson, Rachel. **Silent Spring** (Boston: Houghton-Mifflin Co., 1962). An emotional call to action, still very worth reading.

Casida, John E., ed. **Pyrethrum** (New York: Academic Press, 1973). A comprehensive book, covering the history, chemistry, and applications of this botanical insecticide.

DeBach, Paul. **Biological Control of Natural Enemies** (New York: Cambridge University Press, 1974). A good review of biological control: what has been accomplished, research going on today, and methods you can put to use.

Disease and Insect Problems in The Commercial Orchard. Pennsylvania State University. A correspondence course book for course 173, describing disease cycles and suggesting both chemical and cultural controls, including resistant varieties. Comprehensive and illustrated. Available from Penn State University, University Park, PA 16802.

Handbook on Biological Control of Plant Pests (Brooklyn, NY: Brooklyn Botanic Garden, 1960). This booklet is most valuable for its illustrations and descriptions of many beneficial insects. It is available from the Brooklyn Botanic Garden at 1000 Washington Avenue, Brooklyn, NY 11225.

Hunter, Beatrice Trum. **Gardening Without Poisons.** 2nd ed. (Boston: Houghton-Mifflin, 1971). Although the second edition has added little, the original stands up well, more than a decade after it was printed. This was the first valuable book on non-toxic controls for the garden. It is very well researched, and worth reading for both specific controls and background information.

Knorr, L. C. **Citrus Diseases and Disorders** (Gainesville: University Presses of Florida, 1973). Offers cultural and chemical controls, and illustrated with many halftones.

Olkowski, Hellga. **Common Sense Pest Control** (1971). A cursory discussion of pests, indoors and out, and how to live with or control them. This pamphlet champions the notion that "the best thing to do may be nothing." Available from Consumers Cooperative of Berkeley, Inc., 4805 Central Avenue, Richmond, CA 94804.

Painter, Reginald H. **Insect Resistance in Crop Plants** (Lawrence: University Press of Kansas, 1951). Not of general interest to the gardener, as it is heavy reading and is concerned with crop plants, not garden vegetables. Painter does a good job of explaining the mechanisms of plant resistance.

Philbrick, Helen and John. **The Bug Book** (Charlotte, VT: Garden Way Publishing, 1974). The Philbricks, followers of the Bio-Dynamic method, give chatty instructions for controlling the more common pests of the garden and orchard.

Philbrick, Helen and Richard B. Gregg. **Companion Plants and How To Use Them** (New York: Devin-Adair, 1966). Details, without explaining, the mysteries of companion planting, with many applications to plant protection.

Rudd, Robert L. **Pesticides and the Living Landscape** (Madison: University of Wisconsin Press, 1966). An interesting account of how pesticides affect the environment. As *Audubon Magazine* describes it, Rudd's book is ". . . a worthy sequel to *Silent Spring*."

Swann, Lester A. **Beneficial Insects** (New York: Harper & Row, 1964). Covering microbial control as well as insect predators and parasites, this is a comprehensive text on biological control. The book should be very interesting to the concerned lay reader, even though it is a bit dated.

van den Bosch, Robert and P. S. Messenger. **Biological Control** (New York: Intext Educational Publishers, 1973). A brief survey of biological control research.

Weeds of the North Central States (Urbana: University of Illinois Agricultural Experiment Station, 1960). An excellent and inexpensive field guide. Control methods are not given, and the reader is referred to agricultural experiment stations and county agents.

Westcott, Cynthia. **The Gardener's Bug Book.** 4th ed. (New York: Doubleday, 1973). Although she mentions just about every bug you'll ever run into, Ms. Westcott favors chemicals to biological, cultural, and other non-toxic ways of plant protection. Still, the book can serve as a comprehensive field guide, and the color plates by Eva Melady are helpful.

————. **Plant Disease Handbook.** 3rd ed. (New York: Van Nostrand Reinhold, 1971). An exhaustive catalog of diseases, some discussed and some not. Both cultural and chemical controls are given.

INDEX

The word *color* in brackets [ ] following an entry indicates that the item is illustrated in the color plate section of the book. Bold-faced page numbers indicate the main pages where the insect or disease is discussed.

I

ichneumonid wasps, description of, 82
imported cabbageworm, [*color*], 250-253
  varieties resistant to, 531
imported currant worm, 329, 330
inchworms, trees, 621
injury, winter. See *winter injury.*
insect barriers, 105, 106
insect predators, function of, 68, 69
insect repellents, 111-132
insect traps. See *traps.*
insecticides, 111-132. See also name or
  type of insecticide.
  use of, reasons for, 4, 5
insects. See also *bugs* and name of insect.
  attractants for, pheromones as,
    106-110
  barriers against, 105, 106
  beneficial, help for, 72, 73
    monocultures discourage, 70, 71
  borders against, 104, 105
  BT against, 213, 214
  clean cultivation against, 71, 72
  definition of, 10, 11
  developmental stages of, 11, 12
  diseased plants vulnerable to, 25
  harvesting to discourage, 72
  lures for, 100
  nerve-winged, description of, 78-80
  organic soil repellent to, 24-27
  parts of, 12, 13
  pathogens, 83-91. See also type of
    pathogen; e.g., *bacteria, fungi,* etc.
  plants resistant to, 52-58
  repellent plants for, 42-50
  scale, citrus fruits, 300-303. See also
    type of scale.
  soil moisture's effect on, 38
  trees, 620-624
  varieties resistant to, 530-539. See also
    name of insect or plant.
instinct, insects, 13
integrated control, 91-98
interplanting, nematode control by, 448
iris, **390-392**
  leaf spot, [*color*]
  resistant varieties of, 542
iris borer, 390
iris thrips, 390
iris weevils, 390, 391
iron, plants' need for, 27
  tomatoes' need for, 600
ivy, **392, 393**

J

Japanese beetle, [*color*], **393-396**
  blueberries, 242

control of, 394-396
grapes, 369, 370
lawns, 407
life cycle of, 393, 394
okra, 455
repellent plants for, 43
roses, 552
soybeans, 563
traps for, 100
turpentine against, 118
Japanese leafhoppers, apples, 183
jassid, bean, 222
jays, blue, as predators, 150, 151
jelly-end rot, potatoes, 513
juncos, as predators, 154
June bug grub, 235, 319
juniper, **396-398**
  bagworms, 350
juniper scale, 396, 397
  arborvitae, 197
juniper webworm, 397

K

kale, **399**
  planting time for, 63
  resistant varieties of, 534
kelp, as fertilizer, 36
knot, black. See *black knot.*
  olive, 458
kohlrabi, **399**
  planting time for, 62

L

lacebug, azalea, [*color*], 209, 210
  chrysanthemum, 291
  damage from, on azaleas, [*color*]
  eggplant, 341, 342
  hawthorn, 379
  rhododendron, 209, 546
  sycamore, 584
  trees, 623
lacewing, description of, 78, 79
  mealybugs controlled by, 439
ladybird beetles. See *ladybugs.*
ladybugs, **399-401**
  as predators, 69
  care of, 400, 401
  description of, 74
  life cycle of, 400
  Mexican bean beetle controlled by,
    440
lampyrid beetle, description of, 76
larch, **401-403**
larch case-bearer, 401
larch sawfly, 401, 402
larger elm leaf beetle, [*color*]